LISTEN HERE

"*Listen Here* is a virtual key to the treasury of writing on Appalachia by the women whose knowledge of the region stands out most prominently. Nowhere else can you find in one volume so much biographical and bibliographical information on more than a hundred creators of fiction, nonfiction, poetry, and drama from the Southern mountains. This is a long-needed resource that will be indispensable from the day of its publication. I hope and expect it will become a primary reference that steers readers not only to the most famous women writers of Appalachia, but to the lesser-known ones as well."

—John Egerton, author of *Generations: An American Family*

"This is the culmination of long dedication and a big vision and has been much anticipated. We all owe Sandy Ballard and Pat Hudson huge thanks for compiling such a compelling and necessary addition to our collective literature."

—Jerry W. Williamson, Appalachian State University

"It is common knowledge that women have been instrumental in shaping genres and creating traditions in Appalachian writing for well over a century and a quarter, but when their contribution is viewed comprehensively, a collective genius, which is not to deny any individual genius, shines through, creating not merely surprise but a shock of recognition . . . of the range and quality of their writing. Remedies of all kinds form a substantial part of Appalachian folklore. *Listen Here* is also a remedy, not for aches and pains, but for oversight or indifference of much of our cultural and literary heritage. The store of jewels in our own house, we come to realize in reading it, is greater than many of us ever realized. The symbol for the selections here is a garden with diversity and beauty for many tastes. Here is the perfect illustration of the flowering of Appalachian writing where the blooming itself has not been late, but only the critical recognition of it."

—Robert J. Higgs, East Tennessee State University

LISTEN HERE

Women
Writing
in
Appalachia

EDITED BY SANDRA L. BALLARD
AND PATRICIA L. HUDSON

THE UNIVERSITY PRESS OF KENTUCKY

Publication of this volume was made possible in part by a grant from
the National Endowment for the Humanities.

Editorial and Sales Offices: The University Press of Kentucky
663 South Limestone Street, Lexington, Kentucky 40508–4008

03 04 05 06 07   5 4 3 2 1

Library of Congress Cataloging-in-Publication Data

Listen here : women writing in Appalachia / edited by
Sandra L. Ballard and Patricia L. Hudson.
p. cm.
Includes bibliographical references and index.
ISBN 0-8131-2283-X (hardcover : alk. paper)

1. American literature—Appalachian Region, Southern.
2. Women—Appalachian Region, Southern—Literary collections.
3. Women and literature—Appalachian Region, Southern.
4. Applachian Region, Southern—Literary collections.
5. American literature—Women authors.
I. Ballard, Sandra L. II. Hudson, Patricia L.

PS554.L57 2003
810.8′09287′0975—dc21
2003012680

This book is printed on acid-free recycled paper meeting
the requirements of the American National Standard
for Permanence in Paper for Printed Library Materials.

Manufactured in the United States of America.

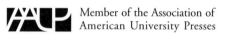 Member of the Association of
American University Presses

Contents

Chronology of Works

Anne Newport Royall
from *Sketches of History, Life, and Manners . . .* (1826)
Rebecca Harding Davis
from *Life in the Iron Mills* (1861)
Mary Noailles Murfree
from *In the Tennessee Mountains* (1884)
Frances Courtenay Baylor
from *Behind the Blue Ridge* (1887)
Will Allen Dromgoole
from *The Heart of Old Hickory* (1895)
Sarah Barnwell Elliott
from *The Durket Sperret* (1898)
Emma Bell Miles
from *The Spirit of the Mountains* (1905)
Corra Harris
from *A Circuit Rider's Wife* (1910)
Mary Johnston
from *The Long Roll* (1911)
Lucy Furman
from *Sight to the Blind* (1914)
Ann Cobb
from *Kinfolks: Kentucky Mountain Rhymes* (1922)
Edith Summers Kelley
from *Weeds* (1923)

NIKKI GIOVANNI
Griots, from *Racism 101* (1994)
JANE WILSON JOYCE
from *Old Wounds, New Words* (1994)
LLEWELLYN MCKERNAN
from *Many Waters: Poems from West Virginia* (1994)
BARBARA PRESNELL
from *Snake Dreams* (1994)
MEREDITH SUE WILLIS
My Boy Elroy, from *In the Mountains of America* (1994)
SHEILA KAY ADAMS
The Easter Frock from *Come Go Home With Me* (1995)
LISA ALTHER
from *Five Minutes in Heaven* (1995)
DORIS DAVENPORT
from *Soque Street Poems* (1995)
SIDNEY SAYLOR FARR
from *Headwaters* (1995)
NIKKY FINNEY
from *Rice* (1995)
LYNN POWELL
from *Old & New Testaments* (1995)
RITA SIMS QUILLEN
from *Counting the Sums* (1995)
LEE SMITH
from *Saving Grace* (1995)
DANA WILDSMITH
from *Alchemy* (1995)
LISA COFFMAN
from *Likely* (1996)
NIKKI GIOVANNI
from *The Selected Poems of Nikki Giovanni* (1996)

MAGGIE ANDERSON
  from *Windfall: New and Selected Poems* (2000)
LISA COFFMAN
  from *Meridian* (2000)
LEATHA KENDRICK
  from *Heart Cake* (2000)
BARBARA KINGSOLVER
  from *Prodigal Summer* (2000)
ELAINE FOWLER PALENCIA
  Briers, from *Brier Country: Stories from Blue Valley* (2000)
JAYNE ANNE PHILLIPS
  from *Motherkind* (2000)
ADRIANA TRIGIANI
  from *Big Stone Gap* (2000)
PAULETTA HANSEL
  from *Divining* (2001)
SHARYN MCCRUMB
  from *The Songcatcher* (2001)
JEANNE MCDONALD
  from Up the Hill toward Home, *Breathing the Same Air* (2001)
MARIJO MOORE
  Rumors, from *Red Woman with Backward Eyes and Other Stories* (2001)
CATHERINE LANDIS
  from *Some Days There's Pie* (2002)
KAREN SALYER MCELMURRAY
  from *Mother of the Disappeared: An Appalachian Birth Mother's Journey* (2003)

ACKNOWLEDGMENTS

The editors want to thank the writers whose work is contained in this book. Their generosity and encouraging words have inspired us throughout this project.

We are grateful to editor Nancy Grayson, who encouraged us to submit our initial proposal to University Press of Kentucky, and to editors Jennifer Peckinpaugh and Nichole Lainhart, whose persistence and cheerful good work have seen the book through to completion. We appreciate the National Endowment for the Humanities Summer Stipend that helped to launch this anthology.

Thanks also to the Carson-Newman College students who helped with the research, photocopying, and typing: Kara Roach Davis, Nicole Drewitz Crockett, Angela Ellis Roberts, Courtney Turnbow, Amy Hartman, Melanie Johnson Daugherty, and Joy Hayes. Special thanks to Nichole Stewart for typing much of the first draft. We thank the students at Appalachian State University who helped in the creation of the final manuscript of this book: Jenny Trest, Cassie Robinson, Ruthie Blakeney, Trish Kilby, Heather Robbins, Carl Larsen, Erin Casto, and Kathy Duffala. Your enthusiasm and energy for this project kept us going. Thanks as well to ASU colleagues Lynn Moss Sanders and Grace McEntee for being such a wonderful writing group.

We especially thank Toney Frazier, Sam Stapleton, and Elizabeth and Erin Stapleton for their loving support and patience.

ABOUT THE EDITORS

Sandra L. Ballard and Patricia L. Hudson are co-authors of *The Carolinas and Appalachian States* in the Smithsonian Guides to Historic America series. Sandy Ballard is the editor of the *Appalachian Journal* and Professor of English at Appalachian State University. Formerly on the faculty at the University of Tennessee as a reference librarian, Pat Hudson is a freelance writer whose work has appeared in *American Heritage, Appalachian Heritage, Americana* and *Southern Living*.

INTRODUCTION

"I'm a hillbilly, a woman, and a poet, and I understood early on that nobody was going to listen to anything I had to say anyway, so I might as well just say what I want to."[1]

—Irene McKinney, West Virginia Poet Laureate

The 105 writers in this collection are women who have spent their writing lives saying what they want to; the goal of this anthology is to ensure that more people have the opportunity to listen. As a group, these writers have been relegated to the fringes of the American literary community, largely because their "place"—Appalachia—continues to be viewed as outside the American mainstream.

Appalachian author Lee Smith has examined the general public's perception of the region and concluded that "Appalachia is to the South what the South is to the rest of the country. That is: lesser than, backward, marginal. Other. Look at the stereotypes: 'Hee Haw,' 'Deliverance,' 'Dogpatch,' and 'The Dukes of Hazzard.' A bunch of hillbillies sitting on a rickety old porch drinking moonshine and living on welfare, right? Wrong."[2]

If the region itself can be dismissed as "other," then it is hardly surprising that the region's literature has suffered the same fate. Indeed, the deprecating label of "regionalist" is often assigned to writers who set their fiction in Appalachia, as if any work depicting the land, people, and culture of a particular place must be provincial and limited in appeal.

New York writers are not labeled as "regional" writers, even when their locale—Manhattan and its environs—suffuses their work. "All American fiction, it seems to me," says writer Leigh Allison Wilson, "is circumscribed by place; I have the feeling that my work ends up being labeled regional simply because fewer people come from my particular place."[3]

As editors of this anthology, we set out to create a collection of creative writings by women whose identities have been marked by life in the Appalachian mountains, because we discovered that their voices are missing from our national literature. Their absence from most of the standard literary reference books was brought into focus in 1998 when the University Press of Kentucky published *Bloodroot: Reflections on Place by Appalachian Women Writers*, edited by Joyce Dyer. The collection of autobiographical essays written by some of the region's most prominent writers holds enough warmth and intimacy, hope and humor, to make readers feel they have received an unexpected inheritance. But when we searched for these writers in standard literary reference books, we found only an empty-room echo.

None of the thirty-five authors in *Bloodroot* appear in the 1996 *Norton Anthology of Literature by Women*. None of them.

We then searched *The Oxford Companion to Women's Writing in the United States* (1995), a massive reference book of more than 1,000 pages, and discovered that only eight women from the Appalachian region were included: Olive Tilford Dargan (1869–1968), Mary Noailles Murfree (1850–1922), Elizabeth Madox Roberts (1881–1941), Harriette Simpson Arnow (1908–1986), Marilou Awiakta (1936–), Nikki Giovanni (1943–), Lee Smith (1944–), and Annie Dillard (1945–).

It is our hope that this book will spread the word that Appalachia has many women writers who are worthy of recognition. Some have gone unnoticed, some have been discovered and then forgotten, and some have gained recognition, only to have their ties to the region ignored. As writer Wilma Dykeman said, Appalachian literature includes "experiences as unique as churning butter and as universal as getting born."[4]

When writers such as Lee Smith, Annie Dillard, or Barbara Kingsolver receive national attention, reviewers rarely highlight their Appalachian roots or acknowledge the rich heritage that nurtured them. But the voices of all of the women in this book were developed within earshot of good storytellers. "Sooner or later," says folksinger Jean Ritchie, "memories would call forth a story—a tale not to be sung but told, with much laughing, and joining in, maybe a tear or two—and life would stretch broader for a while as older generations lived again."[5]

The absence of Appalachian women's voices in American literature, though lamentable, is understandable when we realize that much of the work by these writers has remained uncollected or is no longer in print. The inaccessibility of much of the best Appalachian literature means that students from Appalachia who study American literature rarely find their "place" depicted in textbooks. While they can see the relevance of literature set in other places, it is easy for them to come to the conclusion that writers come ONLY from other places.

It is important for both writers and readers not to cut themselves off from their roots. As Nobel Prize–winning poet Seamus Heaney said, "for words to have any kind of independent energy, in some way they have to be animated by the first place in ourselves."[6]

Appalachian author George Ella Lyon reminds us that "where you're from is not who you are, but it's an important ingredient . . . you must trust your first voice—the one tuned by the people and place that made you—before you can speak your deepest truths."[7]

"I suspect," echoes author Lisa Koger, "that trying to separate a writer's work from his background is a little like trying to separate a turtle from its shell. . . . Remove home and its influence from my back, and I will have lost not just shelter but an essential part of me."[8]

Despite numerous obstacles, a number of women writers from the region have found critical and commercial success. This collection includes the work of nominees and recipients of the Pulitzer Prize, National Book Award, and Newbery Award. Some lived nearly a century; others died young. Most live, or have lived, the life of a writer while also being mothers, parental caregivers, and workers of day jobs to support themselves and their families.

Unlike Carl Sandburg and Ernest Hemingway whose wives brought them breakfast on a tray and set it outside the door so as not to disturb them, most of these writers have had no such emotional or physical "elbow room" in which to create. Yet this anthology makes it impossible to deny their creativity.

While working on this project, we occasionally were asked why we chose to focus exclusively on the region's women writers. Our answer is both political and practical. The late Appalachian scholar, Jim Wayne Miller, addressed the political reasons behind this collection when he wrote in support of our proposal: "The Appalachian region is still seen as the site of an unmitigated patriarchy, with the result that the region's women writers and the impressive body of work they have created is not sufficiently visible, recognized, or appreciated. This collection can make a significant contribution toward correcting this misperception." The practical consideration is that Appalachia's wealth of literary talent has yet to be collected in a single volume. We leave it to others to expand the canon further.

Having convinced ourselves of the need for an anthology of this nature, we proceeded to hammer out the guidelines that would shape this book.

First, we decided the collection should include writings by women who have lived in Appalachia for a significant period of their lives, who identify themselves with the region, whose lives have been influenced by the region, and/or whose writings concern Appalachian experiences.

Second, we defined "Appalachia" as the southeastern mountains and foothills—from the mountainous parts of Pennsylvania and southwest Virginia to West Virginia, eastern Kentucky, East Tennessee, western North Carolina, upstate South Carolina, and northern Georgia and Alabama.

Third, we decided the anthology would include writers who have published at least one book-length work, who are widely published in the region, and/or who have contributed in a significant way to the writing of the region. (Because we found more writers than would fit in this anthology, we have included a list entitled "More Women Writing in Appalachia" to document the range and variety of voices who also deserve to be heard.)

And finally, we believed the collection should highlight the fact that many of the women writing in Appalachia work and publish in multiple genres. Fiction writers also write poetry; poets also write short fiction, etc. The willingness of individual writers to cross from one genre to another suggests that they are more concerned with exploring their creativity than with publication and recognition. This collection includes excerpts from novels, short stories, poetry, drama, creative nonfiction, and children's books.

The majority of the writers included in this anthology are contemporary. We contacted the writers or the heirs of those writers who are deceased. Our correspondence with many of these writers began in the late 1990s; we introduced ourselves, explained the project, and invited them to complete a biographical form if they were interested in being included. As a result, much of the information in this book—birthdates, education, thoughts on the writing process, and ties to the region—has been provided by the authors.

The initial correspondence was followed by several years of research; there was always one more interview to do, one more article to track down, one more book to read. We never dreamed the project would span almost a decade. Fortunately, we had collaborated previously on a book, *The Smithsonian Guide to Historic America: The Carolinas and the Appalachian States*, so we knew we could work together.

What we did not know was that one of our family members would be seriously injured in a horseback riding accident; that there would be a series of surgeries and hospital stays spread between our families; that we would go through three computers apiece and our word processing program would become obsolete. In the midst of all this, one of us changed jobs and moved to a different state, which complicated the collaborative process considerably.

We are deeply indebted to the authors for their patience, as well as their many supportive letters and e-mails. They embraced this project and its two harried editors with tremendous generosity of spirit. We have been privileged to cross paths with these writers, and we continue to marvel at their creativity and their impressive ability to capture and interpret the endless variety of human experience.

In Joanna Russ's book, *How to Suppress Women's Writing*, she writes:

Of those [women] who are not ignored completely, dismissed as writing about the 'wrong' things, condemned for (whatever passes for) impropriety (that year), . . . condemned for writing in the wrong genre, or out of a genre . . . It is still possible to say, quite sincerely: She wrote it, but she doesn't fit in. Or, more generously: She's wonderful, but where on earth did she come from?

Sometimes she comes from Appalachia.

NOTES

1. Quoted by Maggie Anderson in "The Mountains Dark and Close Around Me," *Bloodroot*, ed. Joyce Dyer (Lexington: University Press of Kentucky, 1998), 39.

2. "White Columns and Marble Generals," www.leesmith.com/columns.html 13 Dec. 2002.

3. *Contemporary Authors*, Vol. 117, 487.

4. Quoted by Jim Wayne Miller in "A Note to the Student," *I Have A Place*, ed. Jim Wayne Miller (Pippa Passes, KY: Alice Lloyd College, 1981), x.

5. "The Song about the Story—The Story behind the Song," *Bloodroot: Reflections on Place by Appalachian Women Writers*, ed. Joyce Dyer (Lexington: University Press of Kentucky, 1998), 226.

6. Quoted by George Ella Lyon in "Voiceplace," *Bloodroot*, ed. Joyce Dyer (Lexington: University Press of Kentucky, 1998), 169.

7. "Voiceplace," *Bloodroot*, 169.

8. Koger, Lisa. Letter to editors.

$\mathcal{S}$HEILA $\mathcal{K}$AY $\mathcal{A}$DAMS
(March 18, 1953–)

Sheila Kay Adams is a seventh-generation ballad singer who has participated in the tradition of learning and singing English, Irish, and Scottish ballads from her ancestors who arrived in North Carolina in the late 1700s. Adams and her family live in Madison County, North Carolina, where she was born. She has three children and is passing the ballad traditions to them. Her primary teacher was her great aunt Dellie Chandler Norton, her "Granny," who said about Sheila, "She may not always know where she's going, but she sure knows where she comes from."

After completing her B.A. in education at Mars Hill College in 1974, she worked for seventeen years in Madison County public schools as a schoolteacher, like her mother Neple Norton. In 1991, she quit teaching to begin a career as a musician, storyteller, and writer. She has traveled widely, performing at music festivals and university campuses all over the United States. She served as singing coach for the film *Songcatcher*, and most of the ballads performed are her versions.

Encouraged by novelist Lee Smith to write her collection of stories, *Come Go Home with Me*, she won the 1997 North Carolina Historical Society's award for historical fiction. In 1998, she received the North Carolina Folklore Society's prestigious Brown-Hudson Award for her contributions to the study of North Carolina folklore.

About her longtime love of writing songs, poems, and stories, she says, "I love writing, using the language of my home. I get lost for hours in the rhythm, the lyrical sound of the mountain dialect. And there's such a richness of material just waiting to be plucked from the strong oral tradition . . . in my family." She is currently at work on a novel.

Other Sources to Explore

Primary

Short stories: *Come Go Home with Me* (1995). **Folk music and storytelling recordings:** *What Ever Happened to John Parrish's Boy?* (2002), *My Dearest Dear* (2000), *Christmas on the Mountain* (1998), *Don't Get Above Your Raising* (1993), *A Spring in the Burton Cove* (1991), *Loving Forward, Loving Back* (1985). **Autobiographical essay:** "Flowering Ivy," *Bloodroot* (1998), ed. Joyce Dyer, 17–20.

Secondary

Fred Brown, "Echoes from the Past," *Knoxville News-Sentinel* (24 January 1999), E1, E5. Joyce Dyer, "Sheila Kay Adams," in *Bloodroot*, 16.

FROM *COME GO HOME WITH ME: STORIES BY SHEILA KAY ADAMS* (1995)

The Easter Frock

Bertha Franklin used to love to sit on her porch and tell me stories about what Sodom was like back when she was a girl. I was always spellbound. Bertha was a great storyteller, and she was the same age as my mother. Her stories formed a window for me, a window I could look through back into the times of my mother as a young girl and young woman.

Evidently, Bertha's mother told her stories about what it was like growing up in Sodom back at the turn of the century. This is a story Bertha told me that her mother, Tootie, told her.

Back then, a peddler drove a horse-drawn wagon around to the different communities, and you could buy just about anything you needed off his wagon. You could get nails, buckets, and dry goods. You could even buy cloth.

Before Easter one year, Tootie managed to save up enough money to buy a pretty piece of filmy material to make herself an Easter frock to wear to church. Now, back then, the dresses had a bustle on them that stuck out over the hind end. If you could afford it you could buy a wire frame to make it stand out, but if you couldn't, well, you just stuffed it with rags.

Tootie spent a lot of time working on her frock and finished it the Saturday night before Easter Sunday. She hung it on the back of the door and went on to bed thinking how pretty she'd look next day at church.

She got up late the next morning and realized she had forgotten to stuff her bustle the night before. She hurriedly reached in the rag bag, pulled out an old flour sack, and commenced to stuffing that bustle.

She got to church and swept right down to the front, holding that dress tail out, nodding and smiling and speaking to everybody.

As soon as folks stood for the first hymn, Tootie heard some snickering behind her. And every hymn thereafter, it seemed like the snickering spread till it was all the way to the very back of the church.

When the last amen was said, Tootie hit the door. She checked to see if her slip was hanging or if all her buttons were buttoned, but she couldn't find a single thing undone. She stiffened her spine and stormed off down the road.

About halfway home, her brothers caught up with her and just set into horse laughing, all doubled over holding their sides. Tootie, who had a temper to match her shining red hair, had suffered enough in silence. She wheeled around on them boys with a vengeance.

"I want to know what's so damn funny?" she said. "Folks has laughed at me all morning in church, and I'm about sick of it!"

But you know how brothers are (and Tootie was blessed with eight of them). They just laughed even harder and ran off down the road with Tootie chucking rocks at them as hard as she could.

By this time I reckon Tootie was livid! She charged down the road, marched up the hill to the house, and slammed through the door, banging it closed behind her hard enough to rattle all the window glasses in the house. She started down the hall to her room and spied the hall chair sitting there—the one with the mirror on the wall above it. She climbed up on the chair, positioned herself so she could look over her shoulder, and there across her bustle you could read, plain as day: "50 LBS. OF THE VERY BEST."

DOROTHY ALLISON
(April 11, 1949–)

Born in Greenville, South Carolina, Dorothy Allison began to receive recognition for her work as a poet and short story writer in the 1980s. Her first collection of stories, *Trash,* published by Firebrand Books in 1988, won the Lambda Literary Awards for Best Small Press Book and Best Lesbian Book.

In a 1992 interview with National Public Radio's Terri Gross, Allison explained some of the autobiographical elements of her best-known work, *Bastard Out of Carolina*, a National Book Award finalist in 1992. Allison's birth was traumatic. Her mother, who was barely fifteen, was pregnant when she suffered a concussion during an automobile accident. Thrown through the windshield, Allison's mother was unconscious for three days, during which time Allison was born, and because her grandmother and aunt did not adequately prepare their stories about her young mother's plans to marry, Allison says that she was literally born a "bastard."

Allison's mother, a hard-working waitress all her life, was married three times before Allison was five years old. Her third husband was the man who became Allison's abuser. The complex relationship between abuser and victim form the crux of the partly autobiographical novel.

Allison's central character, Ruth Anne Boatwright, nicknamed "Bone," narrates the devastating story, giving readers a vivid and compelling account of her life with her mother, Anney, and her stepfather, Daddy Glen.

OTHER SOURCES TO EXPLORE

PRIMARY

Novels: *Cavedweller* (1998), *Bastard Out of Carolina* (1992). **Poetry:** *The Women Who Hate Me: Poetry, 1980–1990* (1991). **Short stories:** *Trash* (1988). **Essays:** *What It Took for Me to Get Here: Young Writers on the Journey through Life* (1999),

Two or Three Things I Know for Sure (1995), *Skin: Talking about Sex, Class & Literature* (1993).

SECONDARY

Blanche McCrary Boyd, "Dorothy Allison, Crossover Blues," *The Nation* (5 July 1992), 20–22. *Contemporary Authors*, Vol. 140, 9–10. *New York Times Book Review* (5 July 1992), 3. E.J. Graff, "Novelist out of Carolina," *Poets & Writers* (January/February 1995), 41–49. Michael Rowe, "We're as American as You Can Get," *Harvard Gay and Lesbian Review* 2:1 (winter 1995).

BASTARD OUT OF CAROLINA (1992)

from Chapter 1

I've been called Bone all my life, but my name's Ruth Anne. I was named for and by my oldest aunt—Aunt Ruth. My mama didn't have much to say about it, since strictly speaking, she wasn't there. Mama and a carful of my aunts and uncles had been going out to the airport to meet one of the cousins who was on his way back from playing soldier. Aunt Alma, Aunt Ruth, and her husband, Travis, were squeezed into the front, and Mama was stretched out in back, sound asleep. Mama hadn't adjusted to pregnant life very happily, and by the time she was eight months gone, she had a lot of trouble sleeping. She said that when she lay on her back it felt like I was crushing her, when she lay on her side it felt like I was climbing up her backbone, and there was no rest on her stomach at all. Her only comfort was the backseat of Uncle Travis's Chevy, which was jacked up so high that it easily cradled little kids or pregnant women. Moments after lying back into that seat, Mama had fallen into her first deep sleep in eight months. She slept so hard, even the accident didn't wake her up.

My aunt Alma insists to this day that what happened was in no way Uncle Travis's fault, but I *know* that the first time I ever saw Uncle Travis sober was when I was seventeen and they had just removed half his stomach along with his liver. I cannot imagine that he hadn't been drinking. There's no question in my mind but that they had *all* been drinking, except Mama, who never could drink, and certainly not when she was pregnant.

No, Mama was just asleep and everyone else was drunk. And what they did was plow headlong into a slow-moving car. The front of Uncle Travis's Chevy accordioned; the back flew up; the aunts and Uncle Travis were squeezed so tight they just bounced a little; and Mama, still asleep with her hands curled under her chin, flew right over their heads, through the windshield, and over the car they hit. Going through the glass, she cut the top of her head, and when she hit the ground she bruised her backside, but other than that she wasn't hurt at all. Of course, she didn't wake up for three days, not till after Granny and Aunt Ruth had signed all the papers and picked out my name.

I am Ruth for my aunt Ruth, and Anne for my mama. I got the nickname Bone shortly after Mama brought me home from the hospital and Uncle Earle announced that I was "no bigger than a knucklebone" and Aunt Ruth's youngest girl, Deedee, pulled the blanket back to see "the bone." It's lucky I'm not Mattie Raylene like Granny wanted. But Mama had always promised to name her first daughter after her oldest sister, and Aunt Ruth thought Mama's child should just naturally carry Mama's name since they had come so close to losing her.

Other than the name, they got just about everything else wrong. Neither Aunt Ruth nor Granny could write very clearly, and they hadn't bothered to discuss how Anne would be spelled, so it wound up spelled three different ways on the form—Ann, Anne, and Anna. As for the name of the father, Granny refused to speak it after she had run him out of town for messing with her daughter, and Aunt Ruth had never been sure of his last name anyway. They tried to get away with just scribbling something down, but if the hospital didn't mind how a baby's middle name was spelled, they were definite about having a father's last name. So Granny gave one and Ruth gave another, the clerk got mad, and there I was—certified a bastard by the state of South Carolina.

Mama always said it would never have happened if she'd been awake. "After all," she told my aunt Alma, "they don't ask for a marriage license before they put you up on the table." She was convinced that she could have bluffed her way through it, *said* she was married firmly enough that no one would have questioned her.

"It's only when you bring it to their attention that they write it down."

Granny said it didn't matter anyhow. Who cared what was written down? Did people read courthouse records? Did they ask to see your birth certificate before they sat themselves on your porch? Everybody who mattered knew, and she didn't give a rat's ass about anybody else. She teased Mama about the damn silly paper with the red stamp on the bottom.

"What was it? You intended to frame that thing? You wanted something on your wall to prove you done it right?" Granny could be mean where her pride was involved. "The child is proof enough. An't no stamp on her nobody can see."

If Granny didn't care, Mama did. Mama hated to be called trash, hated the memory of every day she'd ever spent bent over other people's peanuts and strawberry plants while they stood tall and looked at her like she was a rock on the ground. The stamp on that birth certificate burned her like the stamp she knew they'd tried to put on her. *No-good, lazy, shiftless.* She'd work her hands to claws, her back to a shovel shape, her mouth to a bent and awkward smile—anything to deny what Greenville County wanted to name her. Now a soft-talking black-eyed man had done it for them—set a mark on her and hers. It was all she could do to pull herself up eight days after I was born and go back to work waiting tables with a tight mouth and swollen eyes.

Mama waited a year. Four days before my first birthday and a month past her sixteenth, she wrapped me in a blanket and took me to the courthouse. The clerk was polite but bored. He had her fill out a form and pay a two-dollar fee. Mama filled it out in a fine schoolgirl's hand. She hadn't been to school in three years, but she wrote letters for everyone in the family and was proud of her graceful, slightly canted script.

"What happened to the other one?" the clerk asked.

Mama didn't look up from my head on her arm. "It got torn across the bottom."

The clerk looked at her more closely, turned a glance on me. "Is that right?"

He went to the back and was gone a long time. Mama stood, quiet but stubborn, at the counter. When he came back, he passed her the paper and stayed to watch her face.

It was the same, identical to the other one. Across the bottom in over-sized red-inked block letters it read, "ILLEGITIMATE."

Mama drew a breath like an old woman with pleurisy, and flushed pink from her neck to her hairline. "I don't want it like this," she blurted.

"Well, little lady," he said in a long, slow drawl. Behind him she could see some of the women clerks standing in a doorway, their faces almost as flushed as her own but their eyes bright with an entirely different emotion. "This is how it's got to be. The facts have been established." He drew the word out even longer and louder so that it hung in the air between them like a neon reflection of my mama's blush—*established.*

The women in the doorway shook their heads and pursed their lips. One mouthed to the other, "Some people."

Mama made her back straighten, bundled me closer to her neck, and turned suddenly for the hall door. "You forgetting your certificate," the man called after her, but she didn't stop. Her hands on my body clamped so tight I let out a high, thin wail. Mama just held on and let me scream.

She waited another year before going back, that time taking my aunt Ruth with her and leaving me with Granny. "I was there," Aunt Ruth promised them, "and it was really my fault. In so much excitement I just got confused, what with Anney here looking like she was dead to the world and everybody shouting and running around. You know, there was a three-car accident brought in just minutes after us." Aunt Ruth gave the clerk a very sincere direct look, awkwardly trying to keep her eyes wide and friendly.

"You know how these things can happen."

"Oh, I do," he said, enjoying it all immensely.

The form he brought out was no different from the others. The look he gave my mama and my aunt was pure righteous justification. *"What'd you expect?"* he seemed to be saying. His face was set and almost gentle, but his eyes laughed at them. My aunt came close to swinging her purse at his head, but Mama caught her arm. That time she took the certificate copy with her.

"Might as well have something for my two dollars," she said. At seventeen, she was a lot older than she had been at sixteen. The next year she went alone, and the year after. That same year she met Lyle Parsons and started thinking more about marrying him than dragging down to the courthouse again. Uncle Earle teased her that if she lived with Lyle for seven years, she could get the same result without paying a courthouse lawyer. "The law never done us no good. Might as well get on without it."

· · ·

Mama was working grill at the White Horse Cafe the day the radio announced that the fire downtown had gone out of control, burning the courthouse and the hall of records to the ground. It was midway through the noon rush. Mama was holding a pot of coffee in one hand and two cups in the other. She put the cups down and passed the pot to her friend Mab.

"I'm going home."

"You what?"

"I've got to go home."

"Where's she going?"

"Trouble at home."

The cardboard box of wrinkled and stained papers was tucked under the sheets in the bottom of Aunt Alma's chifforobe. Mama pulled out the ones she wanted, took them into the kitchen, and dropped them in the sink without bothering to unfold them. She'd just lit a kitchen match when the phone rang.

"You heard, I suppose." It was Aunt Ruth. "Mab said you took off like someone set a fire under you."

"Not me," Mama replied. "The only fire I got going here is the one burning up all these useless papers."

Aunt Ruth's laughter spilled out of the phone and all over the kitchen.

"Girl, there an't a woman in town going to believe you didn't set that fire yourself. Half the county's gonna tell the other how you burned down that courthouse."

"Let them talk," Mama said, and blew at the sparks flying up. "Talk won't send me to jail. The sheriff and half his deputies know I was at work all morning, 'cause I served them their coffee. I can't get into any trouble just 'cause I'm glad the goddam courthouse burned down."

She blew at the sparks again, whistling into the phone, and then laughed out loud. Halfway across town, Aunt Ruth balanced the phone against her neck, squeezed Granny's shoulder, and laughed with her. Over at the mill, Aunt Alma looked out a window at the smoke billowing up downtown and had to cover her mouth to keep from giggling like a girl. In the outer yard back of the furnace works, Uncle Earle and Glen Waddell were moving iron and listening to the radio. Both of them grinned and looked up at each other at the same moment, then burst out laughing. It was almost as if everyone could hear each other, all over Greenville, laughing as the courthouse burned to the ground.

$\mathcal{L}$ISA $\mathcal{A}$LTHER
(July 23, 1944–)

Novelist Lisa (pronounced "LIE-za") Reed Alther was born in Kingsport, Tennessee, and spent her childhood there. She left the region to attend Wellesley College, graduating in 1966 with a B.A. That same year, she married Richard Alther, a painter; the couple had a daughter, Sara, and later divorced. Alther has lived most of her adult life in New England; she presently divides her time between Hinesburg, Vermont, and Jonesborough, Tennessee. "I get labeled a Southern writer, woman's writer, feminist, gay, Appalachian, sometimes a New England writer," Alther says. "I'm happy to be included in any of those groups. I don't know if being in one excludes you from the others or not."

Alther worked briefly in New York at Atheneum Publishers before moving to Vermont where she and her husband "did the whole back-to-the-land thing. We had huge vegetable gardens, and we froze and dried and canned our own food. . . . I had a lot of friends in communes. . . . I remember fretting because everybody else was doing drugs and having sex and all I was doing was canning and freezing."

Alther's early attempts at fiction resulted in a stack of 250 rejection slips. "I started thinking I needed a new career, but I could tell I was getting better at it as a craft. Also I used writing to explore what was going on around me, in the world and in my life, that I couldn't understand."

Characterizing herself as a slow writer, Alther labors over four or five drafts before she feels her work is ready for publication. It took six years for her to write her first novel, *Kinflicks*. The book became a best-seller. Set in an East Tennessee town some say is modeled on Kingsport, *Kinflicks* chronicles the misadventures of Ginny Babcock.

"Everybody thought Ginny Babcock was me," says Alther. "When they finally met me, they'd say, 'You're not Ginny. You're really boring.' I created her [Ginny] as dumb enough to participate in all those fads of the 60s and 70s. If I'd been doing all that stuff, I wouldn't have had time to write five novels."

Alther's blunt examination of the spectrum of human sexuality discomforts some of her critics. "It seems to me that the whole subject of sexuality in our culture is pretty fraught," says Alther. "You're supposed to choose a category and stay in it. The main character [in *Kinflicks*] has a lesbian episode, but it was treated as humor. With subsequent books, I've tried to take the issue deeper."

Author Marilyn French says Alther "writes with a profound acceptance of human variety and vagary that is rare in this mean age." A reviewer in *Publisher's Weekly* notes, "Alther is a wry satirist. She can be, and almost always is, wildly, ribaldly funny. . . . And with what a cool, clear eye she observes us all."

Alther's novel *Five Minutes in Heaven* follows Jude, a motherless girl, in a haunting search for love that takes her from Tennessee to Paris. In this scene, Jude struggles to accept changes in her relationship with Molly, her childhood soul mate.

OTHER SOURCES TO EXPLORE

PRIMARY

Novels: *Five Minutes in Heaven* (1995), *Bedrock* (1990), *Other Women* (1984), *Original Sins* (1981), *Kinflicks* (1975). **Autobiographical Essay:** "Border States," in *Bloodroot* (1998), ed. Joyce Dyer, 22–30.

SECONDARY

Contemporary Authors, Vol. 65–68, 20. Joyce Dyer, "Lisa Alther," in *Bloodroot*, 21. Carol E.W. Edwards, "Interview with Lisa Alther," *Turnstile* 4:1 (1993), 34–50. Mary Anne Ferguson, "Lisa Alther," *Contemporary Writers of the South* (1993), 22–31. Don Williams, "Writing on a Continuum" [Interview], *Knoxville News-Sentinel* (16 June 1995), B1–B2.

Five Minutes in Heaven (1995)

from Chapter 7

"So if you keep your knees together tight, girls, and smile up at your date while you swing your legs under the dashboard, you can get into any sports car, no matter how small, without displaying all your worldly treasures." Miss Melrose was demonstrating her technique in her desk chair as she talked. The Charm Class was assiduously copying her movements, even though none of the boys they knew could drive.

As Jude secured her worldly treasures beneath her imaginary dashboard, she noticed that Molly had painted her fingernails pink. Now that Jude was in junior high, she, too, shaved her armpits as well as her legs. And she put on lipstick, eyeliner, and mascara every morning. Thanks to Miss Melrose, she knew never to wear white shoes before Easter or after Labor Day and not to make chicken salad with dark meat. But Molly was always one step ahead.

Except in the classroom. Despite her efforts to score poorly on the placement exams, Jude had been assigned to a special seminar, along with the nerds who played slide-rule games in the lunchroom while all the cool kids did the Dirty Shag in the gymnasium to raise money for cerebral palsy. Jude had also been elected seventh-grade representative to the student council, which was dominated by classmates who were Episcopalian and Presbyterian and who lived in the big, fancy houses of the Yankee mill executives along Poplar Bluff.

But Molly never even congratulated her on her student council victory. And if Jude tried to explain some of the ideas she was learning about in the seminar, Molly would just shrug and say, "Afraid you've lost me again, brainchild."

Some afternoons after school now, instead of racing Flame through the Wildwoods, Jude sat with Sandy in his upstairs bedroom discussing the big bang theory and natural selection and relativity. Out the window, they watched Noreen coaching Molly in Noreen's backyard for the upcoming cheerleader tryouts. Sometimes their lyrics reached Jude and Sandy through the open windows:

> "Well, down my leg and up my spine!
> We've got a team that's mighty fine!"

She and Sandy would pause in their discussion of Hegel's dialectic to giggle. Then Jude would frown at herself, feeling disloyal.

As they strolled home from Charm Class through the twilight, allowing their kilted hips to sway with every step, Jude said, "My dad said he'd teach us to drive the jeep down that hill behind the cemetery on Saturday afternoon."

"Oh, Jude, I'm afraid I can't."

"But it would be really neat to be able to drive, wouldn't it?"

"I'm afraid I'm tied up on Saturday afternoon."

"Doing what?"

"Jude, I'm not your slave. You don't need to know my every move."

"Sorry."

They walked in silence past yards full of tulips. Ever since Jude had realized that her experience on the raft with Molly had been just a dream, she hadn't known how to behave with her. It seemed impossible to recapture the unselfconscious accord of their childhood, but no guidelines for their distressing new separateness had emerged. So they often experienced awkward silences or irritated outbursts, followed by frantic attempts to backpedal to the harmony they used to take so effortlessly for granted.

"I like the white tulips best, don't you?" Molly finally said.

"Me, too," said Jude, accepting the apology.

"Actually, I'm going to the lake with Ace Saturday afternoon. To ride in his father's motorboat." She was trying to sound casual.

Jude glanced at her. Molly and Ace often danced together at the noon-time sock hops. And although Molly never admitted it, Jude suspected that they talked on the phone a lot at night. Occasionally, the three of them sat together on the bleachers at lunch to watch intramural basketball. Ace and Molly weren't going steady, and they never went out on dates, but Jude could tell that Molly was sometimes preoccupied with him.

"But why Ace?" she finally asked, genuinely curious. "I just don't get it. Have you forgotten how mean he was to us?"

"There's a really sweet side to him that you've never seen, Jude. He may act tough, but inside he's just a sad, scared little boy." She was smiling fondly, as though describing the antics of her dog.

"Please spare me the details."

"Besides, there are reasons why he was so mean."

"Such as?"

"His father isn't a nice man."

"His father is the best lawyer in town. My dad says he was a big hero in the war."

"I can't say any more."

Jude studied her from the corner of her eye. "We've never had secrets,

Molly." They were passing more tulips. Jude decided she hated them, especially the white ones.

"I promised Ace."

"So Ace is more important to you now than I am?"

"No, of course not, Jude. But he needs me. I think I can help him."

Reaching the crack in the sidewalk marking the boundary between their yards, they turned to face each other. Molly's shirt collar was peeping out from beneath her sweater. On it, Jude spotted a tiny dagger made from a straight pin, a piece of red plastic cord, and some multicolored beads the size of BBs. Noreen had started this fad, which had swept the halls of the junior high school. She and the other cheerleaders made sets consisting of a miniature dagger and sword. The boys bought them, and the cheerleaders donated the money to muscular dystrophy. The boys wore them crossed on their collars until they wanted to go steady, at which point they gave their girlfriends their daggers.

"What's that?" asked Jude, pointing at Molly's dagger as though at a scorpion.

Molly started, then looked quickly away. "Ace asked me to wear it today."

Jude said nothing for a long time. She was losing this battle, but she was damned if she'd make it easy for either of them. "What about me?"

"But Jude, you're a girl," said Molly gently. "You're my best friend, but Ace is my boyfriend. Why don't you get a boyfriend, too? Then we can double-date to the movies. What about Jerry Crawford? Ace says he really likes you."

"What about our cabin?" Jude asked doggedly. She didn't want Jerry Crawford. She wanted Molly.

"What cabin?"

"The cabin we were going to build on the ridge above the cave. With the paddock for Flame and Pal."

"But we were just kids then, Jude. It was like playing house." She was gazing at Jude with loving concern.

Jude felt the bottom drop out of her stomach, like a trapdoor to hell. She had known she was losing, but she hadn't realized that she'd already lost.

ᴍAGGIE ᴀNDERSON
(September 23, 1948–)

Maggie Anderson inherited Appalachian connections from both sides of her family. Her mother's family was from Jefferson, Pennsylvania, on the West Virginia border near Morgantown; her father's family was from Preston County, West Virginia. The only child of teachers, Anderson grew up around aunts and uncles who worked in mines, mills, and on the railroad.

She was born in New York City. Her mother died when she was nine, and when she was thirteen, she and her father moved back to West Virginia. Her West Virginia connections have been the subject of her creative work as a poet, a teacher, and an editor. As she explains, "The hills are in *everything* I write."

She has four books of poetry, including her most recent, *Windfall: New and Selected Poems*. She is also the editor of *Hill Daughter (New and Selected Poems)* by West Virginia's former Poet Laureate Louise McNeill (1911–1993). Anderson's poetry has appeared in *American Poetry Review, Northwest Review, Poetry East*, and other magazines.

Her work has been supported by fellowships from the National Endowment for the Arts and the Pennsylvania Council on the Arts. She has been a Resident Fellow at the MacDowell Colony. For a decade (1978–1988), she worked with the Artists-in-the-School-and-Communities Program in West Virginia and has served as Poet-in-Residence in Marshall, Mercer, and Jackson counties. She has also taught poetry writing in rehabilitation centers, senior centers, and prisons, as well as at Hamilton College, the University of Pittsburgh, and the University of Oregon.

Director of the Wick Poetry Program, she is a professor of English at Kent State University, where she has been honored with a Distinguished Teacher Award. Through Kent State University Press, she edits a chapbook poetry series and a first-book series. She is also the co-editor of *A Gathering of*

Poets (1992), a collection of poems commemorating the shootings of students at Kent State and Jackson State in May 1970. She has co-edited an anthology of poems about the school experience, *Learning by Heart: Contemporary American Poetry about School* (1999).

Poet George Ella Lyon observes that "Anderson's work often walks the line between poetry and prose, but it is generally a taut line, more like a highwire than a fence, and there is energy in the balance." Anderson explains that her writing process is in a constant state of flux: "Just as I learn one way of writing, it changes, or I change, and everything must be relearned or learned fresh again. . . . I like to think of my work as a garden with some things newly sown, some germinating, some which need to be weeded or pruned, and some ready to harvest."

OTHER SOURCES TO EXPLORE

PRIMARY

Poetry: *Windfall: New and Selected Poems* (2000), *A Space Filled with Moving* (1992), *Cold Comfort* (1986), *Years That Answer* (1980). **Autobiographical essay:** "The Mountains Dark and Close Around Me," in *Bloodroot* (1998), ed. Joyce Dyer, 32–39. "Comments," in *Her Words* (2002), ed. Felicia Mitchell, 10–16.

SECONDARY

George Brosi, "New Appalachian Books," *Appalachian Heritage* 15:3 (summer 1987), 91. Catherine Daly, review of *Windfall*, *Valparaiso Poetry Review* (30 September 2002), http://www.valpo.edu/english/vpr/dalyreviewanderson.html. Joyce Dyer, "Maggie Anderson," in *Bloodroot*, 31. Ellesa Clay High, "Maggie Anderson: Two Languages," in *Her Words* (2002), ed. Felicia Mitchell, 3–9. Jane Wilson Joyce, review of *Cold Comfort*, *Appalachian Heritage* 15:1 (winter 1987), 63–67. Gerry LaFemina, review of *Windfall*, *Poetry International* 5 (2001), 184–88. George Ella Lyon, review of *Years That Answer*, *Appalachian Journal* 8:3 (spring 1981), 217–20. Sandra Meek, "Poetry from the Pitt Poetry Series: Connie Voisine, Daisy Fried, Maggie Anderson, and Robin Becker," *Arts & Letters: Journal of Contemporary Culture* 5 (spring 2001), 205–15. Edwina Pendarvis, review of *Windfall*, *Journal of Appalachian Studies* 17:1 (spring 2001), 153–54.

ONTOLOGICAL

from *Windfall: New and Selected Poems* (2000)

This is going to cost you.
If you really want to hear a
country fiddle, you have to listen
hard, high up in its twang and needle.
You can't be running off like this,
all knotted up with yearning,
following some train whistle,
can't hang onto anything that way.
When you're looking for what's lost
everything's a sign,
but you have to stay right up next to
the drawl and pull of the thing
you thought you wanted, had to
have it, could not live without it.
Honey, you will lose your beauty
and your handsome sweetie, this whine,
this agitation, the one you sent for
with your leather boots and your guitar.
The lonesome snag of barbed wire you have
wrapped around your heart is cash money,
honey, you will have to pay.

Poet's note: "Ontological" adapts the phrase ". . . when you go looking for what is lost, everything is a sign" from Eudora Welty's story "The Wide Net."

LONG STORY

from *Windfall: New and Selected Poems* (2000)

> To speak in a flat voice
> Is all that I can do.
>
> —James Wright, "Speak"

I need to tell you that I live in a small town
in West Virginia you would not know about.
It is one of the places I think of as home.
When I go for a walk, I take my basset hound
whose sad eyes and ungainliness always draw
a crowd of children. She tolerates anything
that seems to be affection, so she lets the kids
put scarves and ski caps on her head
until she starts to resemble the women who have to dress
from rummage sales in poverty's mismatched polyester.

The dog and I trail the creek bank with the kids,
past clapboard row houses with Christmas seals
pasted to the windows as a decoration.
Inside, television glows around the vinyl chairs
and curled linoleum, and we watch someone old
perambulating to the kitchen on a shiny walker.
Up the hill in town, two stores have been
boarded up beside the youth center and miners
with amputated limbs are loitering outside
the Heart and Hand. They wear Cat diesel caps
and spit into the street. The wind
carries on, whining through the alleys,
rustling down the sidewalks, agitating
leaves, and circling the courthouse steps
past the toothless Field sisters who lean
against the flagpole holding paper bags
of chestnuts they bring to town to sell.

History is one long story of what happened to us,
and its rhythms are local dialect and anecdote.

In West Virginia a good story takes awhile,
and if it has people in it, you have to swear
that it is true. I tell the kids the one about
my Uncle Craig who saw the mountain move
so quickly and so certainly it made the sun
stand in a different aspect to his little town
until it rearranged itself and settled down again.
This was his favorite story. When he got old,
he mixed it up with baseball games, his shift boss
pushing scabs through a picket line, the Masons
in white aprons at a funeral, but he remembered
everything that ever happened, and he knew how far
he lived from anywhere you would have heard of.

Anything that happens here has a lot of versions,
how to get from here to Logan twenty different ways.
The kids tell me convoluted country stories
full of snuff and bracken, about how long
they sat quiet in the deer blind with their fathers
waiting for the ten-point buck that got away.
They like to talk about the weather,
how the wind we're walking in means rain,
how the flood pushed cattle fifteen miles downriver.

These kids know mines like they know hound dogs
and how the sirens blow when something's wrong.
They know the blast, and the stories, how
the grown-ups drop whatever they are doing
to get out there. Story is shaped
by sound, and it structures what we know.
They told me this, and three of them
swore it was true, so I'll tell you
even though I know you do not know
this place, or how tight and dark the hills
pull in around the river and the railroad.

I'll say it as the children spoke it,
in the flat voice of my people:
down in Boone County, they sealed up
forty miners in a fire. The men who had come

to help tried and tried to get down to them,
but it was a big fire and there was danger,
so they had to turn around
and shovel them back in. All night long
they stood outside with useless picks and axes
in their hands, just staring at the drift mouth.
Here's the thing: what the sound must have been,
all those fire trucks and ambulances, the sirens,
and the women crying and screaming out
the names of their buried ones, who must have
called back up to them from deep inside
the burning mountain, right up to the end.

SONNET FOR HER LABOR

from *Windfall: New and Selected Poems* (2000)

My Aunt Nita's kitchen was immaculate and dark,
and she was always bending to the sink
below the window where the shadows off the bulk
of Laurel Mountain rose up to the brink
of all the sky she saw from there. She clattered
pots on countertops wiped clean of coal dust,
fixed three meals a day, fried meat, mixed batter
for buckwheat cakes, hauled water, in what seemed lust
for labor. One March evening, after cleaning,
she lay down to rest and died. I can see Uncle Ed,
his fingers twined at his plate for the blessing;
my Uncle Craig leaning back, silent in red
galluses. No one said a word to her. All that food
and cleanliness. No one ever told her it was good.

A PLACE WITH PROMISE

from *A Space Filled with Moving* (1992)

Sometimes my affection for this place wavers.
I am poised between a vague ambition
and loyalty to what I've always loved,
kedged along inside my slow boat
by warp and anchor drag. But if I imagine
seeing this for the last time,
this scruff of the borders of West Virginia,
Pennsylvania, and Ohio, shaped by hills
and rivers, by poverty and coal,
then I think I could not bear to go,
would grab any stump or tree limb
and hold on for dear life.

I keep trying to say what I notice here
that's beautiful. There's the evening star
riding the purple selvage of the ridges,
and the flat shine of the Ohio where men
in folding chairs cast their lines out
toward the backwash of the barges.
There are the river names: the Allegheny,
the Monongahela, and the names of the tributaries,
Fish Creek, Little Beaver; the towns named
for function, Bridgeport, Martins Ferry,
or for what the early settlers must have
dreamed of, Prosperity and Amity.

Why can't we hold this landscape in our arms?
The nettle-tangled orchards given up on,
the broken fence posts with their tags
of wire, burdock taking over uncut fields,
the rusted tipples and the mills.
Sometimes I think it's possible
to wash the slag dust from the leaves
of sycamores and make them green, the way
as a child, after lesson and punishment,

I used to begin my life again.
I'd say a little "start" to myself
like the referees at races, then
on the same old scratchy car seat,
with the same parents on the same road,
I could live beyond damage and reproach,
in a place with such promise,
like any of the small farms among the wooded hills,
like any of the small towns starting up along the rivers.

$\mathcal{A}$NNE $\mathcal{W}.$ $\mathcal{A}$RMSTRONG
(September 20, 1872–March 17, 1958)

Born in Grand Rapids, Michigan, Anne Wetzell Armstrong was the daughter of Lorinda Snyder Wetzell and Henry B. Wetzell. She moved with her family to Knoxville, Tennessee, when she was a girl. Having spent part of her youth as her father's hiking partner in the mountains of Tennessee, North Carolina, and Kentucky, she returned to these mountains throughout her life, finally retiring to Sullivan County, in upper East Tennessee where she wrote her best-known novel, *This Day and Time.*

Educated at Mt. Holyoke College and the University of Chicago, Armstrong spent part of her life blazing trails as a businesswoman. After holding management positions with the National City Company on Wall Street (1918–1919) and Eastman Kodak Company in Rochester (1919–1923), she became the first woman to lecture before the Tuck School of Business at Dartmouth and at the Harvard School of Business Administration. She wrote of her business experiences in a number of articles for *Atlantic Monthly, Harper's Monthly, Forbes, New Republic,* and published other works in *Saturday Review of Literature* and *Yale Review.*

She knew fiction writers Thomas Wolfe and Sherwood Anderson and began her own writing career with a novel, *The Seas of God,* in which she used Knoxville as a setting. An unpublished manuscript titled "Of Time and Knoxville, Fragment of an Autobiography" focuses on her memories of growing up in Knoxville from 1885 to 1902. This manuscript of more than 350 pages is located in the Archives of Appalachia at East Tennessee State University.

Though she received little recognition as a novelist, *This Day and Time,* set in upper East Tennessee in the 1920s, preserves the mountain culture that has virtually disappeared with the industrialization of the region. Her central character, Ivy Ingoldsby, a single mother, ultimately rejects dehu-

manizing factory work and returns to the family farm in an effort to find a
better life for herself and her son, Enoch.

This excerpt from chapter 3 recounts Ivy's courtship and marriage, along
with her struggles to make a living in town.

OTHER SOURCES TO EXPLORE

PRIMARY

Novels: *This Day and Time* (1930), *The Seas of God* (1915). **Essays:** "As I Saw
Thomas Wolfe," *Arizona Quarterly* 2:1 (spring 1946), 5–15. "The Southern Moun-
taineers," *Yale Review* 24 (March 1938), 539–54. "Have Women Changed Busi-
ness," *Harper's Monthly* 158 (December 1928), 10–16. "Are Business Women Getting
a Square Deal?" *Atlantic Monthly* 140:1 (July 1927), 28–36. "Fear In Business Life,"
Harper's Monthly 154 (April 1927), 607–14. "Seven Deadly Sins Of Woman In
Business" *Harper's Monthly* 153 (August 1926), 295–303. "A Woman In Wall Street
By One," *Atlantic Monthly* 136:2 (August 1925), 145–58. **Autobiographical essay:**
"The Banner House," *Yale Review* 27 (March 1938), 587–600.

SECONDARY

David McClellan, "A Note on the Life and Works of Anne W. Armstrong" and "A
Personal Reminiscence," in *This Day and Time* (reprint, 1970), ix–xvii. Danny L.
Miller, "Mountain Gloom in the Works of Edith Summers Kelley and Anne W.
Armstrong," in *Wingless Flights: Appalachian Women in Fiction* (1996), 53–68.

THIS DAY AND TIME (1930)
from Chapter Three

As she lay beside Enoch [Ivy's son] on the pallet, huddled close to him for warmth, Ivy tried to stop thinking, but the old question was again hammering in her brain: "Why did Jim leave me? Oh, Lord God, why did he do me that-a-way?"

Her childhood came back to her, the cabin, far from any others, in Rocky Hollow where she had been born, the seventh of twelve—born when laurel was in flower, so that her mother had named her for the rosy cloud of bloom she had looked out on through the little window beside her bed; for the "ivy" that came each May to lighten the deep shadows of Rocky Hollow—ivy, the first thing her mother's tired eyes had rested upon after the granny-woman had lifted her head from lower down the bed. "Hit's a gal, Mis' Buckles, another fine little gal!"

Ivy's thoughts dwelt softly on her mother, a kindly, dragged-out woman, often sick, but always struggling for a semblance of decency and order in the swarming cabin. Her mother would plant a few flower seeds every spring, zinnias or marigolds, touch-me-nots, and bleeding-hearts. "Seems like," she could hear her mother saying, "flowers keeps a body from bein' so lonesome." Ivy could see her mother squatting beside the branch that tumbled down past the cabin, straightening her back from time to time, trying to get enough clean clothes together so that some of the children could go to Sunday-school two or three times at least in the course of the year.

Ivy remembered the daily squabbles; remembered a brother killed by a falling tree; a little sister burned to death, little Dee, left alone in the cabin and trying to start a fire as she had seen the older ones do, by pouring oil on the green wood. She could still hear the screams of little Dee, a sheet of flame, running frantically towards the field where the rest of them were dropping corn. She could see herself on one of the steep slopes that wedged in Rocky Hollow, grubbing sprouts on a piece of "new ground"; she could see a stranger passing up the hollow and all of them stopping, her father and mother too, resting on their hoes or mattocks, staring after the stranger to whom her father had called down a low half-hostile "Howdy." Ivy could scarcely remember a time when she had not handled a hoe.

There were moments of delight Ivy remembered of her childhood; the time she had uncovered the pheasant's nest in the leaves; the little terrapin she had made a pet of; the Indian arrow-heads she had turned up with her hoe; times she had played house under a great sycamore that overspread the log spring-house, with acorn-cups for dishes, with tufts of moss, bits of broken crockery. Her childhood, when she thought of it, did not seem to her to have been an unhappy one. Her father, if high-tempered, had not been brutal, or only occasionally, when he was drunk and might beat her mother or kick one of the boys. There had been the fun of going up on the mountain every summer for huckleberries—the whole troop of them, and other families too—the fun of going down the river each spring to the sugar-orchard, sleeping in the sheds left there from year to year among the sugar-maples.

Then her mother had died, leaving her, the oldest girl at home, to mother the family till her father had married again, within the year. Then, in the spring that followed, back at the sugar-orchard, all of them helping make sugar and syrup again, and people coming to trade with her father for the thin sappy syrup, carrying it away in the buckets they had brought.

And then one day, as she had been carrying a bucket of sap to the fire, a young man standing in her path, teasingly, as if to block the way; a tall, straight, very clean young man, with very short hair, in soldier clothes, and the young man laughing: "Don't be scared! You've growed a right smart since the time I saw you last, at the burying-ground, when they put your Grandpap Buckles away. Well, you ain't gettin' any worse-lookin', I'll swear you ain't!" and then Jim laughing again—Jim was always laughing—"Ivy, I swore to Gawd, first time I ever laid eyes on you, I'd come and steal you some day!"

And then Jim and her "a-talkin'," while the sugaring went on, and Jim helping her as she trudged to and from the fire, or to and from the spring, some distance away. And then a dusk when Jim had caught her and kissed her.

She liked to dwell on the memory of Jim's going to town and bringing her back a pair of slippers, the first she had ever owned, town slippers to replace the clumsy outgrown shoes of her brothers which she had worn before, when she had worn any at all. She saw Jim and herself standing up before the preacher in the sugar-orchard, "of a Sabbath, the prettiest day hit were." She could recall in sharp detail the look and feel of that day, bluets twinkling up from the turf under their feet—those wee "forget-me-nots" her mother had loved—the mountains blue-black, ragged fringes of snowy cloud half hiding their tops; and a red-bird, like a drop of blood, against the bare ghostly branches of a giant sycamore on the river-bank, the red-bird whistling its throat out from the topmost branch of the sycamore.

She could still see Jim's father, Uncle Jake, hobbling down the steps to meet them, his unsmiling deep-plowed face, his faded and patched overalls hanging loosely on his once powerful figure— her and Jim coming through the gate at sundown, Jim laughing, his head high, her own cheeks burning. She had wanted to hide, to streak away like a rabbit when the dogs were after it. . . . She could still hear Uncle Jake's harsh grating voice: "Proud to know ye, Ivy. I know your pap. Me an' him was raised up together." And then Aunt Jane, bleached and gentle, in her clean gray print, shyly, from the doorway: "I reckon you're plumb beat out, Ivy, honey. Hit's a right smart piece from the sugar grove."

She could still see Uncle Jake's and Aunt Jane's cabin as it had first looked to her—the two beds, in opposite corners, the few straight splint-bottom chairs, the wide boards of the floor white as she had never seen before; white spreads on the beds; a clock. Not ten miles from Rocky Hollow, but a strange new world. Someone passing every day, up or down the road; people to shout to and who shouted down to them: "How air ye? How air you-all? Reckon hit'ull fair off?" Other cabins; Big Bill Byrd's down below, on the river; Doke Odum's on down the road; and up it, hardly more than half a mile in the opposite direction, the Philipses'.

Ivy liked to dwell on the memory of Jim's going to town and bringing her home a pink chambray dress and some pretty chemises. Jim was "free-hearted." Jim had money saved from his three years in the army; he had bought a cow and two shotes. Days of plenty. Jim had made the crop by himself. "Pap, you ain't a-goin' to raw-hide these here knobs whilst I'm here. Ivy, do you guess I'm goin' to have *my* woman workin' in the sun? Well, you've got another guess." Days of plenty—sweet milk every day, and butter on the table.

Then winter. Jim walking back and forth to town, twenty miles away, for something to do. Jim's money all spent. Jim sitting by the hearth day after day, smoking cigarettes, getting up to stretch himself now and then, yawning. Uneasy days. And then Jim going off to a logging camp, coming home every week or so with a sack of flour over his shoulder, shoes for Ivy and his mother. Jim laughing again, but talking, while at home, of the army, not such a bad life for a man. "A sight easier 'an loggin', or tryin' to grub a livin' off o' these here worn-out old knobs." Not a bad life, pool, movies—something to do of an evening.

And then bluets twinkling up from the grass again, red-birds whistling from the sycamores. Jim restless again. He had "quit off loggin'." He would look for a job in town. Maybe he would rent a house there, take them all into town to live; no more grubbing. And Ivy whispering to him at the gate: "Could you git me a few yards of nice domestic, Jim, ef your money holds out? An' some pretty soft flannel-cloth or like o' that? Reckon you know what I want 'em fer. I'll be down afore long."

And then a package coming in the mail; some little dresses, a hood, and a white coat, embroidered, everything very fine. But no word. Days of looking and waiting, the days lengthening out to months, the months to years.

. . .

At last, after four years of this struggle, after months of thinking of little else, Ivy had decided on the move to town. . . .

. . .

. . . Before, much of her work had been done outdoors and no two days had been alike. Now, all day long feeding a pair of overalls through a machine, with a dusty window beyond the machine, and through it, if she had looked off her work, a brick wall across an alley, and other dusty windows facing her.

If she had worked hard before, she had stopped to visit with anyone who passed. In the factory, at first, Ivy had stopped to talk to one girl after another along the row of machines where her own was, but they had been quick to warn: "Watch out, forelady's lookin'!" They had been anxious to resume their stitching of pockets and leg seams, and Martha had told her frankly: "You can't never in God's world make it at piece-work, Ivy, if you stop to talk," adding: "Don't none of 'em like to be stopped, Ivy. A body cools off like, when they stop, and it takes a right smart time, *you* know, till they can get up their speed again." Later Martha had cautioned: "Law, Ivy, you got to do more dozens a day 'an that, to live in town."

Ivy herself had begun to long with the whole strength of her being to return to the place whence she had come. Her thoughts had gone back to a hawk that Doke Odum had caught once in a trap and, chained to a stick, brought to show her and Enoch. She remembered the look of fear and anxiety in the hawk's eyes, the hawk's thrusting its head suddenly forward, looking off towards the mountains with its wide-apart far-seeing eyes. Ivy imagined she was the hawk. Following a line of white stitching across blue denim hour after hour, day after day, the eyes of her mind had always been looking far off, to the mountains—those mountains to which, like the hawk, she belonged. . . .

ℋARRIETTE ℐIMPSON ℛRNOW
(July 7, 1908–March 22, 1986)

Harriette Simpson Arnow, the second oldest child of six, grew up in the south-central Kentucky town of Burnside, located on the South Fork of the Cumberland River. Her mother, Molly Denney Simpson, and her father, Elias Simpson, had both been schoolteachers before their marriage, and her mother wanted her daughters also to become teachers.

After graduating from Burnside High School in 1924, Arnow attended Berea College in Kentucky (1924–26) and earned her teaching certificate. She then began a job as the teacher of a one-room school in Pulaski County, Kentucky. While there, she took a correspondence course, the only creative writing class she ever had. From childhood, Arnow wanted to be a writer.

When she had enough money to return to school, she enrolled in the University of Louisville and soon graduated with a B.S. in education. She taught again near her hometown and in Louisville before abandoning the profession, declaring that she would "rather starve as a writer than as a teacher."

In 1934, she moved to Cincinnati, Ohio, where she worked a number of "day jobs"—waitress, typist, and clerk—that allowed her to devote much of her time to writing. Her first short stories and her first novel, *Mountain Path*, were published to favorable reviews. While working on a Works Progress Administration (WPA) historical guidebook, she met Harold Arnow, a Chicago journalist whom she married in 1939.

The couple shared a dream of owning a farm and bought land in Keno, Kentucky, where they lived from 1939 to 1944. Three of their four children were born there, although a son and daughter died as infants.

Arnow continued to write, and the family moved to Detroit's wartime housing in 1944. As she completed *Hunter's Horn,* her life in Detroit offered ideas for her classic novel of the Appalachian migration experience, *The*

Dollmaker. After World War II, the Arnows bought a home in Ann Arbor, where they lived for the rest of their lives.

Her second and third novels were best-sellers; each was nominated for the National Book Award. She received awards for her fiction and nonfiction from the Friends of American Writers (1955) and the American Association for State and Local History (1961), as well as honorary degrees from Albion College (Michigan, 1955), Transylvania University (Kentucky, 1979), and the University of Kentucky (1981). The Margaret King Library of the University of Kentucky preserves her manuscripts and papers in its Arrow Special Collection.

Arnow's fiction treats mountain people with notable authenticity, creating particularly complex and resilient characters. The excerpt from chapter 21 of *Hunter's Horn* focuses on Milly Ballew, pregnant for the eighth time and worried about her children and her husband, Nunn, a foxhunter obsessed with catching an elusive, destructive fox he's named King Devil. Their daughter, Suse, and neighbor, Lureenie, long to leave the Kentucky hills.

The excerpt from Arnow's social history book, *Seedtime on the Cumberland,* reveals her fascination and personal connections with Appalachian history.

The short story "The First Ride" takes the reader along in a pregnant woman's fevered dream.

OTHER SOURCES TO EXPLORE

PRIMARY

Novels: *Between the Flowers* (1999), *The Kentucky Trace* (1974), *Weedkiller's Daughter* (1970), *The Dollmaker* (1954), *Hunter's Horn* (1949), *Mountain Path* (1936). **Nonfiction:** *Old Burnside* (1977), *Flowering of the Cumberland* (1963), *Seedtime on the Cumberland* (1960).

SECONDARY

Hacja K. Chung, cd. *Harriette Simpson Arnow: Critical Essays on Her Work* (1995). Wilton Eckley, *Harriette Arnow* (1974). Glenda Hobbs, "Harriette Simpson Arnow," *American Novelists Since World War II: Dictionary of Literary Biography* (1980), Vol. 6, ed. James E. Kibler, Jr. 3–8. Alex Kotlowitz, "At 75, Full Speed Ahead," *Detroit News* (4 December 1983), 14+.

HUNTER'S HORN (1949)

from Chapter 21

By December, Milly was slow in all her movements, her days long reaches of time that somehow must be got through, with work done in spite of backache and toothache, puffed feet and hands, and the bigness of her body that seemed to hinder her in all things, be it sweeping under the stove or squatting to milk Betsey. But no matter how slowly she might walk to the spring or the milking or on other outdoor errands, the pups followed at her heels, matching their swift pace to her slow one, sometimes running round and round her, but never leaping on her as from sheer exuberance they sometimes jumped on Nunn and the children. And she would smile on them and know they understood how things were with her better than any of her human family; and with her own feet slow and heavy, she would joy in their swiftness, think how good it was that something on this earth could run light-footed and free, running freest and fastest and gayest when it did what God had meant it to do—hunt.

She wished she could be certain that catching King Devil was God's will for Nunn; more and more as he hunted alone through the fall it seemed as if he went against all things: his own body that needed sleep, the weather, the opinion of the neighbors, and God's will. Often in the black time before dawn, when he was not yet home, she would sit shivering by the fire, or move from first one window to the other, listening, staring out into the dark or the cloudy moonlight. Suse would awaken and come to her and say, "Your back hurten you bad, Mom? Could I rub it?"

She would shake her head and tell Suse to go back to bed, but Suse would linger with her by the fire, studying her sometimes with big sorrowful eyes, full of a pity and an understanding that Milly would as lief not have had from her own child. Suse knew it wasn't her back that drove her to walk the floor in misery.

All the warnings and portents of the year would come back into her mind: in October a bird flew into an upstairs room, and a bird in the house was a certain sign of death; last fall, in potato-digging time, Lee Roy had brought a hoe into the house, and that was a sign of trouble; the last two new moons she had first seen barred by the leafless branches of the walnut tree; Deb's tizic tree had done but poorly in the hot dry summer, and now he was taller than the measure of his head last year—that could mean he was going to die, outgrowing his tree like that; worse than anything was the memory of

Sue Annie's face, witchlike and full of mysteries, as she nodded her white-turbaned head and declared that King Devil would never be taken until he had had man blood; oh, he wouldn't kill the man himself; he'd never killed a hound, but many was the one he'd led to its death, and he'd never be satisfied till he had led a man to his death.

And Milly, remembering, would shiver and think of all the ways a man could die: pneumonia fever in the cold damp weather, the cliffs where a man numb with cold or not too wide-awake could, with one false step in the dark, kill himself. On and on her mind would go, until all the future was a black burden in her heart and on her head.

And Suse would watch her mother and envy Lureenie, who was going to a place where men never hunted and women had doctors in childbirth.

But it was near mid-December before Lureenie came running home from the mail, laughing and chattering, her arms spilling packages and a letter from [her husband] Rans clutched in one hand. "I can go now," she cried, and her voice was thin and breaking, as if she were ready to cry. "Rans sent me a money order big enough to come on, an the youngens' coats has come."

She was suddenly silent, looking around the kitchen, the Montgomery Ward package forgotten in her arms; her glance wandered through the window to the hills across the creek, their pine- and cedar-covered slopes gray-black in the dusk. She drew a long sigh and said with a slow shake of her head, "It's th onliest thing I've ever wanted that's come to pass—gitten away. I cain't believe it yit. It's like I was dreamen that in two, three days I'll be in a place where I can see people, hear em talk; th nights won't be so still—I hate th pines at dusty dark an on windy nights, an I'm sick a th hills around th house, shutten out th sun—an all th light I want at night—it's so dark in that house, an so still since—"

She stopped, ashamed even now to give herself away, as if she knew that Milly and others of the neighbor women had pitied her, off by herself like that, with no man person on the long dark nights of the fall.

Suse, too, looked out the window at the hillside; she liked to look at the hill; like the rest of the woods, it was for her full of more change and excitement than any other part of her life; it was fun in spring to leave the corn planting and hunt flowers in the woods or wild greens by the river, and the long grape hunts in the fall—a sudden and unreasoning fear of the future filled her for an instant with a painful doubt.

It was hard enough to be a girl child shut off from the world. How would it be to be a woman like Lureenie, married with little youngens, but wanting still the outside world, tied down to a house and youngens, with one baby in your arms and another big in your belly like Milly—and always the knowing that you could never get away until you were dead?

She shrugged her shoulders and smiled at the hill as the strong smile at the threats of the weak; she wouldn't be like Milly and she wouldn't be like Lureenie; she'd make her own life; it wouldn't make her.

FROM *SEEDTIME ON THE CUMBERLAND* (1960)

Times and places were mingled in my head; the past was part of the present, close as the red cedar water bucket in the kitchen, or the big cherry press put together with pegs, or the parched corn a grandmother now and then made for us. This was the same as the parched corn from the old days, or the cornmeal mush we sometimes ate, no different at all from the mush in the stories. An old shirt in a trunk upstairs, square-armholed, stitched by hand, of cotton grown and woven and spun on the Big South Fork of the Cumberland, could have been the same as that worn by some old granpa with many greats before his name. My people loved the past more than their present lives, I think, but it cannot be said we lived in the past. Two things tied all time together; these had run through most of the old stories to shape the lives of men, and so did they shape our lives and the lives of the people about us. These were the land and the Cumberland.

There was at the head of our stairs a window; and always at night, no matter what the weather, I pulled the curtain; and if I carried a lamp, I pushed my face close against the glass to shut out the light in order the better to see. Many times during the day just passed I would have seen the same thing, but still I looked. Our house rose gaunt and white and high on the western side of a hill above the Cumberland; east were the hills and from our eastern windows we could see nothing save our own hill rising, but west past the river lay a wide sweep of hilly to gently rolling country. The Highland Rim it is called in Tennessee, Pennyrile in Kentucky, and a kind of no man's land between the Bluegrass and the Cumberland Plateau or hills.

Living so at the meeting place of Highland Rim and hill was like having a prize seat in some vast amphitheatre. We could, on fair days or on the white moonlit nights of winter, see for miles and miles across the old high valley of the Cumberland, and past this rows of low hills until earth and sky met in a dark nothingness. Northward we could see at night the lights from the county seat town of Somerset; nearby was Ferguson with its railroad shops and roundhouse where the big double headers were hooked up for the long pull over the mountains and into Tennessee. South and west all set about in the dark, so dim at times there was wonder if it be light or low star, were the lighted windows of farm homes, many at that time yellow-gleaming from coal oil lamps, for electric lights like many other things, including roads, were slow in coming to our part of the country.

Closer, were the brighter lights of Burnside that, after pausing on a narrow bench of level land at the point where the Big South Fork met the Cumberland, rose step-like over limestone bluffs and ledges to a hilly bench of higher land where the churches, the school and most of the homes, all painted white, were gathered. Even in its boom days during my early childhood when all the business life of the town was gathered in the lowland by the river, the place had hardly more than a thousand people; but in it were five churches, five lumber mills, several stores, a Masonic Temple, the brick building housing both elementary and high schools, a bank, and a frame hotel with more than seven gables.

I remember the mules pulling the heavily loaded wagons up from the ferry or the steamboat landing. I remember the stagecoach that ran between Burnside and Monticello until 1915; and all about me were people like my grandmothers and Cousin Dora Taylor who remembered well the days before the coming of the railroad in '78 when the Cumberland was the only highway, and most things from pianos to candy came from Nashville.

There was a varied life in the town, though many now would make of us all one, for all of us were native born, white, and Protestant when we got religion. I do recall that once I heard talk of a foreigner. He dealt in meat, and his speech was strange; worse, nobody had so much as seen his father, or even knew where he had been born—Cincinnati some said. In any case he was not one of our people. There were others not of us exactly—some of the mill owners and managers, but they had been there many years; every one knew from where they came and they had relatives.

The scarcity of nearby relatives troubled me at times as a child, and often I felt a stranger there, though I can recall no one unknown to me as I went about the innumerable family errands. There was in the town a good handful of people, including teachers in school and Sunday school, to be cousined. Still, we were strangers; many of our classmates such as the Newells and the Richardsons lived on land heired down from first settlers who had come at the close of the Revolution.

I could not from the window see even the lights of our country—a part of the adjoining county of Wayne, hidden behind hills to the south; for we were hill people. I had been born there, the fifth of most of my generations, and it was from Wayne that most of the stories came. No horses of my childhood could ever be so fine as the five-gaited saddle horses that took prizes at the Wayne County Fair, nor mules so strong and sleek and black and big, hickories so straight and tall, nor Teachers' Institutes so filled with romance and leg o' mutton sleeves. I knew the big hickories were gone like the chestnut oak, skinned for its tanbark and left to die; the big chestnuts were dying with blight, oxen were seldom seen, metheglin never brewed at all any more, and most of our kin were gone away.

Still, it was there, a place in the geography of time, built on the same things that shaped our lives—the land and the river. Everybody owned at least a little land, and the expression "land poor" was common. Many families of the town had at least a vegetable garden and a family cow, daily twice-driven to and from some pasture field nearby. "He comes of good farming stock," was enough said of the birthright of a man, and earthly dreams were not of mink coats and Cadillacs or of vice-presidencies in great industrial establishments, but to own a good farm with a big stretch of bottom land and a fair boundary of timber.

THE FIRST RIDE (1989)

Note: This story was written in the late 1930s and posthumously published in *Appalachian Heritage*.

She heard her mother's voice hoarse, with fright pressing it into a flat stream of sound, "You'll have to hurry." And then her husband's call, "I've fin'ly got him saddled," while Rebel the big gray stallion neighed and pawed by the porch steps as if he too knew the joy of the long wild ride that lay ahead. Her husband came to the door, and her father turned slowly away and then back to her so that she saw his old face, puckered into pale lines of fright and sorrow. She smiled at him and saw thoughts written into his eyes plain like words. He was loath to have her go and feared for her the long ride. She laughed to show him that she was not afraid, but her tongue seemed heavy and useless for words so that she made them no answer as she galloped away.

Behind her she heard their calling and the crying of the child. She did not turn her head or hesitate. Her name on their tongues was enough; they wished to advise her thus and so and warn her of this and that and maybe tell her again of the need for haste. Soon the wind had blown their cries away, and the road, white sand on the ridge crest now, ran smooth and straight between the black trunks of the high pine trees whose deep moon shadows lay like black bars across the silver of the sand.

She raised one hand and half rose in the stirrups and pretended to snatch at a twig on a black gum tree as they flew past, and dropped again to the saddle and laughed to herself as the wind quickened about her ears and raised her hair like the horse's mane. That was the way to make Rebel fly, Luke her brother had once said. She too had wanted to make Rebel fly, but her mother would never let her ride as she had always wanted to ride; her mother lived for the neighbors and God. The neighbors and God, but tonight she could laugh at the neighbors and God. This night was not like other nights, there was the road and the moon and the wind and the ever-quickening need for haste. She thanked the woman sick and about to die who gave the reason for this ride, and sorrow for the woman lay vague and weightless in the back of her mind behind the half-believing wonder that it was she who rode so, riding as she had always wanted to ride, with trust for her body in the horse's feet, and her soul flung to the moon or maybe to the wind. Tonight the wind came neither west nor south, but out of the neverland that lay between and held the freedom and strength of the west and the lazy whispering laughter of the south. The wind was the smell of spring with lark-spur and wild roses by the creek and the clover in the hill field and the pine scent sharp through the sweetness, and over it all was the sound of the great trees on Fiddle Bow Mountain and the willows by Laurel Run and the simple wail of hills against the beating, rushing waves of air.

The big horse went like a brother of the wind and seemed to know the need that made her drive him so. He went like a horse undriven, like a horse of God with wings and a dragon for his heart. He did not pause when the road curved and swooped down a hill, black in the shadow with white rocks glimmering and sparks from his iron shoes rising and dying like hasty fire-flies. She laughed as they went sliding down into deeper darkness, and knew that she could go there and home again in time. The woman would not die, and she would have this ride, wild and heedless and free as she had always wanted.

She laughed to think she was a woman now with heedless ways and causeless, senseless laughter gone behind her. In the last spring, early when the first wild iris came and she was sixteen, she had married Rufe, and her mother had said, "He'll keep you straight," and her father had said, "It's better that you marry now and never give the neighbors cause to talk," and Rufe had said, "You'll never go hungry."

Rebel was by the creek now, and did not pause to sniff the water, but plunged right in and where his feet struck, the water rose in a flowering spray that stood for a moment clear of the shadow until it seemed that when it fell silver had touched her hair. The creek was deep but clear and the gray horse swam and she trailed her fingers by his side and watched the fan-shaped ripples grow and fade. They crossed the creek and Rebel arched his neck and tossed his head and neighed and snorted with a great trumpeting and flung the water from his sides, and leaped away up the hill and under the beech trees and past the place where the sweet william grew. Their odor rose and mingled with the wind and she thought that some time she might return this way and walk all day on the hill and see the flowers and maybe pick a few to carry home; no, not home; Rufe did not like flowers. Better that a woman spend her time in the garden than with the foolishness of flowers.

They came to a level rutted road with a zigzag rail fence on one side and a rolling pasture field beyond. She saw the field open and wide and inviting with the high grass bowing and whispering in the wind. It would be the shorter way, and she wanted to ride across the field and see Rebel race against his black shadow as it flew over the grass. She drew on the bridle rein and the great horse swerved and she felt his body rise in a flying lunge, and for an instant the rail fence in its mat of persimmon bush and red thorn lay below her, and then they were over and Rebel's front feet were striking the ground and he had fallen to his knees, but he was up again and away, and she was laughing and never looking back, her body one with the horse's body that skimmed over the field lightly as foam on swirling creek water.

She dropped the rein across the saddle and gave the horse his head and looked up at the moon that seemed to ride across the cloud-flecked sky in the same glory of reckless joy with which she rode the field. She remembered the woman sick and like to die, and sorrow for the woman sharpened her own joy in the world. Tonight she thought that she loved the moon and the wind-torn feathers of cloud more than yesterday or any of the days before yesterday; though always she had loved light and darkness and rain and sun and snow and the red leaf-whispering dawns of autumn and the half-sad half-sweet twilights of spring when the whippoorwills began their plaintive callings and the short gray days of winter with the hills secret and shut into themselves against the shrieking, clawing wild beast of the wind. But tonight the world seemed even better and more worthy of her love.

On one side of the hill pasture lay a field of knee-high corn, the freshly plowed dark earth glistening with drops of dew, fine like seed pearls she had read about in school. She smelled the earth and the sweetish smell of the growing corn and loved that too, even as she remembered that sometime, once a long while ago in some vague, formless past when she was heavy and tired from the work she did in the corn rows and some great weight that had pulled against her back and pressed against her heart, the smell of the corn had sickened her nigh unto death it seemed and she had hated the corn and the earth and cried out against them. She bent low over Rebel's flying shoulders and felt a shame and a wonder at the memory, and joy in the lightness of her body and the goodness of the world made her wish to ask forgiveness of something for that faint memory of hatred and pain.

They crossed the pasture and she saw the dark woodland sloping away over the hill down into a narrow valley and up another hill, and past that hill she could see nothing, for it was higher than all the other hills, so high it was like a mountain with its crest hidden in shifting shimmering fog. That, she knew, was where she must go, and by the length of Rebel's flying shadow she knew that she had not been long on the road and would be there on time.

They leaped another fence and plunged into a wood where the wind sang loud in the leafing trees with no sobbing as in the pines, and drops of dew, heavy as rain, fell from the leaves onto her face and hair. Rebel leaped a moss-grown log and leaped through a moonlit glade, cleared a low limestone crag, and plunged again into the deeper darkness of close-growing trees. He went less swiftly now and above the slower beat of his heavy hoofs she heard the roar of a creek and trembled with hungry eagerness for the battle with swift white water coiling in darkness and moonlight.

Heavier drops of dew fell on her face and she impatiently flung them back and glanced up to search out the mountain, for it was dark here and she feared she had lost her way. But it was there, higher and brighter and more beautiful, like the Big Rock Candy Mountain it was a sin to sing about because the singing made you want to dance. She sent Rebel crackling through a prickly grove of holly bush. The ground was soft and the horse's feet sank deep and made no sound, and it was then she heard their calling, louder and more insistent. She checked the horse and paused to think. Their call puzzled her, and she wondered that they could have followed all this way and carried the crying child. She saw them then by scarcely turning.

There was her mother with a glass of water in her hand as she stood and looked down at something that seemed to be just behind her own eyes. There was her father, and Rufe too with his muddy shoes and the overalls she had forgotten to mend. His face looked pale under the sunburn, tight and hard as if he were afraid to come farther than the door where he stood with one foot on the sill. She did not want to look at him. He seemed a man in trouble, and with the joy of the good ride still upon her she had no wish for trouble.

She looked down and saw a hand, small and thin and brown, cupped like a fallen leaf, and as she stared at the hand she wondered at the dew. There was dew on the hand just as on the corn, great drops of it shining yellow in some light that did not come from the moon. She wondered if the dew had fallen on all things and moved her eyes slowly and saw a little mound of patchwork quilt like a hill made small by distance. Her glance which seemed heavy and tired came slowly away from the hill, drew nearer and fell upon a strip of white cotton nightgown with pearl buttons winking in the light. The buttons troubled her—they were so much like some she had once had with four eyes and sewn with coarse white thread. She puzzled over the buttons and heard rain roar on the roof boards, and thought that the next creek would be yellow instead of white.

She heard Rebel's impatient angry neigh and the thud of his pawing feet against the ground. She heard the planks of the floor creak with the weight of heavy hesitating feet, but she did not lift her eyes. It was such a deal of trouble. She heard her mother cry in a thin hoarse croak, "Don't go away, Paw. It's we've waited too long," and then her father's voice, flat and unlike his own, "Yes. No man could ever a made it over th' creek anyhow."

She knew he was wrong about the creek, and hated herself for this waste of time when now they seemed so troubled by the time that had gone. Her thoughts churned in a panic of thinking that she might have lost her way and would maybe be too late. She looked again and smiled to herself for it was still there, high and wreathed in a white fire of moonlit fog. She heard the child crying in another room and Rufe's calling of her name, and there was pity in his call, something more than pity—like terror almost. She saw tears falling on the cupped leaflike hand, and then Rufe's head bent over the buttons on the nightgown. Maybe he had taken her buttons and put them on the nightgown and now was sorry and ashamed. She wanted to tell him that he could have the buttons; there were so many things out there in the night for her to love. It was all so good—she remembered the need for haste and knew that she must wait until another time. Rufe called again, and as she rode away she wondered at the pity in his call.

Sylvia Trent Auxier
(December 28, 1900–December 4, 1967)

Sylvia Trent Auxier was the eldest of sixteen children born to Dollie Blaine May Trent and T.J. Trent. She grew up in Pike County, Kentucky, attending a one-room log school. She went on to Pikeville College Academy, where she graduated at the head of her class.

She was a teacher for two years before earning an R.N. degree at the University of Cincinnati Nursing School. She began her career as a public health nurse in eastern Kentucky, traveling by horseback to patients in Pike, Knott, Perry, and Leslie counties.

In 1928, she married Jean Auxier, a lawyer, and they lived in a rustic log and stone house in Meta, Kentucky. The couple had one son.

Her family has claimed that "the first sentence she spoke was in iambic pentameter and the second rhymed with it." Long before her first book was published, her poems appeared in a number of publications, including the *Saturday Evening Post, Christian Science Monitor*, and *Progressive Farmer*. Auxier's first collection of poetry, published in 1948, was followed by five additional volumes, with the final one published posthumously by Pikeville College Press. She died near Pikeville in an automobile accident.

On the book jacket of *With Thorn and Stone*, Pulitzer Prize–winning poet Gwendolyn Brooks praised her work: "The poetry of Sylvia Auxier is sane as well as beautiful. In it are to be found balance, a tenderized exaltation, and a comprehensive clarity."

Auxier paid attention to the women in her life and to everyday activities—and she paid tribute to them in her poetry.

OTHER SOURCES TO EXPLORE

PRIMARY

Poetry: *With Thorn and Stone: New and Selected Poems* (1968), *Green of a Hundred Springs* (1966), *No Stranger to the Earth* (1957), *The Grace of the Bough* (1957), *Love-Vine* (1953), *Meadow-Rue* (1948).

SECONDARY

Dorothy Edwards Townsend, *Kentucky in American Letters*, Vol. 3 (1976), 21–24.
William S. Ward, *A Literary History of Kentucky* (1988), 344–45.

Neighbors

from *With Thorn and Stone:*
New and Selected Poems (1968)

They saw her walk a quiet way
Of household tasks from day to day;

They saw her tend her flower plots
Bordered with blue forget-me-nots;

And thought that all her footsteps went
On paths of peace and deep content.

They did not know that in her heart
Were lands no human hand could chart,

An alien land; rebellion-fed,
Where wild plum blossoms rioted.

When Grandmother Wept

from *With Thorn and Stone:*
New and Selected Poems

When my grandmother wept she did not weep
Head on her folded arms, but all the while
She'd go about her work, and tears would creep
Slowly as though an inch a hard-won mile.

Their passing made no inroads on her face:
Her cheeks were smooth, the lips firm to her will;
And inked in her eyes' blackness, one could trace
The spirit yielding but unbroken still.

She spoke no word. She seemed to go away
Within herself to some deep silver well

Hewed in the granite years of yesterday,
Water of wisdom pooled in memory's spell.

From this deep well, to which each one must go
Alone . . . alone return, she came back to us then
The smile triumphant on her face—as though
Tears never were . . . would never be again.

CICADA'S SONG

from *With Thorn and Stone:*
New and Selected Poems (1968)

Above the crested waves of summer heat
Cicada's needles dart unceasingly,
Threading a strand of beaded notes complete
And sparkling as a jeweled rosary,
Along the Nile a thousand years ago,
Sifting its sands, children would stop at play
And root brown feet to hear this tremolo
Of needles clicking—as I do today.

And all who will may hold this jeweled strand
And thread the maze of vanished years to find
That always-summer, ever-childhood land
Within the meadow reaches of the mind
Where golden moments float, untold, along
Uncharted channels—timeless as this song.

SOMEDAY IN A WOOD

from *With Thorn and Stone:*
New and Selected Poems (1968)

Death never was a match for me,
So light my feet, so river-strong
My coursing blood. My enemy,
As life and I rushed on headlong,
Could only follow, dark and grim,
Because I could outdistance him.

But someday in a haunted wood
Of fog and twilight days, when Time
Has blanched my flesh and slowed my blood,
Death will outrun me on the climb.
Then I will face him, take his hand,
Murmur his name, and call him friend.

THE STAIR

from *Love-Vine* (1953)

A thousand times I've climbed this curving stair;
A thousand times, a hundred moods and more:
Climbed it in hate, in sorrow and in prayer—
The heart low kneeling, or on wings that soar.
I climbed it on my wedding day, the night
Death made his call, as though to Calvary;
And for such simple things as a better sight
Of dawn or sunset gilding earth for me.

And one would almost think this curving stair
Would show the scars, some crying evidence
Of all the hundred moods it was made to share:
Keen, piercing grief, or joy, deep and intense.
But all it shows of my life's sun and shade
Are smooth-worn treads my climbing feet have made.

MARILOU AWIAKTA
(January 24, 1936–)

A seventh-generation Appalachian native who was born in Knoxville, Tennessee, Marilou Awiakta grew up in Oak Ridge, Tennessee, with a unique heritage that places her mountain and Cherokee roots in the context of the birthplace of atomic energy. Her earliest experiences, she explains, helped her to blend her love of nature with the nuclear science of her hometown community, which was an exciting "frontier environment where anything seemed possible. . . . I could study molecules one morning and pick blackberries the next." She gives her parents credit for helping her learn to value family stories, Appalachian traditions, and classic literature. She currently makes her home in Memphis, Tennessee.

Earning her B.A. degree in French and English at the University of Tennessee in Knoxville, as well as living in France from 1964 to 1967 (where she was an interpreter and her husband, Paul Thompson, was a medical officer for the United States Air Force) honed the poet's sensitivity for language. She has been a prolific writer of poetry, fiction, and nonfiction since the early 1960s. Her prose and poetry have appeared in many magazines, literary journals, and a number of literary anthologies both in America and abroad. Awiakta has received the Distinguished Tennessee Writer Award (1989), the Award for Outstanding Contribution to Appalachian Literature (1991), the Award for Educational Service to Appalachia (1999), and the *Appalachian Heritage* Writers Award (2000). *Selu* was a 1994 Quality Paperback Book Club Selection. An audio tape of *Selu*, read by Awiakta with music by Joy Harjo, received a Grammy nomination in 1996.

She is a longtime advocate of mixing poetry, prose, music, and graphic art. As she explained in 1977, "I believe the day will come when we will simply behold a work of art and not be concerned whether it is a poem, a sculpture, a painting or even a machine, like a space rocket. Everything becomes poetry on the highest level of consciousness. And humanity may reach that level—if we don't blow ourselves up first!" Central concerns in her writing include ecology, preservation of Native American and Appalachian cultures, feminism, nuclear energy, cultural diversity, and family.

Awiakta is the author of a poetry collection and a novella. Her third book, *Selu: Seeking the Corn-Mother's Wisdom,* combines poetry and prose. Like a Cherokee basket, it weaves together history, autobiography, native legends and traditions, poetry, and themes of environmentalism, science, botany, gender issues, politics, and spirituality. Celebrating the interconnectedness of life, Awiakta advocates that readers relate the wisdoms of the Corn-Mother Selu (pronounced "say-loo") to similar wisdoms in their own cultures and return to a relationship with earth and with each other that provides more "balance and harmony" in our lives. Her book offers us "seed thoughts" for the twenty-first century.

OTHER SOURCES TO EXPLORE

PRIMARY

Novella: *Rising Fawn and the Fire Mystery* (1983). **Poetry and prose:** *Selu: Seeking the Corn-Mother's Wisdom* (1993), *Abiding Appalachia: Where Mountain and Atom Meet* (1978). **Autobiographical essay:** "Sound," in *Bloodroot* (1998), ed. Joyce Dyer, 41–51.

SECONDARY

Thomas Rain Crowe, "Marilou Awiakta," *Interviewing Appalachia* (1994), 215–35. Joyce Dyer, "Marilou Awiakta," in *Bloodroot*, 40. Grace Toney Edwards, "Marilou Awiakta: Poet for the People," in *Her Words* (2002), ed. Felicia Mitchell, 19–34. Ruth Yu Hsiao, "Awiakta," *The Oxford Companion to Women's Writing In the United States* (1995), 90. Parks Lanier, Jr. review of *Selu, Appalachian Journal* 21:3 (spring 1994), 326–27. Jerold J. Savory, review of *Selu, Southern Humanities Review* (spring 1995), 198–200. Alexander Vaschenko, review of *Selu, North Dakota Quarterly* (summer 1995), 229–32. John W. Warren & Adrian McClaren, *Tennessee Belles-Lettres* (1977), 109–13.

WOMEN DIE LIKE TREES

from *Abiding Appalachia:*
Where Mountain and Atom Meet (1978, 1995)

Women die like trees, limb by limb
as strain of bearing shade and fruit
drains sap from branch and stem
and weight of ice with wrench of wind
split the heart, loosen grip of roots
until the tree falls with a sigh—
unheard except by those nearby—
to lie . . . mossing . . . mouldering . . .
to a certain softness under foot,
the matrix of new life and leaves.
No flag is furled, no cadence beats,
no bugle sounds for deaths like these,
as limb by limb, women die like trees.

WHEN EARTH BECOMES AN "IT"

from *Selu: Seeking the*
Corn-Mother's Wisdom (1993)

When the people call Earth "Mother,"
they take with love
and with love give back
so that all may live.

When the people call Earth "it,"
they use her
consume her strength.
Then the people die.

Already the sun is hot
out of season.
Our Mother's breast
is going dry.

She is taking all green
into her heart
and will not turn back
until we call her
by her name.

ANOREXIA BULIMIA
SPEAKS FROM THE GRAVE

from *Selu: Seeking the*
Corn-Mother's Wisdom (1993)

Young women, listen to me—
I'm talkin' to you.
Don't come down here before your time.
It's dark and cold.
Nothin' doin' down here
but the Grandmothers sayin'

"Anorexia Bulimia!
Tell the young women this for us:
They bound our feet
and our toes busted out—
to travel on, test new waters.
They bound our breasts . . .
our nipples busted out,
infra-red eyes to take in
what the other two miss.
When they bound our middle
rib 'n hip busted the stays
    took the waist with 'em—
    free as they were born.

But now, young women—*now* . . .
They've got your soul in a bind,
    wounded, wound up
in electronic wire and hard paper twine
that cut images into your brain,

unnatural images sayin'
'Starve yourself to suit us.
Starve your body.
Starve your power.
Starve your dream—
thinner and thinner—
until YOU vanish.'

They want you to do that
'cause if you was to take on weight
you might start throwin' it around.
No way can They handle
a full-grown woman
with a full-grown dream. No way."

Listen young women,
the Grandmothers and Anorexia Bulimia
are talkin' to you—
  Feed your body.
  Feed your soul.
  Feed your dream.
  BUST OUT!!!
  —For Judy (1966-1992)

FROM *SELU: SEEKING THE CORN-MOTHER'S WISDOM* (1993)

A Time to Reweave*

Note: "A Time to Reweave" and "A Time to Study Law" are excerpts from "Womanspirit in the High-Tech World," an address given at the First National Women's Symposium, 1989, sponsored by the Cherokee Nation of Oklahoma and Northeastern State University.

The 1990s will be the decisive decade, when humanity will either call Earth "Mother" again or perish. To survive, we must reconnect the Web of Life. People of reverent spirit everywhere are saying it: scientists, theologians, educators, artists, poets, sociologists, the man and woman next door, the kindergarten child who, when asked his greatest wish, said "I don't want to die." It is a time to reweave, a time when women are coming into our own. As Native people often say, "The Grandmothers are coming back."

Whatever our ethnic, cultural or religious roots may be, women since the beginning of time have been "weavers," weavers who work from a spiritual base. We know how to take diverse strands of life and spin them into a pattern. How to listen to the whole web at once and mend small tears that occur. If the web should be damaged beyond repair, women, like our sister the spider, know how to ingest the remaining strands and spin a new web.

We *are* doing that. Consider women across the country who represent major strands of the web: women working in health, history, government, law, literature, family, holistic healing, spirituality, economics, education, art, conservation, and so on. Diverse in many ways, we are unified in our determination to ensure the continuance of life. There are men who support us in our work, as we so often support them in theirs. This cooperative trend among women and between genders is a hope for the future.

But in the world's society at large, people who call Earth "it" are still dominant and still rending the web at a deadly rate. Contending with them, with their disdain virus and the damage it causes, can be very wearying. That's why I've given you a corn seed for remembrance—a gift from Selu, the strong, who fed the people in body and in spirit. Although eternally giving, she brooked no disrespect, not even inappropriate curiosity (much less sexual harassment). When disrespect occurred, she quit cooking and gave the law instead. This is a principle worth pondering for women today.

FROM *SELU* (1993)

A Time to Study Law*

As women work for the good of our people and move into positions where we help make governing policies, it is useful and strengthening to study the Creator's laws and precedents for their application. Most people now call these laws "natural." Native people have traditionally called them "sacred." In either case, the laws are immutable and inexorable. And they are good guides for keeping focused and centered in our efforts.

My parents used a real spider's web, one that I could see and touch, to teach me the laws. Two that are especially appropriate for women to study are these:

The Creator made the Web of Life and into each strand put the law to govern it. Everything in the universe is part of the web. Stars, trees, oceans, creatures, humans, stones: we are all related. One family. What happens to one will happen to all, for the Creator's laws function this way. They teach us to cooperate and live in harmony, in balance. Ignorance of the laws is no excuse, because through Mother Earth the Creator reveals them continually. If we are reverent toward her and take only what we need, she will sustain us. If we are irreverent and take too much, we separate ourselves from her power and we will die.

A similar law governs all warm-blooded species, including the human. The gender that bears life must not be separated from the power to sustain it. From the eagle to the mouse, from the bear to the whale, the female has the power to nurture and protect her young. A complementary law governs the siring gender, who ranges farther and is more changeable and transitory. Together, the laws make a balance, which provides for continuance in the midst of change—and for the survival of the species.

For centuries American Indians studied the Creator's web and wove the sacred laws into their own cultures, each tribe according to its customs. The welfare of children was paramount.

Imagine that the Grandmothers of these cultures—the female ancestors—have returned to sit in council and consider the dilemmas of American society. Undoubtedly, they would put these questions first on their agenda:

"Who will take care of the children? Who will feed, clothe, shelter, educate, protect—nurture them to maturity?" They would insist that the issue of children's care be resolved before the issue of birth is even considered. To do otherwise is unconscionable. "Children are the seeds of the people. Seed corn must not be ground," is the ancient tribal wisdom for survival.

Suppose we then take the Grandmothers to our cities and show them microcosms of the "grinding of children" that is a national disgrace: physical and sexual abuse, economic exploitation through drugs and the sex industry, the steady descent of women and children into poverty, the violence toward women of all ages. "Although we've had the vote for sixty-five years," we explain, "until recently women have been barred from policy-making bodies that govern life in America. Even now, on a national level, our power is weak: one in nine on the Supreme Court, 4 percent in the Congress and about the same in the state legislatures. We do not have equal representation in making any laws, not even those that affect our children and our own bodies. We are being undermined, disenfranchised, disempowered. . . ."

Calm and steady, the Grandmothers have listened intently. "We've heard this story before. Remember what happened then to the people. . . ."

Native women, especially, do remember.

I'd thought it would never come to this—again. Seemingly, the women's movement was mending the Creator's law that was broken in the Grand-mothers' time. I'd thought my daughters—and surely my granddaughters—would serve with men on the councils of the land, resuming their ancestors' place as "Mothers of the Nation." I'd thought they and my son and their children would live in a society restored to the balance that ensures survival. . . .

"Seed corn must not be ground."

What can women do to prevent our disempowerment and the "grinding" of our children?

For myself, I am a poet, a writer. I have no political clout, no big money to roll. But I do have faith in the Creator. And I do remember the Grandmothers' stories, especially the Cherokee one. I must *tell* it to my children, for it has been erased from most books. Hearing it, they will better understand the Web of Life and their places in it. Science teaches them the web's pattern, but not that the laws holding it in place are sacred. The story will also help my children realize how crucial it is to keep any issue within its context when making a decision. An issue, too, is part of a web. And many of our society's negative attitudes toward women and children have deep roots in the past.

The story of the Cherokee Grandmothers shows how the people interpreted the Creator's law for the female—making the welfare of children central—and of what happened when that law was broken. This story was repeated in many Indian nations.

As I have described previously, when the European men first arrived, Cherokee women had been the center of the family and the center of the Nation for about two thousand years. When the Cherokee men asked, "Where are your women?" the Europeans said, "What are your women doing here?" To their minds, it was "pagan" and "uncivilized" to have women in places of power. Besides, the Europeans followed the laws of property, and the property they wanted was the land. To get it, it was evident they would have to upset the tribal balance. A primary way to do that was to undermine the power of women. No rocks at first. Just steady pressure for decades. They refused to deal with women in treaty negotiations. They called the Cherokee system a "petticoat government" and insisted on their own way. They introduced alcohol to the people. And within the wholesome teachings of Christianity, which the Cherokee found familiar and sound—God is Creator of all, love God and your neighbor as yourself—many missionaries also brought the concept that woman is unclean (because of menses) and the cause of the fall of man. This teaching alarmed the people, for it was well known that "a people cannot be conquered until the hearts of its women are on the ground." Meanwhile, on diplomatic and military levels, the men fought losing battles. Word came back along the great trade routes that the process was everywhere the same in Indian country.

But there was hopeful news from the Iroquois in the North. As a primary model for their constitution, Benjamin Franklin and his colleagues were studying the League of the Iroquois and its Great Law of Peace, which by the late 1700s had united five, then six nations for centuries. Based on equal representation and balance of power, the Great Law had been codified long before European contact by Hiawatha and the Peacemaker, with the support of Jikonsaseh, the most powerful of the clan matrons. The Iroquois system was (and is) spirit-based. The Council of Matrons was the ceremonial center of the system as well as the prime policy maker. Only sons of eligible clans could serve on the councils at the behest of the matrons of their clans, at the executive, legislative and judicial levels. Public and private life were inseparable and the matrons had the power to impeach any elected official who was not working for the good of the people.

But when Franklin and others incorporated the Iroquois model into the U.S. Constitution, they omitted women *as a gender,* as well as men of color and men without property. Within fifty years, indigenous people were forced onto reservations, declared "alien and dependent" by the U.S. Supreme Court, decimated.

In the time of crisis, bereft of political power and disenfranchised in their own land, the Grandmothers felt their hearts sink low. But they did not allow them to be "on the ground." Instead, they took them *underground,* where they joined with wise men, Grandfathers, who accepted women's power as a complement to their own. By restoring the balance of the Creator's law for survival as well as by keeping faith with other sacred laws, American Indians have slowly and patiently rewoven their lives and are emerging with renewed strength.

In most other surviving cultures, deep below the turmoil of historical events, there have been counterparts of the Indian Grandmothers and Grandfathers who, according to their customs, have found ways to ensure that the gender that bears life is not separated from the power to sustain it.

Many institutions in America are trying to bring gender balance into their structures—churches, synagogues, universities, corporations. The U.S. Congress is not among them. Two hundred years have passed since the U.S. Constitution was adopted, fifty-one years since the Equal Rights Amendment was first introduced for debate. Congress remains adamant in refusing to mend the Creator's law, as well as reluctant to make complementary, *enforceable* laws for the siring gender's responsibilities for children.

In some other sectors of society, also, the attitude toward women coming into the public sphere is, "What are you doing here?"

We know why we're here. We're doing our part to get the job done. Keeping our government and our society in balance requires the minds and energies of two genders. The more America is in harmony with the Creator's laws, the better off our people will be.

You and I are sisters but different. Yet we have common ground in an old saying, "There are many paths up the mountain." If we take the mountain to be Womanspirit rooted in the sacred, there is honor to your path and honor to mine. We are one in our calling to bring Womanspirit into balance with Manspirit in our world. We must continue in our paths and resume our rightful places on the councils that govern our land and its people. Otherwise, our Mother Earth will die. And all that lives will die with her. Peace to your path and peace to mine. On our way up the mountain, we'll call to each other: "Keep going. We'll make it. We'll make it. Sure we will. . . ."

Womanspirit is coming back!

A corn seed for remembrance.

Out of Ashes Peace Will Rise

from *Selu: Seeking the Corn-Mother's Wisdom* (1993)

Our courage
is our memory.

Out of ashes
peace will rise,
if the people
are resolute.
If we are not
resolute,
we will vanish.
And out of ashes
peace will rise.

In the Four Directions . . .
Out of ashes peace will rise.
Out of ashes peace will rise.
Out of ashes peace will rise.
Out of ashes peace will rise.

Our courage
is our memory.

ARTIE ANN BATES
(July 20, 1953–)

Eastern Kentuckian Artie Ann Bates was born in Blackey, where she now lives with her husband and son in one of the Letcher County homes where she grew up. The daughter of Eunice Cornett Bates, an elementary school teacher, and Bill Bates, a coal miner, she was the fifth of six children in her family.

During her childhood, she explains, she rarely saw anyone she didn't know. "My first experience living among strangers occurred when I began college at the University of Kentucky in the summer of 1971. These strangers thought *I* was the stranger." Homesickness drove her home for a term at Hazard Community College, but then she returned to Lexington, where she earned her undergraduate degree in nursing in 1976 and took some influential courses in Appalachian history (with Harry Caudill) and in writing (with Gurney Norman). She is now a medical doctor who completed her training at the University of Louisville in 1986. She has also completed a residency in child psychiatry at the University of Louisville, where she has been working with sexually and physically abused children.

While a medical student, she wrote in personal journals, began a novel about a young woman in medical school, and had a son before moving back home in 1987 to practice medicine in eastern Kentucky.

On being a wife and mother, she writes, "raising kids is the most important work we ever do." Being a parent, she continues, "causes me to reach to depths of my selfish self and come out with forgiveness. The romance with my husband is a life-sustaining energy source." A community activist who opposes dams on Linefork Creek and who participated in the local PTA, she often contributed letters to the editor and essays on local politics and the environment to newspapers. She explains that "Appalachia has taught me to survive wherever I land, especially on a little piece of rocky land. It has given me a conscience to write some of its history, one of making do."

OTHER SOURCES TO EXPLORE

PRIMARY

Books for children: *Ragsale* (1995). **Autobiographical essay:** "Root Hog, or Die," *Bloodroot* (1998), ed. Joyce Dyer, 55–60. **Essays:** "I'd Sharpen Your Ax," *Appalachian Heritage* 21:2 (spring 1993), 26–30. "Belinda, Our Tremendous Gift," *Appalachian Heritage* 19:2 (spring 1991), 3–6. "Heirlooms," *Appalachian Heritage* 18:2 (spring 1990), 26–31.

SECONDARY

William T. Cornett, review of *Ragsale*, *Appalachian Heritage* 23:4 (fall 1995), 70–71. Joyce Dyer, "Artie Ann Bates," in *Bloodroot*, 54.

BELINDA, OUR TREMENDOUS GIFT
from *Appalachian Heritage* (1991)

When Belinda Ann Mason is introduced as a member of the prestigious National Commission on AIDS it goes something like this: "Mother of two children who contracted AIDS through a blood transfusion during childbirth." Belinda thinks that is not very telling and would prefer to rewrite it, since there seems to be a subliminal message that anyone who contracted AIDS by other means did so by choice. Her rewriting would say that she is from a rural area and that she loves Conway Twitty. Also it would say that more than anything she loves sitting at her Granny's house watching *All My Children* with her.

Being fellow Letcher Countians and college buddies at the University of Kentucky ten years ago, I have rediscovered my old friend through her writings. Because we live six hours apart and because we are both extremely swamped with work and family, we have had to visit by telephone. Yet I now know her better than when we were in college because her work is so expressive and clear.

After reviewing a large amount of Belinda's creative writing and work with AIDS, my conclusion is that she is a genius, and strikingly similar to Harriette Arnow. She is a master storyteller and playwright, an eloquent speech writer and orator. She is a thinker who takes command of an audience and holds them in the strong web of her words.

A large part of Belinda's writing is present in her hometown of Whitesburg, Kentucky. At Appalshop, the well-known media center, her plays are under contract with Roadside Theater. A video tape in progress consisting of a speech to Southern Baptist Ministers, an informal interview at her home, and a speech to a group of doctors and medical students at the University of Kentucky was recorded by Herb E. Smith and Anne Johnson. This will be shown as part of the Headwaters series on Kentucky Educational Television (KET).

Another large segment of Belinda's work is being archived in the Special Collections of the M.I. King Library at the University of Kentucky in Lexington. This includes numerous short stories and poems as well as a novel in progress about a young boy, Merle, who contracts AIDS through a blood transfusion.

As I plug in the VCR tape entitled "Belinda Excerpts" I feel a quiet excitement as if my friend will jump out of the television. How I wish it were possible. Though we have talked by phone, I have not seen Belinda since early 1987, three months after she was infected with HIV.

Belinda comes onto the screen penetrating my eyes, ears, and chest with her presence and her words. She has changed a bit, I think, as she talks with her same mountain drawl. She is more beautiful than I remembered, perhaps because she is dressed for a crowd. Her heart-shaped face and soft lisp deliver words of great weight.

Belinda is speaking to a group of Southern Baptist Ministers in the first part of this tape. Her message is clear and precise, her mission as a spokesperson for AIDS is unmistakable. "AIDS is a test, not for the people who are infected but for the rest of society. Will we extend the hand of compassion and touch of Christ to others? . . . We must put away the label of victim of AIDS, there are no innocent or guilty victims, nobody planned to get it. . . . AIDS can be less about dying than about choosing how to live. . . . Nothing can ever separate us from the love of God. Nourish and cherish the people in your life, they are lessons for you."

Her voice in this speech is unrelenting. Because she is a person with AIDS quite different from the norm, she is easier to accept. Because of her race, financial status, private pay insurance, family and church support, she is one of the privileged.

Belinda delivers the serious message that we have lost more people to AIDS than to the Vietnam War. Blacks, Hispanics, homosexuals, and drug users suffer a social prejudice that numbs us from the seriousness of AIDS. Yet "we are all God's children. We must not be judgmental, we must not blame or shame, we must practice what we say."

Belinda became infected with HIV during an obstetrical emergency in the birth of her second child, Clayton. She recalls driving to the hospital with her husband Steve, feeling "poised on the edge of something." She thought that "something" was another wonderful chapter in the family life they shared with their daughter Polly. She thought the recovery from the obstetrical emergency would be the worst she would have to suffer, only to find later that a unit of blood was contaminated with HIV.

Belinda's words in speaking for people with AIDS reminds one of her character Enoch's words in her play *Gifts of the Spirit*. Enoch says that "Working on a building is what living is. And just like wood working, you got to have things to believe in before you can build something that'll stand. A house that'll keep the wind off of you. A life where doors is hung right and the roof won't bow. The Lord's give us plenty to delight in and a whole lot to believe. If they is a day of judgement coming as some says, I don't think we'll be faulted much for drinking or gambling nor none of the other things you've heard is a one-way ticket to hell. If He's got a quarrel with us, it'll be for us not laying ahold of our tools. Not trusting our materials."

Among Belinda's best tools are her oratory skills, social conscience, will to help others, and her creative writing ability. In taking up her tools Belinda Mason is a prolific writer of Appalachian literature. Her ear for the music of language immortalizes Appalachian speech and culture. She says she "gave back what I heard," the "poetry that other people speak in restaurants."

Of Belinda's short stories appearing in print, one of them was taken as fact. "A Christmas Lesson" was in *Appalachian Heritage*, Vol. 15, No. 4, 1987. Country music singer Naomi Judd, who had recently subscribed, read the story and thought the two women *were real*. She said the characters "feel like my family." Naomi felt compassion for the women in the story trying to find Conway Twitty and wanted to personally introduce them. After talking with the Hazard, Kentucky, telephone operator and finding that they were not real people, Naomi called the editor and got Belinda's address and telephone number. Later she wrote to Belinda. She arranged a private meeting, praised her for the excellent writing, and has kept in touch with Belinda ever since.

In addition to *Gifts of the Spirit*, Belinda has another play produced by Roadside Theater called *War on Poverty*. Centered around the local shooting of a Canadian filmmaker in the late 1960s, the play encompasses Appalachia's image of itself from within and from the eye of the outside cameras.

To outsiders the shooting incident reiterated stereotypes of Appalachians as impulsive gun wielders. It also lifted the valve of pent up resentment from the influx of those who came to help us poor mountaineers. Belinda's play shows "the other side of the coin besides the crazy hillbilly." It uses slides and "family pictures" to show how we see ourselves and explores significant events that led up to the shooting and beyond. The play is a composite of every Appalachian's frustration in loving the homeland only to discover pity and shame by the outside world.

Belinda Mason's interest in the common person captures us as we feel at home with her characters. She has always been fascinated with the women who follow country music stars like Conway Twitty. Her characters speak our language, struggle our hardships, share our passions. Gid, at his friend Hargis' funeral in *Gifts of the Spirit*, says of having to live in the city, "All that traffic, sirens a blowing, lay down at night with nary a thing between you and a total stranger but a wall. Step outside and cars and people darting ever which way. Like a gang of diddle chicks."

Belinda's zest for life, like her writing, is that of seizing the moment. She resents editors' suggesting that she rewrite things since, "I never do anything that I can do better." She often answers people who ask how she feels about having AIDS with, "I'd rather have a broken leg." She noticed one of her medical records narratives described her as a "32 year old black woman . . ." and said "Well, well, I've been black all these years and didn't even know it." She says the great division in humankind is "not race or religion but those who are able and those who are not."

Belinda Mason is quietly determined. From the days [as] Miss Whitesburg High School, or running track and jumping hurdles, she is writing as a journalist. From newspaper work and freelance creative writing she is being featured in the American Medical Association's newspaper *The AMNews,* publishing articles on AIDS in the *Boston Globe,* medical journals such as *Primary Care* and various AIDS journals. Her travels take her from coffee with President Bush and, at his request, accepting a coveted seat on the National Commission on AIDS, speaking to ministers' groups, Congress, AIDS activists and to medical grand rounds at the University of Kentucky.

It is to a group of doctors and medical students at the University of Kentucky that Belinda is speaking in the second speech of this video tape from Appalshop. Her message to doctors about AIDS is a serious charge since "doctors, like journalists and media people, have the most to learn and are in the best position to institute real attitude changes, to lead people to water if not to knock them over the head and make them drink."

She serves up to them a "scrubbed clean Southern style AIDS which allows listeners to avoid examining their own feelings about otherness." In discussing the method by which she became infected with HIV, people are "spared confrontation with the messy realities of sex and drugs." She drives home the message that "puritanical squeamishness" and "racism and homophobia" prevent this society, both professionals and the lay public, from effectively facing AIDS.

The demands for Belinda to speak became so numerous that she dreaded getting on an airplane because it meant separation from her family. Belinda's daughter, Polly, tiring of her mother's absences asked her how one gets to be "unfamous." Then, when her mother was asked to speak at one more meeting, said, "I thought you weren't going to be famous anymore."

Belinda's family is very dear to her. She has Polly who is 8 and Clayton who is 4. Her husband Steve, a musician, teaches at a local community college. He speaks of her in a soft voice as "articulate, a very unusual person." She comes from an east Kentucky mountain family, the oldest of Barbara and Paul Mason's three children, having two younger brothers.

In the time before AIDS the Rainbow Room, her son's green and yellow painted nursery, was a place where any dreams could come true. Now that is a "distant and receding memory," as she is "one of the people whose life I used to write about as a small town journalist." Belinda carefully describes to these medical students that having AIDS gives one both "devastation and exhilaration in equal measure." Devastation at the "wreckage of a simple and satisfying life with my family, exhilaration at finding myself alive at all." With springtime coming, her children healthy and playing, the family safe, she says, "The grace of it all sustains me."

As I remove the tape I think of Belinda's words during a recent telephone conversation. She talked about the irony of "the terrible beauty of AIDS. I have new eyes. I can see things different. Life is precious and rich. It's a tremendous gift."

Then I think of this powerful little woman, her green eyes and childlike hands, and of her contribution to people with AIDS and especially to people without AIDS. Her plays and short stories have opened Appalachia to us, to the charm of our culture and a deeper way of viewing life. Her writing shows us who we are and from whom we came, and that as common people we are okay. She encourages us to live a passionate, caring life, to make the most of every moment, and to nurture a healthy sense of humor.

Belinda, a flower of life, is our tremendous gift. She lives one of her favorite Native American sayings, "The quality of life is not measured by length but by the fullness with which we enter into each present moment."

Note: For more on Belinda Ann Mason, see the biographical note and sample of her work on pp. 386–90.

ℱRANCES ℭOURTENAY ℬAYLOR
(January 20, 1848–October 19, 1920)

Frances Courtenay Baylor was born in Fort Smith, Arkansas, the daughter of Sophie Baylor Dawson, from Winchester, Virginia, and army officer James Dawson.

Educated by her mother, Baylor spent most of her childhood on army posts. She lived in San Antonio and New Orleans. Around 1865, when her father died (or left), her mother resumed using her maiden name and returned with Frances to live with family in Virginia. At the end of the Civil War, they traveled to England with Frances's sister, who had married Confederate general J.G. Walker, and lived there for several years before returning to Winchester, Virginia.

Baylor drew on her travel experiences for a number of newspaper sketches that appeared in papers from London to New Orleans under the name of a male relative. Her first success was a novel, *On Both Sides*, in which she combined two popular sketches she had written for *Lippincott's Magazine*—the first focused on the social life and adventures of an American family in England and provided the counterpoint for a corresponding tale of an English family in America. "Miss Baylor" (as she signed her work) also became well known for her patriotic poetry. Though her poetry has not been collected, her collected stories were published in *A Shocking Example, and Other Sketches*.

Of her many novels written for children, *Juan and Juanita*, focusing on the capture and escape of two Mexican children, received widest acclaim. At the heart of many of her books are characters who struggle with clashing cultures.

Baylor's second novel, *Behind the Blue Ridge: A Homely Narrative*, focuses on mountain people of Virginia and follows in the local color tradition of Mary Noailles Murfree, recording the dialect and regional customs of people Baylor observed.

In 1896, she married George Sherman Barnum. She was widowed by 1900 and returned to her mother's home in Winchester, where she spent the remainder of her life.

In this excerpt from *Behind the Blue Ridge*, John Shore, who has never been a devout churchgoer, "married the prettiest girl on the mountain" and briefly becomes a church member.

OTHER SOURCES TO EXPLORE

PRIMARY

Novels: *A Georgian Bungalow* (1900), *The Ladder of Fortune* (1899), *Miss Nina Barrow* (1897), *Claudia Hyde* (1894), *Juan and Juanita* (1888), *Behind the Blue Ridge: A Homely Narrative* (1887), *On Both Sides* (1885). **Short stories:** *A Shocking Example and Other Sketches* (1889).

SECONDARY

Dictionary of American Biography, Vol. 1 (1964), 76. C. Carroll Hollis, "Frances Courtenay Baylor," *Southern Writers: A Biographical Dictionary* (1979), 20–21. *The National Cyclopædia of American Biography* (1898), 366.

Behind the Blue Ridge (1887)

from Chapter 1

Unfortunately, John Shore's connection with the church was of the briefest. There are Pharisees in every fold, and that ancient element of all the churches was represented in this one by certain well-to-do farmers' wives who generally sat together, and somewhat apart from all the others, in the chief seats. In the course of the next "protracted meeting" a very poor, and particularly frowsy, unkempt, but reputable young girl imprudently took a seat on the end of one of these benches, tacitly reserved for the elect ladies; and that from sheer embarrassment and not from any desire to intrude upon her neighbors. Up rose the leading lady of the party, and, seizing a blue parasol, and a magenta fan, and a gilt-edged hymn-book, she swept ostentatiously across the aisle and took up a fresh position where paupers could not come between the wind and her nobility, bridling haughtily as she did so, and saying, "I can't get religion with no such people." John Shore heard her, and felt as if he had received a blow in the face; but the forlorn girl accepted the insult meekly, and when "the mourners" were invited to go up she rushed forward and fell weeping on her knees beside her fellow-sinners in a tumult of feeling that made her oblivious of the fact that religion was intended exclusively for the rich and respectable. To John Shore's amazement she was not allowed to stay there. Her tattered robe was not the robe of pharisaic righteousness at all, and, unobserved by the preacher, certain of the elders went up to her, said something to her, and then half led, half hustled her to the back of the church, where she was allowed to drop into a seat near the door. On seeing this, John Shore, who was singing a hymn, suddenly closed first his lips and then his book, and, turning, marched fiercely down the main aisle and out of the church, followed by his wife's startled gaze and the eyes of the whole congregation. "Ef *that's* religion, I've got no use for it!" he said, hotly, when explaining his defection to his wife afterwards. "She had as good a right to be there as anybody. I'll not set foot in meetin' agin, and it's no use askin' me."

And so snapped one of the cables that might have held this soul in the storm that was to beat upon his house and make his heart desolate; nor is it only simple and ignorant folk who make the mistake of confounding Christianity with Christians—so-called. . . .

Sᴜᴇ Éʟʟᴇɴ Bʀɪᴅɢᴇʀs

(September 20, 1942–)

Fiction writer Sue Ellen Bridgers grew up in Pitt County, North Carolina, and moved to Jackson County, North Carolina, in 1971. She was the middle child of the three children of Elizabeth Abbott Hunsucker and Wayland Hunsucker. While her father struggled periodically with depression, her mother encouraged her ambitions to be a writer. "She knew instinctively the value of story. She knew how it brought light into the shadows, meaning to the ambiguous, shape to the fears and delights in daily life. Her encouragement strengthened my resolve to find meaning in the world through language."

Bridgers earned her B.A. from Western Carolina University in 1976, the same year her first novel, *Home Before Dark*, was published. It was named *New York Times* Outstanding Book of the Year. She is best known for her novels for young people and adults, including *All Together Now*—which was named Library of Congress Book of the Year, recipient of the *Boston Globe–Horn Book* Honor Book Award, and the Christopher Award. Her earliest novels, as well as *Notes for Another Life*, *Sara Will*, and *Permanent Connections*, all won the American Library Association's Best Books for Young Adults award.

She and her husband, Ben Oshel Bridgers, live in Sylva, North Carolina, and have three children and six grandchildren.

Her writing process "usually begins with a visual impression of a person," she says. Her central character's identity takes shape as she goes through "a time of questioning, of being receptive to everything I see, hear, read,"—a period of "creative awareness" that can last for months, during which time she takes notes and writes the opening scene.

All of her books are set in North Carolina, though not all are set in the mountains, as are *Sara Will, Permanent Connections,* and a series of short stories about the same characters.

In this excerpt from *Sara Will*, the title character is experiencing an upset in the quiet, routine life she's had with her sister, Swanee. Sara has never married and has never lived anywhere except in the ancestral home she shares with her sister. They have recently taken in several relatives, including a young woman with an infant, who arrived on their doorstep with no place else to go. Sara has been reluctant to open her life to the visitors, and she balks at the idea of babysitting while the rest of the family goes to church.

OTHER SOURCES TO EXPLORE

PRIMARY

Novels: *All We Know of Heaven* (1996), *Keeping Christina* (1993), *Permanent Connections* (1987), *Sara Will* (1985), *Notes for Another Life* (1981), *All Together Now* (1979), *Home Before Dark* (1976). **Autobiographical essays:** "Notes from a Guerrilla," *English Journal* 88:6 (July 1999), 41–47. "Writing for My Life," *ALAN Review* (fall 1995), 1–6.

SECONDARY

Pamela S. Carroll, "Southern Literature for Young Adults: The Novels of Sue Ellen Bridgers," *ALAN Review* (fall 1990), 10–13. *Contemporary Authors* (1977), Vols. 65–68, 79. *Contemporary Authors, New Revision Series* (1992), Vol. 36, 49–52. Ted Hipple, *Presenting Sue Ellen Bridgers* (1990). *Something About the Author* (1981), Vol. 22, 56.

SARA WILL (1985)

from Chapter 11

So they went, leaving her on the porch with Rachel cradled to her chest. She pulled the blanket snugly around the small body everywhere cold could seep in and walked out into the yard. The baby was quiet, fed, groggy, content. She didn't seem to know or care in whose arms she nestled. Held out at arms' length she would have screamed, panicked by instinctive fear of falling, but secure within a boundary, any boundary, she was at peace.

It's the same with me, Sara thought. Here in her front yard staring at the receding bubble of dust behind the truck, she felt herself standing on the edge of her life looking out into what she had always imagined was a rocky place, treacherous with slippery boulders and rising water.

She had seen the valley flooded, had stood alone on the ridge every evening for a month and watched the rising water enveloping familiar places. The water had been alive and powerful. She had been careful not to slip. It was the same with her life; she had thought she would drown out there among people, pushed under by obligations, held fast by concerns she would collect like stones. She had hung back, clinging to the old and familiar which, although chipped, faded, practically useless, offered no resistance. She had fashioned the shape of things, her life here, Swanee's there, the two connecting only at mealtimes or when some minor dilemma faced them simultaneously. She had controlled all the possibilities except natural disasters, illness, and death and had not wanted to look beyond the solitary confinement she faced each morning.

Now, expecting the worst, she was forced to see in place of her dark vision, her own landscape painfully ragged and in need of repair. She saw dilapidated gates, the dry pond bed grown up, the scraggly garden. She saw things Fate Jessop and Michael could do. These intruders might have brought the world with them to ravel her seams, but their damage seemed slight, almost imperceptible, amid the oversights she'd made herself.

Still, she didn't regret her old life. What had been wrong with it? She couldn't think what. She had earned a living, had salvaged her family heritage in ledger books, photographs, household goods, cemetery markers. She had kept the land safe, drawing from it only those resources essential to its maintenance. She had repaired and refurbished when nothing else would do. She had had good friends once, before family took precedence. She had had her share of dates, all local boys she'd been in school with who remembered the awkward girl she'd been and didn't expect any handholding or obligatory smooching, just a screaming ride on the county fair bullet or a willingness to sit through a double feature of gangster movies. She had liked to dance and to play bridge. She had liked Frank Settlemyer but not enough to marry him. Was that true? Had it really been a lack of affection that made her hesitate until it was too late? Surely she had once dreamed of a life different from the one she now led, but she couldn't remember the particulars of it. It had been, after all, a dream, a fantasy saved for sleep. She hadn't let foolishness interfere with the day-to-day practicalities of her life, and she'd managed to accomplish all she'd intended, except for a road cut through the woods and the bridge.

But now the boundaries weren't so clear. Lately, she'd awakened shuddering on the edge of fragile dreams, and the days were dense with emotion. She couldn't quite identify the dread that followed her about, pushing against her, prodding until she felt as though she were again leaning from the ridge toward the dark water. She recognized the panic, though. Its dark familiarity clung to her like a cloak knotted at her throat. Resignation spread across her shoulders.

What was even more strange was the tenderness she had begun to feel. Seeing her life becoming different—every day of this week had presented itself embroidered with a new quirky stitch in someone's personality, some unforeseen glimpse into past lives that astonished her with their richness—she felt only slightly unhinged. She had expected peculiarities. That had been her most persuasive mental argument against letting them stay. What she didn't understand, what truly baffled her, was the feeling of tenderness, of melting inside, that came when she was least prepared for it and which released her briefly and without warning from the tightly held terror she'd felt when she first saw the truck bouncing up the lane.

This morning she'd felt that tenderness while Swanee Hope stood in the hall before the speckled mirror and nervously tucked gray wisps under the edges of her ancient hat. She was wearing her finest, but even that seemed tattered and shabby, out of fashion. Swanee was pretty—why had she always tried to deny that?—but the drab fading blue of her coat and hat defeated her gentle baby features. Swanee is a person meant for pastels, Sara had thought, watching her sister lift on her toes in excitement, poised like a dancer anticipating the sound of music.

At that moment, Sara Will had felt something. Love, perhaps? Surely she had always loved her sister, yet she couldn't bring herself to speak of it. How could she? How did you say I love you to someone you'd known all your life? It would seem so sudden, so impulsive, wouldn't it? Such an embarrassing oversight of feeling all these years. Besides, she couldn't undo, could she, make amends for neglect, for all the years of belittling sarcasm Swanee had seemed to ignore? Swanee had probably deserved every derogatory remark Sara Will ever sent in her direction. Still, Sara regretted cattiness and jokes made at Swanee's expense. With all that, perhaps even because of her sister's endurance, she knew she loved her. Surely she always had.

The baby stirred under the blanket, stretching into sleep. I need to finish dinner, Sara Will thought, moving toward the house. The roast was in the oven but there was corn to put on, fruit to chop for the salad, the table to set. She had plenty to keep herself busy while the house was empty. If nothing else, she could work one of the crossword puzzles she'd been saving from the paper.

But instead of doing any of those things, she sat down in the parlor with the baby in her arms and pushed back the blanket from Rachel's head so the soft fuzz was under her hand. The baby's cheek was against her breast as soft as cotton. Her mouth bubbled a film of moist milky breath onto Sara Will's dress. The warmth seeped in. Sara sat there in the silence, not thinking about anything, not moving.

She'd never felt this calm before, although she'd always considered herself a staid person, reserved, even locked inside herself. This was a new kind of quiet. It seemed to flow between herself and the sleeping baby. After a while she stood up as if startled by her own heartbeat and, cradling Rachel's head against her shoulder to keep the child steady, went up the stairs to put her in the crib. I have to finish dinner, she thought, folding the blanket over the sleeping infant. I can't just sit about all day.

Rachel, startled by the cool flat bed after Sara Will's warm closeness, tensed in a shiver, and Sara touched her back to comfort her. What brought you here to change me? she wondered. The baby relaxed, fingers unclenched, lips parted, eyelids still. I don't want this to happen, Sara Will said silently, but then she could hear the words in the room. They seemed to echo around her, bouncing off the papery walls, resounding as they struck the pine floor, dull from so many years without wax. She had neglected so many things. She had never even listened to her own voice until now.

"I don't want to care about you, Rachel," she said, this time aloud, as if the spoken words could free her. She knew they could not. There was no way to be free again. She turned away from the sleeping baby, went softly to the door, left it partly open so that from the kitchen she could detect the slightest sound. Going down, her arms felt empty.

FLORENCE COPE BUSH
(March 29, 1933–)

Florence Cope Bush is the daughter of Dora ("Dorie") Woodruff Cope and Fred Cope. Born in Tremont, Tennessee, a small community between Townsend and Cades Cove, she lived there only three years before her parents' land was claimed by eminent domain to create the Great Smoky Mountains National Park. "I have no memory of ever having lived in the misty, blue mountains," she writes. "But everything about the Smokies fascinates me, and I'm ever drawn back to the place of my birth."

She spent many summers on her grandparents' farm in Sevier County, Tennessee, and to preserve something of their way of life, which she saw disappearing, she wrote the story of her mother's life, *Dorie: Woman of the Mountains.* Bush spent nine years collecting information from her mother and from libraries. She wrote the manuscript "as a gift" to her daughter and her mother. When a friend convinced her to publish two thousand copies, it sold well because "Dorie came to represent a female relative in almost everyone's life." She often hears, "You wrote about my mother, my grandmother, my aunt."

A former newspaper reporter and freelance writer in Knoxville, Tennessee, Bush has written an appealing account of her family's transitions in southern Appalachia in the early twentieth century. The book's six chapters cover the years from 1898 to 1942. In 1993, Bush won the Tennessee History Award, jointly sponsored by the Tennessee Library Association and the Tennessee Historical Association.

In this excerpt from chapter 1, the writer records her mother's memories of the family's Cherokee neighbors.

OTHER SOURCES TO EXPLORE

PRIMARY

Nonfiction: *Dorie: Woman of the Mountains* (1992), *If Life Gives You Scraps, Make a Quilt* (1992), *Ocona Lufta Baptist: Pioneer Church of the Smokies, 1836–1939* (1990).

SECONDARY

George Brosi, "Booklist and Notes," *Appalachian Heritage* 20:3 (summer 1992), 73. Jane R. Wilson, review of *Dorie: Woman of the Mountains*, *Appalachian Heritage* 21:3 (summer 1993), 68–69.

FROM *DORIE:*
WOMAN OF THE MOUNTAINS (1992)

In the early spring of 1899, Pa decided to move closer to his job. He rented a small farm near the Cherokee reservation. They loaded their few pieces of furniture on a wagon and moved in time for spring planting. Ma worked along beside him until her time to give birth. I was born May 8, 1899, almost an anniversary gift to them.

The Cherokee women were very curious about Pa and Ma. Many times Ma would look up and see a silent, unsmiling Indian looking in the window or open door. Sometimes, when working outside, she'd catch a fleeting glimpse of them behind the trees. They watched while she boiled and washed the clothing in a big, black wash kettle. The kettle sat on three rocks, over a fire. Ma would bring water from the river to fill the kettle and then build a fire under it.

Pa had driven two posts into the ground and stretched rope between them to hang the clothing out to dry. Some of the articles of clothing fascinated the Indians. They'd touch the white bran-sack sheets and wonder about the use for such a big piece of cloth. Indian women washed their clothes in the river and dried them by draping them over rocks and bushes. It wasn't long before Ma could see clotheslines beside the Indians' cabins. They learned fast.

Ma made friends with some of the women. They taught her how to make Indian bean bread and chestnut dumplings. The bread was made of cornmeal, like cornbread, with cooked dried beans mixed into the dough. Chestnut dumplings were chestnuts covered with cornmeal dough, shaped into a ball, rolled in corn shucks, tied on each end with a strip of shuck, and dropped into boiling water.

The Cherokees had many ways to eat corn. It was roasted, boiled, stewed, ground up, parched, popped, mixed with other vegetables and meat, and baked in many kinds of bread. Over half of the Indians' food was plant food. They favored deer meat and bear meat and caught fish with their bare hands.

They tapped maple sugar trees for sweetening. This, along with wild honey was used for trade. Scuppernong grapes, strawberries, huckleberries, gooseberries, crab apples, and persimmons were staples of their diet in the summer months. Persimmons were used with the corn to make a slightly sweet, cakelike bread.

There was one Cherokee delicacy Ma never tasted—they had a fondness for roasted wasp larvae. Finding a new wasp nest just before the young were hatched, they'd take a small stick and remove the white larvae and roast them over an open fire. It was considered an act of bravery to steal a nest from an angry swarm of wasps.

In the early 1900s it was still common for an Indian man to have more than one wife. Ma knew several families where there were three wives for one husband. The census taker said he had found one man with six wives. Two seemed enough for most men.

After Ma had won the friendship and respect of the Cherokee women, they began to share their legends with her. One woman told her:

> At one time all living things were in the sky, on the sky rock, and this was before the world was made. All the animals could understand man; and man could understand them. Then man dishonored the privilege and was striken deaf to the talk of animals and birds. The Great One who was over the sky rock punished man so that he could only understand the talk of his own kind.

Ma loved to hear these stories. She had great admiration for the Indians and said you could learn patience from them. They never hurried with anything. They knew it took time for the giant white oak to grow from a tiny acorn. There was nothing man could do to rush the growth of the seed planted in the ground. Time meant nothing to them. Man must wait for some things to happen. Worry and work could only accomplish so much; the rest was left to the Great One in the sky.

KATHRYN STRIPLING BYER
(November 25, 1944–)

The daughter of a homemaker and a farmer, Kathryn Stripling Byer grew up in southwest Georgia. She graduated from Wesleyan College in Macon, Georgia, in 1966 with a B.A., and earned her M.F.A. in 1968 at the University of North Carolina in Greensboro, where she studied with Allen Tate, Fred Chappell, and Robert Watson. While there, she won the Academy of American Poets Student Prize for the University of North Carolina system.

"Most of my poetry is rooted in the earth of two poetic landscapes," Byer explains, "each with its own particular voice and rhythm. One is the flatlands of Georgia, where I was born and grew up [in Camilla]. The other is the mountains of western North Carolina and Tennessee. . . . If the Deep South is a dusty plain haunted by childhood, these mountains are a crazy quilt of trails haunted by women's voices." Byer describes the particular influence of her paternal grandmother, born in the Blue Ridge, who told her stories of belonging there and wanting to be there when she died. A persona named Alma speaks to Byer as a poet and "seems, in some ancestral way, to be speaking as a kinswoman, harking me back to those grandmothers and great-grandmothers whose stories I grew up hearing." Her 1983 chapbook, *Alma*, reveals the importance of women's voices, as does much of her other work.

For *The Girl in the Midst of the Harvest*, Byer received a 1986 citation from the Associated Writing Programs Award Series. *Wildwood Flower* received the 1992 Lamont Award from the Academy of American Poets. Byer has also received the Anne Sexton Poetry Prize (1982) and the Thomas Wolfe Award (1992). She has received writing fellowships from the National Endowment for the Arts and the North Carolina Arts Council. Her collection *Black Shawl* is dedicated to novelist Lee Smith and the late photographer Sharon Anglin Kuhne, a native of Kentucky. It was selected for the Roanoke-

Chowan Award and the Brockman-Campbell Award. *Catching Light* won the 2003 Southeast Booksellers Award in Poetry. Composer Harold Schiffman has set *Wildwood Flower* to music in a cantata titled *Alma,* commissioned by the Hungarian National Symphony.

She served on the faculty of the M.F.A. Writing Program at the University of North Carolina in Greensboro in 1995 and as Poet-in-Residence at Western Carolina University in Cullowhee, North Carolina, from 1990 to 1999. In 2001, she received the North Carolina Award in Literature.

OTHER SOURCES TO EXPLORE

PRIMARY

Poetry: *Catching Light* (2002), *Evelyn* (1999), *Black Shawl* (1998), *Wildwood Flower* (1992), *The Girl in the Midst of the Harvest* (1986), *Alma* (1983), *Search Party* (1979). **Selected essays:** "Deep Water," in *Bloodroot* (1998), ed. Joyce Dyer, 62–70. "Turning the Windlass at the Well: Fred Chappell's Early Poetry," in *Dream Garden: The Poetic Vision of Fred Chappell* (1997), ed. Patrick Bizzaro, 88–96. "The Wind Passing Through," in *Writing Fiction and Poetry* [Boson Books online, an e-book], ed. Sally Sullivan (1995).

SECONDARY

Contemporary Authors (1994), Vol. 142, 56–57. Joyce Dyer, "Kathryn Stripling Byer," in *Bloodroot*, 61. Robert E. Hosmer Jr. "Poetry Roundup" [review of *Wildwood Flower*] *America* (13 November 1993), 17–18. "Kathryn Stripling Byer Issue," *Iron Mountain Review* Vol. 18 (spring 2002). Ann F. Richman, "Singing Our Hearts Away: The Poetry of Kathryn Stripling Byer," in *Her Words* (2002), ed. Felicia Mitchell, 38–48.

WILDWOOD FLOWER

from *Wildwood Flower* (1992)

I hoe thawed ground
with a vengeance. Winter has left
my house empty of dried beans
and meat. I am hungry

and now that a few buds appear
on the sycamore, I watch the road
winding down this dark mountain
not even the mule can climb
without a struggle. Long daylight

and nobody comes while my husband
traps rabbits, chops firewood, or
walks away into the thicket. Abandoned
to hoot owls and copperheads,

I begin to fear sickness. I wait
for pneumonia and lockjaw. Each month
I brew squaw tea for pain.
In the stream where I scrub my own blood
from rags, I see all things flow
down from me into the valley.

Once I climbed the ridge
to the place where the sky
comes. Beyond me the mountains continued
like God. Is there no place to hide
from His silence? A woman must work

else she thinks too much. I hoe
this earth until I think of nothing
but the beans I will string,
the sweet corn I will grind into meal.

We must eat. I will learn
to be grateful for whatever comes to me.

BITTERSWEET

from *Wildwood Flower* (1992)

Under the thin flannel nightgown,
my daughter's ribs: frail
harp I stroke
as if I might make some lovely sound
of those bones. At my breast

she would cling to the nipple,
my milk like a sudden thaw straining
the downspout let down, oh
the stony earth blossomed, I saw
my pots brimming, my skirts full
of apples. I rocked her to sleep
singing, "Little bird,
little bird under my wing." Hear

my voice crack! I cough
and keep silent. Now she is the one
in this house who sings, crooning
like wind in the chimney. My sweet songs
have all blown away,
one by one, down the mountain.

LINEAGE

from *Wildwood Flower*

This red hair
I braid while she
sits by the cookstove
amazes her. Where
did she get hair the color
of wildfire, she wants to know,
pulling at strands of it
tangled in boar-bristles.

I say from Sister, God knows
where she is, and before
her my grandmother you
can't remember because
she was dead by the time
you were born, though you hear
her whenever I sing,
every song handed down
from those sleepless nights
she liked to sing through
till she had no time
left for lying awake
in the darkness and talking
to none save herself.
And yet, that night
I sat at her deathbed
expecting pure silence,
she talked until dawn
when at last her voice
failed her. She thumbed out
the candle between us
and lifted her hand
to her hair as if what
blazed a lifetime might still
burn her fingers. Yes,
I keep a cinder of it
in my locket I'll show you
as soon as I'm done telling
how she brought up from
the deep of her bedclothes
that hairbrush you're holding
and whispered, "You
might as well take it."

EASTER

from *Wildwood Flower* (1992)

Where my father's house stood
at the edge of the cove is a brown church
the faithful call Bosom of God.
I have come back to sit at the window
where I can see apple trees bud
while the preacher shouts death has no victory.

Everywhere dogwoods are blooming
like white flesh this man claims
is devil's work: woman who tasted
the apple and disobeyed God. But for Christ
we are doomed to the worms waking under
these hills I would rather be climbing

again with my father's goats bleating
so loud I can't hear this man say
I must ask the Lord pardon for what
I've come back to remember—the sun
on my neck as I shook loose my braids
and bent over the washpot. My bare feet

were frisky. If wind made the overalls
dance on the clothesline, then why
shouldn't I? Who's to tell
me I should not have shouted for joy
on this hill? It's the wind I praise God for
today, how it lifted my hair like a veil.

MOUNTAIN TIME

from *Black Shawl* (1998)

News travels slowly up here
in the mountains, our narrow
roads twisting for days, maybe years,
till we get where we're going,
if we ever do. Even if some lonesome message
should make it through Deep Gap
or the fastness of Thunderhead, we're not obliged
to believe it's true, are we? Consider
the famous poet, minding her post
at the Library of Congress, who
shrugged off the question of what we'd be
reading at century's end: "By the year 2000
nobody will be reading poems." Thus she
prophesied. End of that
interview! End of the world
as we know it. Yet, how can I fault
her despair, doing time as she was
in a crumbling Capitol, sirens
and gunfire the nights long, the Pentagon's
stockpile of weapons stacked higher
and higher? No wonder the books
stacked around her began to seem relics.
No wonder she dreamed her own bones
dug up years later, tagged in a museum somewhere
in the Midwest: American Poet—Extinct Species.

Up here in the mountains
we know what extinct means. We've seen
how our breath on a bitter night
fades like a ghost from the window glass.
We know the wolf's gone.
The panther. We've heard the old stories
run down, stutter out
into silence. Who knows where we're heading?
All roads seem to lead

to Millennium, dark roads with drop-offs
we can't plumb. It's time to be brought up short
now with the tale-teller's *Listen*: There once lived
a woman named Delphia
who walked through these hills teaching children
to read. She was known as a quilter
whose hand never wearied, a mother
who raised up two daughters to pass on
her words like a strong chain of stitches.
Imagine her sitting among us,
her quick thimble moving along these lines
as if to hear every word striking true
as the stab of her needle through calico.
While prophets discourse about endings,
don't you think she'd tell us the world as we know it
keeps calling us back to beginnings?
This labor to make our words matter
is what any good quilter teaches.
A stitch in time, let's say.
A blind stitch
that clings to the edges
of what's left, the ripped
scraps and remnants, whatever
won't stop taking shape even though the whole
crazy quilt's falling to pieces.

$\mathscr{C}$ANDIE $\mathscr{C}$ARAWAN
(December 27, 1939–)

Cultural educator Candie Anderson Carawan has been at the forefront of social change in Appalachia since the 1960s. A native Californian, Carawan first came to the South as a college art major on an exchange program from Pomona College in Claremont, California, to Fisk University in Nashville.

Shortly after her arrival in Tennessee, she was caught up in the fledgling civil rights movement, becoming one of the first whites arrested in the lunch counter sit-ins to protest segregation. She met her husband, musician and folklorist Guy Carawan, at a civil-rights workshop; together, they have devoted their lives to preserving grass roots culture and furthering causes of social justice.

In 1963, the Carawans went to Birmingham, Alabama, to record the songs of the civil rights movement, and they were arrested by the infamous police chief Bull Connor for attempting to enter a black church. Carawan recalls, "We could see the demonstrators as they came from one of the mass meetings . . . fire hoses were turned on them. We could see this from the jail cell."

Over the years, Carawan has used the Highlander Research Center in New Market, Tennessee, as her home base. Dedicated to empowering the disenfranchised, Highlander offers leadership training and community building workshops. Through books and recordings, Carawan and her husband have documented the songs and stories of a number of America's major social movements. "We've worked not only in the civil rights movement," says Carawan, "but with coal miners, migrant workers, and on women's issues."

Now retired, the Carawans live in East Tennessee in a cabin adjacent to the Highlander Center. Candie Carawan is a potter who continues to write, make music, and remain active in issues of social justice.

Carawan was an exchange student at Fisk University in the spring of 1960. In the following excerpts from *Sing for Freedom,* she recalls her experiences.

OTHER SOURCES TO EXPLORE

PRIMARY

Nonfiction: *Sing for Freedom: The Story of the Civil Rights Movement Through Its Songs* (1990), *Voices from the Mountains: Life & Struggle in the Appalachian South* (1982), *Freedom is a Constant Struggle: Songs of the Freedom Movement* (1968), *Ain't You Got a Right to The Tree of Life?: The People of John's Island, South Carolina, Their Faces, Their Words, and Their Songs* (1966). **Folksong recordings:** *Sparkles and Shines* (1999), *Tree Of Life=Arbol de la vida* (1990), *High on a Mountain* (1984), *Birmingham, Alabama 1963* (1979), *Green Rocky Road: Songs & Hammer Dulcimer Tunes From Appalachia & the British Isles* (1976), *Music from the People's Republic of China Sung and Played on Traditional Instruments* (1976), *Been in the Storm So Long: Spirituals, Folk Tales and Children's Games from John's Island, South Carolina* (1960).

SECONDARY

Fred Brown, "Eyes on the Prize," *Knoxville News-Sentinel* (2 May 1999), E1–E2. *Contemporary Authors, First Revision* (1976), Vols. 17–20, 125.

FROM *SING FOR FREEDOM: THE STORY OF THE CIVIL RIGHTS MOVEMENT THROUGH ITS SONGS* (1990)

INTRODUCTION

In the spring of 1989, Appalachian miners striking the Pittston Coal Company were singing "We Shall Overcome." In China, where a massive campaign for democracy by students and workers has just been put down, students were photographed with "We Shall Overcome" on their headbands and T-shirts. Bishop Desmond Tutu has used the song as he tries to help people in the United States envision what his country is going through in its painful struggle toward equality and justice. This powerful song, which came originally out of the black church in the southern United States, was adapted and used in the labor movement, and rose to international prominence as the theme song of the civil rights movement. It lives today. It is but the best known of more than eighty songs which were developed and spread in the South and around this country between 1960 and 1965.

The civil rights movement has been described by some as the greatest singing movement this country has experienced. The freedom songs came out of the historical experience and the creativity of southern black communities. There are many kinds and ranges of moods. Two especially important ones are the old, slow-paced spirituals and hymns that sing of hope and determination, and rhythmic jubilee spirituals and bright gospel songs that protest boldly and celebrate victory. Many of these songs have new or revised words to old tunes.

Having witnessed the civil rights era, most of us take for granted the notion of adapting well-known songs to situations of the present. It wasn't always so.

. . .

So how did this begin to happen? One place it happened was at the Highlander Folk School in Monteagle, Tennessee. Highlander was one of the gathering places during the early days of the movement. Weekend after weekend in the early 1960s, community leaders and activists from across the South came to share information, to strategize and to plan, to bolster each others' spirits as they returned home to confront segregation.

We were based at Highlander for those years and could build on what had been learned there during the Labor Movement—that singing could be a strong unifying force in struggle, and that commonly known songs, particularly southern gospel and religious songs with repetitive stanzas adapted to the situation, were most effective. For many years Zilphia Horton had worked with grassroots community people coming to Highlander. She drew from them their favorite songs and helped them change a word or two or shape them slightly differently to fit the situation in their home community (often a union campaign). She also taught songs that she knew from different parts of the South, from around the country and from abroad. In the 1940s and '50s she carried songs from Highlander out to picket lines across the South and brought songs back from various union struggles.

. . .

Pete Seeger had been in contact with Zilphia and with Highlander. His repertoire, as he sang with progressive movements in the North, included many songs from the South. He came to Highlander to share his music, and in 1945 carried away from the school a labor version of "We Shall Overcome" which had been used by striking Food and Tobacco Union workers in Charleston, S.C.

Guy had been greatly influenced by Pete, struck by his exciting way of playing the banjo and his collection of songs from grassroots Americans. In 1959, on Pete's suggestion, he came to work at Highlander and tried to carry on Zilphia's way of working with people. He met with groups gathered there and learned their songs, helping to adapt them to the movement activity in their communities. He also began to travel out to visit the people he had met and found himself leading singing in mass meetings and at civil rights conferences. It did not take long for the notion of adapting songs to catch on and to hit its stride.

. . .

As the movement spread, the songs began to spread. Nashville had one of the first citywide campaigns against segregation, and songs emerged there to suit the sit-ins. . . . Candie was an exchange student at Fisk University in the spring of 1960 and learned firsthand about the power of singing in tough situations, including jail cells.

. . .

"My stomach always hurt a little on the way to a sit-in. I guess it's the unexpected. There was so much we didn't know early in February 1960, when the sit-ins first started in Nashville. Will the sit-ins accomplish anything? Will non-violence work? What happens when demonstrators are put in jail?

"I was an exchange student at Fisk, living in the dorms and attending classes with Negro students. The biggest question for me was the rather lonely one of what can a white student do? What would my presence at the lunchcounter mean? Would I alienate and enrage the community to a greater extent than the Negro students? Or would it show that this is more than a Negro problem? I didn't know . . .

"During the demonstrations I found myself and the other few white students singled out by the crowds, called different names and eventually even segregated in the Nashville City Jail. Eighty of us were arrested the first time. It was one of the first instances where large numbers of students went behind bars, and we found that singing was truly good for the spirit. For two white girls, alone in a cell and only in sound's reach of the other students, the music offered a bond of friendship and support."

. . .

"We were crammed into a narrow hallway to await booking and I studied the faces around me. Many were calm and serious, some were relaxed, smiling, several were openly belligerent and a few were really frightened. But there was a unity—a closeness beyond proximity.

"It was a shock then to be suddenly removed from this large coherent group and thrust into a lonely cell with only one other girl, the only other white female. We protested and inquired why we could not join the large group of Negro girls across the hall. The entire jail was segregated. Through our own small diamond-paned window we could see the corresponding window in the fellows' cell. There were nearly sixty boys crowded in there—a cell the same size as ours which held two. When a face would smilingly press up against that window, we had our only visual contact with the group which had been so close that afternoon, and the previous Saturday afternoons when there had been sit-ins.

"The contact which became more real then was vocal. Never had I heard such singing. Spirituals, pop tunes, hymns, and even slurpy old love songs all became so powerful. The men sang to the women and the girls down the hall answered them. They shouted over to us to make sure we were joining in. Some songs that the kids had written or revised came out—notably some rock-and-roll protests composed by four young Baptist preachers. Calypso songs and Ray Charles numbers made us dance in our roomy quarters and then all of us were singing spirituals—'Amen-Freedom.'

"We sang a good part of our eight hour confinement that first time. The city policemen seemed to enjoy the singing. They even came up with a few requests. Our wardens actually welcomed us back when we returned to jail in a few days, going off our bond. We were a change from the Saturday night drunk who rarely sang."

. . .

"The day of the first trials in Nashville a crowd of 2,500 people gathered around a city court house. Mostly they were Negroes who simply wanted to state by their presence there that they were behind the students and that they wanted justice. As we waited to go inside we sang:

'Amen, amen, amen, amen . . .

Freedom, freedom . . .

Justice . . .

Civil Rights . . .' etc.

"I looked out at the curb where the police were patrolling, and caught one burly cop leaning back against his car, singing away—'Civil Rights' . . . He saw me watching him, stopped abruptly, turned, and walked to the other side of the car."

Jo Carson
(October 9, 1946–)

~

Jo Carson is a native of Johnson City, Tennessee, where she makes her home. A poet, a playwright, a short story author, and an actress, Carson graduated from East Tennessee State University in 1973 with a degree in speech and theater. In addition to writing and acting, Carson has been an occasional commentator for National Public Radio's *All Things Considered*.

Carson first began writing poems around the age of ten, which got her in trouble, she says, because she ignored her schoolwork. "I was a terrible student, and I hated school. . . . I took a long time getting through college because I did other things. I was still writing in college instead of doing other homework."

Many of Carson's plays have received national recognition, including *Daytrips*, which won the Kesselring Award; *Preacher with a Horse to Ride*, which won the Roger L. Stevens Award from the Fund for New American Plays; and for *The Bear Facts*, Carson received a National Endowment for the Art's Playwright's Fellowship.

Her collection of poems, *Stories I Ain't Told Nobody Yet*, was selected for the American Library Association's recommended list for 1990, as well as *Booklist*'s Editor's Choice. The poems in *Stories I Ain't Told Nobody Yet* form the basis of *People Pieces*, a one-woman stage production Carson has taken to theaters and colleges throughout the United States and abroad. "The pieces all come from people," Carson explains. "I never sat at my desk and made them up. I heard the heart of each of them somewhere." Carson describes the poems as "distillations" which remain "true to the thoughts and rhythms" of the original speaker. Carson says, "Everything I write is to be spoken aloud."

In her review of *Stories*, George Ella Lyon noted, "What we hear . . . is not the poet's voice but what she listens to. We are made listeners by our reading, hauled within earshot of voices. . . . Fundamental to *Stories I Ain't Told Nobody Yet* is the belief that all lives speak truths worth listening to."

In the opening scene from her short story "Maybe," from her collection *The Last of the 'Waltz Across Texas' and Other Stories,* Carson's three narrators—Dessa, Brenda, and Harry—take turns sharing their thoughts on love and marriage.

In the excerpt from her play *Daytrips,* Carson examines the impact of Alzheimer's disease on a mother, Ree, who has the disease, and her daughter, Pat, who has to deal with the consequences.

OTHER SOURCES TO EXPLORE

PRIMARY

Selected Drama: *Whispering to Horses* (1996–97), *The Bear Facts* (1993), *Daytrips* (1991), *Preacher with a Horse to Ride* (1990). **Books for children:** *The Great Shaking: An Account of the Earthquakes of 1811 and 1812* (1994), *You Hold Me and I'll Hold You* (1992), *Pulling My Leg* (1990). **Poetry:** *Stories I Ain't Told Nobody Yet* (1989). **Short stories:** *The Last of the 'Waltz Across Texas' and Other Stories* (1993). **Interview:** with Jo Harris, *Appalachian Journal* 20:1 (fall 1992), 56–67. **Autobiographical essay:** "Good Questions," in *Bloodroot* (1998), ed. Joyce Dyer, 72–79.

SECONDARY

Kathie deNobrogia and Valetta Anderson, eds., *Alternate Roots: Plays from the Southern Theater* (1994), 338–39. Joyce Dyer, "Jo Carson," *Bloodroot,* 71. "Jo Carson Issue," *Iron Mountain Review* 14 (summer 1998). Jennifer Mooney, "'Room Is Made for Whoever': Jo Carson and the Creation of Dialogical Community," in *Her Words* (2002), ed. Felicia Mitchell, 50–65. George Ella Lyon, review of *Stories I Ain't Told Nobody Yet, Appalachian Journal* 17:2 (winter 1990), 204–5. James S. Torrens, "Trying Them Out Off Broadway [review of *Daytrips*]," *America* (8 December 1990), 453.

40

from *Stories I Ain't Told Nobody Yet: Selections from the People Pieces* (1989)

The day I married, my mother
had one piece of wedding advice:
"Don't make good potato salad,"
she told me, "it's too hard to make
and you'll have to take something
every time you get invited somewhere.
Just cook up beans; people eat them too."

My mother was good at potato salad
and part of the memories of my childhood
have to do with endless batches made
for family get-togethers, church picnics,
Civitan suppers, Democratic party fund raisers,
whatever event called for potato salad.
I'd peel the hard-boiled eggs.
My mother would pack
her big red plastic picnic bowl
high with yellow potato salad
(she used mustard),
and it would sit proud on endless tables
  and come home empty.

What my mother might and could have said is:
Choose carefully what you get good at
'cause you'll spend the rest of your life doing it.
But I didn't hear that.
I was young and anxious to please
and I knew her potato salad secrets.
And the thousand other duties
given to daughters by mothers,
and sometimes I envy those women
who get by with pots of beans.

49

from *Stories I Ain't Told Nobody Yet:*
Selections from the People Pieces (1989)

I am asking you to come back home
before you lose the chance of seein' me alive.
You already missed your daddy.
You missed your uncle Howard.
You missed Luciel.
I kept them and I buried them.
You showed up for the funerals.
Funerals are the easy part.

You even missed that dog you left.
I dug him a hole and put him in it.
It was a Sunday morning, but dead animals
don't wait no better than dead people.

My mama used to say she could feel herself
runnin' short of the breath of life. So can I.
And I am blessed tired of buryin' things I love.
Somebody else can do that job to me.
You'll be back here then; you come for funerals.

I'd rather you come back now and got my stories.
I've got whole lives of stories that belong to you.
I could fill you up with stories,
stories I ain't told nobody yet,
stories with your name, your blood in them.
Ain't nobody gonna hear them if you don't
and you ain't gonna hear them unless you get back home.

When I am dead, it will not matter
how hard you press your ear to the ground.

The Last of the 'Waltz Across Texas' and Other Stories (1993)
from Maybe

[Dessa:] I am not telling this for sympathy. I don't like sympathy and I don't want any of it. Harry'll say I made my own bed and I now have the honor of lying down in it. Well, maybe I did. If I did, what I'm doing right now is tucking in the corners like they ought to be tucked in. No call for sympathy here. A body feels sorry for somebody, they feel like they're better than that somebody, that's the truth. Now, I might feel different if Harry had died, but Harry didn't die. Harry got mad at me, went to Nashville, stayed two weeks and come home married to somebody else. What I get is "Oh, poor Dessa, I feel so sorry for you . . ." Well, don't. Feel sorry for Brenda if you want to feel sorry for somebody. She married Harry.

[Brenda:] There probably isn't much I can say to keep from looking pretty crazy. Meeting a man in a bar and drinking and talking and after two weeks tying the knot is not what anybody I know thinks Dear Abby might call a good idea, me included, so I knew it was a tomfool thing to do and it was. But I'm not sorry I did it and if I was still just hanging out in Nashville, giving up whatever hopes I had—I am 37—I'd do it again in a minute. Don't get me wrong, marrying was not what I was hoping for, I don't know if I can say what I was hoping for, hope's such a mess spreading all over everything, but I was lonely and sick of trash jobs like waiting tables and getting up the next day and doing the same thing and then there was Harry and marrying Harry was the gift horse that stood grinning at me. I think I was sort of a gift horse for Harry too, and a couple of gift horses that are given to one another know better than to look each other in the mouth.

[Harry:] Now, I am not real proud of myself. What I did was half-cocked and I knew Dessa wasn't going to like it. Even standing there in Nashville at the justice of the peace, I was thinking Dessa ain't gonna like this much. And then driving back up the interstate, Brenda's stuff in the back of the truck, I was doing strict 55. I never drove 55 since the law went in, but I did it coming north on I-81 'cause it takes longer. I was driving with Brenda sitting next to me, and I was saying things a man says to a woman that just married him and he's taking her home, things about the house and who she's gonna like in the neighborhood, things like if she wants to go to church, I reckon we could do that for awhile. But I'm thinking about what I really ought to be telling Brenda and 55 ain't slow enough to get it out. How do you say you have a common law wife you haven't talked about yet and you're getting a common law divorce right as you sit here saying it, only the common law wife doesn't know it yet? And then I'm thinking about how Dessa probably ain't gonna like Brenda even a little bit and she probably ain't gonna be very happy about my getting married. Dessa don't take up with people easy like I do. I stopped at one of those rest stops and I called her. I was going to say it but I couldn't think of how to start. She said "hello" and I couldn't push out a word. I just hung up.

[Dessa:] Marriage is not what it's cracked up to be. I knew that right from the beginning. I knew what I was supposed to think it was and I knew what me and my friends wanted it to be. We wanted romance. Well, my mother made sure a youngun didn't get out of her house without hearing something different. She had this list of names for daddy that began with hard-headed and ended with son-of-a-bitch and got pretty hot in between. But you didn't have to hear the names. You could look at my mother and see her life wasn't much to brag about and daddy was part of the problem and the name calling didn't help. So I knew about that marriage. I just figured I'd be different.

My mother knew when Harry first started talking about getting married. She could tell, I swear she could smell it and she started in on what she called woman-to-woman talks. They were not about the facts of life, she never did get to that. I could have told her stuff. These were talking-tos, they were what I got when I was in trouble right before I got the real punishment. They started the minute Harry knocked on the door to pick me up for a date. They included Harry sometimes, not that he was a volunteer, but then, I wasn't either. They began with "Now Dessa, you are not old enough . . ." To be seeing one boy regular. To be going out as much as I was. I was old enough and we both knew it. I was eighteen. It was like she was talking to take up time. The more she did of it, the worse I wanted out. So I told her I'd find out if Harry was as bad as she thought before I did anything to make it permanent—she didn't like it but she thought I meant sleeping with Harry when I said that about making it permanent and anything was better to her than running away and getting married so she didn't disown me or anything. And I told Harry maybe I'd marry him but I didn't see no reason to rush into things and why didn't we just move in with each other for awhile and see how it worked.

[Harry:] You fall in love like I did, you decide you want to live with a person and you ask that person to marry you and she either does or she don't, right? That's how I see it now. There ought not be no halfway about it and Dessa and I were halfway. All Dessa would go was halfway. Dessa'd stop halfway to the gates of heaven, turn around and tell the angel Gabriel maybe she'd go on but maybe she's just gonna sit here for awhile. She said maybe to me and she never got around to saying yes. It ain't no way to live together, it makes a man uncomfortable, like he ain't welcome to pull his shoes off. It did me. I pulled my shoes off when I wanted to, I don't mean I didn't ever do that, but I never felt halfway about Dessa and Dessa was halfway about me. She had to be. Why else would she stop halfway? Ask yourself that. I asked myself. Over and over and over again, driving somewhere in the truck, even with Dessa sitting there. I couldn't help it. And I asked Dessa. She'd say "Harry, I'm not with you because I'm tied to you so it must be because I want to be here. You should be pleased by that."

[Dessa:] Moving in together was fine with Harry then. He told everybody he knew that he'd hooked up with a swinging woman. "Knows her own mind" he said. I didn't think I was so swinging or so smart either. At first I was worried and I didn't want it to be awful or expensive if it turned out like my mother was so sure it was going to. But it turned out to be almost easy and I thought we did all right.

[Harry:] For a while, I was satisfied. Took the "being with you" bait hook, line and sinker. But people say more than that to one another. Dessa said you can't say more than that, but I know you can. People get married to each other and marrying is deciding I do or I don't, I am or I ain't, it's drawing some lines. Marrying is not having to sit with your back to the wall anymore. I would have married Dessa right up to the minute I married Brenda and been happy as a bug in a rug, but Dessa wouldn't do it and I could not stand all the maybes any more.

[Dessa:] I thought Harry proved my mother wrong. Turns out he proved her right. What I did was different from my mother but it didn't work and what's funny is that after fourteen years, it's not gonna cost much money to get out. It's hard to say what it is costing. I think what mother was trying to tell me is that loving somebody costs, costs in ways you never know it's gonna cost, costs in ways you never think to think about. Loving daddy cost my mother years of her life. I don't know how many but I'd bet it's true. I don't think loving Harry cost me years—Harry wasn't as hard to love as my daddy—but loving Harry cost me more than loving me cost Harry. I'm the one that got the surprise. "Surprise! I married somebody else!" I wouldn't have ever, ever done that to Harry. I wouldn't have even thought of it.

FROM *DAYTRIPS* (1991)

CHARACTERS

NARRATOR/PAT—Pat is forty or so. They are the same person and *two people play her.* Pat is caught in these stories. The Narrator has the perspective to tell them and to comment. The Narrator speaks with the audience.

REE/IRENE—They are the same person and one person plays them both. Ree, 60 or so, is a victim of Alzheimer's Disease. Irene is younger and healthy. Ree/Irene is the mother of Pat.

ROSE—is old. She is not steady but she does not shake, she stares at things to see but she does not squint. She needs more light, not less. She resists the easy sort of help that is an affront to her dignity. She's hard for the social graces age sometimes strip from people, but she is not mean. Rose is the mother of Irene and Helen, the ghost.

. . .

At the open.

Ree is onstage lost. After a moment, Pat enters holding a jacket.

PAT.   Hey, buddy, I got your jacket.

REE.   Am I going home, Olivia?

PAT.   You are home.

REE.   My mother lives at home.

PAT.   You live with your husband. Remember good old Price?

REE.   I know Price, I married him. And there's a man who says he's Price but he isn't. He's one of the Carter boys but he's not the one I married. It's that other man . . .

PAT.   Ree. Don't start.

REE.   Price does whatever that other man says, he told Price not to let me have another dog. . .

PAT.   We have to put your jacket on.

REE.   And he told him not to let me drive and Price won't let me. I can drive. Oh Olivia, you don't know what it's like not to have a car. And he said I couldn't have a dog. He calls Price and Price just goes wherever that other man wants.

PAT.   Ree! Your jacket.

REE.   Oh.

PAT.   OK. Other arm.

REE.   Olivia, you've got to help me with my money.

PAT.   Your arm buddy.

REE.   Price takes it.

PAT.   Price does not take your money.

REE.   He spends it on that other man and they play golf and they won't take me home. Are you going to take me home?

PAT.   Bend your arm! *(Pat gets the jacket on Ree.)* Good. We're going to see your mother.

REE.   My mother . . .

PAT.   In Kingsport.

REE.   My job is to take care of my mother and Price won't let me drive. *(Ree shucks the jacket as if it were connected to "that other man" and leaves it laying in the floor. Punctuate this change.)*

. . .

(Narrator enters. Pat retrieves the jacket and puts it on Ree with no struggle at all.)

NARRATOR.   *(To audience.)* This is Ree. She used to be Irene. Irene was my mother.

REE.   *(To Pat.)* I don't have children.

NARRATOR.   She has Alzheimer's now.

REE.   My brain is turning into jelly.

NARRATOR.   This is her joke.

REE.   Grape.

NARRATOR.   This is my grandmother, Rose.

REE.   Rose is my mother, I take care of her.

NARRATOR.   Rose's mother was Patricia. I am named after Patricia. I am—

NARRATOR and PAT.   We are Pat.

ROSE.   You are Helen. I know Helen.

PAT.   Helen is dead.

REE.   This is Olivia.

ROSE.   It is not.

NARRATOR and PAT.   Pat.

REE.   Olivia.

NARRATOR.   There is a real Olivia, my great aunt Olivia. Ree confuses me with her. I am gone from Ree's memory but I fit somehow in her memory of Olivia. Tomorrow or next month, I will be somebody else. Ruth, Bernice, Elaine, who knows. Someday she will call me mother because her mother will be all she remembers. *(During the speech, Rose hunts for and finds a box of matches.)*

PAT.   What was she like, Grandmother?

ROSE.   Who?

PAT.   Your mother.

ROSE.   She was a mule. All she knew to do was work.

NARRATOR.   Old age has fragile flesh that makes it hard to pull on shoes or unlock doors or stand up from sitting or bend over. (*Rose lights a match and looks for an electric socket with it.*) Old age hurts in the joints of bones. Old age cannot see except at a certain distance.

PAT.   Grandmother, you light matches to plug the heater in?

ROSE.   You have to be so careful of the juice.

NARRATOR.   She used to be afraid electricity ran out of sockets if they didn't have something in them. (*Rose is a fire hazard with the match. Pat puts it out, takes the box of matches.*) Old age cannot or will not hear.

ROSE.   What'd you say?

REE.   Mother, this is Olivia.

ROSE.   You mean Helen. What does she want?

PAT.   I said you are confused sometimes.

ROSE.   Your time's 'a comin'.

PAT.   Is this a prophecy?

NARRATOR.   She and her husband bought the second model T in Hancock County, Tennessee. She drove it down Clinch Mountain with no brakes but the hand brake. It was the only time she ever drove. They kept their horses to pull it with when it wouldn't start.

ROSE.   Or Floyd ran it out of gas.

NARRATOR.   She is old enough to have been old already when men landed on the moon.

ROSE.   Old enough I shouldn't be livin' alone. Say that and see if it don't stick in your craw, Princess Helen.

. . .

PAT.   (*To Helen, a ghost she cannot see.*) "Too old to be living alone!" Is this what you hear?

NARRATOR.   My aunt Helen has been in her grave 40 years. I speak to her ghost.

PAT.   She gave you birth, she held you as you died. Are you back to take care of her? (*Ree sees a ghost.*)

. . .

NARRATOR.   Ree speaks to the ghost of Burkett.

REE.   Ohhh . . . You pulled my ears, I loved you.

NARRATOR.   Ree speaks with ghosts every chance she gets. Burkett is a favorite uncle also years dead. He pulled my ears too, said it made more room for brains.

REE.   And Margaret! She's not bent. Margaret!

PAT.   Where, buddy?

REE.   (*Points to a place.*) Margaret, you want to dress up paperdolls? (*A transformation, Ree becomes Irene.*)

. . .

PAT.   Mother?

IRENE.   Pat?

PAT.   Which jacket do you want?

NARRATOR.   Irene, my mother speaks of her favorite jacket.

IRENE.   The one that makes me look like Grace Kelly, the one that was much too expensive so I charged it, the one that makes me feel as if I received a Nobel Peace Prize for last week in that library and I am on my way to meet the king of Sweden instead of being on my way to take the queen of East Center Street to the grocery store. (*She has it on. It is the jacket from the opening scene.*) This one. You should try it on sometime. (*A second transformation. Irene to Ree. There are not big physical changes, there is an uncertainty in her bearing and an edge in her voice that turns to panic.*)

NARRATOR.   Ree, my patient, speaks of her clothes.

REE.   Where did I put . . . I swear people take things. Pat takes my clothes, I used to have good clothes, I had a jacket that I really liked and I now see her with it on like I wasn't even here and she just walks around in it. What have you done with my jacket? Why did you take it? (*Pat shows Ree the jacket she has on, then hugs Ree. A third transformation begins from the hug, Ree wants loose, Pat lets go. Ree struggles with the jacket. There are physical changes. Ree has a tilt, her eyes don't focus. She tries to get the jacket off. Same as the end of the opening scene.*) Olivia . . .

PAT.   Leave it on, buddy, you'll need it. We're going to Kingsport.

. . .

ROSE.   (*She was on this subject last time she spoke.*) I need somebody to live with me. Helen.

PAT.   You don't want me, you don't like the way I live, Grandmother.

ROSE.   You'll change.

PAT.   When I change, I'll come live with you.

ROSE.   Lord, just take me home.

PAT.   You are home.

ROSE.   I want to go back to Kyles Ford. You reckon anybody's still alive?

cREBECCA cCAUDILL
(February 2, 1899–October 2, 1985)

Rebecca Caudill was a teacher, an editor, and an author of more than twenty books for young adults and children, many of which were set in Appalachia. Caudill was born in Harlan County, Kentucky, to Susan Smith Caudill and George W. Caudill, who were both teachers. Rebecca was educated at Wesleyan College (A.B., 1920) in Macon, Georgia, and Vanderbilt University (M.A., 1922). After graduate school, she traveled and taught in Brazil, Canada, Russia, and Europe. She met her husband, editor James S. Ayars, in Turkey. The couple was married in 1931 and made their home in Urbana, Illinois. They had two children.

Caudill was in her forties when her first book, *Barrie & Daughter*, was published. One of her early works, *Tree of Freedom*, was runner–up for the 1949 Newbery Award. Her Christmas story, *A Certain Small Shepherd*, was set near Pine Mountain, Kentucky, and was honored as an American Library Association Notable Book in 1965. Seven of her books were Junior Literary Guild selections.

"My roots are in Appalachia," Caudill wrote. "Appalachia has . . . provided me with certain values in writing—simplicity, integrity, exactness. I write slowly, and by hand. I also do a great deal of rewriting. This exercise in revising and finding the exact word and phrase is one I greatly enjoy."

Caudill's Quaker faith is a thread that runs through much of her work. Recurring themes are tolerance, the value of the individual, and a search for peaceful solutions to life's conflicts.

One of Caudill's most enduring books is *My Appalachia*. The nonfiction work couples Caudill's reminiscences of her childhood with social commentary on regional problems. In this excerpt, Caudill describes her return to her childhood home.

OTHER SOURCES TO EXPLORE

PRIMARY

Books for children: *Somebody Go and Bang a Drum* (1974), *Did You Carry the Flag Today, Charley?* (1966), *A Pocketful of Cricket* (1964), *Far-Off Land* (1964), *The Best-Loved Doll* (1962), *Higgins and the Great Big Scare* (1960), *Schoolroom in the Parlor* (1959), *Time for Lissa* (1959), *Susan Cornish* (1955), *The House of the Fifers* (1954), *Saturday Cousins* (1953), *Up and Down the River* (1951), *Schoolhouse in the Woods* (1949), *Tree of Freedom* (1949), *Happy Little Family* (1947), *Barrie & Daughter* (1943). **Nonfiction:** *My Appalachia: A Reminiscence* (1966). **Essay:** "A Child and His Books," *PTA Magazine* 64 (February 1970), 28–29. **Poetry:** *Come Along* (1963).

SECONDARY

Kate Black, "Untapped Resources in the Appalachian Collection: Rebecca Caudill's Papers," *The Kentucky Review* 8:3 (autumn 1988), 73–75. *Contemporary Authors*, Vols. 5–6, 83. *Contemporary Authors*, Vol. 117, 76. *Something About the Author*, Vol. 1, 50–52. *Something About the Author*, Vol. 44, 61.

FROM *MY APPALACHIA: A REMINISCENCE* (1966)

On a summer Sunday morning in 1938 in Harrodsburg, Kentucky, where I had been doing historical research, I glanced idly at the eastern section of a road map of Kentucky.

"Poor Fork!" I thought. "While I'm so near, why not go back to Poor Fork?"

Since I did not need to hurry home, I would go to see the place of my birth and early childhood.

Remembering vividly that other summer morning when our family had set out so blithely across Big Black Mountain, I searched the map for Poor Fork, but in vain. Never mind, I decided recklessly. It had to be there, and it was time I went back.

At the bus station, when I asked for a ticket to Poor Fork, the agent eyed me quizzically between the bars of the window separating us.

"Poor Fork, ma'am? Poor Fork's gone," he said. "Been gone a long time."

"Where did it go?" I asked.

"You ever been there?"

"Once." Then, to keep him from saying it, I added, "A long time ago."

"Well," he said, "if you're still a thinkin' of it as Poor Fork, you're in for a shock when you see it. Gone up in the world. Got a railroad through there and ever'thing. Changed its name to Cumberland. Them big coal mines in Harlan County, they've changed ever'thing. Anyway, can't sell you a ticket to Cumberland. Bus don't go there. Can sell you a ticket to Harlan."

Harlan! The word itself frightened me. I could think nothing good of Harlan. I had never even been there, I recalled. Moreover, so many years had passed since we had moved away from Harlan County that I wasn't sure who of my relatives, if any (they would be on my mother's side) still lived there.

"You want a ticket to Harlan?" the agent prodded me.

"All right," I said, feeling this trip was not turning out to be the carefree adventure I had thought I was planning, "give me a ticket to Harlan."

The bus had no sooner started rolling between the pampered, undulating fields around Harrodsburg than my mind began reviewing all I knew about the trouble in the Harlan County coal fields.

Miles later, as the bus labored up steep slopes into the high mountains, I peered out the window. There stood the massive ranges, majestic and ongoing, dressed in the dark lusterless green of midsummer. Were the trees thinner on the high slopes? Some slopes, I noticed, were almost denuded of large trees and were covered instead with scrubby second growth.

The rivers beside the highway seemed much narrower and shallower than I remembered them. They were muddy, too, though I remembered them as running clear and clean. I recalled the first time I had gone home from college and had found the town near which I then lived looking only half as big as I had remembered it, the streets much narrower, the houses not grand at all but quite ordinary. Could it be, I wondered, that childhood memories are always tinged with romance—that nothing looked at through mature eyes can ever equal in grandeur one's childhood impressions?

I looked out the bus window again. This time I looked especially for the tulip poplar trees. In my childhood I had always thought of the tulip poplars as being the most queenly of trees because they stood so erect and shapely among the gnarled oaks, the crooked wild cherry trees, and the tattered and sprawling sycamores. Even in late fall, when most of the leaves on the mountainside forest had fallen, the poplars were still etched in gold by the few remaining leaves outlining their graceful shapes. But something, I saw, had happened to the poplars. I was not imagining now. The tall poplars I had known were gone from the lower slopes. I knew the chestnut trees had died of a blight, but I had not heard that a blight had attacked the poplars. I was to learn that there are other blights than natural ones, and that no blight is so deadly as that conceived in the calloused human mind.

My spirits were steadily sinking when the driver pulled up to a dirt road and opened the door of the bus. An elderly woman collected her bundles and paper pokes and started down the aisle. As she reached the door, she turned, and, including every passenger in her backward look, said invitingly, "You folks better come home with me for dinner."

In that instant time turned backward straight to my childhood in Poor Fork. How long had it been since I had been treated to openhanded, openhearted, innate courtesy such as this old woman of the mountains was proffering? Not since I had left Poor Fork.

Like a tree in springtime when the sap begins to rise, I felt renewed and warmed and nourished, as if I had actually sat at the old woman's dinner table and partaken of her corn pone and beans. The courtesy and kindness and the helpful ways of people among whom I had lived for a few early years, and had taken for granted at the time, made me forget momentarily the ugly face that in my mind Harlan County now wore. Not everything good and lovely in these people had been destroyed, I contented myself. The certainty buoyed me up.

An hour later the bus driver pulled up in front of a drugstore and called out "Harlan!" I got off the bus and looked around me. The town was as quiet as if it were napping on a lazy summer afternoon. Only a few persons were on the streets. Three men sat on a bench in front of the drugstore, whittling and telling tales.

I went into the drugstore and inquired of the druggist if he knew Conway Smith, a cousin of mine. Yes, said he, he knew him well, and he would put me in touch with him on the telephone.

Shortly thereafter Conway arrived to take me to his house. Obviously the grapevine, originating in the drugstore, went to work, and that evening Conway's house was filled with people. Not only is blood relationship a strong tie in the mountains. Mountain origin itself admits into a close-knit circle all who are mountain born. Until late in the evening we sat talking. Among those present, one had gone to school to my father; another, the son of John Yearey, the other Democrat in our voting precinct at Poor Fork, recalled the rugged times our fathers had had on election days; another recalled our house as the meeting place for all who enjoyed singing to the accompaniment of my mother's little organ.

As we talked leisurely, their soft quiet mountain speech fell on my ears like a lullaby, and their flavorsome mountain words and phrases awoke in me memories of things I had not thought of in years. All about me were warmth and kindness. I began to wonder if the accounts I had read of Harlan County lawlessness could be true.

"What about all the trouble in the Harlan County mines a few years ago?" I asked.

"Oh, it was pretty rough around here for a while," someone said, "especially when all those meddlers from the outside came in here to push us around."

"And you didn't get involved?" I asked, remembering all the influential men who had turned down Dreiser's invitation to involve themselves.

"Oh, no, we weren't involved in any way," they assured me. "So long as nobody bothered us, we didn't bother anybody."

As I lay in bed in my cousin's house that night, I wondered who in the human race is an outsider, and when is a person concerned for human suffering a meddler; wondered if I would have had the courage to involve myself on behalf of free speech and free assembly in Harlan County in 1931; wondered if I would have helped to feed the miners in spite of threats; wondered if I had within me the spirit of reconciliation that the Quakers had within them.

But things were different now, I could see. World War II was in the making. Already the hot winds of coming holocaust were blowing across Europe. Soon would come the bang. Operators and miners were tooling up for the boom.

As I lay and wondered, I also made a discovery. The friends who had filled my cousin's house that evening had not come out of mere curiosity to see one who, starting life among them, had gone over the high rim of the mountains and out into the world. They had come out of affection and respect to see the daughter of George and Susan Caudill.

$\mathscr{L}$ILLIE $\mathscr{D}$. $\mathscr{C}$HAFFIN
(February 1, 1925–October 27, 1993)

Lillie Dorton Chaffin Kash grew up in eastern Kentucky, the daughter of Fairy Belle Kelly Dorton and Kenis Roscoe Dorton. A graduate of Pikeville College (B.S., 1956) and Eastern Kentucky University (M.A., 1966), she began her career as an elementary school teacher and a librarian. In the 1960s, she became a freelance writer of poetry and books for children. As a wife, a mother, a teacher, and a writer, she explained, "I do most of my creative writing at 'odd' hours, mostly from two a.m. to six a.m."

From the beginning, Chaffin (pronounced CHAY-fin) received wide recognition and a number of awards for her writing, including first prize from the National League of American Pen Women for the picture book *A Garden is Good* in 1964, the International Poetry Prize for *A Stone for Sisyphus* in 1967, the Child Study Association Children's Book Award for *John Henry McCoy* in 1971, and a Pulitzer Prize nomination for *8th Day, 13th Moon* in 1975. More than three hundred of her poems appear in anthologies and journals, including *Jack and Jill, Child Life, Humpty Dumpty,* and *Prairie Schooner*. She served as poetry editor to the literary magazine *Twigs* and as fiction editor for *American Pen Women*.

After the death of her first husband, Thomas W. Chaffin, in 1981, she married Vernon O. Kash, who died in 1985. She is survived by one son and four grandchildren.

She described herself as "a child of local economics tied to coal mining, part of everything ever seen, heard, read, and imagined." Having focused her writing on natural subjects and on motherhood, she hoped to be accepted by readers as "regional in the best sense of the word."

OTHER SOURCES TO EXPLORE

PRIMARY

Books for children: *Freeman* (1972), *John Henry McCoy* (1971), *A World of Books* [Autobiography] (1970), *I Have a Tree* (1969), *In My Backyard* (1968), *Bear Weather* (1968), *America's First Ladies* (1968), *Tommy's Big Problem* (1965), *A Garden is Good* (1963). **Poetry:** *Appalachian History and Other Poems* (1980), *Love Poems* (1976), *Star Following* (1976), *8th Day, 13th Moon* (1974), *First Notes* (1969), *A Stone for Sisyphus* (1967), *Lines and Points* (1966).

SECONDARY

Contemporary Authors, First Revision, Vols. 33–36, 180–81. *Something About the Author*, Vol. 4, 44–46.

SECOND CHRISTMAS

from *8th Day, 13th Moon* (1974)

Much has been made of gifts—
Sheba, Wise Men, shepherds, kings
have chosen only the best and traveled far
making delivery—and always, perhaps, a little
selfishly, knowing of whatever joy given they were truly
the recipients.

And so it is with me. I sift store shelves, inspecting
first for safety, discarding all with implications
of war, illness or dependence. And settle for a book
without words. It is shaken, squeezed, left unclaimed
until balls have rolled away, planes have lost rudders.
Then book in hand, child on my lap, gift and giver are complete.

SPENDING THE NIGHT

from *8th Day, 13th Moon*

The child who once magnified
my body's special, dark processing
room, who absorbed his substance from
my chemistry, now is his own—
would wrench himself from affection's
hold.
      Let him be free. I have been
what I must—brief room and board—
hostess to a growing miracle. I will
be what I can.

Discipline

from *8th Day, 13th Moon* (1974)

Loneliness will come. Surrounding yourself
with friends is no insurance; some morning
they will all sleep late or have chores to do,
or you may hear them suddenly speaking
a foreign language, and you with no
interpreter. Some day their tongues could be
whips chasing you. Or you could one night find all
the luxurybound books had the pages clipped
at climaxes or you've read everything,
and setting out to borrow see yourself
the only person on the street, in town.
In times like these don't panic; go as straight
into yourself as you can; and since
this is an alien place, explore, search out.
Better a strange friend in an unknown place
than none, and one you meet at least halfway.

THE GLAD GARDENER

from *Appalachian Heritage* (1987)

When morning comes, I rise
Up like a crocus
Bright and frost free.

Earth that slept beneath
My feet wakes in day lilies
Greening, blossoming.

A one man crusade,
I plant strawberries and
Asparagus for the future.

Like a clump of honeysuckle,
I am filled with art
And with music.

My address is green,
My hands are in the earth
Planting, growing, harvesting.

I learn from crickets
Each autumn to sing
Of last rituals.

$\mathscr{L}$OLETTA $\mathscr{C}$LOUSE
(October 17, 1948–)

Novelist Loletta Clouse spent her childhood in Cumberland Homesteads, a New Deal community in middle Tennessee that was designed to give destitute workers both employment and the opportunity to own a thirty-acre farm. "My grandparents were original Homesteaders," says Clouse. "Before that, they had lived in a coal mining camp, which is where my mother grew up; her childhood stories left a deep impression on me."

After earning a B.S. in education from Tennessee Technological University, in Cookeville, Tennessee, Clouse spent a year driving a bookmobile in rural Appalachia. She then went back to school and earned a Master's degree in Library Science from Peabody College at Vanderbilt University in Nashville. Clouse is currently a library branch manager with the Knox County Public Library system in Knoxville, Tennessee.

"Writing offers that rare, intoxicating moment of being totally engaged in what I am doing," says Clouse. "I have had moments when the words rushed through me faster than I could think. I have had moments when I had to pull the words out of my brain like splinters. Ironically, I have gone back and tried to detect this in my work and I can't tell the inspired words from the words produced through slow agony. Inspired was just a lot more fun."

Clouse's novel, *Wilder*, is set in 1932 and is based on her grandfather's memories of a strike in the Cumberland Plateau mining town of Wilder, Tennessee. In this scene from chapter 6, Lacey Conners struggles with her feelings for two very different men, steady John Trotter and unpredictable Coy Lynn Wilson.

OTHER SOURCES TO EXPLORE

PRIMARY

Novel: *Wilder* (1990).

SECONDARY

George Brosi, "New Appalachian Books," *Appalachian Heritage* 20:1 (winter 1992), 72. Review of *Wilder*, *Library Journal* 115 (1 October 1990), 112.

WILDER (1990)

from Chapter 6

Lacey filled two plates with mounds of food and carried them to a large oak where John was already spreading a quilt. The preaching had been going on for over three hours, and the crowd was drained. They eagerly filled their plates with food the women had brought in covered dishes and spread on long tables covered with white tablecloths. People made their way to the shade of the trees to stretch out, eat their dinners, and rest.

The women were already forcing second helpings on Brother Roberts, the traveling preacher. He had drawn quite a crowd with his talk of hellfire and brimstone and was no doubt entitled to second helpings for the souls he had worked so hard to save, Lacey thought. His face, so recently puffed and mottled with the heat, had gone slack. With his thin, white hair smoothed back into place and the sleeves of his white shirt rolled up, he looked like anyone's favorite uncle, smiling and nodding as the womenfolk flocked about preening and pandering.

In spite of all his descriptive talk of the fate that would befall those who did not heed the Word, many of the men had wandered in and out of the brush arbor during the long sermon to gather in small groups to whittle and talk of other things. However, the women had sat in rapt attention, their faces turned upward at the preacher's heavenly words, glancing down only to shoot meaningful looks at the men and children.

Lacey looked at John who was attacking his food with relish. He glanced up, his mouth full, and grinned sheepishly. It was a look so sweet and familiar it tugged at her heart and sent a spasm of guilt to her stomach. She had spent most of the last three hours trying to keep her mind on the sermon. Secretly, she searched the crowd for Coy. She realized it was a most unlikely place for him to be, but she could not keep her thoughts off him. It had been four days since she had faced him on the back porch and heard him say he had come back for her. By now she was sure that she had imagined it or that he had been making a fool of her again. It confused her more with each rethinking. She had never been so angry with anyone in her life. Most likely he wouldn't even remember what he had said. He was the type, she reasoned, that said whatever struck his fancy without thought to what folks might think, least of all her. Still, he'd had a look about him standing there in the mist, his brow creased, his eyes shadowed, like he had suddenly come to some realization.

Law' me, Lacey, she thought, *you surely are the craziest thing! Coy Lynn Wilson couldn't be nothing but trouble. He just seems bent on destroying everything in his path.* It made her think of a storm that had set down on the Runion place once. The force of the high winds had swirled and twisted the tall grass into tight masses and bowed the heads of the trees. And even then she had wondered why. It was such a senseless striking out. Coy was like that: powerful and beautiful and dangerous. Like a raging storm, he would move on until he burned himself out. Speaking up to him had been like throwing herself in the path of that storm. She had been surprised when her words had stopped him short. His fierce dark eyes had widened, and for a moment his body had stiffened in surprise.

"You haven't touched your food, Lacey," John admonished.

"Too many goings on, I recken," Lacey mumbled. Slowly she came to the realization that she was still at the brush arbor with John. She had the feeling that hours or even days had passed and John had been sitting patiently waiting for her return. "I see you done all right for yourself," she said, noticing his empty plate. "Would you like me to get you some more to eat?"

"No thanks. Guess I done eat a cow's bait, at that. Being outside must give me an appetite. That sure was good huckleberry pie. I notice you brung it."

"You don't have to say so just 'cause I brung it."

"I wouldn't. You know that."

Lacey smiled her thanks, and they sat in silence. John didn't seem to have much need to talk, and she couldn't think of any news to tell him. He hadn't brought up the matter of them getting married, and she was relieved. She needed to bring up the subject of Will, but she wasn't sure how. John had never discussed any of the problems in the mines with her, and she didn't know how much she should know. Her pa had always talked to her like she was a man. It might have been little more than his way of worrying out loud, but he was always telling her about the daily goings on in the mines and about the true working of things. He talked about the men who made the decisions that affected their lives and the way they worked. Because he understood power, he knew how little of it the miners had, and it had made him a cautious man.

"John, Pa says there may be trouble again in the mines," she ventured, cautiously.

"I recken. Your pa's got reason enough to believe it."

"What reason you got to believe it, John?"

"Oh, they's been talk of another wage cut. Won't be no trouble if we accept what they give us." John kept his voice low and glanced over his shoulder before continuing. "They been cheating on their agreements for some time now. We the same as don't have no contract. If we accept this next cut, they as same as broke the union in this county."

Lacey was struck by the hardness in his voice. "You sound like you're not planning on accepting it."

"Look around that table over there, Lacey. How many women you think pulled out the last of their canned stuff to set that spread? How many families you think'll have to scrape by tomorrow on fatback and greens? And it ain't just that. We've had three men killed in the mines in the last two years. They don't care nothin' about our safety. The mine inspectors just look the other way while the miners cut corners trying to make a living wage. They don't have time to set timbers and shore up walls. And all the time the mine owners yelling they're losing money."

Lacey had never heard John talk so, and she wondered if he was thinking of his father. "You believe in the union, don't you, John?"

He looked at her with veiled eyes that revealed only the seriousness of his intentions, then looked around cautiously to see if her voice had carried. "A lot of good men believe in the union, Lacey. I'm just one of them. This here is the only miner's union south of the Ohio River. I just happen to believe that's worth fighting for. I know your pa thinks it's a chancy thing, and I want you to know I wasn't the one that brought Will into it. He done that on his own. I know one thing. There comes a time when a man stands to lose it all, no matter which way he sides. I'm a miner, and I'll always be one."

"Pa's not against the union. He's just seen a lot of hard times that made him cautious."

"Hard times is what the union is all about. The union give us the only say-so we've ever had in the mines on how things was to be. Joining up is something a man's got to do of his own free will, or it don't mean nothing, especially when the going gets rough."

"I don't think I've ever heard you talk so serious, John." In fact, she had never heard him speak so many words on any subject.

"I always wanted to live out my life in Wilder. I thought you felt the same way."

"It's my home, John. You got no call to think you care more about it than I do."

John looked at her shamefaced. "No, I ain't got no call. I know how you feel about this town. The truth is, ain't none of this belong to us. No matter how hard the folks here work, they ain't never going to own the house they live in or the land it's on. The coal company owns it. Lock, stock, and barrel. They do things to suit theirselves. If they took a notion to fire a man and throw him out of his house, it wouldn't matter if he'd worked ever day like a dog in the mines and lived in that house for ten year. They could do it 'cause they got the power to say what goes. I recken that's why I get worked up when I think of the union. The union seems like the only chance we got to hang on to what we got, to build any kind of life here." John scratched at the soft ground with a twig, making circles in the dirt. Without looking up, he whispered, "I'm doing this for you, too, Lacey."

She looked at his veiny hand, the coal-stained fingernails nervously pushing at the ground. It was the first hint of his plans for their future. "John, you're into this deep, ain't you?"

John gave her a sidelong glance.

"What'll the company do to you if they find out?"

Shrouding his eyes with a hand, John stroked his forehead and spoke softly. "Everything they can, Lacey. Everything they can."

ℐNN ℰOBB
(September 15, 1885–January 12, 1960)

A native New Englander, Ann Cobb arrived in Kentucky in 1905 at the invitation of May Stone, a former classmate at Wellesley College. Stone and a fellow teacher, Katherine Pettit, had established the Hindman Settlement School (a school for mountain youth) in eastern Kentucky in 1902. Cobb was so impressed with the fledgling school that she joined the Hindman staff and remained there until her retirement in 1957.

Cobb's poetry, based on her experiences with mountain people, appeared regularly in national magazines such as the *Saturday Evening Post* and *St. Nicholas*. In 1922, the Houghton Mifflin Company published *Kinfolks*, a collection of Cobb's poetry about mountain life. The book's heavy reliance on dialect (which was much admired by critics in the 1920s) makes the material rather ponderous to modern ears. However, scholars continue to regard *Kinfolks* as a groundbreaking work, and Cobb is generally credited with having produced one of eastern Kentucky's earliest collections of poetry.

OTHER SOURCES TO EXPLORE

PRIMARY

Books for children: *An English Christmas* (1978). **Poetry:** *Kinfolks & Other Selected Poems,* ed. Jeff Daniel Marion (2003). *Kinfolks: Kentucky Mountain Rhymes* (1922).

SECONDARY

Kentucky in American Letters 1913–1975, Vol. 3 (1976), ed. Dorothy Townsend, 77–81. Jess Stoddart, *The Quare Women's Journals* (1997), 28, 36, 300. Jeff Daniel Marion, Introduction, *Kinfolks & Other Selected Poems* by Ann Cobb (2003), ix–xi. William S. Ward, *A Literary History of Kentucky* (1988), 89–90.

THE BOY

from *Kinfolks:*
Kentucky Mountain Rhymes (1922)

Everything's predestined,
  So the Preachers say—
Wisht I'd been predestined
  To be my brother Clay.

He's the only man-child
  Mammy ever bore.
Four of us that's older,
  Sev'ral young-uns more.

Eats with Pop and Grandsir',
  While we women wait.
Has his wings and drumsticks
  Waiting, if he's late.

Rides behind with Poppy,
  When he goes to mill,
Fun'ral-meetings, anywhar
  Hit suits his little will.

Folks delight to sarve him,
  Let him come and go,—
No! he's not so pettish,
  Hit's a marvel, though.

Everything's predestined,
  And hit's not so bad.
We'd 'a' been right lonesome
  With nary little lad.

HOSPITALITY

from *Kinfolks:*
Kentucky Mountain Rhymes (1922)

Put your purse up, woman,—you'll never need hit here.
Lees don't foller selling a mouthful of good cheer.

We'll not miss the chicken, nor yet the bite of cake.
(Sence my baby married I throw out half I bake!)

"Hit don't cost you nothing," I was raised to say,
"Nothing but the promise to come again and stay."

THE WIDOW MAN

from *Kinfolks:*
Kentucky Mountain Rhymes

I've brung you my three babes, that lost their Maw a year ago.
Folks claim you are right women, larned and fitten for to know
What's best for babes, and how to raise 'em into Christian men.
I've growed afeard to leave 'em lest the house ketch fire again.
For though I counsel 'em a sight each time I ride to town,
Little chaps get so sleepy-headed when the dark comes down!

A body can make shift somehow to feed 'em up of days,
But nights they need a woman-person's foolish little ways
(When all of t'other young things are tucked under mammy's wing,
And the hoot-owls and the frogs and all the lonesome critters sing).
You'll baby 'em a little when you get 'em in their gown?
Little chaps get so sleepy-headed when the dark comes down!

KIVERS

from *Kinfolks: Kentucky Mountain Rhymes* (1922)

Yes, I've sev'ral kivers you can see;
'Light and hitch your beastie in the shade!
I don't foller weaving now so free,
And all my purtiest ones my forebears made.
Home-dyed colors kindly meller down
Better than these new fotched-on ones from town.

I ricollect my granny at the loom
Weaving that blue one yonder on the bed.
She put the shuttle by and laid in tomb.
Her word was I could claim hit when I wed.
"Flower of Edinboro" was hits name,
Betokening the land from which she came.

Nary a daughter have I for the boon,
But there's my son's wife from the level land,
She took the night with us at harvest-moon—
A comely, fair young maid, with loving hand.
I gave her three—"Sunrise" and "Trailing Vine"
And "Young Man's Fancy." She admired 'em fine.

That green one mostly wrops around the bread;
"Tennessee Lace" I take to ride behind.
Hither and yon right smart of them have fled.
Inside the chest I keep my choicest kind—
"Pine-Bloom" and "St. Ann's Robe" (of hickory brown),
"Star of the East" (that yaller's fading down!).

"The Rose?" I wove hit courting, long ago—
Not Simon, though he's proper kind of heart—
His name was Hugh—the fever laid him low—
I allus keep that kiver set apart.

"Rose of the Valley," he would laugh and say,
"The kiver's favoring your face to-day!"

Author's note: In the Kentucky mountains for generations the chief outlet for the artistic sense of the women has been the weaving of woolen coverlets, many of them of elaborate pattern and rare beauty.

LISA COFFMAN
(August 14, 1963–)

Poet Lisa Coffman grew up in East Tennessee. Her mother's family lived in Glenmary, Tennessee, a once bustling logging and mining town. She completed her B.A. in computer science and English at the University of Tennessee in 1985, spent a year in Germany as a Rotary Exchange Scholar at Universität Bonn, and then earned an M.A. in English from the creative writing program at New York University in 1989.

Her first book of poems, *Likely*, won the 1995 Stan and Tom Wick Poetry Prize, a national first-book competition sponsored by Kent State University Press and judged by Alicia Ostriker. Coffman has received fellowships from the National Endowment for the Arts, the Pew Charitable Trusts, the Pennsylvania Council on the Arts, and Bucknell University, where she was resident poet. The Pew grant allowed her to spend six months in Rugby, Tennessee, studying family history and writing. Her poems have appeared in numerous anthologies and literary magazines, including the *Southern Review* and the *Philadelphia City Paper*.

She has worked as a staff writer for the *North Jersey Herald & News* (1989–1990), as a freelance writer (1990–1998, 2001–present), and as an English professor at Pennsylvania State University, Altoona College (1998–2001). She has been writing poetry for more than fifteen years. She says, "Place and landscape are enormously important in my poetry, and no place more so than the Southern Appalachian Mountains, where I grew up and lived until I was 21. When I'm away from the mountains—which has been for most of my adult life—I'm often trying to conjure the place in my poems, to fasten down what it is that I love about the region, perhaps so that I won't miss it too badly. The color and cadence of Southern Appalachian speech has been the strongest influence so far on the lines of my poems."

Other Sources to Explore

Primary

Poetry: *Likely* (1996).

Secondary

Scott Barker, "Poet sings songs of human heart" [review of *Likely*] *Knoxville News-Sentinel* (22 June 1997), F7. Patricia M. Gantt, "A Level Gaze Trained at Life: The Poetry of Lisa Coffman," in *Her Words* (2002), ed. Felicia Mitchell, 69–81.

IN ENVY OF MIGRATION

from *Likely* (1996)

1.

The new American Fabricare laundromat
built from an out-of-business ribs place
keeps its lights on until late
and fans flicking underneath the lights
and women outside leaned against the thick storefront glass
and children orbiting those women's laps.

2.

I was home when the starlings crossed over.
The flock settled and lifted off the yard as it passed.
Always they were calling ahead, behind.
They seemed to have great news.
I think it is pride iridescing their black wings,
pride of the Many-in-One,
like the stand of oaks when the wind starts
or the many impeccable bones of the foot.

3.

The femur prepares for journey
for years: long mineral additions in secret.
Then it can slacken over the shapes of car seats
or chairs in offices
or porch stairs during a joblessness,
or I have seen it part the china color of streetlight
under one left walking when the night is on us.

MAPS

from *Likely* (1996)

FOR CURTIS O. ROBERSON (1906-1994)

In 1960, my grandmother's cousin Curtis Roberson was one of two men assigned by the Appalachian Power Company to find and move all graves in a four-county area near Roanoke, Virginia, that would subsequently be flooded by the Smith Mountain Dam Project. Over the next two-and-a-half years, Curtis and his partner Herbert Taylor, both APCo employees since the 1930s, supervised the relocation of 1,361 graves.

1.

Rely on old maps: they hold a place
just as our faces retain who we have been
and will shine with us now in who we will be,
so dearly does the flesh love us—

its palm lines are said to be a map
of our wanderings under the stars,
then into the root-starred earth.

2.

Ah, lo—
What was the little song you would sing at evening
free from the burden of work
when all paths led endlessly into the green ease of the world?

lo lo Lord—
Did you sing of the good Christians going to heaven?
Of the sweet one leaned forward on the porch
until all but your white shirt was gone in the dark?

Lord, Lord, Lord—
Or did you sing of the forgotten dead
pocketed in the green hills of Bedford County
of Franklin and Roanoke Counties?

Some later resting above the flexing rim of Smith Mountain Lake
some dissolving with the soft lake bed
most the Company moved—

some having left as witness loose buttons,
teacups alongside a thigh, wedding bands,
some unmarked, attended by periwinkle

said to grow of its own accord over the dead.
But by then you were getting on,
a good Company man, instructed to watch

each moved to a two-by-two-by-one-foot box.

    3.

My father is photographed above lit-up Roanoke Valley,
age fourteen. This face shows up later in my brother.
Curtis is photographed with his prize roses.
Smith Mountain Dam floods more light into Roanoke.
Maps are changed. And so on.
Proof of the grave is a stain left in the earth
from the corpse, the clothes it wore. Sure, girl
all the grave holds is a little colored soil
he says, peace of old men on him,
straightens his prize roses. Old maps, inaccurate,
still tell the sites of graves. But flesh maps
what we lose, and all traces of a body's music.

ABOUT THE PELVIS

from *Likely* (1996)

Pelvis, that furnace, is a self-fueler:
shoveler of energy into the body.

It is the chair that walks. Swing
that can fire off like a rocket.

It carries the torso, it sets the torso down.
It connects the brother legs, and lets them speak.

Trust the pelvis—it will get everything else there:
pull you onto a ledge, push you into a run.

It is the other spine, prone, like the fallow field.
Here are the constellations of the pelvis:

Drawn Bow, Flame-of-One-Branch,
Round Star, and Down-Hanging-Mountains.

Here is the dress of the pelvis: crescent belly,
and buttocks shaken like a dance of masks.

Forget the pelvis, and you're a stove good for parts:
motion gone, heat gone, and the soup pots empty.

TICK

from *Meridian* (2000)

"Adults find hosts, suck blood, and mate. . . . Mating usually takes place on the host before feeding."

—from *Ticks and What You Can Do About Them*
by Roger Drummond, Ph.D.

Harpoon-lipped wicked French kisser,
you near-do-nothing fattening
at someone else's board. How come
no heart beats all that blood, heat drop,
balloon thirst, all lust? If our lives
are wrought by curse, who thought up yours
and for what crime? You do not ask
not to be hated, but approach
with galley-slave rowing motion
to your stubble legs, your slowness
not from indecision, not fear.
You scale the biggest predator,
risk a six-figure inflated
desk-bound mammal same as the cur
he's just kicked, and grip your beach ball
bodied mate, a mangy hide bed
as good to you as my white skin
for fornication. You'd bite God!
Not daunted by coagulant,
not ashamed to hide your head
in rusty rivers everyone shuns,
you spit cement instead of fire,
a neat eater for a glutton.

Homely stigmata non grata,
we are not spared the cruelty
of mashing you with a brick edge,
a letter file, or, with tweezers

holding you to the thin match flare
until you pop. You do not go
easily, but ride the toilet's
tipped flush, upright as a captain
around and around, out of sight.

A wasp dangles legs delicate
as kite tails, the spider crochets
circular doilies, why do we
see in you nothing to admire,
nothing of ourselves? Heat seeker,
the places sweet to us are sweet
to you: neck, waist, the feathery
clefts of the crotch, taut soft hinges
where you plunge, hang head down, succumb.

AMY TIPTON CORTNER
(June 22, 1955–)

Amy Tipton Cortner is a writer and a teacher who grew up in Johnson City, Tennessee. She is the daughter of Anne Grafton Tipton, a homemaker "whose profession continues to be caring for all of us—not an easy task," says Cortner. Cortner traces her maternal heritage to South Carolina from the 1640s and her paternal connections to East Tennessee from 1768. Her father, Kermit Tipton, is a retired coach and teacher.

She has an undergraduate degree in American Studies (1977) and an M.A. in English (1983) from East Tennessee State University. She has taught Tennessee literature and traditional dance in the Tennessee Governor's School, and, since 1985, has taught a variety of English courses at Caldwell Community College in Hudson, North Carolina.

A popular essayist about her home region of Appalachia, she says that "being an educated, middle-class woman from Appalachia garners exactly the same reaction Samuel Johnson had to the 'woman who preaches.'" [He said, "a woman preaching is like a dog's walking on his hind legs. It is not done well; but you are surprised to find it done at all."] She goes on to explain that "Walker Percy once said, in essence, that writers have to get mad about something before they can strike a lick. That isn't always so, but much of my writing has sprung from a profound irritation at those who will not let me have a say in defining who and what I am."

She is the author of a number of essays about living in the region; "Eminent Domain" has often been reprinted. She is the author of a poetry chapbook, *The Hillbilly Vampire.*

OTHER SOURCES TO EXPLORE

Poetry: *The Hillbilly Vampire* (1990). **Selected essays:** "Fred Chappell's *I Am One of You Forever*: The Oneiros of Childhood Transformed," *Poetics of Appalachian Space* (1991), ed. Parks Lanier, 28–39. "Eminent Domain," *Now & Then: The Appalachian Magazine* (summer 1989), 6–8. "How I Lost My War with *National Geographic*," *In These Times* (14 December 1997), 39–40.

THE HILLBILLY VAMPIRE

from *The Hillbilly Vampire* (1990)

Many people
      are confused about hillbilly vampires.

They think:
      a hillbilly vampire should look like
      George Jones in a cape
      or Ricky Skaggs with fangs
      or Lyle Lovett, period.

They think
      the hillbilly part comes first—
      the feeder, not the fed upon.

They do not understand
      that this
      is another outside industry
      come down to the hills in the dark
      for raw material.

The Vampire Ethnographer

from *The Hillbilly Vampire* (1990)

The hillbilly vampire lived in a condo
      called Mountain Heritage Estates.
He had many degrees
      and many publications in small magazines.
Garlic didn't faze him, nor did the crucifix;
      pintos and streaked meat and kraut would, however,
      turn him in an instant.

Prowling the bars and back roads
      looking for fresh informants
      whose heart-blood of mountain lore
      had not yet been discovered
      and sucked dry,
      tape recorder fanged and to the ready,
      he worked hard at blending in
      while maintaining the mystique
      of his authority.
He bought sharp work pants from Sears
      plaid flannel shirts from Woolrich
      shoes from L.L. Bean and Timberline.

He didn't fool anybody.

As soon as he sat down
      they pulled their collars up
      and started talking copyright
      and photo-session and P.M. Magazine.

His bitterest complaint
      as he moved from place to unsatisfying place
      pale and eager to feed
      was of how thoroughly the folk
      had been corrupted by
      electronic media.

NO MINORITY

from *The Hillbilly Vampire* (1990)

There is no name
    (so she was told)
    for what you are.

Two generations into town
    is one too far.

One generation still
    retains some authenticity:
    a measure of—veracity.
Legitimacy, if you will.

It's either or—it's town or hill.

Just listen to the way you speak.

You bought a book to learn to play.
You took a class to learn to dance.
That hardly is the mountain way.

No. There isn't any more to say.
There is no name for what you are.

It is, however, plain to see
    that you are no
    minority.

LOU V.P. CRABTREE
(March 13, 1913–)

Born in Washington County, Virginia, Lou Crabtree has spent most of her life in Appalachia. She credits her mother for teaching her to love words. "She loved to read and she taught me to love literature when I was real young." Her father attended Milligan College in Tennessee. Although he never went to law school, he served as a "squire" who officiated over local disputes and trials for forty years.

Lou Crabtree explains that her father had two families. The children from his first marriage lived with her family, though, she says, "we never got along." She graduated from Greendale High School and from Radford University (B.S., cum laude). Then she left for New York, where she studied at the American Academy of Dramatic Arts and the Faegin School of Drama. She served for years as regional auditioner for the American Academy.

She married a farmer, Homer Crabtree, and without a doctor, gave birth to "five children who grew to be adults." After her husband died in 1960, she moved to Abingdon, where she retired after teaching in Virginia public schools for thirty-five years. During that time, she also taught adult education classes for Venuzeulan, Indian, and Vietnamese students working to earn G.E.D. high school equivalency certificates. She also worked with the Mount Rogers Area Commission on Aging.

From 1975 to 1985, she directed and performed with the band Rock of Ages, a group of musicians over age sixty-five. After Lee Smith helped her to get her stories published, *Sweet Hollow* was nominated for the PEN/Faulkner Award, and it won the Highlands Festival Award for Creative Writing.

"During the first sixteen years of my life," she said, "my company was mostly the animals and the flowers and the trees," and she delighted in their company. "We named everything. I tried to get that feeling into my stories. I have the little girl in 'Homer-Snake' do that, because that was what we did."

OTHER SOURCES TO EXPLORE

PRIMARY

Drama: *Calling on Lou* (1984). **Poetry:** *The River Hills & Beyond* (1998). **Short stories:** *Sweet Hollow* (1984). **Autobiographical essay:** "Paradise in Price Hollow," in *Bloodroot* (1998), ed. Joyce Dyer, 81–86.

SECONDARY

Timothy Dow Adams, "Juxtaposition, Indirection, and Blacksnakes in Lou Crabtree's *Sweet Hollow*: A Review Essay," *Southern Quarterly* 23:4 (summer 1985), 90–93. Edwin T. Arnold, "Lou Crabtree Addresses the Mysteries of Life," *Appalachian Journal* 14:1 (fall 1986), 56–61. Joyce Dyer, "Lou V.P. Crabtree," in *Bloodroot*, 80. Roy Hoffman, review of *Sweet Hollow*, *New York Times Book Review* (March 4, 1984), 22. Judy K. Miller, "What Kind of Egg Are You? A Profile of Lou V. Crabtree," in *Her Words* (2002), ed. Felicia Mitchell, 85–93. Jean Tobin, review of *Sweet Hollow*, *Studies in Short Fiction* 22:2 (spring 1985), 243–44.

Homer-Snake

from *Sweet Hollow* (1984)

Old Marth claimed all the blacksnakes as hers. She tongue-lashed the roving Murray boys, who went into people's barns and caught snakes and took them by their tails and cracked them like whips. This cracking broke the body of the snake and sometimes snapped off its head. It was terrible to see the Murray boys wring a snake around a few times, then give a jerk and off snap the head.

Old Marth lived in her cabin next to our cabin down in the hollow of the river hills. She pinned her gray hair with long wire hairpins. I watched her stick the wire hairpins into her hair with little flicks of the wrist. It hurt her head, I thought. Only when she was bothered did her hair escape the pins and fall in gray wisps about her face. Bud, my brother younger than I a few years, thought it his mission in life to trail me, to spy, and to report on me to Maw. Some things Bud would tell but not many. Only things on me. Bud said I told everything I knew. Maw said it, too. Because of this, Bud never let me trek over the hills with him.

He said, "She just can't keep from talking. She talks all along the trace. If you talk, you don't get to know anything."

Old Marth leaned down close to Bud. "Blacksnakes are best of friends. Come down to my house and I'll show you Homer-snake."

I had seen Homer-snake many times. Bud had, too. Homer had lived for years back of Old Marth's house in the corner of the outside rock chimney. A hole was visible, where for warmth Homer crawled in the winter.

I once asked Old Marth, "Did Homer-snake dig his hole by himself?"

Old Marth replied, "I expect it is a once frog hole."

What Old Marth told Bud next was not news to Bud or to me. We had both seen it a million times.

"Homer-snake likes milk to drink. I put out milk for him in his saucer every day. Best of all he likes cream, which I don't give him but ever once in a while. He might get too fat to go in his hole." Old Marth laughed, then fiercelike advanced close to Bud. "Don't you ever come to be tormenting blacksnakes. I'll be wastin' my breath if you come to be like them rovin' Murray boys. Come to my house soon and get better acquainted with my Homer-snake."

Old Marth wouldn't have liked what Bud was carrying around in his pocket. I asked him what the small white rocks were that looked like they were rolled in salt.

"Blacksnake eggs. I found them under a rock up the ridge."

Old Marth was always asking me to go home with her to spend the night. She never asked Bud. He tried to devil me behind Old Marth's back.

"How would you like to turn down your bed covers and there would be Old Homer all curled up warming your bed?"

Then I accused Bud of being jealous, and we got into one of our many spats until Maw moved in, saying, "Old Marth just don't like boys. She is suspecting on account of them Murray boys."

Bud never was known to give up. He used to slink around the house as I was leaving, and peep around the corner, and hiss, "Don't sit down on Homer-snake."

Behind Old Marth's house and up a little rocky path was her vegetable garden. To one side was her little barn where she kept her cow, some hens, and a red rooster. The rooster did not like Homer and gave him many a good flogging. He raked Homer with his spurs until Homer fled from the barn, leaving the rooster and hens alone.

Nevertheless, on the sly, Homer would steal into the barn where he unhinged his jaws and swallowed whole one of the hen's nice eggs. Then off he would sneak, toward the rocky path, where he knocked and banged himself against the rocks until the prongs on his ribs crushed the shell of the egg. Once I saw Homer with a huge knot along his body, and I rushed to Old Marth, alarmed.

Old Marth answered in a knowing way. "Most likely an egg. Could be a mouse or a baby rabbit. Homer-snake is having his dinner."

Once the Murray boys were out "rogueing"—knocking off apples and stealing eggs. Homer was in the warm hen's nest where the hen had just laid a nice egg. Homer liked the warmth and was nestling down and warming himself before swallowing the egg, which was sort of an ordeal for him. A rude hand, reaching into the nest, and pulling out Homer, let go quickly. Even the Murray boys didn't like surprises like Homer.

"Homer is my protection," cackled Old Marth as the Murray boys skirted her place, skulking about carrying an old sack they put their loot into. Old Marth guessed that the Murray boys were out to get Homer. Twice they were almost successful.

Homer loved to climb trees. There were young birds and other delights. He played hide and seek up in the sycamore tree down by the little springhouse. He climbed to the very tiptop and out of his snake eyes viewed the world. I liked to watch him hang like a string and swing in the sycamore tree.

On this particular day, Old Homer had left the sycamore and was up in the tree that had the squirrel's nest. It had once been a crow's nest, but the squirrels had taken over for the summer. In the winter they had a fine home in a hole just below the crow's nest.

Homer liked young squirrels almost as much as young rabbits.

The Murray boys almost got Homer that time. They spotted him up in the tree that had the squirrel's nest. Climbing a tree was nothing to the Murray boys. They could climb to the top of any tree in the Hollow. Homer-snake was in a predicament. The leanest of the Murrays was coming right on up the tree with no problem. Homer couldn't see Old Marth anywhere. It would be too late in a minute. A rough hand would be reaching for him.

There were some small limbs, too small to hold the weight of a boy, and farther on, still smaller limbs that just possibly could hold up a snake. Out crawled Old Homer and with great care coiled himself round and round the smallest ones.

The Murray boy was plain mad. The limb would not hold up his weight. He ventured out as far as he could and leaned out and down and stretched his arm toward Homer.

"Shake him loose. Shake hard."

Round and round the tree looking up, calling louder and louder, went the rest of the boys until the red rooster brought together his pack of hens and they all set to cackling, which caused the hogs to trot around the pen, grunting. Just in time, out of the house, like a whirlwind, came Old Marth. The Murray boys knew to make themselves scarce and they hightailed it, except the one caught up in the tree who tried to skin down fast. Old Marth got hold of his hair and yanked him about, and when he left, he left a piece of his shirt with Old Marth.

Laughter floated backwards as the Murray boys hightailed it, putting distance between them and Old Marth's screeching.

"Rogues! Torments! Thieves!"

So Homer was saved this first time.

Another time, the Murray boys were watching Old Marth's house and knew she was away. They were walking around looking at the roots she had tied up to the rafters of her porch. They had been down to the hogpen and down to the springhouse and had drunk out of the gourd. They spied Homer, who was coming from the garden. He barely got halfway in his door when one of the Murrays got him by the tail, straining and tugging to pull him out. What they did not know was that no one, not anyone, can pull a snake out of his hole, once he gets part way in. The snake swells up and spreads his scales and each scale has a tiny muscle. The snake may be pulled into two parts, but he will never be moved. The Murray boys did not give up easy as they pulled and tugged.

"Pull harder. Yank him outa there."

Homer was about to come apart when he felt footsteps coming along on the ground. Old Marth, home early, came upon the scene and chased off the Murrays with a tongue-lashing they would remember. Homer-snake was saved the second time, but there was to be a third.

In the late summer, Homer got a new skin. He molted. He had a bad case of lassitude. Then his whole body was itching so he could not rest. His lips began to split and his eyes turned milky. He was milky-looking all over. He made trip after trip up into the garden, ate a big lunch of snails and bugs, and lazed back down over the rocky path.

One day there was his old skin beside the path in the rocks. Of course he knew all along what he was doing and just how to do it. He rubbed and rubbed himself against the rocks until his old skin loosened and he rolled it off wrong side out. Just like Bud shed his clothes.

Old Marth found the skin and tied it with several others to the rafters of her porch. When the wind rattled them, they scared me, but not Homer's old enemies, the Murrays.

Old Marth said to Bud after Homer shed his skin, "I will make you acquainted with the new Homer. Don't you like him? Ain't he handsome? Like a new gun barrel, he is."

With his new skin, Homer was so shiny and new, I think Bud almost liked him. Homer looked "spit shined," like Paw said about his shoes from his old army days.

Homer got along real well with the cow. She ignored him and never got ruffled if she came upon him suddenly. Homer only had to watch her feet. She did not care where she stepped. Four feet were a lot to watch and one day Homer got careless. One of the cow's feet came down hard on about three inches of Homer's tail. When Homer looked back, the end of his tail was broken off and sticking out of the mud in the cow's track. His beautiful tail. So for the rest of his life he went about trailing his blunted tail, and after a while he didn't seem to miss it.

Bud said, "I can always tell if it is Homer trailing through the sands and dust. Among the squiggles you can see where his old stepped-on tail went."

Down in the springhouse Old Homer guarded the milk crocks. He would curl around a crock like giving it a good hugging. Old Marth had to keep the lids weighted down with heavy rocks so Homer wouldn't knock the covers off and get in the milk.

Looking back, behind the springhouse, was a swath of daisies with bunches of red clover marked here and there, winding all the way to the top of the ridge. This swath was Homer-snake's special place. He liked to lie and rest and cool off among the daisies. He played all the way to the top of the ridge, got tired and slept, had lunch along the way, slithered down when he chose, spending the whole of a summer's day to arrive back home in the cool of the evening. The daisies gave Homer-snake a nice feeling.

The Murray boys were Homer's end. This was the third encounter.

"All things have an end," Maw said later.

Maw sent me down to Old Marth's place to swap some quilt pieces. Going to her house was all right if I could locate Homer. Sitting on Homer or having him swing down from a rafter and touch me on the shoulder never got any less upsetting. But something bad was waiting for us all that day at Old Marth's place.

Homer was fat and lazy and full of cream.

"I'll put in a spoon of jelly for you, Homer." Old Marth put the jelly in Homer-snake's saucer and went on her way. She was going over the hill to visit and take a sample of the jelly.

Homer loved the jelly. Then I know he began feeling lonely. Loneliness led to carelessness. He failed to notice that everything was too quiet. The birds were quiet like the Murray boys were in the vicinity. The chickens were quiet like a hawk was circling. Homer decided to slip past the rooster and go into the barn to rest.

The Murray boys were out "funning" all day all over the hills. They were stirring up bees' nests beside the trace and getting people stung. They were running the cows so they wouldn't let their milk down. They were riding the steers and tormenting the bull.

They saw Old Marth going over the ridge and grinned at each other and jammed down their old hats over their ears and hitched up their britches. Preparing themselves. Preparing to steal eggs out of the hens' nests, they went into the barn. Bud saw it all and told Maw.

Maw said to me, "There is such a thing as keeping your mouth shut."

Bud was watching the Murray boys that day. He had trailed them and watched from the far edge of the woods on the top of the hill. Bud was always watching. I saw him in the plum grove. He was no partner in what happened.

The Murray boys went into the barn with their everlasting sack, stayed a few minutes, rushed out toward the hogpen, pitched the sack, and whatever was in it, over to the hogs. Then they laughed and shouted and hightailed it.

I saw it. Bud saw it. I ran to tell Maw.

"They threw the sack and Homer in it into the hogpen. The hogs will eat up Homer." I was running, screaming wild, and blubbering.

I was so excited with telling the tale that I had not had time to feel sorry for Homer. The hogpen was one place Homer never fooled around. Even Homer knew that hogs ate up blacksnakes.

Bud had come up. "How are you going to keep her from blabbing?" Bud thought he was the world's best at keeping his mouth shut. He gloried in keeping secrets.

I wanted to talk about what I saw, and I wanted to bring it up ever afterwards and keep asking questions. There was so much to wonder about.

"She will tell her guts," Bud said.

"Let Homer bide," was what Maw said to me and meant it. I could tell for her mouth was a straight line across.

Old Marth came home, missed Homer and looked everywhere. Bud and I stood around and watched her. Her eyes were on the ground looking for some sign, trying to find a trail.

I mooned around and was about sick seeing Old Marth with her graying hair stringing and wisping about her face. Until one day, Old Marth said, "If Homer were alive, he would show up. I know when to give up hopes. I resign myself."

Determined not to let anything slip about Homer, for a while, it helped to clap both hands over my mouth when questions began popping in my head. I didn't want ever to be the first one to tell about Homer being eaten by the—I must not say it now.

Maw kept saying, "Let it bide a while."

Old Marth came back to our house to churn. Her hair like a cap was pinned up with long hairpins. Maw required neat hair around the butter, for a hair found in the butter made a bad tale up and down the Hollow.

I kept holding both hands over my mouth to keep from telling until one day Old Marth noticed and said, "You are acting funny." Turning to Maw, she said, "The child is sick. Goes around all the time about to vommick holding her hands over her mouth. Just might be she is wormy and needs a dose."

I wasn't sick. Maw knew it. Bud knew it.

Days went by, to a day when I went down for a look in the hogpen. The hogs grunted, pointed their ears, and looked up at me with their little pig eyes close together.

There under the slop trough I saw it. The proof I was not seeking. I saw a piece of old sack. I screamed what the whole world already knew. "They threw the sack and Homer in it into the hogpen. The hogs ate up Old Homer." I leaned against the pen and I retched until I spit up. I was really sick. The hogs saw it. Bud did, too, for he was in the plum grove, spying as usual. I started running, jumped some puddles, got tired, and came to stop where some daisies covered with dust were beside the road.

I began feeling nice. The daisies were nice. Old Marth's place behind me was nice. Up overhead the fleecy sheep clouds stood stock still to become masses of daisies. Over to the left was a patch of red sky clover. Then the sheep clouds moved together and formed a maze and across the sky was a swath of daisies. Just like the swath Homer had traveled up the trace to the top of the ridge. I was delighted and looked a long while. I know I saw it. There placed in the maze of daisies he loved so well was Homer-snake. He stood upright on the end of his blunt tail and looking over the daisies, he laughed at me.

I laughed and went home.

Maw's kitchen was nice with smells of sassafras tea, spicewood, ginger-root, milk cheeseing, and cold mint water fresh from the spring.

Bud came in the door, reporting on me. "Maw, I saw her. She has been down to Old Marth's hogpen."

"Whatever for, child?"

Maw didn't expect an answer, and I had already turned my back on Bud. I felt something new in my life. The day was coming soon when I could handle Bud. Maw refers to it as *patience*. Patience was something Bud did not have. Bud hung around, waiting on me to start talking and telling everything. I sat until Bud gave up and left, then I told Maw, "I saw Old Homer-snake among the daisies in the sky. He stood up on his blunt tail and laughed at me."

Maw left her dough-making and with flour up to her elbows, she took my head in both hands. "Precious. You saw what you hoped for, for Homer. Homer-snake is all right. You are all right. Find your little pan. You can come help me make up this bread."

SISTER

from *The River Hills & Beyond* (1998)

It was not that I minded
        being old
I just never thought of her
        that way
She came and found my bed
        to talk
She said of old sad things
And scars left on us all
My arm found the curve
        of her
And we were young again
In a cold bed on a cold night
My cold feet moved away
        from hers
It was not I minding
        being old
That I shivered as my
        little sister slept
And in the dark she did not know
        I wept.

Sports Widow

from *The River Hills & Beyond* (1998)

Got anything you want to say
*   before the season starts?*

Ball one. Ball two. Three games going
        Two tv's and a radio
        My God there are reruns

Boredom. Trouble, you light
        on the sports widow

Bring me a beer
        in his stocking feet
        he stomps his hat upon the floor
Kill the umpire
        O God he is killing me

Rattle pans   slam the door
        step on the dog's tail
How do I like trying to talk
        to a peacock

Sam, I am going to leave you
how would you like to
        kiss a crocodile
You know what I am telling
        you to kiss
He won't move out

OLIVE TILFORD DARGAN
[FIELDING BURKE]
(January 11, 1869–January 22, 1968)

Olive Tilford Dargan's literary career spanned half a century and embraced numerous genres, including poetry, drama, short stories, and novels. Dargan was born on a farm near Litchfield, Kentucky, and spent her early childhood there. When she was ten, her schoolteacher parents moved the family to Missouri. Dargan earned a degree from Peabody College in Nashville and subsequently taught in Arkansas, Texas, and Nova Scotia.

From 1893 to 1894, she attended Radcliffe, where she met Harvard student Pegram Dargan, whom she married in 1898. While in Boston, Dargan worked as a secretary for the president of a small company being taken over by the United States Rubber Company. The experience gave her an insider's view of big business, and the material she gathered during this time figures prominently in her fiction.

In 1906, Dargan and her husband bought a farm in Swain County, North Carolina, which was paid for by income from her writing. Dargan's reputation was initially based on her poetry, including *Path Flower* and *The Cycle's Rim*, a tribute to her husband, who drowned in 1915.

A recurring theme in Dargan's later work was the exploitation of Southern workers by American industry. In the 1930s and 1940s, using the pen name Fielding Burke, she wrote several novels exploring the inhumanity of America's economic system. As *New York Times* literary critic Donald Adams noted, "there is no hatred of capitalists in her conviction that the capitalist system must end; simply an overwhelming sympathy for those whom the system crushes."

From 1925 until her death in 1968, Dargan made her home in Asheville, North Carolina, though she continued to travel extensively in the United

States and Europe. Dargan's final book, *Innocent Bigamy and Other Stories*, was a short story collection published when she was ninety-six.

In her novel *Call Home the Heart* (written under her pseudonym, Fielding Burke), Dargan describes the plight of Ishma Waycaster, a mountain woman who, along with her husband, Britt, struggles valiantly to make a living on her mother Laviny's worn-out family farm. Ishma, who is expecting her first child, resents the lazy ways of her brother-in-law Jim, her sister Bainie, and their seven children.

OTHER SOURCES TO EXPLORE

PRIMARY

Novels: *Sons of the Stranger* (1947), *From My Highest Hill* (1941), *A Stone Came Rolling* (1935), *Call Home the Heart* (1932), *Highland Annals* (1925). **Drama:** *The Flutter of the Goldleaf, and Other Plays* (1922), *The Mortal Gods and Other Plays* (1912). **Poetry:** *The Spotted Hawk* (1958), *The Cycle's Rim* (1916), *Path Flower and Other Verses* (1914). **Short stories:** *Innocent Bigamy and Other Stories* (1962).

SECONDARY

Contemporary Authors, Vol. 111, 132. Nancy Carol Joyner, "Olive Tilford Dargan," *Oxford Companion to Women's Writing in the United States* (1995), 233–34. Virginia Terrell Lathrop, "Olive Tilford Dargan," *N.C. Libraries* 18 (spring 1960), 68–76. *New York Times* [obituary] (24 January 1968), 45, col. 1. Richard Walser, "Olive Tilford Dargan," *Southern Writers: A Biographical Dictionary* (1979), 113–14.

CALL HOME THE HEART (1932)
from Chapter 3

When that first year's crop was harvested it proved as abundant as its promise. Britt walked among his neighbors feeling their commending eyes upon him. Gaffney [the storekeeper] shook his hand when he brought his first load of corn down to pay on the family debt. That debt was larger than Britt expected to find it. There were twelve in the household, not counting the company that Jim's affliction brought in, and four of the children were going to school. However inexorably they limited their spending, some needs had to be met. And Gaffney, always liberal of heart, had met them. Britt and Ishma decided to pay him in full, and do without any new winter clothes. They had to buy a cow, but cows were cheap that year, and Abe Marsh let them have one with a heifer calf for thirty bushels of corn. That was as far as the crop would stretch, aside from the part they must keep for bread and feed. But Jim was getting well, and wouldn't need any more money for medicine and liniment and invalid's kickshaws. The doctor had told them two months before that he wouldn't have to come again, and that immense drain was stopped. Britt sold his gun and laid the money away for the time when Ishma would need it. They felt even with the world, and were not afraid to start a new debt at Gaffney's. This was necessary because Britt intended to put in most of the winter clearing new-ground. They knew that the old fields would not repeat their generosity another year. It wasn't possible to put all of the "stalk land" in orchard grass and sweet clover as they had planned, for seed was too costly. Orchard grass would make good summer pasture, and when it died down there would be the green winter clover for the cattle. They expected to have their own ox-team to feed the next year, and not be dependent on neighbors for plough-brutes. But it would take fifty dollars to seed the land. That would have to wait.

It was February and bitter cold when Edward Britton Hensley was born. Ishma knew she would never forget how cold it was, and how cramped they were for room. She had wanted Laviny to give up her bed in the middle room and let her be sick there, but her mother said there was no use beginning to humor her, she'd have to get used to things like any married woman. So Ishma kept her own bed in the corner of the big room where Jim and Bainie, with their two least ones, occupied another corner, and Sam, Andy and Ben, another. Nettie and Ellie slept with Laviny in the middle room. When Ishma's hour approached, the children all were sent off to the neighbors for a day and night. But they trooped back too soon for Ishma's peace.

"Can't you send them out a little while?" she asked Bainie, feebly hopeful.

"They've jest been out. I kain't send 'em right back an' the air hangin' with ice. They're all keepin' back there in the kitchen. I reckon you don't want the whole house."

"Sounds like they're right on the other side o' the wall, banging and yelping."

"You'll have to git aholt o' yersef, Ishmalee," said her mother, "an' not let Britt make a fool o' ye."

Britt went up to the barn where he could swear unimpeded. He wouldn't let Ishma sit up for two weeks, although Laviny insisted on her "comin' out of it" the ninth day. He and Laviny had their first quarrel, but Britt suddenly became very quiet when he saw tears pushing from under Ishma's eyelashes. He went to her and whispered, "Next time we'll be to ourselves," and with a vehemence that bewildered him she had answered, "There'll be no next time!"

Ned was the finest baby that had ever come into the family. Laviny admitted it, and when he was old enough to return her attachment, she pushed Ishma aside and took possession of him. "You'll have plenty more," she said. "I'll look out fer this'n."

Within a month after his birth, Ishma had regained her bloom and her strength, though she was a little confused in her thinking. Life, the future, her plans, were not so clear as they had been. She felt mentally clamped down, in the way that she had felt physically cramped the night Ned was born. How she had wanted room for her body! The walls had pressed in against her, the presence of the people, taking up good space, smothered her.

Jim, who could hobble about by February, came in one night saying that he had fastened the cow in a stall where she couldn't thrash around. She'd find a calf before morning, and if they left her out she'd go to the very top o' the pasture and they'd have a masterous time getting her down. Cows always wanted the whole earth an' sky too when they's droppin' a calf. He'd shore fixed this'n until she couldn't more'n switch her tail.

That night, while Jim and Bainie were snoring, Ishma slipped from the side of Britt, climbed up to the barn, and let the moaning cow out of the narrow, unclean stall. Next morning the cow was found with her calf at the head of the pasture, and great was the stir over the trouble she gave them. Jim had a mind to give her one good lashing, but he didn't; and it was Britt who finally coaxed her down to the barn lot. Ishma sat by the fire, holding Ned, and smiling.

Doris Davenport
(January 29, 1949–)

Born in Gainesville, Florida, Doris Davenport lived in Cornelia, Georgia, from age five until age fifteen, when people, experiences, and landscapes of northeast Georgia began to shape her identity. The oldest daughter of Ethel Mae Gibson Davenport and Claude Davenport, she attended the "Cornelia Regional Colored High School, one 'magnet' school which included grades one through twelve and all the African American children from five adjoining counties (bussed in, daily)."

She began college at sixteen and graduated in 1969 with a B.A. in English from Paine College in Augusta, Georgia. She earned her M.A. in English from State University of New York in Buffalo in 1971, and completed her Ph.D. in African American literature at the University of Southern California in 1985.

She describes herself as a "lesbian-feminist anarchist" and an "Affrilachian" (Southern Appalachian African American) poet. She has taught at colleges and universities in California, Iowa, Ohio, North Carolina, and Alabama. Her work has been supported by the Kentucky Foundation for Women, the North Carolina Arts Council, the Syvenna Foundation for Women, and the Georgia Council for the Arts. She is a performance poet and a member of Alternate ROOTs, an Atlanta-based organization for artists/activists.

OTHER SOURCES TO EXPLORE

PRIMARY

Poetry: *madness like morning glories: poems* (2004), *Soque Street Poems* (1995), *voodoo chile: slight return* (1991), *eat thunder & drink rain* (1982), *it's like this* (1980). **Autobiographical essay:** "All This, and Honeysuckles Too," in *Bloodroot* (1998), ed. Joyce Dyer, 88–97.

SECONDARY

Joyce Dyer, "Doris Diosa Davenport," in *Bloodroot*, 87. James A. Miller, "Coming Home to Affrilachia: The Poems of doris davenport," in *Her Words* (2002), ed. Felicia Mitchell, 96–106.

COUNTRY

from *Soque Street Poems* (1995)

Country: a rural, rather uncivilized area of the USA especially in the South. One who acts backwards, as in, 'country.' No sophistication or knowledge of the outside, the real world. Provincial, limited, myopic, and zenophobic in language, appearance, actions, customs, and belief systems (superstitions, myths, folktales & collective lies).

In photos, they freeze
stiff & formal
shyly dressed in
their country dress-up
clothes. Their faces freeze
into the camera like it might
bite, all emotion erased except
for strong country personalities
too strong to be erased.

Faces un-animated.
Shoulders erect & stiff.
Sunday-best, if possible;
if not, a pose saying "Well, this me.
Take it or leave it."
Every now and then
a face, a child, still grins
an adult caught
about to get stiff
characters so
strong they defy
attempts to make
them one-dimensional, flat . . .

FOR DR. JOSEFINA GARCIA & THE "TISSUE COMMITTEE" (7.1.90)

from *voodoo chile: slight return* (1991)

(Dr. Garcia continually delayed my operation because
of the "laws" of her profession—i had to have a
"second opinion," twice. i was told that no one could
just "request" a hysterectomy. That if there was no
"pathology in the uterus," my doctor, Dr. Garcia
could be de-doctored [never allowed again to
practice] by the tissue committee. a committee, she
explained, of all elderly white males, who would
examine my uterus for pathology, and decide whether
or not she should have done the operation. they could,
then, decide her life, like they had been attempting to
run my life . . . not to mention, the irony that in the
old days, when any womon of color cld., get a hyst.
FREE w/out even asking for it . . .)

ignoring the fact that **i**
asked for the hysterectomy
apart from the indirectly connected
issue of who
my "tissue"—my uterus—belongs to,
since, after all, it *was* in
my body, it was a part of this
body that i fed, bathed, nurtured, &
paid rent on for
40 years, 7 months, and the last few days and
minutes too,   apart from the
major issue of
control over my own female body &
female parts but connected to my
right to control my life,
i, too, have a few concerns:

1) those white male things
on the committee

never had PMS, vicious cramps, hemorrhages and
chafing between upper thighs. but
according to Chango,
at the next full moon,
they will (& one will be impregnated
against his will).

2) that hysterectomy, Dr. Garcia,
made me the happiest non-bleeding womon
in the midwest or maybe the world. additionally,
you, indirectly, saved
several lives
& enriched *many* besides mine/but
back to the
issue   at hand:

when the committee inspects my
uterus for its pathology, (instead of
inspecting their   inspection for
their pathology) &
can only see it's healthy (the uterus)
pure, even pretty, if they can't *see*
anything
that was wrong
but therefore decide
you   are
(apart from the
question of who
owns my body / who makes
its *ultimate* decisions)
then, what they gone do?

make you
put it back?

ZORA NEALE

from *eat thunder & drink rain* (1982)

in a world of
six million dollar men

and two dollar women,
psychedelic pain

and plastic people,
synthetic eggs and soybean beef,

miseducated educators and sex machines,
there is no place for

mambos.

REBECCA HARDING DAVIS
(June 24, 1831–September 29, 1910)

Rebecca Blaine Harding Davis was the first of five children of Rachel Leet Wilson Harding and Richard Harding. She was born at the family home of her mother's Irish grandparents, the first white settlers in Washington County, Pennsylvania.

In 1837, her parents moved from Big Spring (now Huntsville), Alabama, to Wheeling, Virginia (now West Virginia). Her education was guided by her mother and private tutors until she was enrolled at the Washington [Pennsylvania] Female Seminary, from 1845 to 1848, where she graduated with highest honors. She then returned home to Wheeling to help her mother with the education of her younger siblings.

Davis is best known for her first publication, *Life in the Iron Mills*, a powerful story that exposed the inhumane working conditions of mill workers. Living in Wheeling introduced her to immigrant workers and their families, and she drew on her experiences to write *Life in the Iron Mills*. Published a decade before the French writer Emile Zola's naturalistic fiction, the novella movingly depicts the struggle of characters trapped in their circumstances.

In the summer of 1862, on her way home from a trip to Boston, during which she met Nathaniel Hawthorne, Oliver Wendell Holmes, Ralph Waldo Emerson, and Louisa May Alcott, she also met the lawyer Lemuel Clarke Davis, an admirer who was so impressed by *Life in the Iron Mills* that he had written to her and requested that they meet. They married on March 5, 1863, and eventually had three children: two sons and a daughter.

After their marriage, Rebecca and Clarke Davis moved to Philadelphia, where she worked as an associate editor for the *New York Tribune* (1869–1875) and her husband became a prominent journalist. Their son, Richard Harding Davis, also became an influential journalist.

In this excerpt from *Life in the Iron Mills*, the writer addresses the reader directly and introduces the story of Hugh Wolfe, an iron worker with artistic sensibilities, and his self-sacrificing cousin Deb. Although the setting is not named, the place is much like Wheeling, West Virginia, the novelist's hometown.

OTHER SOURCES TO EXPLORE

PRIMARY

Novels: *Frances Waldeaux* (1897), *Doctor Warwick's Daughters* (1896), *Silhouettes of American Life* (1892), *Kent Hampden* (1892), *Natasqua* (1887), *A Law unto Herself* (1878), *Kitty's Choice: A Story of Berrytown* (1874), *John Andross* (1874), *Pro Aris et Foci: A Plea for Our Altars and Hearths* (1870), *Dallas Galbraith* (1868), *Margaret Howth: A Story of To-Day* (1862). **Novella:** *Life in the Iron Mills, Atlantic Monthly* 7 (April 1861), 430–51. **Autobiography:** *Bits of Gossip* (1904).

SECONDARY

Dictionary of Literary Biography, Vol. 74, 92–96. Tillie Olsen, "A Biographical Interpretation," *Life in the Iron Mills* (1972), 69–156. Harold Woodell, "Rebecca Harding Davis," *Southern Writers: A Biographical Dictionary* (1979), 118–19.

FROM *LIFE IN THE IRON MILLS* (1861)

My story is very simple,—only what I remember of the life of one of these men,—a furnace-tender in one of Kirby & John's rolling-mills,—Hugh Wolfe. You know the mills? They took the great order for the Lower Virginia railroads there last winter; run usually with about a thousand men. I cannot tell why I choose the half-forgotten story of this Wolfe more than that of myriads of these furnace-hands. Perhaps because there is a secret underlying sympathy between that story and this day with its impure fog and thwarted sunshine,—or perhaps simply for the reason that this house is the one where the Wolfes lived. There were the father and son,—both hands, as I said, in one of Kirby & John's mills for making railroad-iron,—and Deborah, their cousin, a picker in some of the cotton-mills. The house was rented then to half a dozen families. The Wolfes had two of the cellar-rooms. . . .

. . .

I want you to come down and look at this Wolfe, standing there among the lowest of his kind, and see him just as he is, that you may judge him justly when you hear the story of this night. I want you to look back, as he does every day, at his birth in vice, his starved infancy; to remember the heavy years he has groped through as boy and man,—the slow, heavy years of constant, hot work. So long ago he began, that he thinks sometimes he has worked there for ages. There is no hope that it will ever end. Think that God put into this man's soul a fierce thirst for beauty,—to know it, to create it; to *be*—something, he knows not what,—other than he is. There are moments when a passing cloud, the sun glinting on the purple thistles, a kindly smile, a child's face, will rouse him to a passion of pain,—when his nature starts up with a mad cry of rage against God, man, whoever it is that has forced this vile, slimy life upon him. With all this groping, this mad desire, a great blind intellect stumbling through wrong, a loving poet's heart, the man was by habit only a coarse, vulgar laborer, familiar with sights and words you would blush to name. Be just: when I tell you about this night, see him as he is. Be just,—not like man's law, which seizes on one isolated fact, but like God's judging angel, whose clear, sad eye saw all the countless cankering days of this man's life, all the countless nights, when, sick with starving, his soul fainted in him, before it judged him for this night, the saddest of all.

I called this night the crisis of his life. If it was, it stole on him un-awares. These great turning-days of life cast no shadow before, slip by un-consciously. Only a trifle, a little turn of the rudder, and the ship goes to heaven or hell.

. . .

[A group of wealthy visitors touring the ironworks encounter a sculpture created by Hugh Wolfe, an iron worker who has used korl, a by-product of the ore, for his art work.]

Mitchell started back, half-frightened, as, suddenly turning a corner, the white figure of a woman faced him in the darkness,—a woman, white, of giant proportions, crouching on the ground, her arms flung out in some wild gesture of warning.

"Stop! Make that fire burn there!" cried Kirby, stopping short.

The flame burst out, flashing the gaunt figure into bold relief.

Mitchell drew a long breath.

"I thought it was alive," he said, going up curiously.

The others followed.

"Not marble, eh?" asked Kirby, touching it.

One of the lower overseers stopped.

"Korl, Sir."

"Who did it?"

"Can't say. Some of the hands; chipped it out in off-hours."

"Chipped to some purpose, I should say. What a flesh-tint the stuff has! Do you see, Mitchell?"

"I see."

He had stepped aside where the light fell boldest on the figure, looking at it in silence. There was not one line of beauty or grace in it: a nude woman's form, muscular, grown coarse with labor, the powerful limbs instinct with some one poignant longing. One idea: there it was in the tense, rigid muscles, the clutching hands, the wild, eager face, like that of a starving wolf's. Kirby and Doctor May walked around it, critical, curious. Mitchell stood aloof, silent. The figure touched him strangely.

"Not badly done," said Doctor May. "Where did the fellow learn that sweep of the muscles in the arm and hand? Look at them! They are groping,—do you see?—clutching: the peculiar action of a man dying of thirst."

"They have ample facilities for studying anatomy," sneered Kirby, glancing at the half-naked figures.

"Look," continued the Doctor, "at this bony wrist, and the strained sinews of the instep! A working-woman,—the very type of her class."

"God forbid!" muttered Mitchell.

"Why?" demanded May. "What does the fellow intend by the figure? I cannot catch the meaning."

"Ask him," said the other, dryly. "There he stands,"—pointing to Wolfe, who stood with a group of men, leaning on his ash-rake.

The Doctor beckoned him with the affable smile which kind-hearted men put on, when talking with these people.

"Mr. Mitchell has picked you out as the man who did this,—I'm sure I don't know why. But what did you mean by it?"

"She be hungry."

Wolfe's eyes answered Mitchell, not the Doctor.

"Oh-h! But what a mistake you have made, my fine fellow! You have given no sign of starvation to the body. It is strong,—terribly strong. It has the mad, half-despairing gesture of drowning."

Wolfe stammered, glanced appealingly at Mitchell, who saw the soul of the thing, he knew. But the cool, probing eyes were turned on himself now,— mocking, cruel, relentless.

"Not hungry for meat," the furnace-tender said at last.

"What then? Whiskey?" jeered Kirby, with a coarse laugh.

Wolfe was silent a moment, thinking.

"I dunno," he said, with a bewildered look. "It mebbe. Summat to make her live, I think,—like you. Whiskey ull do it, in a way."

The young man laughed again. Mitchell flashed a look of disgust some- where,—not at Wolfe.

"May," he broke out impatiently, "are you blind? Look at that woman's face! It asks questions of God, and says, 'I have a right to know.' Good God, how hungry it is!"

They looked a moment; then May turned to the mill-owner:—

"Have you many such hands as this? What are you going to do with them? Keep them at puddling iron?"

Kirby shrugged his shoulders. Mitchell's look had irritated him.

"*Ce n'est pas mon affaire.* I have no fancy for nursing infant geniuses. I suppose there are some stray gleams of mind and soul among these wretches. The Lord will take care of his own; or else they can work out their own salvation. I have heard you call our American system a ladder which any man can scale. Do you doubt it? Or perhaps you want to banish all social ladders, and put us all on a flat table-land,—eh, May?"

The doctor looked vexed, puzzled. Some terrible problem lay hid in this woman's face, and troubled these men. Kirby waited for an answer, and, receiving none, went on, warming with his subject.

"I tell you, there's something wrong that no talk of '*Liberté*' or '*Égalité*' will do away. If I had the making of men, these men who do the lowest part of the world's work should be machines,—nothing more,—hands. It would be kindness. God help them! What are taste, reason, to creatures who must live such lives as that?" he pointed to Deborah, sleeping on the ash-heap. "So many nerves to sting them to pain. What if God had put your brain, with all its agony of touch, into your fingers, and bid you work and strike with that?"

"You think you could govern the world better?" laughed the Doctor.

"I do not think at all."

"That is true philosophy. Drift with the stream, because you cannot dive deep enough to find bottom, eh?"

"Exactly," rejoined Kirby. "I do not think. I wash my hands of all social problems,—slavery, caste, white or black. My duty to my operatives has a narrow limit,—the pay-hour on Saturday night. Outside of that, if they cut korl, or cut each other's throats, (the more popular amusement of the two,) I am not responsible."

The Doctor sighed,—a good honest sigh, from the depths of his stomach.

"God help us! Who is responsible?"

ANN DEAGON
(January 19, 1930–)

The daughter of Robert and Alice Webb Fleming, Ann Deagon was born in Birmingham, Alabama. She earned her B.A. from Birmingham-Southern College in 1950 and her doctorate in classical studies from the University of North Carolina in 1954. In 1951 she married Donald Deagon and is now the mother of two daughters.

After beginning her career as a classics professor at Furman University in Greenville, South Carolina, she joined the faculty at Guilford College in Greensboro, North Carolina, in 1956 and served as Professor of Humanities and Writer-in-Residence there until her retirement in 1992.

Beginning her writing career in 1970, Deagon worked actively with regional and national writers' groups and in 1980 founded Poetry Center Southeast, a forerunner of the North Carolina Writers' Network. She was editor of *The Guilford Review* from 1976 until 1984, and in 1981, received a National Endowment for the Arts Literary Fellowship.

She and her husband spent a dozen summers during the 1950s and early 1960s on the Qualla Reservation in Cherokee, North Carolina, working on *Unto These Hills*, an outdoor drama about the forced removal of the Cherokee to Oklahoma over the infamous Trail of Tears. She wrote her first book-length poem, *Indian Summer*, to honor Jonah Feather and to pay tribute to "the humane vigor of the Cherokee people as well as to the humor and stubborn dignity of one man."

OTHER SOURCES TO EXPLORE

PRIMARY

Novel: *The Diver's Tomb* (1984). **Poetry:** *The Polo Poems* (1990), *There is No Balm in Birmingham* (1978), *Women and Children First* (1976), *Indian Summer* (1975), *Poetics South* (1974), *Carbon 14* (1974). **Short stories:** *Habitats* (1982).

168

SECONDARY

Contemporary Authors, Vols. 57–60, 161–62. James F. Mersmann, "Erotic Hyphens: Ann Deagon's Centers That Hold," *Poets in the South* 1:1, 72–83. A. McA. Miller, "Conversation with Ann Deagon," *Poets in the South* 1:1 (1977), 67–71.

GIVING THE SUN

from *Women and Children First* (1976)

Having readied our instrument
(a cardboard box, white paper
taped inside, two pinholes)
we lead the children
warily into the un-
expected twilight. Not
looking up, we are aware
of a great absence. Its chill
silences the jays. We show
each child the obscured sun
in camera obscura. See:
I give you the sun in a box—
a small love inside four walls.

THE HOLE

from *Women and Children First*

At nine I dug a hole behind
the rabbit hutch, four feet
across and getting deeper. I didn't
want to find China, only
to dig in. Every red
shovelful unmade Alabama.
Squatting in the clay chalice
its tight horizon all mine
I drank the sky, the sky
drank me. Between my toes
I felt dirt quiver, felt
an hour-glass running suck me
through earth's center out
onto a blue beach. It never
happened. So how did I
get here on the other
side of the world, my childhood
under my feet?

TWINS

from *Women and Children First* (1976)

Sears' Dial-Your-Twin Dress Form duplicates
your figure with amazing accuracy. Simply use
any suitable coin or screwdriver to adjust screws
at bust, waist, and hips . . .

When I moved out, back in '50,
my twin stood in for me at home. Clothed
in a tasteful smock she always fitted
in. Over the years (twenty-five)
she kept her figure. (Someone with
an unsuitable implement had screwed
mine out of shape.) To compensate
they taped shoulder pads under her breasts,
diapered her hips and belly. By slow
accretion Art kept pace with Life.

Sears' Best is better, allows
instant adjustment to reality.
An extra slice of cheesecake, or conception—
insert a coin and twist to FULL.
Diet or abortion—a turn of the screw
pulls us back in shape. Say cancer—
screw the left breast till it buckles.
Say you don't make it—the next
wife has only to readjust the screws:
bust, waist, and hips. What other
dimensions does a woman have?

POETICS SOUTH

from *Poetics South* (1974)

You flat poets
grey on grey
in magazines like long front porches
rock chaw whittle
sometimes spit
alike as board and board—

you listen now:
in Centreville I saw a billy goat
a yearling flush with foraging cavort
maverick down a porch of country cousins
propped to the wall, and on that primal stage
kicking his heels between panic and April
let loose a hail of planetary pellets
hot tumbling in orbit reeking of creation,
vaulted the rail and left those whittlers gasping
a universe of stink.

That's poetry, boys—
like it or lump it.

IN A TIME OF DROUGHT

from *Poetics South* (1974)

My grandpa hollowed
like a gourd
beside the produce counter.
Disdaining chairs
he propped his eighty years'
fragility
against a grocery cart
for grandchildren
to drink of dignity.

I hang him hollow
in the wind of memory
for poems to nest in.

[BROADSIDE (1983)]

I never lust
after a man
as much as
before one.

ANGELYN DEBORD
(December 7, 1949–)

Playwright, actress, and storyteller, Angelyn DeBord grew up in western North Carolina. "The music and language of Appalachia has been the inspiration for all of my writing," says DeBord. In an interview in the Appalshop film *Strangers and Kin*, she tells of moving to the North Carolina Piedmont for her dad to find work when she was a child. The whole family suffered from such homesickness that they soon moved back to the mountains.

A founding member of Appalshop's Roadside Theater, based in Whitesburg, Kentucky, DeBord has spent the past twenty-eight years performing and leading workshops all over America and Europe. She has performed at the London International Theater Festival, Lincoln Center, and Kennedy Center.

DeBord views her writing as a means of "examining in a microscopic way, the fabric, texture, weaving and stitches that hold together the patterns of this Appalachian world I've always inhabited. Coming from a background with a very strong oral tradition, my work centers around the importance of being able to tell your own story with pride and confidence."

Her critically acclaimed play *Praise House* was featured at Charleston, South Carolina's Spoleto Festival in 1990. DeBord wrote the play for the Urban Bush Women, a New York City theatre group. "I pulled so much of the information for this play from extended family stories," says DeBord.

In the following scene from *Praise House*, we see three generations of African American women from the same family. Moma is a domestic worker trying very hard to deal with daily realities of survival. Her daughter, Hannah, has visions, sees angels. Hannah's grandmother, Granny, born in Africa, is a freed woman who totally understands young Hannah's absorption in the spiritual world. DeBord explains, "Most of us can choose whether to see or hear angels. Some of us have no choice. This play is about those who have no choice."

Other Sources to Explore

Primary

"The Making of *Praise House*," *Spoleto Festival U.S.A. 1990 Souvenir Program*, 36–39. **Videotaped performances:** *Praise House* (Third World Newsreel, 1991), *Strangers and Kin* (Appalshop, 1984), *Three Mountain Tales* (Appalshop, 1982). **Drama:** *Lessons on Becoming a Woman* (1996), *Homeade Tales: Songs and Sayings of Florida Slone* (Appalshop, 1993), *Stubborn Memories* (1993), *Praise House* (1990).

Secondary

Adora Dupree, review of *Homemade Tales*, *Now & Then: The Appalachian Magazine* 11:3 (fall 1994), 39.

FROM *PRAISE HOUSE* (1991)

MOMA *(Enters, normal weary posture)*: What are you, goin on about your purple dress. You sure don't need your purple dress TONIGHT!
Lord, it is HOT!
(Moment of silence as MOMA fans, GRANNY rocks, HANNAH stands uncertainly)
Mother, you remember that purple dress you made me when I was little?
GRANNY: I remember a pretty little girl out in that yard, her purple skirttail aflyin.
MOMA: I thought I's a whirlwind in that dress.
GRANNY: My sweet little lilac.
MOMA: I liked to flip the skirttail til my drawers would show.
HANNAH: MOMA!
GRANNY: Never still one minute!
MOMA: And I still don't stop and my feet, they ache.
GRANNY *(Studies MOMA as she rubs her feet):* That weren't the only purple dress I ever made you.
MOMA: O, yeah. That un. That was later.
GRANNY: For your grownup self.
MOMA: I only wore that dress one time.
HANNAH: Why, Moma?
MOMA *(ignoring Hannah)*: My, it's a hot night. Reckon it's EVER gone rain?
GRANNY: It was a pretty dress. And you was just flickerin.
MOMA: Flickering?
GRANNY: From a child to a woman and back again. You was on the edge. I would just stare and stare at you. Wonderin which side you'd land on. Flickerin. Like heat lightnin. You wuz somethin in that purple dress. It was the strangest color. Like the sky of a summer's night . . .
MOMA: When the stars first come out.
GRANNY: You wuz all ready for the world.
MOMA: And the world, it come straight to me that night. He moved right out of them shadows . . .
ANGEL VOICE *(singing):* Purple shadows of a summer night.
MOMA: Tall, quiet man . . .
hands like . . . satin . . .
ANGEL VOICE *(sings):* Satin, he has hands like satin
Make you feel like they're made
to make you feel fine
Kisses like juice running out of a cauldron

Run down your throat and set you on fire.

GRANNY: You was on the edge. Just flickerin.

MOMA: In a flash it wuz decided. I was a woman. I didn't hardly know what hit me . . . a flash like . . .

HANNAH: Like a shooting star.

MOMA: He was there and then gone.

ANGELS: Gone. Gone.

GRANNY: A dark empty sky.

MOMA: And I was back at my Moma's again. A little girl again.

GRANNY: You wuz just a child.

MOMA: But there was a child within this child.

GRANNY: Another little shinin star soon shone.

MOMA: Little Hannah. Is she the daughter of a star? A fast-shooting, son-of-a-gun-disappearing-type star? Are you a little star?

GRANNY: A rising star. So bright.

ANGEL I: A child comes from a child.

ANGEL II: Where does the first child go?

ANGEL III: Right up into heaven.

ANGEL I: Maybe.

ANGEL II: Maybe.

ANGEL III: Who knows.

MOMA: Do I still flicker, Moma?

Do I ever still shine?

Who knows.

Who cares. There is so much to do.

HANNAH: Do you ever hear the stars asingin at night?

I do.

ANGELS: I do. I do.

MOMA: Lord child. Why don't you go in yonder and wash them dishes. That'll get them feet of yours back down to this ground. Give you a good job to do.

GRANNY: God give everbody a job but not the same job.

Give us a time.

Backwards and forwards

It's all one time.

One long string of beads.

HANNAH: A string a stars.

GRANNY & HANNAH: All shining.

MOMA: O, you two! Mother, you're as bad as she is. You could help me make this child see . . .

GRANNY: The child has a gift. Hannah CAN see.
MOMA: She can see herself in yonder and wash them dishes. I swear to my soul.

Annie Dillard
(April 30, 1945–)

Annie Dillard grew up in Pittsburgh, Pennsylvania. Her memoir, *An American Childhood,* focuses on her early years and her parents. She attended Hollins College in southwest Virginia and earned her B.A. in 1967 and her M.A. in 1968, both in English literature.

Dillard spent what she describes as "twelve wonderful years" in Roanoke, Virginia, where, in 1973, she wrote *Pilgrim at Tinker Creek,* which won the Pulitzer Prize in nonfiction in 1975. In addition to *Pilgrim at Tinker Creek,* her nonfiction narratives include *For the Time Being* (favored by critics), *Holy the Firm*, *The Writing Life*, and *Encounters with Chinese Writers*. She has two books of poetry, and *Teaching a Stone to Talk* is a collection of her narrative essays.

In 1975, she moved to coastal Washington state and later set *The Living*, an historical novel, there. *The Living* made the Century's Best 100 Western Novels list. Her books have appeared on four separate lists of the 100 Best Books of the Century: western novel, nonfiction, essays, and spiritual writing.

She married Gary Clevidence in 1980 and had a daughter, Rose. She also has mothered part-time for many decades two daughters, Corinne and Shelley.

In 1988, Dillard married author Robert D. Richardson. She now lives in Hillsborough, North Carolina, and in Wythe County, Virginia. She avoids publicity and appearances. She is a member of the Academy of Arts and Sciences, Phi Beta Kappa, and the Key West Saturday Morning Volleyball Association.

Other Sources to Explore

Primary

Novel: *The Living* (1992). **Nonfiction:** *For the Time Being* (1999), *The Annie Dillard Reader* (1994), *The Writing Life* (1989), *An American Childhood* (1987), *Encounters with Chinese Writers* (1984), *Teaching a Stone to Talk: Expeditions and Encounters* (1982), *Living by Fiction* (1982), *Holy the Firm* (1977), *Pilgrim at Tinker Creek* (1974). **Poetry:** *Mornings Like This: Found Poems* (1995), *Tickets for a Prayer Wheel* (1974).

Secondary

Carol Schaechterle Loranger, "Dillard, Annie," *Oxford Companion to Women Writing in the United States* (1995), 249–50. Nancy C. Parrish, *Lee Smith, Annie Dillard, and the Hollins Group: A Genesis of Writers* (1998). Grace Suh, "Ideas are tough; irony is easy: Pulitzer Prize-winner Annie Dillard speaks," *The Yale Herald* (4 October 1996).

FROM *Pilgrim at Tinker Creek* (1974)

I live by a creek, Tinker Creek, in a valley in Virginia's Blue Ridge. An anchorite's hermitage is called an anchor-hold; some anchor-holds were simple sheds clamped to the side of a church like a barnacle to a rock. I think of this house clamped to the side of Tinker Creek as an anchor-hold. It holds me at anchor to the rock bottom of the creek itself and it keeps me steadied in the current, as a sea anchor does, facing the stream of light pouring down. It's a good place to live; there's a lot to think about. The creeks—Tinker and Carvin's—are an active mystery, fresh every minute. Theirs is the mystery of the continuous creation and all that providence implies: the uncertainty of vision, the horror of the fixed, the dissolution of the present, the intricacy of beauty, the pressure of fecundity, the elusiveness of the free, and the flawed nature of perfection. The mountains—Tinker and Brushy, McAfee's Knob and Dead Man—are a passive mystery, the oldest of all. Theirs is the one simple mystery of creation from nothing, of matter itself, anything at all, the given. Mountains are giant, restful, absorbent. You can heave your spirit into a mountain and the mountain will keep it, folded, and not throw it back as some creeks will. The creeks are the world with all its stimulus and beauty; I live there. But the mountains are home.

. . .

Like the bear who went over the mountain, I went out to see what I could see. And, I might as well warn you, like the bear, all that I could see was the other side of the mountain: more of same. On a good day I might catch a glimpse of another wooded ridge rolling under the sun like water, another bivouac. I propose to keep here what Thoreau called "a meterological journal of the mind," telling some tales and describing some of the sights of this rather tamed valley, and exploring, in fear and trembling, some of the unmapped dim reaches and unholy fastnesses to which those tales and sights so dizzyingly lead.

I am no scientist. I explore the neighborhood. An infant who has just learned to hold his head up has a frank and forthright way of gazing about him in bewilderment. He hasn't the faintest clue where he is, and he aims to learn. In a couple of years, what he will have learned instead is how to fake it: he'll have the cocksure air of a squatter who has come to feel he owns the place. Some unwonted, taught pride diverts us from our original intent, which is to explore the neighborhood, view the landscape, to discover at least *where* it is that we have been so startlingly set down, if we can't learn why.

So I think about the valley. It is my leisure as well as my work, a game. It is a fierce game I have joined because it is being played anyway, a game of both skill and chance, played against an unseen adversary—the conditions of time—in which the payoffs, which may suddenly arrive in a blast of light at any moment, might as well come to me as anyone else. I stake the time I'm grateful to have, the energies I'm glad to direct. I risk getting stuck on the board, so to speak, unable to move in any direction, which happens enough, God knows; and I risk the searing, exhausting nightmares that plunder rest and force me face down all night long in some muddy ditch seething with hatching insects and crustaceans.

But if I can bear the nights, the days are a pleasure. I walk out; I see something, some event that would otherwise have been utterly missed and lost; or something sees me, some enormous power brushes me with its clean wing, and I resound like a beaten bell.

I am an explorer, then, and I am also a stalker, or the instrument of the hunt itself. Certain Indians used to carve long grooves along the wooden shafts of their arrows. They called the grooves "lightning marks," because they resembled the curved fissure lightning slices down the trunks of trees. The function of lightning marks is this: if the arrow fails to kill the game, blood from a deep wound will channel along the lightning mark, streak down the arrow shaft, and spatter to the ground, laying a trail dripped on broadleaves, on stones, that the barefoot and trembling archer can follow into whatever deep or rare wilderness it leads. I am the arrow shaft, carved along my length by unexpected lights and gashes from the very sky, and this book is the straying trail of blood.

Something pummels us, something barely sheathed. Power broods and lights. We're played on like a pipe; our breath is not our own. James Houston describes two young Eskimo girls sitting cross-legged on the ground, mouth on mouth, blowing by turns each other's throat cords, making a low, unearthly music. When I cross again the bridge that is really the steers' fence, the wind has thinned to the delicate air of twilight; it crumples the water's skin. I watch the running sheets of light raised on the creek's surface. The sight has the appeal of the purely passive, like the racing of light under clouds on a field, the beautiful dream at the moment of being dreamed. The breeze is the merest puff, but you yourself sail headlong and breathless under the gale force of the spirit.

$\mathscr{H}$ILDA $\mathscr{D}$OWNER
(August 27, 1956–)

Hilda Downer was born and raised in the small western North Carolina community of Bandana, a place so named because a red bandana tied to a laurel signaled the train where to leave the mail. Her birthplace is crucial to her poetry, providing its remote settings, natural imagery, and indigenous language.

She graduated from Appalachian State University with a double major in English and biology in 1978. After completing a nursing degree in 1983, Downer earned an M.A. in English from Appalachian State University in 1989 and an M.F.A. in poetry from Vermont College in 1996. Having worked as a newspaper editor, a waitress, a children's room librarian, a home health nurse, and, for more than a decade, a psychiatric nurse, she continues to practice nursing and to teach English classes at Appalachian State University.

"Just as I have come full circle, moving from being ashamed of the shack I grew up in to being proud," she explains, "I have had to move from feeling that writing meant there was something wrong with me to feeling that it is the main thing right with me." For a decade she almost gave up writing, she says, "to devote time to my children and mostly to trying to make an awful marriage work." Because of her personal struggle, she says, "I feel a responsibility to younger writers to encourage them to never allow the same strange ideas that people in the mountains transferred to me—that you should never get divorced, for instance—to interfere with what is right with them." She lives in Sugar Grove, outside of Boone, North Carolina, with her two sons.

OTHER SOURCES TO EXPLORE

PRIMARY

Poetry: *Down to the Wire* (forthcoming), *Bandana Creek* (1979). **Autobiographical essay:** "Mutant in Bandana," in *Bloodroot* (1998), ed. Joyce Dyer, 99–104.

SECONDARY

Fred Chappell, "Double Language: Three Appalachian Poets," *Appalachian Journal* 8:1 (autumn 1980), 55–59. Joyce Dyer, "Hilda Downer," in *Bloodroot*, 98. Judy Jones, review of *Bloodroot*, *Lexington Herald-Leader*, 3 May 1998. Anna Dunlap Higgins, "'To Walk These Hills': Poetic Inspiration for Appalachian Poet Hilda Downer." *North Carolina Literary Review* 12 (2003), forthcoming.

THIS IS WHAT HISTORY IS

from *Bandana Creek* (1979)

Grey house in which grandparent
would have grown, where a
wife may have taken for granted
what I watch once—
man shaving in porch dark.
All that matters is his back, naked.

Downed in bed,
his feet extend drawerknobs over edge.
The cliff of his side,
too big to feel my presence,
everyone he has ever touched
touches me.

A WOMAN IS SEGMENTED
AS AN ANT

from *Bandana Creek*

I crawl into bed as a woman,
and lay thinking as a woman.
Quilt covers and reveals.
I want to express the soft of my mouth,
that a dead poet knows me.
Blue pains and tight fears
embraced with sky of quiet,
I wait as a woman waits.
I like my own smell.
No man has known me beautiful
when I am alone and woman,
still or stirring,
a drawing power in the shoulders,
waist hidden from vertical glance,

breast to hip.
And between the ticking hips,
springs and cogs,
scraping and bleeding,
pain compensation for kicking,
how would this child have been?
Imagined no less than noble,
souls subtly pass through.
I must feel their lives for them.
And however I see myself,
connector for man,
reporter for God,
the most I could be is woman.

EVERY OPEN SPACE FILLS WITH SKY

from *Appalachian Journal* (1993)

Tooth of my son,
its pale body slides loose in its coffin,
the bright orange treasure chest
the dentist provided.

Where the gum ignited and swelled the eyes closed,
the empty place, left sunken as red soil,
haunts with the whistling
of a gaped toothed graveyard
and how smiling in moonlight.

Tooth of my son,
cradled so fragile I cannot touch
and so alone in its whiteness,
proves braver than its biggest rattle.
Its small body of a stone christening gown,
I think of antique pictures of still babies
in handmade white dresses
propped for viewing in their darkest wood embrace.
This tooth is a smaller heaviness
though continuous like the gift of loneliness,

and it hurts just the same.
After marriage and mortgages,
the value of this tooth may go unrecognized,
that once was the dagger in the mother's heart.
It will be lost as my own ashes,
a false pollen sifted onto butter-and-eggs
by honeybees of Bandana.

Long before this loss, long before I lost baby teeth,
I trembled into solemn woods
with wondering how we could live forever and ever and ever
or who made God?
Now I anticipate that my son might be wasp-stung
in his lifetime, and sometimes I cry
imagining a fall out of a tree or a bicycle wreck.
I try to bite off some of my death each day.

Tooth of my son,
little death embalmed in hard fact,
what will you remember of us?
Incisor like the hitchhiker behind the windshield
of a stranger's truck,
what was your view of the world each time my son smiled?
And, my son, what will you remember of childhood?
What do you think of your mother pressing her hands to a great
        rock
until I turn to you with tears of joy?
Will these tears sink pebbles in your memory's well?
Will one of those memories become my tombstone
as a lost baby tooth of your child will become yours?

ℳURIEL ℳILLER 𝒟RESSLER
(July 4, 1918–February 27, 2000)

Poet and lecturer Muriel Dressler was born in Kanawha County, West Virginia, in a small community southeast of Charleston called Witcher. She told editor William Plumley that she didn't finish high school. "Her real education, she was fond of saying, came at the heels of her mother in the cornfield, where she heard Shakespeare, Milton, Chaucer, and the Bible recited," Plumley said.

Dressler's goal as a writer, she once said, was to "record Appalachia without the sensationalism given it by writers outside the hills." Popular as a lecturer on college campuses in the 1970s, she gave a reading at Harvard University in 1976.

Her first published poem, "Appalachia," appeared in 1970, in the Morris Harvey College publication *Poems From the Hills*, edited by William Plumley. Her poem "Mountain Sarvis" appeared in the first issue of *Appalachian Journal* (1972). Her first poetry collection, *Appalachia, My Land,* contains her best-known poems, including her frequently cited poem "Appalachia," for which she won the Appalachian Gold Medallion from Morris Harvey College (now the University of Charleston, West Virginia).

William Plumley writes that "Elegy for Jody" was "the centerpiece for the hour-long television drama *Morning Star, Evening Star,* written by Earl Hamner [creator of *The Waltons*] and produced by Lorimar in the 1980s." Her papers are collected at West Virginia University in Morgantown.

OTHER SOURCES TO EXPLORE

PRIMARY

Poetry: *Appalachia* (1977), *Appalachia, My Land* (1973).

SECONDARY

Frances Carnahan, "Mountain Friends," *Early American Life* 8:4 (August 1977), 32–33. Avery Gaskins, "Notes on the Poetry of Muriel Miller Dressler," *Things Appalachian* (1976), ed. William Plumley, Marjorie Warner, Lorena Anderson, 142–49. **Documentary film:** *Behold the Land,* Public Broadcasting WPTV, Beckley, West Virginia.

APPALACHIA

from *Appalachia* (1977)

I am Appalachia! In my veins
Runs fierce mountain pride: the hill-fed streams
Of passion; and, stranger, you don't know me!
You've analyzed my every move—you still
Go away shaking your head. I remain
Enigmatic. How can you find rapport with me—
You, who never stood in the bowels of hell,
Never felt a mountain shake and open its jaws
To partake of human sacrifice?
You, who never stood on a high mountain,
Watching the sun unwind its spiral rays;
Who never searched the glens for wild flowers,
Never picked mayapples or black walnuts; never ran
Wildly through the woods in pure delight,
Nor dangled your feet in a lazy creek?
You, who never danced to wild sweet notes,
Outpourings of nimble-fingered fiddlers;
Who never just "sat a spell" on a porch,
Chewing and whittling; or hearing in pastime
The deep-throated bay of chasing hounds
And hunters shouting with joy, "he's treed!"
You, who never once carried a coffin
To a family plot high upon a ridge
Because mountain folk know it's best to lie
Where breezes from the hills whisper, "you're home;"
You, who never saw from the valley that graves on a hill
Bring easement of pain to those below?
I tell you, stranger, hill folk know
What life is all about; they don't need pills
To tranquilize the sorrow and joy of living.
I am Appalachia: and, stranger,
Though you've studied me, you still don't know.

ELEGY FOR JODY

from *Appalachia* (1977)

O, wear a crimson shawl, my child,
Put on a scarlet hood,
And make a point of being brave
When you explore the wood.

But when harsh winds denude the trees,
Fall leaves on cryptic ground
Will write your childhood's prophecy
In syllables of brown.

When dark clouds scud against the sky
And greening trees are gone,
I'll weave for you an ebon rug
For you to walk upon.

Then child, don heavy armor
Against the heart's wild pain;
Try as I may, I cannot bring
Fair April back again.

WILL ALLEN DROMGOOLE
(October 25,1860–September 1, 1934)

Will Allen Dromgoole was a poet, local color fiction writer, and playwright from Rutherford County, Tennessee. She served as Poet Laureate of Tennessee, and in 1930 she was appointed Poet Laureate of the Poetry Society of the South. A Boston editor asserted that "her love of the South is only surpassed by the affection she feels for the mountains and valleys of her dear old Tennessee." Her work was popular in Boston and New York, as well as in the South.

Her parents, Rebecca Mildred Blanch Dromgoole and John Easter Dromgoole, moved to Tennessee from Brunswick County, Virginia, after their marriage. Her father wanted their seventh child to be a son and did not change his mind about the name William when he had a daughter. Dromgoole was born in Murfreesboro, Tennessee, and named William Anne. She used "Will Allen" as her pen name for her first book and Will Allen Dromgoole for most of her other publications. Many readers assumed she was a male writer.

She graduated from the Female Academy of Clarksville, Tennessee, and worked for a while as a clerk for the Tennessee Senate. According to Boston's *Arena* editor, B.O. Flower, her first publication attempt won a prize from *Youth's Companion*.

By one count, Dromgoole wrote 7,500 poems, 14 books, and a number of short stories. For nearly three decades, she was literary editor and author of the column "Song and Story" for the *Nashville Banner*. Her papers are collected at the University of Tennessee in Knoxville. Her collection *The Heart of Old Hickory and Other Stories of Tennessee* is available on-line at http://docsouth.unc.edu/southlit/southlit.html or http://docsouth.unc.edu/dromgoole/menu.html.

OTHER SOURCES TO EXPLORE

PRIMARY

Fiction: *Short Stories* (1970), *The Island of Beautiful Things: A Romance of the South* (1912), *Harum-Scarum Joe* (1899), *Cinch, And Other Stories: Tales of Tennessee* (1898), *Hero-Chums* (1898), *A Moonshiner's Son* (1898), *Rare Old Chums* (1898), *The Valley Path* (1898), *The Heart of Old Hickory and Other Stories of Tennessee* (1895), *The Malungeons* (1891), *The Sunny Side of the Cumberland* [published under the name Will Allen] (1886).

SECONDARY

B.O. Flower, "Preface," *The Heart of Old Hickory and Other Stories of Tennessee* (1895). Vicki Slagle Johns, "Written With A Flourish: Tennessee's local color writers . . ." *The Tennessee Alumnus* (winter 1996), 18–20. Kathy J. Lyday-Lee, "Will Allen Dromgoole: A Biographical Sketch," *Tennessee Historical Quarterly* 51 (summer 1992), 107–12.

THE HEART OF OLD HICKORY
AND OTHER STORIES OF TENNESSEE (1895)
from Fiddling His Way to Fame

We had fallen in with a party of Alabama boys, and all having the same end in view—a good time—we joined forces and pitched our tents on the bank of the Clinch, the prettiest stream in Tennessee, and set about enjoying ourselves after our own approved fashion.

Even the important-looking gentleman, sitting over against a crag where he had dozed and smoked for a full hour, forgot, for the nonce, that he was other than wit and wag for the company; the jolly good fellow he, the free man (once more), and the huntsman.

Our division had followed the hounds since sun-up; the remainder of the company were still out upon the river with rod and line. The sun was about ready to drop behind Lone Mountain, that solitary peak, of nobody knows precisely what, that keeps a kind of solemn guard upon the wayward little current singing at its base. Supper was ready; the odor of coffee, mingled with a no less agreeable aroma of broiling bacon, and corn cake, was deliciously tantalizing to a set of weary hunters. But we were to wait for the boys, that was one of our rules, always observed. The sun set, and twilight came on with that subtle light that is half gloom, half glow, and mingled, or tried to, with the red glare of the camp-fire.

While we sat there, dozing and waiting, there was a break in the brush below the bluff upon which we were camped. "A deer!" One of the boys reached for his rifle, just as a tall, gaunt figure appeared above the bluff, catching as he came at the sassafras and hazel bushes, pulling himself up until he stood among us a very Saul in height, and a Goliath, to all seeming, in strength.

He took in the camp, the fire, and the group at a glance. But the figure over against the crag caught his best attention. There was a kind of telegraphic recognition of some description, for the giant smiled and nodded.

"Howdye," he said; and our jolly comrade took his pipe from between his lips and returned the salutation in precisely the same tone in which it was given.

"Howdye; be you-uns a-travelin'?"

The giant nodded, and passed on, and our comrade dropped back against the crag, and returned to his pipe. But a smile played about his lips, as if some very tender recollection had been stirred by the passing of the gaunt stranger.

It was one of the Alabama boys who broke the silence that had fallen upon us. He had observed the sympathetic recognition that passed between the two men, and had noted the naturalness with which the "dialect" had been returned.

"I'll wager my portion of the supper," he said, "that he is a Tennessean, and from the hill country." He pointed in the direction taken by the stranger. He missed, however, the warning—"Sh!" from the Tennessee side.

"A Tennessee mountaineer—" he went on. "His speech betrayeth him."

Then one of our boys spoke right out.

"Look out!" said he, "the Governor is from the hill country too."

The silence was embarrassing, until the man over against the crag took the pipe from between his lips, and struck the bowl upon his palm gently, the smile still lingering about his mouth.

"Yes," he said, "I was born among the hills of Tennessee. 'The Barrens,' geologists call it; the poets name it 'Land of the Sky.' My heart can find for it no holier name than—home."

The Governor leaned back against the crag. We knew the man, and wondered as to the humor that was upon him. Politician, wit, comrade, gentleman; as each we knew him. But as native, mountaineer, ah! He was a stranger to us in that rôle. We had heard of the quaint ease with which he could drop into the speech of his native hills, no less than the grace with which he filled the gubernatorial chair.

He had "stumped the state" twice as candidate, once as elector. His strange, half-humorous, half-pathetic oratory was familiar in every county from the mountains to the Mississippi. But the native;—we almost held our breath while the transformation took place, and the governor-orator for the moment became the mountaineer.

"I war born," he said, "on the banks o' the Wataugy, in the county uv Cartir,—in a cabin whose winders opened ter the East, an' to'des the sunrise. That war my old mother's notion an' bekase it war her notion it war allus right ter me. Fur she was not one given ter wrong ideas.

"I war her favorite chil' uv the seven God give. My cheer set nighest hers. The yeller yarn that slipped her shiny needles first slipped from hank ter ball across my sunburnt wrists. The mug uv goldish cream war allus at my plate; the cl'arest bit uv honey-comb, laid cross the biggis' plug uv pies war allus set fur me. The bit o' extry sweetnin' never missed my ole blue chiny cup.

An' summer days when fiel' work war a-foot, a bottle full o' fraish new buttermilk war allus tucked away amongst the corn pones in my dinner pail.

"An' when I tuk ter books, an' readin' uv the papers, an' the ole man riz up ag'inst it, bekase I war more favored ter the book nor ter the plough then my old mount'n mammy, ez allus stood 'twixt me an' wrath, she riz up to, an' bargained with the ole man fur two hours uv my time. This war the bargain struck. From twelve er'clock ontil the sun marked two upon the kitchen doorstep I war free.

"Ever' day fur this much I war free. An' in my stid, whilst I lay under the hoss apple tree an' figgered out my book stuff, she followed that ole plough up an' down the en'less furrers across that hot ontrodd'n fiel'—in my stid.

"I've travelled some sence then, ploughed many a furrer in the fiel' o' this worl's troubles, an' I hev foun' ez ther' be few ez keers tur tek the plough whilst I lay by ter rest.

"An' when the work war done, an' harvest in, I tuk ter runnin' down o' nights ter hear the boys discuss the questions o' the day at Jube Turner's store over ter the settlemint.

"'Twar then the ole man sot his foot down.

"'It hev ter stop!' he said. 'The boy air comin' ter no good.'

"Then my ole mammy riz agin, an' set down ez detarmint ez him; an' sez she:—

"'He be a man, an' hev the hankerin's uv a man. The time hev come fur me ter speak. The boy must hev his l'arnin'—books his min' calls fur. He aims ter mix with men; an' you an' me, ole man, must stand aside, an' fit him fur the wrestle ez be boun' ter come. Hit air bespoke fur him, an' ther' ben't no sense in henderin' sech ez be bespoke beforehan'.'

"She kerried, an' I went ter school."

WILMA DYKEMAN
(May 20, 1920–)

A native of Asheville, North Carolina, Wilma Dykeman inherited a deep love of the written word and the natural world from her parents, Bonnie Cole Dykeman and Willard Dykeman. The family spent evenings reading aloud, and Dykeman describes her childhood home as "a bounty of woods and wildflowers . . . a pool and stream, gnarled apple trees. Seventeen acres of past and present."

After graduating from Northwestern University in Evanston, Illinois, with a B.S. in Speech and Drama, Dykeman had a job in radio waiting for her in New York City, but her plans changed abruptly when Thomas Wolfe's sister introduced her to poet James R. Stokely Jr. The couple married after a two-month courtship and made their home in Newport, Tennessee. They have two sons. Their partnership flourished until Stokely's death in 1977.

Throughout her career, Dykeman has possessed an uncanny ability to discern and anticipate the critical issues confronting society, making her a prophetic voice in such areas as race relations, feminism, population control, and especially environmentalism.

Dykeman's first book, *The French Broad*, a volume in the Rivers of America series, was published in 1955 and has never been out of print. She and her husband collaborated on several nonfiction works, including a landmark study of racism called *Neither Black Nor White*. Dykeman's first novel, *The Tall Woman*, was published in 1962 and has remained in print for more than four decades. Her articles have appeared in dozens of national publications, including the *New York Times*, *Harper's*, *Reader's Digest*, and *Fortune*.

She has received numerous awards, including a Guggenheim Fellowship, the Distinguished Southern Writer Award for 1989, and the Hillman Award for Best Book of the Year on World Peace, Race Relations and Civil Liberties. In 1985, she was named Tennessee State Historian.

Summing up Dykeman's influence on the region, North Carolina novelist John Ehle says, "Teller of stories, writer of nonfiction and fiction books, reviewer, teacher, friend of writers, she has become the first lady of Appalachia."

In the excerpt from *Return the Innocent Earth*, Jon Clayburn, a busy executive with the Clayburn-Durant canning company, has returned to the Tennessee farm where the family business began, and where the company has been testing an experimental chemical. A farm worker, Perlina Smelcer, has died suddenly, and Jon has been dispatched by his profit-conscious cousin, Stull Clayburn, to deflect speculation that the chemical might be to blame.

The excerpt from the nonfiction book *The French Broad* introduces an eighty-four-year-old midwife, one of the hundreds of Tennessee and North Carolina inhabitants Dykeman interviewed for this classic work on the history of a river.

OTHER SOURCES TO EXPLORE

PRIMARY

Novels: *Return the Innocent Earth* (1973), *The Far Family* (1966), *The Tall Woman* (1962). **Biography:** *Too Many People, Too Little Love; Edna Rankin McKinnon: Pioneer For Birth Control* (1974), *Prophet of Plenty: The First Ninety Years of W.D. Weatherford* (1973), *Seeds of Southern Change: The Life of Will Alexander* (1962). **Nonfiction:** *Tennessee Woman: An Infinite Variety* (1993), *Tennessee: A History* (1984), *At Home in the Smokies: A History Handbook for Great Smoky Mountains National Park, North Carolina and Tennessee* (1984), *With Fire and Sword: The Battle of Kings Mountain, 1780* (1978), *Highland Homeland: The People of the Great Smokies* (1978), *The Border States: Kentucky, North Carolina, Tennessee, Virginia, West Virginia* (1970), *Neither Black Nor White* (1957), *The French Broad* (1955). **Essay collections:** *Explorations* (1984), *Look To This Day* (1968). **Autobiographical essay:** "The Past is Never Dead. It's Not Even Past," in *Bloodroot* (1998), ed. Joyce Dyer, 106–10.

SECONDARY

Joyce Dyer, "Wilma Dykeman," in *Bloodroot*, 105. Bernadette Hoyle, *Tar Heel Writers I Know* (1956), 56–59. Lina Mainiero, ed. *American Women Writers: A Critical Reference from Colonial Times to the Present* (1979), Vol. 1, 555–57. Scott J. Sebok, "Wilma Dykeman—A Bibliography," *Appalachian Journal* 29:4 (summer 2002), 460–92. "Wilma Dykeman Issue," *Iron Mountain Review*, 5:1 (spring 1989).

RETURN THE INNOCENT EARTH (1973)

from Chapter 1

We came from the airport to the factory, stopping only at the gleaming new motel on the south edge of town to leave my two-suiter. (There are so many who would have claimed me if they had known I was coming: my brother, Monty, Aunt Nettie Sue, and others. But this time I needed the loneliness of a purchased room. There are some things money can buy and loneliness is one of them.) Price brought me up-to-date on inventory in our Churchill warehouses, told me of plans to cut back to winter production of dry-pack foods. And when he spoke of "Burl Smelcer's wife" he kept his eyes on the road, staring straight ahead. "She never pulled out of the coma after her last convulsion. After all, she was sixty-nine years old."

"Probably looked ninety-nine," I said.

He nodded vigorously. "Old Burl's already given up trying to figure out what killed her off." When I didn't push him he glanced at me briefly. "Her kinfolks will be sitting up with the body tonight and funeralizing tomorrow. Outside of that, everything's quiet as cat fur." Price Sims' effort to talk like a mountain man seemed to me to degrade the poor old woman who had died so agonizingly, who—despite Stull's and Price's efforts to keep her anonymous—had a personality, an entity.

At the factory trucks were unloading the last crop of beans. Late limas, shed of their thick tough pods, and long stringless green beans, as prolific and standard-length as years of cross-breeding could make them, were pouring down the chutes into the washing vats, onto the conveyor belts where rows of women inspected them. Once in the cans, and in the big iron retorts, high-pressure cooking would tenderize them, making them seem young and delicate.

"We sprayed these?" I asked Price.

He nodded. "We're keeping this pack separate, at least for the time being." He picked up a handful of the bright emerald beans. His voice was a low awed whisper. Even I could barely hear it. "They held at this stage of their growth for a whole week. Damnedest thing I ever saw. Right at their prime. And their flavor is the finest we've ever packed, at least since I've been around Clayburn-Durant." In a few minutes we went up to the offices, leaving behind the curious stares of the weather-worn women on the inspection line, and in Price's office we talked with one of the plant superintendents and the sales chief for this region.

Later I borrowed Price's car and in the falling part of the afternoon, as old Cebo used to say, I came out here to the fields. Alone. The gigantic bean pickers were just moving off. I watched them roll out of the fields with the massive tread of dinosaurs, their long mechanical necks (for spitting out vines and stalks and leaves) weaving slightly like the necks of those prehistoric animals, sluggish and cumbersome. A stench of oil and fuel trailed behind them like offal. Where they passed the vines are strewn and crushed, the earth packed hard as asphalt.

I try to stir the dirt with the toe of my shoe. It is as unyielding as the concrete of streets I have just left. When we tended this land we were careful to keep it loose and loamy, never plowing too wet for fear it would bake into clods, making sure it could breathe. I can remember hearing about the day Elisha Clayburn, my grandfather, stood not far from where I am tonight and let the rich black dirt filter through his hands, saying, "The land outlives us all—" and within the month he was dead. Now Clayburn Foods has just about come full term. Now our tractors and cultivators and planters gouge up the earth, turn it to rows, beat the clods to dust, feed it, irrigate it, make it yield whatever those gleaming cans demand. I can trace the ridges of the departed dinosaur's tracks even in the early darkness. Once the Clayburns treated the land as if it were a deep, warm, fertile woman worthy of all the care they could lavish. Now the using is all.

Lightning scrawls across the sky like a match struck against the darkness. It has been a long day. Suddenly it is night and the river below me is drowned in shadows. The distant mountains loom dark and threatening as the hump-backed forms of half-submerged whales. The fields are stripped and deserted.

I should go back into town and phone Ellie. I should go to Burl Smelcer's and talk about Perlina. Above all, I should call Deborah. But I do not leave this narrow strip between the bean field and the river for a few more minutes. Some information fed into my system a long time ago holds me here. It has been years since I have walked these fields.

Thunder rumbles off in the west. Pumpkin wagons rolling, the old farmers used to say. Freshness of approaching rain rides the new wind.

The river down below me murmurs in the darkness. Where it reaches under the banked roots of a gaunt old water oak it gurgles strangely, gradually tearing away the earth supporting those aged roots.

Summer has lingered into autumn this year and only today the giant bean-picking machines finished harvesting this field. It is almost time for killing frost. Trunks of the sycamores along the river shine like bleached skeletons under the fitful moonlight that comes and goes in the stormy sky. Starvation moon, the Cherokees who were once here called it.

I have been a company man for a long time but not so long, quite, that I have lost myself, although I learned yesterday that there is much I have buried and need to remember, for the company, for myself.

The river has made this earth I'm standing on, dragging topsoil and debris down from the uplands to enrich it for generations. And land such as this across America has made Clayburn-Durant Foods, which has been my life. None of the Clayburns has been here in a long while, too damn long.

On the plane this morning coming down the great mid-continent flyway I watched the warrens and hives and colonies of cities and suburbs dwindle and disappear as the mountains thrust up their peaks and labyrinths, and I wondered if there are many others in chrome and steel and styrofoam labyrinths today who know bone-deep, as I, the transition from an old land-locked earth to passage through air.

My boyhood boots pulled against the suck of mud; my present British walkers have been jetted across continents of space and time. Down these muddy rows I used to drag battered crates and baskets; now my Gucci brief-case waits on the seat of the car at the edge of the field. I have two urbane children full of supplementary vitamins and enriched cereals but I remember yanking stubborn beets out of this ground, wringing off the purple-green tops and stems which bled a resplendent juice more royal than blood, bending until my back was an aching stiffness and the smell of roots was bitter in my nostrils.

Canning is part of two worlds and there is no escaping either. Land and computers. Seeds and machinery. Weather and sales charts. The gone-before and the yet-to-come are by-products of every can we fill. Yet in those big, sleek central offices in the midwestern metropolis where I live, we lose touch. Yesterday I learned how incredibly we lose touch.

A nightbird calls from one of the beech trees. Unthinking, I reach for pockets—it is chilly and I am wearing a topcoat—hearkening back to the time when old Cebo, whose face was dark and wrinkled and tough as walnut bark, muttered that a screech owl's forebodings could be canceled only by turning all our pockets inside out. Standing in the deepening darkness, many distances from where I began this day, I wonder if the owl speaks of life or death, the present or future. Or perhaps the past. The past has been thick around me all day, like one of the fogs that sometimes sweeps across these Smoky Mountains, smothering all the familiar landmarks, changing contours, obscuring here and revealing there, until the oldest places are new and the new is made ancient, or seems so.

It is the old past in that scent of ketchup which is here, waiting in the silent furrows, passing like the river in its wrenching, ceaseless course. But only yesterday is still raw within me. I'll have to settle many ghosts while I am here.

In the distance, Burl Smelcer's unpainted house squats on a treeless rise. I must go there. But not tonight, not with the dead woman lying in the narrow room fetid with visitors and heat and food and curiosity—and, yes, mourning. I can see the light from the house, no larger than a firefly in the distance.

I hear the screech owl again. Its quavering cry comes from a nearer tree this time. It makes me apprehensive. I do not seem to myself the same man who left the city this morning, brisk and businesslike even though in revolt. Here I know that the past is not dead. Or is it even past? Like all the data programmed into George Hodges' computers, it waits raw and formless. And no one remembers more of it happening here than I do.

Blood soaked into the ground. Sweat mixed with mud and crates of tomatoes and machine grease. Tears and terror and waste, hurt too deep for scars, pure joy, gall of mistakes, the sweet balm of success, and the reach out. And out. And out.

I come from a line of remembering people. In generations past we built churches and ballads and a way of life out of our remembering, handing down words the way others pass along designs woven into coverlets, carved into wood, or worked into clay. But now that is going, too—the woven words and the cloth and all.

Another slash of lightning breaks as I leave the field and the deep-running river and walk along the rutted road toward the car. Does anyone else care about Elisha Clayburn's violent death in these dark mountains or the inheritance he left Mary Clayburn and seven children? Does anyone know of his son Jonathan's improbable journey—so unlike most Clayburn ventures—to unravel the secret of Elisha's death? Does anyone recollect how another son, Daniel Clayburn, with the strong black arm of Lonas Rankin beside him, dreamed and pounded into being machines that made a little plant into a company?

Does anyone recall the face or form of all those anonymous figures—black and white—who gave strength and substance to the Clayburns and their dream through patient, wrenching years and lifetimes? Does anyone at all remember Josh Clayburn's voice, the wounded look in his eyes as he broke before the ultimatum delivered by his own son, Stull? Or the ultimatum itself by which the company became larger than any Clayburn or all the family? And above all, does anyone remember (or can anyone who knew forget?) Jonathan Clayburn, carrying them all by his will and muscle?

This is the memory I have come back to claim. My father. Shape of a world of love-honor-and-obey, of a-man's-word-is-his-bond, of love-thy-neighbor-as-thyself, of something far and lost, abandoned.

I arrive at my car and climb in, turn the key with stiff fingers, head toward town. The first drops of rain fall. Their freshness mixes with the old and acrid smell of mulch and silt left by many floods covering these level plains below the mountains. The dark land stretches around me.

The cold autumn rain is slashing hard against my windshield as I watch the road from the farm into Churchill. A car behind me pulls out to pass in an explosion of impatience. Its tires hiss on the wet pavement and its motor churns. As it cuts back into the right lane ahead of me the rear wheels slip. The driver brings it out of the skid. I wonder if the boy I glimpsed knows how narrowly he escaped plunging down the steep bank to our right. I watch his red tail-light fade into the distance. How did Dan Clayburn feel that long-ago day when his new car stalled in gravel and would not start again?

We are fearfully and wonderfully made, my God-fearing, church-going father and mother told me. Is the foolish boy in that souped-up car? Does he know? Was Perlina Smelcer? Is Stull Clayburn and does he know? Do I know?

No superman of sex or finance or honor. Six-feet-two with hair still dark brown and belly not yet flabby and not-quite twenty-twenty vision. My tennis and love-making are not so unyielding as when I was twenty but they have gained something in form and finesse and enjoyment. I still struggle to keep up with news of neighborhood, city, industry, country, world. The result: frustration, and a dozen riptides pressing in.

A search began for me yesterday: for Jonathan Clayburn, Jr., Jon, in my early fifties, widower, father, business executive, fringe participant in religion and politics and sports and society, secret dreamer at intervals, occasional lover now in love. I ask only to be whole. And I realize the arrogance and impossibility of my asking.

By the time I arrive at the motel the rain has settled to a steady downpour. I stop at the desk to pick up my room key and the clerk makes me welcome. Her formal greeting has been memorized from some innkeeper's manual but as I thank her she adds, "Turning cold yet? I heard thunder a little while ago. My grandpa always said autumn thunder meant a cold spell to come."

I smile at her and nod. All at once I love her. Her hair is set in beauty-parlor majesty and her dress is a wholesale replica of some high-fashion design shown in a slick magazine, her eyes even bear standard Cleopatra outlines and shadows. But the adaptation has not yet been total. It has not reached all the way inside. "My grandpa always said . . ."

We can still remember.

And I need to remember because I must go on. Without yesterday Clayburn-Durant Foods would not be here. The question is, will any of us—on foot or hoof or wing or fin or root—be here tomorrow?

FROM *THE FRENCH BROAD* (1955)

On the opposite side of the French Broad watershed, where bold Allen's Creek rushes down out of the Balsams, anyone you talk with up or down that creek and many adjoining ones can tell you who Granny Sarah McNabb is and where she lives. In a weathered little house yon side of the creek. There are still pockets of snow high up in the mountains around the narrow valley, but the buds on the cherry trees in Granny's yard are swelling toward spring. There are shocks of fodder and stacks of green wood in the yard too, for a son and his family live in part of Granny's house. Nevertheless, she does all her own cooking and keeping in the two front rooms she set aside for herself after she'd finished her life work as a midwife and divided up the farm among her children. Her face is round and webbed with fine lines and full of light. Its strength of character matches her lean body's strength of muscle.

"Law, child, I've had to be strong. I'm eighty-four years old now and I've catched babies ever since I was twenty. The last one was when I was eighty. I slipped out in the night, none of the family knew about it, and I got back before morning. None of them know about it to this day.

"I waited on two or three doctors at different times while I was growing up—everybody always said I had the turn to be a nurse—and after a while women started sending for me if they couldn't get the doctor, and pretty soon some of them wanted just me, wouldn't hear to a doctor looking after them. I couldn't count all the babies—five, six, seven hundred?—there was over a hundred I guess, that I never turned in at Raleigh. It was before I ever had those forms to fill. But out of all that number, over all those years, I never lost a baby or a mother. Oh, it wasn't none of my doing. It was the work of the Lord. I was just an instrument for Him to use.

"During those years I got married and had children myself. There was ten of them, five boys and five girls, all still living today but one, and I've got forty grandchildren and fifty-two great-grandchildren and four great-great-grandchildren. And my husband was only fifty-two years old when he died. My baby was under five and there was four of the younguns just tots. It was hard going for me, sometimes we went short, but I never begged for anything. We always made a crop. I never stopped under a thousand cans of food, not counting pickles and jellies, and we had apples in the cellar.

"And for thirty years I made wreaths for the Farmer's Federation over at Asheville. They'd ship them up North and all around. I'd go up on the Balsams and get my green stuff. I'd hitch up my wagon and team and put the children in and go up into the mountains and gather greens all day long. The Federation furnished me all the wire and materials I needed. I'd get a dollar a wreath.

"But many's the time I've put it aside to go on a call. One of my boys asked me once, 'Mama, what if you had a contract for a hundred wreaths and they was due the next morning and you were running short, but someone came asking you to go to a woman whose time had come, what would you do?' 'Why, I'd lay them wreaths down,' I told him. 'Wreaths can wait. A woman can't.'

"There's no time in the world like the hour a woman's bringing a baby. There's nothing like somebody coming into the world, a new life. And nobody ever come and knocked on my door and asked me to look after their wife that I didn't go. Snow or rain or cold, it never hurt me to go out in weather when I went on a case. I remember one electric storm, the man led the way up over a high ridge, the thunder was crashing and the lightning was so close the horse would just squat and tremble every time it come. But we made it through all right.

"One of the hardest and pitifulest places I ever went was to a lumber camp way back there in the Balsams. The man come after me and we rode just about all night before we got to the house, one of those poor little throwed-together lumber shacks and it already full of babies. The woman was having a hard time. I straightened up the house and took care of the children and gave the mother a little quinine in two ounces of castor oil—that's all the medicine I ever gave, and the best doctor I ever waited on showed me about using that if the baby was lingering. But I stayed a week there. I always saw my woman through, no matter how long it took, and there wasn't a scrap to cover the baby's nakedness whenever it did come. So while I waited I had to make it a belly band and some little shirts and gowns. I'd always take flannel in my bag and if they didn't have any fixings, I'd make what they needed. Sometimes I'd take food too, if I knew it to be a place where the folks were in need. There was seven babies I caught in that lumber camp before I was through there.

"Pay? Once in a while they'd pay me. That wasn't what I went for. At first I charged ten dollars. Later on I asked twenty. But mostly it was just whatever they could give, and I never dunned anybody in my life. They never paid in produce, though, 'cause usually I had more than they did. I'd be carrying them food.

"One of the doctors let me read up in his books and after a while I signed up in Raleigh to be a midwife. They sent out somebody to teach us and give us a test. From that time on, I always got my Permit, and with a Grade A on it too. I carried all my necessaries in a denim bag with a draw-string top: washbasin and handbrush, nail file, soap, Lysol, cotton cord tape and dressing, boric acid and eyedrops, two pad covers, four towels, a white coverall apron and cap and the birth certificate and report cards on the mother and baby. It had to all be boiled in disinfectant water and wrapped in clean rags. And I always kept my special dress and slip and shoes and stockings cleaned and ready at hand for me to step right into night or day whenever a call came."

Granny McNabb leaves for a moment and goes into the next room. She walks slowly because in the past year she's broken both hips. When she comes back her bright blue eyes are shining above the faded blue denim of the bag she's clutching. On her lap she sorts through the remnant of necessaries left in the little bag that has gone with her over so many lonely trails during so many strange hours, helping deliver life in the French Broad country. The white cap that folded to cover her head, crowned by a bit of yellowed lace sewed with tiny stitches. As she handles the flannels and cottons and bottles, a smile creeps across her face.

"Some folks think the moon changing has something to do with the time a baby's born. It don't have anything to do with it. When the apple's ripe, it'll fall. The baby wasn't got in the moon, it'll not be had there, neither." Remembering something else, her face sobers. "A few times I had to tend a girl as young as fourteen. That's not right. A man ought to stay off that marriage till the girl's of age to have a baby. No matter what age, a man can't ever be too good to a woman has had his children. I've seen them come to their time and I know. I remember once a father came after me to help his daughter. She wasn't married, but her folks were looking after her all right. They don't always, when it's like that. I went and stayed with her and when her baby come, it was black. What'd I do? Just what I did for every one of my babies. Spanked the breath of life in it and put drops in its eyes, give it a bath and dressed it and put it to the breast. It was another soul, and its mother was another mother. I'd never lower her name none either. But I watched that baby grow up, and sometimes it pretty near broke my heart seeing him neither black nor white and neither side claiming him. He went away from North Carolina finally. I don't know where he is now but I hope he's found his Lord, wherever he is.

"My babies are scattered all over. Whenever I go to our church up here I can sit and count folks I helped bring in the world. That was my talent. I never had an education but the Lord give me my talent. And I never heard a knock come on that door at night that I didn't start talking to the Lord. He can do anything. He made the leaves of the herbs for the healing of the nations, and He can carry a body through any trial. I'd ask Him to help me. I'd tell Him it was a mother I was going to help and He'd have to show me what to do. All the way going, on horseback or walking, riding behind mules or maybe even oxen, I'd call on the Lord. This was my mission in life and I did it with His help the best I could. Because there's nothing on this earth like seeing a new life come into the world."

ℐARAH ℬARNWELL ℰLLIOTT
(November 29, 1848–August 30, 1928)

Sarah Barnwell Elliott was the daughter of Charlotte Bull Barnwell Elliott and Bishop Stephen Elliott, one of the founders of the University of the South at Sewanee, Tennessee. Born in Georgia, Elliott spent most of her life at Sewanee, with the exception of a year at Johns Hopkins University (1886), and seven years in New York City (1895–1902).

Elliott was part of the nineteenth-century local color movement, a genre which flourished after the Civil War and was based on the ideal that the local fiction writer could interpret her own area better than someone from the outside. One of the genre's trademarks is the heavy use of dialect. Most critics find Elliott's handling of dialect inferior to that of fellow local color writer, Mary Noailles Murfree.

Known primarily as a novelist, Elliott also published a collection of short stories, *An Incident and Other Happenings*, and a biography, *Sam Houston*. She is credited with introducing feminist views into the local color genre, most notably in her novel *The Durket Sperret*. Her most critically acclaimed work was the novel *Jerry*, which opens in the Tennessee mountains but is primarily set in a western mining town; it was originally published as a serial in *Scribner's Magazine* (1890).

Elliott returned to Sewanee in 1902 and, in later life, was known as much for her suffragist activities as for her writing. She was president of the Tennessee State Equal Suffrage Association and vice-president of the Southern States Woman Suffrage Conference.

The main character of *The Durket Sperret* is Hannah Warren, a poor but proud mountain girl who defies her grandmother's demands that she marry "well." A reviewer for *The Nation* noted that Hannah "is made to pass through an improbable experience, but she herself is never improbable."

In this scene from *The Durket Sperret*, Hannah has ventured into Sewanee to peddle produce and encounters the townsfolks' underlying prejudice towards the mountaineers.

OTHER SOURCES TO EXPLORE

PRIMARY

Novels: *The Making of Jane* (1901), *The Durket Sperret* (1898), *John Paget* (1893), *Jerry* (1891), *A Simple Heart* (1887), *The Felmeres* (1879). **Short stories:** *Some Data and Other Stories of Southern Life* (1981), ed. Clara Childs Mackenzie. *An Incident and Other Happenings* (1899). **Biography:** *Sam Houston* (1900).

SECONDARY

Clara Childs Mackenzie, *Sarah Barnwell Elliott* (1980). Review of *The Durket Sperret*, *The Nation*, 19 May 1898, 389. "Sarah Barnwell Elliott," *American Authors*, ed. Stanley Kunitz and Howard Haycroft (1938), 251. Robert M. Willingham Jr. "Sarah Barnwell Elliott," *Southern Writers: A Biographical Dictionary* (1979), 143–44.

THE DURKET SPERRET (1898)
from Chapter II

At the time this story opens, the railway station, known as Sewanee, consisted of a few shops, the post-office, and one or two small houses, built about a barren square. From this a broad road led to the "University," and the other end of Sewanee. Up this road the butcher and shoemaker had planted some locust trees in front of their shops, and beyond them the confectioner had laid a stone pavement for the length of his lot, and planted some maple trees, that, in the autumn, burned like flames of fire. Beyond the confectioner's the road was in the woods for a short space, then more houses. About a half mile from the station this road ended in another road that crossed it at right angles, and up and down this the University town was built.

Between the houses, between the public buildings, wherever any space was left free from carpenters and stone masons, the forest marched up and claimed its own, while the houses looked as if they had been convinced of their obtrusiveness, and had crept as far back as possible, leaving their fences as protection to the forest, and not as the sign of a clearing.

Very still and bare the little place looked on the gray March morning, when, under Mrs. Wilson's guidance, Hannah made her entrance as a peddler. Down the road, beaten hard by the rain, and dotted here and there with clear little pools of water, Hannah led old Bess, bearing the long bags, in the ends of which were bestowed the apples and potatoes, the bucket of butter being fastened to the saddle.

They had not stopped at the station, for Mrs. Wilson said the people in the town paid better prices.

"They don't know no better than to tuck frostbit 'taters," she explained, "an' they'll give most anything fur butter jest now. All the 'versity boys is come back, an' butter's awful sca'ce. To tell the truth," pushing her long bonnet back, "thar ain't much o' *anything* to eat right now. What with layin' an' scratchin' through the winter fur a livin', the hens is wore out, an' chickens ain't in yit, an' these 'versity women is jest pestered to git sumpen fur the boys."

Hannah listened in silence. She had her own ideas about trading, and besides had very scant respect for Mrs. Wilson, either mentally or morally. She knew that her things were good, but she was determined to ask only a fair price for them. It was bad to cheat people because they were simple or "in a push." She was in a push herself, and felt sorry for them.

"An' ax a leetle moren you 'llows to git," Mrs. Wilson went on, "kase they'll allers tuck some off. Thar *air* a few that jest pays what you says, or don't tuck none, an' I axes them a fa'r price." They stopped at a gate as she finished, and she directed Hannah to "hitch the nag an' stiffen up."

"I ain't feared," Hannah answered, while she made old Bess fast, "but I ain't usen to peddlin', an' I don't like hit, nuther."

Mrs. Wilson laughed. "Youuns Granny keeps on a-settin' you up till nothin' ain't good enough," she said. "Lots o' folks as good as ary Warren hes been a peddlin' a many a year."

"Thet don't make hit no better fur me, Lizer Wilson, an' nothin' ain't agoin' to make hit better; any moren a dog ever likes a hog-waller," and she took down the bucket of butter with a swing that brought her face to face with her companion. One glance at Hannah's eyes, that now looked like her grandmother's, and Mrs. Wilson changed the subject.

"Leave the sacks," she said roughly; "hit'll be time to pack 'em in when they're sold." She led the way in along a graveled walk, Hannah looking about her curiously, and trying to conquer her rather unreasonable anger against Mrs. Wilson, before she should meet the people about whom she had heard such varying reports.

At the front piazza Hannah paused, and Mrs. Wilson laughed exasperatingly.

"Lor, gal!" she said, "these fine folks don't ax folks like weuns in the front do'; weuns ain't nothin' but 'Covites come to peddle'; come to the kitchen."

That people lived who thought themselves better than the Warrens or Durkets was a new sensation to Hannah, and she wondered if her grandmother knew it. Her astonishment stilled her wrath until the thought overwhelmed her, that perhaps these people would look on her and Lizer Wilson as the same! She had followed mechanically, and before she had reached any conclusion they were at the back door.

A negro woman stood wiping a pan, while a lady, holding an open bucket of butter, was talking scoldingly to a woman who, as Hannah saw instantly, looked very different from the lady, and very much like Lizer and herself. There was a moment's silence as the newcomers appeared; then the negress spoke.

"Mornin', Mrs. Wilson," she said familiarly.

"Mornin', Mary," Mrs. Wilson answered, in an oily tone; then to the lady she said: "Mornin', Mrs. Skinner."

"Good-morning, Mrs. Wilson," the lady answered, while the woman she had been scolding turned, and Hannah recognized a person who lived near the Durkets, and who was looked down on by them just as Lizer Wilson was by the Warrens. They did not greet each other, but Hannah felt the woman's stare of wonder, that "John Warren's gal" should peddle with Lizer Wilson! She seemed to hear the story being told to the Durkets, and repeated to her grandmother by Si. Things seemed misty for a moment, then, through the confusion, she heard Lizer's voice. "No, I ain't got nothin' left but a few aigs; but this gal has a few things she'd like to get shed of 'fore we starts home."

Hannah listened, wondering, and remembered a saying of her grandmother's, that Lizer could "lie the kick outern a mule."

"What has she?" questioned Mrs. Skinner.

"Taters, an' apples, an' butter," Lizer answered; "nothin' much to pack back if the price ain't a-comin'."

"What is the price of the butter?"

"Thirty cents; I've done sold mine at thet; the taters is a dollar an' a heff a bushel, an' the apples a dollar."

"I have just paid twenty cents for butter; why are your things so high?" was questioned sharply.

"Ourn is extry good," Lizer answered. The negro woman smiled. Hannah's indignation was gathering, but she did not speak. Mrs. Wilson must know the ways of the place—she would wait.

"I'll take the apples," the lady began compromisingly, "but I will *not* take the butter nor the potatoes. How many apples have you?" to Hannah.

"A bushel," Hannah answered quickly, afraid that Lizer would say a cartload.

Mrs. Skinner looked at her keenly. "I have never seen you before," she said.

"She ain't never peddled befo', an' ain't got no need to come now," Lizer struck in, looking straight at the woman from the other valley. "She jest come along fur comp'ny, an' brung a few things fur balance—she ain't pertickler 'bout sellin'."

The first part of this speech soothed Hannah's feelings somewhat, but the final clause, representing her as coming for the love of Lizer Wilson, was worse than the peddling.

SIDNEY SAYLOR FARR
(October 30, 1932–)

〜

A native of eastern Kentucky, Sidney Saylor Farr is a poet, an essayist, an editor, and a writer of short fiction. A graduate of Berea College (B.A., 1980), Farr grew up near Pine Mountain, Kentucky, an experience she shares in her books, *More Than Moonshine: Appalachian Recipes and Recollections* and *Table Talk: Appalachian Meals and Memories*.

She married at the age of fifteen, in part, she says, because the nearest public high school was fifteen miles away and her family didn't have the money to send her to boarding school. Determined to graduate, Farr took courses by mail and eventually earned her diploma.

In the early 1960s, Farr, her husband, Leon Lawson, and their two sons moved to Indianapolis, then to Berea, Kentucky, where she earned a degree in English. She and Lawson divorced in 1967; in 1970 she married Grover Vernon Farr, a counselor.

Farr was the associate editor of *Mountain Life & Work* from 1964 to 1969. In 1976, she became the assistant to the Special Collections librarian at Berea College and served as the editor of *Appalachian Heritage* from 1985 until her retirement in 1999. Farr's groundbreaking annotated bibliography, *Appalachian Women*, was published in 1981 by the University Press of Kentucky, and it remains an indispensable guide to the region's literature.

Farr's autobiographical essay "Shall We Gather in the Kitchen" appears in her collection *More Than Moonshine: Appalachian Recipes and Recollections*.

OTHER SOURCES TO EXPLORE

PRIMARY

Nonfiction: *Tom Sawyer and the Spiritual Whirlwind* (2000), *Spoon Bread Cookbook* (1997), *Table Talk: Appalachian Meals and Memories* (1995), *What Tom Sawyer Learned From Dying* (1993), *More Than Moonshine: Appalachian Recipes and Recollections*

(1983), *Berea's Appalachian Ballad Collectors: James Watt Raine, John F. Smith, Katherine Jackson French, and Gladys V. Jameson* (1980). **Poetry:** *Headwaters* (1995). **Bibliography:** *Appalachian Women: An Annotated Bibliography* (1981). **Autobiographical essay:** "Women Born to Be Strong," in *Bloodroot* (1998), ed. Joyce Dyer, 112–19.

SECONDARY

Contemporary Authors, Vol. 114, 154. Joyce Dyer, "Sidney Saylor Farr," in *Bloodroot,* 111.

FROM *MORE THAN MOONSHINE: APPALACHIAN RECIPES AND RECOLLECTIONS* (1983)

I read the other day that a cook in an old-time country kitchen walked at least 350 miles a year preparing three meals a day. My mother, grandmother, and Granny Brock, as well as other women in the Appalachian Mountains, probably walked three times that distance as they scoured the garden rows and hunted the hills to get food. They did not have cash to buy much, and the corner grocery was miles away. They did not own a cookbook among them, just ancient knowledge and skillful hands, and an instinct born out of desperate need to feed their hungry children.

Families ate what they grew on the place or found in the hills. Busy from dawn to dusk, buying nothing that could be raised, cooked or handmade at home, Mother worked as her mother and grandmother worked before her. Father did outside chores, using handmade tools and methods that Grandpa and his father used.

In the years before and during the Second World War, the hills had plenty of huckleberries, blackberries, raspberries, elderberries, mulberries, strawberries—until timber and coal companies came and stripped the land. There were both orchard-grown and wild fruits: apples, plums, grapes, persimmons, and pawpaws. The trees in the mountains produced black and white walnuts, hazelnuts, beechnuts, and hickory nuts. Father hunted rabbits, possums, coons, squirrels, and groundhogs. He brought in wild ducks, geese, grouse, and quail. There were rock bass, trout, catfish, and other varieties of fish in the streams and rivers. Wild bees swarmed and settled, reswarmed and settled again, until numerous colonies were to be found in hollow trees. The honey was taken for use on the table, the bees put into new bee gums to start all over. The men planted cane and made molasses. They raised crops of white and sweet potatoes, squash, pumpkin, corn, and beans.

Each little homestead had its cornfield, its patch of cane, and its bee gums (hives). Somewhere along the creek there would be a watermill where corn was ground into meal. And somewhere in the hillside thickets there would be moonshine stills where corn was bottled, sold, and drunk.

The kitchen has been central to my life as a mountain woman. I was born and raised in Appalachia—on Stoney Fork in southeastern Kentucky. Straight Creek, one of many creeks and small rivers in eastern Kentucky, has its beginning on Pine Mountain near where Harlan and Leslie Counties join. For thirty miles or more it is fed by smaller streams and gets deeper and wider before it is lost in the Cumberland River at Pineville. Stoney Fork is one of the little creeks running into Straight Creek. From where it merges with the latter up to its headwaters at Peach Orchard, Stoney Fork is about ten miles long.

. . .

Wilburn and Rachel, my parents, lived on Coon Branch until they had three children; I was the firstborn. When I was five they moved a mile below the mouth of Stoney Fork and the one-room school we children later attended. Father bought logs and lumber at Sonny LeFever's sawmill and built a house in the center of an old orchard near a sulfur spring. Pine Mountain rose up steeply from our back yard.

Pine Mountain is one hundred miles long, running through three counties in Kentucky and on into Tennessee. It is filled with limestone caves and covered with scrub trees. A footpath ran up in front of our house across the mountain to the Cumberland River side. A cliff hugged the highest peak near the footpath, and from a crevice a pine grew, gnarled and twisted from endless winds. I loved to stand or sit on the rock, feel the sun on my face, the wind blowing through my hair, and listen to the sound in the pine branches. Far below, Straight Creek was a crooked silver ribbon and the buildings seemed like doll houses scattered along the road. On the Cumberland side, the railroad played a steel counterpoint to the river. Long trains filled to overflowing with Harlan County coal shuttled along to Pineville and points north and east, blowing their whistles at every small crossing.

When the train whistle sounded clearly on our side of the mountain, Mother said, "Children, it's going to rain." Late that afternoon or early the next day it would cloud up and rain. I never questioned the relationship of the train whistle to the rain until I moved to Indianapolis in 1960. We lived near a railroad yard across White River in West Indianapolis. For the first week or so every time I heard a train I thought, "It's going to rain," but the rain did not come. Finally I stopped expecting rain every time I heard a train. Mountain customs die hard.

Mountain people are criticized for leaving the industrial cities where they live and work and heading home almost every weekend. What people who live in today's transient society don't seem to understand about us mountain folks is that it's possible to put one's roots down so deeply they cannot be satisfactorily transplanted anywhere else. People who have lost an arm or a leg complain that they still feel phantom pain. I used to fancy it was that way for us mountain people. Take us anywhere in the world and there will always be pain in the missing part buried so deeply in hillside soil. Mountain people have a strong sense of place; they know where they belong.

It is always a joy to me to leave cities behind, to travel through the Bluegrass section of Kentucky and on to the hills. As the mountains unfold for me I have a feeling of belonging, of being protected, of wanting to settle down and stay forever.

My friend Jane Wilson, an East Tennessee woman, says it well: "I can walk back home from just about anywhere." She and I both have a sense of place—a knowing that if all else fails, we can always walk back home and there will be space for us, and people who care about us.

GRANNY BROCK

from *Headwaters* (1995)

"Granny, is it gonna rain?"

"My bees worked in the clover early and late,
and the moon had a ring around it these past few nights.
There were red clouds in the sky this morning,
the wind turned tree-leaves underside over,
and redbirds called 'wet, wet, wet' all day long.
That's a sure sign of rain," she says.

"Granny, is it gonna snow a lot?"

"The woolly worms done give us their opinion,
and crickets're singing their lonesome winter song.
The cornshucks're thick and stiff this year,
and moss is growing on the north side of trees.
That's a sure sign of a bad winter," she says.

"Granny, why's there so much trouble?"

"The east wind of trouble travels far and near,
and bad times come but they do go away.
Once I was younger in older times,
when a good day's work brought a good day's pay.

Back then was the dayburst,
now it's coming down dusky,
but it's not yet plumb dark in our land—
that's a sure sign," she says.

MOUNTAINS FILL UP THE NIGHT

from *Headwaters* (1995)

I know the mountains covered with snow,
and misty green of earth's awakening,
when they are drenched in summer storms,
painted with master colors
softened with Indian Summer smoke.

Mountains, so steady, and yet they change
when each determined morning climbs.
Some of night sneaks into hollows
but noonday sun blasts it out,
gold heat here but up there—trees.

I know the mountains when heat is gone
and sun challenges the regal night.
I know them when raindrops fall
and break, and wet the silver lichen;
and white mist tassels the trees.

Then dusky dark, its curtain silent;
the mountains grow star-ward
around us, and over us and
under. Even inside us.
Where do the mountains stop?

Appalachia, Where are your Hills?

from *Headwaters* (1995)

Thank God for the mantling snow
He sends to caress the ravaged hills.
It covers the smell of the slag heap burning,
it hides the scars that mar the mountains,
and makes a shroud for murdered trees.
I wish the snow would never stop.

When father was a young boy
the mountains were like nurseries
for the creeks and the young rivers.
They were rich in green-gold bounty
and strong with wide black bones.
They held and nourished our people.

Now the people sit, slack-handed,
from chill, dark drawn to hopeless night.
They sit, dreamless and passive,
waiting for a sedative sleep
to come riding down on the snowfall—
I pray the snow will never stop.

𝒩IKKY 𝒥INNEY
(August 26, 1957–)

Nikky Finney is a founding member of the Affrilachian poets, a community-based group of Appalachian writers of African descent living in and around Lexington, Kentucky. Born in Conway, South Carolina, she is the only daughter of parents who both grew up on farms. Her mother, an elementary school teacher, grew up in Newberry County, South Carolina, and her father, a civil rights lawyer, grew up in Virginia. She was raised in South Carolina and graduated from Talladega College in Alabama.

Her poems have been published in a number of journals and anthologies, including *In Search of Color Everywhere, I Hear a Symphony,* and *Spirit and Flame.* She contributed to Kentucky's New Books for New Readers series, creating the stories in *Heartwood* for an adult literacy program. The author of two books of poetry, *On Wings Made of Gauze* and *Rice,* she has two books in progress: a collection of poetry, *The World is Round,* and her first novel. Finney received the Pen American Open Book Award in 1999.

Finney began teaching and writing in California, where she lived for nearly a decade. Since 1991, she has been a faculty member in the Creative Writing Program at the University of Kentucky. She frequently gives readings at schools, colleges, universities, and writers' workshops across the country.

OTHER SOURCES TO EXPLORE

PRIMARY

Poetry: *Rice* (1995), On *Wings Made of Gauze* (1985). **Short stories:** *Heartwood* (1997). **Autobiographical essay:** "Salt-Water Geechee Mounds," in *Bloodroot* (1998), ed. Joyce Dyer, 121–27. **Video:** *Coal Black Voices: A Documentary* (2001). **Script:** *For Posterity's Sake: The Story of Morgan and Marvin Smith* (PBS documentary, 1995).

SECONDARY

Kwame Dawes, "Reading Rice: A Local Habitation and a Name," *African American Review* 31:2 (summer 1997), 269–79. Joyce Dyer, "Nikky Finney," in *Bloodroot*, 120. Sally Lodge, review of *On Wings Made of Gauze, Publishers Weekly* 228 (12 July 1985), 53. Louis McKee, review of *On Wings Made of Gauze, Library Journal* 110 (1 September 1985), 202.

HEARTWOOD (1997)

from Queen Ida's Hair-Doing
House of Waves

Lots of black women did hair in Luketown. Most of them did it just as a favor for a girlfriend, just because they were good at it, and some did it just for fun. They would sit a sister, a niece, or some other family member down in the middle of their kitchen, in the middle of an easy Saturday, laugh, talk and just do hair.

Ida Sims, who had always been known as "Queenie," was the only one of them to own her own beauty shop. Queenie Sims was serious about the beauty business. But everybody knew she was more serious about the beauty part than the business part. She had been Luketown's first female business owner. For thirty years now, her Hair-Doing House of Waves was where the women of Luketown and a few other towns came to treat themselves when they had a few extra dollars and felt like being served by the Queen of Deep Down Beauty.

On those days when life had been just a bit too hard and the women of Luketown had taken perfect care of everybody else except themselves, they came to Queen Ida's for some relief. Usually Fridays and Saturdays, when they needed just a little extra attention, they called up the Queen and asked if she had any space in her afternoon for them. The women would walk a few doors down the street or drive from somewhere close by to sit and talk and let the Queen of Hair wash and set their blues away and turn their sweet curly naps into endless oceans of waves.

Queen Ida's Hair-Doing House of Waves might have looked like just a hole in the wall to a stranger passing through Luketown, but inside she had built a place of honor for black women and their many different kinds of hair. She had decorated her one-room shop just like something out of those old black and white movies.

Miss Ida was always saying she wanted to make the women who dropped by feel like royalty themselves. Mr. Andy from down the street had covered her two swivel chairs in purple velvet, just for added effect.

Hanging from every wall were soft spotlights, clean sparkling mirrors, and photographs of women who, Miss Ida said, were "some of the most beautiful black women ever born." And in between all the pretty pictures she had small signs printed up with what she called her "words to be beautiful by." One of her favorites was "Beauty is not something your Mama and

Daddy gave you, beauty is something you must give yourself permission to have. So get to work!"

Queenie Sims believed in making her women feel like each and every one of them had finally won the black woman's lottery jackpot! She had the idea, years ago, that black women needed some special love and attention after all their years of having to take care of everybody else. So she decided to go into the business of treating them like queens every chance she got. That's how Miss Queenie got and kept her name.

Even though the sign said "Hair-Doing House of Waves," to each and every black woman who went there each week, it also became a private rest stop, vacation, hot tub, emergency room, and restaurant, all in one. Not only did their scalps benefit from Ida's homemade creams and conditioners, but the good and honest talk they got back from her helped them work out some important things they were battling in their own private lives.

When Ida Sims got through with her customers, not only did she have the women of Luketown looking good, but she also had one or two of them thinking and believing something good about themselves as well. Her beauty shop wasn't just about fixing up what was on top of the head, it was also about cleaning out the years of dust hidden inside the deep corners of their lives.

After every head had been brushed and styled, and before anybody ever thought about leaving, she offered each customer a cup of tea as well as a slice of homemade coconut creme pie. And each customer who stood up to leave always got a little surprise box of something. A gift wrapped up in leftover Christmas paper. Something sweet secretly tucked down in their handbags with a little note attached. With that kind of special attention, no wonder Ida Sims had been in business thirty years. There were other shops in other towns nearby, but no one had ever opened up another beauty shop in Luketown to compete with the Hair-Doing House of Waves.

Ida Sims worked three shifts a day with two customers at a time. Each shift lasted about two hours, depending on the length and thickness of the hair. But as busy as she was, she never thought about getting a bigger place or hiring on more help. She said she could only give quality care to the hair and heads of two women at a time and no more than six per day. Quality was more important to Queenie Sims than making more money.

Women who came to Queen Ida's were never sure who would come in at the same time. They never knew which two would arrive and sit side by side for at least two hours with only each other as company. Some of them might have been friends before, but some others might never have spoken to each other before that day. That was part of the beauty of Ida's place, never being sure of just who you might be getting your hair done beside.

Miss Ida always believed that they would talk and by the end of the day make friends with each other. And because of that, they would have more to share the next time they saw each other out in the world doing something else.

There was no waiting room in the House of Waves. There was no room for anybody to avoid somebody else's eyes. There were no magazines, and it was rare to hear any music. It was Queen Ida's mission to get people to talk to each other. The rest of that stuff, Ida said, "you can do anytime." This was the sacred beauty hour.

Her grandmother told her way back when she first started her business to always remember that there were some black women who never got the free time that other women got in their lives to make and keep friends. These were the black women who for all their time on earth had worked two and three jobs. These women had taken care of their own children and somebody else's too. Ida Sims decided way back then that bringing black women together to be friends was an important part of her all-round beauty work. This was where she started making the women of Luketown pay attention to their inside beauty.

No matter what day it was and no matter which two customers came in, there was always a lively conversation going on inside the House of Waves. In this relaxed time of working and talking, a lot more than hair-doing went on. In fact, nine times out of ten, somebody stood up to leave with a new, five-dollar hairdo and a million-dollar attitude. Queen Ida softly preached that creating outside beauty only lasted a week but inside beauty lasted for as long as the head itself stayed around.

IRONS AT HER FEET

from *Rice* (1995)

from the coals
of her bedroom fireplace
onto the tip
of my grandmother's
december winter stick
for fifteen years
hot irons traveled
into waiting flannel wraps
and were shuttled
up under covers
and inbetween quilts
where three babies lay shivering
in country quarter
night time air
hot irons
wrapped and pushed
up close
to frosting toes
irons instead of lip kisses
is what she remembers
irons instead of carmel colored fingers
that should have swaddled shoulders
like it swaddled hoes
and quiltin' needles
and spongy cow tits

everytime
i am back home
i tip into her room
tip again into her saucering cheeks
and in her half sleep
my mother reads her winters
aloud to me
her persimmon whispers are deleriously sweet
to this only daughter's ear

when you are home
she says
the irons come back
every night
i know the warm
is coming

$\mathscr{L}$UCY $\mathscr{F}$URMAN

(June 7, 1870–August 26, 1958)

Short story writer Lucy Furman was born in Henderson, Kentucky, and was orphaned when she was young. An aunt took her into her home and sent her to school in Lexington's Sayre Institute, from which Furman graduated at the age of sixteen. She lived with her grandparents for several years, before completing a secretarial course and working as a court stenographer in Evansville, Indiana. In Evansville, she began to write stories.

By the time Furman was twenty-three, her stories were being published in *Century Magazine,* and soon after, her first book of stories, *Stories of a Sanctified Town*, was accepted for publication.

After a decade of poor health, Furman moved in 1907 to eastern Kentucky and became a teacher at the Hindman Settlement School. There, she joined Sayre classmate Katherine Pettit, who had founded the school on Troublesome Creek in Knott County, Kentucky. Furman lived on campus and worked as a teacher, houseparent, and gardener, and gained strength enough to resume writing. "I have charge of the gardening and outdoor work at the Settlement School," she wrote, "but the happiest part of my life is my residence at the small boys' cottage, about which I have told in the 'Perilous' stories, and in which I find endless pleasure and entertainment. Here I hope to spend the remainder of my days." *Mothering on Perilous* was published in 1913, and she continued to write stories for *Century Magazine.* Although she moved from Knott County in 1924, the years she spent at the Hindman Settlement School were her most prolific years as a writer.

After leaving Knott County, Furman returned to her hometown, Henderson, for a decade before moving to Frankfort, Kentucky, until 1954, and spent her final years with her nephew in Cranford, New Jersey.

In this excerpt from the opening of *Sight to the Blind,* a settlement school nurse encounters a woman blinded by cataracts who has been told by her community that her blindness is the result of her questioning God's will after the death of her daughter.

OTHER SOURCES TO EXPLORE

PRIMARY

Novels: *The Lonesome Road* (1927), *The Glass Window* (1925), *The Quare Women* (1923), *Sight to the Blind* (1914). **Stories:** *Mothering on Perilous* (1913), *Stories of a Sanctified Town* (1897).

SECONDARY

"Miss Lucy Furman [obit]," *New York Times* (26 August 1958), 29. Ish Richey, *Kentucky Literature, 1784–1963* (1963), 83–84. John Wilson Townsend, "Lucy Furman," *Kentucky in American Letters*, Vol. 2 (1913), 247–48. William S. Ward, "Lucy Furman," *A Literary History of Kentucky* (1988), 86–88.

FROM *SIGHT TO THE BLIND* (1914)

One morning in early September, Miss Shippen, the trained nurse at the Settlement School on Perilous, set off for a day of district-visiting over on Clinch, accompanied by Miss Loring, another of the workers. After riding up Perilous Creek a short distance, they crossed Tudor Mountain, and then followed the headwaters of Clinch down to Skain's Fork, where in a forlorn little district-school-house the trained nurse gave a talk on the causes and prevention of tuberculosis, the spitting of tobacco-juice over the floor by teacher and pupils abating somewhat as she proceeded. Two miles farther on she stopped at the Chilton home for a talk to half a dozen assembled mothers on the nursing and prevention of typhoid, of which there had been a severe epidemic along Clinch during the summer.

Afterward the school-women were invited to dinner by one of the visiting mothers. Mrs. Chilton at first objected to their going, but finally said:

"That's right; take 'em along with you, Marthy. I allow it'll pyeerten Aunt Dalmanuthy up to hear some new thing. She were powerful' low in her sperrits the last I seed."

"Pore maw!" sighed Marthy, her soft voice vibrant with sympathy. "It looks like things is harder for her all the time. Something new to ruminate on seems to lift her up a spell and make her forget her blindness. She has heared tell of you school-women and your quare doings, and is sort of curious."

"She is blind?" inquired the nurse.

"Blind as a bat these twelve year'," replied Mrs. Chilton; "it fell on her as a judgment for rebelling when Evy, her onliest little gal, was took. She died of the breast-complaint; some calls it the galloping consumpt'."

"I allus allowed if Uncle Joshuay and them other preachers had a-helt off and let maw alone a while in her grief," broke in Marthy's gentle voice, "she never would have gone so far. But Uncle Joshuay in especial were possessed to pester her, and inquire were she yet riconciled to the will of God, and warn her of judgment if she refused."

"Doubtless Uncle Joshuay's high talk did agg her on," said Mrs. Chilton, impartially, "but she need n't to have blasphemed like she done at Evy's funeral occasion."

Marthy covered her face with her hands.

"Oh, that day!" she exclaimed, shuddering. "Will I ever forget it? John and me had got married just a month before Evy died in October, and gone to live up the hollow a small piece from maw, and even then she were complaining of a leetle scum over her eyes. Losing Evy, and rebelling like she done atterward, and Uncle Joshuay's talk, holp it along fast, and it were plain to all before winter were over that he had prophesied right, and her sight were a-going. I would come down the branch of a morning and beg her to let me milk the cow and feed the property and red up the house and the like, but she would refuse in anger, and stumble round over chairs and table and bean-pot and wash-kittle, and maintain all spring and summer her sight were as good as ever. Never till that day of the funeral occasion, one year atter Evy died, did she ever give in."

Here Marthy again covered her face with her hands, and Mrs. Chilton took up the tale:

"I can see her now, up thar on the hill-shoulder, betwixt you and John on the front log, by Evy's grave-house, and Uncle Joshuay a-hollering and weeping and denouncing like he does, and her setting through it like a rock. Then finally Uncle Joshuay he thundered at her the third time, 'Hain't it the truth, Sister Dalmanuthy, that the judgment and the curse of God has fell on you for your rebelliousness, like I prophesied, and that you hain't able to see John thar or Marthy thar or the hand thar before your face thar?' when Aunt Dalmanuthy riz up sudden, and clinched her hands, and says slow and fierce: 'Man it *is* the truth you speak. The curse *has* fell; and I hain't able to see John here or Marthy here or the hand here before my face here. But listen what I got to say about it. I'm able to hate and to curse as good as God. And I do! I hate and curse the Hand that, after taking all else I loved, snatched from my bosom the one little yoe lamb I treasured thar; I hate and curse Him that expected me to set down tame and quiet under such cruelty and onjestice; I hate and curse and defy the Power that hated and spited me enough, atter darkening the light of my life, to put out the sight of my eyes! Now,' she says, 'you lay claim to being mighty familiar with the Lord; take that message to Him!' she says.

"Women, that whole funeral meeting kotch its breath at them awful words, and sot there rooted and grounded; and she turnt and looked around defiant-like with them sightless eyes, and strode off down the hill, John and Marthy follering."

After a somewhat protracted silence, Marthy's gentle voice resumed:

"And from that day to this John and me hain't left her sence. We shet up our house and moved down to hern; and she tuck to setting by the fire or out on the porch, allus a-knitting, and seldom speaking a word in all them years about Evy or her sorrow or her curse. When my first little gal come along, I named it Evy, thinking to give her some easement or pleasure; but small notice has she ever showed. 'Pears like my young uns don't do much but bother her, her hearing and scent being so powerful' keen. I have allus allowed if she could get her feelings turnt loose one time, and bile over good and strong, it might benefit her; but thar she sets, day in, day out, proud and restless, a-bottling it all up inside."

ᗔENISE ᵍIARDINA
(October 25, 1951–)

Born in Bluefield, West Virginia, Denise Giardina (pronounced jar-DEE-na) is the daughter of Leona Whitt Giardina, a nurse who grew up in eastern Kentucky, and Dennis Giardina, an accountant whose family came from Sicily to work in the mines. She grew up in the coal mining camp of Black Wolfe in McDowell County, West Virginia, where most of the men in her family worked for the mining companies. Her grandfather and uncles were miners; her father was a bookkeeper for Page Coal and Coke Company. When she was thirteen, the mine that employed her father closed, and she witnessed the dissolution of the community. Her family moved to Charleston, West Virginia.

She earned her B.A. from West Virginia Wesleyan College in 1973 and spent several years in Washington, D.C., as part of the ecumenical Christian activist community known as the Sojourners Fellowship. In 1979, she completed a Master of Divinity from Virginia Theological Seminary and was ordained by the Episcopal Church as a deacon. During her ministry in McDowell County, West Virginia, a bishop tried to discourage her from becoming involved in political issues like speaking out about absentee landowners not paying property taxes, and such censure helped her decide to channel her creative energy into becoming a writer and activist.

She describes herself as "an Appalachian writer, interested in the affinities between Appalachia and other exploited places like Poland and Central America," and she adds, "I am also interested in writing that includes the political and spiritual dimensions in life and am not much interested in fiction that pretends these areas do not exist."

Her first book, *Good King Harry*, is an antiwar novel set in fifteenth-century England, exploring crises of conscience faced by young Henry V and introducing moral dilemmas that are a hallmark of Giardina's fiction.

Storming Heaven focuses on West Virginia and Kentucky mining communities and the conflicts between coal companies and miners that led to the Battle of Blair Mountain in 1921, when coal barons convinced President Harding to send U.S. troops to put down the union. This novel was a Discovery Selection of the Book-of-the-Month Club and received the 1987 W.D. Weatherford Award for best book published about the Appalachian South.

She uses multiple narrators in *Storming Heaven* and in its sequel, *The Unquiet Earth,* to span the years from the 1890s to 1990 and explore the public and private crises of the generations of characters in World Wars, mining strikes and layoffs, and the War on Poverty in her fictional Justice County, West Virginia. For *The Unquiet Earth*, Giardina received an American Book Award and the Lillian Smith Award for fiction.

Saints and Villains takes readers from West Virginia mountains to European ones, examining the life of Dietrich Bonhoeffer and its moral complexities. For it she won the 1999 Fisk Fiction Prize awarded by the *Boston Book Review.*

Giardina is the only writer in this book to have been a candidate for governor. In 2000, her gubernatorial campaign as a candidate for the Mountain Party in West Virginia succeeded in establishing a third party based on environmental and community-based issues.

OTHER SOURCES TO EXPLORE

PRIMARY

Novels: *Fallam's Secret* (2003), *Saints and Villains* (1998), *The Unquiet Earth* (1992), *Storming Heaven* (1987), *Good King Harry* (1984). **Selected essays:** "No Scapin the Booger Man," in *Bloodroot* (1998), ed. Joyce Dyer, 129–31. "Appalachian Mirror," *New York Times* (31 October 1992), L21. "Solidarity in Appalachia," *The Nation* (3 July 1989), 12–14. **Interviews:** W. Dale Brown, "True Stories: A Conversation with Denise Giardina," *Carolina Quarterly* 47:1 (fall 1994), 40–51. Thomas E. Douglass, "Interview: Denise Giardina," *Appalachian Journal* 20:4 (summer 1993), 384–93. Susan Koppelman and Janet Mullaney, "Belles Lettres Interview: Denise Giardina," *Belles Lettres* (spring 1989), 11, 21.

SECONDARY

Tim Boudreau, "Fighting Back: Denise Giardina talks about *Storming Heaven*," *Now & Then: The Appalachian Magazine* 5:1 (spring 1988), 9–10. Aviva L. Brandt, "Region's Untold Tales Bring Writer Home," *Charleston* [WV] *Gazette* (16 May 1993), E9. *Contemporary Authors* (1987), Vol. 119, 118–19. Joyce Dyer, "Denise Giardina," *Bloodroot*, 128. "Denise Giardina Issue," *Iron Mountain Review* Vol. 15 (spring 1999). Laurie K. Lindberg, "An Ethical Inquiry into the Works of Denise

Gardina," *Appalachia Inside Out,* Vol. 2, 664-72. Lillian S. Robinson, *Coal Miner's Daughter* [review of *The Unquiet Earth*], *The Nation* (28 December 1992), 816–18. Teresa K. Weaver, "Moving Mountains: West Virginia Novelist Runs for Governor . . . ," *Atlanta Journal-Constitution* (24 October 1999), M1, M3. Meredith Sue Willis, review of *The Unquiet Earth*, *Appalachian Journal* 20:2 (winter 1993), 204–6.

STORMING HEAVEN (1987)

from Chapter 3

CARRIE BISHOP

You have seen old photographs, brown and sweet-looking, as though dipped in light molasses. My memories of the Homeplace in Kentucky are like that. Sweet, bitter-sweet.

When I was ten years old, Ben Honaker lent me his copy of *Wuthering Heights*. I loved it, just for the name of it, even before I read it. It has the sound of a lost and precious place, Wuthering Heights. I learned from that book that love and hate are not puny things. Nor are they opposed. Everything in this world that is calculating and bloodless wars against them both, wars against all flesh and blood, earth and water.

Even now, when I whisper that name, Wuthering Heights, it is the Homeplace I see. My people crowd around me, Ben and Flora, Miles, Daddy, Aunt Jane and Aunt Becka. And I see myself, waiting for Heathcliff, waiting for someone to come from outside, bearing with him both passion and menace.

I knew he would come from the outside, because Daddy and Aunt Becka said I would never find a man on Scary Creek or Grapevine. I was too forward, they said, too stubborn. I was not pretty like Flora. Flora looked like the princess in children's stories old folks tell—white skin, rosy cheeks, and black hair. She took after Daddy and Aunt Becka's side of the family, which was part Cherokee. I took after my dead mother's side. Freckles splashed my face, my shoulders, my arms. My nose was a trifle large, my hair drab brown.

"Carrie takes after the Mays," Aunt Becka said to Daddy one night when we were in bed before the hearth and supposedly asleep. She was Daddy's oldest sister. "She's even got her Papaw Alec's nose, poor child. Hit wouldnt look so bad on Miles."

I couldn't sleep for worrying and went straightway up the river the next morning to the Aunt Jane Place. Aunt Jane May lived at the mouth of Scary Creek where it flowed into Grapevine. Aunt Jane was both my grandmother and my great-aunt. She was Daddy's aunt who had married Alec May, and their daughter Tildy was my mother.

I cried out my hurt feelings to her. She sat composed, her hands laid flat on her lap so the blue veins stood up in ridges.

"Dont you pay no mind to your Aunt Becka," she said. "That woman will wrap her tongue around any kind of silliness. You're the picture of your mother, and I love to gaze on you for it."

"Am I ugly?"

"Course you aint ugly. You favor your Papaw Alec a heap, too. His face had character. They wasnt no forgitting what he looked like, no more than you could forgit the mountains. When I stand on my porch and look at those mountains, I still yet see him everywhere."

Uncle Alec had been dead for a long time, killed in the War Between the States.

"You think he's a ghost?" I asked. "You think he still yet comes around here, and that's why you cant forgit him?"

Aunt Jane smiled. "Maybe. Sometimes I feel him close. But ifn he's a ghost, he's a contented one. He walks for joy, not for disquiet."

I began to watch for him then. I thought he walked abroad in the fog. The mists rose from the river each morning to cling to the mountaintops, and in the evenings, after a rain shower, patches of fog ran like a herd of sheep up the hillsides. I would go out then, breathe the air and feel it clean the bottom of my lungs. A path wandered behind the cabin down the riverbank. Grapevine was broad and green, slow running, never more than waist deep on a grown man save during the spring thaw. I waded into the water, my skirt hiked to my thighs. Silver explosions of trout churned the water and minners darted fearlessly about my legs. I came abreast a stand of cattails and halted. The sweep of Grapevine curved away north, its path to Shelby and the Levisa hidden by the far mountains layered one after another, the mist dancing up their flanks. Every way I turned the lush green peaks towered over me. Had it been winter or spring, they would have been iron gray, or dappled with pink and white dogwood, sarvis, and redbud, but always they would be there, the mountains, their heights rounded by the elements like relics worn smooth by the hands of reverent pilgrims.

I swept my arm up and flung water like beads of glass.

"Hey, Uncle Alec," I whispered.

THE UNQUIET EARTH (1992)
from The Ice Breaks, 1930s

DILLON FREEMAN

When my daddy died I was an infant, lying on his chest with his thumb caught tight in my fist. I try to remember properly. I try to remember to hold on tighter to that thumb, to keep the warmth from seeping out. If I squeeze hard enough I'll recreate him, thumb first, then the rough hand, the forearm with its thick brown hair, the soft fold of skin over his throat, the chin stubbled coarse with beard. But I stop there because it is all I can bring to life. I don't know his face. And the quickening wanes again until only the thumb is warm, and then not even the thumb.

Me and Mom still live in the cabin where he died. She dragged the deathbed outside and burned it like a funeral pyre. He was already buried in the Homeplace cemetery with the rest of her people. But it was like she had to see something go up in flames. She wouldn't have dreamed to throw herself on the fire, though, like Teacher says those women do over there in India. My mother, Carrie Freeman, wouldn't turn her back on life for nobody, not even a man she loved so desperate she slept with him and them not married and traipsed over mountains to be with him.

I am the child of that love. A woods colt, as we say in these Kentucky mountains. Nobody troubles me over it. Nobody dares because I am a steady fighter. People here don't get het up over such things anyway, except a few of the meanest church women. Besides, my mother was married to a preacher before she and Daddy made me, and I ended up with the preacher's last name, so that as good as sanctified the whole proceedings.

My daddy was a union organizer over in the West Virginia coalfields, and he was in a battle with the state police and company thugs and took a bullet that snapped his spine clean in two. That's how he came to die slow and in bed with me sprawled atop him. Rachel, who is my cousin, says she recalls him. I don't believe she could recall much, she was barely two. But she says she remembers being scared of the Aunt Jane Place because a mean man lived there. Mom says Daddy was bad-tempered for being paralyzed and Rachel was skittish of him. It does put me in awe of Rachel a little, it makes me jealous because I should be the one to remember him. I should remember grabbing onto that thumb. But I don't hold Rachel's memory against her. I just stay as close to her as I can.

Rachel gets uncomfortable when I talk about Mom and Daddy making me. She was raised more proper. Rachel is a Honaker, and she lives on the Homeplace just down Grapevine nigh to the shoals. We are first cousins—our mothers are sisters, Carrie and Flora. Me and Mom live at the Aunt Jane Place. It is all the same land, just two different houses, theirs the white wood farmhouse, ours the cabin that creaks in the wind and smells of woodsmoke. Uncle Ben says move down to the Homeplace, he'll build on an extra room and the older younguns will be moving out soon, but Mom won't hear of it. I think she wants to stay in the house of Daddy's last breathing.

Uncle Ben is worried about whether we can live on our land at all. He says the taxes have gone up because the coal companies are buying land, and he has taken out a mortgage to pay them. Then he opened a general store at the mouth of Scary to help pay the mortgage but the store is not doing any good. Mom says Ben would pick the depths of the Depression to open up a store. Uncle Ben is a smart man but him and Aunt Flora have got no business sense, Mom says, and they give too much credit. In these times we are living in, lots of folks need credit. So the sacks of flour disappear from the dusty shelves as soon as they are set out, and Ben cannot keep the pokes of already baked-and-sliced lightbread that caused such a stir when they first arrived. A poke of sliced lightbread is prized, for it means you can afford to spend money to replace the biscuits and cornbread people bake themselves, but Ben even gives credit for lightbread, so everyone is the same.

At school Rachel has fried egg sandwiches on lightbread with store-bought mayonnaise or sometimes mayonnaise by itself which nobody else has. She doesn't take on about it. Mom will not have lightbread in the house, she says even if we had the money it's just as tasty as a handkerchief and she sends me to school with yellow cornbread. Some younguns who bring cornbread hide what they have because they are embarrassed to be poor but I won't do that because it would shame my Mom.

Mom says she gives the store less than a year, then she smiles and says, "That Ben, he'll feed the hollow while it lasts." There's things we don't get from the store. We grow our corn and vegetables and raise our own pigs and chickens and milk cows. We put up preserves in mason jars for the winter, or I should say the women do. They stand over the cast-iron stoves in the heat of summer and stir the great boiling pots of tomatoes and beans, dip their ladles into the roiling red and green liquid, and wipe the sweat from their faces with one corner of their aprons. They slice the apples and sun-dry them into leather-sweet strips. They take a needle and thread to the beans and hang them in rows to dry from the porch rafters. Me and Uncle Ben and his big boys plow and hoe and plant and haul. Rachel tends the chickens and cows.

But we get lard and salt from the store, and baking soda and flour, and nails and needles for piercing. And Goody's Headache Powder that Aunt Flora eats like it is candy.

Sometimes when the hens are laying good, Rachel has two eggs to trade at the store. Aunt Flora makes her trade even though the store is theirs, because she says it is proper. Rachel trades for a Three Musketeers. Each of us pops one chocolate Musketeer in our mouths and we break the third exact down the middle. I like to see the nougat heart. Or Rachel trades for a CoCola in a little green bottle, what some call a dope and others call a sodypop but Rachel always calls by its right name. Ben's store has a big metal sign nailed to the front wall with a raised red oval that reads Coca-Cola in curlicued white letters. The red paint has faded in the sun and there are dents where younguns throw pebbles to hear the clang. The best sodypops come from Ben's ice chest and you sit on the front stoop where the bottle catches glints of sunlight and you look at the green mountain that hovers over the store. It is best when your feet are dusty from the road. Rachel and I share sodypops and the neck of the bottle is warm and tastes the way I guess her mouth would taste.

A long time ago Uncle Ben was the teacher at the Scary Creek School. I am glad he doesn't teach anymore because I despise school and if he was the teacher I'd have to despise him. I am not a bad student, I learn what I am supposed to, but still I don't care for it. You have to hold your pencil a certain way even though it's cramped as hell and if you don't do it right, Teacher wraps your fingers around the pencil hard and like to breaks every bone in your hand. You learn spelling rules and grammar rules and that the way you talked all your life is ignorant even though it seems to suit most people fine, and when Teacher goes on and says we live in a free country it's just a little hard to believe. Nobody admits it but school is to teach you how to get bossed. I reckon I could read some books on my own and learn what I want, but my mom sets a store by school.

Rachel is the best student. She is sixteen and I am only fourteen-and-three-quarters. But I am right behind her at school. Rachel is very thin and has wavy light-brown hair that come to her shoulders. She wears very nice clothes because Aunt Flora cuts pictures from the mail-order catalog and makes dresses to look like them. My mom says it's a good thing I'm a boy because she can't sew and she would send me to school in potato sacks. Most of what I wear is hand-me-downs from Uncle Ben's boys.

Once Aunt Flora got hold of some old window drapes and clothes from a missionary box. Missionaries from up North are always sending us boxes of old things like we aren't even Christian. I wouldn't touch a thing in those boxes nor my Mom neither, but Aunt Flora says why waste, she can make the things nicer than when they were sent. She took some drapes of slick red material and made Rachel a coat that looked like the Chinese wear. Then she cut down a big white wool skirt and jacket into a dress with a high collar and red buttons down the front. Rachel wore the red coat and white dress to school on Class Day when we all had to recite poems. Rachel's dress had long narrow sleeves and a long skirt down to her boot tops. When she stood up to recite, she looked like a queen.

$\mathscr{J}$ANICE $\mathscr{H}$OLT $\mathscr{G}$ILES
(March 28, 1909–June 1, 1979)

A native of Arkansas, Janice Holt Giles attended the University of Arkansas, as well as Transylvania University in Lexington, Kentucky. Her first marriage ended in divorce in 1939, and in 1945 she married Henry Giles, a Kentuckian whose family had settled in the state during the eighteenth century. The couple made their home on the Giles family farm near Knifely, Kentucky.

A prolific writer, Giles contributed short stories to *McCall's*, *Good Housekeeping*, and *Woman's Day*. Her first book, *The Enduring Hills*, was published in 1950. For the next decade and a half, Giles produced nearly a book a year, both fiction and nonfiction.

Her most popular works were a series of extensively researched novels about the American frontier. The first in the series, *The Kentuckians*, depicts the struggles of the earliest settlers who pushed westward into the Kentucky wilderness through the Cumberland Gap. It was followed by *Hannah Fowler*, which examined the harsh reality of frontier women's lives. *The Believers* depicted the communal life of Kentucky's Shakers.

Giles wrote, "If I only enjoyed writing these books as much as I do the research all would be well, but alas, the writing is a heavy piece of work."

Two autobiographical works, *A Little Better Than Plumb* and *Forty Acres and No Mule*, detail life on the Giles's remote ridge farm. One reviewer declared that *Forty Acres and No Mule* did more "to bring alive the section of country now known as Appalachia than a half a dozen surveys."

In 1996, the Giles Foundation was established to preserve Giles's literary legacy and to restore her log home. The Foundation plans to preserve the home as a museum and a writer's retreat.

In the following scene from *Hannah Fowler*, Hannah and her injured father, Samuel, have been befriended in the Kentucky wilderness by a woodsman named Tice who happened upon them. Because of the threat of Indian attack, Hannah and Tice take turns standing guard through the night.

OTHER SOURCES TO EXPLORE

PRIMARY

Novels: *Act of Contrition* (2001), *Shady Grove* (1978), *The Believers* (1976), *Wellspring* (1975), *The Kinta Years* (1973), *Miss Willie* (1971), *Six-Horse Hitch* (1971), *The Great Adventure: A Novel* (1966), *Run Me a River* (1964), *Voyage to Santa Fe* (1962), *Savannah* (1961), *Johnny Osage* (1960), *The Land Beyond the Mountains* (1958), *Hannah Fowler* (1956), *Hill Man* (1954), *The Plum Thicket* (1954), *The Kentuckians* (1953), *Tara's Healing* (1951), *The Enduring Hills* (1950). **Nonfiction:** *The G.I. Journal of Sgt. Giles* (1965). **Autobiography:** *A Little Better Than Plumb* (1962), *Forty Acres and No Mule* (1952).

SECONDARY

Contemporary Authors (1967), Vols. 1–4, 368. *Contemporary Authors*, New Revision Series, Vol. 3, 228. Bonnie Cox, "Kentucky Women Writers: Lost, Forgotten, Overlooked, and Acclaimed," *Belles Lettres* (spring 1991), 12–14. Dianne Watkins Stuart, *Janice Holt Giles: A Writer's Life* (1998). Dianne Watkins, "Foreword," *Hannah Fowler* (1992). Dianne Watkins, *Hello, Janice* (1992).

HANNAH FOWLER (1956)

from Chapter 3

It was black dark when she awakened. She rolled over and edged to the front of the lean-to, looked at the sky. She judged it was near midnight. Certainly the dawn was several hours off yet. She shivered as she crawled out of the warm bed and reached back for the blanket to wrap about her shoulders, yawning. Tice heard her and called out softly in the darkness, "You needn't to git up."

She found her gun and made her way over to him. "I'd ruther to," she said. "If you're aimin' to hunt in the mornin', you'll need a mite of rest yerself."

He grunted and she could see a blur of movement by the trees. He was standing. "If they's e'er trouble," he told her, "hit'll come from acrost the river. I don't look fer it, understand. Hit's jist best to take keer. You got yer gun?"

"Yes."

"Well, then. . . . Yer pa ain't stirred. Reckon that rum purely knocked him out."

"Hit must of. The sleep'll do him good."

"Yes . . . well, come daylight, if I don't stir, call me. If *he* c'n stand bein' moved, we'd best make camp further away from the river."

"Ain't you aimin' on takin' the raft on up the river?"

"No, ma'am. That would be the last thing I'd aim on doin'. We'll move an' camp an' wait till yer pa c'n travel. Then we'll strike out through the woods. Well, I'll lay awhile now."

Hannah settled herself by the tree. She was fully awake now, felt fresh and rested. There was an open spot in the trees just over the camp and by leaning her head back and resting it against the trunk of the tree she could see the stars, and a little, pale disk of moon off in the west. You could tell, she thought, the time of night by the stars and moon, when the night was clear. And you could tell, too, that the winter was over and summer coming on. They moved, the stars did, changing places in the sky with the hours, and changing places as the seasons passed them by. She thought about it, wondered about the stars and moon, wondered why they'd been put there to shine in the night . . . why they moved. It wasn't a thing she could study out, though. It was past e'er *human* body's knowing, she guessed. There were some things that couldn't be studied out.

She felt a breath of wind on her cheek. There, now . . . wind was one of them. What was it? Where did it come from? What moved it unseen around the world and across the land? It would stir through the night, ruffle the leaves and shake them, bend the limbs—but when the dawn was near, when the dark was just beginning to lift, not light yet but just ready to be, it would quieten as if it listened for the sun. As still as death it would be then, at that time just before the light streaked into the sky, so still that, if you were stirring then, you could hear your own breath coming and going in your throat, and hear your own heart beat. The way of wind . . . it went queer and odd to a human body.

And the way of rain, blowing up in the clouds, the clouds splitting and pouring it down. She named over to herself the things she could in no way study out . . . wind, the moon and stars, rain, sunlight, clouds, storm, the fall of rivers down the land, the rise and flow of water. There was a power of things, she told herself, no human body could ever know the straight of. You could, in time and with study, know the ways of birds and animals, and even folks. They had life inside them, they all bled and their hearts beat and they breathed in the air. One way or another they all moved, flew or walked, swam or ran. They all died, too. The sun, now, and the stars, the wind and the rain, the water in the rivers, those things went on forever. How could it be, she wondered, that a thing that lived should come to the end of its living, and those things that had no life in them should go on forever? "Hit ort," she told herself, "to be the other way round, looks like." Then she laughed, to think of the sun and stars and moon dying. "The folks would die fer sart'n, then," she said.

She never talked about such thoughts as these. Once when she was a child she had tried to tell Samuel about the sound the branch back of the house made, running over the rocks. It went, she had told him, like singing, real soft. "You c'n hear the words, I reckon," Samuel had said, grinning at her.

"I kin," she had told him stoutly. "Hit's a singin' 'Go to sleep, go to sleep, go to sleep.'"

Sam had not laughed then. Sternly he had bade her to keep such foolish talk to herself. "Hit ain't nothin' but water runnin' over the rocks," he'd said. "Don't go gittin' foolish fancies in yer mind, Hannah. They'll make you go quare in the head . . . folks'll think you're tetched, an' they'll mistrust you."

So she had never again named the things she thought to Samuel, or to anyone else. But she was always thinking them, just the same. It did no harm to *think*, as far as she could see.

Samuel moved in his sleep, stirred and muttered, threw one hand from under the blanket. She watched until he had settled, her thinking distracted, and when he was quiet again she thought about moving camp tomorrow . . . today, now. Wondered where Tice would pick. Wondered if Samuel could be moved. Thought of the problems and shook her head. Below, she could hear the liquid sound of the river, running shallow around the tongue of the beach. She smiled in the dark. In spite of Samuel, running water *did* make a singing sound.

eNikki Giovanni

(June 7, 1943–)

Nikki Giovanni was born in Knoxville, Tennessee, into a close-knit African American family. Although her parents moved the family to Cincinnati when Giovanni was an infant, she returned frequently to Tennessee to be with her grandparents, and she attended Austin High School in Knoxville.

Giovanni entered Fisk University in Nashville at the age of seventeen but was expelled after her first semester for leaving campus without permission. She returned to Fisk in 1964 and became an activist, leading two hundred students in a demonstration that forced the reinstatement of a campus chapter of the Student Nonviolent Coordinating Committee. In 1967, she graduated, magna cum laude, with a B.A. in history.

After attending the University of Pennsylvania's School of Social Work, Giovanni enrolled in Columbia University's M.F.A. program for creative writing but left without completing her degree after publishing her first book of poetry in 1968 entitled *Black Feeling, Black Talk*. Hailed as a unique voice, Giovanni's revolutionary rhetoric won her many fans.

Over the years, Giovanni's poetic vision has grown to include themes of love and creativity alongside those of anger and revolution. Her son, Thomas, was born in 1969; since then, many of her works, beginning with *Spin a Soft Black Song*, have been for young readers. Once, when questioned about this transformation, Giovanni replied, "Only a fool doesn't change."

She is the author of numerous books of poetry and essays, holds honorary doctorates from more than a dozen institutions (including Smith College and Indiana University), and has been given the keys to more than three dozen cities, including New York City. Giovanni is the first African American University Distinguished Professor at Virginia Tech in Blacksburg, Virginia, an honor bestowed upon only one-half of one percent of the faculty. She is "Hokie proud."

In her essay "Griots" from the collection *Racism 101*, Giovanni examines the interplay of family and memory. The term "griot" refers to an African elder who preserves a community's oral history.

OTHER SOURCES TO EXPLORE

PRIMARY

Poetry: *Quilting the Black-Eyed Pea* (2002), *The Love Poems of Nikki Giovanni* (1997), *The Selected Poems of Nikki Giovanni* (1996), *Those Who Ride the Night Winds* (1983), *Vacation Time: Poems for Children* (1980), *Cotton Candy on a Rainy Day* (1978), *The Women and the Men* (1975), *Ego-tripping and Other Poems for Young People* (1973), *My House: Poems* (1972), *Spin a Soft Black Song: Poems for Children* (1971), *Re:Creation* (1970), *Black Feeling, Black Talk* (1968). **Essays:** *Racism 101* (1994), *Sacred Cows—and Other Edibles* (1988), *Gemini* [autobiography] (1971). **Autobiographical essay:** "400 Mulvaney Street," in *Bloodroot* (1998), ed. Joyce Dyer, 133–39. **Nonfiction:** *A Poetic Equation: Conversations Between Nikki Giovanni and Margaret Walker* (1974), *A Dialogue: James Baldwin and Nikki Giovanni* (1973). **Editor of anthologies:** *Grand Fathers: Reminiscences, Poems, Recipes and Photos of the Keepers of Our Traditions* (1999), *Shimmy Shimmy Shimmy Like My Sister Kate: Looking at the Harlem Renaissance Through Poems* (1996), *Grandmothers: Poems, Reminiscences, and Short Stories About the Keepers of Our Traditions* (1994), *Appalachian Elders: A Warm Hearth Sampler* (1991), *Night Comes Softly* (1970). **Illustrated poems for children:** *The Genie in the Jar* (1996), *The Sun is So Quiet* (1996), *Knoxville, Tennessee* (1994).

SECONDARY

Alex Batman, "Nikki Giovanni," *Dictionary of Literary Biography: American Poets Since World War II* (1980), Vol. 5, 286–89. *Contemporary Authors* (1978), Vols. 29–32, 237–38. Joyce Dyer, "Nikki Giovanni," in *Bloodroot*, 132. Virginia C. Fowler, "And This Poem Recognizes That: Embracing Contrarieties in the Poetry of Nikki Giovanni," in *Her Words* (2002), ed. Felicia Mitchell, 112–35. Joanne V. Gabbin, "Giovanni, Nikki," *The Oxford Companion to Women's Writing in the United States* (1995), 349–50. *Great Women Writers* (1994), Vol. 2, 135–37. Lillie P. Howard, "Nikki Giovanni," *American Women Writers* (1980), Vol. 2, 135–37. *Something About the Author* (1981), Vol. 24, 120–21.

Griots

from *Racism 101* (1994)

I must have heard my first stories in my mother's womb.

Mother loved a good story and my father told good jokes, but it was her father, Grandpapa, who told the heroic tales of long ago. Grandpapa was a Fisk University graduate (1905) who had majored in Latin. As he sometimes told the story, he had intended to be a diplomat until he met Grandmother, but that is probably another story altogether, he being Black and all in 1905 or thereabouts.

Grandpapa loved the stars. He knew the constellations and the gods who formed them, for whom they were named.

Grandpapa was twenty years the senior of Grandmother, so he was an old man when we were born. Grandmother's passion was flowers; his, constellations. One needn't have a great imagination to envision this courtship: the one with her feet firmly planted on earth, the other with his heart in the sky. It is only natural that I would love history and the gossip of which it is composed.

Fiction cannot take the place of stories. Aha, you caught me! Fiction is stories, you say. But no. Stories, at their best, pass along a history. It may be that there was no Ulysses with a faithful Penelope knitting and unraveling, but something representative of the people is conveyed. Something about courage, fortitude, loss, and recovery.

I, like most young ladies of color, used to get my hair done every Saturday. The beauty parlor is a marvelous thing. Every Saturday you got the saga of who was sleeping with whose husband; who was pregnant; who was abused by whose boyfriend or husband. Sometimes they would remember the children were there, but mostly the desire of the women to talk without the presence of the men overcame their desire to shield us from the real world.

My mother's family is from Albany, Georgia, but Grandmother and Grandpapa had moved to Knoxville, Tennessee. We four grandchildren spent our summers with Grandmother.

At night, when we were put to bed, my sister Gary and I would talk and sing and sometimes read under the covers using our Lone Ranger flashlight rings. Of course, we were caught. Grandmother would threaten us and take our rings. We would sneak out of our room, wiggling on our stomachs, to reach the window under which we sat and listened to Grandpapa and Grandmother talk.

Sitting under that window I learned that Eisenhower was not a good president; I learned that poll taxes are unfair. I heard Grandmother berate Grandpapa for voting Republican when "Lincoln didn't do all that much for colored people." I heard assessments of Black and white people of Knoxville and the world. No one is enhanced by this. I'm not trying to pretend they were; there were no stories of "the African" in my family, although I am glad there were in Alex Haley's.

We were just ordinary people trying to make sense of our lives, and for that I thank my grandparents. I'm lucky that I had the sense to listen and the heart to care; I'm glad they talked into the night, sitting in the glider on the front porch, Grandmother munching on fried fish and Grandpapa eating something sweet. I'm glad I understand that while language is a gift, listening is a responsibility. There must always be griots . . . else how will we know who we are?

KNOXVILLE, TENNESSEE

from *The Selected Poems*
of Nikki Giovanni (1996)

I always like summer
best
you can eat fresh corn
from daddy's garden
and okra
and greens
and cabbage
and lots of
barbecue
and buttermilk
and homemade ice-cream
at the church picnic
and listen to
gospel music
outside
at the church
homecoming
and go to the mountains with
your grandmother
and go barefooted
and be warm
all the time
not only when you go to bed
and sleep

REVOLUTIONARY DREAMS

from *The Selected Poems of Nikki Giovanni* (1996)

i used to dream militant
dreams of taking
over america to show
these white folks how it should be
done
i used to dream radical dreams
of blowing everyone away with my perceptive powers
of correct analysis
i even used to think i'd be the one
to stop the riot and negotiate the peace
then i awoke and dug
that if i dreamed natural
dreams of being a natural
woman doing what a woman
does when she's natural
i would have a revolution

A POEM OFF CENTER

from *The Selected Poems of Nikki Giovanni*

how do poets write
so many poems
my poems get decimated
in the dishes the laundry
my sister is having another crisis
the bed has to be made
there is a blizzard on the way go to the grocery store
did you go to the cleaners
then a fuse blows
a fuse always has to blow
the women soon find themselves

talking either to babies or about them
no matter how careful we are
we end up giving tips
on the latest new improved cleaner
and the lotion that will take the smell away

if you write a political poem
you're anti-semitic
if you write a domestic poem
you're foolish
if you write a happy poem
you're unserious
if you write a love poem
you're maudlin
of course the only real poem
to write
is the go to hell writing establishment poem
but the readers never know who
you're talking about which brings us back
to point one

i feel   i think   sorry for the women
they have no place to go
it's the same old story blacks
hear all the time
if it's serious a white man
would do it
when it's serious
he will
everything from writing a poem
to sweeping the streets
to cooking the food
as long as his family doesn't eat it

it's a little off center
this life we're leading
maybe i shouldn't feel sorry
for myself
but the more i understand women
the more i do

GAIL GODWIN
(June 18, 1937–)

Gail Godwin grew up in Asheville, North Carolina, with her mother and her maternal grandmother. In her essay "On Becoming a Writer," Godwin explains that her grandmother took care of their domestic life, while her mother, Kathleen Godwin, who had earned an M.A. at the University of North Carolina at Chapel Hill, divided her days between teaching English at a local college and working as a newspaper reporter with the *Asheville Citizen*. Godwin has strong memories of her mother typing her own stories on the weekends. By the time she was five, Godwin says, "I had allied myself with the typewriter rather than the stove."

After attending Peace Junior College (1955–1957) and graduating from the University of North Carolina in 1959, Godwin worked as a journalist for two years at the *Miami Herald*. She married and divorced a *Herald* photographer.

From 1961 to 1965, she worked with the United States Travel Service in London, before beginning her master's degree at the University of Iowa. "London is where I really got my education," she explains. "It was the perfect job for someone in her early twenties who wanted to write but needed money and experience." While she lived abroad, she read novels and wrote her first novel. She also married again and, within a year, divorced a second time.

By 1971, she completed her Ph.D. in Iowa, where Kurt Vonnegut was one of her teachers, and John Irving and Jane Barnes were among her classmates.

A Mother and Two Daughters, one of her most popular novels, was on the *New York Times* Best-Seller List for most of 1982. She has received a grant from the National Endowment for the Arts, a Guggenheim Fellowship, the Thomas Wolfe Award for *A Southern Family*, and three of her novels (*The Odd Woman*, *Violet Clay*, and *A Mother and Two Daughters*) have been nominated for National Book Awards.

In this excerpt from *A Southern Family*, two childhood friends, Julia and Clare, a writer who has returned home for a visit, share a mountain hike during their annual reunion.

OTHER SOURCES TO EXPLORE

PRIMARY

Novels: *Evenings at Five* (2003), *Evensong* (1999), *The Good Husband* (1994), *Father Melancholy's Daughter* (1991), *Remembering Felix* (1989), *A Southern Family* (1987), *The Finishing School* (1985), *Mr. Bedford and the Muses* (1983), *A Mother and Two Daughters* (1982), *Violet Clay* (1978), *Dream Children* (1976), *The Odd Woman* (1974), *Glass People* (1972), *The Perfectionists* (1970). **Nonfiction:** *Heart* (2002). **Autobiographical essays:** "Becoming a Writer," *The Writer on Her Work* (1980), ed. Janet Sternburg, 231–55. "A Novelist Breaches the Border to Nonfiction," *New York Times* (15 Jan. 2001). "Uncle Orphy," in *Bloodroot* (1998), ed. Joyce Dyer, 141–45.

SECONDARY

Joyce Dyer, review-essay on *A Southern Family*, *Appalachian Journal* 15:4 (summer 1988), 382–86. Joyce Dyer, "Gail Godwin," in *Bloodroot*, 140. Dannye Romine Powell, "Love and Order" [Interview with Gail Godwin], *Charlotte* [NC] *Observer* (16 October 1994), F1, F5. Mary Ann Wimsatt, "Gail Godwin" in *Contemporary Fiction Writers of the South: A Bio-bibliographical Sourcebook* (1993), 193–201. Mary Ann Wimsatt, "Gail Godwin's Evolving Heroine: The Search for Self," *Mississippi Quarterly* 42:4 (winter 1988–89), 27–45.

A SOUTHERN FAMILY (1987)

from Chapter II

"How did you ever find this place, Julia? A meadow on top of a mountain? The air up here is like champagne. Why didn't we know about this spot when we were growing up?"

"It's called Pinnacle Old Bald by the locals, but it still goes by its unpronounceable Indian name on the maps. So when people come asking for it, of course, the locals can't—or won't—tell them where it is. And you know as well as I do that there are a whole lot of things we didn't know about when we were growing up."

"You said a mouthful there, honey." Clare clapped her friend jovially on the arm as the two of them, Julia in front, hiked up a wide path in noon sunshine towards a dome-shaped golden meadow sticking right up into the blue sky. Clare was lighter of heart since Julia had driven her away from Quick's Hill this morning. The frown lines between her brows had disappeared and her shoulders had sprung back, as if released from an invisible load. She grew more confident and relaxed with every breath she took of the invigorating air.

"The spirits are pretty friendly up here," Julia said, "if you come with the right attitude. It's supposed to have been an Indian burial ground once. A retired Navy officer owns it now. But he allows hikers and picnickers, as long as they clean up after themselves and don't bring guns. Anyway, he's not here very much. I think it's just an 'investment' for him. That's a Christmas tree farm, all those little spruces in rows on that sunny slope. The caretaker was one of my students, that's how I know about it."

"Well, I love it. There's something . . . sacred about it. I wouldn't mind being buried up here."

"I think you'll enjoy it much more being alive, dear." But Julia was pleased with Clare's enthusiasm. She liked to show her new places, places in these mountains they had never dreamed existed when they were growing up. It had become a self-imposed commission for Julia to be able to produce a different hiking and picnic spot every year when Clare visited. It was Julia's way of reminding her old friend that there were rewards for those who returned to live in the place where they were born. Perhaps it was also, Julia thought, a way of reassuring herself that the old and familiar harbored special revelations for those who hung around faithfully and stayed alert. "I was going to take you up to Mount Mitchell, but George and I drove up there in

August for a hike, and when we got there and saw what had happened to it, we just turned the car around and went somewhere else."

"God! It's terrible. I saw a picture of it; it made the front page of the *Times*. All those noble red spruce woods where we used to camp out as Girl Scouts look like some blasted peak in Hell. Acid rain. All the way from Ohio, the article said. From smokestacks of coal-burning furnaces. I got very depressed when I read it. One more old landmark gone. Just like the old St. Clothilde's getting torn down board by board when I was away in England. But Mount Mitchell, you would have thought, was inviolable. Do you remember that year, when we were camping out and everybody started blowing on the fire, only the air was so thin we couldn't get our breaths properly and Freddy Stratton just sank in a heap all of a sudden and that good-looking forest ranger had to pick her up in his arms and carry her to the station wagon so they could get her back down to the camp infirmary?"

Julia laughed. "I'll bet she wasn't so far gone that she couldn't enjoy it."

"You know, I've about got up my courage to phone Freddy. I've been working up to it for years. I want to test whether I'm over that terrible sense of inferiority she could make me feel just by looking at me. It's been over twenty years since I last saw her."

"I wish you *would* call her. It's time you realized she's not the arch-rival you always made her into. I saw her a couple of weeks ago, out at that new crafts center they've made out of the old railway depot. At first I didn't recognize her; I thought it was just one more tense society matron in her Talbots catalogue clothes. She nursed her mother at home through the last stages of lung cancer, you know. Yet, the whole time we talked, Freddy was chain-smoking."

"What did you talk about?" Clare's voice, suddenly regressing to its anxious adolescent pitch, reminded Julia how jealous Clare had been of Freddy Stratton's sudden courting of Julia when they had reached the age when it was time to meet the right kind of boys and there was Julia's family conveniently living on the Belvedere School grounds.

"Well, her mother, of course. I said, 'It must have been awful for you,' and she said, 'No, I was really *glad* to be able to do it.' And she asked about you. I told her you'd be coming down to visit your family."

"What did she say about me?"

"Well, she asked how I felt about your using my family in your novel."

"What did you say?"

"I said that I had known you were doing it, that we had even corresponded about it, but that, really, it wasn't my family when you got through with us. I explained to her that was the way writers work. You made up your own Richardson family and called them the Taylors. You idealized us into a sort of generic genteel Southern family."

"Oh, do you think so?" Clare sounded annoyed.

"More or less. But what does it matter? It's a fine book. And it's given my father's ego a boost. Not that my father's ego exactly *needs* a boost, but—"

"So how is George?" Clare changed the subject abruptly. "Is that still on, then?"

"I'm not sure 'on' is the word for it— I mean, we were never on fire, or anything— but we're not altogether *off*, so I guess it'll do. We both like to walk, and eat good food, and complain about how they overwork us at North State. We make love once a week, on Friday nights, when I stay over at his house. He's very . . . punctilious. And on Saturday morning we have a big celebratory breakfast because we've acquitted ourselves like a normal couple, and then he starts looking wistfully towards his study—he's doing a book on medieval French monasteries—and I rinse the dishes and put them in his dishwasher and go home and do my own laundry. Actually we suit each other very well. He would have made a perfect Jesuit if God hadn't been so inconsiderate as to cause him to be born into a Protestant family, and I . . . well, I've had the feeling lately that I'm just marking time until I reach the age when I can dispense with the social necessity of having a boyfriend."

"Julia, do you really feel that way?"

"I'm exaggerating a little, but I *can* imagine how it would be. It wouldn't be so different from our early adolescence, when we were just . . . ourselves. Before we got infected with the notion that we'd better go hide in our closets if we didn't have a man to go out with on Saturday night. You know, I counted it up the other night: it's been fifteen years since I was a married person, and I was married only four years. Even counting live-in lovers, by far the greatest portion of my adult life has been spent alone. It may well be that solitude is my most natural state."

"I used to think that, before I met Felix. Now I don't know. I think my talent for living alone may have atrophied. Funny, isn't it, you're the one who's been married and you're talking like a spinster; whereas I'm the real spinster, I'll probably never marry, but I can't imagine life without Felix."

CONNIE JORDAN GREEN
(February 4, 1938–)

Born in West Virginia, children's author Connie Jordan Green moved to the wartime development of Oak Ridge, Tennessee, in 1944. Although Green spent her childhood in the "Atomic City," her connection to a more traditional Appalachia remained strong.

"On visits to my grandparents' home in the mining area of southeastern Kentucky, I fell asleep to the lullaby of adult voices discussing everything and everybody. I believe it's both the substance of the stories and the sound—the rhythm of the speech, the cadence of the language—that propel my writing.

"In subject matter, both my young adult novels concern families living in Appalachia. *Emmy* used stories from my mother's childhood . . . and *The War at Home* is about a young girl growing up in Oak Ridge. . . . I also feel the poetry I write is greatly influenced by my present life on a farm in East Tennessee, by my years growing up in Appalachia, and by my Appalachian ancestors."

Green received her B.S. in education from Auburn University in 1960, and an M.A. in creative writing from the University of Tennessee in 1987. She has been a teacher for most of her professional life and is currently working as an adjunct instructor in English at the University of Tennessee.

Concerning the writing process, Green says, "I just begin writing and see what happens. Writing helps me think. Not only do I think better with a pen in my hand, I remember more and I perceive more in the world around me. Without writing, I would go blindly through the world."

The following scene is the opening of *The War at Home*, Green's young adult novel set in the newly created town of Oak Ridge, Tennessee, during World War II.

257

OTHER SOURCES TO EXPLORE

PRIMARY

Novels: *Emmy* (1992), *The War at Home* (1989).

SECONDARY

Reviews of *The War At Home*: Susan M. Harding, *School Library Journal* 35 (June 1989), 105. *Horn Book Magazine* 65 (1989), 482–83. Denise Wilms, *Booklist* 85 (1 June 1989), 1722.

THE WAR AT HOME (1989)

from Chapter 1

"Cat got your tongue, Virgil?" Mattie asked. Then she hated herself for saying the words that made her sound just like Gran.

But Virgil wasn't paying any attention to her. He hunched low in the car seat as the armed guard walked toward them. With World War II raging across the oceans, the guards checked everyone who came in or out of the newly built city of Oak Ridge, Tennessee. Mattie didn't understand what was so important about the city, but she had learned to live with the fences surrounding it and with the guards at all the exits. Now she couldn't help grinning as she thought how wonderful it would be if Virgil had to have a pass and couldn't get one.

But, of course, that wouldn't happen. Kids came into Oak Ridge with adults and left with them anytime. It was only grown-ups who had to wear the numbered plastic cards with their pictures in order to get in or out of the city.

The man in the crisp khaki-colored shirt and pants, pistol buckled at his waist, flicked his eyes from the badge Daddy held up back to Daddy's face. Then he bent over and stared into the car. He looked at twelve-year-old Virgil in the front seat, at thirteen-year-old Mattie as she tried to appear nonchalant in the corner of the backseat, and at the empty seat beside her.

Mattie thought of how scared she'd been last summer when the family had entered Oak Ridge for the first time. The guard had told Daddy to open the trunk of the car. Then Daddy had taken out their suitcases and opened them, one by one. The guard had looked casually at the piles of neatly folded clothes. Then he let them go.

But even though he hadn't messed with their clothes, Mother still didn't like the search.

"Nosey, isn't he," she said, as they drove away.

"Now, Lucy, he's just doing his job."

"I guess his job is to insult innocent people."

"Most of the time they just look at your badge and wave you on. But they have to check about every ninth or tenth car just to keep everybody honest." Daddy reached over and patted Mother on the knee. "It wasn't anything personal."

"Personal or not, I don't like the idea of somebody checking us."

Mattie had leaned forward, eager to hear how Daddy would reassure

Mother. Months had passed from the time he had applied for the job until he had been hired. And the neighbors had all told them they'd been questioned about Daddy by FBI agents. She hadn't given much thought to the questioning; however, the sight of Oak Ridge and its tight security made her wonder.

But Daddy was not very comforting. "All I know," he said, "is that whatever is going on has something to do with the war effort. None of us know what we're working on, and we're warned not to say a word about our jobs."

"What was the guard looking for in our suitcases?" Mattie had asked.

Daddy had only shrugged. Ever since, Mattie had wondered what sort of thing she might have innocently brought along that would have caused the guard to keep them from entering Oak Ridge.

Now, as Daddy drove the car away from the gates, Virgil resumed his talking.

Mattie sighed loudly. Her cousin had talked nonstop during the six-hour drive from the mountains of eastern Kentucky to east Tennessee. The crooked roads were enough to make her feel half sick, and keeping all the windows closed against the damp March air hadn't helped. The sound of Virgil's voice had almost finished the job. After the first hour she'd grown tired of turning her head from Daddy to Virgil and back again in order to follow their conversation. She had tucked her feet up on the seat, leaned her back into the corner, and pretended she was on a bus going to a place she'd never seen. Might as well actually be going, she thought. Daddy and Virgil wouldn't have noticed anyway if she'd vanished into thin air.

And here they were taking up where they'd left off a few minutes earlier. As they drove along the Turnpike, the main street in Oak Ridge, toward the west end of town, Virgil wanted to know what each building was, why the people were standing in line, and why the buses and buildings were all the same drab green.

And, of course, Daddy answered the questions in his usual cheerful voice. To listen to him, you'd think Daddy was glad Virgil was coming to live with them for a while.

Well, Mattie hoped someone was glad. When she was younger, she had liked having Virgil as a playmate. But he had changed during the last year or two. Now he drove her crazy with his talk about how much better boys were at everything than girls. And whenever Daddy was around, Virgil monopolized him.

When Mattie could stand the front-seat conversation no longer, she interrupted.

"I hope Mother has supper ready. I'm starving to death."

Daddy nodded to her. "I don't doubt she'll have fried chicken and mashed potatoes ready for a celebration."

"What celebration?"

"Why, us bringing Virgil down to Tennessee."

Virgil twisted in his seat and grinned at her. Mattie wanted to cross her eyes and stick her tongue out, but she saw Daddy watching her through the rearview mirror. So she turned her face to the window and concentrated on the colorless scene sliding by.

Finally they left the Turnpike, followed Illinois Avenue up a hill, and turned left onto West Outer Drive. Mattie could see the Cumberland Mountains rising to the west. They were gentle mountains, etched in purple against the setting sun or tipped with white against a bright winter sky. They were not like the mountains she'd lived among in Kentucky. There, the valley between the ridges was so narrow there was room only for the dirt road bordering the creek and for the houses with their tiny lawns. Eastern Kentucky mountains were so crowded together that the valleys received direct sunlight only during the midpart of the day.

"Here we are," Daddy said, as he pulled the gray Ford off the gravel road onto the edge of their lawn.

Mattie looked at her home. The land surrounding the house required a great deal of imagination to be considered a lawn. The yard was rocky red clay with oaks stretching overhead thirty feet before they branched out into limbs and leaves. Like the rest of the recently built city, the yard was muddy in the March rains.

"Gol-ol-lee," Virgil said, as the three of them stepped from the car. "What a long house you've got, Uncle Omer."

Daddy laughed. "We'd be in fine shape if we could just live in all of it. Nope, Virgil, this is what the government calls a T.D.U., a Twin Dwelling Unit. Only, everybody who lives in one hopes it's a *Temporary* Dwelling Unit."

"Yeah, real temporary," Mattie muttered. At least for you, Virgil, she wanted to add.

$\mathscr{V}$IRGINIA $\mathscr{H}$AMILTON
(March 12, 1936–February 19, 2002)

Virginia Hamilton was the first African American writer to win the Newbery Medal, one of the most prestigious awards in children's literature. A native of Yellow Springs, Ohio, Hamilton's lifelong interest in African American history grew from the tales told by her maternal grandfather, who was born a slave and managed to escape. "In the background of much of my writing is the dream of freedom tantalizingly out of reach," Hamilton said.

She attended Antioch College and Ohio State University, but left school and moved to New York to pursue a writing career. In 1960, she married Arnold Adoff, a well-known white anthologist of African American poetry. The couple, who had a son and a daughter, lived in Hamilton's Ohio hometown until her death.

Critics credit Hamilton with having raised the standards of American literature for younger readers; her books are often challenging both in style and theme. "What is transformed from myth, history, and family narrative in my own fictions is not a play-pretty to be held in the hands of children," says Hamilton. "My fictions for young people derive from the progress of Black adults and their children across the American hopescape. Occasionally, they are light-hearted; often they are speculative, symbolic and dark."

During the course of her career, Hamilton's work garnered not only critical acclaim but also a long string of awards.

Her best-known novel, *M.C. Higgins the Great,* won the Newbery Medal, the National Book Award, and the *Boston Globe–Horn Book* Award. In 1992, she was awarded the Hans Christian Andersen Medal for her contributions to children's literature.

Set in the Appalachian foothills, *M.C. Higgins the Great* depicts the life of an African American teenager (M.C.) who loves his home on Sarah's Mountain, yet lives in fear of the seemingly inevitable day when the strip-mining "spoil" from the mountain above them slides down and buries the family home. M.C.'s place of refuge is a forty-foot-tall steel pole that towers above his house. From the top, M.C. surveys the valley below, a world beyond his own troubles.

In the scene below, M.C. tries to make his father, Jones, realize the danger the family faces from their beloved mountain.

OTHER SOURCES TO EXPLORE

PRIMARY

Books for children: *Time Pieces: The Book of Times* (2002), *Sweet Whispers, Brother Rush* (2001), *Wee Winnie Witch's Skinny: An Original Scare Tale For Halloween* (2001), *The Girl Who Spun Gold* (2000), *Bluish: A Novel* (1999), *Plain City* (1998), *Second Cousins* (1998), *The Magical Adventures of Pretty Pearl* (1997), *Many Thousand Gone: African Americans From Slavery to Freedom* (1997), *Primos* (1997), *The House of Dies Drear* (1996), *When Birds Could Talk & Bats Could Sing: The Adventures of Bruh Sparrow, Sis Wren, and Their Friends* (1996), *Her Stories: African American Folktales, Fairy Tales, and True Tales* (1995), *Drylongso* (1992), *Cousins* (1990), *Anthony Burns: The Defeat and Triumph of a Fugitive Slave* (1988), *A White Romance* (1987), *On Being a Black Writer in America* (1986), *The People Could Fly: American Black Folktales* (1985), *A Little Love* (1984), *Willie Bea and The Time The Martians Landed* (1983), *The Gathering* (1981), *Dustland* (1980), *Justice and Her Brothers* (1978), *M.C. Higgins the Great* (1974), *The Planet of Junior Brown* (1971).

SECONDARY

Contemporary Authors (1977), Vols. 25–28, 299. *Contemporary Authors,* New Revision Series (1999), Vol. 73, 217–21. Martha E. Cook, "Virginia Hamilton," *American Women Writers* (1980), Vol. 2, ed. Lina Mainiero, 232–34. *Something About the Author* (1989), Vol. 56, 60–70.

M.C. HIGGINS THE GREAT (1974)
Chapter 4

It wasn't often that he and Jones could sit down together without Jones having to test him or think up a game to see if he could win it. He knew Jones only wanted to have him strong and to have him win. But he wished his father wouldn't always have to teach him.

Just have him listen to me, M.C. thought. Have him hear.

Maybe now he and Jones were sitting without a war between them. Maybe he could speak about what was on his mind.

"Daddy?" he said, "you taken a look up there, at the spoil heap behind us?"

"Way behind us," Jones said, easily and without a pause. He was looking off at the hills he loved and at the river holding light at the end of the day. He was thinking about his wife, his Banina, who would not have had time yet to concern herself with coming home. But in another hour or so, she would think about it. She would say to herself, *It's time!* No clock was needed to show her. From where she was across-river, she could look away to these hills. She might even be able to see M.C.'s needle of a pole. No, not likely. But maybe a sparkle, maybe a piercing flash in the corner of her eye. She would have to smile and come on home.

Jones sighed contentedly.

"Daddy," M.C. said, "it can cause a landslide. It can just cover this house and ground."

"That's what's bothering you?" Jones asked. "That's why you were standing tranced in the cave. You thought I didn't know but I did. You worry about everything you don't need to worry from."

A shudder passed over M.C. like a heavy chill. Jones studied M.C.'s face. M.C. was so skilled at living free in the woods, at reading animal signs, at knowing when the weather would change even slightly. Jones could convince himself at odd moments that the boy had second sight. And now, half afraid to ask but worried for his children on their way to Harenton, his Banina, he said, "What is it you see?"

M.C.'s eyes reflected light bouncing green and brown from one hill to another. Deep within the light was something as thick as forest shadow.

"Just some rain coming from behind us," M.C. said. "You listen and you can maybe hear it come up Sarah's other side." There was more. It was a feeling M.C. hadn't known before. He kept it to himself.

Jones stepped off the porch and turned around in order to see behind him. Beyond the rim of the outcropping, he saw Sarah's final slope with shade slanting halfway across it, and trees, made more dense with late-day shadow. As the trees appeared heavier this time of day, Sarah's seemed to pierce the sky.

Jones gazed at the spoil and beyond it to the bare summit where he had spent so much time with M.C. when the boy was small. Looking, he remembered how he had taught M.C. all he knew about hunting bare-handed. He recalled Sarah's cut, trees falling.

Now he listened. He saw the sky grow heavy with mist as he watched. It turned gray and, finally, dark. He heard sound coming. Rain, like hundreds of mice running through corn. He watched it come over the mountain and down the slope in a straight line.

M.C. hadn't bothered to move from the step. He had already felt the rain, seen it without seeing.

Wind hit Jones first. It ran before the rain. Jones didn't want his clothes soaked, so he stepped onto the porch while rain came full of mist, but hard all the same.

They watched it. The rain marched down Sarah's and on across, turning hill after hill the same shade of silver mist clear to the river. Then it was gone from the mountain. As it had come, clawing through cornstalk, it vanished with the same familiar sound.

"Huh," Jones grunted. "That will cool it off maybe a minute. Wish it would rain hard enough to fill up that gully. Then I could take me a swim without sweating a mile to do it."

M.C. had his mind on the spoil heap. He couldn't see it but he could feel it, the way he felt Sarah's above him pressing in on him when he lay in his cave room.

"It holds the water," he told his daddy, "just hanging on up there. It'll rain again and it'll grow just like it's alive."

"Now why did you have to catch hold of that all of a sudden?" Jones asked him. "You get something in your head, I swear, you don't let it go. Glad when school gets going. Catch hold of your math work like that one time. Don't talk to me no more," he added and sat down again on the step.

The step was wet. So was M.C., who seemed not to notice. The rain was just dripping now. The mist had grown intense with light.

"It already cover all the trees they root up," M.C. forced himself on. "It'll tear loose, maybe just a piece. But without a warning. Maybe a roar, and sliding into the yard and trying to climb my pole."

"Quit it," Jones said. "Just . . . don't talk to me."

M.C. couldn't tell if there was any worry in his father's face. He could see only an intensity of anger at being bothered.

Suddenly the sun came out. M.C. bowed his head until the light leveled off, softened and shaped by the green of hills.

Doesn't even hear me, M.C. thought. Fool, Daddy. All at once, he wanted to be back up on his pole.

Dude'll have to tell him. He'll have to listen.

Bright sunlight began to dry up the truth seen so easily in the rain.

"These old mountains," Jones said. He looked out over the side of Sarah's and beyond. "They are really something."

M.C. stayed quiet. Sullen.

"It's a *feeling*," Jones said. "Like, to think a solid piece of something big belongs to you. To your father, and his, too." Jones rubbed and twisted his hands, as if they ached him. "And you to it, for a long kind of time." He laughed softly. To M.C., it sounded full of sadness.

PAULETTA HANSEL
(August 29, 1959–)

~

Poet Pauletta Hansel is one of three children of Larnie Lewis Hansel and Charles Hansel of Somerset, Kentucky. Born and raised in eastern Kentucky, she began writing when she was a child and became a published poet (in *Mountain Review*) when she was a teenager. At age sixteen, while still in high school, she was recruited to enroll at Antioch College. She attended Antioch's Appalachian campus in Beckley, West Virginia, and graduated in 1978 with a B.A. in human services. Her master's degree, with a concentration in Montessori education, is from Xavier University (1980).

In 1976, Hansel's work was featured in *Ms.* magazine in an article on Appalachian women poets. At age fifteen, she told the *Ms.* reporter that both her grandfathers were miners, but "home" for her "meant one mountain community college town after the other, wherever her father happened to be teaching philosophy. 'The outside,' she says, 'never did seep in all that much.'"

She was instrumental in organizing early networks of Appalachian writers, including the Soupbean Poets, a politically active writers group she co-founded at Antioch; Street Talk, a theater collective that wrote, produced, and performed plays locally and nationally from 1980 to 1984; and the Southern Appalachian Writers Cooperative (SAWC), which is still active today.

Since 1980, Hansel has worked in Cincinnati, first as a teacher at a Montessori school, then as a paralegal for the Legal Aid Society of Cincinnati, then as an administrator for the Urban Appalachian Council, where her main responsibilities focused on community arts programs and community development. She is currently a teacher and administrator at Women Writing for (a) Change, a feminist creative writing center.

She gave up writing from 1984 to 1994, in part, she says, because "in my early years I tried too hard to be an 'Appalachian writer,' and lost the sound of my own voice in trying to blend with others. My work now is definitely influenced by my Appalachian roots . . . but the stories and language reflect not just my past but my present as an urban dweller for more than half my life." Her poetry has appeared in *Appalachian Journal*, *Adena*, *Twigs*, *Wind*, *Pine Mountain Sand and Gravel*, and in anthologies including *New Ground*, *A Gathering at the Forks*, and *Old Wounds, New Words*.

OTHER SOURCES TO EXPLORE

PRIMARY

Poetry: *Divining* (2001). *We're Alright but We Ain't Special* (1976), with Gail V. Amburgey, Mary Joan Coleman. *What's a Nice Hillbilly Like You . . . ?* (1976). *Some Poems by Some Women* (1975).

SECONDARY

Jacqueline Bernard, "Mountain Voices: Appalachian Poets," *Ms.* 5:2 (August 1976), 34–38. Jackie Demaline, "The Arts Life: Desk doesn't bind this poet," *Cincinnati Enquirer*, 30 July 2000.

WRITING LESSONS (I.)
from *Divining* (2001)

I look for the way
things will turn
out

—Poetics, *A.R. Ammons*

I am trying to find the shape of things,
to find where words might go
without the prodding of my pen,
left to their own devices:
startled sliding up
as if unnoticed,
nestling in the curve
of *century's* end;
places I have never seen—
Niagara Falls, Lookout Mountain—
sliding down
between the floorboards
of my mother's kitchen, 1962.

I am trying to find the shape of things,
to let them unfold
without my restless hands forever
moving, pressing up or down
into the patterns
so familiar they are all I ever
dare to sew;
to let this life unfold:
a bolt of cloth spilling
from a tall shelf,
haphazard by its own design;
a liar's yarn spinning out
incredulously true.

SHE

from *Divining* (2001)

That spring
she let herself go,
uncoiled the cord
and slipped out through
the crack in the window.

She was unleashed.
Even her hair sprung
free of curl.
Her clothes
would not stay put.

She spoke too loudly.
Sentences ran on
ahead of her.
She followed
when she chose.

When people said
they didn't know her
anymore,
she did not
hear them.

WRITING LESSONS (II.)

from *Divining* (2001)

You really only need to breathe,
as long as you breathe
with everything,

the way your hand breathes in
the shape of a baby's head
as you cradle the soft

green scent of his neck,
and your ears breathe in the teeming
silence of the forest's edge,

and how your eyes breathe in the day
as it cracks wider open
all the way until you see

its fiery center
pushing out the night,
and how your very heart

breathes all you
cannot bear to know
with eyes or ears or skin alone.

Breathe in and hold until your
center burns and swells
but does not crack.

Breathe out.

TO HER MOTHER, LYING IN STATE

from *Appalachian Journal* (1982)

At least that's what they say,
in state.
I say he's the one who's in a state, daddy
now can't use you like a cane.
He lies without you for a pillow,
eyes open and not able to believe
that you aren't standing in the door.

Lying in state.
What do they know
about the states you've lain in?
One had the mountain you were born on,
where you lay screaming in a midwife's arms,
on your mother's breast,
by the willow, up creek
and in his arms,
or the state you were in
when you left, screaming inside,
to come up north
to this state without mountains.
You lied then
that first night when he asked
if things would be all right there.
He lied too
when he believed you.

Lying in state.
What a state you both were in
when I lay inside you,
him without a job,
you without him, half the time,
or anything you knew back home.
Then I was there,
screaming in a doctor's arms,
who got paid by the state.

You worried then
the state would take me.
You would've hid, you said,
or run back home,
but stayed thinking times get better soon.
You told me this,
me with my daughter in me,
and so scared.
Times changed,
but not enough to keep me here.
Just like you,
I left,
like my girl will leave me,
coming back
only now to see you
lying in state.
You would be in a state
to see me here, too late
and with this girl, eyes black like coal,
like dirt,
like yours.
But they don't know that.

$\mathscr{C}$ORRA $\mathscr{H}$ARRIS
(May 17, 1869–February 7, 1935)

Corra Mae (or Mary) White Harris was born in Elbert County, Georgia. She married Lundy Howard Harris, a Methodist clergyman, in 1887 and began writing in an effort to eke out a living after her husband suffered a nervous breakdown and was forced to resign his professorship at Emory College. She became a regular contributor to a New York journal, the *Independent*, tackling everything from book reviews to editorials.

Her novels were extremely popular during the first half of the twentieth century. Her first novel, *The Jessica Letters*, was followed by her best-known work, *A Circuit Rider's Wife*, a novel set in rural Georgia which was serialized in the *Saturday Evening Post*. The book, based on her husband's experiences in the ministry, was a witty critique of the Methodist Church and its underpaid emissaries in rural mountain communities. A film version of the novel was released in 1951 under the title *I'd Climb the Highest Mountain*.

Harris published a total of fourteen novels and spent the final years of her life writing a column for the *Atlanta Journal*. Her papers are at the University of Georgia.

In this scene from *A Circuit Rider's Wife*, a novel based on Harris's own experiences as a minister's wife, the female narrator ponders the fate of a "fallen" woman in a turn-of-the-century mountain community.

OTHER SOURCES TO EXPLORE

PRIMARY

Novels: *The Happy Pilgrimage* (1927), *Flapper Anne* (1926), *As a Woman Thinks* (1925), *My Book and Heart* (1924), *A Daughter of Adam* (1923), *The House of Helen* (1923), *The Eyes of Love* (1922), *My Son* (1921), *Happily Married* (1920), *From Sunup to Sundown* (1919), *Making Her His Wife* (1918), *A Circuit Rider's Widow*

(1916), *The Co-Citizens* (1915), *Justice* (1915), *In Search of a Husband* (1913), *The Recording Angel* (1912), *Eve's Second Husband* (1911), *A Circuit Rider's Wife* (1910), *The Jessica Letters* (1904).

SECONDARY

Grace Toney Edwards, "Foreword," *A Circuit Rider's Wife* (1998). *National Cyclopædia of American Biography* (1937), Vol. 26, 380–81. L. Moody Simms Jr., "Corra Harris," *Southern Writers: A Biographical Dictionary* (1979), 205–6. John E. Talmadge, "Harris, Corra May White," *Notable American Women 1607–1950: A Biographical Dictionary* (1971), Vol. 2, 142–43.

A CIRCUIT RIDER'S WIFE (1910)

from Chapter 5

I have often wondered what would have happened if the prodigal son had been a daughter. Would the father have hurried out to meet her, put a ring on her finger and killed the fatted calf? I doubt it. I doubt if she would ever have come home at all, and if she had come the best he could have done would have been to say: "Go, and sin no more."

But "go," you understand. And all over the world you can see them, these frailer prodigals, hurrying away to the lost places.

In a rotting cabin, in an old field five miles from Redwine, lived one of them. Once a week she walked fourteen miles to the nearest large town to get plain sewing, and with this she supported herself and child. The field was her desert. For eight years no respectable woman had crossed it or spoken to her till the day William and I and the redheaded horse arrived at her door. She stood framed in it, a gaunt figure hardened and browned and roughened out of all resemblance to the softness of her sex; her clothes were rags, and her eyes like hot, dammed fires in her withered face. William sprang out of the buggy, raised his hat and extended his hand.

"My wife and I have come to take dinner with you," he said.

"Not with me! Oh, not with sech as me!" she murmured vaguely. Then, seeing me descend also, she ran forward to meet me, softly crying.

We stayed to dinner, a poor meal of corn hoecake, fried bacon and sorghum, spread upon a pine table without a cloth. But of all the food I ever tasted that seemed to me the most nearly sanctified. It was with difficulty that we persuaded the lost Mary to sit down and partake of it with us. She was for standing behind our chairs and serving us. After that she sat, a tragic figure, through every service at Redwine, even creeping forward humbly to the communion. She was not received, however, in any of the homes of the people. She might "go in peace"—whatever peace her loneliness afforded—that the Scriptures might be fulfilled, and that was all. They would have none of her. This was not so bad as it seemed. She was free, indeed. Having no reputation to win or lose she could set herself to the simple business of being good, and she did. The time came when the field changed into a garden and the cabin whitened and reddened beneath a mass of blooms.

MILDRED HAUN
(January 6, 1911–December 20, 1966)

East Tennessean Mildred Eunice Haun was one of three children of Margaret Ellen Haun and James Enzor Haun. As the writer explained, "My mother was a Cocke County Haun and married a Hamblen County Haun." Mildred grew up in the Hoot Owl District of Cocke County, Tennessee, and attended public schools there.

Deciding that her community needed a doctor, Haun went to live with an aunt and uncle to further her education. After graduating from Franklin High School in 1931, she was admitted to Vanderbilt University. She gradually abandoned her dream of medical school and took an advanced composition course with poet John Crowe Ransom, who encouraged her to write. After she graduated, she continued to write stories about her native Cocke County while she taught high school in Franklin and began graduate school. Donald Davidson directed her 440-page M.A. thesis "Cocke County Ballads and Songs," a valuable collection of East Tennessee folklore. She also studied writing, supported by a fellowship, at the University of Iowa. When she completed her collection of stories, *The Hawk's Done Gone,* it was accepted for publication by Bobbs-Merrill in 1940.

Throughout her life, she supported her mother and herself with work as a writer and an editor. She was book review editor for the Nashville *Tennessean* (1942–1943), an editorial assistant to Allen Tate on the *Sewanee Review* (1944–1946), and an information specialist who lived in Memphis and then Washington D.C., and wrote and edited press releases, speeches, and technical information for military personnel and the Department of Agriculture.

Haun's stories show her keen ear for dialect and the oral tradition that surrounded her at home, as well as her willingness to explore the dark side of human nature. Regarding the subjects of her stories, critic Hershel Gower asks, "How does one account for the intense absorption in somber, discomfiting themes—witchcraft, incest, miscegenation, infanticide . . . ?"

In her story "The Hawk's Done Gone," the family matriarch, Mary Dorthula White, is counting her losses, because her husband Ad and stepson Linus have been selling her valuables to antique dealers.

OTHER SOURCES TO EXPLORE

PRIMARY

Short stories: *The Hawk's Done Gone* (1940), *The Hawk's Done Gone and Other Stories* (1968).

SECONDARY

Hershel Gower, "Introduction," *The Hawk's Done Gone and Other Stories* (1968), ix–xxv. Stephen Glenn McLeod, "Bottom of the Night: A Study of Mildred Haun," M.A. Thesis, Vanderbilt University, 1973. *Mossy Creek Reader* [Carson-Newman College, Jefferson City, TN] 3 (spring 1993) [entire issue devoted to Mildred Haun includes previously unpublished stories, photographs, and essays: Fred Chappell, "New Stories by Mildred Haun," 35–37. Amy Tipton Gray, "The Perfect Hell of 'The Hawk's Done Gone,'" 40–47. Robert Morgan, "This Page of Names: The Narrative Art of Mildred Haun," 38–39. Karen Travis, "Adventure Begins at Home," 49–56].

The Hawk's Done Gone (1940)

from The Hawk's Done Gone

Mary Dorthula White (born January 6, 1847)

I wonder why Ad and Linus never tried to sell me off to them hunters for old things. I would be a sight for somebody to look at. Big and motley and rough-looking. Old and still strong for my age. I miss the things they have sold. These new-fangled things are weak. They make me feel weak too. But I ought not to be setting here nursing this old Bible. I ought to get out and pick some sallet for supper.

The Bible is about the only old thing I have left, though. I thought I couldn't thole it when Ad and Linus first started selling off my stuff. I hate them folks that come around hunting for things to put in the Smoky Mountain museum. And I nigh hate Linus for letting them have my things. Linus is Ad's youngest boy by his first old woman and he has been spoiled rotten. Ad is the one that spoiled him too. Ad has turned everything over to him and let him run it to suit hisself—my own stuff too.

William Wayne was the only one of them antique hunters that was decent. Him and that painted-up woman he called Miss Robinson come together. I recollect that first day when they come. I was bent over the tub washing. Miss Robinson, she strutted up like she thought she was something on a stick, all dyked out in a purple silk dress and spike-heeled shoes. The first thing she did was to commence complaining about having to walk through the mud.

Miss Robinson's old hawk eyes seed everything I had. She got around Linus and got nigh everything I wanted to keep. She picked out the things she wanted. Looked at both of my corded bedsteads. One of them wasn't in very good shape, she said, and she didn't know whether she would take it or not. I felt like giving her a piece of my mind. And I did flare up a little. I looked at her straight and I said, "Who said anything about you taking either one of them? Them is the first bedsteads my pa ever made—made them for him and Ma to start housekeeping on. I was born in this one hyear and all my youngons were born in it."

I recollect the way I said it to her. I recollect the way William Wayne looked—almost like the soldier boy looked at me that day—that first day. William Wayne had brown eyes—big brown eyes that smiled as much as his mouth did. He put me in mind of the soldier, smiling all the time and talking so gentle. But Charles would be old by now. Old enough to be dead. He was older than me back then. I was just fifteen year old and he was a full-grown man. At least he was old enough to be out fighting the Yankees. At first I thought William Wayne might be Charles's boy maybe. But then I knowed Charles wouldn't ever have any other boy. William Wayne had pity for me and he hated to take my bedsteads away.

It didn't matter who had pity, though, for Linus and Miss Robinson made the bargain. The very next day Miss Robinson would send a wagon up here with two brought-on bedsteads, pretty ones, she said, to swop for my two wild-cherry ones.

And nigh all my quilts too. That huzzy said she would take all the pretty ones. Said some of them were mighty dirty but she could have them cleaned. My "Harp of Columbia." Of course, Miss Robinson's hawk eyes got set on it the very first thing. The one I was piecing on when Charles come.

I was setting in here in the big house piecing on it when I heard the soldiers walk up into the yard—setting here in the old hickory rocking chair with Ma's red-and-tan checked homespun shawl around my shoulders. I kept it in my hand when I started to get the water for them. I held it all the time while Charles went to the spring. He looked at the quilt when he come back.

"What's that you are making there?" he asked. He took hold of it and fingered it like it was a piece of gold. "I never could handle them little squares and three-cornered pieces with my big fingers," he said. And his hands were big. But I knowed right then I wasn't afeared of Charles.

I could tell from the way he kept looking at me he thought I was pretty too. He didn't tell me till all the other soldiers went over in the horse lot to catch up Old Kate. He didn't come right out plain and tell me then. "I'll bet your name is Edith—or Mary one."

"Huh uh—Mary's just part of it."

"Mine is Charles—Charles Williams. What is the rest of yours?"

"Hit's Dorthula—Mary Dorthula White."

"It's pretty too." In that deep voice. He kept feeling of the quilt. And looking at me. "Does that little red blanket on your shoulders keep you warm?"

That "Harp of Columbia" quilt was the one I always held in my lap and worked on when anybody come to see me during the while Joe was growing inside me. I told Joe about using it to hide him. Joe thought a heap of that quilt. I think it was the prettiest one I ever made. With Joe's stitches on it. My stitches—short and straight. And Joe's over there in the corner— long and crooked. Miss Robinson didn't take notice of them, I reckon. But somebody took Joe's stitches out, I know, before they hung it up for folks to look at. Nobody else would care. But I would rather had the hair pulled out of my head than had Joe's stitches pulled out of that quilt. The way he looked up at me with them eyes he had—Charles's eyes—and begged me to let him quilt. I couldn't help but let him do it. "And you won't pull mine out, will you, Ma?" I promised him his stitches never would be pulled out.

That night, after Miss Robinson and William Wayne left, while Ad and Linus were both out of the room, I set there on the bed and run my fingers over Joe's stitches. I reckon they wouldn't be counted pretty stitches by anybody else. I felt like getting inside the feather tick and being took off too. I couldn't sleep that night. I laid awake and squeezed that quilt in my hand.

It was lucky for me the next day. Ruby Arwood was called to straw and I had to be over there with Ruby all day. When I come in that night it seemed more different from home than ever. Nearly all my things gone—spinning wheel, warping bars and everything. Even my big bone knitting needles, and my tatting shuttle that I made myself. I didn't give up then and I'm not going to give up now. Dona Fawver will be dying pretty soon and Dona couldn't stand for anybody to lay her out save me. I ought to go see her today.

I couldn't help but see the bedsteads the first thing when I come into the room that evening. There was that big old brass bed, all scarred up, setting over there in the corner, and that little old rickety bent up green one in front of the window. Both of them had the rods so scarred up they looked like they had been through the war. No telling who had used them. No telling what kind of old dirty folks had been sleeping in them. But Linus was setting in there bragging about them being so pretty. New stuff, he said, brought-on stuff. One of them was worth a dozen home-made things, he said.

I didn't look at them any more than I had to. I went on and got supper. When I turned the beds down I seed they had some big old dirty-looking gray blankets on them. I felt of them. They weren't even wool—just plain cotton. They were somebody else's old things too. I would rather sleep on the floor than to sleep on them old pads with cotton all wadded up in them. Ad and Linus said they were what all folks used that weren't old fogies. But I ought to be hunting the guineas' nestes. And I promised Mollie McGregor my receipt for corn relish.

It didn't seem right with them bedsteads in the room. And my little green and gold mug gone. It was my ma's mug. I used to think it so pretty. The time I had the measles Ma let me drink water out of it. I got thirsty every few minutes till Ma caught on and took to bringing it in the dipper. . . .

ELLESA CLAY HIGH
(December 23, 1948–)

Ellesa Clay High was born and raised in Louisville, Kentucky, but has chosen to reside in Appalachia for most of her adult life. Her mother was a teacher and poet who, High says, "grew verse as abundantly as the beans she raised in her garden," and was a major influence on her daughter's lifelong love of words.

High received a B.A. from Butler University in 1970 and an M.A. from the University of Louisville in 1972. She completed her Ph.D. at Ohio University in 1981.

A writer of poetry, fiction, and nonfiction, High's best-known work, *Past Titan Rock,* weaves all three genres together to tell the story of a remote section of eastern Kentucky called the Red River Gorge. Her work has won numerous awards, including a James Still Fellowship in Appalachian Studies and an Andrew W. Mellon Foundation Award.

High is an Associate Professor in the English Department at West Virginia University, where she teaches courses in creative writing and Appalachian literature. She is also the coordinator for the university's Native American Studies Program.

High lives on an eighty-five-acre farm in Preston County, West Virginia, with her son. "Grounding in this place now called Appalachia always has been central to my work," she says. "Who I am, what has influenced me, and where I'm going might best be understood by a walk around this farm."

In this scene from *Past Titan Rock,* High recounts the beginning of her sojourn into a section of Kentucky known as the Red River Gorge.

Other Sources to Explore

Primary

Books: *Past Titan Rock: Journeys into an Appalachian Valley* (1984). **Autobiographical essay:** "The Standing People," in *Bloodroot* (1998), ed. Joyce Dyer, 147–52. **Essays:** "A Tribute to Lily May Ledford," *Appalachian Heritage* 14 (spring 1986), 5-6. "The Coon Creek Girl from Red River Gorge: An Interview with Lily May Pennington," *Adena: A Journal of History and Culture of the Ohio Valley* 2:1 (spring 1977), 44-74.

Secondary

Joyce Dyer, "Ellesa Clay High," in *Bloodroot*, 146. Norman Julian, "Purest Water, 18th century spring house shows perfect stonemasonry," *The Dominion* [WV] *Post* (8 July 2001).

FROM *PAST TITAN ROCK* (1984)

June 14, 1979

Time depends on the river here. To go where I want in the Gorge usually doesn't take long in the bone white heat of summer. You follow the asphalt highway through part of the Gorge, then veer onto a graveled, one lane road with passing places. If you know where to look, after a while you'll see a wash with tire tracks leading between two corn fields. When it's dry, you can skid down this gulley to a ford in the river. Once across, you're on the farm I'm aiming for, and it's only a few minutes before you pull up next to the yard.

But this summer has begun as the wettest on record, and the river is in no mood to be driven through. Its currents are quarrelling with its banks, the banks rank and feisty in return. So Red River is named after mud, I think, watching the clay-thick water sweep by. I don't dare try it. Though my Volkswagen bus sits high off the ground, today it's loaded with supplies. My dog, a black-and-white Llewellyn setter, is pacing the middle seat, tired of being cooped up. If I could just use what's left of this old country road which passes through the farm and beyond it, my trip would be finished. I look once more at the far bank, less than twenty feet away, and wonder how long it will take me to reach the other side.

Using high weeds for traction, I turn back on the gravel road and swing past the farmer's other house, the convenient one where he lives. He's not home. My only guide will be the instructions in his letter. I anxiously check them and the sky. Much of the afternoon is gone, and the sun doesn't linger in the hollows. I stay on this road until it crosses the river at Bowen, then head east, passing through the next jumble of houses called Nada, and up Snakey Holler to Nada Tunnel. Driving through the tunnel is like being swallowed whole by the mountain, with barely enough room to squeeze through. Cars at the other end, seven hundred feet away, must wait or back up. But today I'm alone in this unlit passage. I flash on my headlights and the mountain crowds in, its jagged sides playing tricks with my eyes. The ceiling seeps water and seems barely high enough for a van like mine.

Originally built for a standard gauge railroad, the tunnel was constructed some seventy years ago by logging companies eager to reach the vast forest in the lower half of the Gorge. This signalled a boom period for the area, opening jobs for loggers, blasters, railroaders, mechanics—virtually anyone willing to work for twelve or more hours a day. As the railroad grades and tracks were laid and the forest cut, shanties and log houses cluttered the new clearings and relatively prosperous times prevailed until the logging operations were finished. Then the tracks were removed, though the tunnel remained open to foot and wagon traffic. I remember once hearing a man say that he had driven through the tunnel with fireflies for lights and mud up to his team's knees. Aside from asphalt replacing the mud, little else has changed in the tunnel, conditions which excite tourists and create traffic jams on weekends.

I've got a feeling I won't have to worry about traffic where I'm going. I pass Titan Rock, a hulk of stone jutting from a ridge like the prow of a ship, and take what I hope is the right turnoff. This narrow road climbs a ridge so steep my van barely tops it in first gear. Then I'm in part of the Gorge I've never visited before. The road descends close by the river, its asphalt crumbling to gravel. In a mile or two it shrinks to a dirt path bristling with rocks and pocked with mud holes. I stop and recheck my instructions. I haven't seen a house in quite a while, but this might be right. I creep forward again, slow enough not to rip the car bottom on rocks, though I hope fast enough not to get stuck in the mud. Anyway, that is my strategy.

Now it's the forest that squeezes close, branches slapping my windshield. If there were a place to turn around, I would, but there is none. The road is dangling on a ridgeside which drops some fifteen or twenty feet to the river. Just in front I see a slippage. There is still space to pass, I judge, though no room for error. Despite the slick mud, I decide to try it. Crossing over, I glance down. Toward the bottom a car lies half-buried, half-pillowed in the slide. Corroded and crumpled, it looks as if it's been there for a long time, but who can tell.

All now is trees, or the shadows of trees. And mud and gloom. I'm sure I've made a terrible mistake, and one I can't back out of. The trees thin, and up ahead the road looks blocked by a massive cliff. This miserable path must dead-end there, and I name the place "Face to the Wall." Finally, I see where the road eases past to the left. I follow, and the land spreads out again. I drive through an open gate and over a cattle guard. A hay field extends to one side and around one more curve a barn and house swing into view. As I stop by the yard fence, a big, fleshy man pushes to his feet from the front porch steps. It's the farmer. I open the car door, hot and relieved, and my dog jumps out to explore the new territory.

The farmer walks toward the gate, a deliberate, slow smile on his face. He says, "I just about gave up on you. What took you so long?" And he chuckles, because he knows. This man I've quickly met twice and not seen for a year, but he nevertheless will generously let me use his tenant house on the far side of his property. I can see that already I amuse him, provide a pleasant interruption to his routine—one reason I imagine he's letting me stay. Another is as a favor to Lily May Ledford, an old friend of his and of many people still living in and around the Gorge. Without her introduction, I wouldn't be here.

He shows me around the yard. It is neat and uncluttered. The grass has been freshly mowed, some weeds giving off a strange skunky smell. The house looks well cared for on the outside, its wood protected by clean white paint. He points out the well and nods toward the privy, which totters on the hillside beyond the fence. Then his eyes return to me, slow and brown as molasses, yet sharp. I doubt that he misses much. He says, "This house has been empty for seventeen years. Sometimes people get back in here that got no business poking around. I figure it wouldn't hurt having somebody watch the place for the summer." He pauses. "If you think you can handle that," he adds, chuckling again.

I assure him that I'll manage.

"That's good. That's real good," he says.

Mary Bozeman Hodges

(July 1, 1944–)

Mary Bozeman Hodges grew up in Jefferson City, Tennessee, the daughter of Charlie Mae McGill Bozeman and Paul Bozeman. She credits both her parents with influencing her love of language. "My mother always read to me from the classics. Even when there were words I didn't understand, she read with so much feeling and expression that there was no question as to the meaning. Very early in my life, I read Dickens, Mark Twain, Tolstoy, Alcott, and others, at her insistence." Hodges adds, "She was a secretary and a stickler for correct grammar." But Mary Hodges's father was the family's oral storyteller: "He saw everything as a story." From him, she learned family history, stories of the Civil War, his stories of the Depression, of World War II days, of work on the farm and in the local zinc mine. "I realize now how much my parents helped me to become a writer."

Through the mining company where her father worked, she got a scholarship to Washington University in St. Louis, Missouri, where she graduated in 1966 with a B.S. in English and secondary education. She earned a Master's degree in English at the University of Tennessee in 1971.

She taught secondary education classes in Tennessee, South Carolina, Florida, and Hawaii, as her husband's job with the federal government required transfers and relocation until he retired, and the couple then returned home to East Tennessee. Mary Hodges lives with her husband, James, in Talbott, Tennessee, and since 1990, she has taught English at Carson-Newman College. They have two grown children and a granddaughter.

"Most of my writing reflects the region I grew up in," she says, "but I didn't write seriously about it until I had lived away from it for many years and returned there to live with a renewed appreciation for its natural beauty, its culture, and its people."

OTHER SOURCES TO EXPLORE

PRIMARY

Short Stories: *Tough Customers and Other Stories* (1999), includes "An Interview with Mary B. Hodges" 141–51.

SECONDARY

Gurney Norman, "Introduction," *Tough Customers and Other Stories* (1999), 7–11.

Ms. Ida Mae

from *Tough Customers and Other Stories* (1999)

What do I want you to call me? Why, everybody just calls me Ida Mae. "Mrs." kinda runs against my grain right now, don't you know. And, course, I ain't no "Miss." But, you can tell that from my ring, can't you? Or maybe you got that off the form your nurse had me fill out. The one you got there in front of you. I do kinda like that new "Ms." Maybe you can just call me Ms. Jenkins—no, make it Ms. Ida Mae. Call me Ms. Ida Mae. Jenkins ain't the name I was born with, noway.

I guess you're wondering what I'm doing here. I mean, it's obvious I ain't crazy or nothing. I guess you must see some real lulus. But, I'm not sick, you understand. Course, I know you ain't no real doctor, neither, even if I was sick. But, anyway, I just want you to know. I don't need no—no—well, doctor. It, uh, it is okay if I parked down the street at the Bigger Better Burger, ain't it? I mean they won't tow my car or nothing like that, will they? I think it ought to be okay. Course, I know they's parking out front of your office; but, well, you know, I just thought I'd park down there. And, after all, I am going in there when I leave here. They can't tow my car if I go in there when I leave here, can they? Have you ever had one of their bigger better bacon burgers? You ain't lived till you have.

Well, anyway, about why I'm here. It all boils down to this: I got to have me somebody to talk to, you know? I can't talk to my folks. On the other hand, maybe I should talk to Mama; she'd certainly have all the answers. She'd sure enjoy telling me what I shoulda done different, namely not to a married Hubert. Hubert, that's my husband. And then she'd know what I ought to do now, and that would be to get rid of him, like she's been telling me for years. The way I see it, if she'd a done everything right herself, she'd have something better to do than preach to me, wouldn't you think so? Anyway, I ain't listening to that. And Daddy, well, let me tell you. Daddy's solution would be to blow Hubert's head off. Now, that'd really help a lot, wouldn't it? Then, instead of having an unfaithful husband, I'd have a dead one—and a convict for a Daddy to boot.

I used to tell everything to Imogene. Imogene, she's my best friend. Well, except for Hubert. I guess he's my really best friend, but he's my husband. Imogene's my best girl friend. Well, she's also Hubert's best friend—girlfriend, if you know what I mean. It's hot in here, ain't it? Maybe you ought to adjust the thermostat. It ain't healthy to be in a room that's too stuffy. Anyway, can you believe that they both talk to me. Like I'm just some person sitting between them in a movie and they're explaining the show. And then there's Imogene's husband George. You want to talk stupid—he's just like the three monkeys—See Nothing, Do Nothing, and Know Nothing. Well, you can see as how I can't talk to Imogene. You know, you really ought to consider changing this chair. It's not very comfortable. I'd think it'd be important for folks to be comfortable when they—when they, well, you know, come in here. I thought you was supposed to have a couch. Why don't you have a couch?

Actually, you know, I ought to just go talk to Brother Shepherd. He's our preacher. I've thought of that. He's been our preacher for some fifteen years. Ain't that funny? Shepherd—you get it? Like with sheep, and he's the pastor. Just like Jesus in the Bible. He's the Shepherd. And his name is Shepherd. And he's the pastor of the sheep. I mean, you just know this man was meant to be a preacher.

Well, ah, anyway. I can't go talk to him cause Imogene, she goes to talk to him all the time. She does. Talks to him, right there in his office in the church. At least once a week. Can you believe it? Just baring all our dirty laundry to God and all. Course, she talks to him cause she knows he won't say nothing to nobody, and he don't cost her nothing. And she just talks to him like it's perfectly all right and like all her sins are forgiven, washed away. Poor man, he's just too nice and won't say nothing. She's hoping he'll sympathize with her and tell her love is from God and all that, make her feel better. Well, let me tell you, there's love and then there's love. Anyway, she says he just nods and don't really make no comment one way or the other.

She thinks cause he don't directly tell her she's going to hell—do not pass go, do not collect $200, for a breaking one of them ten commandments—that she ain't going. She thinks it's one of them things in the Bible that you ain't supposed to take literal—like Jesus turning the water into wine. Well, I know you ain't supposed to take that literal. Of course, Jesus didn't make no wine, but them ten commandments—now I don't know no way they can mean nothing other than what they say, "Do not commit adultery." That's what it says. Plain as the nose on your face.

Lord, bless us all, you can see I can't go talk to Brother Shepherd. Mercy, I can't even look the man in the eyes at church anymore. All through the sermon I have to look over his head at the plastic clock with Jesus in the middle. The minute hand and hour hand is nailed in at his nose, you know, and a different miracle is on each hour. And I just watch that slow little hand creep like Methuselah from the miracle of loaves and fishes to the miracle of the turning the water into wine. But you can't really tell about the wine on the clock. You just see Jesus with a pitcher in one hand and a cup in the other. Anyway, all the time while I'm sitting there a watching the miracles and a worrying about the wine, she sits up in that choir loft just as big as Ike. Like it's all okay, cause she talks to Brother Shepherd ever week. Just like she wasn't going to hell in a handbasket and taking my Hubert right along with her.

Well, I tell you what, this conversation has done me a world of good. I guess there is something to having a—professional person—tell you what to do about your problems. Course I don't know if I can do what you would do. I know I should dump Hubert, but, well, we been married a right long time. And, I know I should tell Imogene to jump right on that express train to the lower regions, but, you know, we been friends since we been in diapers.

Anyway, I know I don't need to come back here no more. I reckon I'll live through this, and Hubert will, too, if I don't kill him. But, let me tell you, you really ought to get you a nice couch for in here—you know, for your real patients.

GLORIA HOUSTON

Children's author and educator Gloria Houston is a native of Marion, North Carolina. Her parents ran a country store near Spruce Pine, North Carolina, and, Houston says, she was "saturated with language, almost from birth. I heard the language of every stratum of society as customers came and went."

By the age of seven, she knew she wanted to be a writer, but an aptitude for music led to a bachelor's degree in music education from Appalachian State University in 1963, and a subsequent series of teaching positions. Houston earned an M.Ed. in curriculum and instruction in English education in 1983 and a Ph.D. in curriculum and instruction in interdisciplinary studies in 1989, both from the University of South Florida. The emphasis in each graduate degree was on writing and children's literature.

Houston's first book, *My Brother Joey Died*, was rejected fifty-four times before its publication. It went on to win numerous awards, including an American Library Association (ALA) Notable Book citation. "Life is revision," says Houston. "You do it until you get it right. I learned to revise sitting at the piano. The toughest part of writing is putting your fanny on the chair and keeping it there."

Houston's other books have won awards as well, including an ALA designation as a Best Book of the Decade for *The Year of the Perfect Christmas Tree* and an ALA Notable Book Award for *My Great-Aunt Arizona*.

"I believe that children are the most important audience for which to write," says Houston. "No book will influence the adult reader as profoundly as the right book at the right time when read by a child reader." Houston says she hopes to "provide a mirror for the children of Appalachia to help them see the beauties of their culture and way of life."

Since 1994, Houston has been on the faculty of Western Carolina University in Cullowhee, North Carolina, as Author-in-Residence.

What follows is excerpted from Houston's picture book *My Great-Aunt Arizona*, which portrays the life of a dedicated teacher in the Blue Ridge Mountains.

OTHER SOURCES TO EXPLORE

PRIMARY

Books for children: *Bright Freedom's Song: A Story of the Underground Railroad* (1998), *Littlejim's Dreams* (1997), *Littlejim's Gift: An Appalachian Christmas Story* (1994), *Mountain Valor* (1994), *My Great-Aunt Arizona* (1992), *But No Candy* (1992), *Littlejim* (1990), *The Year of the Perfect Christmas Tree* (1988), *My Brother Joey Died* (1982).

SECONDARY

Contemporary Authors (2000), New Revision Series, Vol. 86, 130–33. Roberta Herrin, "Gloria Houston and the Burden of the 'Old Culture'," *Appalachian Journal* 24:1 (fall 1996), 31–44. Rob Newfeld, "Gloria Houston's Avery County Universe," *Asheville* [NC] *Citizen-Times* (3 February 2002), B4. "Sunny Brook Store," [web site] www.sunnybrookstore.com

FROM MY GREAT-AUNT ARIZONA (1992)

My great-aunt Arizona
was born in a log cabin
her papa built
in the meadow
on Henson Creek
in the Blue Ridge Mountains.
When she was born,
the mailman rode
across the bridge
on his big bay horse
with a letter.

. . .

Arizona had a little brother, Jim.
They played together on the farm.
In summer they went barefoot
and caught tadpoles in the creek.

In the fall
they climbed the mountains
searching for galax and ginseng roots.

In the winter they made snow cream
with sugar, snow, and sweet cream
from Mama's cows.
When spring came,
they helped Papa tap
the maple trees
and catch sap in buckets.
Then they made maple syrup
and maple-sugar candy.

Arizona and her brother Jim
walked up the road
that wound by the creek
to the one-room school.
All the students
in all the grades

were there,
together
in one room.
All the students
read their lessons
aloud
at the same time.
They made
a great deal of noise,
so
the room was called
a blab school.

When Arizona's mother died,
Arizona had to leave school
and stay home to care for Papa
and her brother Jim.
But she still loved to read—
and dream
about the faraway places
she would visit one day.
So she read and she dreamed,
and she took care of Papa
and Jim.

Then one day
Papa brought home a new wife.
Arizona could go away to school,
where she could learn to be a teacher.
Aunt Suzie invited Arizona
to live at her house
and help with the chores.
Aunt Suzie made her work very hard.
But at night Arizona could study—
and dream of all the faraway places
she would visit one day.

Finally, Arizona returned
to her home on Henson Creek.
She was a teacher at last.

She taught in the one-room school
where she and Jim had sat.

. . .

She grew flowers in every window.
She taught students about words
and numbers
and the faraway places
they would visit someday.
"Have you been there?"
the students asked.
"Only in my mind," she answered.
"But someday you will go."

Arizona married the carpenter
who helped to build the new Riverside School
down where Henson Creek joins the river.
So Miss Arizona became Mrs. Hughes,
and for the rest of her days
she taught fourth-grade students
who called her "Miz Shoes."

. . .

The boys and girls
who were students in her class
had boys and girls
who were students in her class.
And they had boys and girls
who were students in her class.

For fifty-seven years
my great-aunt Arizona
hugged her students.
She hugged them
when their work was good,
and she hugged them
when it was not.
She taught them words
and numbers,
and about the faraway places
they would visit someday.
"Have you been there?"

the students asked.
"Only in my mind,"
she answered.
"But someday you will go."
                    . . .
My great-aunt Arizona died
on her ninety-third birthday.
But she goes with me
in my mind—
A very tall lady,
in a long full dress,
and a pretty white apron,
with her high-button shoes,
and her many petticoats, too.
She's always there,
in a sunny room
with many flowers
in every window,
and a hug for me every day.

Did she ever go
to the faraway places
she taught us about? No.
But my great-aunt Arizona
travels with me
and with those of us
whose lives she touched. . . .

She goes with us
in our minds.

$\mathscr{L}$EE $\mathscr{H}$OWARD
(January 30, 1952– April 25, 2003)

Eastern Kentucky native Lee Howard was a poet and short story author. "My mountain voice is my first and true voice," wrote Howard. "The thing I tell people after giving my name, is that I'm from the mountains in East Kentucky."

Howard's ancestors arrived in Kentucky even earlier than Daniel Boone, and have lived there ever since. Howard, who spent the last years of her life in the Pacific Northwest, noted wryly, "I am the only member of my clan living on the other side of the continent. Much of my family believes I've moved to Japan."

Howard earned a B.A. in sociology from George Washington University in 1976 and an M.A. in comparative religion from Marylhurst University in Oregon in 1999.

Although she lived in Oregon for years, Howard observed that "my poetry and stories are in the narrative voices and narrative style of Appalachia. It is the particular voice that allows me a specific means to say what is universally true for many. I cannot imagine how I would write or what I might say if I came from anywhere else."

OTHER SOURCES TO EXPLORE

PRIMARY

Poetry: *The Last Unmined Vein* (1980).

SECONDARY

George Ella Lyon, "The Poet's Job," *Appalachian Journal* 8:3 (spring 1981), 217–23.

MOMMA'S LETTER

from *The Last Unmined Vein* (1980)

Not much to say
Orville and Neva put out their garden
well at least the onions and tater part of it
and it only the first of March
I hope and pray it does not freeze
but you can't count on March
anymore than you can on a man
Might do it—might not
Of course John and Re are just the same
John a spewing over
Re spending time with Ruth
and mind you she's there at Ruth's gas station
most ever' night
not to mention all day Sunday
and so she's been doing for years
and John has been fussin' just that long
It's raining on today of all days
You know of course it is Mammy's birthday
She's laid dead now these last 5 years
and I cannot say that it seems
like more than yesterday
that I saw her
rocking on the front porch
round evening time
and complaining about
how fast George Cope's boys drive
like the devil by
I wished I had made more time to be with her
You don't realize what your mother means to you
til there's no one there
to call you home
But I was married
and full of being so
and of course you children
did need so much watching after

May she be in God's Glory
and waiting for me
Your Daddy is fine
and working sun up to down
and quite happy doing so
His little church is not setting the world on fire
but then he had no mind for it to
I suppose 25 or 30 counting children
come for Sunday morning
and then about ½ that at night
And he preaches just like it were a whole tent full
and he was Billy Graham
Well I am at the beauty shop
and my hair is about dry
So I will close
This finds me well and happy
and missing you
Count the mistakes as love

THE LAST UNMINED VEIN

from *The Last Unmined Vein* (1980)

Now it's neither here nor there
to most folks
but then I've never figured myself
to be like many
much less most
I know what they do
no matter what they say
I know how they come
with trucks bigger than ary road
can hold
and drive her through yer yard
and right up on the porch
and park her next to yer rocking chair
and you ain't got a howdy-do
to say about it neither
once you put yer name

to that paper
that's it

Now my daddy and me
we used to dig a little coal
out of that vein across the bottom
Just a pick and shovel
and what could be wheelbarrowed
out of there
was all that was took
and didn't hurt nothing
and kept a fire real good
and that's it
but that ain't what they got in mind
They wanting to make steel in Ohio,
turn on the lights in New York City
and heat houses in Detroit
Shoot—I don't know a soul
in the whole state of Michigan
but that ain't really it
It ain't my business what they do with it
but this farm and everything that's in it
is plenty my concern
and I know how they come
with their mouths full of promises
and leaving with every one
of your fields full of ruts
and the mud sliding down the hillside
right onto your back steps
and there ain't a creek left
what would hold a living thing
and that's it
and the money
just don't mean that much to me
I done seen all I need to see
about where that money goes
and what's got with it
Last thing this county needs
is another new mobile home
with a four-wheel drive truck

parked on a mudbank in front of it
and that's it
and not another thing to show
for where and what your mammy and pappy
and their mammy and pappy
not to mention your own self and family
always had
So when that man in his new suit
and smooth as silk talking
came to my door
I didn't even ask him in
Said I wasn't interested
He laughed and said he wasn't selling
Said I didn't figure I was either
and that was it
Of course, I know he'll be back
but probably after I'm dead and gone
and if the children want to be so foolish
as to put an end
to what came long before them
ain't nothing I can do about it then
but I been laying plans
to remind them
of what it's gonna cost them
I done got my marker
and laid out the lines for my grave
right smack in the middle
of that vein
They gonna have to chip out the coal 6 foot by 6
and then put her right back on top of me
and that will be the end of that

ℳARY ℐOHNSTON
(November 21, 1870–May 9, 1936)

Mary Johnston was born in Buchanan, Virginia, the daughter of a Confederate veteran. The eldest of six children, she was schooled at home until the age of sixteen, when her mother's death forced her to take over the management of the Johnston household. The family moved to New York City for a time, and though Johnston later traveled extensively in Europe and the Middle East, western Virginia remained her home for most of her life.

Johnston published poetry, short stories, a drama, and even a volume of history, but she was best known as a historical novelist. Her most popular novel, *To Have and to Hold*, set in colonial Jamestown, Virginia, was the country's number one best-seller in 1900. Profits from the book enabled her to build a large country home in Warm Springs, Virginia. In her later years, Johnston turned from writing historical fiction to writing novels that highlighted her feminist and suffragist views.

Critics disagree on the quality of Johnston's work. Some call her plots melodramatic and her characters limited, but others praise her narrative power, as well as her attention to historical detail. Battle descriptions in her Civil War novels are so accurate that one reviewer referred to them as "military history," rather than fiction.

In this scene from *The Long Roll*, Johnston describes General Stonewall Jackson on the eve of his 1861 campaign in the Shenandoah Valley. In a note to her readers, Johnston explained that the incidents in the book "were actual happenings," adding that she had "changed the manner but not the substance."

OTHER SOURCES TO EXPLORE

PRIMARY

Fiction: *Drury Randall* (1934), *Miss Delicia Allen* (1933), *Hunting Shirt* (1931), *The Exile* (1927), *The Great Valley* (1926), *The Slave Ship* (1924), *Croatoan* (1923), *1492* (1922), *Silver Cross* (1922), *Sweet Rocket* (1920), *Michael Forth* (1919), *Foes* (1918), *Pioneers of the Old South: A Chronicle of English Colonial Beginnings* (1918), *The Wanderers* (1917), *The Fortunes of Garin* (1915), *The Witch* (1914), *Hagar* (1913), *Cease Firing* (1912), *The Long Roll* (1911), *Lewis Rand* (1908), *The Goddess of Reason* (1907), *Sir Mortimer* (1904), *Audrey* (1902), *To Have and To Hold* (1900), *Prisoners of Hope, A Tale of Colonial Virginia* (1898).

SECONDARY

Dorothy M. Scura, "Mary Johnston," *American Women Authors*, Vol. 3 (1980), 416–19. Cratis Williams, "The Southern Mountaineer in Fact and Fiction," abridged in *Appalachian Journal* 3:3 (spring 1976), 236.

THE LONG ROLL (1911)

from Chapter VI

It was the middle of July, 1861.

First Brigade headquarters was a tree—an especially big tree—a little removed from the others. Beneath it stood a kitchen chair and a wooden table, requisitioned from the nearest cabin and scrupulously paid for. At one side was an extremely small tent, but Brigadier-General T.J. Jackson rarely occupied it. He sat beneath the tree, upon the kitchen chair, his feet, in enormous cavalry boots, planted precisely before him, his hands rigid at his sides. Here he transacted the business of each day, and here, when it was over, he sat facing the North. An awkward, inarticulate, and peculiar man, with strange notions about his health and other matters, there was about him no breath of grace, romance, or pomp of war. He was ungenial, ungainly, with large hands and feet, with poor eyesight and a stiff address. There did not lack spruce and handsome youths in his command who were vexed to the soul by the idea of being led to battle by such a figure. The facts that he had fought very bravely in Mexico, and that he had for the enemy a cold and formidable hatred were for him; most other things against him. He drilled his troops seven hours a day. His discipline was of the sternest, his censure a thing to make the boldest officer blench. A blunder, a slight negligence, any disobedience of orders—down came reprimand, suspension, arrest, with an iron certitude, a relentlessness quite like Nature's. Apparently he was without imagination. He had but little sense of humour, and no understanding of a joke. He drank water and sucked lemons for dyspepsia, and fancied that the use of pepper had caused a weakness in his left leg. He rode a rawboned nag named Little Sorrel, he carried his sabre in the oddest fashion, and said "oblike," instead of "oblique." He found his greatest pleasure in going to the Presbyterian Church twice on Sundays and to prayer meetings through the week. Now and then there was a gleam in his eye that promised something, but the battles had not begun, and his soldiers hardly knew what it promised. One or two observers claimed that he was ambitious, but these were chiefly laughed at. To the brigade at large he seemed prosaic, tedious, and strict enough, performing all duties with the exactitude, monotony, and expression of a clock, keeping all plans with the secrecy of the sepulchre, rarely sleeping, rising at dawn, and requiring his staff to do likewise, praying at all seasons, and demanding an implicity of obedience which might have been in order with some great and glorious captain, some idolized Napoleon, but which seemed hardly the due of the late professor of natural philosophy and artillery tactics at the Virginia Military Institute. True it was that at Harper's Ferry, where, as Colonel T.J. Jackson, he had commanded until Johnston's arrival, he had begun to bring order out of chaos and to weave from a high-spirited rabble of Volunteers a web that the world was to acknowledge remarkable; true, too, that on the second of July, in the small affair with Patterson at Falling Waters, he had seemed to the critics in the ranks not altogether unimposing. He emerged from Falling Waters Brigadier-General T.J. Jackson, and his men, though with some mental reservations, began to call him "Old Jack." The epithet implied approval, but approval hugely qualified. They might have said—in fact, they did say—that every fool knew that a crazy man could fight!

MARY HARRIS "MOTHER" JONES
(May 1, 1830?–November 30, 1930)

Mary Harris "Mother" Jones, labor organizer and union gadfly, was born in Ireland in the 1830s. Her father's anti-British activities forced the family to flee to the United States where Jones worked as a schoolteacher in Memphis, and later, as a dressmaker in Chicago. In 1861, she married George E. Jones, an iron molder and staunch unionist.

When a yellow-fever epidemic swept Chicago in 1867, Jones's husband and all four of her children died. Five years later, her home and dressmaking business were destroyed in the Great Chicago Fire.

Made homeless by circumstance, she remained homeless by choice, dedicating her life to improving the working conditions of America's laborers. She helped organize rail strikes in Pittsburgh and Birmingham, a textile strike in Philadelphia, and coal strikes in Pennsylvania and West Virginia. When asked where she lived, Jones replied, "Wherever there is a fight."

Dubbed "Mother" Jones by union members, she grew adept at staging events which garnered national attention, such as a 125-mile march across New Jersey and into New York City to protest the textile industry's exploitation of child workers.

Because of her activities in a 1912 United Mine Workers' strike, Jones, at the age of eighty-two, was labeled "the most dangerous woman in America" by a West Virginia prosecutor who complained, "She comes into a state where peace and prosperity reign . . . crooks her finger [and] twenty thousand contented men lay down their tools and walk out."

Sentenced to twenty years in prison by a West Virginia court, Mother Jones was pardoned by the governor after the U.S. Senate threatened an investigation.

Her autobiography retains a great deal of the passion that made her such an effective orator. Although critics contend that her memory for dates was suspect, most agree her writings offer an invaluable look behind the scenes at the struggles of American workers in the late nineteenth and early twentieth centuries.

The following excerpt is from *The Autobiography of Mother Jones,* published near the end of Jones's life.

OTHER SOURCES TO EXPLORE

PRIMARY

Books: *The Speeches and Writings of Mother Jones* (1988), ed. Edward M. Steel. *The Correspondence of Mother Jones* (1985), ed. Edward M. Steel. *The Autobiography of Mother Jones* (1925), ed. Mary Field Parton.

SECONDARY

Helen M. Brannan, "Mary Harris Jones," *American Women Writers* (1980), 422–24. Elliott J. Gorn, *Mother Jones: The Most Dangerous Woman in America* (2001). Joseph Gustaitis, "Mary Harris Jones: The Most Dangerous Woman," *American History Illustrated* (22 Jan. 1988), 22–23. Edward M. Steel, ed. *The Court-Martial of Mother Jones* (1995).

THE AUTOBIOGRAPHY
OF MOTHER JONES (1925)
Chapter III: A Strike in Virginia

It was about 1891 when I was down in Virginia. There was a strike in the Dietz mines and the boys had sent for me. When I got off the train at Norton a fellow walked up to me and asked me if I were Mother Jones.

"Yes, I am Mother Jones."

He looked terribly frightened. "The superintendent told me that if you came down here he would blow out your brains. He said he didn't want to see you 'round these parts."

"You tell the superintendent that I am not coming to see him anyway. I am coming to see the miners."

As we stood talking a poor fellow, all skin and bones, joined us.

"Do you see those cars over there, Mother, on the siding?" He pointed to the cars filled with coal.

"Well, we made a contract with the coal company to fill those cars for so much, and after we had made the contract, they put lower bottoms in the cars, so that they would hold another ton or so. I have worked for this company all my life and all I have now is this old worn-out frame."

We couldn't get a hall to hold a meeting. Every one was afraid to rent to us. Finally the colored people consented to give us their church for our meeting. Just as we were about to start the colored chairman came to me and said: "Mother, the coal company gave us this ground that the church is on. They have sent word that they will take it from us if we let you speak here."

I would not let those poor souls lose their ground so I adjourned the meeting to the four corners of the public roads. When the meeting was over and the people had dispersed, I asked my co-worker, Dud Hado, a fellow from Iowa, if he would go with me up to the post office. He was a kindly soul but easily frightened.

As we were going along the road, I said, "Have you got a pistol on you?"

"Yes," said he, "I'm not going to let any one blow your brains out."

"My boy," said I, "it is against the law in this county to carry concealed weapons. I want you to take that pistol out and expose a couple of inches of it."

As he did so about eight or ten gunmen jumped out from behind an old barn beside the road, jumped on him and said, "Now we've got you, you dirty organizer." They bullied us along the road to the town and we were taken to an office where they had a notary public and we were tried. All those blood-thirsty murderers were there and the general manager came in.

"Mother Jones, I am astonished," said he.

"What is your astonishment about?" said I.

"That you should go into the house of God with anyone who carries a gun."

"Oh, that wasn't God's house," said I. "That is the coal company's house. Don't you know that God Almighty never comes around to a place like this!"

He laughed and of course, the dogs laughed, for he was the general manager.

They dismissed any charges against me and they fined poor Dud twenty-five dollars and costs. They seemed surprised when I said I would pay it. I had the money in my petticoat.

I went over to a miner's shack and asked his wife for a cup of tea. Often in these company-owned towns the inn-keepers were afraid to let me have food. The poor soul was so happy to have me there that she excused herself to "dress for company." She came out of the bedroom with a white apron on over her cheap cotton wrapper.

One of the men who was present at Dud's trial followed me up to the miner's house. At first the miner's wife would not admit him but he said he wanted to speak privately to Mother Jones. So she let him in.

"Mother," he said, "I am glad you paid that bill so quickly. They thought you'd appeal the case. Then they were going to lock you both up and burn you in the coke ovens at night and then say that you had both been turned loose in the morning and they didn't know where you had gone."

Whether they really would have carried out their plans I do not know. But I do know that there are no limits to which powers of privilege will not go to keep the workers in slavery.

JANE WILSON JOYCE
(July 17, 1947–)

~

Poet Jane Wilson Joyce grew up in Kingsport, Tennessee. Her mother is a painter and a native of England, and her father spent his entire life in upper East Tennessee. "What with his stories, and her habit of looking, I found a lot of what I needed in their relationship to the region—how they helped me see and be there," says Joyce.

Joyce earned a B.A. in Latin from Bryn Mawr College in 1969, an M.A. in Greek from the University of Texas in 1972, and her Ph.D. in classics from the University of Texas in 1982.

Her poetry collection *Beyond the Blue Mountains* follows "the journey of an imaginary family travelling from Kentucky to Oregon in 1852." The original publication of her collection *The Quilt Poems* was by Mill Springs Press. These poems appear in *Quilt Pieces* by Gnomon Press, along with a short story by Meredith Sue Willis.

She has been on the faculty of Centre College in Danville, Kentucky, since 1978. "I teach a wide range of courses in the Classics—language, literature, culture," says Joyce. She was instrumental in the establishment of Centre's major in the classics, and has been awarded the designation of Distinguished Professor of Humanities. Currently, she is the Luellen Professor of Literature.

OTHER SOURCES TO EXPLORE

Poetry: *Beyond the Blue Mountains* (1992), *The Quilt Poems* in *Quilt Pieces* (1992).

LIFE AND ART
IN EAST TENNESSEE

from *Old Wounds, New Words:*
Poems from the Appalachian Poetry Project (1994)

I had read in National Geographic
how in Alaska, or some places like it
where chill mysteries winter,
people stand on ice ten months thick
and see fish glint far beneath
shivering the deep green with their speed.

I stood on creek ice
one windfall of a subzero day
skating thin and bladeless
on a dare. Dreaming of parkas,
the huskies' bark, a fish-hook gleaming
carved from a fat walrus tusk,
I saw only the bent brown ribs
of the old year's reeds
like a kayak skeleton
breaking up in the backwater.

Whatever I saw or didn't in the mud,
come spring and full summer
the creek overflowed
with tadpoles, snapping-turtles, water-bugs,
the green wink of a lizard disappearing.
I kept one eye peeled
in hopes of cottonmouth, water-moccasin
as I kneeled in the weeds, sleeve hiked,
feeling in water brown as tobacco
for the least thrill of minnows
shimmering between my fingers.

Hooked Album Quilt, 1870

from *Quilt Pieces* (1992)

Mama, I finished your quilt
but my heart wasn't in it
like yours was
so my work stands out—
plain crochet, thin and poor
alongside of yours.

I watched you
cut up the uniforms
they shipped home from Virginia,
sliding your big scissorblades
up the trouserlegs
like a doctor
slicing open a boot
when the leg inside is broken.

You sat, skeins striping
your black skirt
green, yellow, red,
tugging heavy yarns
through the dense weave of dull cloth
strand by strand,
shearing them down
just so: 33 squares
you worked this way,
never saying a word
that wasn't bright,
while the blisters came up on your hand,
broke, and wept.

I finished the quilt—
counterpane, you called it—
rolled it up and packed it away
in the cedar chest in the attic,
touching the rounded bunches

of cat-tails, tulips,
the one sunflower,
repeating fields of moss rose.
Why would you want to sleep
under such a weight
of remembering.

*M*AY *J*USTUS
(May 12, 1898–November 7, 1989)

A prolific writer of children's books, May Justus was born in Del Rio, Tennessee. "I am a Smoky Mountaineer, born and bred, and proud of it," wrote Justus in the 1950s. "The mountain culture of the past is fading. . . . The old customs, the folk speech, the ballads, the fiddle tunes, the play party singing games, the herb lore, the weather signs, the nonsense rhymes, the tall tales, even the riddles—you'll find them in the books I've written for a quarter of a century."

Justus attended the University of Tennessee, then taught school in rural Tennessee and Kentucky. A community activist, she sought to improve not only educational opportunities, but health care and nutrition as well. She was affiliated with the Highlander Center during its early days and espoused such "liberal" ideas as integration.

She began writing stories for her students who were "always eager for the next adventure." Her first book was published in 1927, when she was twenty-nine. One of her books, *New Boy in School*, was on the *New York Times* Best Book list for 1963, and Justus considered it one of her most significant, because it was one of the first children's books to deal with integration.

Justus's writing career spanned nearly six decades, and during that time she produced more than fifty books. The University of Tennessee's May Justus Collection contains all her books, many manuscripts, and an extensive correspondence.

Justus chose the title of her collection of folklore, *The Complete Peddler's Pack*, because of a childhood memory: "To those of us who lived far removed from the stores and shops of a city, the visit of a peddler was a thrilling event. . . . When the peddler loosened his load and spread its treasures on the floor, it was a sight to behold." In the excerpts from *The Complete Peddler's Pack*, we glimpse the region's folk wisdom as recorded by Justus.

OTHER SOURCES TO EXPLORE

PRIMARY

Books for children: *Jumping Jack* (1974), *Surprise for Perky Pup* (1971), *Tales from Near-Side and Far* (1970), *Eben and the Rattlesnake* (1969), *The Wonderful School of Miss Tillie O'Toole* (1969), *It Happened in No-End Hollow* (1969), *The Complete Peddler's Pack: Games, Songs, Rhymes, and Riddles from Mountain Folklore* (1966), *A New Home for Billy* (1966), *Tale of a Pig* (1963), *New Boy in School* (1963), *Smoky Mountain Sampler* (1962), *Winds A'Blowing* [poetry] (1961), *The Right House for Rowdy* (1960), *Lester and His Hound Pup* (1960), *Then Came Mr. Billy Barker* (1959), *Barney Bring Your Banjo* (1959), *Let's Play and Sing* (1958), *Jumping Johnny and Skedaddle* (1958), *Big Log Mountain* (1958), *Peddler's Pack* (1957), *Use Your Head, Hildy* (1956), *Surprise for Peter Pocket* (1955), *Little Red Rooster Learns to Crow* (1954), *Peter Pocket and His Pickle Pup* (1953), *Whoop-ee, Hunkydory!* (1952), *Children of the Great Smoky Mountains* (1952), *Lucky Penny* (1951), *Luck for Little Lihu* (1950), *Toby Has a Dog* (1949), *Susie* (1948), *Mary Ellen* (1947), *Sammy* (1946), *Hurray for Jerry Jake* (1945), *Fiddlers' Fair* (1945), *Lizzie* (1944), *Banjo Billy and Mr. Bones* (1944), *Jerry Jake Carries On* (1943), *Bluebird, Fly Up!* (1943), *Step Along and Jerry Jake* (1942), *Nancy of Apple Tree Hill* (1942), *Fiddle Away* (1942), *Dixie Decides* (1942), *Cabin on Kettle Creek* (1941), *The Mail Wagon Mystery* (1941), *Mr. Songcatcher and Company* (1940), *Here Comes Mary Ellen* (1940), *The House in No-End Hollow* (1938), *Near-side-and-far* (1936), *Honey Jane* (1935), *Gabby Gaffer's New Shoes* (1935), *Peter Pocket's Book* (1934), *The Other Side of the Mountain* (1931), *At the Foot of Windy Low* (1930), *Gabby Gaffer* (1929), *Betty Lou of Big Log Mountain* (1928), *Peter Pocket* (1927).

SECONDARY

Contemporary Authors (1974), Vols. 9–10, 246. *Something About the Author* (1971), Vol. 1, 127–29. John W. Warren and Adrian W. McClaren, *Tennessee Belles-Lettres: A Guide to Tennessee Literature* (1977), 218. Eliot Wigginton, ed. *Refuse to Stand Silently By: An Oral History of Grass Roots Social Activism in America, 1921–1964* (1991), 75–88, 266–72, 334–40.

WEATHER RHYMES

from *The Complete Peddler's Pack: Games, Songs, Rhymes, and Riddles from Mountain Folklore* (1966)

Between twelve o'clock and two,
You'll see what the day will do.

> Rain before seven,
> Quit before eleven.

When the wind's against the sun,
Trust it not, for back 'twill run.

When the smoke bites the ground,
Bad weather will be found.

Hoar frost on mornings twain,
On the third look for rain.

When the wind is in the north,
Man nor beast should venture forth.
When the wind is in the east,
It's good for neither man nor beast.
When the wind is in the west,
This for man and beast is best.

If the moon changes on Sunday,
Weather change is sure on Monday.

Onion skin very thin,
Pretty winter coming in.
Onion skin thick and tough,
Winter mighty cold and rough.

When April blows his horn (*thunder*)
It's good for hay and corn.

Mist in May,
Sun in June,
Makes the harvest ripen soon.
Change not a clout (*winter garment*)
Till May be out.

If the oak is out
Before the ash,
There'll be a summer
Of wet and splash.

If a cow beast scratch her ear,
Stormy weather's very near.

ÉDITH SUMMERS KELLEY
(April 28, 1884–June 9, 1956)

The youngest child of Scottish immigrant parents, Edith Summers was born and raised in Toronto, Canada. By the age of thirteen, she had sold her first story to a local newspaper. She received a scholarship to attend the University of Toronto and graduated with honors in 1903.

Eager to pursue her ambitions as a writer, she moved to New York City, settled in Greenwich Village, and took her first job on the staff of Funk & Wagnall's *Standard Dictionary*. In 1905, she answered a newspaper ad and began work as secretary to novelist Upton Sinclair, author of *The Jungle*. She eventually joined his experimental commune in New Jersey, a place which attracted a number of writers and thinkers—including Charlotte Perkins Gilman and Sinclair Lewis. When fire destroyed their communal home, Helicon Hall, Summers returned to Greenwich Village and supported herself by writing stories and poems for magazines. After breaking her engagement with Sinclair Lewis, she married his roommate and friend, Allan Upderdraff, in 1908. They had two children, a daughter and a son, before divorcing three years later.

Soon after she began to live with sculptor C. Fred Kelley, they moved in 1914 to a seven hundred-acre tobacco farm in Scott County, Kentucky, a farm they rented and planned to manage, though they knew little about tobacco farming. There, where she lived as a tenant farmer—"in a three-room tenant shack"—she received the inspiration for her novel, *Weeds*.

After several financially unsuccessful farming ventures and the birth of another son, the family moved to Imperial Valley, California. She began writing *Weeds* and contacted Sinclair Lewis, who helped her to secure his own publisher for her manuscript. She never found in California the supportive community of writers and intellectuals that had surrounded her in the East, but she remained in California until her death.

319

Though *Weeds* received favorable reviews from well-known critics, its sales were never good. Kelley attributed the poor sales to weak promotions and to American readers' tastes, which preferred romantic stories to "realistic" ones. Rediscovered in the 1970s and praised for its feminist themes, the novel focuses on Judith Pippinger, an artistic tomboy in the rural hills of Kentucky, who struggles unsuccessfully to overcome the oppressive roles assigned her as a woman when she becomes a wife and mother.

This scene is from the opening of chapter 3 of *Weeds*.

OTHER SOURCES TO EXPLORE

PRIMARY

Novels: *The Devil's Hand* (1974), *Weeds* (1923).

SECONDARY

Charlotte Margolis Goodman, "Afterword," *Weeds* (1996). Danny L. Miller, "Mountain Gloom in the Works of Edith Summers Kelley and Anne W. Armstrong," in *Wingless Flights: Appalachian Women in Fiction* (1996), 53–68.

WEEDS (1923)

from Chapter III

But with the growth of this harmony with natural things, Judith developed a constantly growing tendency to clash with the life of the school and the home kitchen and the kitchens of the various relatives with whom the Pippingers visited. She was considered by her aunts and other female relatives "a wild, bad little limb," and her contempt for the decent and domestic scandalized them more and more as she grew older. Lena Moss could not for her life understand how it was that Judith had learned to read and write and figure better than almost any other child in the school; for she was anything but studious. In fact she never seemed to pay the slightest attention to her studies. She flatly refused even to try to learn Lena's long and carefully prepared list of counties and county towns in Kentucky; and the battles of the Revolutionary and Civil wars, with their accompanying dates, found no lodgement in her mind. Instead of applying herself to these, she munched apples, chewed slippery elm and sassafras, stared idly out of the window, bedeviled the child who sat in front of her, cut folded bits of paper into intricate designs or drew pictures on her slate, the desk, the seat, the floor, the back of the pinafore of the girl in front, any available space within her reach.

These pictures were the curse of Lena's existence. They were to be found everywhere: on the desks, the walls, the floor, the blackboard, the window casings. Outside they decorated the whitewashed wall of the school building, the tops of big flat stones, the fences, the trunks of trees where the bark had been stripped away, every place where a piece of chalk or a bit of black crayon could function.

The pictures, invariably of human beings or animals, were usually comic, satirical or derisive. That they showed great vigor and clarity of vision would have meant nothing to Lena even if she had known it. They were, in her phraseology, "not nice!" They were frequently disrespectful. The morning after the visit of the county superintendent, a large picture in white chalk was found on the blackboard wickedly caricaturing the features of that august personage. The picture was done in profile and exaggerated irreverently the large, bulbous nose, the receding forehead, and the many chins reaching around to a fleshy, pendulous ear. Poor Lena was hard put to it to find a way to control this unruly member of her school. Having much less force of character than her pupil, the advantage of years and vested authority availed her little.

When asked why she had done thus and so, Judith's almost invariable reply was: "Cuz I had to."

"Judy, why hain't you a better gal at school?" Bill asked one morning, trying to look sternly at his favorite daughter across the mush and milk. "Lizzie May says the teacher has a heap o' grief with you. Why don't you mind the teacher, Judy?"

"I do mind her, dad—all I can," Judith returned without looking up. She had the syrup pitcher in her hand and was absorbed in pouring sorghum onto her plate in a very thin stream. Presently she set the pitcher down and handed the plate across the table to her father.

"There, dad, ain't that a good mule? I drawed 'im with the blackstrap. Lizzie May couldn't draw a mule like that."

"Ner I don't want to neither," put in Lizzie May disdainfully. "You otta see, dad, sech pitchers as she draws all around the school, an' makes fun of everybody: the teacher an' the sup'rintendent an' her own relations an' all. She'd otta think shame to herse'f!"

Bill was proud of his girl's ability to draw, but felt it his duty to discourage her choice of subjects, seeing that the same seemed to be so universally condemned.

"What makes you draw them kind o' pitchers, Judy?" he asked.

"Cuz I want to," replied Judith a little sullenly. "I see things; an' when I see 'em I want to draw 'em."

"O law, she don't see no sech things, dad! Haow kin she? Nobody else sees 'em!" exclaimed Lizzie May, outraged. "Why, the idea of her sayin' she sees sech things!"

"Aw, shet up, Liz, an' tend yer own business!" snapped Judith, flushing red with sudden anger. "Jest cuz you don't see nuthin don't mean nobody else does."

$\mathscr{L}$EATHA $\mathscr{K}$ENDRICK
(June 27, 1949–)

Poet Leatha Kendrick was born in her mother's hometown of Granite City, Illinois, but spent most of her childhood in her father's native Kentucky. "I have always had this dual sense of 'home,'" says Kendrick. "I come from farming people, so I felt rooted in both the red clay of Kentucky and the black loam along the Mississippi."

Kendrick earned a B.A. in English, Phi Beta Kappa, from the University of Kentucky in 1971, and an M.A. in English from the University of Kentucky, in 1977. In 1994, she received an M.F.A. in poetry from Vermont College.

Kendrick has taught at Morehead State University and at the University of Kentucky, and has been active in the Kentucky Peer Advisory Network, a network of arts consultants created by the Kentucky Arts Council. She has also developed a course called "Writing Through Crisis," which reflects her "experience with writing during my cancer diagnosis and treatment."

She has been the recipient of numerous grants and awards, including a poetry grant from the Kentucky Foundation for Women, and the Al Smith Fellowship in Poetry from the Kentucky Arts Council.

"Family, home, and relationships ground the Appalachian culture—as they do my poems," says Kendrick. She and her husband, Will, a lawyer, have three daughters. They make their home on George's Branch in East Point, Kentucky.

In this excerpt from her essay "No Place Like Home," Kendrick examines the tension between family and a woman's need for self-expression.

OTHER SOURCES TO EXPLORE

PRIMARY

Poetry: *Heart Cake* (2000). **Autobiographical essay:** "No Place Like Home," *The American Voice* 49 (1999), 96–106. **Co-edited book:** *Crossing Troublesome: 25 Years of the Appalachian Writers Workshop* (2002).

SECONDARY

Michael McFee, "'The World So Vivid, Nothing Ends': A Conversation with Leatha Kendrick," in *Her Words* (2002), ed. Felicia Mitchell, 152–64.

FROM NO PLACE LIKE HOME
The American Voice (1999)

It's August now. Two months since I started this essay. My daughters are home, briefly, between summer commitments and school. I cook. I wash. I set my real work of writing aside. Devoured by the all-consuming work of "caring-for"—that gaping maw of giving, a mouth like those eager ones that once enclosed my breast—I know again both the peace of self-forgetting and the *waiting* that lies within it. "Home" suddenly seems a frayed and frowzy imitation of its former self. "Home-making is no longer my number one occupation," I laughingly apologize to an old friend who stops by to stay overnight. She and I both remember other days when keeping house battled with our need to prove we were more than "just housewives," even when that was what we mainly were. Without those struggles and the friendships forged with women during my children's infancies, however, I might still be very much the arrogant woman I was as a graduate student, unable to embrace the mundane messiness of mothering without feeling diminished by it.

During the weeks when the girls are home, I write in thirty-minute snatches and jot in the margins of newspapers or on the back of envelopes in the kitchen. I read a lot (as if I were more "available" when absorbed in a book!). I am reminded of my high school days and my mother's absence, her body going through the motions. Books, alcohol, sadness, sleeping—there are plenty of ways to leave without going anywhere. Plenty of ways to be alone and have no solitude. My mother lived in a kind of vibrating stasis— keeping a grip on herself so tightly the strain told on all of us. She didn't allow herself to consider what kind of life she might really want to have. Adrienne Rich says in *Of Woman Born*, "The quality of the mother's life . . . is her primary bequest to her daughter." It reminds me of Jung's statement that there is no more powerful influence on any of us than the unlived life of our parents. Most of us daughters struggle under the weight of the unlived lives of our mothers and of their unacknowledged woman-hating (a form of self-hatred), which are their primary bequests to us.

I remember another August and my "beanfield epiphany": the smol- dering weight of damp air, the falling dusk in the garden that seemed like an encroaching blindness, the sense of lifting something with my back as I stood up between rows and declared, "I've got to *do* something! I want to get an MFA." My husband, Will, picking beans a few rows over, was puzzled by this outburst. "Why would you want to do that?" he asked. Though I don't think

I ever adequately wove together all the strands of regret I felt for my mother's life, and the fears for our daughter's future (that weight of my unlived life which I did not want any of us to bear), he did eventually understand that for me, at least, this was a life-and-death decision—it was my very existence at stake.

And so I started off to seek my fortune—which for women is too often characterized as running away from home. I managed to keep all the balls in the air, to live my double life (writer/mother) without breaking apart (at least on the outside) or breaking anyone else. The benefits? Though I have gained no certain answers as to "the self," for my daughters at least there was some freedom from the demand that they justify my existence with their own. Each of them has ended up choosing to go away to boarding school to finish high school—partly because my leaving convinced us all that there were many possible opportunities which had seemed beyond our reach before. Perhaps they will have the freedom and the courage to find their real work, to find a self and love her more quickly than I have been able to.

Meanwhile, when we are together I experience moments of real, unconstrained joy—all of us around the table some nights, the imagined weight of them in their beds, and those few unexpected moments of talk at odd times through the day. Even the endless laundry comforts me and makes me laugh at its recalled dominance—a real weight to be lifted over and over. I know it's only temporary this time. The beginning of school, like a door at the end of this hallway of time, promises release, focuses my attention. Even in the most serene of moments, though, inside me the writer woman fidgets. The purity of my love affair with words wrestles with the daily demands of my equal love of the girls. Unwilling, almost unable, to shut the door to her children's presence, my writer self is just as incapable of closing off to the needs of the solitary me. I cannot quite shake the guilt that says I should not want to have a life that does not center on (or even include sometimes) my family, nor can I go back to being the woman who had not realized that she needed a life of her own.

THE FAMILIAR LEVEL

from *Heart Cake* (2000)

She shows us how to stretch paper so light
it should have torn, and how to tie the rags
in tails to make the weight that keeps the flying
true. At first our kites will fall.
"Too long," she says. Then we untie some strips,
speechless against the wind
that whips her hair around her face,
and uneasy with her giddiness.

She stumbles often, even falls,
but smiles! in this field that is our father's place,
as if she rides a bubble rising through her,
a buoyancy that cannot gather
inside the kitchen walls.

"I was born on the equinox," she says
above the wind. It seems some light place,
this point on which the year is held—
balance of daylight and night.
(An egg will stand up by itself that day.)

Feet planted wide on rough clods,
Mother stands at last, the kite held firm
in air. Wind fills our open mouths. We rise
on tiptoe—*Fly!!* we want to scream. Gravity's string
slings a low curve toward earth. *Hold on.*
We know that tug, that lift, and we're afraid.
Her lightness frightens us. We crave
the familiar level of the kitchen floor.
She motions to us—hands across the line.

REFUSING A SPINAL

from *Heart Cake* (2000)

Six years old and pale that night, I was already experienced
in surgery—days in my father's clinic,
evenings when he let me ride along.
This night the cow stood quiet,
straining and her backside bulging as if to split. I screeched,
"Something's wrong!" I knew something had to be
sideways when she hadn't waited for Dad to cut
the clean window in her side and pull out
the soaking calf and neatly sew the edges
like two halves of a blanket
hem-stitched. Not this mix
of shit and straw, cobwebs greasy with old dust
the one raw bulb hanging brown
with fly droppings, her baby falling finally
onto the slime.

                        No wonder
the doctor said to me twenty-one years later
when I requested natural childbirth
(me in the chair and him behind the square
expanse of desk in the right
angles of his well-lit office, walls
blazing with white rectangles)—no wonder
he said to me that he could not understand
why some women wanted to have their babies
like cows in a barn. It was then
I saw again the liquid gleaming
globe of the cow's eye, the patient
rhythm squeezing her sides, the calm
heaving and the pale tips
of the calf's hoofs tender as tulips
as he left her, the swell
and rush of water, the newborn swimming
out into the half-dark of the barn.

                    I could not speak
in that white room, was sobbing so hard as I left
that my friend had to ask, "What's wrong? Did the baby die?"
I could see my father watching from the shadows,
hear the rough scraping of the cow's tongue,
regular as a heart urging the newborn
onto his feet, her sudden lowing,
so loud it startled me. My father
loved to blast our ignorance, loved to laugh
at any fear whiting our eyes. Running
his hand along the sharp ridge of her spine,
he said, "*This* is how things get born."

BARBARA KINGSOLVER
(April 8, 1955–)

Barbara Kingsolver was born in Annapolis, Maryland, but spent most of her childhood in eastern Kentucky. In 1977, she graduated, magna cum laude, from DePauw University in Greencastle, Indiana, with a degree in biology, then earned an M.S. in Ecology and Evolutionary Biology from the University of Arizona in 1981. After graduate school, Kingsolver worked at the University of Arizona as a technical writer and, later, worked as a freelance journalist, writing for magazines ranging from *Redbook* to *Smithsonian*. She is married to musician and biologist Steven Hopp and has two daughters.

Beset with insomnia while pregnant with her first child, Kingsolver spent her nights writing what became her first novel, *The Bean Trees*. On the day she brought her daughter home from the hospital, she got a phone call from New York with the news that her manuscript had been accepted for publication.

The Bean Trees received glowing reviews. Margaret Randall, in *The Women's Review of Books*, said the story was "propelled by a marvelous ear, a fast-moving humor and the powerful undercurrent of human struggle." Jack Butler in the *New York Times Book Review* felt the novel was "as richly connected as a fine poem, but reads like realism." Subsequent Kingsolver novels, as well as collections of short stories and essays, have been equally well received. In 2000, President Clinton awarded Kingsolver the National Humanities Medal.

Themes which run through Kingsolver's work include the tension between individualism and one's need for community, the search for justice in an often unjust world, and the need for reconciliation between humans and the natural world.

"The natural history and culture of southern Appalachia were the most appealing and defining elements of my childhood," says Kingsolver. "Southern Appalachia remains the region that feels like home to me, and although I've lived and worked in Arizona for twenty years, my family now spends a large part of each year back 'home' in southern Appalachia. To my mind, it's the only place on earth where the birds sound right, and people do too."

The opening scene of *The Bean Trees* introduces the reader to Missy Greer (who soon changes her name to Taylor Greer) a Kentucky high school student who's determined to escape the sort of life many of her classmates have heedlessly embraced.

The narrator in the scene from *Prodigal Summer* is Deanna Wolfe, a biologist who's employed as a United States Forest Service ranger in the Appalachian highlands. She has just encountered a hunter named Eddie Bondo who has asked her to accompany him on the trail.

OTHER SOURCES TO EXPLORE

PRIMARY

Novels: *Prodigal Summer* (2000), *The Poisonwood Bible: A Novel* (1998), *Pigs in Heaven* (1993), *Animal Dreams* (1991), *The Bean Trees* (1988). **Nonfiction:** *Last Stand: America's Virgin Lands* (2002) *Small Wonder* (2002), *High Tide in Tucson: Essays from Now or Never* (1995), *Holding the Line: Women in the Great Arizona Mine Strike of 1983* (1989). **Poetry:** *Another America/Otra America* (1992). **Short stories:** *Homeland and Other Stories* (1989).

SECONDARY

Contemporary Authors, Vol. 134, 284–89. "Messing with the Sacred: An Interview with Barbara Kingsolver," [transcription of KET, The Kentucky Network's 1997 *Signature: Barbara Kingsolver* program, produced & directed by Guy Mendes], *Appalachian Journal* 28:3 (spring 2001), 304–24. Amy Pense, "Barbara Kingsolver" [Interview], *Poets & Writers Magazine* (July/August 1993), 14–21. Meredith Sue Willis, "Barbara Kingsolver, Moving On," *Appalachian Journal* 22:1 (fall 1994), 78–86.

THE BEAN TREES (1988)

from Chapter One,
The One to Get Away

I have been afraid of putting air in a tire ever since I saw a tractor tire blow up and throw Newt Hardbine's father over the top of the Standard Oil sign. I'm not lying. He got stuck up there. About nineteen people congregated during the time it took for Norman Strick to walk up to the Courthouse and blow the whistle for the volunteer fire department. They eventually did come with the ladder and haul him down, and he wasn't dead but lost his hearing and in many other ways was never the same afterward. They said he overfilled the tire.

Newt Hardbine was not my friend, he was just one of the big boys who had failed every grade at least once and so was practically going on twenty in the sixth grade, sitting in the back and flicking little wads of chewed paper into my hair. But the day I saw his daddy up there like some old overalls slung over a fence, I had this feeling about what Newt's whole life was going to amount to, and I felt sorry for him. Before that exact moment I don't believe I had given much thought to the future.

My mama said the Hardbines had kids just about as fast as they could fall down the well and drown. This must not have been entirely true, since they were abundant in Pittman County and many survived to adulthood. But that was the general idea.

Which is not to say that we, me and Mama, were any better than Hardbines or had a dime to our name. If you were to look at the two of us, myself and Newt side by side in the sixth grade, you could have pegged us for brother and sister. And for all I ever knew of my own daddy I can't say we weren't, except for Mama swearing up and down that he was nobody I knew and was long gone besides. But we were cut out of basically the same mud, I suppose, just two more dirty-kneed kids scrapping to beat hell and trying to land on our feet. You couldn't have said, anyway, which one would stay right where he was, and which would be the one to get away.

Missy was what everyone called me, not that it was my name, but because when I was three supposedly I stamped my foot and told my own mother not to call me Marietta but *Miss* Marietta, as I had to call all the people including children in the houses where she worked Miss this or Mister that, and so she did from that day forward. Miss Marietta and later on just Missy.

The thing you have to understand is, it was just like Mama to do that.

When I was just the littlest kid I would go pond fishing of a Sunday and bring home the boniest mess of bluegills and maybe a bass the size of your thumb, and the way Mama would carry on you would think I'd caught the famous big lunker in Shep's Lake that old men were always chewing their tobacco and thinking about. "That's my big girl bringing home the bacon," she would say, and cook those things and serve them up like Thanksgiving for the two of us.

I loved fishing those old mud-bottomed ponds. Partly because she would be proud of whatever I dragged out, but also I just loved sitting still. You could smell leaves rotting into the cool mud and watch the Jesus bugs walk on the water, their four little feet making dents in the surface but never falling through. And sometimes you'd see the big ones, the ones nobody was ever going to hook, slipping away under the water like dark-brown dreams.

By the time I was in high school and got my first job and all the rest, including the whole awful story about Newt Hardbine which I am about to tell you, he was of course not in school anymore. He was setting tobacco alongside his half-crippled daddy and by that time had gotten a girl in trouble, too, so he was married. It was Jolene Shanks and everybody was a little surprised at her, or anyway pretended to be, but not at him. Nobody expected any better of a Hardbine.

But I stayed in school. I was not the smartest or even particularly outstanding but I was there and staying out of trouble and I intended to finish. This is not to say that I was unfamiliar with the back seat of a Chevrolet. I knew the scenery of Greenup Road, which we called Steam-It-Up Road, and I knew what a pecker looked like, and none of these sights had so far inspired me to get hogtied to a future as a tobacco farmer's wife. Mama always said barefoot and pregnant was not my style. She knew.

It was in this frame of mind that I made it to my last year of high school without event. Believe me in those days the girls were dropping by the wayside like seeds off a poppyseed bun and you learned to look at every day as a prize. You'd made it that far. By senior year there were maybe two boys to every one of us, and we believed it was our special reward when we got this particular science teacher by the name of Mr. Hughes Walter.

Now *him*. He came high-railing in there like some blond Paul McCartney, sitting on the desk in his tight jeans and his clean shirt sleeves rolled up just so, with the cuffs turned in. He made our country boys look like the hand-me-down socks Mama brought home, all full of their darns and mends. Hughes Walter was no Kentucky boy. He was from out of state, from some city college up north, which was why, everyone presumed, his name was backwards.

Not that I was moony over him, at least no more than the standard of the day, which was plain to see from the walls of the girls' bathroom. You could have painted a barn with all the lipstick that went into "H.W. enraptured forever" and things of that kind. This is not what I mean. But he changed my life, there is no doubt.

He did this by getting me a job. I had never done anything more interesting for a living than to help Mama with the for-pay ironing on Sundays and look after the brats of the people she cleaned for. Or pick bugs off somebody's bean vines for a penny apiece. But this was a real job at the Pittman County Hospital, which was one of the most important and cleanest places for about a hundred miles. Mr. Walter had a wife, Lynda, whose existence was ignored by at least the female portion of the high school but who was nevertheless alive and well, and was in fact one of the head nurses. She asked Hughes Walter if there was some kid in his classes that could do odd jobs down there after school and on Saturdays, and after graduation maybe it could work out to be a full-time thing, and he put the question to us just like that.

Surely, you'd think he would have picked one of the Candy Stripers, town girls with money for the pink-and-white uniforms and prissing around the bedpans on Saturdays like it was the holiest substance on God's green earth they'd been trusted to carry. Surely you would think he'd pick Earl Wickentot, who could dissect an earthworm without fear. That is what I told Mama on the back porch. Mama in her armhole apron in the caned porch chair and me on the stepstool, the two of us shelling out peas into a newspaper.

"Earl Wickentot my hind foot" is what Mama said. "Girl, I've seen you eat a worm whole when you were five. He's no better than you are, and none of them Candy Stripers either." Still, I believed that's who he would choose, and I told her so.

She went to the edge of the porch and shook a handful of pea hulls out of her apron onto the flowerbed. It was marigolds and Hot Tamale cosmos. Both Mama and I went in for bright colors. It was a family trait. At school it was a piece of cake to pick me out of a lineup of town girls in their beige or pink Bobbie Brooks matching sweater-and-skirt outfits. Medgar Biddle, who was once my boyfriend for three weeks including the homecoming dance, used to say that I dressed like an eye test. I suppose he meant the type they give you when you go into the army, to see if you're color blind, not the type that starts with the big E. He said it when we were breaking up, but I was actually kind of flattered. I had decided early on that if I couldn't dress elegant, I'd dress memorable.

Mama settled back into the cane chair and scooped up another apronful of peas. Mama was not one of these that wore tight jeans to their kids' softball games. She was older than that. She had already been through a lot of wild times before she had me, including one entire husband by the name of Foster Greer. He was named after Stephen Foster, the sweet-faced man in the seventh-grade history book who wrote "My Old Kentucky Home," but twenty-two years after naming him that, Foster Greer's mother supposedly died of a broken heart. He was famous for drinking Old Grand Dad with a gasoline funnel, and always told Mama never to pull anything cute like getting pregnant. Mama says trading Foster for me was the best deal this side of the Jackson Purchase.

She snapped about three peas to every one of mine. Her right hand twisted over and back as she snapped a little curl of string off the end of each pod and rolled out the peas with her thumb.

"The way I see it," she said, "a person isn't nothing more than a scarecrow. You, me, Earl Wickentot, the President of the United States, and even God Almighty, as far as I can see. The only difference between one that stands up good and one that blows over is what kind of a stick they're stuck up there on."

I didn't say anything for a while, and then I told her I would ask Mr. Walter for the job.

There wasn't any sound but Henry Biddle using a hay mower on his front yard, down the road, and our peas popping open to deliver their goods out into the world.

She said, "Then what? What if he don't know you're good enough for it?"

I said, "I'll tell him. If he hasn't already given it to a Candy Striper."

Mama smiled and said, "Even if."

PRODIGAL SUMMER (2000)

from Chapter 1

PREDATORS

The trail ended abruptly at the overlook. It never failed to take her breath away: a cliff face where the forest simply opened and the mountain dropped away at your feet, down hundreds of feet of limestone wall that would be a tough scramble even for a squirrel. The first time she'd come this way she was running, not just her usual fast walk but *jogging* along—what on earth was she thinking? And had nearly gone right over. Moving too fast was how she'd spent her first months in this job, it seemed, as if she and her long, unfeminine stride really *were* trying to leave the scene of a crime. That was two summers ago, and since that day her mind had returned a thousand times to the awful instant when she'd had to pull up hard, skinning her leg and face in the fall and yanking a sapling sourwood nearly out of the ground. So easily her life could have ended right here, without a blink or a witness. She replayed it too often, terrified by the frailty of that link like a weak trailer hitch connecting the front end of her life to all the rest. To *this*. Here was one more day she almost hadn't gotten, the feel of this blessed sun on her face and another look at this view of God's green earth laid out below them like a long green rumpled rug, the stitched-together fields and pastures of Zebulon Valley.

"That your hometown?" he asked.

She nodded, surprised he'd guessed it. They hadn't spoken for an hour or more as they'd climbed through the lacewinged afternoon toward this place, this view she now studied. There was the silver thread of Egg Creek; and there, where it came together like a thumb and four fingers with Bitter, Goose, Walker, and Black, was the town of Egg Fork, a loose arrangement of tiny squares that looked from this distance like a box of mints tossed on the ground. Her heart contained other perspectives on it, though: Oda Black's store, where Eskimo Pies lay under brittle blankets of frost in the cooler box; Little Brothers' Hardware with its jar of free lollipops on the dusty counter— a whole childhood in the palm of one valley. Right now she could see a livestock truck crawling slowly up Highway 6, halfway between Nannie Rawley's orchard and the farm that used to be hers and her dad's. The house wasn't visible from here, in any light, however she squinted.

"It's not *your* hometown, that's for sure," she said.

"How do you know?"

She laughed. "The way you talk, for one. And for two, there's not any Bondos in Zebulon County."

"You know every single soul in the county?"

"Every soul," she replied, "and his dog."

A red-tailed hawk rose high on an air current, calling out shrill, sequential rasps of raptor joy. She scanned the sky for another one. Usually when they spoke like that, they were mating. Once she'd seen a pair of them coupling on the wing, grappling and clutching each other and tumbling curvewinged through the air in hundred-foot death dives that made her gasp, though always they uncoupled and sailed outward and up again just before they were bashed to death in senseless passion.

"What's the name of that place?"

She shrugged. "Just the valley. Zebulon Valley, after this mountain." He would laugh at Egg Fork if she declared its name, so she didn't.

"You never felt like leaving?" he asked.

"Do you see me down there?"

He put a hand above his eyes like a storybook Indian and pretended to search the valley. "No."

"Well, then."

"I mean leaving this country. These mountains."

"I did leave. And came back. Not all that long ago."

"Like the mag-no-lia warblers."

"Like them."

He nodded. "Boy, I can see why."

Why she'd left, or why she'd come back—which could he see? She wondered how this place would seem to his outsider's eye. She knew what it *sounded* like; she'd learned in the presence of city people never to name her hometown out loud. But how did it look, was it possible that it wasn't beautiful? At the bottom of things, it was only a long row of little farms squeezed between this mountain range and the next one over, old Clinch Peak with his forests rumpled up darkly along his long, crooked spine. Between that ridge top and this one, nothing but a wall of thin blue air and a single hawk.

$\mathscr{L}$ISA $\mathscr{K}$OGER

(September 6, 1953–)

One of three children of Anne Vannoy Jones, a teacher and homemaker, and Eldred Jones, a welder, Lisa Koger grew up in Gilmer County, West Virginia. She married Jerry L. Koger, an engineer, in 1974, the same year that she graduated with honors from West Virginia University with a bachelor's degree in social work. She studied journalism at the University of Tennessee, earning a master's degree in 1979, and an M.F.A. from the Iowa Writers' Workshop at the University of Iowa in 1989.

She has received awards for her writing from James Michener and the Copernicus Society of America (1989), the Kentucky Arts Council (1999, 1996, 1995), the Kentucky Foundation for Women (1987), and the Appalachian Writing Association (1988, 1987). Her first collection of short stories, *Farlanburg Stories*, was a Barnes & Noble Discover Great New Writers selection in 1990.

A freelance writer since 1980, Koger is best known for her short fiction. Having worked as a newspaper journalist and as a teacher of creative writing in workshops across the country, she is currently at work on a novel. She lives with her husband and two children in Somerset, Kentucky.

When her first published story appeared in *Seventeen* magazine in June, 1985, she remembers, "a familiar voice inside my head told me that the only reason they'd accepted my story was that their regular writers had gone on vacation or had died." Though she had worked on it for three years, she was dissatisfied with it, as she reports she always is when she reads her published work.

She explains the importance of her home in her work, set in the rural southern Appalachian Mountains: "I suspect that trying to separate a writer's work from his background is a little like trying to separate a turtle from its shell. . . . Remove home and its influence from my back, and I will have lost not just shelter but an essential part of me. I grew up in a community where people had meat on their bones, physically and spiritually. As a reader I like fiction with heft and heart rather than fiction that is fashionably thin. I like 'necessary' fiction, stories that feel as if they were born because they had to be born, to give life to a character who had begun to kick and thrash about because he knew his incubation period was up."

Stories from *Farlanburg Stories* appeared originally in *Seventeen*, *Kennesaw Review*, *American Voice*, and *Ploughshares*. The ten-story collection won acclaim from Anne Rivers Siddons, Lee Smith, Mark Childress, and Madison Smartt Bell, among others, who praised her storytelling skill, wit, humor, and compassion for her characters.

In these scenes from "Extended Learning," Della Sayer relishes spending time with her grandson, T. Barry, and his parents who have come for a summer visit.

OTHER SOURCES TO EXPLORE

PRIMARY

Short stories: *Farlanburg Stories* (1990). **Autobiographical essay:** "Writing in the Smoke-House" in *The Confidence Woman: 26 Women Writers* (1991), ed. Eve Shelnutt, 353–66; rpt. in *Bloodroot* (1998), ed. Joyce Dyer, 154–66.

SECONDARY

Atlanta Journal and Constitution (15 July 1990). *Charleston Gazette* (26 August 1990). *Chattanooga Times* (16 July 1990). *Chicago Tribune* (29 July 1990). Mark Childress, review of *Farlanburg Stories*, *New York Times Book Review* (August 19, 1990), 16. *Cleveland Plain Dealer* (19 August 1990). *Contemporary Authors* (1991), Vol. 133, 216–17. Joyce Dyer, "Lisa Koger," in *Bloodroot*, 153. *Newsday* (12 August 1990). *Philadelphia Inquirer* (22 July 1990).

FARLANBURG STORIES (1990)

from Extended Learning

At eleven o'clock the next morning, Frank and Marjorie were still asleep. The sun had completed half its arc across the sky, and Della's dogs, two male mongrels, had already lumbered off to find shade. Silvervine, the cat, just returned from hunting, sat licking her paws and sunning herself on the walk.

Della had been up since five. When she was younger, she used to crave sleep. She dreamed of going to bed before dark and nesting there until noon the next day, but now that she had the opportunity, she had lost the inclination, which was just as well, she supposed, considering she had a grandson to attend to and a turn of light bread to make.

T. Barry sat beside her on the back porch steps, hands on his knees, a wrinkled bag full of hickory nuts in his lap. Della had gathered the nuts last fall from the big shagbarks that lined the road below her house and had stored them in a box on the top shelf of her cupboard until the insides were sweet and chewy, the shells the color of clean sand. She had saved them for this occasion, and at the end of the week, she planned to send what was left home with T. Barry with the hope that each time he cracked one, he'd remember the fun they'd had. She scooped a handful from the bag, tapped one with her hammer, then dropped the kernel into her grandson's open mouth. "So," she said. "Tell me again what the T. stands for. It's Timothy or Terrence or Tutwyler. My memory's not as good as it used to be, you understand."

The boy chewed steadily and looked at Della out of clear, deep-set gray eyes. He was a quiet kid with thick, blond hair cut so his head appeared peanut-shaped and difficult to balance. His arms and legs were remarkably unscarred and new looking, as though he hadn't figured out what to do with himself from the neck down. "It stands for Thurman," he said, shyly. "You know that."

Della nodded and cracked another nut, this time for herself. "Maybe," she said, "and maybe I just wanted to see if *you* did. I knew a man once, a pitiful fellow, who got kicked in the head by a horse and couldn't remember his own name. He went crazy trying to remember it, so they locked him in a corncrib and kept him there till he died."

T. Barry frowned and studied Della's crib. The rock supports at the two front corners had crumbled during the years, allowing the north side of the building to sit down, but the south side was still stable and several feet off the ground. Della liked her corncrib, though she had to admit it was hazardous. It reminded her of the hotrods the young boys drove through town.

"I don't believe that," said T. Barry. "It's against the law to lock some-one in a corncrib."

"They abolished that law," said Della. "I guess you're not familiar with the Corncrib Act."

Behind them, inside the kitchen, Snapper whined and dug at the screen. Della had walked him earlier and would have let him out to run in the yard, but Marjorie had forbidden it. "Not as long as your dogs are home," she'd said. "Fleas."

T. Barry bit down hard on an unshelled nut. "What's 'abolish'?"

"It means to do away with, to get rid of. Don't worry about it though. I still think you're plenty smart."

"I'm in the E.L.P."

"Sorry," said Della. "I didn't know." She tilted her head and looked at her grandson through her bifocals. "What's the E.L.P.?"

"Extended Learning Program. It's a thing for smart kids at my school."

"Oh," said Della. "Are you smart?"

T. Barry shrugged. "They say I am."

"They say a lot of things," said Della.

"I'm smart enough not to believe everything you tell me. Mama and Daddy say you have a bad habit of making things up."

Della laughed. "I don't know why grown-ups do that."

"Do what?"

"Try to keep things from kids." Della shook her head. "Fifty cents says they'll tell you there's no such thing as the Corncrib Act."

"I'll ask them," said T. Barry, rising.

"Go ahead. I guess I'd better hurry inside and fix their breakfast. But I must say I was having fun sitting out here cracking nuts and talking to you."

T. Barry rolled a nut with the toe of his shoe, then sat down again. "Is it true about that crazy man? I want you to tell me the truth."

"Of course it is," said Della.

"Tell me his name, then."

"Can't do that."

"Why not?"

"If he didn't know it, how do you expect me to?"

The day turned out to be a scorcher. By three o'clock that afternoon, the temperature had reached the mid-nineties, and the cows had wandered off the hills and stood under the apple trees below the house, chewing cuds and flicking matted tails at the flies.

Della's house had no air-conditioning, but she kept fans in most of the windows. On humid days, the only really cool spot on the place was the cellar because it was partially under the hill, and occasionally, Della would pull a chair in there and relax or take a flashlight and admire the variety of colors in her canned fruits and vegetables. Earlier, she had mentioned the cellar to Frank and Marjorie, but neither of them took her up on it, so she assumed they weren't too uncomfortable with the heat. She had also suggested they all get in her car and go for a drive to enjoy the countryside, maybe get an ice cream cone, her treat, but no one had seemed especially wild about that idea.

"Don't think you have to entertain us," said Frank. "You just go on and do your thing, and so will we, and that way we can all relax."

"I *am* relaxed," said Della. "I just thought you might enjoy getting out and seeing the sights."

"I grew up around here, Mom. Remember?"

"Things change," said Della. "You've been gone a long time."

Della stood in her kitchen, rolling and cutting egg noodles. She had the radio on to help pass the time. Frank was asleep, Marjorie was reading, and T. Barry lay stretched out on the living room floor doing his homework. It was their first full day of vacation, and Della wanted it to be memorable and exciting.

"Homework?" she had said when Marjorie told T. Barry it was time to get his books. "It's summer."

"He takes a test in three weeks when school starts. He has to have a high score if he wants to stay in the E.L.P. That's a program for gifted kids at his school."

Della looked at her daughter-in-law over the top of her glasses.

"He enjoys it," said Marjorie. "At home, he'd much rather be inside reading or fooling with his computer than outside with the other kids playing in the street."

"You think that's normal?"

"What's normal?" said Marjorie.

"Homework," Della said to herself as she picked up a big knife and sliced off sections from the roll of noodle dough. Frank had never done homework during the summer, and as far as school went, he had certainly done all right.

At the moment, he was snoring in the front porch swing. He had eaten his breakfast a little after noon and had gone upstairs and prowled through some boxes of old books. He was asleep again when Della went to check on him at two. The noodles were for him; Della hoped they might enliven him. When he was a boy, his favorite dish had been a concoction of homemade egg noodles and beans. In those days, he liked to fish and hunt, and he spent hours walking the creek banks or just wandering over the hills. Back then, he'd come home with burrs in his socks and a craving for noodles, and Della had wound up fixing them once or twice a week. Now, he insisted they weren't worth the trouble it took to make them. Della loved her son dearly and was proud of his accomplishments, but there were moments when she was struck by the unmotherly thought that, at some point, he had turned into one of the most boring people she knew.

He had done well in high school and had earned a scholarship to the state university. Four years had turned into six, six into ten; more than half his life had been spent in school. He had knocked off all the rough edges, but in the process, something else had been knocked off, too. Though he could tell her there was a statistically significant correlation between canopy tree mortality and drought-induced stress, he could not tell her how to save her wild chestnut trees. And Della was surprised and, secretly, a little disappointed the first time she discovered that, unlike his father, he could not recognize a white oak suitable for veneer from one destined for crossties.

Neither she nor Royce had any education beyond high school, and Royce had always been proud that his son was smart and had done so well at books. "It's the way the world's goin'," he had said when Frank finished his Ph.D. "Gettin' an education is the ticket to a better life." There was a slightly wistful tone to his voice that Della hadn't heard before.

"Oh, I don't know about that," she said. "I don't have an education, and I'm happy with my life." She laughed. "Why, I don't know as I could stand it if it got any better."

Royce smiled, patted her shoulder, and said, "Some are just easier satisfied than others," which caused Della to wonder for weeks whether he knew something about their life that she didn't.

Della lifted the noodle sections, combing with her fingers until the yellow strips unwound and lay like a pile of shorn curls. Through the kitchen window, she had a clear view of Marjorie, who was stretched out in a lawn chair in the backyard. She was a good visitor, really, no more trouble than the cows. She did not hang around the kitchen and get in the way by trying to be useful, nor did she rattle on about the food and interrupt Della's work by asking for recipes. All she wanted was to be left alone with her book, and occasionally, she would look up and inquire whether there was any iced tea.

She was Frank's wife, and Della wanted to like her, but Frank's wife or not, she wasn't very lively, and Della often wondered how she worked up enough energy to pull a tooth. Della recalled having a tooth pulled by a dentist, a Dr. Weeble, when she was a child, and what she remembered most about the experience was not the pain or the blood but the look on Dr. Weeble's face as he rolled up his sleeves, rubbed his hands together, and told her to say, "Aaahhh." It was an eager, alive look, one that said, "I am *passionate* about teeth!" To be good at anything, you had to feel passionate about it, Della had always believed, the way she felt about the people she loved, the way Royce had felt about trees.

"If you had only ten minutes left on earth, how would you spend them?" she once asked Royce, and, without hesitation, he told her he'd go to the woods, lie on his back, and look at trees. At the time, she was hurt because he hadn't said he'd spend his last moments with her. Looking back on it, she thought she recognized a rare, uncalculating honesty and a genuine love of nature in his answer, and she wished he were around to instill a little of that love in their grandson.

When she had finished with the noodles, Della washed her hands and tip-toed into the living room. T. Barry lay on his stomach, studying. Seeing him like that took Della back almost thirty years. He looked so much like Frank from certain angles.

"Psstt," she said.

He glanced up.

"You don't look like you're having much fun," she said. "Are you having fun at Grandma Della's house?"

He wrinkled his nose. "You've got something awful in your carpet," he said, pointing at a dark spot in the pile.

Della knelt and examined it. "That's not something awful," she said. "It's a mashed raisin. Your better brand of carpets come that way."

T. Barry looked skeptical.

"It's true," said Della. "The manufacturers put little pieces of food in there so the people who buy the carpets will have something to fall back on in case of hard times."

T. Barry put his face closer to the raisin and peered at it. "You're making that up," he said. "I bet it doesn't say that in any carpet books."

"Just because it's not written down somewhere doesn't mean it's not true. Grandma Della loves T. Barry. True or false?"

He shrugged. "True."

"See," said Della. "You believe that without reading it." She untied her apron and took it off. "Are you finished with your homework?"

He shook his head.

"Too bad. I was looking for someone to take a walk with me."

"I've got to do my math," said T. Barry.

Della picked at the raisin. "What's nine plus nine?"

He rolled his eyes and looked insulted. "That's easy. Eighteen."
Della held up her hand. "Ding-a-ling-a-ling."
"What's that?"
"A bell," she said. "School's out. You already know more than me. . . ."

CATHERINE LANDIS

(June 9, 1956–)

~

Novelist Catherine Landis is a native of Chattanooga, Tennessee. After graduating from Davidson College in 1978 with a B.A. in English, she spent several years as a newspaper reporter in New Bern, North Carolina, before moving on to a job in the promotions department at Kentucky Educational Television (KET). She resides in Knoxville, Tennessee, with her husband and two sons.

Landis's first novel, *Some Days There's Pie*, was published in 2002, to critical acclaim. Fred Chappell wrote, "With its strongly engaging characters, suspenseful story, and limpid, evocative style, Catherine Landis' novel is first-rate. . . . Landis should take pride—and prizes." Reviewer Pam Kingsbury described the fried pies sold at the local hardware store in the novel as "a mouth-watering metaphor for the surprises of life in a small Southern town."

"I consider myself more of a re-writer than a writer," says Landis. "The first draft of any project is merely a tool for writing . . . the real writing unfolds only when I dig deeper into the material. . . . One minute I feel like a genius, the next, a deluded pretender. I have found both 'voices' unhelpful and have learned to tell both to, 'Sit down and be quiet.' The only 'voice' I listen to is the one that tells me, 'Okay, it's not right, but here's how to make it better.'"

Landis says the music of the region has been a major influence on her work. "Writing my first novel, I found that, when I got stuck, the way to 'unstick' was by listening to this music. It gave me voice, rhythm, tone, humor and an efficient way of telling a story. I sometimes am amused to hear people deliberate at length on what makes Southern writing. I want to say to them, 'Listen to the way I talk and ask yourself, what else would you expect?'"

The opening chapter of *Some Days There's Pie* is set in the North Carolina mountains, where Ruth Ritchie, a young woman searching for herself, has been befriended by the aging Rose.

OTHER SOURCES TO EXPLORE

PRIMARY

Novel: *Some Days There's Pie* (2002)

SECONDARY

Pam Kingsbury, "A sweet and sassy slice of life," http://www.bookpage.com/0205bp/fiction/some_days_there's_pie.html. *Library Journal* (15 March 2002), 105.

SOME DAYS THERE'S PIE (2002)

Chapter 1,

ON MY WAY TO THE
REST OF MY LIFE

Rose is dead. I am sorry for it but not surprised; she's been dying for years now. I found her lying on the roll-away in Room 12 of the Little Swiss Inn in Mount Claire, North Carolina. It's just like Rose to have left me the double bed. *I don't want to be any trouble,* was what she said all the time, but there's a lot of people who say that kind of thing who are loads of trouble. Rose never was.

We had been driving since that morning, starting in Lawsonville, where it was hot. It was not hot in Mount Claire. It was chilly, and I had already started worrying that this damp air was not going to do a thing for her but make her sicker. We were on our way to Texas because Rose was born in Texas, in a little town on the Gulf of Mexico, to a mother who claimed to have a little Cajun in her and a daddy who ran a printing press, which was why Rose swore she had ink in her blood. Cajun or ink, either one could account for a lot. When I met her, she was seventy-nine years old but looked older, bent over like the letter C, which made it so she peered up at you when she talked, like a turtle out of its shell, craning its neck to see the sky. Her skin was wrinkled and pale, and her voice had gone rusty from too many cigarettes. Rose claimed she had aged early, but her hair was still the color of mountain clay; she was named for it, red on the day she was born, the only one in the family, Red Rose.

The Little Swiss Inn had no restaurant, and I had gone looking for supper. "You want to come?" I had asked Rose.

"No, Ruthie," she said. "I think I'll just lie down for a minute."

"I'll bring you back something."

"I'm not all that hungry right now, thank you."

"What do you want?"

"Whatever you get, hon. You decide."

I let it go at that, because I knew she was telling the truth. Rose did not care about food. She said she never did, and I believed her, because food and clothes and houses and all those things that keep a body together were things Rose never thought about, which can be an admirable quality in a person, but sometimes I wondered if it didn't make her do dotty things, like when she left half-eaten sandwiches on other people's desks, or buttoned her shirts up crooked. Her house reminded me of Durwood's, the hardware store next door to where I grew up, which was a mess, partly because that's what happens when something gets old, when it moves through time holding on to things, not because some things are worth holding on to, but because it takes too long to sort through them. Durwood had boxes of Christmas ornaments older than me on the shelves, but he saw no reason to buy more until those were gone. Year by year they had dwindled until there came a time when nobody wanted to hang anything that old on their Christmas tree. So there they sat, next to the hammers, which were mixed in with screwdrivers, which were mixed in with drill bits, which were mixed in with extension cords. If you were wanting nails, you had to scoop them out of a wooden keg and weigh them on a rusting scale, and there were cats everywhere. I worked over there at Durwood's, selling his wife's homemade fried pies, something you might not expect to find in a hardware store. People would come in wanting plumbing fixtures and a pie; I never got over that.

What you expected to find in a place like Durwood's was a potbellied stove in the middle of the floor, where men and near-men gathered to commiserate over the state of the world or the state of their lives, sometimes without words, just a look between fellows who know you and know what you mean. I used to imagine my daddy in a place like that. I used to imagine he would wink at me from across the store as if right there in Durwood's was where we belonged. I had no way of knowing if he was that kind of man, but that's how I pictured him.

Now, I never saw evidence of any such a stove in Durwood's, which tells you to look out; I'm likely to blow things up bigger than they are; but this much is true: Durwood's was a place where people went for more than what they could buy. You can go down to Kmart for a box of nails if that's all you want.

As for Rose's house, if I had suggested we straighten it up, she would have looked at me as if I'd gone crazy. Most everything she owned was given to her anyway, which was one thing about Rose; if somebody gave her something, she did not throw it away, so there were odd things, like dead house plants, and seashells sitting in little piles of sand, and the two Chinese dolls on top of the refrigerator, one jade green, the other robin's-egg blue, whose heads bobbed up and down when you opened the door. Sometimes I wanted to shake her. I did not care what she wore or how she kept her house, but I hated that other people did. They had made her into a town character, the eccentric old lady, "old" being the key word, as if there is a point you can cross and lose your place in the world. Everybody loved Rose, but no one paid any attention to her anymore. People talked to her the way you talk to a child. They acted as if she were already dead.

The Little Swiss Inn was surrounded by woods with no sign of a restaurant anywhere. The office was in a trailer next to the highway, the front stoop covered with bright green indoor/outdoor carpet. I had to pry open the metal screen door and, instead of a bell, a tinny music box played the first two lines of "On Top of Old Smoky." I found the manager in the office flipping through a model-rocket catalogue. He was a large man who wore glasses too tiny for his head, and he did not look up when I walked in.

"So," I said. "Where in the world is Big Swiss?"

He frowned, stuck a finger in the page to save his place, then looked up. He did not laugh.

"Any chance of getting something to eat around here?" I asked.

"Sam's Deli. About a quarter mile down the road. They got pizza, too." He said I could walk. "No problem."

A sidewalk followed the road through the woods, crossed a large creek, then led to the town of Mount Claire. I passed a couple of gas stations, a 7-Eleven, a bank, and a post office before reaching the main part of town, where crowds of people were dressed in shorts and golf shirts, their children wearing T-shirts that said *Hilton Head* and *Grand Caymen Island* and *Ski Aspen*. They were buying corncob pipes and bird feeders and wooden bear statuettes with *Mount Claire* burned into their sides. I passed by stores that sold shuck dolls made by mountain people, which was probably true, if you were talking about the mountains of China. There was a snack shop making out like there's something so special about ice cream you had to pay three dollars a scoop to find out what it was. I didn't linger. I found Sam's Deli and bought two turkey subs and chips then stopped by the 7-Eleven. I got us some Cokes and a couple of candy bars: Butterfinger for Rose, a Bit-O-Honey for myself.

I had not wanted to stop in Mount Claire. My idea was to keep going, drive on past sundown into the night, eating up the miles in darkness. I liked that vision of myself, tough night driver, cigarettes and coffee keeping me awake, a sad song on the radio. My car did not have a radio, but that's beside the point. What I wanted was to feel like an outlaw, which was not so far-fetched since me and Rose had snuck away from Lawsonville without telling anybody. I wanted it to be me and Rose and the truck drivers and their headlights and the night sky and the sound of my wheels going faster than the speed limit, but Rose insisted she had to rest, so we stopped. If we hadn't, Mount Claire, North Carolina, would have stayed forever a tourist town I passed through once, a dot on a map that meant nothing to me.

When I got back to the room, Rose was lying on her back as if she were sleeping, but dead people don't really look like they are sleeping. There's something wrong.

"Rose?"

The only light in the room came from what spilled through the blinds, throwing stripes across the floor. They fell across the roll-away and Rose. I sat down next to her and held her hand. It was still warm, enough to make you think for a minute anyway, that what was happening wasn't really happening.

"Oh, Rose."

I sat there for a long time.

I don't know how long, but the first thing I remember noticing was the sack from Sam's Deli. I was holding it without knowing I was holding it, when all of a sudden I looked and remembered it was there. Then I understood; Rose was dead. More than the way her arm was stiff when I shook it, more than the pulse I could not find; this simple fact: Rose was never going to eat that sandwich.

I did not know a lot of dead people, unless you want to count my daddy, but I did not remember him. I knew Marianne Johnson, a girl from school who was killed in a head-on collision with a lumber truck when she was sixteen. She had a locker near mine and once had asked to borrow my hairbrush, and I had said no. Marianne had hair that fell down her back like black satin ribbons. The strange thing was, after she died I found myself thinking about her all the time. It came to me at odd moments, like a dream that lingers in the back of your mind long past the time it should have faded away. I see the man who drove the truck. He is standing at his kitchen counter, eating a honey bun. He burns his mouth on coffee, which he drinks from a plastic travel cup as he walks out the door. It is dark still. When he pulls onto the highway I see a single stream of light, heading east. Then I see Marianne. She gets out of bed, drops her nightgown on the floor, gets dressed, and combs her satin hair. She eats nothing before getting into her small, white car, the envy of those of us who did not get cars for our sixteenth birthday. I see a single stream of light heading west, and I wonder. Was there a line between them, drawn before they were born, a line they raced along until that morning, or was it, simply, that one of them looked down to change the radio?

The part that gets to me is the nightgown. Because there is something about dropping your nightgown on the floor that says, I'm coming back.

I'm coming back.

But she didn't. Marianne Johnson was never going to pick up her nightgown, and Rose. She was never going to eat that sandwich.

It was not fair that Rose had died, and not just to her but to me, too. I am not going to pretend otherwise, because it is the truth. No matter what happens to somebody else, you are still thinking about what's happening to you, and what had happened to me was that the first purely noble thing I had ever done in my life had just come to an end.

$\mathscr{L}$ILY $\mathscr{M}$AY $\mathscr{L}$EDFORD
(March 17, 1917–July 14, 1985)

Lily May Ledford, author, musician, and storyteller, was a founding member of the Coon Creek Girls, the country's first all-woman string band. The seventh of fourteen children born to an eastern Kentucky farm family, Ledford's childhood was filled with traditional mountain activities—ginseng digging, berry picking, fodder pulling, and making music.

Ledford learned to play a groundhog hide banjo when she was seven. A couple of years later, she traded everything she owned (an old flashlight, a sweater, a sling-shot, and a box of crayons) for a broken fiddle. She whittled new parts for it, then fashioned a bow out of a willow stick and hair from the tail of the family's plow horse.

In 1935, Ledford auditioned for and won a regular job with a Chicago radio show, the WLS National Barn Dance, where she played fiddle, banjo, and guitar. In 1937, the Coon Creek Girls, composed of Lily May, her sister Rosie, and two other female musicians, was formed. Eleanor Roosevelt invited the group to the White House in 1939 to play for the King and Queen of England. The group performed together until 1957.

In 1968, Lily May was "rediscovered" at the Newport National Folk Festival, and from then on was in demand as a solo performer at folk festivals throughout the United States and Canada. Shortly before her death, she was awarded a National Heritage Fellowship, the nation's highest honor for traditional artists.

Ledford's brief autobiography, *Coon Creek Girl*, describes her childhood in Kentucky's Red River Gorge as well as her life as a musician during the early days of radio.

OTHER SOURCES TO EXPLORE

PRIMARY

Autobiography: *Coon Creek Girl* (1980).

SECONDARY

Ellesa Clay High, *Past Titan Rock: Journeys into an Appalachian Valley* (1984), 67–106, 169–83. Ellesa Clay High, "A Tribute to Lily May Ledford," *Appalachian Heritage* 14:2 (spring 1986), 5–6.

COON CREEK GIRL (1980)
from Chapter II

Off on my first train trip to my first job in radio at nineteen, I had with me my home-made fiddle case, shaped like a coffin, and my pasteboard suitcase packed with odds and ends of home-made clothing, hand-me-downs and borrowed clothes (everybody had tried to help me out). I had about $9 in my pocket.

Mr. Lair [talent manager at WLS] greeted me warmly, and as we started on our drive straight to WLS, he began to tell me of his plans for a barn dance of his own, to originate in Cincinnati, Ohio, and about his plans for an all-girl band of which I could be the leader. He told me of a couple of girls he had auditioned and was saving till the right time came to bring together this act. He thought it would all happen within a year and again warned me against signing any kind of contract with WLS. We reached the station on Washington Boulevard about a mile or two from the Loop and its rattle and clatter of elevated trains, buses, street cars and thousands of people of every race, creed and color, all talking and gesturing in all kinds of languages.

Oh how frightening, yet how exciting it all was. "Lord have Mercy," I said, "Mr. Lair, I'll never learn how to get to and from work." He then told me that he and Mrs. Lair had already planned to keep me in their home for a while. How grateful I was when I heard this. I felt among friends. Mr. Lair had briefed most everybody about me, and as we walked into the station a tall gentleman was introduced to me, a Kentuckian, Red Foley! I grew to depend upon this gentle-natured person, as a defender against the teasing I later was to receive from the others. I finally got to know the others and liked them very much too, for if they hadn't liked me they wouldn't have bothered to tease me about the way I talked and my old-fashioned music.

Most everyone was at the station each day and all day when not on the road with a show. The heads of WLS, said to be the greatest hillbilly station on the map, encouraged this. Many rehearsal rooms were provided, along with a billiard room, and a rec room for off-hours. All this resulted in a family atmosphere all over the 4 or 5 floors. The station was owned and sponsored by *Prairie Farmer*, a weekly magazine that was published on one of the lower stories.

After I had met everybody on our floor, including the many office workers with their smiling welcome, I was led on a tour of all the other floors, and oh Lord! so much of everything and so many nice people to take in, in an hour's time. Gradually my fears and apprehensions melted away and I began to feel proud and sure of myself. More than once Mr. Lair remarked that I had shown poise that no one would have thought a mountain girl could have possessed.

. . .

One night on the barn dance, a little boy was brought out on stage with an old fiddle. He was wearing shabby clothes and I watched, almost in tears (he looked so much like my brother Coyen) to see what they would do with him. They interviewed him briefly and put him on to play, calling for back-up guitars. That little boy rared back and just made that fiddle talk with a couple of fast breakdowns. By then I was crying a little. The MC called me up, introduced me to the boy, and asked me what did I think of this little fiddler, hitch-hiking from way down in Southern Indiana. I was putting my arm around the boy's shoulder and starting to tell him how proud I was of him when I burst into uncontrollable crying, tears streaming and splashing on the stage. I had to turn and hurry off stage, embarrassed to death, and get to the dressing room and cry it out. When I went back on stage, now composed, Red, Lulu Belle and a few others were crying. I was neither scolded nor teased about this. Everyone at home who had been listening in wrote letters to cheer me up, realizing that I was homesick. Poor old Mama dressed a chicken and sent it, thinking that it being winter it would reach me without spoiling (it did spoil). She also sent a few jars of blackberry jam, molasses and pickles. Bless her heart. She had been touched deeply by my crying spell on the air and I'll never forget her for it, for she was a person that believed in no pampering. All my life she had scolded and lectured me saying, "Toughen up! If the rest can make it you can! You let people lead you around by the nose too much!"

By Christmas of 1936, I had gained a good solid popularity with my listeners, and also the friendship of my co-workers. Patsy Montana was one of my best friends, always wearing her leather western costume and big white hat, taking me home with her. Dolly and Millie did the same, and Lulu Belle to her nice apartment, for a good home cooked meal. I also remember the hospitality of Red and Eva.

I shopped and shopped for Christmas, for the family and for the "Skiddies," as I loved them and owed them so much for their great help in the past. I ran my legs off riding street cars and "L's" to the post office, mailing huge packages. Then the fans started mailing stuff, home made cookies, candies, roses, clothes, cosmetics, and finally one that tore the mail room all to pieces. A live crated possum had arrived for me, a baby one. Rev. Sharpe was greatly alarmed but consented to let me keep it. It wouldn't allow itself to be petted, nor would it eat anything I brought to it. It just huddled up and grinned. How I longed for persimmons, favorite food of possums. He finally got out of the crate and crawled into the coal bin and got all black and filthy. Mr. Lair appeared, to take it and donate it to the zoo, so his whole family and I went to the zoo, enjoyed it and donated the possum. I was given a check for $5 for the "donation of one o'possum." I kept this check for a long time before cashing it. I wish I'd kept it. To this day I believe that the sender of the possum was only trying to relieve my homesickness.

GRACE LUMPKIN
(March 3, 1891–March 23, 1980)

Grace Lumpkin usually gave 1900 or 1901 as the year of her birth, though her younger sister, born in 1897, says that Lumpkin was 88 when she died in 1980. Born in Milledgeville, Georgia, to Annette Caroline Morris Lumpkin and William Wallace Lumpkin, a Civil War veteran, she was the ninth of eleven children. Around the turn of the century, the family lived in Columbia, South Carolina. Moving to a farm in Richland County, South Carolina, around 1910, gave Lumpkin firsthand experiences with sharecroppers.

In 1911, after graduating from a teacher's training program at Brenau College in Gainesville, Georgia, Lumpkin spent time in France, taught in a rural school, worked as a home demonstration agent, and spent summers in the North Carolina mountains. She also worked as a secretary for the YWCA and lived in New York City, where she studied writing at Columbia University and became involved in left-wing politics.

Her first novel, *To Make My Bread*, won the Maxim Gorky Award for best labor novel of the year. Chronicling events she had witnessed—mountain people leaving farms for textile mills—it begins in the North Carolina mountains in 1900 and ends with union activities in the 1929 Gastonia strike.

Her second novel also concerns proletarian issues of race, social justice, and union activity. Though a complex web of personal and public events eventually turned Lumpkin away from Marxism and toward more conservative political and religious ideas in her subsequent work, her first novel remains a significant literary contribution to American literature. The principal archive of her papers is in Columbia, South Carolina, at the University of South Carolina.

This excerpt from the first chapter of *To Make My Bread* introduces John McClure, whose difficult birth in a one-room cabin is traumatic for the whole family.

Other Sources to Explore

Primary

Novels: *Full Circle* (1962), *The Wedding* (1939), *A Sign for Cain* (1935), *To Make My Bread* (1932). **Short stories:** "The Treasure," *O. Henry Memorial Award Prize Stories* (1940). "White Man—A Story," *New Masses* (September 1927), 7–8.

Secondary

C. Michael Smith, "Grace Lumpkin," *Southern Writers: A Biographical Dictionary* (1979), 287–88. Suzanne Sowinska, "Introduction," *To Make My Bread* (1995), vii–xliii.

TO MAKE MY BREAD (1932)

from Chapter 1

Granpap Kirkland and Emma McClure's two sons had ventured out to find the steer and cow. When they did not return Emma stood outside the door and screamed to them. She could not stand long against the strong wind. It blew her against the wall of the cabin with the force of a strong man's fist. Leaning over she held to the woodblock that served as a step and kept up intermittent screams until the others returned. They came crawling on hands and knees, and she did not see them until they were right on her, and Granpap called into her ear that they were safe.

She did not learn until later that the steer and cow were lost, for as soon as her anxiety for Granpap and the boys was over, Emma felt a first sharp pain and knew that her time had come. Inside the cabin with the door shut she crouched over the fire trying to get some of the warmth of it into her body. The icy wind had reached the very marrow of her bones.

The hickory log fire shone on her twisted face, and on the form that protruded from her belly in an oval shape. It seemed as if the child in her womb had already been born and was lying wrapped up in her lap asleep.

On the floor at Emma's right eight-year-old Kirk lay and stared into the fire, and between them in a poplar log cradle Bonnie, the youngest, whimpered in her sleep. On the other side of the fire, Basil, who was a year older than Kirk, sat against the chimney, his legs spread out before him on the floor.

The wind sniffed at the doors and blew gusts of icy breath through the cracks of the log cabin. Clothes hanging to pegs on the walls flapped out into the room, making strange balancing movements. If the wind died down for a moment they suddenly collapsed against the wall as a man does who gives up the struggle to keep on his drunken legs.

In the half darkness of the small space between the circle of firelight and the end wall of the cabin, John Kirkland walked the floor. His boots stamped on the split-log flooring regularly, hesitating when he turned at the wall and again when he turned just behind Emma's chair.

Granpap Kirkland's life had been full of varied experiences. A fight with a she bear had left three long scars across his right cheek, and there was a scar on his side from a wound received in battle. He was not a fearful man by nature. But he had known fear and dread in the last few moments since he knew that some time in the night he must deliver Emma of her child.

Emma instructed Granpap. She took his thumb for a measure. The cord must be cut so far from the child. Neither of them had much fear for Emma. She was a strong woman. A few months before, just after Jim McClure died of fever and before Granpap had come to stay with her, Emma, then five months gone with child, had carried the best part of a thirty-pound shoat the twelve miles over steep mountain trails to Swain's Crossing. Nevertheless her children always came hard, and Emma knew there would be plenty of pain even before the child made its final struggle.

Bonnie cried out loud. Emma walked to the wall where the clothes hung and took down a pair of old jeans. She tucked them into the cradle around the child. Back in the chair with her foot against the cradle she set it rocking slowly, and the child quieted for a moment.

The old man came and stood behind Emma. His shoulders were bowed a little, but he was very tall, and stood high above her.

"Do you think it'll be soon, Emma?" he asked. His voice was anxious and querulous.

Emma did not answer. She knew he wanted it over and done with. But so did she. There was no way to hurry the child.

"Are you going to bed?" he asked. She straightened up.

"When hit's time, Pap. Hit's s' cold there."

The wind slapped against the cabin and snarled down the chimney. Snow blew in under the north door and spread over the floor in a hurry and flurry like an unwelcome quest who is trying to make himself at home.

During one of the quiet times between the pains Emma took the coffee pot from the fire and poured out a drink for each one in the tin cups. Above the kerosene lamp on the table strings of dried apples hanging from the rafters stirred and as the lamp flame gutted and flared up the apple strings made long crooked shadows across the bed in the corner.

"Hit'll warm up our backs," Emma said and handed the cups. She walked over and picked up the water bucket that was in a dark corner behind Kirk.

"Here, Kirk," she said. "Hold the pan."

The water was frozen. Emma broke through the ice with her fist. When she poured it out of the bucket it clinked against the bottom of the tin basin. She set the basin down in the ashes against the live embers.

"You'll need the hot water," she said to Granpap. As she gulped down the warm coffee she wished in herself there was a woman who would know what to do without telling. And she wished the men were where they belonged when a woman was in travail—somewhere out on the mountains or at a neighbor's. There was a shame in having her sons near, and Granpap must see her as he had not seen her since she was a naked baby in her mother's arms. Soon, maybe, it would be over. The pains had begun to get worse, as if it was the end.

In the bed away from the others, Emma let go. She was shaking with cold yet the quilts and her cotton flannel skirt were too much and she pushed them off. Sitting up in bed she pressed down slowly with her hands over the great lump stirring inside. Others had done this for her before to help the child come. She found that she could not do it for herself. The hot pulling cramp forced her to lie back and scream again. A bear was gnawing at her belly, pulling at the muscles with its strong teeth. She felt its fur on her face and beat at the fur with her arms.

It was Granpap's beard. He was trying to tell her to keep covered as long as she could. She pushed him off. It was not possible to bear the agony of one hair touching her. There was no Granpap and no children now. Nothing mattered but herself and the pain.

Bonnie kept up a fretful wail, and Granpap walked up and down the room. Outside the storm brushed against the cabin as if all the trees on the mountains had been uprooted and their dry branches were scraping over the roof and against the outside walls.

Kirk was quiet. Now he stood with his back to the chimney, watching the corner with frightened eyes. Suddenly Emma cried out sharply to Granpap. He stooped over the bed and peered down.

"Bring the lamp, Kirk," he ordered. "And you, Basil, put that pan of water and bucket on the table."

He rolled up his sleeves and walking quickly to the fire leaned far over to rub his cold hands in the flames.

Kirk held the lamp over the bed and kept his eyes on his Granpap. On the bed was a woman he did not recognize as his mother. She was a stranger, a sort of beast. Granpap stood between him and the new thing, and he kept his eyes on the wide back where Granpap's old shirt and patched jeans were familiar and safe. Kirk saw the old man bending over working with his hands at Emma's body and he smelled blood. It made a familiar shudder run over him. Granpap bending over the bed was like a man bending over at a slaughtering and Emma's last cries were the same as those of a pig with a knife at its throat.

For a while Kirk had not heard the storm because Emma's cries were closer than the sounds outside. But when they stopped there was the storm again, wheezing around the cabin and pushing at the door. When Granpap at last stood up he held in his hands something that looked to be a mass of blood and matter. But it was really a living thing. For as Granpap shook it the mass made a wailing sound—a sort of echo of the storm outside.

There was washing to be done, and Kirk stood and held the lamp until the old man finished. At last Granpap covered Emma where she lay exhausted on the dry side of the cold bed. Then he put the washed baby in the cradle with Bonnie to keep it warm until Emma would come to and let it suck.

GEORGE ELLA LYON
(April 25, 1949–)

George Ella Lyon, the daughter of Gladys Fowler Hoskins, a community worker, and Robert Hoskins Jr., a savings and loan officer, is a native of Harlan, Kentucky. "I was born with poor vision and a good ear, into a Southern mountain family and culture rich in stories," she says. "Early on, I wanted to be a neon sign maker and I still hope to make words that glow."

Lyon earned a B.A. in English, Phi Beta Kappa, from Centre College in Danville, Kentucky, in 1971. She completed her M.A. in English at the University of Arkansas in 1972, and her Ph.D. in English, with a minor in creative writing, from Indiana University in 1978. While at Indiana, she studied with poet Ruth Stone.

"In 1972 I began trying to publish a collection of poems," says Lyon. "Eleven years later I succeeded." Her first book, *Mountain*, was published in 1983, and a steady stream of publications have followed, including more than nineteen picture books, four novels for young readers, an autobiography, and a second collection of poetry. Her first novel for adults, *With a Hammer for My Heart*, was selected by Borders bookstore for inclusion in its Original Voices series. She designed and hosted a five-program writers' workshop series entitled *Everyday Voices* [for Kentucky Educational Television (KET).]

Lyon's work has won numerous awards, including a Golden Kite Award for *Borrowed Children* and a Best Books of the Year citation from *Publisher's Weekly* for *Who Came Down That Road?* One of her children's books, *Come a Tide*, has been featured on PBS's *Reading Rainbow*.

"Writing," says Lyon, "is not thinking something up and putting it down, like downloading a computer. It's more like offering your clay body to the kiln. Give your heart to writing and your substance will be changed."

Recognized as a nurturer of young talent, Lyon jokes that she "runs a pro bono unemployment agency consulting with writers on how not to take jobs which would preclude writing."

Lyon has taught at a number of universities, but presently makes her living as a freelance writer, lecturer, and workshop leader. She has served as co-editor of three anthologies, including *Old Wounds, New Words: Poems from the Appalachian Poetry Project*. She lives in Lexington, Kentucky, with her husband, Steve Lyon, a musician, and their two sons.

In this scene from *With a Hammer for My Heart*, the reader is introduced to Mamaw, Lawanda's grandmother who lives in the small Appalachian community of Cardin, Kentucky.

OTHER SOURCES TO EXPLORE

PRIMARY

Novels: *With a Hammer for My Heart* (1997). **Novels for young readers:** *Gina.Jamie.Father.Bear* (2002), *The Stranger I Left Behind Me* (1997; originally published as *Red Rover, Red Rover*, 1989), *Here and Then* (1994), *Borrowed Children* (1988). **Picture books for children:** *One Lucky Girl* (2000), *Book* (1999), *Counting on the Woods: A Poem* (1998), *A Sign* (1998), *A Traveling Cat* (1998), *Ada's Pal* (1996), *A Day at Damp Camp* (1996), *Mama Is a Miner* (1994), *Five Live Bongos* (1994), *Dreamplace* (1993), *Who Came Down That Road?* (1992), *Cecil's Story* (1991), *The Outside Inn* (1991), *Come a Tide* (1990), *Basket* (1990), *Together* (1989), *A B Cedar: An Alphabet of Trees* (1989), *A Regular Rolling Noah* (1986), *Father Time and the Day Boxes* (1985). **Poetry:** *where i'm from: where poems come from* (1999), *Catalpa* (1993), *Mountain* (1983). **Short stories:** *Choices* (1989). **Autobiography:** "Voiceplace," in *Bloodroot* (1998), ed. Joyce Dyer, 168–74. *A Wordful Child* (1996). "Story: Making Things Whole," *Hemlocks and Balsams* [Lees-McRae College, Banner Elk, NC] 7 (1987), 47–55.

SECONDARY

Contemporary Authors, Vol. 120 (1987). Roberta T. Herrin, "From Poetry to Picture Books: The Words of George Ella Lyon," in *Her Words* (2002), ed. Felicia Mitchell, 166–77. John Lang, ed. "George Ella Lyon Issue," *The Iron Mountain Review* 10 (summer 1994). Donna Olendorf, ed., *Something About the Author* (1992).

WITH A HAMMER FOR MY HEART (1997)
from Part One

MAMAW: It was at Little Splinter Creek Church that I saw what I saw. It's been thirty-five years and I remember that night like the nights my younguns was born.

Perry Roby had took the Spirit and was shouting "Damnation" up one side of his breath and "Praise Jesus" down the other. August, dusky dark, and the hot church keeping you mindful of the Pit. All of a sudden, a light whipped out like you'd unrolled a bolt of cloth. I couldn't see the church nor nothing in it. I couldn't hear the creek out the window. There was only this lap of light. I didn't know but to climb up into it. That light held me in its arms, it laid my head on its bosom.

And the light had a voice.

"Mother Jesus didn't do your dying," it said. "You'll still have to cross that river, like a child has to learn to sleep in the bed by itself. But of a morning, you'll wake up and I'll be waiting. I'm telling this to your hands. Don't let nobody go to bed before their time."

The light hummed something sweet as rain and it set me down in Little Splinter. My hands was so hot, my sister Gola jumped when I touched her.

"She's with us now!" I shouted, and keeled toward Carla Dixon.

"Praise His name!" I heard, going down, and knew they had it all wrong.

First thing I did was make a sign that said LITTLE SPLINTER CREEK CHURCH OF THE MOTHER JESUS. Made it from boards left over from strengthening the chicken coop. I got me a poker and burnt the words in. Took me two weeks, had to wait till the kids was in bed. John said I was touched.

"More'n touched. I was knocked down," I told him.

"Your insides can knock you down," he said.

"I know that. But my insides never took me nowhere, never told me nothing."

"Yeah?" he said. "Well, your insides ain't never been this old before. You got lights going on where my ma used to have heat waves. She'd call one of us to pump water while she stuck her head under the spout. Maybe you could use a baptizing."

I didn't listen past that. No knot in the end of his string anyhow.

Next church day I went early, learned Sam Wilder was conducting the service, and told him I was aiming to testify. I had my sign under my arm, wrapped up in a quilt.

"You going to beat the Spirit into us?" he asked.

"No. I got something to show."

"More'n I've got," he said, running his hand over what was left of his hair. It was flat and yellow.

So I was called first, after "Precious Memories" and Eugene Coldiron's prayer. As soon as heads went up, Sam looked at me, thinking I would speak right where I was, but I headed up front, struggling past bellies and elbows with my sign.

"Sisters and Brothers of this church," I said, "watered by Little Splinter Creek, baptized in Redfox River, members of this Association, every one of you sons and daughters, some fathers and mothers to boot. I tell you: we have been led, but we have mistook the leading. We've seen a sign and read it clear wrong. Those words you carved on your heart about the Father, those words are lies. 'Jesus is our Brother,' you've been taught, been singing since you was a sprout. 'Father and Son and Their Breath, that good Holy Ghost.'

"Well, I been breathed on, let me tell you. I been lifted up to look Them in the eye. The heart's eye, friends, the One that sees it all. And this is what I'm here to tell you: there ain't no whiskers on Their faces. She ain't our Father. She ain't our Brother. She's our Mother Jesus and she longs to take us in Her arms."

I took the quilt off my sign and held it up.

"Mother Jesus!" I shouted as they drug me out.

. . .

MAMAW: "It was hard being turned out of Little Splinter. I was weaned on that church—it was beans and buttermilk to me. Every time there was service, my mommy had us all there, scrubbed and shiny, with our hair skinned back. I was baptized from that church, married in it, saw my daddy and mommy prayed over there at the once-a-year funeralizing. And biggest thing of all, I saw God Herself in that church, was lifted up just like the old hymn says. And that was the very thing that put me out.

"That Sunday, Lord, I went home so down, I felt I'd never get up again. My sign, which had weighed like the world walking over, I didn't even notice going back.

"Your papaw was out hoeing corn when I got home. He's never been a churchgoer.

"'What are you doing home early, woman?' he hollered. 'And where are them younguns?'

"Younguns? Upon my honor, I had plumb forgot about them! The service was still going when I was thrown out and I had headed home like a horse to the barn.

"Well, I didn't even speak to your papaw. I pitched my sign into a fencerow and took off up the road a-flying. Halfway there, I met them coming home.

"'What happened, Mommy?' June cried. 'Where'd you go?'

"'She was churched,' Burchett said. 'I done told you that.'

"Dolan just stood there with his thumb in his mouth.

"'Hush, Burchett,' I said, scooping Dolan up with one arm and with the other hugging June to my waist.

"'Ain't it true?' Burchett insisted.

"'Can't tell you what's true right now. Let's go home and get some dinner.'

"We did. I watched them all eat hearty while every bite I took tasted like sand.

"For the next weeks, months, I don't know how long, it seemed like there was a skin over everything. Sun was far away; colors was dimmer. I couldn't even hear good. I'd stand at the stove and not smell dinner burning, not hear your papaw a-calling in the yard.

"Then Annie Isom's boy fell on a wagon tongue and Jeb asked me to sit with her while he went to Cutshin for the doc.

"It was a long journey he was starting, and this boy, Jess, was bleeding real bad. Annie had gone cold and dumb in the way people will sometimes. I sent the other younguns to play in the barn. For some cause, I called to Flo as she went out, 'Hunt up a feather and bring it back to me, will you?'

"She did. Brown one, short and wide-splayed, most likely a wren's.

"'Better put on some coffee, Annie,' I said. 'We'll be needing to keep awake.'

"It was full daylight as I said this, but Annie didn't question, just put more kindling on the fire. I didn't question either. I was following something with my tongue and my hands.

"I went over to the bed where Jess was laying, whiter than just-come snow. Ten years old and his breath on my hand no stronger than a baby's, the sheets wadded around him bright with blood.

"'Mother Jesus,' I said, something drawing out my voice, 'let us keep Jess, this boy that's just started to grow. Stop his life from spilling. Let his pain fall away like this old wren's feather. Seal his wounds, Mother Jesus, and heal Sister Annie's heart.'

"I had one hand on Jess's forehead as I said this, and with the other I touched the feather to his shoulder bones, the fork of his legs, his heart. I closed my eyes and laid the feather inside my dress, against the heat of my bosom. And I sang:

'Leave us a while longer
In this earthly light.
Our eyes are not ready
For Your holy sight.
Mother, comfort
Your child and take his ills.
Leave him to work for you
Among these sacred hills.'

"I'd never heard this song, mind you, but I heard my voice singing it, hoarse and flat, like wind whining in a door.

"I opened my eyes, and Jess's eyes were open too. A little color had come to his cheeks and the blood on the sheets had darkened. No new came to keep it red.

"'She's healed him, Annie,' I said. 'Mother Jesus has healed him!'

"Annie rushed over to the bed. She took Jess's hand, stroked his hair, smiled into his face. Then she looked back at me. 'Don't worry, Ada,' she promised. 'I won't never tell.'

"That seemed a shame at the time, but it didn't really matter. What I knew, I knew, and it closed the church hole in my heart. I won't say I don't sometimes grieve for Little Splinter. But all its members call me when the bad times come. Somebody goes for the doc, somebody for Mamaw. There's been many a door opened to Mother Jesus since Sam Wilder and the church shut us out."

WHERE I'M FROM

from *where i'm from:*
where poems come from (1999)

I am from clothespins,
from Clorox and carbon-tetrachloride,
I am from the dirt under the back porch.
(Black, glistening,
it tasted like beets.)
I am from the forsythia bush
the Dutch elm
whose long-gone limbs I remember
as if they were my own.

I'm from fudge and eyeglasses,
        from Imogene and Alafair.
I'm from the know-it-alls
        and the pass-it-ons,
from Perk up! And Pipe down!
I'm from He restoreth my soul
        with a cottonball lamb
        and ten verses I can say myself.

I'm from Artemus and Billie's Branch,
fried corn and strong coffee.
From the finger my grandfather lost
        to the auger,
the eye my father shut to keep his sight.

Under my bed was a dress box
spilling old pictures,
a sift of lost faces
to drift beneath my dreams.
I am from those moments—
snapped before I budded—
leaf-fall from the family tree.

RINGS

from *where i'm from:*
where poems come from (1999)

This poem began one day when I sat down to write and began studying my hands. (In addition to exercises for writing, I have lots of techniques for Writing Prevention!) It happens that I wear three wedding rings: one from each of my grandmothers and one from my great-grandmother, Ella, whose name I share. I chose to wear these, of course, but until that day I had never really thought about what it meant. Sitting on the tawny rug in my mother-in-law's Hialeah Townhouse, it suddenly hit me: I am married to my grand-mothers!

Adrienne Rich said, "The moment of change is the only poem," and this realization was such a moment for me. It was as if, hiking a familiar trail, I spotted a cave I'd never noticed before. The writing that followed was like spelunking: I had no idea what I would find, and I often got lost or stuck. The poem wasn't finished for a long time—months, as I recall. But it started that afternoon with the gleam of Florida sunshine off magic objects: rings.

I married with my grandmother's wedding ring
and wear my great-grandmother's on the other hand,
both too large—the jeweller cut them down.

Mother and daughter bore seven children,
seven times met death inside out.
Each time they rose and grew larger

like trees, ring on ring, thick with time.
Not all the children lived.
Some were put to bed in iron ground

uncovering the bone-ring of the eye.
Death is its hook—together they close the gap.
At my grandmother's house we drank from a dipper

long after the backporch pump was gone,
bent and came face to face with water
mouth to metal rim, ring on ring.

SALVATION

from *where i'm from:*
where poems come from (1999)

What does the Lord want with Virgil's heart?
And what is Virgil going to do without one?

O Lord, spare him the Call.
You're looking for bass
in a pond stocked with catfish.
Pass him by.
You got our best.
You took Mammy and the truck and the second hay.
What do You want with Virgil's heart?

Virgil, he comes in of a night
so wore out he can hardly chew
blacked with dust that don't come off at the bathhouse.
He washes again
eats onions and beans with the rest of us
then gives the least one a shoulder ride to bed
slow and singing
> *Down in some lone valley*
> *in some lonesome places*
> *where the wild birds do whistle . . .*

After that, he sags like a full feed sack
on a couch alongside the TV
and watches whatever news Your waves are giving.
His soul lifts out
like feed from a slit in that sack
and he's gone
wore out and give out and plumb used up, Lord.
What do you want with his heart?

GROWING LIGHT

from *where i'm from:*
where poems come from (1999)

I write this poem
out of darkness
to you
who are also in darkness
because our lives demand it.

This poem is a hand on your shoulder
a bone touch to go with you
through the hard birth of vision.
In other words, love
shapes this poem
        is the fist that holds the chisel
        muscle that drags marble
        and burns with the weight
            of believing a face
            lives in the stone
            a breathing word in the body.

I tell you
though the darkness
has been ours
words will give us
give our eyes, opened in promise
a growing light.

ℒINDA 𝒫ARSONS ℳARION

(February 5, 1953–)

A Tennessee native who grew up in Nashville and has lived in Knoxville for nearly three decades, Linda Marion fondly remembers her maternal grandmother's pivotal role in her early years that were punctuated with frequent moves and an unsettled home life. "I always felt I was in the calm eye of the storm when I was with her."

Marion completed her B.A. (1988) and M.A. (1991) in English at the University of Tennessee, where she works as an editor and policy coordinator for the University of Tennessee's internal audit department. "Although editing provides my bread and butter and occasionally concert tickets," she says, "writing poetry provides something less tangible in my life—but nourishment and music all the same."

She is the mother of two daughters, served as poetry editor of *Now & Then: The Appalachian Magazine*, co-editor of the anthology *All Around Us: Poems from the Valley* (1996), and remains active in the Knoxville Writers' Guild. The recipient of the Associated Writing Program's 1990 Intro Award, she has also been awarded two literary fellowships from the Tennessee Arts Commission, the 1995 Tennessee Poetry Prize, and the Tennessee Writers Alliance Award in Poetry in 1996, 2000, and 2001. Her poetry has appeared in a variety of journals and anthologies.

OTHER SOURCES TO EXPLORE

PRIMARY

Poetry: *Home Fires* (1997). **Nonfiction:** "Listening for the Hello of Home: A Conversation Between Linda Parsons Marion and Jeff Daniel Marion," in *Her Words* (2002), ed. Felicia Mitchell, 178–90. "The Writing Well," *New Millennium Writ-*

ings (1995–2000), "Rescue from Within," *Sleeping with One Eye Open: Women Writers and the Art of Survival* (1999).

SECONDARY

Gina Herring, "'Approaching the Altar': Aesthetic Homecoming in the Poetry of Linda Marion and Lynn Powell," *Appalachian Heritage* 30:2 (spring 2002), 20–30. Linda Lange, "Kindling 'Home Fires,'" *Knoxville News-Sentinel* (17 May 1997), B1.

MULBERRIES

from *Home Fires* (1997)

They fruit themselves into early June
somewhere between the abelias and
the blue-balled hydrangeas. In the backyard
I'm crushing grapes with my skirts held
high, squishing and purpled, the air rife
with ferment. I stand in this kitchen
of smells, the loaded tree a Bordeaux drunk
slowly, burning all the way to my toes.
People say cut it down, it doesn't bloom,
it stains the sidewalk, the rugs, your shoes.
What's a stain but the mark of memory
you hope never fades—a spot of red-eye gravy
from Grandmama's table every Sunday of my life,
the flow of woman's wine telling my age
season after season, as sharp as the yellowing
bouquet I saved from her grave, as delicious
as the first long day when the bikes come out
and kids count off streetlights coming on
from the corner to the bridge, their hands
and mouths black from berry-eating, believing
their wheels can take them anywhere.

To My Daughter Going Off to College

from *Home Fires* (1997)

One day it will not be enough
to make perfect pesto, cinnamon coffee,
and know every little club on Jackson Avenue.
All this you've learned in secret, striking out
on your own. I've said the usual mother things:
There are men downtown who would crack
you open, leave you drying on the curb.
Where will your pearl be then?
I've said, *One day you'll see,*
as you counted your bus tokens.

One day you'll look in the mirror and see
only furniture. You'll feel a great hole
in your heart, a weight in your pocket.
You'll take these crumbs, drop them
by an ancient moon and, in your darkest hour,
find yourself at my door.

I'll take you to the clock on the mantel.
My grandfather used to scavenge the alley
for his clocks. That one's made of bedposts.
He drank, people called him weak.
I watched him work, a carpenter's hands
hiding his bottle when I came too close.
Four daughters, no sons, something less
than a man. As a girl, my mother must've heard
him stumbling in, the raucous chiming
greeting him like children.

Now light the eye of the stove and smell
my grandmother's kitchen. I'd stand shivering
till she struck the long wooden match.

On Saturdays she bought gladiolus
for the altar, for the quick and the dead.
We walked through the hothouse, our palms
brushed yellow for forgiveness.
In the dense geranium air
I clung to her dress like a bud
at the moment of birth.

All week she cut buttonholes
at the Allen Garment Factory.
Thirty years of service,
the diamond pin says.
Up at five, lighting the flame,
her hands planed smooth by the zig
and zag of broadcloth.
I have her hands, people say,
a woman who lived her faith.
She believed in the diamond pin,
in the thirty years. She believed in
his clocks after he died. She forgot
the man who sang to his shadow
and bragged on him finally being saved.

Sometimes I'll turn on the gas, a smell
so sweet I'll turn to hold her dress.
One day all this will be yours:
You'll sit at a vanity, her milk-glass lamps
on either side. You'll take her diamond pin
from the drawer and rub it like a token.
The moon will look new, you'll get up
while your daughter is asleep
to hear the soft ticking.
And with your whole heart
you'll know where you've come.

Welcome to the Other Side

from *Home Fires* (1997)

FOR ELAYNE

This Christmas you came all the way
over. You left the living room minefield
of tissue paper, indestructible playhouse,
Obi-Wan reruns, spilled drinks. With plates
in hand, you crossed over surely as if to another
country. You're with us now, the women
of the kitchen, preparers of bread and bandages,
showers of scars and casseroles, savers
of foil and string. This summer you'll be married,
and while you say no children, no children
for awhile, you'll take what life hands you, a glass
empty or full. You say I'm yin to your yang—
my towels straight, yours crooked—whatever is
opposite or contrary. Still, I see a house
not too far from here. The woman has learned
to put raisins on the baby's tray while she vaccuums.
She gives out the lion's share, but hides
the Swiss chocolate. She dries mittens
on the register, wool scenting the air like soup.
Your hand is in every room, stirring, mending,
shining, coming closer to the words I have folded
in hospital corners all these years. Words
you can pick up like a doll saying *mama*,
whole sentences you never thought possible,
yours from this day forward, to have
and to hold.

GOOD LUCK CHARM

from *Home Fires* (1997)

Our hike all done this perfect morning,
the trail extending its hand to receive us,
the mist in slow descent to our shoulders
like the smoke rings I begged from my grandfather
and his pack of Camels. We went the whole way up
Greenbrier, past the swept floor under hemlocks,
the feathery maidenhairs under poplar, past
the little graveyard, its stones as crusted as moles
on a stooped back—the babies *borned and died*
on the same day in 1890, in 1903, in 1910,
and the women who joined them
the next day in heaven.

Driving down from the trailhead, you saw them:
the orange hulls of buckeye broken by squirrel
or groundhog on a river rock. *We need all the luck
we can get*, you said and stopped the car.
We overturned beds of moss and oak for our
lucky charm, the shiny meat with its dimple
of brown that just fits in your palm. But the bank
was picked clean of its sweetness. We found
no buckeyes to carry home in our pockets,
to ward off rheumatism and old age and keep
the dark nights away.

Over the years we've walked this trail, at times
the exhaustions of love weighed down our pockets.
Though once you peeled back a nest of trillium
to show me Indian pipes, pale and shy in their beauty.
And once I showed you a white mushroom hiding
in the paper roots of birch. It rose as simply as this
perfect morning, beautiful in its maleness, fitting
like you in my palm when you take away
the dark night, bringing me
all the luck I need.

$\mathscr{C}$ATHERINE $\mathscr{M}$ARSHALL
(September 27, 1914–March 18, 1983)

Sarah Catherine Wood Marshall was born in Johnson City, Tennessee, the daughter of Leonara Whitaker Wood, a teacher, and John Ambrose Wood, a minister. Her parents met while working at a mission school in the mountain community of Del Rio, Tennessee, and Marshall used their experiences as the basis for her best-selling novel, *Christy*.

Marshall graduated from Agnes Scott College in Atlanta, Georgia, in 1936, and that same year married a promising young minister, Peter Marshall, a native of Scotland whose powerful sermonizing led to his appointment as the chaplain of the United States Senate.

Peter Marshall served as Senate chaplain from 1947 until his sudden death from a heart attack in 1949. Widowed and with a young son to support, Catherine edited a collection of her husband's sermons and produced a surprise best-seller, *Mr. Jones, Meet the Master*. Encouraged by the response, Marshall decided to pursue a writing career.

In 1951, Marshall published a critically acclaimed biography of her husband, *A Man Called Peter*. The book remained on national best-seller lists for the next three years and also became a popular film. In 1959, Marshall married Leonard LeSourd, the editor of *Guideposts* magazine, and in 1968, the couple became partners in the Chosen Books Publishing Company, based in Lincoln, Virginia.

Marshall's best-known work, *Christy*, is set in the East Tennessee mountains. A fictionalized version of her mother's remembrances, the book sold more than four million copies during the author's lifetime, and remains a perennial favorite on young adult reading lists. Catherine Marshall's collected papers are housed at Agnes Scott College in Atlanta.

In this scene from chapter 38 of *Christy*, Christy is summoned to the cabin of her dear friend Fairlight Spencer, who is seriously ill with typhoid fever.

OTHER SOURCES TO EXPLORE

PRIMARY

Fiction: *Julie* (1984), *Christy* (1967). **Nonfiction:** *Quiet Times with Catherine Marshall* (1996), *Something More* (1990), *Light in My Darkest Night* (1989), *Together With God: Family Stories, Poems and Prayers of the Marshall Family* (1987), *To Live Again* (1957), *The Prayers of Peter Marshall* (1954), *Mr. Jones, Meet the Master: Sermons and Prayers of Peter Marshall* (1950). **Books for children:** *Stage Fright* (1997), *Mountain Madness* (1997), *Brotherly Love* (1997), *Goodbye, Sweet Prince* (1997), *The Princess Club* (1996), *Christy's Choice* (1996), *The Proposal* (1996), *The Angry Intruder* (1995), *Silent Superstitions* (1995), *Midnight Rescue* (1995), *The Bridge to Cutter Gap* (1995), *God Loves You: Our Family's Favorite Stories and Prayers* (1973).

SECONDARY

Contemporary Authors, First Revision, Vols. 17–20, 477–78. *Something About the Author*, Vol. 2, 182–83, and Vol. 34, 149–50.

CHRISTY (1967)

from Chapter Thirty-eight

How can I ever forget that day in early October when Fairlight Spencer sent Zady to tell me that she needed me. Would I please come as soon as possible? No clue was offered as to what the need was. Only Zady's dark brooding eyes and thin face screwed up with worry underscored the urgency.

Nor would the child leave my side until she had seen me saddling Buttons. Then her mission accomplished, without another word she bounded off toward home, streaking across the mission yard, leaping from rock to rock across the creek, running like a brown-legged deer diagonally up across the face of the mountain.

I followed by the more tedious trail, giving Buttons the rein up the low foothills. But as we reached the first heavily wooded spur from which the path rose steeply, my mare was forced to a slow walk. The rhododendron leaves were still straight and shiny, like summer leaves, not beginning to curl as they usually did in the fall. At moments the silence of the woods was so intense that the patter of acorns falling from the oak trees onto the dry leaves sounded like gentle rain.

Though Buttons and I had made this trip often, the mare had never been sure-footed on the heights and she was always skittish about the final ascent to the Spencer cabin. As I rode over the crest of the last rise, I saw that all of the children—except John and Zady—were in the yard watching for me, their faces solemn.

"What a nice welcoming committee," I greeted them. But there was no gaiety in their response.

Clara came to help me dismount. "Been waitin' for you." She spoke softly, taking the reins from my hands. "I'll hitch the post to Buttons."

Such a funny way to say it! "Where's your mother?" I asked.

"Mama's inside." The tall girl's face was expressionless. She would not look me in the eyes. "She's abed."

I hurried on into the cabin. From the open door, brilliant autumn sunlight spilled across the floor. But the cabin, usually noisy with activity—children's voices and laughter, kitchen sounds, Jeb's music—was so quiet it seemed deserted. Then I saw her, Fairlight, lying on the bed, the outlines of her body defined by the quilt tucked in around her.

Her face was flushed with a heavy look about it that changed her features. Her eyes were open but bloodshot and dull, her head moving restlessly from side to side on the pillow. I felt her forehead. Hot! Incredibly hot!

"Christy—" One hand crept across the quilt toward me. "You've come."

"Of course, I've come, Fairlight. Why didn't you send for me sooner?"

"My side hurts—here—so bad."

Her breathing was heavy with such wheezing that I thought she might have pneumonia. *But it was so early in the autumn. We haven't even had any cold weather.*

The children had trailed me into the house and were standing at the foot of the bed, watching me carefully. Their mother held her right hand up in front of her face. "It's bigged. All swelled up. Why is it so big?"

I looked at the hand. Perfectly normal except that the skin was so dry that it was pulled taut. Fairlight's lips, cracked from the fever, were twitching in a strange way.

"Clara, how long has your mother been like this?"

"Mama was ailin', right bad off all last week," the girl answered. "Complained of a-hurtin' in the head. Yesterday had the trembles. Shook all over like an aspen tree in the wind. But she wouldn't take to her bed."

"Where's your father?"

"Took the hound-dogs, went ba-ar huntin'—over Laurel Top somewheres."

"How long has he been gone?"

The girl thought a moment. "I'm not certain-sure. Left at day-bust, 'twas three days ago, reckon."

"Christy—" the voice from the bed sounded desperate. Fairlight raised her head off the pillow to look at me, but I had the feeling that her eyes were not focusing. The pupils looked dilated. "Christy, tell them to take the chairs off'n me. All that house plunder they're a-pilin' on me. The chairs—all them chairs. Tell them— They're a-smashin' me. Tell them—" She began coughing, a deep racking cough, painful to hear.

I pressed her hand reassuringly. "Fairlight, there's no furniture on you, no chairs."

"Off'n me, off'n me. Tell them—*Christy*—"

"Fairlight, I'm here now. Right here. I won't let anybody pile anything on you."

My heart was thumping and my legs trembling. *I must not let the children see my alarm.* I forced myself to speak slowly to try to keep the panic out of my voice. "Clara, hasn't anybody sent for Dr. MacNeill?"

"Mama didn't reckon to need no doctor-medicine."

"How about John? Is he around? Could I send him for the Doctor?"

"Papa carried him ba-ar huntin' too."

At that moment Zady appeared in the doorway, breathless and panting from the long climb from the mission.

What was I to do? For the girls it was too long a journey to Doctor MacNeill's cabin and he might not be there anyway.

"Clara," I said, "we've got to have help. Would you run over to Holcombes' and get one of the men to go fetch the Doctor?"

Already Clara was at the door. "Say they can use Buttons if necessary. And tell them to try the mill first. Usually one of the men there knows where the Doctor is. Oh, and Clara—" The girl stood in the doorway looking at me with large solemn eyes. "Tell them that your mother is really sick. This is an emergency." She turned and in a moment had disappeared over the brow of the hill.

BELINDA ANN MASON
(July 2, 1958–September 9, 1991)

Journalist and short story author Belinda Ann Mason was a native of Letcher County, Kentucky. "I was born with the mountains in my blood," said Mason. "I could hear music when people talked."

Mason earned a B.S. in journalism from the University of Kentucky in 1980, worked in public relations for a time, then settled into a journalism career, writing for two weekly papers: first for the *Ohio County Times-News* in Hartford, Kentucky, and later for the *Appalachian News-Express* in Pikeville, Kentucky. Her short stories appeared in *The American Voice* and *Appalachian Heritage*, and the Kentucky Foundation for Women awarded a grant for Mason to collaborate with the Roadside Theater to produce her play, *Gifts of the Spirit*.

In 1987, Mason contracted AIDS from a blood transfusion following the birth of her second child. Facing her situation with quiet courage, Mason became an AIDS-rights advocate, calling for greater sensitivity toward victims of the disease. "AIDS is less about dying than about choosing how to live," she insisted. In 1989, President Bush appointed her to the National Commission on AIDS.

"One of the most difficult parts of my illness is the loss of my life as a writer," said Mason. "When people talk to me now, they see the disease first. Nobody talks to Belinda Mason the short story writer anymore."

Mason died of AIDS-related pneumonia in 1991 at the age of 33. A play based on Mason's work, *Passing Through the Garden*, was produced by Appalshop's Roadside Theater after her death. Her original manuscripts, including a dozen unfinished stories and a novel in progress, are housed in the Special Collections of the University of Kentucky Libraries.

OTHER SOURCES TO EXPLORE

PRIMARY

Drama: *Gifts of the Spirit, Appalachian Heritage* 16:2&3 (spring/summer 1988).
Short story: "A Christmas Lesson," *Appalachian Heritage* 15:4 (1987).

SECONDARY

Artie Ann Bates, "Belinda, Our Tremendous Gift," *Appalachian Heritage* 19:2 (spring 1991), 3–6 [This essay is reprinted in this volume]. *Belinda*, dir. Anne Johnson (Appalshop documentary film, 1992). Philip J. Hilts, "Belinda Mason, 33, U.S. Panelist and Bush Advisor on AIDS Policy," *New York Times* (10 September 1991), B5, col. 4. Linda Kramer, "AIDS Commissioner Belinda Mason Speaks with Ringing Authority About the Disease," *People Weekly* 32 (11 December 1989), 147–50. "Milestones," *Time* (23 September 1991), 68. Anne Shelby, *Passing Through the Garden*. Jack Sirica, "Woman on AIDS Panel Dies of AIDS," *Newsday* (10 September 1991), 8.

THE GIFTS OF THE SPIRIT
from *Appalachian Heritage (1988)*

The play is set in the present in a rural eastern Kentucky funeral home. The characters are members of a closely-knit mountain community who have gathered for the evening wake of a young man who has died in a car wreck. As it does so many times in this setting, the characters' thoughts and their talk turns away from death to life.

Enoch, this speaker, talks of faith. He is about 70, wears khaki work clothes and wing-tip shoes. He is easy going and has a special kind of humor.

A man's born without a thing and he dies the self-same way. So he's got to make the most of what's in the middle.

Now they's plenty of 'em that would fault me on this, but if the good Lord hadn't a meant for us to enjoy life He'd a took us straight to heaven when we was born and skipped over it.

And look a here what all He's give us:
Children.
Fishin.
Dogwood trees.
Pie.

Them might not be your picks, but they's mine. They's plenty other fine things. Just git ye head out of ye hindend for a minute and think about it.
Music.
Buddies.
Biscuit.

Now I'm not what you'd call a religious man. For I believe religion ain't necessarily limited to the church house. Don't git me wrong though, the church house is good for a lot. When I was a young man I did a sight of courtin at meetings. And in the middle of my years, sometimes there wasn't a thing in the world that was any better than cleanin up, walkin down the creek with Virgie and the younguns and listenin to some preachin. Set of them satiny-smooth benches, spring of the year comin in the winders and the smell of them talcum powders when Virgie'd git that fan goin.

Brother Felix Ison would git wound up. They used to say he preached starvation, instead of salvation. I'd listen to him awhile. Then take note of everbody. My neighbors, I'd think to myself. My family. My friends. Lord, it was sweet. A good feelin. Then maybe I'd put my arm round Virgie and squeeze that soft part of her between the shoulder and the elbow. My hands is old now, but they remember yet holdin that woman's skin.

I've studied on it and I believe now what I loved so good about them times in church is how all of us fit together. As tight and true as a dovetail joint. Must have been somethin to it, for they was certain days in church I even loved my mother-in-law.

Now the truth is that Mag Muncy was a bitch. She worked her husband to death and then set in on her younguns. Cold as ice, that woman. Virgie was her oldest and Mag done her like a pack horse. Course she never could forgive me for takin her. But here I'd set, in back of Mag, filled with somethin that could have been the Holy Ghost for all I know about such matters and they'd be ten minutes spaces of time when I loved Mag. Loved how straight she sat, like she had a poker up her rear. Loved them stringy little plaits around her head. Not seein her old mouth, nothin but a line across her face, and lovin that, too.

But what I meant to say is that they's a lot of 'em that wouldn't pick me for a religious man. I handle bad talk. I'll take a drink. And I ain't never been baptized. Virgie's accused me, more than once, of blasphemin.

Years ago I had Frank Fulton helpin me clear a spot of ground up in the Sandlick Gap. Wadn't nothing up there but a wilderness. We'd worked our tails off, cutting trees, burnin brush, grubbin roots. People thought I'd gone crazy and some said as much. But I knowed underneath all them woods was a fine little house seat. Long about August it started to shape up and it was so pretty I decided I'd build a house for myself.

Little Ted Adams, he was the Presbyterian preacher, he come by one day and was braggin and goin on. I had the footer poured and was fixin to lay the foundation. You could already see what a fine dwellin house I was gonna have. Little Ted said, 'Now just think, Enoch. All this belongs to you and the Lord.' I said, 'Well, preacher. You should a seen it when the Lord owned it by His self.' Frank Fulton, he's dead now, told that all over the country.

Now I'm a carpenter and Jesus was too. And I know if He was any hand at all, He paid mind to how things fits together.

If a man's gonna build for it to stand, they's certain things he's got to believe in. You got to believe in the level. You got to have faith in the chalkline. You have to trust the square.

Workin on a buildin is what livin is. And just like wood workin, you got to have things to believe in before you can build something that'll stand. A house that'll keep the wind off of ye. A life where the doors is hung right and the roof don't bow.

And like I said at the outset. The Lord's give us plenty to delight in and a whole lot to believe. If they is a day of judgement comin, as some says, I don't think we'll be faulted much for drinkin or gamblin nor none of the other things you've heard is a one-way ticket to hell. If He's got a quarrel with us, it'll be for us not layin ahold of our tools. Not trustin our materials.

I'm an old man and I figure now it don't matter so much what you believe. So long as you believe somethin.
The Democrat party.
A good huntin dog.
General Motors products.
The UMW.
They's plenty to pick from.

$\mathscr{K}$ATHY $\mathscr{L}$. $\mathscr{M}$AY
(October 17, 1952–)

Kathy L. May was born in southern Ohio but spent her childhood in Floyd County, Kentucky. "Some of my earliest memories are of the frequent floods that devastated that area of eastern Kentucky," says May. "My first serious poem, 'Rain,' was about those floods."

May earned a B.S. in psychology in 1974 from the University of Louisville, and an M.F.A. in creative writing in 1987 from Indiana University, where she was the recipient of the first Samuel Yellen Fellowship. In 1997, she won the *Wind Magazine* short fiction competition. Other awards include a poetry grant from the Kentucky Foundation for Women, and a fellowship from the MacDowell Colony. May's work has appeared in *American Voice*, *Southern Poetry Review*, *Mississippi Review*, and *Appalachian Heritage*.

She has taught literature and writing at Indiana University, Virginia Tech, and Piedmont Virginia Community College. She currently teaches Appalachian literature and creative writing through the University of Virginia's School of Continuing Education.

Her collection of poems, *Door to the River*, was published in 1992 in the Panhandler Poetry Chapbook series at the University of West Florida. Her first children's book, *Molasses Man*, was published in 2000. May lives in Charlottesville, Virginia, with her husband, Garry Barrow, and their two children.

OTHER SOURCES TO EXPLORE

PRIMARY

Poetry: *Door to the River* (1992). **Books for children:** *Molasses Man* (2000).

SECONDARY

"Kathy L. May's Web Page," Presented by America Writes for Kids, [web site] http://usawrites4kids.drury.edu/authors/may/

RAIN

from *Door to the River* (1992)

The wooden barrel
at the corner of the house
spilled rain in storms
and my mother washed
her brown hair softer.

Cool and wet, she
listened from the window.
Her eyes were brown as the river
while the barrel drowned
in silver light.

I was five when my father
stacked our beds
on towers of blocks,
hoisted tables to the ceiling
and we left the house
riding in a boat.

But we could have perched on the roof
and floated downriver,
water rushing wide and high,
to the top of a mountain
where the house would tangle
sideways in the trees.

For years the scent of rain
flooded my mother's house.
In a dream we swam
from room to room
when she opened the door
to the river.

Saved

from *Door to the River* (1992)

Wearing her best white dress,
she stands unseeing with the others
gathered near the river
where the preacher sways
waist-deep in muddy water,
arms stretched above his head,
eyes closed, chanting.
On the bank the women murmur
in response: *Sweet Jesus, Amen.*

When the preacher calls her name
she drags slowly through water
seeping heavily into her clothes.
The chant comes faster, louder.
She trembles in a fever
of longed-for salvation,
shouts *Yes, Oh yes* and he pulls her
hard into the water and she comes up
thrashing, a long high vowel
torn from her throat.

Arms open wide and dripping,
she walks toward the crowd,
shivers in the grip of something
waiting for her as she rises
from the river, sanctified,
wet cloth clinging to her body.

ASCENSION

from *Door to the River* (1992)

"Woman Survives After Being Carried Away by Tornado"
(newspaper headline, April, 1984)

Easter Sunday walking home
from church in gusty rain,
she saw dogwood blooming
in the hills, white fists uncurling.
Wind twisted her dress
around her legs, tore the raffia
flowers off her purse,
tossed them into the air
like a bridal bouquet.

Running then, she felt a presence
behind her running faster.
Lifted up inside the moving walls
of a tunnel thick with dust,
she flung out her arms
and floated in the current.
From the eye of the storm
the world tilted—
houses, farms, cattle
huddled near the creek.
She watched her shoes fly off
over the trees, crows flapping
toward the horizon.
What was herself soared
out of the body, weightless.

Then drifting down
on a long spiral slide
she dropped to the ground.
Her family climbed out of the cellar,
blind and unbelieving.
They blinked at her

sitting in the dirt,
still clutching her purse,
while all around them
in the swept fields
the wind blew flurries of blossoms.

CRUDA WILLIAMS McCOY
(February 3, 1902–1974)

Truda Williams McCoy was the eldest of seven children of Charlotte Casebolt Williams and James T. Williams. Born in Pikeville, Kentucky, she grew up there and recalled spending much of her childhood helping to care for younger sisters and brothers. She learned to read and write before starting school and wrote her first poem when she was five years old. She graduated from the local high school and Pikeville Teacher's College.

She married Rex Calvin McCoy in 1924, and two years later their son, Rex Samuel, was born. In 1930, she had twins, Paul Ronald and Judith Diana.

A prolific eastern Kentucky poet, she produced three poetry collections, and her poems were published in more than seventy magazines and journals. She was a member of the National League of American Pen Women.

This excerpt from chapter 4 of *The McCoys* offers an account of Johnse Hatfield's introduction to Roseanna McCoy.

OTHER SOURCES TO EXPLORE

PRIMARY

Nonfiction: *The McCoys: Their Story As Told to the Author by Eye Witnesses and Descendants* (1976). **Poetry:** *Till the Frost* (1962). *The Tempter's Harvest* (1954).

SECONDARY

Harold Branam, review of *The McCoys: Their Story . . .*, *Appalachian Heritage* 5:3 (summer 1977), 83–86. *Kentucky in American Letters* (1976), Vol. 3, ed. Dorothy Edwards Townsend, 225–27. Review of *The McCoys: Their Story . . .*, *Appalachian Journal* 4:3–4 (spring-summer 1977), 274–75.

THE McCOYS: THEIR STORY AS TOLD TO THE AUTHOR BY EYE WITNESSES AND DESCENDANTS (1976)

from Chapter 4, Roseanna McCoy

Election day in the hills of Kentucky was always a day to look forward to. It was the only day in the year that everybody met everybody else. Friends and enemies, Republicans and Democrats, the poor and the well-to-do (nobody was considered rich), the respected people of the community and the ones not so well respected. Everybody went to the elections.

Whisky was always plentiful: Sparkling moonshine as clear as the mountain streams, but singing a more potent song. Part of it was brought to the election ground by the voters, but most of it was furnished by the leaders of the two parties in the attempt to influence the voters in their favor. Baskets of food were brought by the womenfolk, so that there was never a lack of something to eat or drink.

By sunup most of the voters (men over twenty-one), and younger men were already gathered, dressed in their best "Sunday go to Meetin" clothes and best felt hats. They came singly or in groups, laughing and bantering good-naturedly.

By noon most of the women had gathered, dressed in gaily colored dresses of print calico and wearing soft woolen shawls when the weather was chilly, the middle-aged and older women wearing huge sunbonnets with tails reaching to their shoulders. The young, or unmarried, women usually went bareheaded.

Always at election time there were a dozen or more women (old or married, which was about the same thing), carrying baskets of gingerbread which they sold "one fer a nickel er three fer a dime" in order to make a little extra money for a few yards of calico, a picture for the wall, a vase to hold their flowers.

Among the crowd of men and women were children laughing, talking and munching ginger cookies. When the men became thirsty, most of them retired to a shade and took a dram of white liquor. Any old timer could hook his forefinger in the handle of a gallon jug and, with a peculiar twist of the wrist, throw the jug over his hand, raising it to his mouth with one movement. Women and children resorted to water to quench their thirst. Respectable mountain women didn't drink whisky except (perhaps a small sip) in the privacy of their own homes. No respectable woman was ever known to become drunk, since drunkenness and respectability did not go together.

A crowd of McCoys were gathered on the election ground at one side of the building, talking with their friends. On the opposite side of the building were the Hatfields. Some were drinking in good fellowship and arguing in a friendly way with each other.

"Hey there, don't be stingy with your likker," called out a voice as a good-looking, sandy-haired young man came up.

"Howdy, Johnse," they chorused, "here's the likker, don't drink it all, though."

Johnse took the jug, hooked his forefinger in its ear, and with one movement had the jug to his mouth. He drank long and deeply.

Old Jim Vance winked at another member of the clan and turning to Johnse said, "You're larnin, Johnse, by heck. Twon't be long till ye can drink with any of us old hands."

Johnse laughed at the praise and asked, "Are ye jealous, Uncle Jim?"

"No," Vance assured him, "but you're too young to be a-drinkin so much. Put too much likker in a young feller and he's liable to start anything. Likker is something you got to let grow on ye. Take a little at first and after awhile ye can take more and more of it. Come to think of it, likker is a lot like women; you don't want to take too many of em right at the start; go slow till ye learn their ways—then spread out. Likker's fun. So's women."

"Likker was made to drink," Johnse replied. "In fact, that's all it is good for, that I've ever heard of."

Several of the crowd laughed loudly and slapped Johnse on the back good-naturedly. "You're right, Boy. Drink the stuff and don't wait for a snake to bite ye for an excuse."

"Or put in bitters like the women folks do."

Johnse was still arguing in a friendly way with Vance when he caught sight of a girl in the McCoy crowd that made him hold his breath in awe.

The girl was tall and slender with a beautiful, proportioned body. She had a fair complexion that had tanned to a pale golden hue during the summer months. Tanned, but her beautiful skin was as soft and flawless as a child's. The most noticeable of all was her hair, red-brown, abundant and wavy. She stood in the path of the sun and the sun turned her hair to a burnished gold.

This was not the first time in his life that young Johnse Hatfield aged nineteen had ever noticed a girl. Far from it. He had been noticing girls all his adult life, but perhaps, this was the first time he had ever really noticed a girl and really wanted her, felt that he needed her and must have her. He did not analyze his feelings at this time, nor say to himself, "Love at first sight." He only knew that he must meet her.

Turning to his uncle, he questioned earnestly, "Who is she, Uncle Jim? The girl with the red hair—the girl there a-talking to Tolb McCoy?"

Vance looked in the direction of the McCoys and his brow puckered with annoyance as he answered, "That's Roseanna McCoy, Ranel's daughter." Then he continued, "Ranel didn't use to let his girls come to the elections. He's mighty tight on em from all accounts and I've heard—"

But Johnse interrupted whatever Vance had started to say. "Roseanna McCoy." He repeated the name softly, musically. "God, ain't she purty!"

"There's other purty girls—," Vance started to say, but without waiting to hear who they were or where they were, Johnse left the group of relatives and crossed the few yards that separated the two clans, and walked up to where Roseanna stood.

The girl looked at Johnse and then she looked toward the group of relatives that he had just left, then back to Johnse. She knew her family and the Hatfields were estranged. Why did he seek her out? Surely he must know they weren't allowed to talk and be friendly together like other people. However, she waited for him to speak. She was twenty-one and had some freedom.

Johnse was smiling in a friendly manner. Stretching out his hand toward her, he said, "Howdy."

Immediately the crowd became tense. Hatfields and McCoys dropped their hands to their pistol holsters. Ranel was some distance away, having a friendly argument over who would be elected and had noticed nothing. Gradually, the crowd relaxed and watched for the outcome. Both McCoys and Hatfields were watching, but without Ranel or Devil Anse would do nothing.

Roseanna looked at her people, saw them watching her with disapproval. She looked at Johnse. He was good looking, she thought, and friendly. He didn't look *bad*—but of course he was. *All Hatfields were bad.* She had always known that, so she hesitated to take the proffered hand.

"I am Johnse Hatfield," he said still holding out his hand. "Won't ye be friends?"

Roseanna didn't hesitate any longer. She took Johnse's hand and stammered, "I guess so—I don't know—I am Roseanna McCoy."

From that moment on, Roseanna's life was different from anything she or anyone else had ever dreamed it would be. From the moment she placed her slender hand into Johnse Hatfield's, she was never the same. Her heart had gone with her hand. . . .

$\mathscr{S}$HARYN $\mathscr{M}$cCRUMB
(February 26, 1948–)

Novelist Sharyn McCrumb grew up in Burlington, North Carolina, but hearing tales of her pioneer ancestors from her father, she became enamored with mountain culture at a young age. "It's in the blood," she says, noting that her father's family settled in western North Carolina in the 1790s. "I found that all the tales and memories of substance come from that side of the family."

McCrumb graduated from the University of North Carolina at Chapel Hill, and received an M.A. in English from Virginia Tech in 1985. She has worked as a newspaper editor and a journalism instructor, but has been a full-time writer and lecturer since 1988. She lives on an estate near the Appalachian Trail in the Virginia Blue Ridge.

"My books are like Appalachian quilts," says McCrumb. "I take brightly colored scraps of legends, fragments of rural life and local tragedy, and I piece them together into a complex whole that tells not only a story, but also a deeper truth about the culture of the mountain South."

McCrumb's Ballad Novels are a highly acclaimed series set in fictional Wake County, Tennessee. Despite a fictionalized setting, the books explore the very real issues facing contemporary residents of Appalachia: pollution, the breakdown of the region's traditional culture, the loss of farmland to strip development, the moral implications of the death penalty.

Her work has appeared on the *New York Times* Best-Seller List and has received numerous awards, including Appalachian Writer of the Year in 1999, the Chaffin Award, the Plattner Award, Best Appalachian Novel in 1983 and 1992, and a citation for Outstanding Contribution to Appalachian Literature in 1997. "McCrumb writes with quiet fire and maybe a little mountain magic," says a *New York Times* reviewer. "Like every good storyteller, she has the Sight."

In this excerpt from *The Songcatcher,* McCrumb introduces her character Baird Christopher, who runs an inn near the Appalachian Trail in North Carolina and calls himself a "Cosmic Possum." McCrumb credits East Tennessee writer Jane Hicks with coining the term "Cosmic Possum" to describe "the child who was born to the first generation out of the holler or off the ridge. Grew up in touch with those past generations who settled these mountains . . . learned the old songs, the old stories, knew how to hand-tie tobacco and kill hogs, but he did not live in that world. He may eat penne pasta instead of fatback and vacation in Aruba instead of Gatlinburg. . . . He lives in the modern world, but he knows what has been lost."

OTHERS SOURCES TO EXPLORE

PRIMARY

Novels (Ballad Series): *Ghost Riders* (2003) *The Songcatcher* (2001), *The Ballad of Frankie Silver* (1998), *The Rosewood Casket* (1996), *She Walks These Hills* (1994), *The Hangman's Beautiful Daughter* (1992), *If Ever I Return, Pretty Peggy-O* (1990). **Novels (Elizabeth MacPherson Series):** *If I'd Killed Him When I Met Him* (1995), *MacPherson's Lament* (1992), *Missing Susan* (1991), *Highland Laddie Gone* (1991), *The Windsor Knot* (1990), *Lovely in Her Bones* (1990), *Sick of Shadows* (1989), *Paying the Piper* (1988). **Novels (Jay Omega Series):** *Bimbos of the Death Sun* (1997), *Zombies of the Gene Pool* (1992). **Short stories:** *Foggy Mountain Breakdown* (1997). **Autobiographical essay:** "Keepers of the Legends" in *Bloodroot* (1998), ed. Joyce Dyer.

SECONDARY

Ethan Fischer, "Highland Mastery: Interview with Sharyn McCrumb," *Antietam Review* 20 (2000), 39–42. David Hunter, "Sharyn McCrumb," *New Millennium Writings* 2:1, 10–14. *From a Race of Storytellers: Essays on the Ballad Novels of Sharyn McCrumb* (forthcoming) Kimberly H. Kidd, ed. Pamela Murray Winters, "A Trip to Appalachia: Sharyn McCrumb" *Dirty Linen* 76 (June–July 1998), 15.

THE SONGCATCHER (2001)

from Chapter 5

On the North Carolina side of the mountain, Baird Christopher was shelling peas and shucking corn for a vegetarian supper for twenty.

The Cosmic Possum Hikers Hostel was a white Victorian mansion dating from the late nineteenth century. Three miles from the Tennessee state line and a mile outside town, the house stood on a hillock overlooking the French Broad River, surrounded by manicured lawns and tall rhododendron bushes, and shaded by oaks and poplars. The mountain mansion had been built in the 1870s when the western North Carolina highlands became fashionable for summer vacationing, because, in a world without air-conditioning, the cool mountain air made southern summers tolerable. When the last of the original owners' family had died or moved out of the country, the farmland was sold at auction, and Baird Christopher bought the remaining acre of land and the big white house. Then, with the carpentry skills he had perfected in the Peace Corps, he set about renovating the elegant old mansion into a dormitory for transient Trail folk. Wallboard partitions split the spacious upstairs bedrooms into two smaller bedrooms, and the chestnut-paneled dining room with its bronze chandelier and ten-foot ceiling was now crammed with homemade pine tables and metal folding chairs set close together to accommodate the twenty or thirty hikers who would turn up for dinner.

Baird usually let one of the hikers do the kitchen cutwork in exchange for a meal, but when he had asked around at lunch today no one seemed to need a free dinner bad enough to work for it, so Baird was doing his own culinary prep work. He took care to station himself in the most conspicuous spot in the garden, however, and he kept another chair close at hand in case a volunteer happened along. Baird wasn't much on chopping vegetables, but he was glad of an excuse to sit out in the shade of the oaks and watch the world go by—migrating monarch butterflies or investment bankers in hiking boots: it was all one to him. With the white plastic colander balanced on his knees, Baird Christopher snapped open pea pods to the steady beat of a tune in his head.

"Need any help?"

A stout middle-aged man with a red face and a Cornell sweatshirt stood over him, glistening with sweat. "This is the hostel, isn't it?" he asked, wiping his forehead with his sleeve. "That potato farmer in the old green truck said it was."

"Potato farmer?"

"Yeah. Guy in overalls hauling bushel baskets of potatoes in bed of his pickup. He offered me a ride, but I told him I just needed directions to a place to stay. Said to tell you hello. Gordon Somebody, I think he said."

"Oh, *Gordon,*" said Baird with bemused smile. "Potato farmer in an old green truck. Right. I'll tell him you said so. He'll be tickled to death." He chuckled. "*Potato farmer.*"

"Well, weren't they potatoes? Or yams, maybe?"

"Well, they might have been yams, but old Gordon is no potato farmer. He's a cardiologist from Charlotte. Likes to come up here to his summer place and play farmer whenever we can. He'll be thrilled that you mistook him for the genuine article. It'll make his day. Now, what can I do for you?"

The man mopped his face with a grubby bandana. "I need a bath. Can I get a room for tonight?"

Baird nodded. "Welcome to the Cosmic Possum Hostel," he said. "I'm just getting the vegetables ready for tonight's dinner. You can help if you're so inclined." He removed the paper bag of corn from the second lawn chair and indicated that the man could sit down. "I'm Baird Christopher. I run this place."

"By yourself?"

"More or less. Every so often one of the Trail puppies will take a break for a couple of weeks or months, either to recuperate from an injury or to earn some cash to take them the rest of the way, and I give them a job helping out around the place, but sooner or later, everybody but me moves along. You should have been here *last* month: The guy working here had been trained as a chef. Used to work at the Four Seasons. He headed out when the weather broke. While it lasted, though, we were eating like kings around here. He even made us call the grits *polenta.*"

The hiker sat down in the extra lawn chair, loosened his boot laces, and sighed. "Feels good to sit," he said. "I'm Stan, but my Trail name is Eeyore. Nice place," he added, looking approvingly at the gingerbread trim on the covered porch, wreathed by the branches of shade trees. He wasn't sure what kind of trees they were. Trees had never played a big part in Stan's life up until now, but in his last few weeks on the Trail he had begun to feel they were old friends. "It's peaceful here."

Baird held a pea pod up to the light and inspected it with the eye of an artist. "There's a serenity about the whole mechanical process of opening pea pods, you know? I was watching the butterflies a little while ago, and I thought: *They know what it's like to be inside a pod, only no one helps them break out. They have to do it on their own.* Now, with people, some folks break their own pods, and some have to be broken out by others, but it doesn't matter which way you're set free. The important thing is that you emerge—get out there into the great world and seek your destiny."

The man blinked. He looked from the colander of peas to the amiable face of his host and back again. After a moment's pause he ventured a guess: "Are you a poet?"

Baird smiled. "Well, we're all poets, aren't we?"

Eeyore shrugged. "I'm a mechanical engineer."

"Yeah,"said Baird, "but the way I see it, just planting those hiking boots of yours on the Trail is a poem to the unspoiled glory of nature. Where are you headed, friend?"

"All the way." Eeyore's face shone with pride. "This is my first time on the southern end of the Trail. I've done short hikes in New England for years now, but this time I'm going to try to make it all the way from Springer to Katahdin."

"Georgia to Maine. Sounds like you're breaking out of the pod, friend." Baird dumped another handful of peas to the strainer. "More power to you."

"Ever hiked it yourself?"

Baird nodded. "Bits and pieces. Mostly North Carolina and Tennessee, and up into Virginia. Pennsylvania is tough going—rocky and steep. Mostly it's a question of time for me—I can't find anybody who'll stay and look after this place for six months while I take off to hike. But you know what Milton said: *They also serve who only stand and wait.*"

The stockbroker, to whom English Literature was a never-opened book, nodded politely, wondering if Milton was another local doctor turned potato farmer. He said, "Hiking the Trail is a great experience. I've already lost eighteen pounds. Feel better than I have in years."

Baird smiled and went on shelling peas. He had this conversation three times a week, but with every hiker who told him this he tried to share the joy of it as if he was hearing it for the first time. "It's a magical place," he said. "The Trail through these eastern mountains follows a chain of a green mineral called serpentine that leads from Alabama all the way to New Brunswick, Canada. The chain breaks off at the Atlantic coast, skips the ocean, and then picks up again in Ireland and snakes it way through Cornwall, Wales, and Scotland, till it finally ends in the Arctic Circle. These mountains here once fit on to the tail end of the mountains over there like pieces of a giant continental jigsaw puzzle. The chain of serpentine is a remnant of that togetherness, and it still links us to the mountains of Celtic Britain, where most of our ancestors came from when they settled here. *Will the circle be unbroken.*"

"Pretty country," Eeyore said. "Great views. I hope my photos turn out."

"Oh, this country is more than pretty. It's elemental. You know, a hiker from Queensland once told me that the aborigine people of Australia believe that their ancestors sang the world into being, and that there are special song paths that those first people took while they were doing it. Singing up the world from out of nothingness. That hiker said he thought this trail was one of them. That wouldn't surprise me at all. If this was one of the creation roads. *A song path."*

Eeyore shrugged. "I didn't think the AT was that old," he said carefully. "Government built it. Maybe forty years ago, something like that?"

"Yes, that's the official word on it, but parts of it follow a much older trail called the Warriors Path. The Indians made that one centuries ago, and they used it for everything from raids on other tribes to trading expeditions." Baird smiled. "And before that the Ice Age animals made trails over the mountains to the salt pools. Who knows how far back this northbound path stretches? All the way to the serpentine chain, I reckon—and that would make it 250 million years old."

"Interesting part of the country. Lots of stories."

"Lots of Celtic bloodlines in the people here. Stories is what we do."

"Well, I'll be interested to hear some stories. This is my first visit to *Appa-lay-chia."*

Baird said gently, "Well, folks in these parts call it *Appa–latch-a."*

Eeyore shrugged, as if the information did not interest him. "In New York we say *Appa-lay-chia."*

Baird had this conversation rather often, too, and in this round he was less inclined to be charitable. The statement *We say it that way back home* sounded like a reasonable argument unless you realized that it was not a privilege Easterners granted to anyone other than themselves. If a Texan visiting New York pronounced "Houston Street" the same way that Texans pronounce the name of their city *back home*, he would be instantly corrected by a New Yorker, and probably derided for his provincial ignorance. But here in rural America, the privilege of local pronunciation was revoked. Here, if there was any difference of opinion about a pronunciation, Eastern urbanites felt that their way was the correct one, or at least an equally acceptable option. One of Baird Christopher's missions in life was to set arrogant tourists straight about matters like this.

"You know," he said to Eeyore, gearing up to his lecture in genial conversational tones. "Over in Northern Ireland once I visited a beautiful walled city that lies east of Donegal and west of Belfast. Now, for the last thousand years or so the Irish people who built that city have called it *Derry,* a name from *darach,* which is the Gaelic word for 'oak tree.' But the British, who conquered Ireland a few hundred years back, they refer to that same city as *Londonderry*. One place: two names.

"If you go to Ireland, and ask for directions to that city, you can call it by either name you choose. Whichever name you say, folks will know where it is you're headed and mostly likely they'll help you get there. But you need to understand this: When you choose what name you call that city—*Derry* or *Londonderry*—you are making a *political* decision. You are telling the people you're talking to which side you are on, what cultural values you hold, and maybe even your religious preference. You are telling some people that they can trust you and other people that they can't. All in one word. One word with a load of signifiers built right in.

"Now, I reckon *Appalachia* is a word like that. The way people say it tells us a lot about how they think about us. When we hear somebody say *Appa-lay-chia*, we know right away that the person we're listening to is not on our side, and we hear a whole lot of cultural nuances about stereotyping and condescension and ethnic bigotry, just built right in. So you go on and call this place *Appa-lay-chia* if you want to. But you need to know that by doing that you have made a po-li-ti-cal decision, and you'd better be prepared to live with the consequences. Friend."

Eeyore blinked at him and took a deep breath. *"Ap-pa. . .latch-ah?"* he said.

"That's right," said Baird. "Appa-latch-ah. Say it a time or two and you'll get the hang of it. Pretty soon any other way of saying it will grate on your ears."

Another long pause. Eeyore peered at his smiling host, who had gone back to shelling peas and humming an Irish dance tune. "Who *are* you?"

Baird Christopher smiled. "Why, I'm a Cosmic Possum."

ᏋᎬANNE ᏟᏟᏟᏟDONALD

(May 31, 1935–)

A native of Norfolk, Virginia, Jeanne McDonald graduated from the College of William and Mary with a B.A. in English and had dreams of being a writer. When some of her early stories were rejected, she settled for occasional writing, coupled with marriage, motherhood, and a career teaching high school English. After raising her three children, she returned to the work force as an editor for the University of Tennessee's Center for Business and Economic Research in Knoxville, Tennessee.

When McDonald signed up for a creative writing class taught by novelist Alan Cheuse at the University of Tennessee, all of her old dreams resurfaced. "I couldn't stop writing," recalls McDonald. "I stayed up until one or two in the morning, and took notes wherever I was—on the backs of grocery lists or sales receipts. All these stories that had been building for years just came out."

In 1989, she won the Alex Haley Literary Fellowship, and in 1995 she was a finalist for the Faulkner Prize. Her stories have appeared in several anthologies, including *Worlds in our Words: Contemporary American Women Writers* (1996) and *Homeworks* (1996). McDonald and her second husband, journalist Fred Brown, have collaborated on two nonfiction works, *Growing Up Southern: How the South Shapes Its Writers,* and *The Serpent Handlers: Three Families and Their Faith.* Her first novel, *Water Dreams,* is to be published in 2003 by the University Press of Mississippi.

"The settings for my stories are often the East Coast," says McDonald, "but the special rhythms of the Appalachian language, and the unabashed humility and humor of the people have drawn me to write more and more about this region."

In the following excerpt from her essay "Up the Hill toward Home," McDonald relates her experiences as a volunteer with a mental health program that assisted patients in gaining independence.

OTHER SOURCES TO EXPLORE

PRIMARY

Novel: *Water Dreams* (2003). **Nonfiction:** *The Serpent Handlers: Three Families and Their Faith* (2000), co-author with Fred Brown. *Growing Up Southern: How the South Shapes Its Writers* (1997), co-author with Fred Brown. **Autobiographical essay:** "Fantasy Meets Reality: Ah, the glamour of a book tour," *Metro Pulse* [Knoxville, TN] (31 August 2000), 23, 30.

SECONDARY

Jenny Nash, "You Never Know" [Interview / profile], *Tennessee Alumnus* (spring 1996), 29–31.

Breathing the Same Air: An East Tennessee Anthology (2001)

from Up the Hill
toward Home

This is a story I've needed to tell for a long time, one that has rolled around in my mind for years now. In many ways it seems like a sad story, but finally I have realized that it has as happy an ending as possible under the circumstances, that it is really a saga of bravery and resilience and just plain determination. It's the story of Mildred Hale, a woman who kept fighting for her life under the most adverse circumstances—parents killed when she was a child, mental breakdown in young adulthood, thirty years in a state mental institution, and then, in the last twenty years of her life the slow, late blooming of the inner woman she had always been meant to be. But there wasn't enough time to reclaim the first sixty years of her life.

Mildred died in 1996, at the age of 84, having lived a long life, some might say, but one that was virtually lost to her because, for most of it, she lived under the influence of numbing medications, terrifying electroshock therapy, and nightmarish phobias. At the end of her life, she lived alone, and that's how she died. Alone. Knowing how frightened she must have been, I've asked myself over and over if I could have done something to save her. I remember my telephone ringing just once that night, in the small dark hours. I didn't realize until a couple of days later that it must have been Mildred.

Mildred was what some people would call a "character." Anyone who saw her walking unsteadily along the street, wearing her polyester dresses and Indian moccasins, with her tightly-waved hair and an overabundance of bright and glittering costume jewelry, would think her odd, to say the least. But to me she was a heroine, because in a sense she was symbolic of millions of people in this country who are mentally ill, whose everyday lives are mired in fear, anxiety, and paranoia, and who, like Mildred, find even the simplest everyday acts painful—even impossible—to perform. Mildred was afraid to look anyone directly in the eye, as if in surrendering herself that way, she would somehow be swept away. She was frightened of new people, new places. She refused even to meet my new husband. And because she feared going to a beauty salon, for fifteen years I gave her home permanents in her apartment, twice a year—June and December. That was her schedule, not mine. Always, on those occasions, she would press a five- or ten-dollar bill into my hand for payment. When I gave it back, she would swear by "hell's fire" in her gravelly, cigarette-tainted voice that she would never speak to me again if I didn't take it. Of course she didn't mean it.

Mildred lived in a squalid apartment with hand-me-down furniture because her Social Security income couldn't buy her anything better. As her eyesight failed, the place became filthy because she couldn't see to clean. Sometimes church volunteers came in and washed floors and curtains and struggled with stains in the bathroom, but finally, they seemed to give up. Roaches, unnoticed by Mildred, scurried boldly in her refrigerator, and at the end of each of my visits, she would insist I take something home for the children. She would reach into the refrigerator and give me uncovered pieces of cake or pie, which I accepted so as not to injure her feelings, but tossed into the garbage once I got home. When mice invaded her apartment, Mildred stuffed steel wool under the molding to keep them out. Plants died on her windowsills and she didn't notice. Friends did her washing, and once I offered to pay for maids to clean her apartment, but she didn't want strangers there, and anyway, they would probably have left immediately when they saw the odds they would be facing.

Over the years Mildred gained the confidence to walk to the bank and the grocery store, where she made friends who helped her balance her account or find things on grocery shelves, and there was always someone in the neighborhood who would notice her struggling up the hill toward home and stop to offer her a ride.

There were happy moments, too. She loved her cigarettes, Moon Pies, Goo-Goo Clusters, chocolate-covered cherries, watching "The Price Is Right" on television, and listening to Red Foley and country music on the radio. She cherished letters and cards from friends and relatives back in West Tennessee, and she loved it when I brought my children to visit. This was Mildred's life, and it mirrored the anguished existence of millions of others like her, not only in East Tennessee, but in the entire country. Like Mildred, most of these victims have to rely on the mercy of social services, state and federal programs, and public agencies. Theirs is a life of waiting for help—in hospitals, in offices of doctors who serve the indigent, and in city and county agencies, always at the mercy of time and the people who are meant to assist them.

I first met Mildred back in 1977, when the government was slashing federal expenditures and one of the solutions was to dump people out of state mental hospitals and into the unforgiving streets of mainstream American life. Mental health officials tried to alleviate some of the trauma by setting up a program called "Community Friends," which called on citizens to help patients become acclimated to living in an open and unprotected environment—in short, the real world. The plan was to help them find housing, teach them how to open bank accounts and write checks, and show them how to buy groceries—basically, to set up a support system to which they could turn for help.

The first meeting for volunteers was held in one of the main buildings at Eastern State Hospital in Knoxville, now called Lakeshore Mental Health Institute. The men and women who showed up that day practiced role playing (I'm still not sure why) and discussed problems the exiles might face outside the environment they were so accustomed to. But nothing prepared us for the tour through the upper floors of the state mental hospital. In that brief walk-through, I experienced an immediate realization of the pain and frustration that mental illness can create not only for patients, but for their families as well. We walked through areas where glassy-eyed men and women constantly shuffled up and down the halls, mumbling to themselves; we entered huge wards where elderly or unmanageable patients were tied to chairs with sheets, and we passed dismal rooms with gray, padded walls and floors, rooms of the last resort. Then, suddenly, I was jolted by a male patient who leaned into my back and pushed his face into my hair. "Don't be afraid," said one of the psychologists leading the tour, "he loves the smell of shampoo." No wonder. The building was permeated by the odors of urine, disinfectants, cooking grease, and—you somehow realize this instinctively—the unmistakable odor of fear. Part of that fear was my own. It was impossible to walk into such a place and not be afraid, not be sickened, not be traumatized by a strange man pushing his face into your hair.

I had a lot to learn.

When we left the building, the psychologists warned us about patients walking in the streets of the hospital complex. "Don't worry," said these jaded caregivers, "they'll move when they see you coming. They're crazy, but they're not stupid." I gradually came to learn that this seemingly careless attitude was a protective shield the doctors used to keep themselves from becoming overcome with despair at the emotional magnitude of their jobs.

My initial meeting with Mildred and three other women who were to begin their outside lives together was more frustrating than traumatizing. It took place in one of the bungalows on the hospital grounds. Those who lived in the bungalows were the luckier patients. To a certain extent, they had learned to take care of themselves—bodily, anyway, although their medication was overseen by an orderly. They had a certain amount of freedom; some of them could even ride the bus in to town. All had some sort of job in the hospital—waiting tables, cooking, cleaning, or washing dishes. They could watch television and smoke—a precious privilege and vice that Mildred had picked up in the hospital. She continued to chain smoke up until the very day of her death, and I was convinced that she would die by setting herself or her rooms on fire. Partly because of her poor vision and partly because of her preoccupation with something I could never see, Mildred always forgot the ash at the end of the cigarette, which grew longer and longer, until finally it surrendered to gravitational pull, dropped and burned yet another hole in her skirt, her sofa, her bed, or the battered secondhand coffee table in her living room. Once, she saw a television program about lung cancer, and at eighty-one or eighty-two, she asked me did I reckon she would die from smoking. I told her no, that if she was going to get lung cancer, she'd surely have contracted it by now, and though I feared her death by fire, I figured that she had had few enough pleasures in this world anyway without taking away her cigarettes. Let her keep smoking.

The meeting with the four women that day was tense, because as they say in the movies, what we had there was a failure to communicate. All of them were frightened about being displaced from the safe and familiar surroundings of the hospital and their now accustomed routines. The women were mostly quiet, and, as was her custom, Mildred exhibited her paranoia by sitting off by herself in a corner of the room, with her back to the wall. She never made eye contact with anyone, not for years, and the first time she looked me directly in the face, I went home rejoicing.

KAREN SALYER McELMURRAY
(September 12, 1956–)

Karen Salyer McElmurray was born in eastern Kentucky, "where my writing began," she says. "When I was nine years old, I'd visit my grandmother in Johnson County during the summers and I became friends with Vicky Cantrell [now Hayes], the girl across the road. She played twelve-string guitar and wrote songs and poems. I wanted to do these things too, so I began to write poetry. Later, after I grew up in Frankfort, Kentucky, in the central part of the state, Johnson County remained my spiritual and emotional homeplace. . . . When I close my eyes and think of 'home,' I think of my grandmother's house. . . . When I dream of houses and home, that's the place my subconscious takes me, the place for which I long."

After earning her B.A. in philosophy and literature at Berea College in 1980, McElmurray earned an M.F.A. in fiction at the University of Virginia in 1986, an M.A. in contemporary fiction writing at Hollins University in 1989, and a Ph.D. in American literature at the University of Georgia in 1997. She has received grants from the National Endowment for the Humanities, the Kentucky Foundation for Women, and the North Carolina Arts Council. She is currently a writing professor at Berry College in Georgia. "I have also worked as a cook, a landscaper, and a waitress," she said. "All my lives have made my writing life."

Her first novel, *Strange Birds in the Tree of Heaven,* is set largely in Inez, a real eastern Kentucky mining town, fictionalized as the home of Ruth Blue Wallen, her husband Earl, and their son Andrew, characters who are searching for God, love, and redemption.

She describes her forthcoming memoir, *Mother of the Disappeared: An Appalachian Birth Mother's Journey,* as "my own story as a mother who relinquished her child to adoption" and as "also my own mother's story." In 2002, McElmurray was reunited with her son, who was born in 1973;

she discovered that his name is Andrew. The excerpt is the opening scenes from her memoir.

OTHER SOURCES TO EXPLORE

PRIMARY

Novel: *Strange Birds in the Tree of Heaven* (1999). **Memoir:** *Mother of the Disappeared: An Appalachian Birth Mother's Journey* (2003). **Essay:** "Minimalism and Maximalism in the Creative Writing Classroom," *Creating Fiction: Instruction and Insights from the Teachers of Associated Writing Programs,* ed. Julie Checkoway (March 1999). In *Leaving the Nest: Mothers and Daughters on the Art of Saying Goodbye* (2003), ed. Marilyn Kallet.

SECONDARY

Reviews of *Strange Birds in the Tree of Heaven*: *Atlanta Journal-Constitution* (14 Nov. 1999). *Chicago Tribune* (30 Jan. 2000), sect. 14: 5. *Lambda Book Report* (Feb. 2000), 18. *Women's Review of Books* (July 2000).

MOTHER OF THE DISAPPEARED: AN APPALACHIAN BIRTH MOTHER'S JOURNEY (2003)

from June 21, 1973

I'm sixteen and I'm on my way to the maternity ward of King's Daughter's Hospital in Frankfort, Kentucky, with a boy I'll call Joe. He's my husband, and we're riding the elevator, which we once skipped school to do all afternoon, for that rush of up and back down and up. Now a nurse with crimson nails is guiding my wheelchair and some woman is holding the hand of a little girl with lace-edged socks and a deep cut on her forehead, stitched at a slant.

Nothing but a baby, says the woman, and she means me. She has cat-eye glasses, and her voice is slurred as whiskey.

Or that's me. I'm buoyant already, with contractions and momentum. The labor isn't much, yet. Physically, there's a pushing down between my legs, a shove at my lower back, an ache, none of it worse than menstrual cramps. It's my image I want to keep intact. I'm with it. I'm moving forward, steady as we go. I'm tough, ready to give birth as if it were an everyday affair, casual as buttered toast or sex.

Nothing but a baby her own self, the woman says, looking at me with a rat-toothed smile.

And she's right. I'm a teenaged girl and I'm married to a teenaged boy and we've decided to give our son away at birth. I'm sixteen and I'm waiting for the future to happen, but it already has, in ways I'll discover for the rest of my life.

These are the facts. My son, relinquished to adoption on the day he was born, was named Brian Keith McElmurray by the Kentucky Department of Social Services in June of 1973. Other than his name, which they later sent to me in a form letter, I know very little about this boy who long ago became a man. I know that he was born very early in the morning, after a hard two days of labor. I know he weighed six pounds and something when he slid from my womb, the only time I ever heard him cry. I know that I was allowed, by law, to refuse to relinquish my son to my father who, two days after the birth, told me how he'd stood looking through the hospital nursery window and wondered that such a new being could so resemble his own father, a Standard Oil service station man who died when I was nine. I know that this is the only second-hand glimpse I have ever had of my son's face.

I know, or I have been told according to what is admissible by Kentucky Adoption Law, that my son was adopted one year after I relinquished him. Twenty-five years after his birth I will finally receive a letter from the Kentucky Department of Social Services, my first irrefutable proof that my son has a life beyond my own imperfect memory. The letter, dated January 15, 1998, states:

Dear Ms. McElmurray:

In response to your request to place information in the adoption/case record of Brian Keith, this is to let you know that your letter/request has been placed in his adoption record. To date, our agency has had no contact with him or the adoptive family since he was adopted by a Kentucky family in 1974. If he should ever contact our agency in the future seeking information about his birth family, we will advise him of your letter/request.

Under Kentucky's current adoption law, KRS 199.570, we can share the following non-identifying information about the adoptive parents.

The adoptive father was born in 1936 and had his Ph.D. in math. He was a professor at a large university. The adoptive mother was born in 1938 and also had advanced degrees in math. She taught part-time at the college level. Both enjoyed good health and had more than adequate resources to provide for a child or children. Brian Keith had adjusted quite well to the adoptive parents and they to him. The adoptive mother enjoyed being a mother and housewife. Our agency has no current information on the adoptive family.

I hope this information is helpful to you. For your information, Brian's birth date as given in our record is June 21, 1973.

Sincerely,
Virginia Nester
Program Specialist

These are the facts I currently possess, accrued like stray traces of dust. A paper trail that might lead, if I knew how to follow it, to irrefutable truths about what it meant to bear a son and give him away on that long-ago day, June 21st, 1973.

On this day of the birth, I woke in a room shadowed by floodlights Joe's father kept on in the dog lot, for his coon hounds. Damian, the Siamese cat, slipped out from the bend of my knees. We both often got out of bed at that time, the cat for a midnight kitchen raid and myself to stand at the window. White and liver-spotted dog coats, night moisture on glass, all of it gleaming and cool. Pain in my lower back woke me this night, a tightness starting in my back and moving down, pulling between my legs. Not for sure yet this was labor, I raised my hand to the window. A thin hand, and in the flood light I saw blue. Pale blue skin, blue bones, right down to the blue, chilled insides of me.

Joe, I said. Wake up. I think it might be time.

Time, he said.

His chubby cheeks were bluish, a two day beard, and his boy eyes were pale blue with bits of sleep in the corners. He rubbed his fists against them hard, and I thought of the times I'd seen those eyes, wide and black, the pupils expanded and electric with acid or speed or whatever else we could drum up from the streets and medicine cabinets of our town. I wished both of us could fall into those pupils, some bottomless and safe place, and never come back again. Instead, I saw blue sparks ignite in the close bedroom air. We were both so small in that light. Blue sparks of fear, his and mine, ignited the scents of socks and sleep. What I didn't imagine yet was the stretching, the slow opening of me.

Oh my god, Joe said.

He was sitting on the edge of the bed, full lips beneath his mustache twitching. He had a habit of drawing his long mustache hairs into his mouth, sucking, especially when he was frightened or angry. I went to him, tucked his head next to my stomach, where he could hear movement. If this child could talk, I wondered, what would be the words? *I'm late, I'm late*, like the rabbit in Alice and Wonderland. I want to stay here, the baby might say, in this soft place of blood.

Joe and I had a plan of sorts down pat. We'd prearranged with his parents, Rose and Joseph, with whom we lived, to use their station wagon for the hospital run—no fooling around in the middle of the night with hot wiring the Duster, which was now our car. We envisioned a back road short-cut to the hospital, a screeching halt at the emergency room, a wheelchair or two and then, in the most undefined part of our plan, a fast-forward version of that thing called *labor*, a painless, tidy version that involved no excretions or wounds, nothing so flesh-like as afterbirth. The real exodus was chaos.

My water had not yet broken, but the pain was shifting lower, and had developed an urgent, burning edge. Joe threw on cutoffs and a rose-colored polyester shirt and, still barefoot, opened the door, flipped on the hall switch and flooded the room with light. Somewhere, in the piles of blue jeans, Marvel Comics and the circuit breakers and boards that were his hobby, lay a spare set of keys to the station wagon, ready for an emergency. I stood in the middle of this emergency, cradling my belly, which was lower than it had been and needed hands to hold it up. . . .

*L*LEWELLYN *Mc*KERNAN
(July 12, 1941–)

Poet and children's author Llewellyn McKernan is a native of Arkansas who has set down roots in West Virginia. She is married to poet John McKernan, and the couple has one daughter. McKernan earned her B.A. in English from Hendrix College in Conway, Arkansas, in 1963, followed by an M.A. in English from the University of Arkansas in 1966. In 1976 she completed an M.A. in creative writing from Brown University. Her thesis was a collection of poetry, *The Blue Ball, and Other Poems.*

Says McKernan, "I have lived longer in Appalachia than anywhere else on earth. It is home to me. Its hills and valleys map my mind. Its creeks and rivers flow through my lines."

She is the author of four books for children and three volumes of poetry, including *Short and Simple Annals: Poems about Appalachia*, and *Many Waters: Poems from West Virginia.* McKernan is currently an adjunct professor of English at Marshall University.

OTHER SOURCES TO EXPLORE

PRIMARY

Poetry: *Many Waters: Poems from West Virginia* (1994), *Short and Simple Annals: Poems about Appalachia* (1983), *The Blue Ball, and Other Poems* (1976). **Books for Children:** *This is the Day* (1994), *This is the Night* (1994), *Bird Alphabet* (1988), *More Songs of Gladness* (1987). **Autobiographical essay:** "Letter from a Poet in West Virginia," in *Bloodroot* (1998), ed. Joyce Dyer, 188–91.

SECONDARY

James Byer, "The Woman's Place Is in the House," *The Poetics of Appalachian Space* (1991), ed. Parks Lanier Jr., 178–82. Joyce Dyer, "Llewellyn McKernan," in *Bloodroot* (1998), 187. Marianne Worthington, "Nothing Must Be Lost: Regional Identity and Dialogue in the Works of Edwina Pendarvis and Llewellyn McKernan," *Appalachian Heritage* 30:2 (spring 2002), 7–19.

MANY WATERS

from *Many Waters:*
Poems from West Virginia (1994)

Nothing in my house
but pale blue foliage
furniture dry as chalk and
dusty, and
tiny paths that lead
to bathroom, bedroom, kitchen,
jammed on both sides
with books opened
by the wind
and mulched by good intentions.

I do not trust
the light that comes through the windows
nor the pantry
where canned goods
are stacked from floor to ceiling nor the one
recipe with "darling
darling" written all over it. I only trust the rain,
how it vanishes

then reappears
the same yet different. Once this spring
after a storm
the basement flooded,
a natural disaster that left in its wake
strange plants
hooded like cobras
and during a cloudburst this summer hail
big as jawbreakers
tumbled down
the chimney (inside them were seeds:
sunflower, alfalfa,
mung bean).

And now that it's fall and I'm a Jill-in-the-Box
whizzing from love letter
to laundry, ironing board
to ironing out the flaws in a real estate contract,
scattering here a toe
there a nipple—
O! Out of a ragtag bobtail sky a hissing and
a murmuring

builds
in the long yellow funnel of a cloud that
swells, pregnant
with strife, and a dark streamlined cry
spreads its wings,
getting louder and louder,
wheeling like a plot,
chockful of the quotidien, getting wild-eyed
and in heat

when it reaches
my level: thundering through trees, crashing
into windows,
spinning rooms
around on their stone foundation. The roof
pops like corks
out of champagne bottles as the rain shouts
down the house with its jiggers
and I rise, drenched to the bone,
luminous, whole,
bringing out from under the lumber
all the family silver.

For My Grandmother Who Knows How

from *Many Waters: Poems from West Virginia* (1994)

In busy hands lie the greatest stillness, in
mountains quilted with rain, where crickets cry
    midnight and noon, I walk, you walk on bane-
laden slopes bathed in green, stroked long ago by
    the steps of the circuit court rider.
We step over his satchel, where tobacco and
    script, paled to the vein of a flower,
lie curled among the vines
    that crush them. (Beside them toadstools push
up their shadows.)
    We step over his saddle, whose cinch broke the
night when attacked by the headless horseman, he
    spurred his fine gray stallion to a stumble.

And perhaps no night goes by but he doesn't rise
from the bones that float their silver from one
    mountainside to another.
The dead laugh knowingly, but can they peel this
    fruit? How the worm removes even the wildest
rose to another country.
    In West Virginia, no one walks on water. A wind
rises as we start to cross the border, and on a road

    that plunges straight down to the flatlands,
narrowing as it goes (like a fountain), farmers
    wade to church on Sunday morning.

THE HOLLOW

from *Short and Simple Annals: Poems about Appalachia* (1983)

Reading Li'l Abner in the Sunday paper, she thinks
   of her grandmother and how she wore her hair:
All coiled, white and gleaming, tucked at the back
   of her head.

She thinks of Al Capp's wit. He spreads it across
   the page in screaming reds and yellows, but it ends
up silent: all coiled, white and gleaming, tucked
   at the back of her head.

Reading Li'l Abner in the Sunday paper, she thinks
   of her sister, who's dumb but sweet; whose vital
statistics like Daisy Mae's are 36-24-36; whose
   husband is some General Motors VIP.

All coiled, white and gleaming, tucked at the back
   of her head are yesterday's dreams, today's poverty,
tomorrow's chores. She bites her fingernails down to
   the quick, and then some more.

Reading Li'l Abner in the Sunday papers, she thinks
   of her husband: his shoulders are narrow. He's smart.
He's an Irish Catholic who shadowboxes with the wall
   and reeks of Scotch.

All coiled, white and gleaming, tucked at the back
   of her head is a vision of her father dead in a
cemetery in West Virginia, is a vision of her mother
   still in bed, sleeping late on Sunday morning.

Reading Li'l Abner in the Sunday papers, she thinks
   of her childhood, lost forever in a hollow overhung
by towering Appalachian beeches. Her tears lie all coiled
   white and gleaming, tucked at the back of her head.

MOTHER MILKING

from *Short and Simple Annals* (1983)

FOR CHRISTINE MCKINNIE

Turn down the brim of your old felt hat
so all I can see are your rosy lips

Chew on them absently
Think thoughts I have no way of hearing

Step carefully through
the muck of the barn

Stop to look at the beginning of sun:
beside each brown slat a blue one

Sigh and rub the ache in the bone
the place over the heart where fullness

has flown like a hen out of a coop go
around the black snake that lies in your path

The eggs inside its belly strung out
like cocoons just before the butterflies

emerge from their safekeeping Shush the hens
that roost in a row on the cow's back

Listen to the soft cooing issuing
from their throats to the ruffling

of their shiny feathers as they rise
to the rafters like powder puffs

Here where nothing moves but the cow chewing
its cud its dull stare turning to rock

Make your hands flash in the dark
make them light up the barn

as they take me back to that moment
in my childhood where nothing belongs but milk

filling the pail inch by inch
with its white froth

warm and sweet
as the breath of a baby

MUSIC

from *Short and Simple Annals* (1983)

The house where I was born had a big front yard.
The porch was blue eye shadow.

The dwarf cedar had eczema. Rain rolled
down it like water off a duck's back.

The moon-faced walk led to a gate
that creaked when the wind opened it.

This music rivaled the bee's tiny bell,
the bird's bubbling promise. Most of the time

I heard it: the iron gate's solo, its dog face
looking both ways, its ears curled up like snails.

Sometimes I made this music myself:
swinging back and forth, listening to

the click and moan that sounded
like my heart in the dead of night

when in the bedroom alone I heard
through the wall the ghost of a quarrel:

mother's dark hair, pressed against the chair's
pale flank, my father's fist raised and juggling

the anger that when it fell smashed
my mother's face in two like precious china.

IRENE McKINNEY
(April 20, 1939–)

"I'm a hillbilly, a woman, and a poet," says Irene McKinney, "and I understood early on that nobody was going to listen to anything I had to say anyway, so I might as well just say what I want to." She has said what she wanted in four collections of poetry. In 1985, she was the recipient of a National Endowment for the Arts Poetry Fellowship. She has also been awarded a West Virginia Commission on the Arts Fellowship in Poetry. In 1994, she was named Poet Laureate of West Virginia.

Born in Belington, West Virginia, where she currently lives, McKinney is the daughter of Celia and Ralph Durrett. She earned her B.A. from West Virginia Wesleyan College, her M.A. from West Virginia University, and her Ph.D. from the University of Utah. She has taught poetry at the University of California at Santa Cruz, the University of Utah, the University of New Mexico, Western Washington University, and Hamilton College. Currently, she teaches English and creative writing at her alma mater, West Virginia Wesleyan College in Buckhannon.

About McKinney's book of poems *Six O'Clock Mine Report*, poet Maxine Kumin has written, "I am grateful for the poems that burst forth from her West Virginia roots to shape this fine collection."

OTHER SOURCES TO EXPLORE

PRIMARY

Poetry: *Six O'Clock Mine Report* (1989), *Quick Fire and Slow Fire* (1988), *The Wasps at the Blue Hexagons* (1984), *The Girl with the Stone in Her Lap* (1976). **Edited book:** *Backcountry: Contemporary Writing in West Virginia* (2002).

SECONDARY

Maggie Anderson, "The Mountains Dark and Close around Me," in *Bloodroot* (1998), ed. Joyce Dyer, 39. Jeff Mann, "A Conversation with Irene McKinney," in *Her Words* (2002), ed. Felicia Mitchell, 194–205.

TWILIGHT IN WEST VIRGINIA: SIX O'CLOCK MINE REPORT

from *Six O'Clock Mine Report* (1989)

*Bergoo Mine No. 3 will work: Bergoo Mine
No. 3 will work tomorrow. Consol. No. 2
will not work: Consol. No. 2 will not
work tomorrow.*

Green soaks into the dark trees.
The hills go clumped and heavy
over the foxfire veins
at Clinchfield, One-Go, Greenbrier.

At Hardtack and Amity the grit
abrades the skin. The air is thick
above the black leaves, the open mouth
of the shaft. A man with a burning

carbide lamp on his forehead
swings a pick in a narrow corridor
beneath the earth. His eyes flare
white like a horse's, his teeth glint.

From his sleeves of coal, fingers
with black half-moons: he leans
into the tipple, over the coke oven
staining the air red, over the glow

from the rows of fiery eyes at Swago.
Above Slipjohn a six-ton lumbers down
the grade, its windows curtained with soot.
No one is driving.

The roads get lost in the clotted hills,
in the Blue Spruce maze, the red cough,
the Allegheny marl, the sulphur ooze.

The hill-cuts drain; the roads get lost
and drop at the edge of the strip job.
The fires in the mines do not stop burning.

DEEP MINING
from *Six O'Clock Mine Report* (1989)

Think of this: that under the earth
there are black rooms your very body

can move through. Just as you always
dreamed, you enter the open mouth

and slide between the glistening walls,
the arteries of coal in the larger body.

I knock it loose with the heavy hammer.
I load it up and send it out

while you walk up there on the crust,
in the daylight, and listen to the coal-cars

bearing down with their burden.
You're going to burn this fuel

and when you come in from your chores,
rub your hands in the soft red glow

and stand in your steaming clothes
with your back to it, while it soaks

into frozen buttocks and thighs.
You're going to do that for me

while I slog in the icy water
behind the straining cars.

Until the swing-shift comes around.
Now, I am the one in front of the fire.

Someone has stoked the cooking stove
and set brown loaves on the warming pan.

Someone has laid out my softer clothes,
and turned back the quilt.

Listen: there is a vein that runs
through the earth from top to bottom

and both of us are in it.
One of us is always burning.

SUNDAY MORNING, 1950

from *Six O'Clock Mine Report* (1989)

Bleach in the foot-bathtub.
The curling iron, the crimped, singed hair.
The small red marks my mother makes
across her lips.

Dust in the road, and on the sumac.
The tight, white sandals on my feet.

In the clean sun before the doors,
the flounces and flowered prints,
the naked hands. We bring
what we can—some coins,
our faces.

The narrow benches we don't fit.
The wasps at the blue hexagons.

And now the rounding of the unbearable
vowels of the organ, the O
of release. We bring
some strain, and lay it down
among the vowels and the gladioli.

The paper fans. The preacher paces,
our eyes are drawn to the window,
the elms with their easy hands.

Outside, the shaven hilly graves we own.
Durrett, Durrett, Durrett. The babies there
that are not me. Beside me,
Mrs. G. sings like a chicken
flung in a pan on Sunday morning.

. . . This hymnal I hold in my hands.
This high bare room, this strict accounting.
This rising up.

THE ONLY PORTRAIT
OF EMILY DICKINSON

from *Six O'Clock Mine Report* (1989)

The straight neck held up out of the lace
is bound with a black velvet band.
She holds her mouth the way she chooses,
the full underlip constrained by a small muscle.

She doesn't blink or look aside,
although her left eye is considering
a slant. She would smile
if she had time, but right now

there is composure to be invented.
She stares at the photographer.
The black crepe settles. Emerging
from the sleeve, a shapely hand

holds out a white, translucent blossom.
"They always say things which embarrass
my dog," she tells the photographer.
She is amused, but not as much as he'd like.

VISITING MY GRAVESITE
TALBOTT CHURCHYARD, WEST VIRGINIA
from *Six O'Clock Mine Report* (1989)

Maybe because I was married and felt secure and dead
at once, I listened to my father's urgings about "the future"

and bought this double plot on the hillside with a view
of the bare white church, the old elms, and the creek below.

I plan now to use both plots, luxuriantly spreading out
in the middle of a big double bed. —But no,

finally, my burial has nothing to do with my marriage, this lying
      here
in these same bones will be as real as anything I can imagine

for who I'll be then, as real as anything undergone, going back
and forth to "the world" out there, and here to this one spot

on earth I really know. Once I came in fast and low
in a little plane and when I looked down at the church,

the trees I've felt with my hands, the neighbors' houses
and the family farm, and I saw how tiny what I loved or knew
      was,

it was like my children going on with their plans and griefs
at a distance and nothing I could do about it. But I wanted

to reach down and pat it, while letting it know
I wouldn't interfere for the world, the world being

everything this isn't, this unknown buried in the known.

LOUISE McNEILL
(January 9, 1911–June 16, 1993)

Poet Louise McNeill was born in Pocahontas County, West Virginia, on a farm that was settled by her ancestors in 1769. She earned an A.B. degree from Concord College in Athens, West Virginia, and, at the age of nineteen, began teaching in a one-room schoolhouse. She later earned a master's degree from Miami of Ohio, and a Ph.D. in history from West Virginia University.

In 1938, McNeill won the *Atlantic Monthly* Poetry Award and was invited to the Bread Loaf Writers' Conference where she studied with Robert Frost. In the fall of 1938, McNeill was awarded a fellowship to the University of Iowa Writers' Workshop.

Her first major collection of poems, *Gauley Mountain,* was published in 1939, after Archibald MacLeish took an interest in her work. In that same year, she married "Yankee schoolteacher" Roger Pease. The couple lived outside the region for many years, but returned to West Virginia in 1959.

For the next twenty years, McNeill taught history and English at various West Virginia colleges and universities. She was named Poet Laureate of West Virginia in 1979 by West Virginia governor Jay Rockefeller.

In McNeill's autobiography, *The Milkweed Ladies,* she reminisces about the West Virginia farm that had been in her family since the eighteenth century.

OTHER SOURCES TO EXPLORE

PRIMARY

Poetry: *Hill Daughter: New & Selected Poems* (1991), *Elderberry Flood: The History, Lore, and Land of West Virginia Written in Verse Form* (1979), *Paradox Hill: From Appalachia to Lunar Shore* (1972), *Time Is Our House* (1942), *Gauley Mountain* (1939), *Mountain White* (1931). **Memoir:** *The Milkweed Ladies* (1988).

SECONDARY

Maggie Anderson, Introduction, *Hill Daughter: New & Selected Poems* (1991), xiii–xxvi. Arthur C. Buck, "Louise McNeill, West Virginia's Hill Daughter," *From a Dark Mountain* (1972), 24–26. Loyal Jones, review of *The Milkweed Ladies, Appalachian Heritage* 17:2 (spring 1989), 63–64. "Louise McNeill," *Appalachian Heritage* 13:4 (fall 1985), 12. "Louise M. Pease, 82, Poet of Appalachia," *New York Times,* 19 June 1993, 10.

THE OTHER WOMAN

from *Appalachian Heritage* (1985)

This windy morning as I stuffed
The rags around my window sill,
I found the strips that she had tucked
Against a wind that now is still.

Her rags were brown, and mine are gray
Hers stained and rotted; mine are new;
And yet, as women learn to stuff
(As once, at least, all women do)
Rags against terror—so she bent—
Then I, and now our rags are blent
Gray in the brown; from hill to hill
My wind goes screaming—hers is still.

AUBADE TO FEAR

(HEAVY WITH CHILD)

from *Hill Daughter* (1991)

Last night as I lay cold with fear
Of my travail now drawing near,
A gray wind I no longer hear
Blew from the darkness over me—
Blew southward from the Norn-white skies
Until I slept with seeing eyes—
Seeing no bauble fit to prize.

Not seeing dawn, its thin gray trace
Turn gold upon the pillow lace
And touch the warm beloved face.
Not seeing all I lived to own:
The torque of rubies, stone by stone,
The living pages touched and known.

Seeing instead that nets are small
Which shield us from the sparrow's fall,
How frail the rooftree and the wall,
How thin the string by which we tie
Our great ships of the wind and sky—
And what a little thing to die.

HILL DAUGHTER

from *Hill Daughter* (1991)

Land of my fathers and blood, oh my fathers, whatever
Is left of your grudge in the rock, of your hate in the stone;
I have brought you at last what you sternly required that I
  bring you,
And have brought it alone.

I, who from the womb must be drawn, though the first born,
  a daughter,
And could never stand straight with the rifle, nor lean with
  the plow;
Here is ease for the curse, here is cause for the breaking of
  silence.
You can answer me now.

It has taken me long to return, and you died without
  knowing,
But down where the veins of the rock and the aspen tree
  run—
Land of my fathers and blood, oh my fathers, whatever
Is left of your hearts in the dust,
I have brought you a son.

ARROW GRASSES
BY GREENBRIER RIVER

from *Paradox Hill* (1972)

Arrow grasses by the river,
Phalanx, spear by spear arrayed,
Teach us that we may remember
Others here have walked afraid.

Teach us—all our generation—
We are not the first to know
Death and war and red transgression
Where these quiet waters flow.

Long ago our father's father
Here in springtime dropped his corn,
Died and fell, an arrow winging
In his heart that April morn—

Dead as you and I will ever
Lie beneath the atom's burst—
Arrow grasses by the river,
Teach us we are not the first,

Nor the last to live in danger,
Live in wonder and in woe,
Here on earth beside the river,
Where the quiet waters flow.

THE MILKWEED LADIES (1988)
from A Patch Of Earth

Until I was sixteen years old, until the roads came, the farm was about all I knew: our green meadows and hilly pastures, our storied old men, the great rolling seasons of moon and sunlight, our limestone cliffs and trickling springs. It was about all I knew, and, except for my father and before him, the old Rebel Captain, all that any of us had even known: just the farm and our little village down at the crossroads, and the worn cowpaths winding the slopes; or we kids driving the cows home in the summer evenings; or the winter whiteness and stillness, Aunt Malindy's "old woman in the sky" picking her geese, the "old blue misties" sweeping out of the north.

Some of our tales were old and old, going back into time itself, American time. Living so long there in the same field under the same gap in the mountain, we had seen, from our own ragged little edge of history, the tall shadows passing by. "Old Hickory" in his coach passed along our dug road one morning; General Lee one evening on his way to the Gauley rebel camps. Then, in 1863, as we watched from our cliff walls and scrub oak bushes, the great Yankee army passed on its way to the Battle of Droop: all day long the clank and spur and roll of their passage, 2,000, 3,000, 4,000, hard, blue Yankees, their bayonet tips made bloody in the sunset.

Grandpa Tom, our "old one," had gone with George Rogers Clark to Kaskaskia and had run the Falls of the Ohio under an eclipse of the sun. Uncle Bill went to Point Pleasant against old Cornstalk and his Ohio Shawnee; then Little Uncle John to the War of 1812; Captain Jim to the Virginia Rebels, his brother Al to the Yankees. My father, in 1906, sailed with Teddy Roosevelt's Great White Fleet; then Cousin Paul and Cousin Coe "to make the world safe for Democracy."

But before I grew up and went out into the world—and a bloody thing I found it—we were all at home there in our faded cottage in the meadow, all of us safe and warm. Sometimes now, a quiet sense comes to me, the cool mist blowing in my face as though I am walking through islands of fog and drifting downhill slowly southward until I feel the mountains behind my shoulder. Walking on, I can see the light in the "big room" window as I come to our cottage standing in the meadow under "Bridger's" Mountain, as it always stands on the fore-edges of my memory, and the old farm where I ran the April fields and pastures to my great rock up in the woodland where the lavender hepaticas grew. Then I knew just the earth itself: the quiet measure of the seasons; the stars in the sky; the wheat field in August, golden: darkness and day; rain and sunlight; the primal certainty of spring. Then we were all there together, the years not yet come on us, these seventy-five years of war and money and roaring turnpikes and torrents of blood.

I know, deep down, that our one old farm is only a ragged symbol, a signet mark for all the others, the old and far older hard scrabble mountain farms of Kentucky, Tennessee, North Carolina, and Virginia, all the briery fields scattered across the mountains south. And how the earth holds us is still a dark question. It is not the sucking deepness that draws us, for the earth is mother, protector, the home; but the oppressor too. It requires, sometimes, the very lifeblood of its own, and imprisons the flyaway dreams and bends the backs of men and women. Yet to love a familiar patch of earth is to know something beyond death, "westward from death," as my father used to speak it.

We could sense, just beyond our broken-down line fences, the great reach of the American continent flowing outward. Because we stood so long in one place, our rocky old farm and the abundant earth of the continent were linked together in the long tides of the past. Because the land kept us, never budging from its rock-hold, we held to our pioneer ways the longest, the strongest; and we saw the passing of time from a place called solid, from our own slow, archean, and peculiar stance.

ꝒANE ꝒERCHANT
(November 1, 1919–January 2, 1972)

Jane Hess Merchant, one of four children of Donia Swann Merchant and Clarence Leroy Merchant, was born in Knoxville, Tennessee, where she lived all her life. Debilitated by a bone disease, Merchant spent her adult life in bed, writing poetry that ranged from humorous reflections to religious meditations. When she became deaf in the final years of her life, she relied on the written word as her primary means of communication.

More than fifteen hundred of her poems have been published in newspapers and magazines in the United States, Canada, and England.

Her talent has been acknowledged by awards from the National League of American Pen Women for *The Greatest of These* and *Blessed Are You*. She received the 1961 Lyric Foundation Citation and Award for Outstanding Achievements in Poetry, and the 1965 Beaudoin Gemstone Award for Poetry.

OTHER SOURCES TO EXPLORE

PRIMARY

Poetry: *Because It's Here* (1970), *Every Good Gift* (1968), *All Daffodils Are Daffy* (1967), *Petals of Light* (1965), *The Mercies of God* (1963), *Blessed Are You* (1961), *In Green Pastures* (1959), *Halfway up the Sky* (1957), *Think about These Things* (1956), *The Greatest of These* (1954).

SECONDARY

Contemporary Authors, New Revision Series, Vol. 4, 416. Lillian Keller, "Through a Poet's Window," *Progressive Farmer* (April 1952). *Publishers Weekly* (January 24, 1972). Grace Watkins, "The Poetry Merchant," *Christian Herald* (November 1954).

LANTERNS AND LAMPS

from *The Greatest of These* (1954)

My parents carried light with them, for they
Lived in the days when people made their own
Or did without. The lantern's frosty ray,
When Dad came late from milking, always shone
As if a star were coming home to us,
And if I called at midnight, goblin-harried,
The shadows fled and night grew luminous
Before the little lamp that Mother carried.

Folk have small need of lamps and lanterns now;
Even on farms the darkness will withdraw
By swift electric magic, but somehow
I always shall be grateful that I saw
My parents' coming make the darkness bright
And knew them as the carriers of light.

FIRST PLOWING IN THE HILLS

from *The Greatest of These* (1954)

When it's too soon for spring, and even too soon
To think of it, you'd think—some afternoon
You're sure to raise your eyes and see them there
Cresting the topmost ridge that tries to pare
Whole sections from the sky; a man and team
Of horses plowing. Cloud and clod would seem
To feel the plowshare equally. You wonder
If the sun itself isn't apt to be plowed under
In that steep enterprise. It makes you proud
Of men who'll start out halfway up a cloud
To sketch designs for summer on a land
That isn't sure of spring. You understand,
Of course, it's hard work plowing on a hill,
And bottom lands grow better crops, but still
There's something useful to the heart and eye
In men who plow the earth, against the sky.

ÉMMA ᘓELL ᘓILES
(October 19, 1879–March 19, 1919)

Writer and painter Emma Bell Miles was born to Martha Ann Mirick Bell and Benjamin Franklin Bell. Her mother was visiting relatives in Evanston, Illinois, away from their home along the Ohio River in Rabbit Hash, Kentucky, when she gave birth to twins. Miles's brother lived only one day. Both parents were teachers and strict Presbyterians. Because of her frail health, Miles was educated mostly at home, where she learned at a young age to read and enjoy nature studies with her mother.

In hopes that a climate change would improve her health, the family moved south in 1891 to Walden's Ridge, Tennessee, near Chattanooga. By 1899, Miles was strong enough to begin attending the St. Louis School of Art, and her father planned to send her to New York to study art. But Miles had plans of her own, and she married mountaineer Frank Miles in 1901. Their twin daughters were born in 1902, and three other children followed by 1909.

Her marriage to Frank was a rocky one with frequent moves and a pattern of separations and reunions. They lived in a tent when they could not afford better housing, and she sold sketches to the summer people to support the family. With her husband often out of work, Miles frequently was responsible for keeping the struggling family finances afloat.

By 1903, Miles had met writers Alice MacGowan and Grace MacGowan Cooke, successful collaborators and sisters who were published authors of novels, stories, and poems. They helped Miles to get her first publications, two poems and a nonfiction article, in *Harper's Monthly* in 1904. The article became a chapter of her first book, *The Spirit of the Mountains*, a landmark study that inspired Horace Kephart's *Our Southern Highlanders* and others with her keen observations and frank admiration of mountain people.

OTHER SOURCES TO EXPLORE

PRIMARY

Nonfiction: *Our Southern Birds* (1919), *The Spirit of the Mountains* (1905). **Poetry:** *Strains from a Dulcimore* (1930).

SECONDARY

Kay Baker Gaston, *Emma Bell Miles* (1985).

THE SPIRIT OF THE MOUNTAINS (1905)

Cabin Homes

"Poor people has a poor way."

Solitude is deep water, and small boats do not ride well in it. Only a superficial observer could fail to understand that the mountain people really love their wilderness—love it for its beauty, for its freedom. Their intimacy with it dates from a babyhood when the thrill of clean wet sand was good to little feet; when "frog-houses" were built, and little tracks were printed in rows all over the shore of the creek; when the beginnings of aesthetic feeling found expression in necklaces of scarlet haws and headresses pinned and braided together of oak leaves, cardinal flowers and fern; when beargrass in spring, "services" and berries in summer and muscadines in autumn were first sought after and prized most for the "wild flavor," the peculiar tang of the woods which they contain.

I once rode up the Side with a grandmother from Sawyers' Springs, who cried out, as the overhanging curve of the bluff, crowned with pines, came into view: "Now, ain't that finer than any picter you ever seed in your life?—and they call us pore mountaineers! We git more out o' life than anybody."

Grandmothers and Sons

"There's more marries than keeps cold meat."

The best society in the mountains—that is to say, the most interesting—is that of the young married men and that of the older women. The young people are so shy that they can hardly be said to form a part of society at all. They are hedged with conventions and meet almost as formally as young Japanese. For example, on entering church the men are expected to turn to the left and seat themselves, and the women to the right. It is permitted a young fellow who is avowedly out courting to sit beside his "gal," but I cannot imagine what would happen if a young woman were to place herself on the men's side of the house.

After marriage something of the young man's shyness wears off; he gradually loses his awe of the opposite sex, and even within the conventions he finds room for intelligent conversation. Then he begins to be interesting, for his twenty-odd years of outdoor experience have really taught him much. As for the woman, it is not until she has seen her own boys grown to be men that she loses entirely the bashfulness of her girlhood, and the innate beauty and dignity of her nature shines forth in helpfulness and counsel.

I have learned to enjoy the company of these old prophetesses almost more than any other. The range of their experience is wonderful; they are, moreover, repositories of tribal lore—tradition and song, medical and religious learning. They are the nurses, the teachers of practical arts, the priestesses, and their wisdom commands the respect of all. An old woman has usually more authority over the bad boys of a household than all the strength of man. A similar reverence may have been accorded to the mothers of ancient Israel, as it is given by all peoples to those of superior holiness—to priests, teachers, nuns; it is not the result of affection, still less of fear.

HEATHER ROSS MILLER
(September 15, 1939–)

Poet and novelist Heather Ross Miller was born in Albemarle, North Carolina. Both her father, Fred Ross, and her uncle, James Ross, were novelists,
and Miller's aunt Eleanor, herself a poet, married acclaimed fiction writer
Peter Taylor. "I took it as natural," says Miller, "this business of finding stories and poems in everyday affairs."

Miller earned her B.A. in English in 1961 and her M.F.A. in 1969,
both from the University of North Carolina at Greensboro. She also did
postgraduate work in modern drama and cinema at the University of London, and taught at several North Carolina colleges, as well as at the University of Arkansas. In 1984, she was awarded an honorary Ph.D. from Methodist
College in Fayetteville, North Carolina.

Her first novel, *The Edge of the Woods*, published in 1964, won the
National Association of Independent Schools Best Book Award for that year.
Critics lauded the novel for its lyrical style. One reviewer wrote, "Hers is a
truly individual style which, though drawing in a rather original manner on
Biblical imagery, in no way suggests any recognizable imitation of her liter-
ary elders."

Miller has gone on to publish more than a dozen books and has contributed to periodicals ranging from the *New York Times* to *Vogue*. Miller
says, "I want the stories, the poems, to be natural. I am a Southern woman,
and I write about the places that flavor me." Since 1992, she has been the
Thomas Broadus Professor of English at Washington and Lee University in
Lexington, Virginia.

In the following scene from *The Edge of the Woods*, Miller's first novel, we
meet Anna Marie Wade, an observant child being raised by her grandparents.

OTHER SOURCES TO EXPLORE

PRIMARY

Novels: *Champeen* (1999), *Gone a Hundred Miles* (1968), *Tenants of the House* (1966), *The Edge of the Woods* (1964). **Stories:** *In the Funny Papers: Stories* (1995), *A Spiritual Divorce and Other Stories* (1974), *Delphi: A Collection of Stories* (1969). **Poetry:** *Days of Love and Murder: Poems* (1999), *Friends and Assassins* (1993), *Hard Evidence: Poems* (1990), *Adam's First Wife* (1983), *Therapia* (1982), *Horse Horse, Tyger Tyger* (1973), *The Wind Southerly* (1967). **Memoir:** *Crusoe's Island: The Story of a Writer and A Place* (2000). **Autobiographical essay:** "A Natural History," in *Bloodroot* (1998), ed. Joyce Dyer, 193–99.

SECONDARY

Contemporary Authors, New Revision Series, Vol. 5, 372–73. Joyce Dyer, "Heather Ross Miller," in *Bloodroot*, 192. Lottie H. Swink, "Heather Ross Miller," *Southern Writers: A Biographical Dictionary* (1979), 307–8.

THE EDGE OF THE WOODS (1964)

from Chapter 1

Here is my name across the top line of my copy book: Anna Marie Wade, born September twenty-third, in the time of the autumnal equinox, when day and night are everywhere on earth of equal length. And winter approaches. In the night, the wind changes and brings frost with morning, turning the songbirds southward. The blood-red bead in the thermometer slowly descends. And Paw Paw will have to poke up the fire, showering the hearth with crimson sparkles.

"Listen! It's a snow fire," he says, holding the poker stiffly upright, like a toy soldier at attention.

My brother and I look up from our lessons and strain our ears to hear the soft crunch, crunch, shoo-ish of the flame that Paw Paw says sounds like a man walking on a crust of snow.

Grandmother is brushing out her hair for bed. Long pearl-grey strands rippling down her shimmy like a dim waterfall, a mist, her brush racing through it, making little electric crackles in the soft, drowsy room.

"Whoo-ee," she says, stopping a moment, the hair floating over her face like a dingy cloud. "I'm all give out in my back. One of you younguns come over here and finish my hair for me. Anna'Ree?"

I close my copy book and put my yellow pencil in the washed-out iodine bottle which holds all our pencils and pieces of pencil, pins, rubber bands, and such. Grandmother's hair feels dry and soft in my hand, strangely impersonal and unalive, like the thick hair of our shaggy shepherd, a cloak that could be thrown off at any moment and reveal the naked flesh beneath. I let it slide through my fingers, grey, white, a few rivulets of dull gold, a mantle of salt-and-pepper, Rapunzel, Rapunzel, let down your golden hair, Rapunzel, Rapunzel, let down your golden stair.

"Comb and brush until it flows like silken threads," sighs Miss Jen, nodding against the wicker chair. "Like silken threads."

She is asleep, dreaming under my hands, swept away on the old grey flood of her hair. An old Rapunzel, with no more flax to spin into gold, no prince to climb again upon her stair, no tower, and no witch of darkness.

In the corner, Paw Paw yawns over his Bible, tracing out each line under a rough old finger, each word flowing under his thick black nail, the flimsy pages pressed under a palm horny with calluses. He dozes, like Grandmother, but swept away on a different flood, just as old and perhaps more turbulent.

Once, when I was still quite young, still in loose ginghams and wearing long yellow braids, back before my brother was really a person, I sat in my grandfather's Sunday School. Cedar Grove had only a one-room, white, wooden, Methodist Church and there were dark heavy curtains, like burlap, strung on rails to divide off the classes. The screech of those curtains rings skittering along the rail would always put my teeth on edge and make the skin of my neck prickle. I sat beside Miss Jen, feeling her bosom blossom and sink under the Sunday voile, the straw buds of her bonnet trembling like tiny yellow cornucopias around the pale flush of her brow. It was quite warm and the windows were open, letting in every fly, wasp, and bumblebee from each mile of thick country garden and crop land that lay spread out like a fan around the church.

I was nervous for Paw Paw. I'd never heard him speak in front of folks before, and he seemed awfully out of place to me, standing up there small and stiff in his black vest, the clump of white hairs that sprouted from a mole on his chin quivering like thistles in dew, and his eyes watering. He took up the Bible and began, something from Psalms.

Blessed *is he whose* transgression *is* forgiven, *whose* sin is covered. . . .

Rejoice in the Lord, O ye righteous, for praise is comely to the upright. Praise the Lord with harp: sing unto him with the psaltery *and* an instrument of ten strings.

He was one of those people who gave deep Biblical emphasis to any words that were printed in italics. He could not have known that the Jacobean translators simply could not render every word of God into the King's English. Paw Paw was unlettered, but not illiterate. He never got beyond the fifth grade in formal schooling. There just wasn't any for him. And the lessons of the land had to be learned first. Before the letters of the alphabet, a man must know seedtime and harvest, the phases of the moon, and how to cure hog meat that would keep through winter. And the mysteries of numbers were to be found in penny nails or bushel baskets, in acres and bales and how much hard cash was tied up in the middle of a greasy handkerchief.

I should have trusted him more that Sunday. His voice was strong and his eye firm. King David himself could have done no better than Paw Paw at Cedar Grove. But maybe I was only a child, and very impressionable, like warm wax.

SEVENTH GRADES

from *Friends and Assassins* (1993)

We spread in the grass and slit clover
with a thumbnail, slid one stem
through another, hinged like long lovers,
locked death mates, sucking
the tight white knots
of dead persistent flowers.
We said we'd have it all,
bridesmaids, babies,
hot abundant nectars
the magazines promised like Aretha
singing off our mother's radios,
chainchain—*chain!*
        chainchain—
chain! Chain of *foooooools!*

That was our flowering period,
unlucky three-leafed,
each one an unwed
troublesome weed
of a girl
growing April through October,
chaining clover, easy as cattle
in good pasture.

BREADSTUFF

from *Hard Evidence* (1990)

I've had enough of making bread go around,
slapping it, pat-a-caking me to death. But.
Nowhere do I find me so painstakingly
real and rising, leavening each hour
but in this salt, yeast, and cool unblanched flour.
Over the dough bowl, my loony face sifts,
takes shape and lifts. My thumbs search
the elements and my fist blends
the taste of a real presence.
I'd like to waste it, starve people,
go to bed and sleep a year. But.
The oven heats up right
and I wait wait wait.
Crumbs and little bones, sweet dark-curling peels
pile my table, seal the plates. I set out more,
pour cups, catch fish, rob bees to fill up
hungrier, hungrier brothers, nursing all these
on my one lovely body. Never enough.
I make myself go around. Starting over,
I measure and stir, punch the blind stuff
to make it grow. Somebody's tears fall in,
teasing the helpless dough.
Stop it, brothers.
I've got life up to the elbow.

ᏤANICE ᏟOWNLEY ᏜOORE
(April 29, 1939–)

Poet Janice Townley Moore has lived in Hayesville, in the western North Carolina mountains, and in north Georgia, where she has taught classes in writing and literature at Young Harris College since 1963. She says, "No matter what the subject, the mountains sometimes slip into my poems. The seasons and moods of this region, along with the native wildlife, have definitely given my poems a sense of place."

She earned her B.A. from LaGrange College in 1961 and her M.A. from Auburn University in 1963. She studied further at Emory University, Georgia State University, University of Virginia, and North Georgia College. From 1985 to 1997, she served as poetry editor for *Georgia Journal* and in 1996 co-edited *Like a Summer Peach: Sunbright Poems and Old Southern Recipes*.

Her work has appeared in a variety of anthologies and literary journals including *The Georgia Review, Southern Poetry Review, Prairie Schooner, When I Am an Old Woman I Shall Wear Purple, The Bedford Introduction to Literature*, and *Old Wounds, New Words*.

OTHER SOURCES TO EXPLORE

PRIMARY

Edited book: *Like a Summer Peach: Sunbright Poems & Old Southern Recipes* (1996).
Poetry: *Windows Filled with Gifts* (unpublished collection).

SECONDARY

Michael J. Bugeja, "Keep Your Senses Alive in Writing," *Poet's Market* (1994).

ALL THOSE NIGHTS

from *Southern Humanities Review* (1982)

What was he looking for
my Father, with his flashlight,
padding up and down the hall,
opening the cellar door
to shine the beam
down the long stairs?

I never heard the noise
that roused him from his bed.

I remember only the sudden light
on the bedroom wall,
how it swept across my face
and my brother's, for love.

Even now in the dark house
I awaken to his flare,
when the moon escapes
from behind a cloud,
breaking against the ceiling.

Under the Earth

from *Southern Humanities Review* (1985)

Where the road slices
through Needle Gorge
animals of stone
root out of the cliff

Their snouts, heads, shoulders
bulge from red clay
as if to catch the scent of
ancient water

Eons piled upon eons
this is the only place
where the mountain lion
will lie with the lamb

Stacked together,
the buffalo, wild boar,
oxen, the goat
with its grassy beard—

Did they all stop
before they reached
the saving water of the river,
caught in their final breath?

THE WAY BACK

from *Negative Capability* (1984)

The mountains are barren
in the season
you would have been born,

their useless bellies push
against Christmas sky.

It is the month of children
like those on the doctor's
bulletin board
in the room where he put me,

the one time I lay
in that room,

his affirmation
attached to my
long night of losing.

A difficult way to daylight
it seems. I find it months later,
kneading dough for a seasonal bread,
the first I have ever made,
awaiting its rise in the oven.

MARIJO MOORE
(August 24, 1952–)

Poet and fiction writer MariJo Moore is of eastern Cherokee, Irish, and Dutch ancestry. She grew up in western Tennessee and says about her childhood, "I grew up in an alcoholic home with a white stepfather who did not like the idea that I had Indian blood. Reading was my only escape as I grew older, and of course, this fueled my love of writing." Her first poem was published when she was sixteen. Her goal as a writer, she explains, is to "make use of all I have survived to give strength and hope to others."

She attended Tennessee State University in Nashville and earned the equivalent of a B.A. in Literature from Lancashire Polytechnic in Preston, England, in 1987.

A self-employed writer, she lives in Candler, North Carolina, where she has formed rENEGADE pLANETS pUBLISHING, a company committed to publishing the writing of Native Americans. She encourages other American Indians to write because, she says, "it is time we begin writing our own literature so that we will not be stereotyped to death."

She was nominated Writer of the Year in Poetry by Wordcraft Circle of Native American Writers and Storytellers (1997) and was named North Carolina Distinguished Woman of the Year (1998) by the Department of Administration, Council for Women, in Raleigh, North Carolina. She has served on the board of the North Carolina Writers' Network, on the Speaker's Bureau and on the board of the North Carolina Humanities Council, and as the project director for the 1997 North Carolina Native American Literary Heritage Conference. In 2000, *Native Peoples* magazine named her as one of the top five American Indian writers of the new century.

Her work has appeared in such publications as *Indian Artist, Indigenous Woman, Native Women in the Arts, Voices From Home: An Anthology of North Carolina Prose,* and *National Geographic.* She has edited a collection of writ-

459

ings by North Carolina American Indians, *Feeding the Ancient Fires* (1999). She is also editor of *Genocide of the Mind: A Collection of Essays by Urban Indians* (2003).

Other Sources to Explore

Primary

Fiction: *Red Woman with Backward Eyes and Other Stories* (2001). **Poetry:** *Desert Quarter* (2000), *Spirit Voices of Bones* (1997), *Tree Quarter* (1997), *Crow Quarter* (1996). **Fiction and poetry:** *Returning to the Homeland—Cherokee Poetry and Short Stories* (1995).

Secondary

Jennifer Hicks, "Profile: MariJo Moore, Survive and Follow Your Heart," http://www.minorities-jb.com/native/marijo9.html

Story is a Woman

from *Spirit Voices of Bones* (1997)

Story is a
woman. Not
long, not short. A
woman with body of
carved petroglyph
tongue of red memories
eyes of dark insight
ears of drummed
legends

hair of ageless ceremony falling onto
her skirt of history woven, tradition colored, many
gathered. Stranded myth beads float over her
breasts like crows float over timeless time.
Scavenging

connecting words
old and new
told and retold
sung and shouted
whispered and chanted
reflecting mirrors in front
scraping medicines from behind.

Listen   children!
Story is   a woman.
Not long,   not short.
A woman.   Respect her.

SOLIDARITY IN THE NIGHT

from *Spirit Voices of Bones* (1997)

This was the night
all the people sang together.

This was the night
all the people dreamed together.

This was the night
all the people danced together.

This was the night
all the people prayed together.

This was the night
all the people began to heal.

Ahlawe Usv' Tsigesvgi

from *Spirit Voices of Bones* (1997)

Usv' tsigesvgi
nigata yvwi duninogisv.

Usv' tsigesvgi
nigata yvwi anasgitskvgi.

Usv' tsigesvgi
nigata yvwi analskvgi.

Usv' tsigesvgi
nigata yvwi anadadolistihvgi.

Usv' tsigesvgi
nigata yvwi anadaleni unidiwisga.

Eastern Cherokee translation
"Solidarity in the Night"

RUMORS

from *Red Woman with Backward Eyes and Other Stories* (2001)

It was rumored that Addy May Birdsong would sneak into your house, touch your forehead with her fingers while you were sleeping, and change the course of your dreams. I had heard this rumor for the first time when I was about thirteen. Lydia Rattler, who sat next to me in Home Room, told me this because she had heard that Addy May was related to me.

"So what?" I had said back to her. "Everybody's related to everybody here." I had never liked Lydia much because she had ugly teeth that stuck way out and because she wanted to gossip all the time like an old woman. But she sat next to me that whole school year and I learned to endure her gossip, if not her buck teeth.

When I had asked my mama about the rumor, she said that lots of things were said about Addy May because she was different than most.

"What do you mean, different?" I asked in total sincerity. It seemed to me that almost every adult I knew back then had some sort of strangeness about them—mostly caused from alcohol, or from running out of it.

"Well," my mama had said thoughtfully as she scratched her chin the way she often did when she was trying to explain something in terms that she thought I might understand, "Cousin Addy May just has a way of stirring people up. She looks all the way into their souls with those black-pitted eyes of hers and it makes people wonder if she knows what they've been up to." I had to agree with the part about the black-pitted eyes. They reminded me of a tunnel a train had just gone through.

"But you don't pay any mind to what you hear about her. She's your cousin and she's had a hard life, harder than most on this reservation, and so she deserves to be a little stranger than most if she wants."

I forgot about my "stranger than most" Cousin Addy May and all the rumors about her until one night it was so hot I was having trouble sleeping and decided to crawl out the bedroom window to get some fresh air. I was careful not to wake my younger twin sisters. Course I loved them with all my heart, but they could be quite bothersome when I wanted some time alone.

The night air was so cool and refreshing I pulled my braids on top of my head and let it touch the back of my neck. It made me feel really good, so I decided to take a walk down the road that led up the mountain to our house. The two other families who lived on the road were at least two miles away, so I felt like I had the road all to myself. I had walked for about ten minutes, staring up at the stars and the full moon, feeling proud that I was so brave to be out by myself that late at night, when I saw Addy May standing there in the middle of the road with the moon shining down on her head like a flashlight. Her hair was long and loose, not braided as usual, and I remember thinking that it looked like a thick, black waterfall flowing down her skinny back. I was totally shocked to see someone standing there in the middle of the night and grateful that she hadn't heard me coming down the road.

She had her back to me, so I stepped into the darkness of the brush beside the road so I could watch her. She was wearing a long cotton skirt that was probably dark blue but looked purple in the moonlight, and a shawl of many colors was draped loosely around her thin shoulders. I watched quietly as she swayed her body back and forth, waving both hands above her head. The more I watched her, the faster my heart beat. And when she started singing, I felt like it would bust right out of my chest. Her voice was beautiful, high pitched and full of rich guttural tones. Over and over she sang her song, swaying there in the moonlight. I could hear her words distinctly:

"First I was woman
then I was mother
now I am woman again."

Mesmerized by her presence and her voice, I had no idea what her song was about, but I knew the words came from way down deep inside her. From the same place my moon time had begun flowing several months back when mama had told me that I had become a woman. Addy May's words came from the connecting source to the earth that every woman has inside her, and my stomach burned way down deep in that spot as I listened.

I must have stood there in the brush for at least half an hour, watching her, listening to her singing, and feeling my heart trying to jump up into my throat. Then something happened that I never would have believed if someone else had told me about it. There were two female spirits come down from the sky and stood right next to Addy May's swaying body. One was real old and the other a young girl just a little older than me. With quick, jerky movements, they began to dance around Addy May, looking kind of like the white curling smoke that dances around a red hot fire, and chanting in Cherokee. I couldn't understand all of what they were saying because I don't speak my native language proper, but I heard a few words I could recognize and realized the gist of their song had to do with sorrow and grief.

As I stood there, squinting my eyes trying to figure out what was in the bundles each spirit woman carried in her arms, and muster up enough courage to stay and see what would happen next, Addy May turned and looked directly at me. I swear she looked directly at me and smiled right into my eyes, never missing a beat to her swaying or a word to her song. When she did that, I ran back home as fast as I could and didn't tell a soul what I had seen than night. Not even my mama. As a matter of fact, I kind of forgot about the incident for a while because my thoughts were on other things. Mostly my new boyfriend, Roger. That is until I heard from Lydia Rattler that Addy May had been arrested for stealing a baby boy.

She had gone into John and Amanda Wolfe's house late one night and taken their baby right from his crib. The baby hadn't cried or made any noise or anything, so the parents didn't know he was missing until his mama woke up the next morning and went to check on him. He was only six months old but he was big for his age. I had seen him in front of the Spirits on the River with his mama the week before Addy May stole him. Amanda had gone in there to apply for a job and asked me and my cousin Lenny, who happened to be walking by at the time, to hold him for her while she went in the restaurant to get an application. It was really curious to me that I had actually held that same baby in my arms just a week before Addy May stole him.

She hadn't tried to hide him or anything, and that's why they found out so quick that she had him. She had just taken him home with her, and when Mavis Rose had passed by Addy May's house on her way to the Tribal Offices as she did every weekday morning, she had seen Addy May sitting there on her front porch in an old rocking chair, holding him. Mavis said later that she thought it was kind of odd, Addy May sitting there on her front porch with a baby and all, but didn't know how odd until she arrived at work and was told that the Wolfe baby was missing. Of course she told all of them at the Tribal Offices what she had seen and they called the Wolfes who had Addy May arrested. The baby wasn't hurt or anything, so the Wolfes didn't press it. The authorities let Addy May go after a good talking to because they didn't know what else to do with her, I guess.

Mama said she probably needed some kind of professional help 'cause she had never got over the death of her two babies who had burned to death that past winter. One was a girl, about a year-and-a-half old, and the other a boy, six-months old. Her old mobile home had caught fire because of bad wiring or something, and she hadn't been able to save them.

I cried after my mama told me that story. I cried like I had never cried for anybody before because I felt close to Addy May somehow. So I went to visit her about a week after that. I just stopped by her house on my way home from school one day to tell her I was her cousin and just to see how she was doing. She didn't talk much, just nodded her head a little, and gave me some water from her well to drink. I can still taste that water now, all fresh and cool and sweet from that dipper gourd she used. I stayed for about an hour I guess, just sitting there on her front porch with her, not talking. And that was OK with me 'cause I felt like I just needed to be there for her. She never mentioned that night I had seen her in the road, swaying and singing, but I knew she knew. And I knew she knew that I cared about her.

I didn't go back to visit her again, but I did see her at different times, walking around, mumbling to herself. She got real crazy after the Wolfe baby incident and people just kind of left her alone and made up more rumors about her to entertain themselves. She wasn't a real threat to anybody, and the Crowe Sisters who lived down the road from her always made sure she had something to eat.

I guess I just grew up and forgot about her for several years. There were my two kids and a husband to worry over, and I hadn't thought about her for a while until Mama told me that Addy May had died. She had gotten the flu or pneumonia or something, and passed to spirit in her sleep one night.

"She's probably better off," Mama had said. I quietly agreed 'cause deep inside I knew that Addy May was with those two spirits who understood the song she was singing that night there in the middle of the road. The night she was swaying and singing in the moonlight, and I stood in the darkness of the brush, quietly watching and listening.

MARY NOAILLES MURFREE
(January 24, 1850–July 31, 1922)

The daughter of Fanny Priscilla Dickinson Murfree, who inherited plantations in Tennessee and Mississippi, and William Law Murfree, a successful attorney and published writer, Mary Noailles Murfree was born in Murfreesboro, Tennessee, a town named for her great-grandfather.

Although a childhood illness had left her lame from the age of four, she enjoyed spending summers in the Cumberland Mountains, at her family's cottage in Beersheba Springs. There, she and her elder sister, Fanny, observed the place and met the mountain people who became the subjects of her local color fiction.

After the family moved to Nashville in 1857, Murfree attended the Nashville Female Academy. She completed her education in a Philadelphia boarding school.

Murfree began to write in the 1870s, with encouragement from her father. Using the pseudonym Charles Egbert Craddock, she published her first important story, "The Dancin' Party at Harrison's Cove" in the *Atlantic Monthly* (May 1878). After her initial success, she signed a number of stories and novels with her male pseudonym. Her first novel, *Where the Battle was Fought*, focuses on the Civil War, an event that drastically affected her family, as their home was destroyed.

Murfree is best known for her contributions to local color fiction about Tennessee mountaineers. After publishing her first collection of short stories, *In the Tennessee Mountains*, she received widespread, favorable reviews and soon thereafter achieved national attention when she revealed her identity. Her literary reputation rests on her work from the 1880s. Her later fiction followed popular trends toward historical romances.

Popular as a lecturer, she was awarded an honorary doctorate from the University of the South during the last year of her life.

The following scenes, excerpted from *In the Tennessee Mountains,* offer examples of some typical features of local color fiction: dense dialect, humor, and descriptions of natural landscapes that use flowery diction and allusions to classical literature.

OTHER SOURCES TO EXPLORE

PRIMARY

Novels: *The Erskine Honeymoon* (published posthumously in the *Nashville Banner,* December 29, 1930–March 3, 1931), *The Story of Duciehurst; A Tale of the Mississippi* (1914), *The Ordeal; A Mountain Romance of Tennessee* (1912), *The Fair Mississippian* (1908), *The Windfall* (1907), *The Amulet* (1906), *The Storm Centre* (1905), *The Frontiersmen* (1904), *The Spectre of Power* (1903), *The Story of Old Fort Loudon* (1899), *The Juggler* (1897), *The "Stranger People's" Country* (1891), *His Vanished Star* (1894), *The Despot of Broomsedge Cove* (1888), *In the Clouds* (1886), *The Prophet of the Great Smoky Mountains* (1885), *Where the Battle Was Fought* (1884). **Short stories:** *The Raid of the Guerilla and Other Stories* (1912), *The Bushwhackers and Other Stories* (1897), *The Phantoms of the Foot-Bridge and Other Stories* (1895), *The Mystery of Witch-Face Mountain and Other Stories* (1895), *In the Tennessee Mountains* (1884). **Books for children:** *The Champion* (1902), *The Young Mountaineers* (1897), *The Story of Keedon Bluffs* (1887), *Down the Ravine* (1885).

SECONDARY

Richard Cary, *Mary N. Murfree* (1967). Allison R. Ensor, "What is the Place of Mary Noailles Murfree Today?" *Tennessee Historical Quarterly* 47:4 (winter 1988), 198–205. Edd Winfield Parks, *Charles Egbert Craddock* (1941). Nathalia Wright, "Introduction," *In the Tennessee Mountains* (1970), 5–33.

IN THE TENNESSEE MOUNTAINS (1884)

from Drifting Down Lost Creek

"Laws-a-me!" she cried, in shrill, toothless glee; "ef hyar ain't 'Vander Price! What brung ye down hyar along o' we-uns, 'Vander?" she continued, with simulated anxiety. "Hev that thar red heifer o' our'n lept over the fence agin, an' got inter Pete's corn? Waal, sir, ef she ain't the headin'est heifer!"

"I hain't seen none o' yer heifer, ez I knows on," replied the young blacksmith, with gruff, drawling deprecation. Then he tried to regain his natural manner. "I kem down hyar," he remarked in an off-hand way, "ter git a drink o' water." He glanced furtively at the girl; then looked quickly away at the gallant redbird, still gayly parading among the leaves.

The old woman grinned with delight. "Now, ef that ain't s'prisin'," she declared. "Ef we hed knowed ez Lost Creek war a-goin' dry over yander a-nigh the shop, so ye an' Pete would hev ter kem hyar thirstin' fur water, we-uns would hev brung su'thin' down hyar ter drink out'n. We-uns hain't got no gourd hyar, hev we, Cynthy?"

"'Thout it air the little gourd with the saft soap in it," said Cynthia, confused and blushing.

Her mother broke into a high, loud laugh. "Ye ain't wantin' ter gin 'Vander the soapgourd ter drink out'n Cynthy! Leastwise, I ain't goin' ter gin it ter Pete. Fur I s'pose ef ye hev ter kem a haffen mile ter git a drink, 'Vander, ez surely Pete'll hev ter kem, too. Waal, waal, who would hev b'lieved ez Lost Creek would go dry nigh the shop, an' yit be a-scuttlin' along like that, hyar-abouts!" and she pointed with her bony finger at the swift flow of the water.

He was forced to abandon his clumsy pretense of thirst. "Lost Creek ain't gone dry nowhar, ez I knows on," he admitted, mechanically rolling the sleeve of his hammer-arm up and down as he talked. "It air toler'ble high,—, higher'n I ever see it afore. . . .

. . .

It was a great opportunity for old Dr. Patton, who lived six miles down the valley, and zealously he improved it. He often felt that in this healthful country, where he has born, and where bucolic taste and local attachment still kept him, he was rather a medical theorist than a medical practitioner, so few and slight were the demands upon the resources of his science. He was as one who has long pondered the unsuggestive details of the map of a region, and who suddenly sees before him its glowing, vivid landscape.

"A beautiful fracture!" he protested with rapture,—"a beautiful fracture!"

Through all the countryside were circulated his cheerful accounts of patients who had survived fracture of the skull. Among the simple mountaineers his learned talk of the trephine gave rise to the startling report that he intended to put a linchpin into Jubal Tyne's head. It was rumored, too, that the unfortunate man's brains had "in an' about leaked haffen out;" and many freely prompted Providence by the suggestion that "ef Jube war ready ter die it war high time he war taken," as, having been known as a hasty and choleric man, it was predicted that he would "make a most survigrus idjit."

"Cur'ous enough ter me ter find out ez Jube ever hed brains," commented Mrs. Ware. "'T war well enough ter let some of 'em leak out ter prove it. He hev never showed he hed brains no other way, ez I knows on. Now," she added, "somebody oughter tap 'Vander's head, an' mebbe they'll find him pervided, too. Wonders will never cease! Nobody would hev accused Jube o' sech. Folks'll hev ter respec' them brains. 'Vander done him that favior in splitting his head open."

. . .

. . . A vague prescience of dawn was on the landscape; dim and spectral, it stood but half revealed in the doubtful light. The stars were gone; ever the sidereal outline of the great Scorpio had crept away. But the gibbous moon still swung above the dark and melancholy forests of Pine Mountain, and its golden chalice spilled a dreamy glamour all adown the lustrous mists in Lost Creek Valley. Ever and anon the crags reverberated with the shrill clamor of a watch-dog at a cabin in the Cove; for there was an unwonted stir upon the mountain's brink.

ÉLAINE FOWLER PALENCIA
(March 19, 1946–)

Having grown up in Morehead, Kentucky, in the 1950s, where her mother taught at the county high school and her father taught at Morehead State College (now a university), Elaine Fowler Palencia recalls receiving very little emphasis on Appalachia in her formal education. When she was sixteen, her family moved to Cookeville, Tennessee. She graduated from Vanderbilt University, magna cum laude, with a B.A. in 1968, where she studied English literature with Allen Tate.

She lives in Champaign, Illinois, with her husband, a professor of comparative literature at the University of Illinois, and her son, who attends special education classes. Their daughter is a doctoral candidate at the University of Missouri. Palencia has taught creative writing at Illinois Wesleyan University and lectured at a number of universities and writers' conferences. She currently works as a freelance writer and editor and as a YMCA aerobics instructor.

She wrote her first story in Spanish, while spending a summer in Colombia with her husband, whose home is in the Andes. But since she became serious about writing fiction, she has written in English spoken by Appalachian characters. Her father's stories of his childhood on farms in West Virginia, on Spurlock Creek and Nine Mile Hollow, provide important background for her fiction.

Equally important, she says, are her Aunt Glenith's stories of leaving the hills (and Brierhoppers) for Ohio cities. She explains, "The main theme of my writing is exile and return: the search for home. It arises from my journey away from eastern Kentucky—first to central Tennessee, then Germany, Boston, Detroit, Colombia, and to end up in the flat Midwest. My sense of story comes from the narrative, anecdotal speech of my Appalachian friends and relatives. I owe my entire writing career to having grown up in the region. Every story I write is a letter to the place I came from."

Palencia has received awards for her fiction and poetry from the Appalachian Writers Association, the Illinois Arts Council, *Iowa Woman*, *Willow Review*, *Appalachian Heritage*, the Kentucky State Poetry Society, and the American Association of University Women. Her poem "Emily Dickinson's Bodyguard Speaks," published in *River King Poetry Supplement*, was nominated for a Pushcart Prize. She has written two poetry chapbooks about her son, *Taking the Train* and *The Dailiness of It*. Under the pseudonym of Laurel Blake, she is also the author of several mass-market romance novels, earning recognition as a finalist for the Golden Medallion Award of the Romance Writers of America.

The author's Aunt Glenith and Uncle Carl inspired the characters of Dreama and Floyd McDonald in *Small Caucasian Woman*, a critically acclaimed collection of interrelated short stories set in an eastern Kentucky town (based on Morehead) and tracing the lives of Appalachian people who migrate to northern industrial cities. They reappear, along with other characters and places in *Brier Country*, her second collection of Appalachian short fiction.

Other Sources to Explore

Primary

Short stories: *Brier Country: Stories from Blue Valley* (2000), *Small Caucasian Woman* (1993), *Heart on Holiday* (1980). **Poetry:** *The Dailiness of It* (2002), *Taking the Train* (1997). **Autobiographical essay:** "Leaving Pre–Appalachia," in *Bloodroot* (1998), ed. Joyce Dyer, 201–8.

Secondary

Pat Arnow, review of *Small Caucasian Woman*, *Now & Then: The Appalachian Magazine* 10:3 (fall 1993). Joyce Dyer, "Elaine Fowler Palencia," in *Bloodroot*, 200. Art Jester, "Morehead Native Writes and Dreams About Kentucky," *Lexington Herald-Leader* (15 August 1993), E4. Marianne Worthington, review of *Brier Country*, *Appalachian Heritage* 28:2 (spring 2000), 66–70.

BRIERS

from *Brier Country: Stories from Blue Valley* (2000)

They came in a shiny new car. Don Fields was waiting for them under the maples, sitting on one of Mr. Forrester's old yard chairs. We supposed they had called Don from the town. We had seen the man before but not the woman, when the man decided to buy the old Forrester place. From the edges of the yard, we watched and waited.

We like Don. Don and his family live by the bridge. Don's granddaddy helped build the bridge. Don's daddy was killed in the Big War.

The new people were wrong for us. We could tell by their smell, a smell of flowers killed in moonshine. We could tell by their soft hands. They were tall and ruddy, matched like a pair of Irish setters.

The man had lightning with him. We could feel it.

Don knew it, too.

"What's that ye got there, a Geiger counter?" he asked.

"It's a laptop computer," said the man.

"Oh, right. My daughter has one of them. She works for the state," said Don.

"Really," said the man, and smiled at the woman.

We do not like lightning.

Don showed them around. He showed them where Mr. Forrester fell in the garden. That was why the Forresters had to go live with their daughter far away. After they left, Charley Carruthers was looking after their farm, but he is not able anymore. He could not keep the renters from throwing their garbage off the back porch and using the henhouse for firewood.

We do not like fire.

Mr. Forrester came back to visit once. He died on Charley Carruthers's porch. Then the Forresters' daughter, Dreama, decided to sell the farm. Long years ago, Dreama liked to come with two buckets and a jug of water and pick all morning. She did not stamp the bushes down but slipped in between the vines. She sang to herself and ate berries until the juice ran down her chin. We miss Dreama still.

We like Charley and his wife. They live above the road. Charley is part Old People. When Charley digs up a ginseng plant to sell, he puts a seed down in the hole to grow a new plant. He shows respect.

Don showed the new people how the cistern collects water from the roof.

"Like I'm going to be drinking out of that," said the woman.

Don said, "As you know, the house has running water, too. In the thirties Mr. Forrester and his boys dug a reservoir up on the hill and ran a pipe down to the kitchen."

"Brilliant," said the woman, turning her sharp hips this way and that like she was handling knives.

Don showed them where the Forresters buried their famous hound Katie, under the lilacs. He walked them over the hillside where Norton Forrester used to grow grapes. We tolerated the Forresters for forty years. They kept the brush cut so we could breathe. But we didn't tolerate the renters, and now we want it all back.

We do not like being tolerant.

Everywhere the new people stepped, there we were.

"These goddamned brambles," said the woman, ripping her sleeve loose.

Don said, "They'll take over a place if you don't keep it cleared. That and the honeysuckle and the laurel. A place like this is a by-God backbreaker if you don't have help."

"Oh," said the man, "we'll have help." He took a deep breath and patted his chest with both hands. "Mountain air. This is so authentic."

That night they slept on the floor upstairs, in sleeping bags.

"Well, what do you think so far?" asked the man.

"Don't ask," said the woman.

"No, this is great. You've got to feel it. The whole ambience is American Primitive. And besides, it's just for one year," said the man. "One year for me to write my book about getting away from it all in a forgotten corner of Appalachia. I'm going to do for this place what Peter Mayle did for Provence. After we sell our little patch of heaven, we can live anywhere. Don Fields would be a fool not to sell, too. People are going to want to build up here. You know what the developer said."

"God, where am I going to get arugula?" wailed the woman.

We bided our time. We watched him write with the lightning. We watched him visit the neighbors with his tape recorder, he called it. We watched the woman smoke and leave for town. She would stay away all day. Inch by inch, by root and tip, we walked toward the house.

One day Elsie Fields brought them a cherry pie. She asked the woman, "Did Don show you Sarah's roses?"

She and the woman went out in the sloping backyard. Elsie knelt down by a rosebush and touched the heavy cream-and-pink blossoms the way she used to stroke her children's hair when they were asleep.

"Even after Sarah Forrester lost her mind, she loved her roses," said

Elsie. "This is a Seven Sisters. That one is a Queen Anne. It looks like the briers are about to take them over, though. And do you know what that is, there?"

She pointed to the apple tree deep in our midst.

"A tree," said the woman bitterly.

"That's a Pound Royal apple tree. You don't hardly ever hear of Pound Royals anymore. In fact, I don't know of another one anywhere. That one's might' near an antique. You ought to take care of it, cut them briers back so's you can pick the apples. They're mighty good eating. So are the berries, for that matter."

After Elsie left, the woman went to find her husband. He was sitting on the breezeporch, plunking on a dulcimer that he ordered from New York. The dulcimer was bright and shiny like it had been dipped in honey.

The woman said, "Elsie Fields says we've got some kind of rare apple tree behind the house. But the yard is so grown up that it's impossible to get to it. I thought you were going to have this place cleaned up."

"Listen to this," said the man, picking out notes. They sounded like rain in a lard bucket.

"You need a shave," said the woman.

"I've decided to grow a beard," he said, plucking away.

"Where's the phone number of that yardman the realtor gave you?" she said.

I've been thinking that I'll clear the yard myself. As part of the whole experience," he said.

Frankly, we were relieved to hear it.

The next day he went to town and bought a hedge trimmer, a hand scythe, and a plastic bucket. The woman went with him and bought a small air conditioner like Burl Corbett has for his son's asthma.

The man put the air conditioner in a window.

"I got the bucket so we could pick berries. You could make jelly in a big iron kettle. If we could find a kettle," said the man.

The woman just looked at him. Then she went in the cool room and shut the door.

The hedge trimmer had a cord for the lightning. But when he plugged it in and brought it outside, the cord was too short to reach us.

He hung the bucket on his left arm. With the scythe in his right hand, he began to cut a path to the apple tree. When he had cleared a space, he would stop to fill the bucket. Slash and pick. Slash and pick. He whistled the tune he had been trying to play. Happy as a hog in clover, he was.

We closed in behind him. If he had looked back, he couldn't have seen the path he'd made. But he never looked back. He edged down the slope, where we grew tall over him. We treated him fairly: We plucked at his clothes. We tangled around his ankles and raked his hair. Thus we spoke a warning to him: go back while you still can.

But he was in a rhythm, like a man who will fish a stream to extinction for the pure joy of killing. He even forgot to pick. Slash slash slash he went, his eyes hot and bright. This was what he had come to the country for: to feel his blood pumping, to feel alive.

He woke up Old Mother. She was sleeping at the base of the apple tree. Raising her weaving head, she looked and listened.

He was working his way around the tree when her swift, dark uncoiling caught his eye. Backwards and forwards he thrashed, screaming, wreathing himself in vines, tearing his flesh on our teeth, which are as numberless as the stars. For a moment after his foot slipped off the rock ledge, we supported his weight as a bird's nest supports a clutch of eggs. Then he fell like a man falling from the sky.

The next day they found his body on the rocks along the creek. He was lying beside the bones of the last renter, a man who had loved Pound Royal apples.

We have reached the back steps now. We can look in the windows. We can see the field mice playing in the breakfast dishes on the table. We can see the camel crickets eating spiders in the corners and the moths flitting in and out of the clothes the woman left behind.

Hissing peacefully to herself, Old Mother lays her eggs in high grass, on a blanket of rose petals.

$\mathcal{J}$AYNE $\mathcal{A}$NNE $\mathcal{P}$HILLIPS
(July 19, 1952–)

Jayne Anne Phillips was born in Buckhannon, West Virginia, the daughter of Martha Jane Thornhill Phillips, a teacher, and Russell R. Phillips, a contractor. Although she left the region after college, much of her work is set in Appalachia. "No one has labeled Phillips as a Southern writer or a woman writer," wrote literary critic Dorothy Combs Hill. "Her relentless intelligence breaks those boundaries. And, although her fiction set in West Virginia is evocative of place, it feels universal."

Phillips graduated, magna cum laude, with a B.A. from West Virginia University in 1974, then earned an M.F.A. from the University of Iowa in 1978. Her first published work, a chapbook entitled *Sweethearts*, won the 1977 Pushcart Prize. Since then, she has won many major American literary awards, including O. Henry and Best American Short Stories awards for her short fiction. She has received Guggenheim and National Endowment for the Arts Fellowships. *Black Tickets* was awarded the Sue Kaufman Prize, and *Shelter*, an Academy Award in Literature from the American Academy and Institute of Arts and Letters. *Machine Dreams* received a National Book Critics Circle Award nomination and was a *New York Times* Best Book for 1984. *Motherkind* won the 2000 Massachusetts Book Award and was nominated for Britain's Orange Prize.

A major theme running through Phillips's work is the human failure to communicate, a failure that is most tragic when it occurs among family members. Phillips's characters are often anguished, isolated, and frequently misunderstood. "I'm interested in what home now consists of," Phillips has said. "Because we move around so much, families are forced to be immediate; they must stand on their relationships, rather than on stereotypes of a common history."

In 1985, Phillips married physician Mark Brian Stockman. The couple and their children make their home in the Boston area where Phillips is Writer-in-Residence at Brandeis University.

In his review of Phillips' novel *Machine Dreams,* Jonathan Yardley notes, "Ordinary people can be extraordinary, she is saying, and what happens to them is terribly important. She is right, and the best parts of *Machine Dreams* do honor to them." In the following scene from *Machine Dreams*, readers enter the thoughts of Danner, a young girl growing up in West Virginia during the 1950s. Through her, we also hear the voices of her parents: her father, Mitch, and mother, Jean.

In the scene from *Motherkind*, Kate, a new mother who is caring for her own mother who is dying, enjoys a serene moment with her infant son.

OTHER SOURCES TO EXPLORE

PRIMARY

Fiction: *Motherkind* (2000), *Shelter* (1994), *Fast Lanes* (1984), *Machine Dreams* (1984), *The Secret Country: Randolph County* (1982), *How Mickey Made It* (1981), *Hometown* (1980), *Black Tickets* (1979), *Counting* (1978), *Sweethearts* (1976). **Autobiographical essays:** "Why She Writes," in *Why I Write* (1999), ed. Will Blythe. "Premature Burial," in *Bloodroot* (1998), ed. Joyce Dyer, 210–17. "Callie," in *Family: American Writers Remember Their Own* (1996), ed. Sharon Sloan Fiffer and Steve Fiffer.

SECONDARY

Adam Begley, "Tales out of Camp," *Mirabella* (August 1994), 56, 59. Joyce Dyer, "Jayne Anne Phillips," in *Bloodroot*, 209. David Edelstein, "The Short Story of Jayne Anne Phillips," *Esquire* (December 1985), 108–12. *Great Women Writers* (1994), 401–3. Dorothy Combs Hill, "Jayne Anne Phillips," *Contemporary Fiction Writers of the South* (1993), 348–59. Jonathan Yardley, "Jayne Anne Phillips: West Virginia Breakdown" *Washington Post Book World* (24 June 1984), 3.

FROM *MACHINE DREAMS* (1984)

The House At Night

DANNER, 1956

In the humid nights her mother let her sleep under one thin sheet, an old one worn soft from many washings, and in the dark of her child's bedroom she turned and sweated until the sheet wrapped her small body like a sour cocoon. Night sounds in the house were shot with lambent silence: rotary blades of the stilled electric fans gathered a fine dust behind the ribs of their metal cages. *Once you're asleep you won't know how hot it is, go to sleep, fans cost money to run;* crickets sounded in the close dark, their throbbing continuous as the running of a high-pitched musical engine. No breeze stirred to break their sounds; Danner drifted, almost sleeping; each shrill vanished faster than the last. She heard faintly her brother breathe and whimper; in these summer days the artificial disruption of school was forgotten and the fifteen months of age separating them disappeared; they existed between their parents as one shadow, *the kids,* and they fought and conspired with no recognition of separation. Doors opened now onto the same unlit hallway; near Billy's room the hallway turned, lengthened past the bathroom and emptied into their parents' bedroom. There the high Grandmother Danner bed floated like an island above its starched white skirt; the row of closet doors slid on their runners, a confusing line of illusions; and the two big bureaus shone. The bank of windows was so high no one could see anything but the branches of the lilacs, branches that now in the August night looked furred with black and didn't stir. By day the leaves were a deep and waxen green. *Jean, come and get these kids, don't either one of you ever stand near the driveway when you see I'm backing the car out, goddamn it, I'll shake the living daylights out of you*: what it meant was the State Road construction and the jackhammer, shaking a grown man's body as he held the handle and white fire flew from the teeth of the machine. Endless repair of the dusty two-lanes progressed every summer, but the roads were never finished; they kept men working who had no other work and Danner liked to watch; at night she saw those men in the dark corners of her room, tall shadows with no faces. *Even if there aren't prisoners anymore the workmen are nearly the same thing,* and they did look different, dangerous, though they wore the same familiar khaki work clothes her father wore to work at the plant. *Your father and Clayton own the concrete company—they don't work for a wage, do you understand what I'm saying?* The workmen were from Skully or Dogtown and their families got assistance, a shameful thing; in those shabby rows of houses on mud roads they kept their babies in cardboard boxes. But that was just a story, Mitch said; they were trying to get along like anyone. *You'd say that about any man who worked on a road, wouldn't matter if he was a lunatic,* and Jean turned back to the stove, always; she stood by the stove, the kitchen cabinets, the sink, the whole house moored to earth by her solid stance, just as the world outside went with Mitch in the car. He carried the world in and out in the deep khaki pockets of his workman's pants. When Danner and Billy were with him and the road crews were out, Mitch waited with no complaint for the flagman's signal and kept the windows rolled down. Yellow dust filled the car and caked everything with a chalky powder. Big machines, earth-movers and cranes, turned on their pedestals with a thunderous grinding as two or three shirtless men pulled thick pipes across the asphalt with chains. Mitch held both children on his lap behind the steering wheel, the three of them crushed together in a paradise of noise. Jackhammers and drills were louder than the heat, louder than sweat and the shattered ground and the overwhelmed voices of the men. Mitch smoked and talked to the foreman, yelling each sentence twice while the children coughed from the dust and excitement. Jean made them stay in the back seat if they had to stop near the construction; she nodded politely to the flagman, kept the car windows rolled up in the stifling closeness *just another minute,* and locked all the doors. At home they weren't allowed to lock doors: *children are safe at home, you should never be doing anything you don't want Mama to see,* but Danner and Billy closed themselves secretly into adjacent closets and stayed there until the dark scared them, tapping messages with their fists on the plyboard between them. Pressed back against clothes and stacked shoe boxes, Billy wore a billed khaki cap like his father's and Danner kept a navy blue clutch purse her mother no longer used; it smelled of a pressed powder pure as corn, and the satin lining was discolored. Danner unzipped it and put her face in the folds; she held her breath just another minute and that made everything lighten: the fields surrounding the house were full of light, scrub grass grew tall, and the milkweed stalks were thick as wrists. Wild wheat was in the fields and the crows fed, wheeling in circular formations. Milk syrup in the weeds was sticky and white; the pods were tight and wouldn't burst for weeks. Where did the crows go at night? They were dirty birds waiting for things to die, Danner was not to go near them; when the black night came she was in her bed to wake in the dark and pretend she saw the birds, rising at night as they did at noon, their wingspan larger, terrifying, a faint black arching of lines against the darker black; even the grasses, the tangled brushy weeds, were black. Danner heard the house settle, a nearly inaudible creaking, ghostly clicking of the empty furnace pipes; her mother, her father, walking the hall in slippers. They walked differently and turned on no lights if it was late. Danner lay listening, waiting, fighting her own heavy consciousness to hear and see them as they really were. Who were they? The sound of her father was a wary lumbering sound, nearly fragile, his heaviness changed by the slippers, the dark, his legs naked and white in his short robe, the sound of his walking at once shy and violent. Danner heard him ask one word and the word was full of darkness: *Jean?* At night her mother was larger, long robe dragging the floor, slide of fabric over wooden parquet a secretive hush. Danner heard her mother up at night. Doors shut in the dark. The bathroom door, click of a lock. Hem of the long robe gliding, a rummaging in cabinets too high for the kids to reach. Jean finds the hidden equipment and pulls out the white enamel pitcher; the metal is deathly cold, the thin red hose coiled inside is the same one she uses, sterilized before and after, to give the children enemas. "Younger than Spring-time" is the song she sings when she rocks Danner to sleep, the child at seven nearly too big to be held like a baby, earaches and sore throats Billy will catch next, and the two of them awake till midnight. She rocks them both at once and reads a thick college text for the classes she takes one at a time. She memorizes everything as though she were a blank slate; next year when Billy's in school she'll do practice teaching and get the certificate, there's never enough money and they meet the bills because she plots and plans, and the smell of her throat and neck as the cane-bottomed rocker creaks is a crushed fragrance like shredded flowers. Danner is the one who won't sleep; she smells her mother and the scent is like windblown seeding weeds, the way the side of the road smells when the State Road mowing machines have finished and the narrow secondary route is littered with a damp verdant hay that dries and yellows. Cars and trucks grind the hay to a powder that makes more dust, swirling dust *softer than starlight;* Danner hears Jean's voice as one continuous sound weaving through days and nights. *Pretty is as pretty does, seen and not heard, my only darling, don't ever talk back to your mother, come and read* Black Beauty, *a little girl with a crooked part looks like no one loves her,* and she cuts Danner's flyaway brown hair to hang straight from the center with bangs, a pageboy instead of braids; that way it takes less time. The chair creaks and Danner is awake until Jean lies in bed with her and pretends she'll stay all night. She calls Danner Princess, Mitch calls her Miss, Billy is called My Man; *who's my best man?* Danner watches Jean pick him up; he's still the smaller one, hair so blond it's white. He stiffens laughing when his mother burrows her big face in his stomach, and he drinks so much water in the summer that he sloshes when he jumps up and down. Runs in and out of the house all day to ask for more and drinks from the big jug. *How can he have such a thirst? Lifting that heavy jug by himself, looks like a little starving Asian with that round belly;* at five he shimmies to the top of the swing-set poles, a special concrete swing-set their father has brought from the plant and built in the acre of backyard down by the fence and the fields. The poles are steel pipes twenty feet high, sunk into the earth and cemented in place; the swings are broad black rubber hanging by thick tire chains. Billy climbs the tall center pole and the angled triad of pipe that supports the set at either end, but Danner prefers the swings, a long high ride if she pumps hard enough, chains so long the swings fly far out; she throws her head back, mesmerized, holding still as the swing traces a pendulum trajectory. Locusts in the field wheedle their red clamor under her; locusts are everywhere in summer, in daylight; she and Billy find their discarded shells in the garden, a big square of overgrown weeds in a corner of the lot. In the tumbledown plot they dig out roads for Billy's trucks, and the locust shells turn up in the earth: they are hard, delicate, empty. Transparent as fingernails, imprinted with the shape of the insect, they are slit up the middle where something has changed and crawled free. Danner throws the shells over the fence. Billy smells of mud and milk, kneels in dirt and sings motor sounds as he inches the dump trucks along. They make more roads by filling the beds of the bigger plastic trucks, pushing them on their moving wheels to the pile of dirt in the center; when they've tunneled out a crisscross pattern of roads, they simply move the dirt from place to place, crawling in heat that seems cooler when they're close to the soil, making sounds, slapping the sweat bees that crawl under their clothes and between their fingers. The stings, burning pinpricks, swell, stay hot, burn in bed at night. Danner sucks her hands in her sleep, and the lights are out, the calls of the night birds are faint, and the dream hovers, waiting at the border of the fields; the dark in the house is black. The bathroom light makes a triangular glow on the hallway floor; the glow hangs in space, a senseless, luminous shape, and disappears. The bedroom door is shut, a lock clicks. Danner lies drifting, hears the furtive sound of the moving bed, the brief mechanical squeak of springs, and no other sound at all but her father's breath, harsh, held back. All sounds stop then in the black funnel of sleep; Danner hears her mother, her father, lie silent in an emptiness so endless they could all hurtle through it like stones. Jean sighs and then she speaks: *Oh, it's hot,* she says to no one. Danner sinks deep, completely, finally, into a dream she will know all her life; the loneliness of her mother's voice, *Oh, it's hot,* rises in the dream like vapor. In the cloudy air, winged animals struggle and stand up; they are limbed and long-necked, their flanks and backs powerful; their equine eyes are lucent and their hooves cut the air, slicing the mist to pieces.

The horses are dark like blood and gleam with a black sheen; the animals swim hard in the air to get higher and Danner aches to stay with them. She touches herself because that is where the pain is; she holds on, rigid, not breathing, and in the dream it is the horse pressed against her, the rhythmic pumping of the forelegs as the animal climbs, the lather and the smell; the smell that comes in waves and pounds inside her like a pulse.

MOTHERKIND (2000)

from Chapter 2

When Kate woke, the bed tray was gone. Her mother was gone, and the house was perfectly quiet. She remembered finishing the food and leaning back in bed, and then she'd fallen asleep, dreamlessly, as though she had only to close her eyes to move away, small and weightless, skimming the reflective surface of something deep.

She heard a small sound. Alexander lay in the bassinette, his eyes open, looking at her. His swaddling blankets had come loose. Propped on his side by pillows, he raised one arm and moved his delicate hand. Kate sat up to lean near him and touched her forefinger to his palm; immediately, he grasped her hard and his gaze widened. "They're your fingers," she told him. "You don't know them yet, but I do." Everyone had told her to leave him be when he was happy, she'd be holding him and caring for him so ceaselessly, but she took him in her arms, propped up the pillows, and put him in her lap. He kicked excitedly and frowned. She bent her knees to bring him closer and regarded him as he lay on her raised thighs; the frown disappeared. "You're like me," Kate said softly. "You frown when you think. By the time you're twenty-five, you'll have two little lines between your eyes. Such a serious guy." He raised his downy brows. He had a watchful, observing look and a more excited look—he would open his eyes wider, compress his lips, strain with his limbs as though he was concentrating on moving, on touching or grasping. He could feel his body but he couldn't command it to move or do; his focus was entirely in his eyes. And he did focus. Kate was sure he saw her. He wasn't a newborn any longer; today he was one week old. Perhaps his vision was still blurry, and that was why he peered at her so intently. His eyes were big and dark blue, like those of a baby seal. One eye was always moist and teary; his tear duct was blocked, they'd said at the hospital, it would clear up.

Now Kate wiped his cheek carefully with the edge of a cloth diaper, then drew her finger across his forehead, along his jaw, across his flattened, broad little nose. "Mister man," she whispered, "mighty mouse, here's your face. Here are your nose, your ears, your widow's peak. Old widower, here are your bones . . ." She touched his collarbone and the line along his shoulder, under his gown. His skin was like warm silk and his names were too big for him; she called him Tatie, for his middle name was Tateman, after her family, her divided parents. She cleaned him with warm water, not alcohol wipes, and used a powder that contained no talc. The powder was fine as rice flour and smelled as Kate thought rice fields might smell, in the sun, when the plants bloomed. Like clean food, pure as flowers. Across the world and in the South, those young shoots grew and moved in the breeze like grass. "Rice fields are like grass in water," she said to him. "We haven't seen them yet. Even in India, I didn't see them." Outside the wind moved along the house; Kate heard it circling and testing. Suddenly a gust slammed against the windows and Tatie startled, looked toward the sound. "You can't see the wind," Kate murmured, "just what it moves." The wind would bring snow again, Kate knew; already she heard snow approach like a whining in the air. Absently she traced the baby's lips, and he yawned and began to whimper. You're hungry, Kate thought, and he moved his arms as though to gather her closer. Her milk let down with a flush and surge, and she held a clean diaper to one breast as she put him to the other. Now she breathed, exhaling slowly. The intense pain began to ebb; he drank the cells of her blood, Kate knew, and the crust that formed on her nipples where the cuts were deepest. He was her blood. When she held him he was inside her; always, he was near her, like an atmosphere, in his sleep, in his being. She would not be alone again for many years, even if she wanted to, even if she tried. In her deepest thoughts, she would approach him, move around and through him, make room for him. In nursing there would be a still, spiral peace, an energy in which she felt herself, her needs and wants, slough away like useless debris. It seemed less important to talk or think; like a nesting animal, she took on camouflage, layers of protective awareness that were almost spatial in dimension. The awareness had dark edges, shadows that rose and fell. Kate imagined terrible things. That he might stop breathing. That she dropped him, or someone had. That someone or something took him from her. That she forgot about him or misplaced him. There were no words; the thoughts occurred to her in starkly precise images, like the unmistakable images of dreams, as though her waking and sleeping lives had met in him. Truly, she was sleeping; the days and nights were fluid, beautiful and discolored; everything in her was available to her, as though she'd become someone else, someone with a similar past history in whom that history was acknowledged rather than felt, someone who didn't need to make amends or understand, someone beyond language. She was shattered. Something new would come of her. Moments in which she crossed from consciousness to sleep, from sleep to awareness, there was a lag of an instant in which she couldn't remember her name, and she didn't care. She remembered him. Now his gaze met hers and his eyelids fluttered; she could see him falling away, back into his infant swoon. His sleep closed around him like an ocean shell and rocked him within it. In this they were alike, Kate thought, though he had no name known to him, no name to forget. He was pure need. She took him from the breast and held him to her shoulder, patting and rubbing him, softly, a caress and a heartbeat.

$\mathscr{L}$YNN $\mathscr{P}$OWELL
(October 11, 1955–)

Poet Lynn Powell grew up in Jefferson City, Tennessee, graduated from Carson-Newman College in 1977 and earned her M.F.A. at Cornell University in 1980. Her first collection of poetry, *Old & New Testaments*, won the Brittingham Prize in Poetry from the University of Wisconsin Press. She is also recipient of the 1996 Great Lakes Colleges Association's New Writers Award.

She has worked as a writer in the schools for twenty years, in Tennessee, New Jersey, and Ohio, in rural, urban, and suburban schools, with residencies ranging from seminars with auditioned high school students to collaborations with a modern dancer in her neighborhood primary school. She and her husband, Dan Stinebring, have two children.

Powell describes the Appalachian influences on her work in this way: "Family, lush landscape, and the Baptist church: those were the defining experiences of my East Tennessee childhood, and they are the preoccupations now of my poetry." She says, "I grew up going to church every Sunday morning for Sunday School; every Sunday evening for Baptist Training Union; every Wednesday night for Fellowship Supper, G.A.'s, and Prayer Meeting; and every night of the week during revivals, helping to pack the pews. So, the Broadman Hymnal, the King James Bible, and Baptist evangelists gave me my native tongue. I am fluent in other cultural languages now, but find myself as a poet often slipping into the language most fragrant with connection and meaning for me."

OTHER SOURCES TO EXPLORE

PRIMARY

Poetry: *The Zones of Paradise* (2003), *Old & New Testaments* (1995).

SECONDARY

Fred Chappell, "Five New Southern Women Poets," *Georgia Review* 50:1 (spring 1996), 174–84. Gina Herring, "'Approaching the Altar': Aesthetic Homecoming in the Poetry of Linda Marion and Lynn Powell," *Appalachian Heritage* 30:2 (spring 2002), 20–30. F.B. Jackson, "Temples of the Holy Ghost: Recent Poetry by Kathleen Norris, Lynn Powell, and Julia Kasdorf," *Shenandoah* 46:4 (winter 1996), 118–29. William Jolliff, review of *Old & New Testaments*, *Appalachian Heritage* 24:3 (summer 1996), 71–73. John Lang, "'Slowly the Heart Revises': Lynn Powell's *Old & New Testaments,*" in *Her Words* (2002), ed. Felicia Mitchell, 209–17.

NATIVITY

from *Old & New Testaments* (1995)

Some parents shy away from the body,
but we hush up about the cross—
rereading our daughter the story about Jesus
we must believe in: mother
and father kneeling after the hard birth,
humbled by the exhaustions of love.

She studies the illustration, loves
the halos wide-brimmed on everybody's
heads. Five pages later, though, it's death
that rivets her—Herod, jealous and cross,
ordering the slaughter. The unnamed mothers
are left out of this version of the Christ,

but our daughter worries if God
warned them in time, too. She senses love,
though fierce, is not omnipotent. *Mommy,*
what's the baddest thing that can happen to somebody?
she asks, remembering the museum, the crosses
hung a step away from the joyful births,

stark scripture plain enough to a child: death
looks back at every birth, even God's.
She punishes the sentries at the cross
in her own drawings, coloring their unloved
faces blue, grinding green into their bodies.
Once I whispered to my mother,

I think God would have picked me as Mother
Mary if He'd sent His Son right now—though birth
and the other secrets of the body
still eluded me. Now my daughter calls, *Jesus!*
to her baby brother, a prop, lovingly
swaddled in blue dish towels, his head criss-crossed

with paisley scarves. As Mary, she crosses
the room regally, diaphanous in her mother's
hemmed-up nightgown. Outside, the snow loves
everything it touches. Suffering and death
keep their distance from the warm house. Jesus
laughs as Mary tickles his brand-new body.

You be the manger, Mom, Mary says. I cross
my legs, sit the baby, fat with love, on the throne of my body,
done with the hard births, the beginnings of God.

ECHOCARDIOGRAM

from *Old & New Testaments* (1995)

An occasional turbulence of the heart—
of no consequence, said the first doctor who heard it,
listening, eyes closed, like a god to a conch.
But the doctor I visit for a sore throat
is less sanguine: *You could drop dead tomorrow.*
He sends me right over to a specialist.

The specialist sits beside me on the narrow bed
and asks about my family.
I tell him of my mother's murmur,
and how my father's father, sick with pneumonia,
slumped as his wife rubbed his head.
I turn away, stretch out on my side, open my shirt.
He circles his arm round my chest, and with cold steel
he roots for my heart.

His electronics amplify the sound of an earnest
washing machine, not the African drum
of the heart I walked through as a child
at the Museum of Science and Industry,
a maze of plush vestibules I lingered in, peering
down the corridors of blood.

And, supposedly, my mother's real mother
died young, I add. "She grieved herself to death."

His eyes stay fixed on the craggy sierra
my heart is etching on the screen: *Hold still.*
I stiffen, stare at the smooth, green, cement block wall.

It's best not to hold a baby you must give away, her
doctor must have said, wrapping it quickly in a white blanket—
though later the nurse brought her a wet, black lock.
Down the hall she could hear a baby crying, crying.
In her own room the radiator ticked its heat
like a trapped cicada.

A slight prolapse,
a valve that lets the blood seep
a little backwards, he says, measuring peak
and ravine, calculating volume per second.
Perfectly innocent.
You can button up your blouse.

Back home, I lift my daughter's shirt and press
my ear to her chest, her pale nipples
small as chamomile—until she giggles.
No murmur, the doctor said when she was born.
No murmur, no murmur, I repeat above her,
her little heart churning out its clear lub
dubs, her valves snapping shut
without a whisper back.

For weeks I browse encyclopedias, unearth old
anatomy texts, then decide to visit
the Philadelphia copy of The Heart.
Inside the Institute, I coax my daughter past
the spinning discs of Optical Illusion,
the button-ready syntheses of Sound.
We round a corner and, just as I've promised,
it's there: tall as our house, a winter clutch
of blue ivy snaking the smooth outside, God's
fist inside pounding the table . . .

Too scary, she cries, clinging to me—
then runs out for comfort toward
the birth of tornados,
the measurement of earthquakes.

THE CALLING

from *Old & New Testaments* (1995)

> But lay up for yourselves treasures in heaven, where neither moth
> nor rust doth corrupt . . .
>
> —Matthew 6:20

Retired missionaries taught us Arts & Crafts each July at Bible Camp:
how to glue the kidney, navy, and pinto beans into mosaics,
and how to tool the stenciled butterfly
on copper sheets they'd cut for us.
At night, after hymns, they'd cut the lights and show us slides:
wide-spread trees, studded with corsage;
saved women tucking T-shirts into wrap-around batiks;
a thatched church whitewashed in the equator's light.
Above the hum of the projector I could hear the insects flick
their heads against the window screens, aiming
for the brightness of that Africa.

If Jesus knocks on your heart, be ready to say,
"Send me, O Lord, send me," a teacher told us
confidentially, doling out her baggies of dried corn.
I bent my head, concentrating hard on my tweezers
as I glued each colored kernel into a rooster for Mother's kitchen wall.

But Jesus noticed me and started to knock. Already saved,
I looked for signs to show me what else He would require.
At rest hour, I closed my eyes and flipped my Bible open, slid
my finger, ouija-like, down the page, and there was His command:
Go and do ye likewise—
Let the earth and all it contains hear—
Every tree that does not bear good fruit is cut
down and thrown into the fire—.

Thursday night, at revival service, I held out through *Trust and Obey,*
Standing on the Promises, Nothing But the Blood, but crumpled
on *Softly and Tenderly Jesus is Calling,*
promising God, cross my heart, I'd witness to Rhodesia.

Down the makeshift aisle I walked with the other weeping girls
and stood before the little bit of congregation left
singing in their metal chairs.

The bathhouse that night was silent,
young Baptists moving from shower to sink
with the stricken look of nuns.
Inside a stall, I stripped, slipped my clothes outside the curtain,
and turned for the faucet—
but there, splayed on the shower's wall,
was a luna moth, the eyes of its wings fixed on me.
It shimmered against the cement block:
sherbet-green, plumed, a flamboyant verse
lodged in a page of drab ink.
I waved my hands to scare it out,
but, blinkless, it stayed latched on.
It let me move so close my breath
stroked the fur on its animal back.

One by one the showers cranked dry.
The bathhouse door slammed a final time.
I pulled my clothes back over my sweat, drew
the curtain shut, and walked into a dark
pricked by the lightning bugs' inscrutable morse.

$\mathscr{B}$ARBARA $\mathscr{P}$RESNELL
(April 8, 1954–)

For generations, Barbara Presnell's family has lived in the rolling hills of Randolph County, North Carolina, where she was born and grew up. "Family," she claims, "both my nuclear and my large, extended family, past and present, is perhaps the most important ingredient to my sanity and success, insanity and failure. My birth family and kin, though many are long dead, continue to inspire and limit me."

She completed two degrees in English from the University of North Carolina at Greensboro: a B.A. in 1976, as well as an M.F.A. in creative writing in 1979. She also earned an M.A. in English from the University of Kentucky in 1989 and has done additional study at the University of Iowa (1989), Lexington Theological Seminary (1991–1992), and the University of Minnesota (1998).

In 1980, she married newspaperman Bill Keesler, and they have one son, born in 1985.

She has taught expository and creative writing and literature in a number of colleges, including Hazard Community College, Lexington Community College, and the University of Kentucky. She has worked as an Artist-in-Residence for the North Carolina Arts Council and the Kentucky Arts Council. Currently, she is a faculty member of the English department at the University of North Carolina in Charlotte, North Carolina.

During the years when she lived in Kentucky, she explains, "after nearly 20 years of prose writing, . . . I began writing poetry, and I don't think it was mere coincidence. Rather, I believe the richness of the land, the language, the stories, and the people—all familiar from my own home in N.C.—metamorphosed my writing into a new form, more natural and far more satisfying." Settings for her work are usually in either her birth home of North Carolina or her "adopted" home of Kentucky.

Her work has been supported by the Kentucky Foundation for Women (1987), the Kentucky Arts Council (1993), the Lexington, Kentucky Arts and Cultural Council, and the North Carolina Arts Council (2001–2002). She describes her first poetry chapbook, *Snake Dreams*, as "a collection of mountain-grown poems." It won the Zoe Kincaid Brockman Award from the North Carolina Poetry Society.

OTHER SOURCES TO EXPLORE

PRIMARY

Poetry: *Los Hijos* (2002), *Unravelings* (1998), *Snake Dreams* (1994), *"Words Are My Only Way To Get Free": A Celebration of Poetry* (1990), *"A Word Explodes": Poems From the Mountains, A Collection of Works By Students in Leslie, Letcher, and Perry Counties, 1988–1989* (1989), *"The Mountains in Winter are Like Mashed Potatoes": Poetry in the Schools: A Collection of Poems by Students in Breathitt, Knott, Letcher, and Perry Counties (1987–1988)* (1988).

SECONDARY

Annalee Allen, "Local Author's Poems Relate to Life's Common Situation," *The Dispatch* (4 February 1999), A5. Juanita Bouser, "Catawba Professor Finds Poetic Bliss," *Salisbury Post* (24 September 1995), B4. Jill Doss-Raines, "Mexico is Focus for Poetry" *The Dispatch* [Lexington, NC] (17 October 2002), A5. Claire Johnston, "UK Instructor Attempts to Bridge Literary Gap" *Kentucky Kernal* (27 April 1995). Ellis Normandi, review of *Snake Dreams*, *Wind Magazine* (1995), 97. Shelby Stephenson, "Presnell Poems Show Her Tar Heel Roots," review of *Snake Dreams*, *The Pilot* [Southern Pines, NC] (27 February 1995).

IN THE KITCHEN
WE STRING BEANS

from *Snake Dreams* (1994)

They mound like a grave on today's front page,
covering the news that a soldier was hung,
strung up like a ham, in some faraway country.
My mother, my grandmother, my aunt, me.
We snip heads from beans,
unthread their sides then snap the green flesh
into finger joints we'll cook for supper.

I listen as they talk of cancer,
how suddenly it comes, how quickly it works,
how Herbert Combs planted his corn
on the slant of his hill two weeks
before he died, how old Ethel,
thin as a vine this Sunday at church,
won't last long.

The soldier's smiling face peeks at me
through beans in my pile. His newsprint eyes
dampen with dew that came in from the garden.
His skin softens. He is a boy,
my son's age, arms and legs
like tender pods, plucking beans
from stems before the season
takes them to seed.

We are a family of women
who grow older than oaks.
Every summer we string beans,
slicing out the imperfections
with a blade. Grandmother strings
slowest of us all, for beans slip
between her thick fingers too often
for speed.

I am waiting to die, she told me
two nights ago. Now she says
how good these beans will taste
with a spoonful of grease and a
bite of cornbread.

CLARISSA AND THE SECOND COMING

from *Snake Dreams* (1994)

An ordinary woman, why her?
she wonders. A sinner, even, not
musically inclined, just one half-tuned
ear and a taste for rock and roll.
But there he is, night black
hair that wind and rhythm wave,
lip snarling when he smiles, eyes pure
and blue as the sky over Graceland.
She watches him, eight-year-old
boy tight as an E string,
riding his bike like any other boy.
He doesn't know who he is,
how he'll change the world,
how already he's changed her,
how at night while he sleeps,
she kneels by his bed
cradling his immaculate hand,
whispering thank-yous for miracles
to the moon and stars
that stud the blue suede sky.

WHEN YOU LOSE A CHILD

from *Snake Dreams* (1994)

At the shopping mall at Christmas,
in a sheet cold hospital bed, or
just to age,
it doesn't matter when or where:
first your breath will stop and
you will think you are going to die.
Your head and face will pound like
someone pummeling you with years,
and though you have been here
a hundred times, you will not know
where you are.

You will gather your wits like deputies
and say, we will find him,
he isn't really gone.
There, peeking in the toy store window,
there, by the fountain,
standing with those shoppers,
moving quick as deer through
red and coated crowds, his hair,
his clothes, his face.

You will imagine that someone else has him,
some other kind mother,
perhaps, some criminal,
you will picture him grown
to manhood without you.

You report that he is missing:
there was a small boy, they tell you,
by himself, in those same clothes.
Your senses are as sharp now
as they will ever be. Your eyes
could see the scar on his chin in Africa,
you could hear his voice calling you

from Mars, and if even one hair
of his arm brushed yours,
you would know it.

Then if you are lucky
you will see him, squatting
by the trains, staring down
at the trains, and just like that,
he will show you how they
go round and round and tell you
again and again how he loves them.

But maybe he will not be there,
and not in the toy store,
not waiting on the sidewalk,
not today, not this week, this
month, this year. Still you search
in the faces of children, you will reach
for his hand as you walk,
in the hollow night
you will hear him cry,
in your dreams, he will sleep
against you, his body
pressed to you, his perfect curve
from now on the perfect curve
of you.

SNAKE DREAMS

from *Snake Dreams* (1994)

Last night I dreamed a rattlesnake
moved into my house like
it was his and he was home at last.
In his slick belly a lump
exactly the shape and size of a
hummingbird throbbed like a heartbeat
and I swear I saw a smile
on those reptile lips. Even the cats,
mean as mountain lions, ducked behind chairs
when he trilled his tongue.
Let's just let him have the place, I said.
I've been wanting a larger house,
a smaller house, whatever.
But my sister stepped toward him,
let him nudge her leg like a colt
then strangled him with her fingers,
pinching just below those green eyes.
He played the tambourine until he dropped.

Now I know there are many things in these mountains
to be wary of besides rattlers.
I know too what they say about
snake dreams, that I am running from
some man, or ought to be.
But it was only yesterday I was thinking,
Spring is coming to these hills.
See how pale green splatters against
winter-burned trees, red Judas bleeds
like birth. Stand at the top
where rattlesnakes are waking up
and look down at the twisting North Fork,
how it yawns and stretches then coils,
pulsing with the overflow of the season,
see how it spills out and moves in,
brown and venomous.

RITA SIMS QUILLEN
(September 8, 1954–)

Poet Rita Quillen's roots go five generations deep in the hills of southwest Virginia. She was born in Hiltons, Virginia, and grew up on the family farm in Scott County first settled by her great-great-grandparents. She received both her B.S. (1978) and her M.A. in English (1985) from East Tennessee State University. Married to her "high school sweetheart," Quillen has two children.

Her M.A. thesis, *Looking for Native Ground: Contemporary Appalachian Poetry*, published by the Appalachian Consortium Press in 1989, remains an indispensable reference work. Other contributions to Appalachian literature include her work as associate editor for *A Southern Appalachian Reader* (1988) and her bibliography "Modern and Contemporary Mountain Poets," published in *Appalachian Journal* (fall 1985).

In 1987, Quillen's chapbook, *October Dusk*, won favorable reviews. "Rita Quillen's poems are the result of her craft chipping away imaginatively at her experience," said Jim Wayne Miller. "Coming on one of her poems is like finding an arrowhead turned up in a freshly plowed field." A second collection of poetry, *Counting the Sums,* elicited praise from Robert Morgan, who said, "Rita Quillen has a voice you will not forget." Fred Chappell observed that "Rita Sims Quillen shines with truth, even in her darkest lines, and what she says is as true as the world's unceasing breath." In her review of *Counting the Sums*, George Ella Lyon says, "She looks at life and herself through the lens of birth-family and marriage-family, building to a conclusion about her job as a writer, the one between generations who must speak for and to them all."

Quillen lives in southwest Virginia and is on the English faculty at Mountain Empire Community College in Big Stone Gap, Virginia. When asked to describe herself, Quillen says, "I can flatfoot, shoot well, burp extremely loud for a girl, have really, really good teeth, and hope I don't look like my driver's license photo."

OTHER SOURCES TO EXPLORE

PRIMARY

Poetry: *Counting the Sums* (1995), *October Dusk* (1987). **Autobiographical essay:** "Counting the Sums," in *Bloodroot* (1998), ed. Joyce Dyer, 219–24. **Essays on poets and poetry:** *Looking for Native Ground: Contemporary Appalachian Poetry* (1989). **Recorded interview:** *Tell it on the Mountain: Appalachian Women Writers* (Appalshop, 1997).

SECONDARY

George Brosi, "Booklist and Notes," *Appalachian Heritage* 26:2 (spring 1996), 74. Joyce Dyer, "Rita Quillen," in *Bloodroot*, 218. Don Johnson, "Staring at the Wind: A Conversation with Rita Sims Quillen," in *Her Words* (2002), ed. Felicia Mitchell, 220–34. George Ella Lyon, review of *Counting the Sums*, *Appalachian Journal* 24:1 (fall 1996), 76–77. Barbara Smith, review of *October Dusk*, *Appalachian Heritage* 15:4 (fall 1987), 67.

July 18, 1966

from *Counting the Sums* (1995)

In the days before air conditioning
we lay in the muggy dark
smelled our own sweat
no hope of sleep
while the fans roared
drowning the night chirp away.
In the next room my mother
lay swollen and weak
with her last child;
my father slept heavy as death
under a blanket of summer heat.

My childhood summers
are not memorable
just images
of swimming in coffee-colored water
sitting like a moth on the front steps
answering my neighbor's cattle call
riding and riding my bike
and long, long nights of heat
staring at the ceiling
trying to accept the idea of eternity
touching myself
fantasizing a life
where I was the star, a hero
not a secondrate extra.

And this:
the sound, an eerie sound
in the night six weeks
before my sister was born
of my mother crying in her bed.
How could my father not hear?
I heard no voice of comfort
I imagined his breath

steady as his will
her tears blown away by the fans.

On July 18, 1966
I learned this
about women and their crying:
tears belong to the nighttime
you must comfort yourself
your daughter will do her own weeping.

WOMAN WRITER

from *Counting the Sums* (1995)

Spending the days attending to bodily functions
our own and everyone else's
gives us a handicap.
Words crawl into the laundry basket
hide among the socks
circle and scream in the toilet
hang in the closet and beg
for freedom.
While my son warms in my arms
a line that could make me famous
leaps up in my face
spits and leaves by the back door.
I cannot throw down my baby
and chase into the air
I am too tired anyway,
too tired.
I dream words that have magic
I dream lines that make my heart
beat faster in the heat of recognition.
Today
a poem becomes a morning song
a psalm almost
but dies after a few verses
drowned in the everyday.

A lost poem swirling down
blurred like the face
of a childhood friend
lands on my doorstep.
In the morning
I open the door
and step on the poem.
Writhing, gasping words
try to cry out,
get off the page.
My children come to hover
while they watch my face
just watch and wait.

I Used To Be A Teacup

from *Counting the Sums* (1995)

I used to be a teacup
bone and gold-rimmed
thin-lipped and light
slim-handled
easy to hold.

Then I became a mug
heavy and practical
people warmed their hands on me
warm steam rising
scented the air
with home and good.

If I live I'll grow to be
a gravy boat
sailing around
smug and self-satisfied
filled with an imperfect, lumpy mixture
comforting and familiar
only brought out on special occasions.

DISCOVERED

from *October Dusk* (1987)

A skinny girl with cornstalk legs
and hair like straw
was mocked by her classmates
for her Goodwill clothes,
her self-pitying seriousness.
While they attended ballgames
and worshipped Max Factor,
she hid safely in her room
reading big thick books
full of questions
and very small print.
Kant, Freud, and Camus,
she still didn't understand
while the flames licked the posters off the wall
and the rug grew too warm for her feet.

At 16 she begged with adolescent fervor
for THE ANSWER
until one Sunday afternoon,
the air wet with tears,
she said no to the easiest one.

It's a good thing—
for a curly-haired boy in overalls
with cat-gray eyes
and a wonderfully hard body
discovered her,
introduced her to the joy of unreserved excess
to a different kind of flames
convinced her
that it was not up to the 16-year-olds of the world
to answer the questions.

How Do You Remember Him?

from *Appalachian Journal* (1997)

(For Jim Wayne Miller)

My students ask.
I only shake my head and stare at the floor.
I think:

He was a scratchy version
of "Cluck Old Hen" on a play-worn fiddle
with a touch of Hank Williams thrown in.

He was a cup of strong black coffee
and a dish of melting ice cream.

He was Rilke's evil twin.

He was the color brown and a throaty laugh.
He was fingers blunt as fenceposts
and wingtip shoes.

But this is poetic pretense that they would
confuse with profundity.
So I say,

Jim was his grandfather resouled.
He moved restless,
free and fluid in his own skin
as the old man's foxhounds,
plowed long, straight deep rows,
burned the ridges by moonlight,
waded hip deep in wild water by day,
walked always with his head down,
lived to fish, fished to live,
died too soon.

ᴊᴇᴀɴ ᴿɪᴛᴄʜɪᴇ
(December 8, 1922–)

The youngest of fourteen children, Jean Ritchie grew up surrounded by music. In the evenings, her family gathered on the porch of their farmhouse in Viper, Kentucky, to sing and to tell tales. Ritchie's father taught her how to play the lap dulcimer when she was only five years old.

Ritchie graduated from the University of Kentucky in 1946 with a degree in social work, then moved to New York City and worked in a settlement house, intending to return eventually to Kentucky to establish much-needed social services in her native state. While in New York, her music brought her to the attention of Alan Lomax, who was collecting recordings of folk artists for the Library of Congress.

Astonished by Ritchie's repertoire of more than three hundred traditional songs, Lomax not only recorded her but encouraged Ritchie to write a book about her musical childhood. *Singing Family of the Cumberlands* was published in 1955 and is still in print almost fifty years later. Said one Chicago critic, "Jean writes with such tenderness at times that one murmurs an apology for intruding on the family circle."

Over the years, Ritchie has made numerous recordings and performed at folk festivals throughout the world with such artists as Woody Guthrie, Pete Seeger, and Doc Watson. In 1977, her album *None But One* was awarded the *Rolling Stone* Critic's Award. Her work is also featured on *Washington Square Memoirs* (2001), and *Contemporary Anthology of Music by Women* (1999).

She is known today, not only as a performer, but as an author, songwriter, and folklorist. Her many awards include a Fulbright, as well as two Honorary Doctors of Letters, one from the University of Kentucky and the other from Berea College. In 2002, the National Endowment for the Arts awarded Ritchie a National Heritage Fellowship: the Bess Lomax Hawes Award "for

508

outstanding contributions as a 'keeper of tradition.'" Ritchie divides her time between her home in Port Washington, New York, and a cabin in Viper, Kentucky.

What follows are the opening paragraphs of Ritchie's *Singing Family of the Cumberlands.*

OTHER SOURCES TO EXPLORE

PRIMARY

Autobiography: "The Song about the Story—The Story behind the Song," in *Bloodroot* (1998), ed. Joyce Dyer, 226–32. **Nonfiction:** *Black Waters* (1983), *Jean Ritchie's Dulcimer People* (1975), *Apple Seeds & Soda Straws: Some Love Charms and Legends* (1965), *Folk Songs of the Southern Appalachians* (1965), *The Dulcimer Book* (1963), *Jean Ritchie's Celebration of Life, Her Songs . . . Her Poems* (1971). *Singing Family of the Cumberlands* (1955). **Selected recordings:** *Mountain Born* (1999), *Kentucky Christmas* (1990), *Jean Ritchie and Doc Watson at Folk City* (1990), *None But One* (1977).

SECONDARY

Beverly Boggs, "Religious Songs Remembered: *Sweet Rivers, Jean Ritchie,*" *Appalachian Journal* 9:4 (summer 1982), 306–10. George Brosi, "New Books," review of *Singing Family of the Cumberlands, Appalachian Heritage* 17:1 (winter 1989), 72. Joyce Dyer, "Jean Ritchie," in *Bloodroot*, 223. Loyal Jones, "Jean Ritchie, Twenty-Five Years After," *Appalachian Journal* 8:3 (spring 1981), 224–29. *Mountain Born: The Jean Ritchie Story* (Kentucky Educational Television [KET], 1996).

SINGING FAMILY OF
THE CUMBERLANDS (1955)

from Chapter One

I was born in Viper, Kentucky, in the Cumberland Mountains, on the eighth day of December 1922. I think I was a little of a surprise to my mother who had thought that if a woman had a baby in her fortieth year it would be her last. Mom had my brother Wilmer when she was forty, and she settled back to raise her thirteen young uns without any more interference. Then when she was forty-four, I came along.

It must have been hardest on Wilmer; he had himself all fixed to be the baby of the family for life. Mom says that the day I was born they found him, in the middle of all the excitement, away out behind the house all alone. He was leaning up against the old June-apple tree just crying his eyes out. He wouldn't tell what was the matter for a long time, but finally he snubbed and said that he never would get to sleep with Mommie no more.

My sisters laughed and made a great joke out of it, and shamed him and said that was a fine way to act when there was a pretty little sister in the house. But Mom told them to hush about it, and she told Wilmer to climb into the bed too. So that first night she slept with her girl babe and her boy babe and my Dad, all three.

Well, that was my introduction to this world, so they tell me, the way families will remember little funny things about a birth or a marrying or even a funeral, and tell about them a thousand times over the years on all those occasions when families start to recall old times. Whenever the Ritchie family falls into one of these sessions of telling tales on one another, it is sure to take up a long evening, because we have so much to remember and so many to remember about.

My very first memory is of our house—filled with crowds and noise and laughing and singing and crying. Beds, chairs, everything full and running over with people. There was never quite enough room even at our long homemade table for all of us to sit and have any elbow room, but we managed to get everybody around it by standing the little ones at the corners. When she saw us all ranged around the table like that, Mom would sometimes say out loud, in a sort of wonder,

'Lordie, it's a mystery to me that the house don't fly all to pieces. I don't rightly know where they all get to of a night.'

Still, our house was thought a big and a fine one in the community, and we were proud of it. My father built it himself with his own hands and the help of the neighbors, and the day he moved his family and his goods and chattels over the ridges with his wagon and team, that was a fine day. Up to this time it seemed he just couldn't find a place he could be satisfied in for long. When they were first married, Mom and Dad went to live in the big old log house with Granny Katty, Dad's mother, on Clear Creek in Knott County, where Dad was born and raised. Two months later Dad finished building their first little house, away up on Clear Creek, and they lived in that until the family got so big that they had to find a place to spread out, farther down the creek. The next move was to the county seat of Hindman, and finally, five or six years before I was born, Dad brought Mom and the big family back to Mom's birthplace, Viper, in Perry County.

Viper is a tiny village whose fifteen or twenty houses string out like a chain around the hillside where it dips inward to follow the curve of the river. There are a few more houses built on the narrow strip of bottom land between the railroad and the river, but not many, for there isn't much bottom land. The mountains are part of the Appalachian chain called the Cumberlands, and in this section they rise in long, gently arching ridges, one following another and one beyond another as far as the eye can see. Because of their shapes they have been given local names like Razorback Ridge, Devil's Backbone, and Longbow Mountain.

To stand in the bottom of any of the valleys is to have the feeling of being down in the center of a great round cup. To stand on top of one of the narrow ridges is like balancing on one of the innermost petals of a gigantic rose, from which you can see all around you the other petals falling away in wide rings to the horizon. Travelers from the level lands, usually the Blue Grass section of Kentucky to the west of us, always complained that they felt hemmed in by our hills, cut off from the wide skies and the rest of the world. For us it was hard to believe there was any "rest of the world," and if there should be such a thing, why, we trusted in the mountains to protect us from it.

The place Dad picked out to build our house was the prettiest piece of level land in the community, about three acres stretched out between the hill and the branch. The house when finished was a three-room frame building in the shape of an L, and then they built a separate kitchen in the back yard. In later years this "old kitchen" was torn down and three small rooms were added onto the long side of the main house, next to the hill, but it was in the first four rooms that the thirteen children were for the most part raised.

We managed it on a sort of dormitory plan. Mom and Dad and the babies slept in the front room that settled back into the hill. The other front room was the girls' room and extended out toward the branch. The boys' beds were in what we called the living room, the third and largest of the three, built onto the back of Mom's room, with a door between. It was here that we received strangers and fine-looking people—peddlers of rugs, herb cures, spices, dulcimers, and tintypes; travelers over the mountains, asking to take the night; and once or twice strange folks from away over the ocean in England, wanting to hear Mom and Dad and the girls sing the old ballads. Then we used the living room. If it was somebody we knew, though, he'd come into Mom's room, first off. That was our real living room.

The very nicest thing about the house to me was the porch that ran all around the house on all sides except the back of the kitchen and the living room where the house settles into the mountain. And my favorite part of the porch was The Corner, where the boys' room met the girls' room and made the ell. The branch, with its water always twinkling and making music, ran parallel to this side of the house, and so did the sledroad up the holler. If you sat in The Corner long, you would most surely see someone go up or down the road, Earl Engle on his mare taking a turn of corn to the mill, or Lee-up-on-the-Branch walking to his house at the head of the holler. He always had a little bagful of something, you never did know what, but it made your mouth water to think what it might be—peppermint or licorice sticks, or hoarhound drops, cinnamon "belly-burners," or big round lemon cookies, maybe. Anyway, it was good fun just to watch folks go by, because they always nodded their heads and said "Howdy-do" to you, same as if you were a grown person.

Mom hated The Corner just about as much as I loved it. It was the handiest place to throw things in passing, and for that reason it was her everlasting despair. She was sure that everybody who passed in the road looked especially into our porch corner and said to himself, "What messy folks the Ritchies are, plum shiftless, to keep a porch looking like that in plain sight of the road."

So, about once a week Mom would roll up her sleeves and call around her three or four young uns, and brooms would swish-swash and dust would boil and dogs would yelp and run, and the family would come and admire the clean, empty Corner. Next day Dad would all unthinking throw down a load of wood in The Corner; the little ones would bring their dolls and use the wood to make a playhouse; the boys, Raymond and Truman and Wilmer, would toss their apple and walnut sacks over behind the wood; and the dogs would come in and have pups on the sacks. It was just the most comfortable place in the whole house, and I loved it in the daytime, but Lord pity the poor chap who had to go past it on the way to bed after a long evening spent listening to Granny Katty and Dad and the old people tell stories of ghosts and hants they had seen in their time. . . .

ÉLIZABETH ⨏ADOX ⨏OBERTS
(October 30, 1881–March 13, 1941)

Poet, novelist, and short story writer Elizabeth Madox Roberts was born in Perryville, Kentucky. She was one of eight children of Mary Elizabeth Brent Roberts, a teacher, and Simpson Roberts, a teacher, a store owner, and a surveyor. Her great-grandmother arrived in Kentucky on the Wilderness Road. When Roberts was three, she moved with her family to the place she considered her home for the rest of her life, Springfield, Kentucky. As poet George Ella Lyon describes her in the introduction to *Old Wounds, New Words* (1994), "Roberts . . . is a central Kentucky native whose work often deals with Appalachian themes and experiences."

After withdrawing from State College of Kentucky (now the University of Kentucky) before completing her freshman year, she eventually enrolled in the University of Chicago in 1917, at the age of thirty-six. She became friends there with the future novelist Glenway Wescott and poet Yvor Winters, who encouraged her poetry. When she graduated cum laude, with a degree in English in 1921, she also received the Fiske Poetry Prize.

After her graduation, she returned home and had these words to say about her native Kentucky: "All young people wish to try the world and to find out adventures, but the young of Kentucky do not seem to look upon their region as a place from which to escape. A pride in the place where they were born stays with them when they go, if they must go, and often they return." Her life reflects these sentiments; she repeatedly left Kentucky, but always returned. Recurrent health problems sent her for visits to Colorado (1910–1916), to the Riggs Foundation in Stockbridge, Massachusetts (1923–1924), and to Santa Monica, California (1927). She was diagnosed with Hodgkin's disease in 1936.

Roberts spent winters in Orlando, Florida, and continued to write until her death in 1941. She is buried in Springfield, Kentucky.

She began her writing career as a poet and was published in Harriet Monroe's *Poetry* magazine, receiving its prestigious John Reed Memorial Prize in 1928. In 1930, she received the O. Henry Award for her short story "The Sacrifice of the Maidens," and she wrote two collections of short fiction. But she is best known for her novels *The Time of Man* and *The Great Meadow*.

Cratis Williams describes *The Time of Man* as "a significant guidepost on the route traveled by regional literature from romantic local color to the more powerful realism of the 1930s." This novel, translated into at least six languages, brought Roberts international acclaim. It is the story of a white sharecropper's daughter, Ellen Chesser. The fourteen-year-old protagonist marries young, bears a child, and manages to see beyond her heartbreaking poverty to the poetry in life. Roberts's stream-of-consciousness narration, her extraordinary female characterizations, and her poetic prose are primary strengths of her fiction.

OTHER SOURCES TO EXPLORE

PRIMARY

Novels: *Woodcock of the Ivory Beak* (1981), *Horse* (1980), *Christmas Morning* (1950), *Black is My True Love's Hair* (1938), *On the Mountainside* (1936), *He Sent Forth a Raven* (1935), *A Buried Treasure* (1931), *The Great Meadow* (1930), *Jingling in the Wind* (1928), *My Heart and My Flesh* (1927), *The Time of Man* (1926). **Short stories:** *Not by Strange Gods* (1941), *The Haunted Mirror* (1932). **Poetry:** *Song in the Meadow* (1940), *Under the Tree* (1922), *In the Great Steep's Garden* (1915).

SECONDARY

Contemporary Authors (1999), Vol. 166, 335–40. *Dictionary of Literary Biography* (1981), Vol. 9, 310–13. Earl Rovit, "Elizabeth Madox Roberts," *Southern Writers: A Biographical Dictionary* (1979), 385–86. Earl Rovit, *Herald to Chaos: The Novels of Elizabeth Madox Roberts* (1960). Anne Rowe, "Elizabeth Madox Roberts," *American Women Writers* (1988), 635–36. *Something About the Author* (1981), Vol. 33, 168–70. William S. Ward, "Elizabeth Madox Roberts," *A Literary History of Kentucky* (1988), 150–59.

THE TIME OF MAN (1926)

from Chapter III

Ellen milked her cow by the little gate which led from the dooryard to the pasture. In three days she had learned to make the milk flow easily, stroking the animal flesh with deft fingers. The cow was a slim tan Jersey with a bright face and quick horns. Her body was bony and full of knots—bone joints, and her sides were unsymmetrically balanced. She had slender short legs and small sharp feet. She seemed to Ellen to be all paunch, a frame skeleton supporting a subtended belly with buds of milk, a machine to produce milk hung under a bony frame. Ellen looked at her each milking time; she knew the wrinkles on her skin around the eyes and her wrinkled neck, her loud breathing, her corrugated tongue and lips, her moist muzzle, and her pathetic mouth with its drooping lower lip. The tight eyelids seemed scarcely large enough to fit over the large round eyes and the hair spread out from a center on her forehead, making a star. Her horns were like dark rough pearl and they slanted up over the big skeleton of her face. She moved about very slowly, turning away from the milking place when she had been drained dry, always humble and enslaved, or she walked off across the pastures joining many others at the feeding rick near the stock barns. . .

. . .

When Henry had burned his plant bed he plowed and hoed the ashes into the soil and made a frame of logs about the whole, a light frame to hold the canvas that would be stretched over the bed when the seeds were sown. There were more stones to gather after the plowing and these Ellen piled outside the bed. The rocks were dark with mould and moss, for this was a virgin hill. It was a mild March day, cool and clear, with winds worrying the hillside brush and leaping off across the farms in a great rush or beating gently now and then at Ellen's garments. Henry nailed at the frame while she worked with the stones.

"No plow iron ever cut this-here hill afore, not in the whole time of man," Henry said.

"The time of man," as a saying, fell over and over in Ellen's mind. The strange men that lived here before our men, a strange race doing things in strange ways, and other men before them, and before again. Strange feet walking on a hillside for some purpose she could never think. Wondering and wondering she laid stones on her altar.

"Pappy, where do rocks come from?"

"Why, don't you know? Rocks grow."

"I never see any grow. I never see one a-growen."

"I never see one a-growen neither, but they grow all the same. You pick up all the rocks offen this-here hill and in a year there's as many out again. I lay there'll be a stack to pick up right here again next year."

"I can't seem to think it! Rocks a-growen now! They don't seem alive. They seem dead-like. Maybe they've got another kind of way to be alive."

"Maybe they have. All I know is they grow."

"Rocks have got shells printed on the sides and some have little snails worked on their edges and some have got little worms-like worked on. But once I found a spider with a dragon beast in a picture on its back. Some rocks, now, are shaped like little silos and some are all marked with little snails and waterbugs and some are open fans and some have little scallops on the edges. Rocks grow in ways that are right pretty now. It's a wonder, really."

"I wish I could see a rock grow," she said again. "I can't think how it is. You could watch a rock for a whole year and you'd never see any sign of it growen. The rock doorstep over at Bodine's didn't grow e'er bit all the time we lived there."

. . .

She was working alone on the hillside. Henry had gone for the seeds and was long in returning. She gathered stones from the plowed soil and piled them in her neat mound, and the wind continued to blow off the hilltop. She found spotted ladybugs hidden under the leaves and the twigs; they shone out like jewels in the brown and black of the earth. Far away toward MacMurtrie's cedar trees doves were crying, and over the plowed field plovers went circling, singing on the wing. To the northeast the hills rolled away so far that sight gave out, and still they went, fading into blue hazes and myths of faint trees; delicate trees stood finer than hair lines on a far mythical hill. She piled stone after stone on the mound, carrying each across crumbled earth that the plow and the hoe had harried. The rocks fell where she laid them with a faint flat sound, and the afternoon seemed very still back of the dove calls and the cries of the plovers, back of a faint dying phrase, "in the time of man." The wind lapped through the sky, swirling lightly now, and again dashing straight down from the sun. She was leaning over the clods to gather a stone, her shadow making an arched shape on the ground. All at once she lifted her body and flung up her head to the great sky that reached over the hills and shouted:

"Here I am!"

She waited listening.

"I'm Ellen Chesser! I'm here!"

ANNE NEWPORT ROYALL
(June 11, 1769–October 1, 1854)

Some sources identify Anne Newport Royall as the first female American newspaper journalist. A dubious legend has it that she once caught President John Quincy Adams skinny dipping in the Potomac and sat on his clothes until he agreed to an exclusive interview. Though their mutual friendship makes the story's credibility questionable, she had a reputation for being a strong-willed woman.

The daughter of loyalist William Newport, she was born near Baltimore, Maryland, before the American Revolution, and grew up on the western Pennsylvania frontier, in Westmoreland County. When her father died, her mother Mary, a Virginia native about whom little is known, remarried, had a son, and lost her second husband. The family then relocated to Monroe County, Virginia, now West Virginia, where her mother found work as a servant in the household of the wealthy Captain William Royall, reputed to be a friend of George Washington.

The teenaged Anne won Royall's attention, though he was at least twenty years her senior. He shared with her his extensive library, his deist ideas, his antislavery sentiments, and in 1797, when she was twenty-eight, they married. When he died in 1813, she decided to move south to the warmer climate of Alabama, where she lived for a decade before Royall's children succeeded in their quest to break his will and left her, at the age of fifty-four, without financial resources.

Had she not been faced with this hardship, she may never have become a writer. Motivated to support herself, Anne Royall began her career as a journalist. She traveled by foot, by stagecoach, and by steamboat in the 1820s, when travel was neither entirely safe nor very comfortable, and took copious notes on nearly every important American city and settlement, producing ten volumes, which sold fairly well. Her travel narratives combined documentary social history with her lively personal opinions and wry observations, spiced heavily by her rather bitter worldview.

Around 1830, Royall settled in Washington, D.C., where she began petitioning the United States Government for her widow's pension from her husband's Revolutionary War service (which she did not obtain until 1848). In the meantime, she acquired a printing press and took in printing jobs before beginning her own weekly newspaper, for which she served as investigative reporter, writer, editor, printer, and subscription manager. It featured political gossip and uncovered graft in public offices, in addition to editorializing for religious tolerance and the separation of church and state, as well as a number of other causes.

In one infamous incident she attacked a local group of Presbyterians, or "Holy Willies" as she called them, and a little-known law was evoked to convict her of being a "common scold." She was fined ten dollars—in lieu of a dunking—and according to at least one source, President Jackson's secretary of war, John Eaton, paid her fine.

Earning both fear and begrudged respect, she boldly lobbied for her causes in her enterprising newspaper, first named *Paul Pry*, and then *The Huntress*, until she was eighty-five.

The first of her travel books continues to be her best known.

OTHER SOURCES TO EXPLORE

PRIMARY

Mrs. Royall's Southern Tour (3 vols., 1830–1831), *Letters from Alabama* (1830), *Mrs. Royall's Pennsylvania* (2 vols., 1829), *The Black Book: A Continuation of Travels in the United States* (3 vols., 1828–1829), *The Tennessean: A Novel Founded on Facts* (1827), *Sketches of History, Life and Manners in the United States by a Traveller* (1826).

SECONDARY

Sarah Harvey Porter, *The Life and Times of Anne Royall* (1909). George S. Jackson, *Uncommon Scold: The Story of Anne Royall* (1937). Russel B. Nye, "Royall, Anne Newport" in *Notable American Women 1607–1950*, Vol. 3, 204–5. Don Dodd and Ben Williams, "'A Common Scold': Anne Royall," *American History Illustrated*, 10:9 (January 1976), 32–38. *Dictionary of Literary Biography*, Vol. 43, 402–8.

SKETCHES OF HISTORY, LIFE, AND MANNERS, IN THE UNITED STATES (1826)

from Kenhawa County

As this famous county is to be a link in the chain which is to connect that part of Virginia east of the mountains with the whole of the western country, I have been at some pains to pick up every thing respecting it. As curiosity leads one to trace things to their origin, such as the history of countries, and remarkable events, I have traced this part of Virginia as far back as the year seventeen hundred and seventy-four, to the memorable battle of the Point [Battle of Point Pleasant, in 1774, a pivotal Revolutionary War battle], fought between the whites and the Indians, at the mouth of this river [the confluence of the Ohio and Kanawha Rivers]. I have seen several men who were in that bloody and hard fought battle, and have just returned from viewing the ground on which it was fought. I have seen that part occupied by the "Augusta militia," commanded by Gen. Lewis, and that by the Indians. I have seen the bones of the latter sticking in the bank of the Ohio river; part of the bank having fallen in where the battle was fought discloses their bones sticking out in a horizontal position: the engagement lasted from sunrise till dark; the victory was claimed by the whites. From this bank, which is a hundred feet, or thereabouts, in height, I had a view of the beautiful river Ohio: at this place it is said to be five hundred yards wide.

This river, which is justly celebrated for its beauty and utility, flows in a smooth current as silent as night; not the least noise can be heard from it; not the smallest ripple is seen. This, and its limpid appearance, the rich foliage which decorates its banks and looks as though it were growing in the water, by reason of its luxuriance, completely conceals the earth, and constitutes its beauty. If the reader can imagine a vast mirror of endless dimension, he will have an idea of this beautiful river. It is so transparent that you may see pebbles at the bottom; not a rock or stone of any size, has a place in the Ohio. Kenhawa is a very handsome river, being generally as smooth as the Ohio, but by no means so limpid; it has a greenish appearance; you cannot see the bottom, except at the shoals. And more than all this. I have seen the celebrated heroine, Ann Bailey, who richly deserves more of her country, than a name in its history.

This female is a Welch woman, and is now very old. At the time Gen. Lewis's army lay at the Point, a station on Kenhawa river, Ann would shoulder her rifle, hang her shot-pouch over her shoulder, and lead a horse laden with ammunition to the army, two hundred miles distant, when not a man could be found to undertake the perilous task—the way thither being a perfect wilderness, and infested with Indians. I asked her if she was not afraid—she replied, "No, she was not; she trusted in the Almighty—she knew she could only be killed, and she had to die some time." I asked her if she never met with the Indians in her various journies. (for she went several times.) "Yes, she once met with two, and one of them said to the other let us kill her, (as she supposed, from the answer of the other). No, said his companion, God dam, too good a soger, and let her pass:" but how said I, did you find the way,—"Steered by the trace of Lewis's army, and I had a pocket compass too." "Well, but how did you get over the water courses?"—Some she forded, and some she swam, on others she made a raft: she "halways carried a hax and a hauger, and she could chop as well has hany man;" such was her dialect. This is a fact that hundreds can attest. A gentleman informed, that while the army was stationed near the mouth of Elk, he walked down that river to where it intersects with Kenhawa, for the purpose of fishing; he had not remained long there before he heard a plunge in the water, and upon looking up, he discovered Ann on horseback swimming toward him; when the horse gained the landing, she observed, "cod, I'd like to a swum." She was quite a low woman in height, but very strongly made, and had the most pleasing countenance I ever saw, and for her, very affable. "And what would the General say to you, when you used to get safe to camp with your ammunition." "Why he'd say, you're a brave soldier, Ann, and tell some of the men to give me a dram." She was fond of a dram. When I saw the poor creature, she was almost naked; she begged a dram, which I gave to her, and also some other trifle. I never shall forget Ann Bailey. The people here repeat many sayings of hers, such as "the howl upon the helm on the bank of the helk"—that is, an owl on an elm upon the bank of Elk river.

$\mathcal{C}$YNTHIA $\mathcal{R}$YLANT
(June 6, 1954–)

Cynthia Rylant was born in Hopewell, Virginia, and grew up in the mountains of Raleigh County, West Virginia, surrounded by the warmth of a family who lived on the edge of poverty. She is the daughter of a nurse, Leatrel Rylant, and an army sergeant, John Tune. Her parents divorced when she was young, and she spent some of her childhood with her grandparents while her mother was in nursing school. "I grew up reading comic books because there was no library in my town or in my school, and I did not enter a public library until I was in my twenties," says Rylant.

Rylant graduated from Morris Harvey College (now University of Charleston) in 1975 with a B.A. in English, then earned an M.A. in English at Marshall University in 1976. After completing a Master's in Library Science at Kent State University in 1982, she worked as a children's librarian in Akron, Ohio, before becoming a full-time writer.

Rylant has won numerous awards, including a Newbery Award in 1993 for her young adult novel, *Missing May*. Her first book, *When I Was Young in the Mountains* was a Caldecott Honor Book, as was *The Relatives Came*. She received the 1991 *Boston Globe–Horn* Book Award for nonfiction for *Appalachia: The Voices of Sleeping Birds*.

Her childhood experiences left her with a special affinity for the underdog. "I get a lot of personal gratification thinking of those people who don't get any attention in the world and making them really valuable in my fiction—making them absolutely shine with their beauty."

Rylant currently lives in Oregon with her son, Nate. Her selected papers, including multiple drafts of many of her works, are held by the Special Collections Department in the university library at Kent State.

The following excerpt is the opening chapter of *Missing May*, in which Summer faces the death of her foster mother, May, and the grief of May's husband, Ob.

OTHER SOURCES TO EXPLORE

PRIMARY

Selected picture books: *Poppleton Everyday* (1998), *Tulip Sees America* (1998), *Bear Day* (1998), *Scarecrow* (1997), *Silver Packages: An Appalachian Christmas Story* (1997), *Cat Heaven* (1997), *An Angel for Solomon Singer* (1992), *Mr. Griggs' Work* (1989), *All I See* (1988), *Birthday Presents* (1987), *Night in the* Country (1986), *The Relatives Came* (1985), *This Year's Garden* (1984), *Miss Maggie* (1983), *When I Was Young In the Mountains* (1982), and more than a dozen books in the Henry and Mudge series. **Fiction for children:** *Missing May* (1992), *Appalachia: The Voices of Sleeping Birds* (1991), *A Couple of Kooks: And Other Stories about Love* (1990), *A Kindness* (1989), *A Fine White Dust* (1986), *Every Living Thing* (1985), *Blue-Eyed Daisy* (1985). **Poetry for children:** *Good Morning Sweetie Pie and Other Poems for Little Children* (2002), *Soda Jerk* (1990), *Waiting to Waltz* (1984). **Autobiography:** "Newbery Medal Acceptance," *The Horn Book Magazine* 69:4 (July/August 1993), 416–19. *But I'll Be Back Again* (1989). Anita Silvey, "An Interview with Cynthia Rylant," *The Horn Book Magazine* 63:6 (November/December 1987), 695–702.

SECONDARY

George Brosi, "New Books," *Appalachian Heritage* 20:3 (summer 1992), 79. *Contemporary Authors*, Vol. 136, 357–58. *Something about the Author* (1991), Vol. 13, 155–63. *Something About the Author* (1992), Vol. 13, 155–63; Vol. 50, 182–88; Vol. 76, 193–99. Diane Ward, "Cynthia Rylant," *The Horn Book Magazine* 69:4 (July/August 1993), 420–23.

MISSING MAY (1992)

Chapter One

When May died, Ob came back to the trailer, got out of his good suit and into his regular clothes, then went and sat in the Chevy for the rest of the night. That old car had been parked out by the doghouse for as long as I could remember, and the weeds had grown up all around it so you didn't even notice it unless you looked, and for years I couldn't understand why Ob didn't just get rid of the awful thing. Until I saw him sitting in it after the funeral. Then I knew that even though nobody in the world figured that old car had any good purpose, Ob knew there was some real reason to let it sit. And when May died, he figured out what it was.

I never saw two people love each other so much. Sometimes the tears would just come over me, looking at the two of them, even six years back when I first got here and was too young to be thinking about love. But I guess I must have had a deep part of me thinking about it, hoping to see it all along, because the first time I saw Ob help May braid her long yellow hair, sitting in the kitchen one night, it was all I could do not to go to the woods and cry forever from happiness.

I know I must have been loved like that, even if I can't remember it. I must have; otherwise, how could I even recognize love when I saw it that night between Ob and May? Before she died, I know my mother must have loved to comb my shiny hair and rub that Johnson's baby lotion up and down my arms and wrap me up and hold and hold me all night long. She must have known she wasn't going to live and she must have held me longer than any other mother might, so I'd have enough love in me to know what love was when I saw it or felt it again.

When she died and all her brothers and sisters passed me from house to house, nobody ever wanting to take care of me for long, I still had that lesson in love deep inside me and I didn't grow mean or hateful when nobody cared enough to make me their own little girl. My poor mother had left me enough love to go on until somebody did come along who'd want me.

Then Uncle Ob and Aunt May from West Virginia visited, and they knew an angel when they saw her and they took me on home.

Home was, still is, a rusty old trailer stuck on the face of a mountain in Deep Water, in the heart of Fayette County. It looked to me, the first time, like a toy that God had been playing with and accidentally dropped out of heaven. Down and down and down it came and landed, thunk, on this mountain, sort of cockeyed and shaky and grateful to be all in one piece. Well, sort of one piece. Not counting that part in the back where the aluminum's peeling off, or the one missing window, or the front steps that are sinking.

That first night in it with Ob and May was as close to paradise as I may ever come in my life. Paradise because these two old people—who never dreamed they'd be bringing a little girl back from their visit with the relatives in Ohio—started, from the minute we pulled up in Ob's old Valiant, to turn their rusty, falling-down place into a house just meant for a child. May started talking about where they'd hang the swing as soon as she hoisted herself out of the front seat (May was a big woman), and Ob was designing a tree house in his head before he even got the car shut off. I was still so sick to my stomach from traveling all those curvy West Virginia roads that all I could do was swallow and nod, swallow and nod. Try to smile without puking.

But when we got inside the trailer, it became plain to me at once that they didn't need to do any great changing to make a little girl happy. First thing I saw when May switched on the light were those shelves and shelves— seemed every wall was covered with them—of whirligigs. I knew what they were right off even though they weren't like any whirligigs I'd ever seen. Back in Ohio people had them hooked to their fences or stuck out in their gardens to scare off the birds. And they'd be mostly the same everywhere: a roadrunner whose legs spun in the wind, or maybe a chicken or a duck. Cartoon characters were popular—Garfield was in a lot of gardens with his arms whirling like crazy in the breeze.

I'd seen plenty of whirligigs, but never any like Ob's. Ob was an artist—I could tell that the minute I saw them—though *artist* isn't the word I could have used back then, so young. None of Ob's whirligigs were farm animals or cartoon characters. They were *The Mysteries*. That's what Ob told me, and I knew just what he was talking about. One whirligig was meant to be a thunderstorm and it was so like one, black and gray, beautiful and frightening. Another was Ob's idea of heaven, and I thought his angels just might come off that thing and fly around that house trailer any minute, so golden and light were they. There was Fire and Love and Dreams and Death. Even one called May, which had more little spinning parts than any of the rest of the whirligigs, and these parts all white—her Spirit, he said. They were grounded to a branch from an oak tree and this, he said, was her Power.

I stood there before those shelves, watching these wonders begin to spin as May turned on the fan overhead, and I felt like a magical little girl, a chosen little girl, like Alice who has fallen into Wonderland. This feeling has yet to leave me.

And as if the whirligigs weren't enough, May turned me to the kitchen, where she pulled open all the cabinet doors, plus the refrigerator, and she said, "Summer, whatever you like you can have and whatever you like that isn't here Uncle Ob will go down to Ellet's Grocery and get you. We want you to eat, honey."

Back in Ohio, where I'd been treated like a homework assignment somebody was always having to do, eating was never a joy of any kind. Every house I had ever lived in was so particular about its food, and especially when the food involved me. There's no good way to explain this. But I felt like one of those little mice who has to figure out the right button to push before its food will drop down into the cup. Caged and begging. That's how I felt sometimes.

My eyes went over May's wildly colorful cabinets, and I was free again. I saw Oreos and Ruffles and big bags of Snickers. Those little cardboard boxes of juice that I had always, just once, wanted to try. I saw fat bags of marshmallows and cans of SpaghettiOs and a little plastic bear full of honey. There were real glass bottles of Coke looking cold as ice in the refrigerator and a great big half of a watermelon taking up space. And, best of all, a carton of real chocolate milk that said Hershey's.

Whirligigs of Fire and Dreams, glistening Coke bottles and chocolate milk cartons to greet me. I was six years old and I had come home.

ℬ𝑒TTIE 𝒮ELLERS
(March 30, 1926–)

Poet Bettie M. Sellers was born in Tampa, Florida, and was raised in Griffin, Georgia. She moved to the Georgia highlands in 1965 when she and her husband accepted teaching positions at Young Harris College in Young Harris, Georgia.

Sellers received her B.A. from La Grange College in 1958, and her M.A. from the University of Georgia in 1966. She was awarded an Honorary Doctorate of Letters from La Grange College in 1991. Sellers retired from the faculty at Young Harris in 1996. In 1997, she was named Poet Laureate of Georgia.

The author of seven books of poetry, Sellers has received numerous awards, including being named Poet of the Year by American Pen Women for *The Morning of the Red-Tailed Hawk*. She also won a Georgia Emmy as scriptwriter for the documentary *The Bitter Berry: The Life of Byron Herbert Reece*. Her work has appeared in a wide variety of publications, including *Georgia Review*, *Chattahoochee Review*, and *Arizona Quarterly*.

Sellers crafts poems from the images that surround her in the mountains of northern Georgia. Many of her poems illuminate the lives of the women of the region. One critic noted that Sellers knows these women "from the heart-side out."

Sellers says, "The language of a transplanted mountaineer is, of necessity, somewhat different from that of one born here. The rural way of life, though, is much the same, and it has been easy for me to think that I truly do belong."

Other Sources to Explore

Primary

Poetry: *Wild Ginger* (1989), *Satan's Playhouse* (1986), *Liza's Monday and Other Poems* (1986), *The Morning of the Red-Tailed Hawk* (1981), *Spring Onions and Cornbread* (1977), *Appalachian Carols: Poems* (1977), *Westward from Bald Mountain* (1974). **Nonfiction:** *The Bitter Berry: The Life of Byron Herbert Reece* (1992), *Beyond Uncle Remus: A Study of Some of Joel Chandler Harris' Negro Characters* (1966). **Autobiographical essay:** "Westward from Bald Mountain," in *Bloodroot* (1998), ed. Joyce Dyer, 234–42.

Secondary

Dorla D. Arndt, review of *Morning of the Red-Tailed Hawk*, *Appalachian Heritage* 13:3 (summer 1985), 75–76. *Contemporary Authors*, Vols. 77–80, 485. Joyce, Dyer, "Bettie Sellers," *Bloodroot,* 233. Robin O. Warren, "Stories of the Land, Family, and God: The Poetry of Bettie Sellers," *Her Words* (2002) ed. Felicia Mitchell, 249–60.

PINK

from *Liza's Monday and Other Poems* (1986)

Her mama called her "Pink" when she was born,
to match a tiny flower pressed in Exodus—
from Charlestown gardens, its like not found
among the blossoms wild in Brasstown soil.

She called the two boys "Flotsam" and "Jetsam,"
having heard such words ring somewhere
with all the strength of heroes: Samson, Saul—
though never could she find them in The Book

no matter if she searched to Revelation's end.
The last child Mama named "Rebecca" to be sure,
make up for giving wrong names to the boys—
and those now stuck too tight to budge.

Then Mama died, not knowing just how right
she'd called her boys, hell-bent to leave the plow
and hoe for parts out West where gold grew common
as the stones they cursed in winding valley rows.

In time, their faces faded as Pink brushed
Rebecca's long red hair, the color of her own.
She washed and cooked, up on a wooden stool
that Papa made so she could reach the tubs and stove.

She stitched the gown for Rebecca's wedding day,
embroidered it with pinks and ragged robins
around the neck and sleeves. In other springs,
she knitted caps for babies never hers.

She did for Papa till his days were through
and kept the cabin neat as Mama ever could.
Alone, she withered slowly, frail and dry
as petals caught and pressed by Exodus.

Mornings, Sheba Combs Her Hair

from *Liza's Monday and Other Poems* (1986)

She watches from the open door, the man
long-legged, tall and straight, his hair aflame
like foxes make as they run through the broom
sedge patch behind her house. This neighbor
passes by each day to climb the slope
of Cedar Ridge, cut logs to build a barn
near where the trail that crosses Unicoi
turns west through Brasstown Gap.
She watches, thinking how her own man,
gone these three years, never had
that loose-limbed stride, that fire atop
his head. Older than she, he never made
her heart run wild and fly across the valley
free as red-tailed hawks rise high
on currents of cold morning air. She watches,
planning how one day she'll walk out, ask him
how his wife does, how his son. She'll wait
beside the big oak, ask him in to warm his hands
before her hearth, to notice how her dark hair falls
as smooth as water in Corn Creek caresses stones.
How she will warm cold fingers in his hair,
and face eternal burning if she must.

LIZA'S MONDAY

from *Liza's Monday and Other Poems* (1986)

She has left her tubs and boiling sheets, fled
north across the woodlot, heard no grumble
from the pigs as she passed, the chicken shed
where eggs wait to be gathered, felt

no pain as December's harsh wind dried
lye soap on her arms, reddened hands held
stiff by her sides, palms forward as to catch
the gusts that sweep the slopes of Double Knob.

Inside the cabin: Ethan's shirt to patch,
the fire to mend, small Issac sleeping
in his crib, soon to wake for nursing.
These and other chores are in her keeping,

but she hurries up the mountainside
as on an April day to search for mint
and cress, to find first violets that hide
in white and purple patches by Corn Creek.

The ridge is steep and rocky, sharp with briars.
Raked inside by gales howling bleak
as northern winds around the cabin whine,
she does not feel the laurel tug her dress,

the briars pricking dark red beads that shine
on bare arms. All winter afternoon she climbs
until she gains the highest rocks, the knobs
where one can look out, trace the spines

of distant mountains, scan the valley floor—
black dots for shed and cabin, smoke only wisps
blown by the wind. Liza sees no more:
not broken stones underfoot, not heavy sky

holding snow. She sits on Double Knob, back
against the ledge, and watches night come by
to close the valley, wipe her clearing out
as though it has never been. Snow clouds

roil around Liza's head, wrap cold arms about
bent shoulders, fill her aproned lap, open hands,
Below, the wash-fire has burned down to embers;
Ethan long begun the search across his lands.

THE MORNING OF THE RED-TAILED HAWK

from *The Morning of the Red-Tailed Hawk* (1981)

In holy books, in church, I hear curses,
see stones hurled at bodies caught in acts
that spurn the law of Moses and of God. I,

like Saul, have judged, held coats in hands
washed clean in the blood of a Bible-belt Lamb.

But, outside my window now, the red-tailed hawk
glides, imperceptibly adjusting to turbulence,
scanning his territory for unwary rodents
in the reaches of tall marsh grass.

I too cruise, needing emotion, words to write.
Today, I intercepted a man's glance, saw his eyes
smoothing the light hairs on another man's arm
as they walked the beach.

These two are lovers in some sheltered cove,
where my claws could intrude, sharp
as the red-tailed hawk, his talons sunk in flesh.

I will not write their names. Deeper than books,
than church, I have caught some ancient pain,
accepting it to cup, as in a chalice,
between my trembling hands.

ALL ON A
SUMMER'S AFTERNOON

from *The Morning of*
the Red-Tailed Hawk (1981)

When my mother had turned her sad
slow heel back into childhood,
she ran away,
for most of a summer's afternoon.

Neighbors with pitying faces came to help
my father search the Flint River bottoms
where she had scratched up arrowheads for us
and told such tales that Creeks were lurking
behind every pine and oak for all our summers.

They combed high grasses skirting the beaver ponds
where she once sat, shushing our very breath
to quietness even the shyest beaver could trust.

They found her in the farthest pasture.
Tugging feebly at her print dress caught
in a tangle of barbed wire, she stood
with wide eyes, watching the Indians
come from behind the trees.

Legacy For Rachel

from *The Morning of the Red-Tailed Hawk* (1981)

I could call you Rachel
though that is not your name.
In the old story, Rachel waited,
watching Leah bear her children,
spun and wove in the corner
of Jacob's tent, hearing babies cry.

Years, you sat at your mother's knee,
wound her wool balls, stacked quilt
scraps in neat piles, cleaned her house.
And Leah came on Sundays, bristling
with young, ate your meals, patted
your thin shoulder, saying:
"What a good sister you are."

While funeral meats still lined
the kitchen cupboard shelves,
she piled up afghans, quilts
for daughters one, two, and three—
drove off toward town, leaving you
cradling balls of wool, picking lint
and scraps nestling under the cushions
of your mother's favorite chair.

MARY LEE SETTLE
(July 29, 1918–)

Born in Charleston, West Virginia, Mary Lee Settle's childhood was divided between West Virginia and eastern Kentucky, where her father worked as a civil engineer. She attended Sweet Briar College from 1936 to 1938, then worked at the Barter Theater in Abingdon, Virginia, where she was "discovered" and sent to Hollywood to be screen-tested for the movie *Gone With the Wind*. After returning from California, she spent a year modeling in New York. In 1942 she traveled to England to join the Women's Auxiliary Air Force, a branch of the Royal Air Force, an experience she recounts in *All the Brave Promises*.

After the war, Settle traveled extensively and made her home in the United States, England, and Turkey. She has returned to West Virginia several times over the years, homecomings that she has fictionalized in *The Killing Ground* and *Charley Bland*.

Settle's most acclaimed work is her 1977 novel *Blood Tie*, which won the National Book Award. Many critics contend, however, that Settle's most lasting literary contribution is the Beulah Quintet, a series of historical novels which begins in seventeenth-century England and ends in twentieth-century West Virginia. *Prisons* provides the prologue to *O Beulah Land*, followed by *Know Nothing*, *The Scapegoat*, and *The Killing Ground*. On publication of the last volume, Settle won the 1983 Janet Heidinger Kafka Award for the best fiction published by an American woman.

Liberty, its use and abuse, is a theme Settle explores throughout the Quintet. Spanning nearly three hundred years of British/American history, the Quintet addresses the uncomfortable truth that freedom for one group of individuals often translates into enslavement for others. Settle's examples range from the uneasy relationship between the British gentry and commoners in Cromwellian England, to the struggles between Appalachia's coal barons and miners.

Settle writes, "What matters . . . in the historical novel is not the retelling of great historical events, but the poetic awakening of the people who figured in those events."

The two following scenes are from *Addie*, Settle's autobiography, in which the author recalls her grandmother's life in the Kanawha Valley of West Virginia. First, Addie recounts her failed marriage to a coal miner. The second scene offers a glimpse of Addie's second marriage to Mr. Tompkins and her support of the legendary Mother Jones, a union organizer active in the West Virginia coalfields at the turn of the century.

In the scene from *The Killing Ground*, the final volume of the Beulah Quintet, Hannah McCarkle, the daughter of a well-to-do West Virginia family, confronts Jake Catlett, a poor mountaineer who killed her brother, Johnny, during a drunken brawl. The Beulah Quintet evolved over a twenty-five-year span, and Settle traced it back to this scene, saying, "I had a picture of one man hitting another in a West Virginia drunk tank one Saturday night, and the idea was to go all the way back to see what lay behind that blow. At first I went all the way to 1755, then I realized that wasn't far enough, and I went back further still, to Cromwell's England in *Prisons*, to trace the idea of liberty from which so much of the American experience sprang" (*Contemporary Writers*, Vol. 89–92, 467).

Other Sources to Explore

Primary

Novels: *Choices* (1995), *The Kiss of Kin* (1995), *Charley Bland* (1989), *The Beulah Quintet* (1988), *Celebration* (1986), *Water World* (1984), *The Killing Ground* (1982), *Know Nothing* (1981), *The Scapegoat* (1980), *Blood Tie* (1977), *The Long Road to Paradise* (1973), *Prisons* (1973), *The Clam Shell* (1971), *Fight Night on a Sweet Saturday* (1964) [revised in 1982 as *The Killing Ground*], *Know Nothing* (1960), *The Old Wives' Tale* (1957), *O Beulah Land* (1956), *The Love Eaters* (1954). **Nonfiction:** *I, Roger Williams: A Fragment of Autobiography* (2001), *Addie* (1998), *Turkish Reflections: A Search for a Place* (1991), *The Scopes Trial: The State of Tennessee v. John Thomas Scopes* (1972), *All the Brave Promises: Memories of Aircraft Woman 2nd Class* (1966). **Autobiographical essay:** "The Search for the Beulah Quintet," in *Bloodroot* (1998), ed. Joyce Dyer, 244–46.

Secondary

Contemporary Authors, Vols. 89–92, 467. Joyce Dyer, "Mary Lee Settle," in *Bloodroot*, 243. George P. Garrett, *Understanding Mary Lee Settle*, (1988). James A. Grimshaw Jr., "Mary Lee Settle," *Southern Writers: A Biographical Dictionary* (1979), 404. Nancy Carol Joyner, "Mary Lee Settle," *Contemporary Fiction Writers of the South* (1993), 393–99. "Mary Lee Settle Issue," *Iron Mountain Review* 7:1 (spring 1991). William J. Schafer, "Mary Lee Settle's Beulah Quintet: History Darkly, Through a Single-Lens Reflex," *Appalachian Journal* 10:1 (autumn 1982), 77–86. Jean Haskell Speer, "Through the Beulah Quintet," *Appalachia Inside Out*, Vol. 1 (1995), 16–30.

FROM *ADDIE* (1998)

Addie had married at fifteen into the Morris family, who were victims of a change that had been going on since 1812, when the salt wells were dug north of the river at Burning Springs, a few miles east of Charleston. Christopher Morris, her husband, like most of the men, had gone into the new mines. He was a drunkard, but then so many of them were. He did beat her, but in that world of coal mining, day long, night long, where petrified tree trunks called kettles could loosen and kill, where the white bones of ancient fish in the coal caught the light from the miners' head lamps, and the crystal skeletons of plants were known as flowers of darkness, where accidents waited for millennia when the earth was disturbed, the men were all edged with fear, like people in a perpetual war who go about their business as best they can.

There were too many shootings on Saturday nights. From the new language of machinery and the railroad they took the phrase "letting off steam." In winter, when he had work, Chris Morris left home before dawn with his carbide lamp lit on his miner's hard hat to show him the way; he made the daily trip by mule-drawn tram into the mine, sometimes as far as two or three miles. When he returned, long after dark, with his lamp lit to show him the way home, Addie heated water on the kitchen range and tried to scrub off the black gold while he sat in the washtub.

You could tell a coal miner by his eyes, and it was still so when I was a child there. They were darkened around the rims with coal dust that never came off—Nefertiti eyes. Yes, he beat her. Yes, he drank. Men then lived hard, died early, carried guns, gambled, and, being so on the tether of some decision made someplace else by men who didn't know their names, they swaggered even more. Those with brains fought their way downriver, to college, but carried the scars of the coal business, and still do. The feudalism. The exploiting of earth and men. Owner and worker, each far from the other, were threatened by the same diseases of danger and indifference, recognized each other as brothers who don't claim kin.

We are all marked, who have lived and been blooded by the coal fields. We never get away because it is deep in us, whether our fathers have worked the coal face, or bought our clothes and our college educations with money that was as black as the rims of coal miners' eyes. We have all been formed long before human ancestry or our culture or kindness or hatred or lack of money has affected us. These are all personal. And they can twist and stunt, or lie fallow in us, or help us grow strong.

But the coal mines, the darkness, like the mark of Cain, are as deep within us as the eons that formed us both, slowly and inexorably, millions of years ago, where patient time has crushed and dried ancient seas, swamps, forests, animals into something mysterious that seduced the world we lived in, made us rich, made us poor, broke the health of some of us, made some of us refugees. Like people who have been deserted by a lover, we may hate it, but we never forget it.

. . .

Mother Jones had left the coal town of Cedar Grove until late in her conquest of Kelly's Creek. It was not completely a company town. The boat yard and the mill were working, and the railroad owned property. All through the growing town there were still areas owned by my grandfather, and he could still say that he had kept the house and the acres around it away from what were being called, by all West Virginians, the "outside interests." "Outside interests" cornered the mines, "outside agitators" were trying to organize them. West Virginians, who had sold to whoever would buy, sat in the middle, innocently claiming that "outside" was ruining their land and starving the miners.

When Mother Jones tried to find a field to have a meeting in the town of Cedar Grove, there was little land that did not belong to the companies or to the local mine owners.

Behind the facade of the Big House, little seemed to have changed. Everybody still had their place at the supper table, and there were still silver napkin rings with their names on them that enclosed damask napkins. By 1902 there were two grown half sisters, Myrtle and Bertha, old enough to court, brother Pressy, two younger brothers, Roger and Bado, two Tompkins girls, my mother Rachel and little Helen, two long-staying cousins of Addie, and a tutor and nurse for the youngest. Mr. Tompkins sat at the head of the table and served the meat. Mrs. Tompkins sat at the foot of the table and served the vegetables. After the long prayer, said by Mrs. Tompkins, there was usually a babble of voices.

At the supper table one winter night in 1902, all the family discussed the terrible Mother Jones who looked like a little old lady and had a mouth like a section foreman. Mr. Tompkins said she had sent him a message that she wanted to use his land to have a meeting but he wouldn't let her, and besides, most of the subsurface had been leased out, so he didn't have the right.

For once, nobody at the table said a word. The only sounds were the scrape of forks, passing of hot potatoes, reaching out by Mr. Tompkins for plates to serve second helpings. The whole table had retreated into a silence where everybody seemed to be someplace else or waiting for someone else to say something. My mother, who was ten, said she had never been in the dining room when it was so quiet.

Finally Addie spoke.

"Mr. Tompkins," she said, "do I own the bull field outright?" He had turned over some of the property to her when there was one of the boom-bust fears of bankruptcy.

"Yes my dear, you know that," he told her, and then, according to my mother, there was another silence.

Then Addie announced, "Then Mother Jones can use my bull field for her speech."

Grandfather forbade the children to go to the meeting, and Addie agreed. "I don't want a single one of you children going out there with that bunch of miners. Those men are armed and dangerous," she told them, laying down the law. "Now I mean it," she added, not trusting them.

My mother was the only one who disobeyed. A few nights later, Mother Jones spoke in the bull field and my mother, thank God, provided me with an eyewitness. She crept down the back stairs and scuttled out through the dark up the creek to the field where the miners' lamps lit the black sky like fireflies mingling with the winter stars. Beyond the dark crowd of men, the famous Mother Jones stood in dirty clothes on a feed box raising hell, so far away that my mother, hiding by the fence so nobody would see her and tell Addie, could only see the shape of her, even though she was lit up with pitchpine torches. But she heard her.

"She was a little tiny woman. She hollered just like a Holy Roller preacher, and she gave the miners hell. She told them they were cowards and didn't have backbones and didn't stand up for each other. I thought she was mean to them," she said, when I asked her years afterwards if she had ever seen Mother Jones. "My God, she used language I never would let pass my lips, and she had grown men crying. I wouldn't have missed it for a farm in Georgia." Then she smiled and said, "I was the only one brave enough to disobey my mother."

The Killing Ground (1982)

from Before the Revolution—1960

For the second time in my life I saw Jake Catlett—not that I knew it. It would take years for me to recall a sixteen-year-old boy, old Jake's least one, who looked, in his Sunday suit, like Ichabod Crane.

At the jail that late afternoon I only saw the back of the man who had murdered my brother, and I wanted, in a surge of hate, to kill him, stamp him out. He was leaning on the jail windowsill, watching downriver through the bars. When Jack opened the cell door he didn't look around or speak, even when Jack said, "Somebody to see you," and then, "Catlett, you got a visitor." I saw his back arch as Jack walked toward him.

"Let me talk to him by myself," I whispered. When I heard his name I only connected it with the Catlett that my mother said brought her papa downriver on a shutter.

He turned around. The man who stood there, watching me, was tall and quiet. The grief in his black eyes under heavy brows was so deep it could have been mistaken for aloofness. His face was gaunt and made without fat, his black hair fell long on his neck, the sideburns made his cheeks hollow. He needed a shave. He was spare-boned, straight, skinny as a rake; his head jutted forward as he took me in slowly, then Jack, and said, low, like a man not used to speaking, "I don't want to talk to nobody."

I was afraid Jack would say something to make the man retreat into the isolated mountain of himself.

"Can I stay for a minute, by myself?" I begged.

Jack knew when he was shut out. He made one last try. "Okay, Catlett, you're in enough trouble."

"I ain't gonna bother no lady," Jake Catlett told him.

We could hear the rattle of Jack's steps as he went across the iron floor and clanged the outside cell door, and sat down within hearing in case I raised my voice.

Like any other cage, the cell had bars; the sun drew them in great shadows across the sleeping face of a man in the next cell. The place smelled of urine and Lysol. We stood, watching each other. What had happened did not show with him. He was just waiting, shut away from the river; he kept on glancing at it, clenching and unclenching his long spare hands.

"You from the newspaper?" he finally asked.

"No." I sank down on the end of the rack, becoming small, obliterating anything that might rouse his distrust, because he had to tell me what he didn't know himself. I was in an agony of guile.

"What did you come for, then?" His voice came on strong. He was rooted out, ground-hog cornered.

"Catlett, shut up." The man in the next cell turned over and went to sleep again.

"Don't pay him no mind. He's full of sneaky pete." Jake Catlett stared at the man's scrap-bag back.

"It was my brother," I whispered.

He looked at me as he would look at a wounded or frightened animal. I, stone-cold, willed him to it harder, using everything I'd lady-learned.

"I never meant to," he muttered. "I never even knowed him. I never knowed he was your brother."

I watched him.

"Look, lady. I never meant it. Why, I'm thirty-eight years old. I never done nuthin' like takin' on to scrap like that since I was a boy. You . . ."

"Tell me!" I had to force him back to where it had to begin, the key, the point, the place.

Jake Catlett sank down on the rack beside me and put his gaunt head between strong hands that could work a coal face, hold a woman hard by the shoulders, or hit Johnny. The black hair on the sunburned back of his fist stood out. That hand was the source—one hand, clenched, one strike—from that one hand, all the questions, a life that would never be the same again, not for him, not for us. I couldn't stop watching it.

We sat so long that the outdoor sounds came in and surrounded us: the beep of a car horn, across the river the whistle of Number 6 as it drew into the station. We were getting used to the smell of each other. The time tightened into the insistence between two people dwelling in the same needs—he to tell, me to learn. I had a dim urge to take his hand.

I broke the tightening stillness. "I heard he said something."

When he did begin to speak his voice was gentle. He was thinking aloud. He seemed to have forgotten who I was. "I been settin' here figurin'—goin' over and over it. He was just standin' there, and that feller kept callin' on Jesus—I figured I had to shut him up, leave me time to think. Gawd knows, I needed it even if I had to get locked up. That old man kept on and on—*he's* just lookin' out through them bars. I seen his face and his clean white coat in the light from the toilet. That was over at the City before they moved me over to the County. This here is the County. I ain't never been to jail before . . . Gawd, when I think about Loretta and Maw and Paw . . ."

He stopped for a minute, then came back from his thinking. "I reckon

I flew red. Couldn't nothin' be done to shut that old feller up. *He's* the only one I could see. I took and hit him one and he—you know, when you shoot, a bird seems to linger in the air for the longest time, only it ain't more than a second. I seen him standin' before he fell and he looked kind of surprised. Then he said, 'Thank you.' He said a real quiet thank you, and just sighed down on the floor and hit that iron rack. Jeez Christ, I hated him when he said that, that thank you, lording it over a goddamn drunk tank. I never hit him hard. Just blowed off the last of my steam. I figured he was makin' fun of the rest of us . . ."

"How long had you been standing there looking at Johnny before you hit him?" It was such a curious question, not what I had meant to ask him. I wasn't seeking the power in one Saturday-night pint, but the power behind that.

"Just about all my life." He looked at me then.

I began to laugh. It insulted him. I managed to stop laughing.

"Y'ought to be ashamed of yourself. Settin' there laughin' with your brother not cold in his grave. I can sure see you two are brother and sister."

"That's the trouble with all you damned people who strike out blind. Your fist is packed for an enemy, so you hit the first person who looks like him." Disgust of the man beside me made me stand up to get away from him.

He looked up at me and studied me for a while as he must have studied Johnny. "You people make me sick. When you spit you hawk coal dust same as us." He was taking the bandage of wariness and grief and surprise from his eyes, and they showed clear, clean hate—lit up with it—something honest to deal with.

"What got you into it, Jake? What put the chip on your shoulder?" I questioned fast, before he could retreat again.

That curious tenderness of quiet men, even with the hate there, made him get up and put his hand on my shoulder. His grip was viselike.

"Now look here, lady. I'm goin' to tell you. It's too late not to, ain't it?"

"Yeah, it's too late not to." Our hands had the same shape. Behind us we could hear Number 6 pull out of the station, going west.

"I've about had enough. Here I end up with ten thousand dollars' bail and I ain't never had nuthin' since we sold the farm but a few acres of ridge land and Loretta's womb and Gawd knows ye cain't borry money on that. Looks like a man works hard all his damn life and things are goin' along all but Loretta's womb."

He sat down and folded his hands in his lap and told himself the story, as he seemed to have told it forever, over and over. "Loretta come to Jesus

and took to gettin' sick along about the same time. She had fifteen operations, that purty little gal; she come from up around Beulah—Slavish people.
Come here in the mines. Ever time she'd get in the hospital she'd get purty as
she ever was. Then she'd come home and get drug down again and takin' to
goin' to bear witness on Wednesdays, gettin' up there in public tellin' how
she had all them operations and come to Jesus and Maw fussin' and fumin'
tell her that kind of carryin' on wasn't like no Jesus she ever knowed. They'd
fight and argue about Jesus never shut up. Maw is Baptist, and that there
womb of Loretta's must'a had a rock in it that couldn't nobody find start in
to draggin' her down again, that thing must'a weighed a ton." He paused
long enough to fetch a deep sigh. "Then this July the union ruled you couldn't
have no Number 8 for the hospital, unemployed over a year. I been out of
work one year last Saturday, that damn Number 8 was all we had worth a red
cent. I was a good coal-face man. I been makin' coal up and down this here
valley since I was fifteen years old." He remembered me and accused, "They
ain't a damn thing, ain't even that dress on your back didn't come off the coal-
face and don't forget it. You people puttin' on to act high and mighty . . ."

From his own coal-face all the way down his life he was getting to
Johnny. But his voice had dropped so low that what he had to say ran out
toward the floor and I had to lean almost into his lap. He didn't even notice,
for he was no longer talking to me.

"We're good people. Come from upriver, up around Lacey Creek. Sold
out up there. We had to. Even Paw saw that. Automation come in and we
read out to move. Ain't nary a thing left now. They done stripped it. We
come down here and Paw bought a little piece of property. Old Carver place
. . . I got me another job."

I could see the hill farm at Beulah, the neglected fall field rippling, the
lespedeza, the orchard covey wurtling in the air, before it was all thrown
away, stripped down to bedrock like the Catlett place on Lacey Creek, or this
man's face, this distant cousin stranger. "You're Mr. Jake Catlett's son," I told
him. "We're kin, a long way back." He didn't even hear me.

*A*NNE *S*HELBY
(September 25, 1948–)

Essayist, poet, children's author, and playwright Anne Shelby is a native of eastern Kentucky. Both of her parents were schoolteachers, and Shelby notes that during her childhood, "Most of the people I knew were schoolteachers or farmers. I didn't know anybody who was a writer."

Shelby received her B.A. in English from St. Andrews Presbyterian College in 1970, and her M.A. in English from the University of Kentucky in 1981. She has worked as an editor of the *Mountain Review* and taught creative writing for the Kentucky Governor's School for the Arts and the Kentucky Arts Council's Artist-in-Residence program. She is the author of several children's books, and her poetry has appeared in a wide range of publications, including *Appalachian Heritage* and *Appalachian Journal*. She was part of a collaborative effort to create the play *Passing through the Garden: The Work of Belinda Mason*, produced at Appalshop (1996) and at Georgetown College (2001). Shelby is also the author of *The Adventures of Molly Whuppie*, a play based on Appalachian folk tales featuring female lead characters.

"My family—on both sides—has lived in southeastern Kentucky for more than two hundred years now," says Shelby. "The history and the landscape and the language of that region are inside me, like water in cells." Shelby and her husband, Edmund, editor of the *Beattyville Enterprise*, live near Oneida, Kentucky, on a farm that has been in her family for generations. They have a son, Graham, who is also a writer.

OTHER SOURCES TO EXPLORE

PRIMARY

Books for children: *The Someday House* (1996), *Homeplace* (1995), *Potluck* (1995), *What To Do About Pollution* (1993), *We Keep a Store* (1990). **Poetry chapbook:** *Lines from Home* (1999). **Drama:** *Passing through the Garden: The Work of Belinda*

543

Mason, The Adventures of Mollie Whuppie, Waiting for Daylight, Storehouse, Lessons. **Autobiographical essays:** "Piddlin'," in *Bloodroot* (1998), ed. Joyce Dyer, 248–52. "The 'R' word: What's So Funny (and Not So Funny) about Redneck Jokes," *Confronting Appalachian Stereotypes: Back Talk from An American Region* (1999), eds. Dwight Billings, Gurney Norman, and Katherine Ledford, 153–60.

SECONDARY

Contemporary Authors, Vol. 151, 393–94. Joyce Dyer, "Anne Shelby," in *Bloodroot*, 247.

WHY I WRITE

from *Pine Mountain Sand & Gravel* (1997)

I.
Because teaching's too hard. I did have a job
as a waitress but I got fired. Can't work
in offices. They wear their clothes too tight.
Too nervous to sit through meetings, too fat
for a ballerina. Awkward and nearsighted,
I read too much as a child. There was a little career counseling
in high school. It's a cover
for excessive behaviors, for appearing late,
ill-mannered and inappropriately dressed,
for hanging out in stationery stores, fondling
the pads and pens. And what is one to do
with experience? It's the only time I feel
I'm doing the right thing. I avoid it when I can.

II.
It's ridiculous, really, filling all these notebooks,
these file drawers and diskettes. Who will read this?
Who will give you money? you could be making
a quilt or something. You could be out doing good.
But here you are again, moving words around,
mostly because it touches that one spot in your head
nothing else does, some microscopic junction of music,
religion and a good joke. There, yes, right there. Please,
don't stop.

III.
So that's it? You write because it feels good
and you can't do anything else? What about the Truth?
What about Helping Others? I don't know
what the truth is, though I've discovered a number
of lies. And don't come to me with a rotten tooth,
leaky faucets or a letter from the IRS. I do love you
and if words can heal you, take them. But I can't
overhaul your engine, set a broken bone or teach you

to forgive. Jimmy Fiechter. In sixth grade you looked
at his hair and knew he was destined to be a dentist.
The artist, at five, wouldn't play outside. He couldn't
stop looking at the Breughel. I stayed in at recess,
to spend more time with the alphabet. We do
what we have to, what we can, our part
of whatever the truth is.
I write.

FAT SESTINA

from *Pine Mountain Sand & Gravel* (1998)

You could run over your television
set with the truck, or pitch it off the mountain
or shoot it like Elvis
or to create an unusual planter, line with gravel,
fill with dirt, peat and sand,
then top with a mulch of wood chips. Pine

is best. When I hear the word *pine*
and think *fresh bathroom scent,* I blame television.
I rest before it like a sand-
bag, like a soft flickering mountain.
I'm cracking my teeth on gravel-
hard popcorn kernels. I'm fat as Elvis

at his last concert. Even then Elvis
could still make me pine
like a teenage virgin parked in a Chevy on a gravel
road. Remember when you first saw him on
        television?
So much for "She'll Be Coming Round the
        Mountain."
So much for "Love Letters in the Sand."

I left the sand-
box, saved my allowance for Elvis
records. We planted an antenna on the mountain,
metal tree from an alien planet, landed among pine

and poplar. We turned on the television
and let it settle over us like fine gravel

dust. Nobody bothered to pick beans or gravel
potatoes anymore, preferring a sandwich in front of the television.
Seasons changed. The Army got Elvis.
I grew up quick but crooked, a pine
in a wet spring. They stripped the mountain.

Now I'm too old and fat for mountain-
climbing. The neighbors' kids throw gravel
at me from my own driveway. I pine
for Lonnie, my high school boyfriend, warm sand
on the riverbank. I mourn for Elvis.
I microwave popcorn and turn on the television.

It said on educational television, gravel
in time turns to sand. When it does
I'll be with Elvis on Pine Mountain.

SPELLCHECK

from *Pine Mountain Sand & Gravel* (1998)

It's handy, but not much account for writing
hillbilly poems with. It won't let you waller,
won't let you foller a feller up the holler,
makes you have titles where titties ought to be.

I'll go along with changing logwoods into dogwoods,
but before I could say Undo it turned
my housecat to a housecoat. Sallet, newground,
Junebug, graveyard—Not in Dictionary.

You can't have a grandbaby on this thing
without special arrangements. One spell
transformed my taters into tatters, served
me subpoenas when I ordered soupbeans.

Now it wants to replace the homeplace
with just someplace. Is this the same spell
that changed proud to poor, turned minnows
into memories? I need flies

buzzin in this poem, cool snap of beans
breakin on the porch, tenor of coonhounds
on a moonlit ridge. Exit.
Float a while on a honeysuckle breeze.

Spell:
How long to set
on a sycamore bank
with your feet in the creek.

ᴹURIEL ᴱARLEY ˢHEPPARD
(1898–1951)

Born in Andover, New York, Muriel Earley Sheppard, an English major with a degree from Alfred University, moved with her mining engineer husband to the mining town of Spruce Pine, North Carolina, in 1927. According to novelist John Ehle, who wrote the foreword to the 1991 edition of her work, *Cabins in the Laurel*, she viewed herself as "progressive." As evidence, he offers that she read the latest magazines, entertained in ways foreign to her North Carolina neighbors, and wore men's trousers. She also had ambitions for a project that few in Mitchell County had ever attempted—she wanted to write a book. Intrigued by her new home, she collected regional history and folklore from friendly locals and wrote feature stories for the *Asheville Citizen*, the closest city newspaper.

By mid-1932, she had completed a manuscript she titled *Kim Thickets*, an early name for the community of Spruce Pine. Collaborating with portrait photographer Mrs. Bayard Wootten (1875–1951), she travelled the backroads to visit the remote homes of mountain families. Where they found people wearing store-bought clothes and using modern cookware, they asked them to change into homespun clothing and bring out their old things for the photographs that would accompany Sheppard's text. Ultimately, this "progressive" writer did not please her local subjects with her retrograde portrayal.

The 1991 edition of *Cabins in the Laurel*, however, has found greater acceptance among natives of the Toe River Valley and has earned comparisons with the landmark works of two other outlanders who attempted non-fiction portraits of the mountain people, Horace Kephart and John C. Campbell. Readers should judge for themselves how Sheppard's work compares to that of Emma Bell Miles.

In chapter II of *Cabins in the Laurel*, Sheppard records multiple accounts of the story of Frankie Silvers.

OTHER SOURCES TO EXPLORE

PRIMARY

Nonfiction: *Cloud by Day: A Story of Coal and Coke, and People* (1947), *Cabins in the Laurel* (1935).

SECONDARY

John Ehle, Foreword, *Cabins in the Laurel* (1991), ix–xi. Charles Alan Watkins, "Merchandising the Mountaineer: Photography, the Great Depression, and *Cabins in the Laurel*" in *Appalachian Journal* 12:3 (spring 1985), 215–38.

CABINS IN THE LAUREL (1935)

from Chapter II

The most sensational murder case in the history of the Toe River Valley was that of Frankie Silvers, accused of killing her husband, Charles Silvers. The defendant, who was tried in Morganton two years before county government was established in the Valley itself, was the first woman hanged in North Carolina. It is an old story of jealousy and revenge, played out in a cabin in the Deyton Bend of Toe River, a story that keeps turning over and over and adding to itself like a snowball. There are half a dozen versions. Here is one recently told to an outsider, which will serve to introduce the story and show how a tale metamorphoses with oral repetition.

. . .

In her ninetieth year Aunt Cindy Norman, sister of the murdered man, gave W.W. Bailey, of Spruce Pine, the following account of the killing.

In the winter of 1831 Charles Silvers was living in the Deyton Bend with his wife, Frankie, and their baby daughter. Very early on the morning of December 23rd Frankie dropped in at her father-in-law's and found the family preparing to wash. "My washing is done and I've scoured too," she boasted, and her mother-in-law marvelled at her smartness to do a day's work before dawn. Frankie went on to tell the reason for her visit. Charlie had gone over the river on the ice the day before for his Christmas liquor, and had not returned. She was worried and begged his people to look at the crossings to see if he had fallen through. They searched the river for a considerable distance, but there was neither trail nor break in the ice. When he was still absent after several days, other families joined in the search. Frankie shook the valley with her lamentations. Word of the strange disappearance seeped into the country around Bear Creek and Art'ur's Knob.

An old man named Jakie Collis determined to go and walk over the ground himself to satisfy his curiosity on certain points. He went first to the father's house, where Cindy Silvers, the eight-year-old sister of the lost man, offered to take him to Charlie's empty cabin. Frankie had by now given up on his return and refused to stay there alone with her grief. At the deserted cabin Jakie and Cindy and others who had joined them scrutinized closely the mantel and sides of the fireplace. There were fresh irregular chippings at intervals over the whole surface where someone had hewn lightly with an axe. It gave Jakie an idea.

"Help me lift the puncheons," he said to one of the men.

The upper surface of the slabs was neatly scoured, but the rounded sides underneath were streaked at the cracks with old blood stains. There was a fresh layer of ashes between the puncheons and the earth. Old Jakie thrust his hand into them and found them clotted with what appeared to be dried blood. Just then Frankie, who had watched from a distance, pushed her way among the men like a mad woman and ordered them off. The men stood still, looking at her with horror in their eyes that told her what they suspected. Then they went on with their work. In a frenzy of despair she wept and swore and made wild protestations while she saw the men sift the ashes in the fireplace and find human teeth and the remains of bones showing hack marks. Somebody realized that the big pile of hickory wood that had stood by the door was gone. When they looked at the axe, its edge was dulled with chopping something other than wood. The facts were plain enough without Frankie's extraordinary behavior. They sent for the sheriff to take charge of her.

More evidence came to light as the weather grew warmer. The investigation of a hollow sourwood where a dog sniffed suspiciously revealed the intestines and other parts of the body that did not burn readily. The horror of the tragedy shook the Valley from end to end.

Judge Donnell sentenced Frankie to death at the June term, 1832. She appealed, but Judge Ruffin sustained the conviction. When there was no hope through the regular channels of the law, her kinfolks took a hand in the affair. They spirited her out of jail and took her through the streets in a load of hay. As soon as they were out of town, Frankie climbed off the wagon. Dressed in a man's clothes and carrying a gun, she tramped behind the hay. The sheriff's posse overtook the suspicious load too quickly for her to crawl back out of sight. She tried to brazen it out.

"Want to buy some hay?" she asked in the deepest possible voice.

"No. We don't want hay," answered the sheriff, helping himself to the gun. "But we do want you, Frankie."

It was no use. She went back to jail. In the beginning she had protested her innocence. Now when there was no hope she made full confession.

According to her story she had been goaded by jealousy to kill her husband, and was awaiting the first opportunity to do it. On the night of December 22nd, he came into the house tired and cold from a day spent chopping wood to last over Christmas. He had a big pile of hickory chunks laid by to show for his labor. After supper he took the baby in his arms and lay down on a sheepskin in front of the fire to get the chill out of his bones. The axe lay handy, and in her anger she longed to seize the chance to kill him. In case she should find courage to go through with it, she gently slid the sleeping baby out of his arms. He did not waken.

At last, to end the torment of indecision, she seized the axe and tried to sever his head from his body in one mighty stroke. The blow glanced, and Charlie, horribly mutilated, sprang up and thrashed about making noises that frightened her half to death. She jumped into bed and covered her head to shut out the sound until he commenced to grow quieter from loss of blood. There was no way but to go on with it now. When she could muster courage, she got out of bed and struck the blows that quieted him forever. The rest of the night she spent dismembering and burning the body. It took a hot fire, and in a single night she used the whole of the Christmas hickory. Then in that blazing, suffocating cabin she carefully whittled away the spatters of blood and grease from the mantel and sides of the fireplace and scoured every stain from the floor that had been generously smirched as the body thrashed about. She washed the spattered bedding. That was the washing of which she boasted to her mother-in-law a few hours later.

Frankie Silvers must have had some feeling, because in the last days of her imprisonment she contrived a long, gloomy poem which she recited from the scaffold before her execution, July 12, 1833.

. . .

The words of the poem were eagerly seized upon by a countryside familiar with the dramatic story. It became a song, but it could be sung only when no members of either family were present, lest they be reminded of the tragedy. This is not a feud country, and while neither family took up the grudge, everyone felt that it was better not to meddle with fresh wounds. The song survives today in an eerie, mournful tune whose urgent minor beat is the restless scurrying of unlaid ghosts in lonely places.

$\mathscr{B}$ETSY $\mathscr{S}$HOLL
(June 12, 1945–)

Poet Betsy Sholl grew up in Brick Town, New Jersey, and was educated at Bucknell University (B.A.,1967), University of Rochester (M.A., 1969), and Vermont College (M.F.A., 1989). In 1976 she moved from Boston to a double-wide trailer on Clinch Haven farm near Big Stone Gap, Virginia, when her husband took a job as a probation officer in Wise County, Virginia. Although her sojourn in Appalachia lasted only seven years, she says the experience was profoundly enriching, both personally and poetically.

"Any growth I've experienced since that time has occurred only because those years prepared me, gave me a sense of depth, an emotional life in three dimensions, rather than the shallow propped-up feelings I experienced in the city."

She is the author of several books of poetry, including *Appalachian Winter*, published in 1978. Her collection, *The Red Line*, won the 1991 Associated Writing Programs' award series, and *Don't Explain* won the University of Wisconsin's 1997 Felix Pollack Prize for Poetry. She has been nominated for several Pushcart Prizes and has received a National Endowment for the Arts Fellowship. Her poems have appeared in a variety of publications, including *Ploughshares*, *Massachusetts Review*, and *Indiana Review*.

She currently lives in Portland, Maine, and teaches at the University of Southern Maine. She is also on the poetry faculty for Vermont College's M.F.A program. She and her husband, Doug Sholl, a family therapist, have two children.

Other Sources to Explore

Primary

Poetry: *Don't Explain* (1997), *The Red Line* (1992), *Rooms Overhead* (1986), *Appalachian Winter* (1978), *Changing Faces* (1974). **Chapbooks:** *Coastal Bop* (2001), *Pick a Card* (1991). **Autobiographical essay:** "Big Stone Gap," in *Bloodroot* (1998), ed. Joyce Dyer, 254–60.

Secondary

Joyce Dyer, "Betsy Sholl," in *Bloodroot*, 251. Richard Jackson, "The Place of the Poet, the Poet's Place: An Interview with Betsy Sholl," in *Her Words* (2002), ed. Felicia Mitchell, 266–73.

APPALACHIAN WINTER

from *Appalachian Winter* (1978)

1

I sit in darkness
beside the stove, rocking

like Gretel come back alone
to the old, tight place—
away from her father and brother now,
lonely as the witch herself.

I stoke the fire.

•

When I close my eyes
the forest returns. Flickers of trail
disappear like snakes under rocks,
ledges drop sudden as guillotines.

I see that others who came here before me
have left no more of themselves than
pieces of chimney crumbling like bread.

2

The change I want I cannot name—
perhaps the ability to live anywhere
not fearing the little shacks
scattered throughout the hollows
where women stare, grim with silence,
growing thinner each year.

I have crawled through briars
until I cannot recognize
the woman on my face.

I have cut stems, set stalks on fire.
Nights I dream of luring children
to join me.

3

These mountains were opened by men
unashamed of slaughter, mapped
by the crisscrossing of bootleggers.
Now night after night, they are held in place
by women left alone, aging too quickly in shacks,
their shotguns pointed at shadows.

Something rustles at my window.

Hansel? Hansel?
I rummage the sheets all night.

In the morning I pull out the vines
that brush and scrape against the glass.
I sift dirt through my fingers.
Learn not to hate myself.

Hansel. Hansel. I continue
to speak out loud for months.

4

When our new mother moved in
she stood in the doorway
staring at the forest that held her
like a madwoman screaming in the attic.
Her face was so hard, Hansel and I
broke just looking at her.

We took off through the flickering of leaves.

At each cabin we came to
she appeared before us, grim, hungry.

Father was a woodsman. He taught us
to cut down everything in our paths
till we were left standing in a clearing.

5

Later, we played house. Hansel deepened
his voice and disappeared through the trees.
He left me raising mine
to screech at our imaginary children
till my face was stiff.

Once I thought I could live forever
tip-toeing on the edge of his shadow.
I tried to burn down the woods for him.

Now I tie bright cloth to branches,
hike in further and further.

Hansel! Do you hear me? I walk alone.
The bushes do not jump out and grab.
I shed layers of anger and fear
as easily as leaves falling
first from the maples on the ridge,
then in flame-colored waves moving down.

6

The sun rises. The ridge
separates itself from the sky,
comes forward with what scant color
the cold has left it.

I see that land has tides.
Our mother sank. The dirt closed over her.
But the waves of disturbance
did not spread out and fade as on water.

Father was the last part of her
I clung to—last root of the pain
that swelled within her, crying
for a life of its own.
I cannot go home.

7

I cut, trowel,
burn my roots like fuses.
I belong in this strip-mined land.

Perhaps it's her death I fear—
that body shriveling before me.

I turned and ran. The flames grew
smaller through the leaves.

Her voice cracked like dry wood.
It hissed, licked through my thoughts.

Now it is gone, that hunger
scorching the tree limbs black.

I heat my oven with sticks.
It is not so hard after all
to keep from burning myself,
to forgive the lonely women
whose love curdled inside me.

As the day warms, I open the house
and step outdoors. Rocking on this porch
rooted in mountains, I stare across the ridge
singing the old hymns I've learned here,
words that say there is nothing to fear.

ELLEN HARVEY SHOWELL
(October 26, 1934–)

Ellen Harvey Showell was born in Kingsport, Tennessee, and grew up in Monroe and Greenbrier counties in West Virginia. The daughter of a teacher, Elizabeth Hudson Harvey, and a cabinet maker, Clarence Ballard Harvey, she married John S. Showell and has one son, Michael, who publishes the *Mountain Messenger*, a weekly newspaper in Lewisburg, West Virginia.

After graduating with a B.A. from Berea College in Kentucky in 1957, she moved several years later to Washington, D.C., and worked as an advertising and a public relations writer. Holding jobs in a housing market research company and in the Federal Office of Economic Opportunity and the Community Action Agency, she spent the turbulent 1960s in Washington, during the War on Poverty, as a feature story writer for the VISTA program from 1963 until 1971.

Known primarily for her writing for children, she began her career as a freelance writer in 1971. Her writing includes award-winning novels, plays, musical plays, screenplays, and chapter books. Her play about the death penalty, *The Executioners*, has been performed by church and community groups. She received the South Carolina Children's Book Award for *The Ghost of Tillie Jean Cassaway*, and a Parents' Choice Award for Literature for *Cecelia and the Blue Mountain Boy*. For her first nonfiction book, *From Indian Corn to Outer Space: Women Invent in America*, she received recognition from the Women's National Book Association. She says she "finds inspiration in her West Virginia childhood" for her stories "of crooked rivers, dark woods and song."

Her chapter book, *Our Mountain*, includes a note on its title page explaining the story is "as told by Jimmy and Corey Allder to Ellen Harvey Showell." These two young brothers describe for the author their home, family, and favorite pastimes.

OTHER SOURCES TO EXPLORE

PRIMARY

Books for children: *The Trickster Ghost* (1992), *Our Mountain* (1991), *Cecelia and the Blue Mountain Boy* (1983), *The Ghost of Tillie Jean Cassaway* (1978). **Plays:** *The Executioners, Cecelia and the Blue Mountain Boy, Twiddelaxadaffy.* **Nonfiction:** *From Indian Corn to Outer Space: Women Invent in America*, with Fred M.B. Amram (1995).

SECONDARY

Contemporary Authors (1980), Vols. 85–88, 538. *Something About the Author* (1983), Vol. 33, 210.

OUR MOUNTAIN (1991)
What Is a Mountain?

When you are far away, our mountain looks like a big round hill covered with trees. But if you climb up, it changes. Our mountain goes up and down and up again and there are high flat parts and ridges and hollows, which are little valleys. You can be in a fairly open and level place, and come to a knob. That is a rounded top of a hill that usually is cleared off. Big knobs always have snow on them in the winter. Little knobs have old structures on them that people built so they wouldn't be surprised by Indians.

Creeks start up high in the mountain and travel down through the forest to the river. They are crooked. Fields and tall grass and farms are on the part of our mountain that's more level. Electric and telephone lines come up through cleared passageways in the woods. The road that goes up to our house is winding and gravelly. There is not very much traffic.

About thirty families live on our mountain. Most people don't live close together, but they are almost all friendly.

The Trouble with Town

We were with some friends in town, at the softball field. Nothing was going on, so we went over to a junkyard where there was a boxcar that used to be part of a train. We were sitting there talking when all of a sudden a police car pulled up. A police lady came toward us. A little girl who was with us started to cry for her mother. The police lady said, "I won't hurt you." She explained to us that people who lived in a nearby trailer said that we were vandalizing city property. We hadn't done anything wrong. She said, "You aren't supposed to be playing here. You could get hurt." So we ended up going back to the softball field and getting bored.

Another time in town we were at Old Stone Presbyterian Church for a pancake supper. We had finished our pancakes, so we went outside in the cemetery. Pinecones were all over the ground. We started throwing them at each other. A pinecone almost hit a car that was driving by. The car backed up. The driver got out. She said to me, "What's your name?"

"Jimmy."

"What's your last name?"

"Allder."

"What's your daddy's name?"

"Bob."

"What's his last name?"

"Allder,"

She said, "Your parents will be hearing from me!" They haven't, though.

A long time ago people who made moonshine hid out on our mountain. I bet we could, too, if we ever have to.

Going to the River

Another day, Corey and I, our cousin Timmy, and Sheba started from our house to go on a hike to the river and have a picnic. We usually go by our creek, but this time we walked through the alfalfa field, then down the mountain through the woods.

We crawled through a thicket of rhododendron and came out on a cliff. We could see the river and far down the Greenbrier Valley. Below us were some houses, and we could see a bridge way upstream.

The only way to get down from there was to slide on a bank of shale rock, so we did. At the bottom, the bank leveled off and sloped into the river. We sat there and ate crackers and cheese.

We began walking upstream, along the trail where the old railroad tracks used to be. We passed where our creek comes down. After a while, we saw some houses on the other side of the river. A woman called to us. "What are you boys doing over there?"

"We came from up on the mountain," we called back. "Where are we and what time is it?"

"Spring Creek Station," she said. "It's near two o'clock!" She told us that the bridge we could see was an old railroad bridge that goes across Spring Creek, not the river. We figured we'd better go back up the mountain by following our creek through the woods.

Part of the way you can walk alongside our creek on a path. Part of the way the bank is too steep and rough, and you have to walk in the creek by stepping on rocks. Sheba walks right in the water. There are many places in the creek where water falls over rocks into little scooped-out areas and makes pools. We decided to take a little bath in one pool because we had dirt on us and blood from cuts from the briers. The water was pretty cold.

We put our socks and shoes back on and climbed on up. Some of the pools we came to were muddy. We lay down on our stomachs and watched crawdads swimming around on the bottom. One was a huge granddaddy. We poked at him with a stick and he disappeared under a rock.

It was hard to walk without stepping on smushrooms, which is a word we made up. There's one mushroom that looks like a messy cow pile on the ground and you'll have to guess what we call it. Some of the mushrooms and other fungi along the creek are bright red, or orange, or polka-dotted. Some are on rocks, some on rotting wood. Some are round, like the puffball, which is a real name. Most puffballs are little, but once we saw one big as a turkey.

When we go walking, we try not to step on Indian pipes. They are flowers that stick up out of the ground and curl down, like real pipes. Some are white, but some are silvery orange.

We saw Sheba over on a big flat rock that has waves on it, just like waves in the ocean. They were made by water going over the rock for hundreds of years. Sheba was playing with something we thought was a snake. Corey jumped over to her and took it away. It was the backbone of some animal.

We were just going along, looking at things, climbing around, like always. Then something happened that made us glad for those natural bathtubs in the creek. Timmy and I had climbed up the hillside to swing on a grapevine. Timmy jumped off and came sliding down the hill. I tried to come down more slowly, but my feet slid over something that looked like a puffy mushroom but it wasn't. Yellow jackets started coming out of it. Timmy yelled and ran for the creek. The bees swarmed around my head. Timmy and I dived into a pool about two feet deep. We came up for air and the bees were still there, so we ducked under again and kept doing that, going under and coming up for air and ducking back under, until they had all gone away. We both got stung in a few places.

We decided to take a shortcut along the path made by the telephone company for telephone poles. We kept going and every time we thought we were real close, it took another five minutes before we thought we were real close again. We came to an old house that nobody lives in anymore. But the flowers in the garden were perfect. There were many, so we each took back some.

We walked to the road and followed it to the lane that goes in to our house. . . .

ℬENNIE ℒEE 𝒮INCLAIR
(April 15, 1939–May 22, 2000)

South Carolina Poet Laureate, Bennie Lee Sinclair, was the ninth generation of her family to live in the mountainous upstate region of South Carolina.

At Furman University, where she graduated Phi Beta Kappa, she met Don Lewis, and in 1958 they married. They built a small cabin on two acres given to them as a wedding present and held part-time jobs in addition to their work scholarships. Sinclair edited Furman's literary magazine, picked peaches, gardened, and collaborated with her freelance photographer husband on occasional projects.

Throughout the 1960s, Sinclair's husband supported them as a professional potter, as she faced the deaths of her father and her brother and began to write poetry. One of the first poets to whom she showed her work was the future United States Poet Laureate Mark Strand, who encouraged her efforts and wrote the introduction for her first collection, *Little Chicago Suite*. Her childhood memories of the South Carolina community of "Little Chicago," a crossroads named during Prohibition when local bootleggers' gunfire there coincided with a shootout in the more famous city, led to the title of her first volume.

The author of four poetry books, a novel (*The Lynching*), a collection of short stories, and the editor of two local history books, she has received the Stephen Vincent Benet Award, a citation from Best American Short Stories, a writing award from Winthrop College, the Appalachian Writers' Association Book of the Year Award, and a Pulitzer Prize nomination for *Lord of Springs,* as well as other awards.

During the early days of *Appalachian Heritage*, she served as an advisory editor and contributor. "Without realizing it," she said, "I was establishing an identity as an Appalachian writer and becoming part of an exciting revival and continuance of Appalachian letters." She described Wildernesse, her home, as "a 135-acre wildlife and wild-plant sanctuary in the southern Appalachian mountains of South Carolina. Remote and beautiful, it affects my life and work strongly."

From the 1970s until her death in 2000, she worked as a Poet-in-the-Schools, served as a Writer-in-Residence, taught creative writing, gave hundreds of readings, and continued to write poetry, fiction, and nonfiction.

OTHER SOURCES TO EXPLORE

PRIMARY

Poetry: *The Endangered: New & Selected Poems* (1992), *Lord of Springs* (1990), *The Arrowhead Scholar* (1978), *Little Chicago Suite* (1971). **Autobiographical essay:** "Appalachian Loaves and Fishes," in *Bloodroot* (1998) ed. Joyce Dyer, 262–71. **Fiction:** *The Lynching* (1992), *Carolina Woodbine I* (1977). **Nonfiction:** *The Fine Arts Center Story* (1980), *Taproots: A Study in Cultural Exploration* (1975).

SECONDARY

Contemporary Authors (1981), New Revision Series, Vol. 1, 601–2. Joyce Dyer, "Bennie Lee Sinclair," in *Bloodroot*, 261. *Furman Magazine* 20:3 (summer 1973). *North Carolina Arts Journal* 4:12 (1979). William B. Thesing and Gilbert Allen, "Stewardship and Sacrifice: The Land and People of Bennie Lee Sinclair's South Carolina," in *Her Words* (2002), ed. Felicia Mitchell, 274–85.

Homecoming

from *The Arrowhead Scholar* (1978)

When I came home
the dogs barked,
and you stepped out to the car
through the dark trees

in a hurry, without your coat;
and when I followed you in
you quickly built me a fire.

Later, while you slept, I lay
and watched the moon through our window
and snowflakes on the glass

until, when the cold came through,
I whispered you awake
that you might make me a fire
more slowly than the last.

Kathy

from *Little Chicago Suite* (1971)

Wearing a crown of curlers,
she steps out on the trailer porch
to feel the sun. The morning
is reflected in her eyes:
mountains coming blue, a trace
of greening in the forest across the road;
the road itself, tarblack and free.

She has never heard of Emma Bovary.
Relinquishing her brief parole,
she sets the ironing board
before the television, props the baby

against a chair and, sighing,
takes the curlers from her hair.
So goes the wonder of her days.

The lineman knows that she is beautiful:
he spent an hour working at the pole
to watch her hanging clothes, but he
will never tell her, and she
will never know why spring;
why the sight of her young ones growing,
makes her sad.

MY FATHER. HIS RABBITS.

from *Lord of Springs* (1990)

In my dreams they return as they should,
my father's rabbits I loosed one day
when I was four, the year
that he, too, left—
not suspecting how wildly they strained

toward field and wood,
or that even our deep yard, rimmed with roses,
seemed merely extension of cage.
They appeared reliable and tame
as I whispered through the wire, worked the latches,

remained with me for awhile
browsing clover—their fur, their markings
intact, in health and lovely.
Perhaps it would not have occurred
to desert roof, kin, feed—pit hunger against hunger

in a dark rife with owls and traps—
if I had not thought to free them.
Most, we never saw again.
But one or two came
back to the edge of our lawn

thinner, harried—like him
to visit, but never quite within.
It is only in my dreams
I welcome them truly home.
Salving their wounded eyes, patching

ears torn by gun and thunder
I lift them into their pens, shut the doors,
making all as it was before.

My father. His rabbits.

BACKWOODS HAIKU

from *Lord of Springs* (1990)

I.   From tree tops
      wisteria seed pods crack,
      pop-guns triggered by fall sun.

II.   Vines thick as trunks
      detail a house once here,
      buried trace of char
      its fate.

III. Dried cones, white pine, drop
      like resinous snow
      I gather to make fires glow.

IV.   Solstice; equinox. They too struggled
      to stay warm: extreme
       and balance.

V.   I take my sack downhill
       against the cold, dreaming
      woodstove elegance.

VERNA MAE SLONE
(October 9, 1914–)

Verna Mae Slone grew up in the mountains of eastern Kentucky, near the town of Pippa Passes. Her formal education ended before she had completed high school because her family needed her to work.

She wrote her first book, *What My Heart Wants to Tell*, when she was in her sixties. The original manuscript was written in longhand and intended for her grandchildren, because "so many lies and half-truths have been written about us, the mountain people."

When excerpts of Slone's reminiscences were read on National Public Radio, an editor at New Republic Books asked to publish the entire manuscript. "I believed you had to have a college education before you would be accepted as a writer," says Slone. "Because I believed that, I was the most surprised person of all that *What My Heart Wants to Tell* did get recognized and published."

Slone is the tenth generation of her family to live in eastern Kentucky, and she bristles at the hillbilly stereotypes so often applied to the region. "These lies and half-truths have done our children more damage than anything else," writes Slone. "They have taken more from us than the large coal and gas companies did by cheating our forefathers out of their minerals, for that was just money. Their writers have taken our pride and dignity and have disgraced us in the eyes of the outside world."

In this scene from her autobiography *What My Heart Wants to Tell*, Slone recounts the life and death of her handicapped sister, Alverta.

OTHER SOURCES TO EXPLORE

PRIMARY

Nonfiction: *What My Heart Wants to Tell* (1979). **Fiction:** *Rennie's Way* (1994).

SECONDARY

"Verna Mae Slone [bio and autobiography]," in *Table Talk: Appalachian Meals and Memories* (1995), ed. Sidney Saylor Farr, 3–17. Carla Waldemar, "Old Kentucky Home," *The Christian Science Monitor* 71:110 (2 May 1979), 19.

WHAT MY HEART
WANTS TO TELL (1979)

Chapter Twenty

Sarah Alverta was my sister's name but I always called her Sissy. She was born with a normal mental capacity, but when she was eighteen months old, she had a fever that lasted six weeks. The doctor called it a brain fever. When she recovered she could not talk and her mind never grew anymore, but remained as the mind of a two year old. She might have been taught some if she had had the right teacher. We ourselves could have done more for her, if we had been rash with her; but we loved her so much we gave her her way in everything. The whole household was run to suit what we thought was best for her. My sister Vada was the one who loved her the most and took constant care of her, sleeping with her at night, washing her clothes, even diapers.

She was a few years older than me, but I soon learned that whatever she wanted of mine, I was supposed to give her. I did not resent this because I had been taught that she was someone very special. I remember once I had a fried egg in my plate and she reached with her hand and took it and ate it. I thought it was a big joke and laughed.

Once we were playing near the chair shop where my father was making chairs. The little nobs or ends of wood that were left as scraps from the ends of the finished chair post made very nice playthings. With a child's imagination they could become anything from a father and mother with a whole family, to a table covered with pots and pans. To me they could be anything. All Sissy liked to do was beat them together to make a loud noise, or pile them up in a large heap and then kick them over.

I can remember many happy hours playing with Sissy and these wooden scraps. But what I am going to tell you next was told to me by my father.

He heard a loud noise, looked out, and found me pulling and tugging at Sissy. She was hitting me and kicking but I would not let go. Both of us were screaming and crying.

My father came running and parted us and demanded, "What are ye doing? Ye know ye must never fight with Alverta."

"But, Papa," I said, "there was a big worm. It might bite Sissy."

He went back to where we had been playing and he found a large copperhead, which he killed.

We did not get much candy, but each time my father went to the store he always brought back three large red and white peppermint sticks of candy, which were called "saw logs." There was one for each of us: Alverta, Edna, and me—the youngest of all the kids. Sissy wouldn't eat candy. I don't know if she just did not like the taste, or if it hurt her several decayed teeth. But she loved the red and white striped color, so she always wanted one, mostly to play with. My father would always tell me, "Now don't ye take Alverta's candy, but ye watch her and when she gets tired of playing with it, you can have it to eat." I would follow her around for hours, and sometimes wait until she took a nap, but sooner or later, I got her candy.

Alverta loved anything that was red. One Christmas my sister Vada got a large apron, which was then known as a coverall. It was something like a sleeveless dress that opened up and down the back. The color was a bright red with a small, springly, flowered design. Alverta fell in love with it at once and Vada cut it up and made a dress for Sissy. She had this pretty red dress on that Easter morning that had such a sad ending.

Several boys had met in the large "bottom" or meadow just across from our home at the mouth of Trace to play a game of "round town," a game somewhat like baseball. Lots of girls had come to watch from our porch and yard. Everyone was having a good time. It was Easter and everyone had on their new clothes for the occasion.

When we heard a terrible scream, everyone ran in the house and found Alverta's clothes on fire. Lorenda ran for the water bucket, which was empty. Vada began tearing at the burning clothes, but before Renda could get a bucket of water from the well, Alverta's clothes were burned.

My father had just been gone for a few hours on his way to Wheelwright, where he had a job as a "planer" in a carpenter shop.

Someone sent for a nurse who stayed at the Caney school. Someone said, "Who will go overtake Isom?" Hazy Caudill said, "I have the fastest mule, so I will go."

In my childish trusting mind I thought "everything will be alright again, when Papa gits here." The next thing I remember was running to meet him, when I saw him coming, and he hugged me until it hurt. I did not know until later that he had been told I had been the one who got burnt.

Sissy lived until about midnight. I can still see my father as he pulled the sheet up over her head and told the nurse, "It's over."

ℬARBARA ᏚMITH

(March 21, 1929–)

Barbara Smith was born in Wisconsin but has lived in West Virginia for much of her adult life. She and her husband moved from New York City in 1960 to take teaching positions at Alderson-Broaddus College in Philippi, West Virginia, "because we both wanted to teach in a church-related liberal arts college away from the city streets."

Smith earned degrees from Carroll College in Waukesha, Wisconsin, and the University of Wisconsin. She has published more than three hundred poems, short stories, and articles in a wide variety of publications including *Antietam Review*, *English Journal*, and *Appalachian Heritage*. She has published seven books of nonfiction.

Smith's first novel, *Six Miles Out*, was published in 1981. A second novel, *The Circumstance of Death*, was published in 2001. Novelist Lee Smith describes Smith as a "fearless writer. She has always been willing to take on the really tough themes, the themes most of us turn away from."

Smith is Emerita Professor of Literature and Writing and former Chair of the Division of Humanities at Alderson-Broaddus College. She makes her home in Philippi, West Virginia, where she works as a freelance writer and editor.

OTHER SOURCES TO EXPLORE

PRIMARY

Novels: *The Circumstance of Death* (2001), *Six Miles Out* (1981). **Nonfiction:** *Community Ministries, Work for Today: Ministering with the Unemployed* (1990). **Poetry:** *Demonstrative Pronouns* (unpublished collection). **Poetry editor:** *Wild Sweet Notes: Fifty Years of West Virginia Poetry, 1950–1999* (2000), *Coming Together* (1995), *Weeping with Those Who Weep: Poems of Bereavement* (1986, 1998), *What the Mountains Yield: A Collection from West Virginia Writers* (1986, 1998). **Plays:** *With Blissful Hope, Miss*

Emma and E.J. **Autobiographical essay:** "Inside Discoveries," in *Bloodroot* (1998), ed. Joyce Dyer, 273–76.

SECONDARY

Joyce Dyer, "Barbara Smith," in *Bloodroot*, 272. Genie Jacobson, review of *Circumstance of Death, Now & Then* 20.1 (spring 2003), 35. Parks Lanier, "A Conversation with Barbara Smith," 21st annual Highland Summer Conference [videorecording], Radford University, 18 June 1998. Felicia Mitchell, "From Image to Epiphany: Barbara Smith's Poetic Moments," in *Her Words* (2002), ed. Felicia Mitchell, 288–97.

BAD NEWS

from *Weeping with Those Who Weep:*
Poems of Bereavement (1998)

So there I was simply filling the gas tank
When you cruised in and calmly reported
You are dying of cancer.

So what was I supposed to do,
Straining to hear your husky words,
Trying not to flicker an eyelid
Nor imagine the bleeding, the vomit, the pain,
While the gas was spilling and filling my shoes?

Well, I'll tell you tomorrow, as I told you today,
We're all dying, some just a little faster than others—
And missing more—
Like singing and watching the children grow up—
And I asked about Martha and paid for the gas,
Registering forever the look in your eyes,
Wanting me to say just something, more,

So I'll tell you tomorrow, as I told you today,
We're all dying. But I won't believe it
As I tear through the gears driving back up the hill
And split the hell out of the firewood in the yard
And scrub floors until my knuckles are red
And as raw as your throat.

Then I'll bake two blackberry pies,
And I'll bring one warm to the shadows on your porch
And offer it, still not saying the words,
But you'll know,
And I'll know.
We're all dying.

And This Is The Way To Be Poor

from *Pine Mountain Sand & Gravel* (1998)

Wearing the same jeans and T-shirt
And the purple plastic earrings
Bought for a quarter at the Salvation Army.
Buying Big League Chew
So your kids will think candy
But won't swallow the bubblegum
And won't cry for hotdogs
For at least ten more minutes.
Asking for gas in one gallon shots,
Pretending you don't want to change a twenty.
Paying the water bill after three warnings
And disconnecting the telephone instead.
Using the food stamps for day-old bread
And year-old sans-label cans of whatever.
Smelling not half as good as the woman in front of you
And wondering why the hell you came
To see the teachers, the principal, who smile tight-lipped
And tell you that Georgie is doing just fine
When you know he can't even read a cereal box
And nobody gives a damn.
That's poor.

The Language of Poetry

from *New River Free Press* (1997)

It has to twang,
Snap back and sting your fingers
When it breaks or gets away from you,
Elastic with emotional pressure,
Its fibers clasping each other,
Reaching for a fit as perfect
As Paul Tillich's grave in Harmony, Indiana,
Where the cedar trees, the native rocks,
The needles that you walk upon
Speak even as they draw you in
And pull you back when you try to walk away.
I feel them, hear them even now,
The syllables of aspen leaves,
The words of waterfalls,
The stanzas of stones.
They make the whole world vibrate.

ÉFFIE WALLER SMITH
(January 6, 1879–January 2, 1960)

Eastern Kentucky poet Effie Waller Smith was the daughter of Sibbie and Frank Waller, former slaves who saw to it that all of their children received an education, even though educational opportunities at the turn of the century for black and white students in Pike County, Kentucky, were extremely limited. Smith and her siblings all attended local segregated state schools and then earned teaching certificates at the Kentucky State Normal School for Colored Persons in Frankfort.

Smith was writing poetry by the time she was sixteen. Her diction reflects her reading of classical literature as well as popular, contemporary writers of the day.

In February 1908, she married Charley Smith, a deputy sheriff. The marriage was an unhappy one, and although it survived the death of a child, it ultimately ended in divorce. Charley Smith later died of a shotgun wound in the line of duty during a moonshine raid.

In 1918, she joined a religious commune in Waukesha, Wisconsin; although she left the commune after four years, she remained in Wisconsin until her death in 1960. Smith was the author of several short stories and three books of poetry.

OTHER SOURCES TO EXPLORE

PRIMARY

Poetry and short stories: *The Collected Works of Effie Waller Smith* (1991). **Poetry:** *Rosemary and Pansies* (1909), *Rhymes from the Cumberland* (1909), *Songs of the Months* (1904).

SECONDARY

David Deskins, "Black Pioneer Poet: Effie Waller Smith," *Appalachian Heritage* (fall 1991), 66. David Deskins, "Effie Waller Smith: An Echo Within the Hills," *The Kentucky Review* 8:3 (autumn 1988), 26–46. David Deskins with Jennifer Kovach, "Introduction," *The Collected Works of Effie Waller Smith* (1991), 3–26.

MEMORIES OF HOME

from *The Collected Works of Effie Waller Smith* (1991)

Thoughts of the dear old homestead
    Haunt my memory to-day;
Thoughts of my home, my childhood's home
    Far away, far, far away.

Far away in East Kentucky,
    There beneath her towering hills,
Rich in forestry and beauty,
    Watered well with brooks and rills,

On a farm—the old, old homestead—
    Which to me is still endeared,
I was born a baby tiny,
    And to womanhood was reared.

Lilacs purple, roses yellow,
    Massive blooms of snow-balls white,
Beautiful the ample door-yard
    In the sunny springtime bright.

Woodbines sweet and morning-glories
    Rife with butterflies and bees
Climbed and clambered round the doorway
    In the sunshine and the breeze.

Often rang through that old farm house
    Childish voices gay and sweet;
Oft its walls of log have echoed
    Patter of the childish feet.

Down below the apple orchard
    From a fern-clad mossy bank
Where the naiads love to linger,
    Where the elders, tall and rank,

And the willows cast their shadows,
    Where the night-birds sweetly sing
To the moonlight and the starlight,
    Bubbled forth a sylvan spring.

Oh, my eyes are getting tear-filled,
    As before my memory come
Those scenes of my early childhood
    In my East Kentucky home.

Which is now fore'er deserted
    By my father's bright household;
It has now been changed and altered,
    Into strangers' hands been sold.

Some of that dear homestead's members,
    Many past-gone years have trod
In a far and distant country:
    Others sleep beneath the sod.

O'er the graves of those dear dead ones
    Marked by moss-grown chiseled stone
All the years in wild luxuriance
    Have the grass and flowers grown.

ℒEE ℐMITH
(November 1, 1944–)

Fiction writer Lee Smith was born in mountainous southwest Virginia, in the town of Grundy, where her family goes back four generations. Her mother, Virginia Marshall Smith, a home economics teacher from eastern Virginia, married Ernest Lee Smith, a businessman who owned a Ben Franklin department store. She went to boarding school at St. Catherine's School in Richmond and then to Hollins College. During the summer of 1966, inspired by Huck Finn, she and thirteen other Hollins College women took a raft trip from Paducah, Kentucky, to New Orleans; the trip was the inspiration for Smith's most recent novel, *The Last Girls*.

Lee Smith says that in college she tried at first to reject the advice to "'write what you know.' I didn't want to write what I knew. . . . I wanted to write in order to *get away from* my own life." Eventually, she admits, she was surprised at the approval she won from her teacher and classmates when she "sat down and wrote a story about some women sitting on a porch all afternoon drinking iced tea and talking endlessly about whether one of them did or did not have colitis." Her study of writers like Eudora Welty, Flannery O'Connor, and James Still helped her to see the artistic value and potential in the details of women's lives. In each of her novels, she creates memorable female protagonists, many of whom live in Appalachia and struggle to discover their identities in the family and community.

She graduated from Hollins in 1967 and married several weeks later. While her sons were young, she worked as a newspaper journalist, an editor, and a teacher. In 1977, she joined the creative writing faculty at the University of North Carolina in Chapel Hill. In 1981, she began work in the English department at North Carolina State University in Raleigh, a job from which she has now retired.

From the beginning of her career as a writer, Smith has received recognition, earning O. Henry Awards for "Mrs. Darcy Meets the Blue-Eyed Stranger at the Beach" (1978) and "Between the Lines" (1981), which appear in her first short story collection, *Cakewalk*. She has also been the recipient of the Sir Walter Raleigh Award for Fiction (1983), the North Carolina Award for Fiction (1984), the John Dos Passos Award for Literature (1987), the W.D. Weatherford Award for Literature (1989), the Appalachian Writers Award (1989), a Lyndhurst Fellowship (1990), the Robert Penn Warren Prize (1991), the Lila Wallace-*Reader's Digest* Writers Award (1995), and a special award in fiction from the American Academy of Arts and Letters (1999).

Lee Smith is the author of ten novels. She and her husband, writer Hal Crowther, live in Chapel Hill and often teach at the Hindman Settlement School Writers Workshop in eastern Kentucky, one county away from her Virginia birthplace.

The excerpt below is from the opening chapter of her novel *Saving Grace*, in which a minister's daughter introduces herself and her family as she narrates the story of her young life.

OTHER SOURCES TO EXPLORE

PRIMARY

Novels: *The Last Girls* (2002), *Saving Grace* (1995), *The Devil's Dream* (1992), *Fair and Tender Ladies* (1988), *Family Linen* (1985), *Oral History* (1983), *Black Mountain Breakdown* (1980), *Fancy Strut* (1973), *Something in the Wind* (1971), *The Last Day the Dogbushes Bloomed* (1968). **Novella:** *The Christmas Letters* (1996). **Short stories:** *News of the Spirit* (1997), *Me and My Baby View the Eclipse* (1990), *Cakewalk* (1981).

SECONDARY

Harriette C. Buchanan, "Lee Smith: The Storyteller's Voice," in *Southern Women Writers: The New Generation* (1990), ed. Tonette Bond Inge, 324–45. Dorothy Combs Hill, *Lee Smith* (1991). Chris Holbrook, review of *Saving Grace*, *Appalachian Heritage* 23:4 (fall 1995), 67–70. Anne Goodwyn Jones, "The World of Lee Smith," *Southern Quarterly* 22:1 (fall 1983), 115–39. "Lee Smith" in *Interviewing Appalachia: The Appalachian Journal Interviews, 1978–1992* (1994), ed. J.W. Williamson and Edwin T. Arnold, 341–62. "Lee Smith Issue," *Iron Mountain Review* 3:1 (winter 1986). Lucinda H. MacKethan, "Artists and Beauticians: Balance in Lee Smith's Fiction," *Southern Literary Journal* 15:1 (fall 1982), 3–14. Nancy C. Parrish, *Lee Smith, Annie Dillard, and the Hollins Group: A Genesis of Writers* (1998). Virginia A. Smith, "On Regionalism, Women's Writing, and Writing as a Woman: A Conversation with Lee Smith," *The Southern Review* 26:4 (October 1990), 784–95. Bonnie Winsbro, "A Witch and Her Curse: External Definition and Uncrossable Boundaries in Lee Smith's *Oral History*," *Supernatural Forces: Belief, Difference, and Power in Contemporary Works by Ethnic Women* (1993), 26–51.

SAVING GRACE (1995)

from Chapter 1

My name is Florida Grace Shepherd, Florida for the state I was born in, Grace for the grace of God. I am the eleventh child of the Reverend Virgil Shepherd, born to him and his third wife, Fannie Flowers. They say I take after her, and I am proud of this, for she was lovely as the day is long, in spirit as well as flesh. It isn't true, however. I am and always have been contentious and ornery, full of fear and doubt in a family of believers. Mama used to call me her "worrywart child."

"You've got to trust more in Jesus, Gracie," she'd tell me again and again in her pretty voice which always reminded me of running water, of Scrabble Creek falling down the mountain beside our house. "You've got to give over to Him," she'd say. "Hasn't He always took good care of us? The Lord will provide," she'd say, smoothing my long yellow hair and pressing me against her bosom where I could smell the familiar smell of cotton dried out on the line. She'd hold me until I quit crying, maybe sing me a little song. Mama was never in a hurry when we were kids. She had all the time in the world for us, putting down whatever she was doing in order to catch us up and comfort us. Mama took good care of us, as good as she could.

This was not true of Daddy, nor of Jesus either, as far as I could see. Daddy and Mama talked about Jesus all the time. I loved Daddy and Mama, but I did not love Jesus. And I actually hated Him when He made us take up traveling in His name, living with strangers and in tents and old school buses and what have you.

I couldn't understand why we had to do this, why this was required of us alone when other children I knew from school got to live in a nice brick house and have Barbie dolls and radios. I was full of resentment and raged against Him in my heart, but I knew better than to say it out loud, for then they might decide I was possessed by the Devil and try to cast him out as directed by Acts 10:38. I had seen this done, and did not want it done to me. But I worried and worried, about everything. I worried that the Devil might really be in me after all, growing like a baby inside of me until I got so big that everyone could see, and everyone would know my awful secret.

When I think on my childhood now, it appears to me as a wild mountainside where I was lost. Often over the years I have dreamed about it. In these dreams I always have a duty—to take something to somebody, to tell somebody something—but the trees are thick and the path disappears beneath my feet. I never know where I'm going, and I never get there.

I reckon I never did get there.

This is why I have had to come back now, traveling these dusty old back roads one more time. For I mean to tell my story, and I mean to tell the truth. I am a believer in the Word, and I am not going to flinch from telling it, not even the terrible things, not even the part about Lamar nor how Mama died nor the true nature of Travis Word nor what transpired between me and Randy Newhouse. I have entered these dark woods yet again, for I've got to find out who I am and what has happened to me, so that I can understand what is happening to me now, and what is going to happen to me next.

My best memories come from Scrabble Creek. This is where we lived the longest, in the house God gave us when I was seven years old. We had come to North Carolina from Georgia in an old car that blew up in the mountains near Waynesville in the summer of 1949. The car was a blue humpbacked Studebaker. A used-car dealer in Stone Mountain, Georgia, had given it to Daddy free for healing his baby daughter of croup. It made a funny noise but it ran pretty good until that August afternoon when it just flat exploded on a high narrow mountain road with Daddy driving of course and Evelyn and Billie Jean and Joe Allen and me crammed in the backseat and Mama nursing Troy Lee in the front. All of a sudden there came a big "pow!" noise and the car lunged over to the left—*away* from the edge of the mountain, thank the Lord—and came to rest at an angle against a rocky cliff. Black smoke poured out from under the hood. We scrambled all over each other trying to get out, which was hard since the left side of the car was pushed against the mountain and the right side was up in the air. One by one we jumped.

"We're wrecked, we're wrecked!" Joe Allen shouted, running around and around.

"Joe Allen, stop that foolishness this minute," Mama directed from inside the car. "Evelyn, come over here and get Troy Lee," she said, and handed him out to my older sister. Troy Lee was crying like crazy, his face bright red. Mama jumped out lightly after him, like she was entirely accustomed to jumping out of burning cars, and took Troy Lee back from Evelyn and comforted him. "Now, now," she said. "There now." I clung to Mama's skirt and wished that Troy Lee had never been born, or that he would die, so that Mama would hug *me*.

My handsome daddy followed Mama out, yelling, "Praise be to Jesus!" as he hit the ground. For traveling, Daddy always took off his jacket and drove in a white shirt with the sleeves rolled up. Daddy was fifty-six then, but he seemed younger, because he was so full of energy. The Holy Spirit kept him hopping, as he said. His eyes were a sharp, bright blue. His long curly hair had been turned pure white by God in a vision on top of Roan Mountain, in Tennessee, when he was twenty-five years old. "All right children," he said calmly, "help me now," and we untied the bundles that were lashed to the top and the back of the Studebaker and got them over to the far side of the road just before the car exploded in earnest, its hood popping off, a great plume of smoke shooting straight up in the air.

"My goodness!" Mama said. Billie Jean was sucking her thumb and Evelyn was crying. "What will we do?" Evelyn sobbed wildly. "What will we ever do now?" Daddy fell to his knees in the road and started praying. I knew he would take the explosion as a sign—Daddy was ever on the lookout for signs and wonders, which were vouchsafed to him accordingly.

"I guess we'll just take to the tent again," Joe Allen said darkly, kicking at our biggest bundle, the green canvas gospel tent which we had slept in before, and plenty of times at that. I wished with all my heart it was burning up in the Studebaker. I hated it when we stayed in the gospel tent. One time we had slept out in that tent in the blowing snow. Another time, in summer, I woke up one morning and found both my eyes swollen shut from bug bites. That was in Dahlonega, Georgia.

Now Mama sat down on the rolled-up tent and unbuttoned her blouse and set in to feeding Troy Lee some more. A piece of her long blond hair had come loose from its bun and it fell in a screen across her face as she leaned over Troy Lee. The rest of us pulled back from the heat of the blazing car but continued to watch it closely as it shimmered and snapped, except for Daddy, who stayed right where he was.

"I'm hungry," Billie Jean said, but nobody answered her.

We were all hungry. We had slept in the car the night before, piled on top of each other, and breakfast had been half a loaf of white bread, hours and hours before. I'd never cry, though. I'd die first. I took pride in not being a whiner like Billie Jean. I ignored my empty stomach and looked up the dark column of smoke, past the tops of the dusty green trees, to a patch of deep blue sky. I wished I could just float away with the smoke, away from there, away from them all. "I'm hungry," Billie Jean said again, and again nobody answered her. We knew there was nothing to eat. Mama buttoned herself back up and placed Troy Lee face down across her lap. Butterflies fluttered around her. She smiled at us. "I'll swear," she said, "if it's not the prettiest day!"

About five minutes later, a gray truck came rumbling along the road and stopped. God had answered Daddy's prayer. The back of the truck held three boxes with hunting dogs in them, and all the dogs started barking at once. A man got out as quick as he was able. He had a long red face and a nose with a knob on it. "You folks okay?" he hollered over the sound of the fire and the barking and Billie Jean's crying and Daddy's praying.

"Why yes, praise Jesus, we are," Mama said sweetly.

The man walked over to get a closer look at Daddy. "Son of a gun," he said. He stood there in the middle of the road and waited until Daddy finished praying and got up.

"Virgil Shepherd, minister of God," Daddy said, grinning his big grin and holding his hand out. "Mighty pleased to meet you."

"Likewise." The man said his name was Carlton Duty, and he was going on to say something else when the other door of the truck swung open and a woman stuck her curly red head out. "And this here is my wife Ruth," he said. We would learn that Ruth Duty loved children, and hadn't ever been able to have any. She had the kindest heart in the world.

"Why this is awful!" she cried. "You poor little things! You all look like something the cat drug up! I tell you what, I've got a coconut cake in here that we was taking over to my sister's." She pointed at me. "Honey, you come on over here and help me."

So I ran right up to the Dutys' truck, and Mrs. Duty handed me a platter holding a great big cake covered all over with little white strings of coconut, which we had never seen before. I took the cake and put it down in the road beside Mama, and then Daddy came over and sat on a rock and cut it up with his pocketknife. Though we were about to faint with hunger by then, we knew better than to start eating before Daddy had said the blessing. He stretched out his arms and set in, "Hallelujah! Oh, He's a good God, that had led us up here from Georgia and give us His sign of holy fire and provided us a feast in the middle of the day. He's a good God, hallelujah!" Daddy went on and on, the way he always did, but I peeped out from under my eyelids to watch Carlton Duty just standing there leaned up against his truck staring at Daddy with his mouth open. Daddy had had this effect on people before. I thought I would die of starvation before he finally hollered, "Amen!" and picked up a piece of cake.

In my whole life, I have never tasted anything to equal Mrs. Ruth Duty's coconut cake. Even today, it makes my mouth water just to think about it! I reckon we ate like we were about starved, which we were. The Dutys came near to watch us eat, Carlton Duty smoking a cigarette and Mrs. Ruth Duty hovering around our little circle like a big old moth. We didn't even have anything to wash the cake down with. We just ate. I thought we had died and gone to Heaven for sure. We ate until every crumb of that cake was gone, and then we stretched out our legs and lay back against the mossy bank and blessed God and watched our car finish burning up, and Daddy told Carlton Duty how we had got there.

"Mr. Duty," he said, "I preach the Gospel of Jesus Christ as it is written in His Holy Bible, amen, and not in no other place, and I am out here on the road follering His divine plan where He said, 'Go ye into all the world, and preach the Gospel to every creature.' My religion is not a mouth religion, Mr. Duty. No sir. I am follering the plan of God. I will do what He tells me to do, I will go where He tells me to go, and stop where He tells me to stop, praise His sweet name."

"But what about all these poor sweet little younguns?" cried Mrs. Duty, looking at us.

"I cannot think of no better plan for them than to foller the plan of God," Daddy said. "These children may not have new clothes on their back nor new shoes on their feet, but they are going to Heaven with me. These children are on the road to salvation. Isn't that right, Fannie?" Daddy asked Mama, not taking his eyes off Carlton Duty's face, not even nodding when Mama smiled and said, "That's right." I snuggled over closer to Mama and the sleeping Troy Lee, while Evelyn held Billie Jean in her lap and Joe Allen poked around in the woods with a stick.

Carlton Duty swallowed hard. "Do you mean to tell me, sir," he said, "that you-uns wasn't even for sure where you was a-going? That you did not have no more definite destination in mind than Heaven?"

"That's right, brother," Daddy said seriously. "As it says in the good Bible, this world is not our home, we're only passing through. We're follering the plan of God, brother, and we have given our lives over to Him. He is leading us where He wants us to go, and today He has brung us to—" Here Daddy paused and narrowed his eyes and asked, "What place is this?"

"Well, you're about nine miles outside of Waynesville," Carlton Duty said.

"Bless Jesus!" Daddy said, reaching his arms up in the air and bowing his white head to the will of God. His left hand was still blue-black and swollen from where he had gotten bit in Clayton. "Bless Jesus," Daddy continued, "who had showed us by the sign of fire in His holy woods nine miles outside of Waynesville, North Carolina, His plan for our life today, by freeing us from the things of this world and casting us wholly on His mercy, amen, and by bringing us His blessing as a gift of food from his good servants Carlton and Ruth Duty, amen."

"Shoot, it's just a *cake*," Ruth Duty said in the silence that followed Daddy's prayer.

But Daddy appeared beatified, gazing around at the smoking skeleton of the car and the thick green woods and the blooming black-eyed Susans beside the road as if he had never seen such sights in his whole life. Bumblebees droned and yellow butterflies fluttered around us.

Carlton Duty cleared his throat. He looked at his wife. "Well," he said, "seeing as how things are, I believe I might be able to help you out. You-uns stay right here, and I'll be back directly."

"God be with you," Daddy told him.

They climbed back in the truck and rattled off down the road with the dogs all barking at once. Mrs. Ruth Duty waved out the window. We sat there and watched them go until there was nothing left of them at all except a puff of dust that hung in the hot, still air above the rutted road.

Then Joe Allen came crashing through the underbrush and reported that he had found a spring, and Evelyn and Billie Jean and I started off down the steep hill after him. Down, down, down we went until we came to a deep shady spot where the spring bubbled up between the mossy rocks like a fountain. We cupped our hands and drank like we were dying of thirst, like it was our last chance for water in the world. The spring water was cool and sweet, delicious. Finally I quit drinking and raised my dripping chin and looked back up the mountain.

And there stood Daddy, black against the sun. His white shirt and his white hair appeared to be shooting off rays of light behind his dark form. I did not wave or holler at him. I started playing with Joe Allen and Evelyn and Billie Jean. We built a dam, and made a little lake, and sailed leaf-boats in it. The whole time we played, I knew that Daddy was watching over us. . . .

JANE STUART
(August 20, 1942–)

Poet, short story writer, and novelist Jane Stuart was born in Ashland, Kentucky, the daughter of well-known author Jesse Stuart. She describes her childhood home in Greenup, Kentucky, as a log cabin which had "ten rooms . . . with books in eight of them." Stuart says, "My writing was always influenced by Appalachia. I never tried to 'get away' or write about anything that did not relate in some way to home."

Stuart earned an A.B., magna cum laude, from Case Western University in 1964, then went on to complete two master's degrees in classical languages, as well as a Ph.D. in medieval and modern Italian literature from Indiana University in 1971. She taught English and creative writing on several faculties, including the University of Florida.

Her multifaceted career has combined writing with teaching, translating, book reviewing, and extensive travel. She's been a contributor not only to numerous scholarly publications, but also to general interest magazines ranging from *Ladies Home Journal* to *National Wildlife*.

In 1992, Stuart won first place in the National Federation Poetry Contest, as well as receiving the Kentucky State Poetry Society's highest honor, the Grand Prix Award for "From Winter Meditations." *Moon Over Miami* received the 1995 *Poetry Forum*'s chapbook contest prize.

Now retired from teaching, Stuart has returned to her childhood home in Kentucky where she plans to "keep an interest in writing and improve my work that has lain untouched and fallow for so many years."

The prose excerpt is taken from *Transparencies*, a book of remembrances about her father.

OTHER SOURCES TO EXPLORE

PRIMARY

Novels: *Land of the Fox* (1975), *Passerman's Hollow* (1974), *Yellowhawk* (1973). **Poetry:** *Journeys; Outward/Inward/Home* (1998), *Moon Over Miami* (1995), *Cherokee Lullaby* (1995), *Passages into Time* (1995), *White Tock* (1994), *The Wren and Other Poems* (1993), *White Barn* (1973), *Eyes of the Mole* (1967), *A Year's Harvest* (1957). **Short stories:** *"Karnak"* (1993), *Gideon's Children* (1976). **Autobiographical nonfiction:** "The House and This World," in *Bloodroot* (1998), ed. Joyce Dyer, 283–88. *Transparencies* (1985).

SECONDARY

Contemporary Authors, First Revision, Vols. 41–44 (1974), 604. Joyce Dyer, "Jane Stuart," in *Bloodroot*, 282.

CYCLES

from *Transparencies* (1985)

It seems strange, looking back, that at the time of death the respectful funeral home silence is punctuated by quiet conversation (relatives) and spurts of nervous laughter (children). I suppose that I was both a child and a relative. When I tired of standing in a long reception-like line, meeting people I had heard of but never seen, seeing people from my own past, seeing people I had just met—I wanted to run away, into the rainy February night. But there was no place to go.

It was an ungentle nightmare, to be lived through again and again in my thoughts and in my dreams. The long line of old and young filing past my father's casket, looking in at the wax figure wearing glasses; the reception line we formed so uncertainly—do you laugh or cry or do both at the same time? Or escape into the room where there are chairs, cold drinking water, and ashtrays?

On the day of the funeral—but I don't want to think about that day— my uncle saw to it that our rental car was parked in my mother's garage. The door was closed and a line of cars blocked its exit. But who would have left? And where was there to go?

It was my duty as a daughter to be present at my father's funeral and to be part of his burial. I was able to perform that duty—not with any pleasure, but glad, so glad, that I could do what must be done.

He had truly gone to earth, after a long, slow, and painful dying.

A part of me went with him.

Perhaps I better understand now the cycle of being. You can be born, and you can die, many times within one lifetime. You can see your father's face in your son's mischievous eyes. You can hear your mother's voice in your sleep. You can determine, by instinct, the day and time of death.

No wonder I am old and being old has made me younger once again. I have passed through several cycles and I have become at last myself again.

I only hope that I will not make the mistakes that I made before. I am on my own. No one of this world can tell me what to do or how to do it. And there is no voice from the grave to guide me.

I am very much alone.

And at times I am still afraid.

WHERE STUARTS LIE

from *Eyes of the Mole* (1967)

If ever fields were flecked with sun-gold green
and hollows high, between tall tree-clumped hills
that, circled with mauve mists, shoulder sky,
it is here, in Shelbyanna, where Stuarts lie.

If pine-cone chimes can sound the evensong,
white wind-fingers pluck the willow harp,
as night-things purr a silver slumber song,
it is here where sleeping earthlings dream of dawn:

of violets and melons wet with dew—
cornfields ripening in lush river beds—
a hummingbird sucking pink hollyhocks—
on hills where they shall no more walk.

Here they are buried with their mighty dreams,
weary giants sleeping in the soil—
in mottled fields of green and sun-flecked gold
and misty hills that echo tales yet told

about the Stuarts.

ROOTS

from *Eyes of the Mole* (1967)

Roots dug in this hungry craw of land
are badly tangled. No resolute hand
can jerk them up from the mesh of grass
that entwines them to languishing eons that pass
in a cloud of grey mildew, clogged with the sperm
of man's endless renewal, from dust unto worm.

COMPOSITION

from *White Barn* (1973)

Wild strawberries,
green apples,
and twilight

taste of the past,
still-life upon the wall.

Last night I heard the wind,

cold, gray, and wet,

whip fragile stars
that had let heaven fall.

ADRIANA TRIGIANI

Adriana Trigiani, the third of seven children in an Italian-American family, moved from Pennsylvania to Big Stone Gap, Virginia, at the age of six, when her parents, Ida and Anthony Trigiani, settled there and opened a garment factory. "She didn't like to weave," notes her mother, "but Adri was creative in different ways." Trigiani had a way with words, and by the age of sixteen, she was a roving reporter for WNVA radio in Norton, Virginia.

Trigiani graduated from Notre Dame/Saint Mary's Theatre Program in South Bend, Indiana, having written and directed her own play, *Notes from the Nile*, as well as being the founder of an all-girl comedy troupe, The Outcasts.

After graduation, Trigiani moved to New York City where she made her off-Broadway debut as a playwright in 1985 with *Secrets of the Lava Lamp*. She then segued into writing screenplays as well and, in 1988, was hired as a writer for *The Cosby Show*. "All my TV experiences were wonderful," Trigiani says. "I learned a lot."

Trigiani is married to Tim Stephenson, an Emmy Award–winning lighting director for *The Late Show with David Letterman*. The couple lives in New York City.

In the opening scene of her novel *Big Stone Gap*, readers are introduced to Ave Marie Mulligan, a thirty-five-year-old, self-proclaimed spinster and owner of a pharmacy in Big Stone Gap, Virginia.

OTHER SOURCES TO EXPLORE

PRIMARY

Novels: *Lucia, Lucia* (2003), *Milk Glass Moon* (2002), *Big Cherry Holler* (2001), *Big Stone Gap* (2000).

SECONDARY

Rebecca Sturm Kelm, review of *Big Cherry Holler*, *Library Journal* 126:9 (15 May 2001), 165. Brad Lifford, "Town inspires novel," *Kingsport* [TN] *Times-News* (7 April 2000), D1, D2. Bella Stander, "A Conversation with Adriana Trigiani," www.bellastander.com/writer/adriana.htm.

BIG STONE GAP (2000)

from Chapter One

This will be a good weekend for reading. I picked up a dozen of Vernie Crabtree's killer chocolate chip cookies at the French Club bake sale yesterday. (I don't know what she puts in them, but they're chewy and crispy at the same time.) Those, a pot of coffee, and a good book are all I will need for the rainy weekend rolling in. It's early September in our mountains, so it's warm during the day, but tonight will bring a cool mist to remind us that fall is right around the corner.

The Wise County Bookmobile is one of the most beautiful sights in the world to me. When I see it lumbering down the mountain road like a tank, then turning wide and easing onto Shawnee Avenue, I flag it down like an old friend. I've waited on this corner every Friday since I can remember. The Bookmobile is just a government truck, but to me it's a glittering royal coach delivering stories and knowledge and life itself. I even love the smell of books. People have often told me that one of their strongest childhood memories is the scent of their grandmother's house. I never knew my grandmothers, but I could always count on the Bookmobile.

The most important thing I ever learned, I learned from books. Books have taught me how to size people up. The most useful book I ever read taught me how to read faces, an ancient Chinese art called *siang mien*, in which the size of the eyes, curve of the lip, and height of the forehead are important clues to a person's character. The placement of ears indicates intelligence. Chins that stick out reflect stubbornness. Deep-set eyes suggest a secretive nature. Eyebrows that grow together may answer the question *Could that man kill me with his bare hands?* (He could.) Even dimples have meaning. I have them, and according to face-reading, something wonderful is supposed to happen to me when I turn thirty-five. (It's been four months since my birthday, and I'm still waiting.)

If you were to read my face, you would find me a comfortable person with brown eyes, good teeth, nice lips, and a nose that folks, when they are being kind, refer to as noble. It's a large nose, but at least it's straight. My eyebrows are thick, which indicates a practical nature. (I'm a pharmacist—how much more practical can you get?) I have a womanly shape, known around here as a mountain girl's body, strong legs, and a flat behind. Jackets cover it quite nicely.

This morning the idea of living in Big Stone Gap for the rest of my life gives me a nervous feeling. I stop breathing, as I do whenever I think too hard. Not breathing is very bad for you, so I inhale slowly and deeply. I taste coal dust. I don't mind; it assures me that we still have an economy. Our town was supposed to become the "Pittsburgh of the South" and the "Coal Mining Capital of Virginia." That never happened, so we are forever at the whims of the big coal companies. When they tell us the coal is running out in these mountains, who are we to doubt them?

It's pretty here. Around six o'clock at night everything turns a rich Crayola midnight blue. You will never smell greenery so pungent. The Gap definitely has its romantic qualities. Even the train whistles are musical, sweet oboes in the dark. The place can fill you with longing.

The Bookmobile is at the stoplight. The librarian and driver is a good-time gal named Iva Lou Wade. She's in her forties, but she's yet to place the flag on her sexual peak. She's got being a woman down. If you painted her, she'd be sitting on a pink cloud with gold-leaf edges, showing a lot of leg. Her perfume is so loud that when I visit the Bookmobile, I wind up smelling like her for the bulk of the day. (It's a good thing I like Coty's Emeraude.) My father used to say that that's how a woman ought to be. "A man should know when there's a woman in the room. When Iva Lou comes in, there ain't no doubt." I'd just say nothing and roll my eyes.

Iva Lou's having a tough time parking. A mail truck has parked funny in front of the post office, taking up her usual spot, so she motions to me that she's pulling into the gas station. That's fine with the owner, Kent Vanhook. He likes Iva Lou a lot. What man doesn't? She pays real nice attention to each and every one. She examines men like eggs, perfect specimens created by God to nourish. And she hasn't met a man yet who doesn't appreciate it. Luring a man is a true talent, like playing the piano by ear. Not all of us are born prodigies, but women like Iva Lou have made it an art form.

The Bookmobile doors open with a whoosh. I can't believe what Iva Lou's wearing: Her ice-blue turtleneck is so tight it looks like she's wearing her bra on the outside. Her Mondrian-patterned pants, with squares of pale blue, yellow, and green, cling to her thighs like criss-cross ribbons. Even sitting, Iva Lou has an unbelieveable shape. But I wonder how much of it has to do with all the cinching. Could it be that her parts are so well-hoisted and suspended, she has transformed her real figure into a soft hourglass? Her face is childlike, with a small chin, big blue eyes, and a rosebud mouth. Her eyeteeth snaggle out over her front teeth, but on her they're demure. Her blond hair is like yellow Easter straw, arranged in an upsweep you can see through the set curls. She wears lots of Sarah Coventry jewelry, because she sells it on the side.

"I'll trade you. Shampoo for a best-seller." I give Iva Lou a sack of shampoo samples from my pharmacy, Mulligan's Mutual.

"You got a deal." Iva Lou grabs the sack and starts sorting through the samples. She indicates the shelf of new arrivals. "Ave Maria, honey, you have got to read *The Captains and the Kings* that just came out. I know you don't like historicals, but this one's got sex."

"How much more romance can you handle, Iva Lou? You've got half the men in Big Stone Gap tied up in knots."

She snickers. "Half? Oh well, I'm-a gonna take that as a compliment-o anyway." I'm half Italian, so Iva Lou insists on ending her words with vowels. I taught her some key phrases in Italian in case international romance was to present itself. It wasn't very funny when Iva Lou tried them out on my mother one day. I sure got in some Big Trouble over that.

Iva Lou has a goal. She wants to make love to an Italian man, so she can decide if they are indeed the world's greatest lovers. "Eye-talian men are my Matta-horn, honey," she declares. Too bad there aren't any in these parts. The people around here are mainly Scotch-Irish, or Melungeon (folks who are a mix of Turkish, French, African, Indian, and who knows what; they live up in the mountain hollers and stick to themselves). Zackie Wakin, owner of the town department store, is Lebanese. My mother and I were the only Italians; and then about five years ago we acquired one Jew, Lewis Eisenberg, a lawyer from Woodbury, New York.

"You always sit in the third snap stool. How come?" Iva Lou asks, not looking up as she flips through a new coffee-table book about travel photography.

"I like threes."

"Sweetie-o, let me tell you something." Iva Lou gets a faraway, mystical twinkle in her eye. Then her voice lowers to a throaty, sexy register. "When I get to blow this coal yard, and have my big adventure, I sure as hell won't waste my time taking pictures of the Circus Maximus. I am not interesed in rocks 'n' ruins. I want to experience me some flesh and blood. Some magnificent, broad-shouldered hunk of a European man. Forget the points of interest, point me toward the men. Marble don't hug back, baby." Then she breathes deeply, "Whoo."

Iva Lou fixes herself a cup of Sanka and laughs. She's one of those people who are forever cracking themselves up. She always offers me a cup, and I always decline. I know that her one spare clean Styrofoam cup could be her entrée to a romantic rendezvous. Why waste it on me?

"I found you that book on wills you wanted. And here's the only one I could find on grief." Iva Lou holds up *As Grief Exits* as though she's modeling it. The pretty cover has rococo cherubs and clouds on it. The angels' smiles are instantly comforting. "How you been getting along?" I look at Iva Lou's face. Her innocent expression is just like the cherubs'. She really wants to know how I am.

My mother died on August 2, 1978, exactly one month ago today. It was the worst day of my life. She had breast cancer. I never thought cancer would get both of my parents, but it did. Mama was fifty-two years old, which suddenly seems awfully young to me. She was only seventeen when she came to America. My father taught her English, but she always spoke with a thick accent. One of the things I miss most about her is the sound of her voice. Sometimes when I close my eyes I can hear her. . . .

$\mathscr{D}$ANA $\mathscr{W}$ILDSMITH
(July 17, 1952–)

Poet Dana Wildsmith was born in Macon, Georgia. She grew up in rural Georgia, the daughter of a Methodist minister who was a social activist. She married at nineteen and attended Tusculum College, the University of Tennessee, and Virginia Wesleyan College, moving as often as her husband's duties with the Navy required. She graduated from Virginia Wesleyan College with a B.A. in sociology in 1986. She and her husband now live in north Georgia on her family's land, where their home is a one-hundred-year-old converted cotton barn.

She has worked as a writer, an editor, and a workshop leader throughout the Southeast. She has been a poetry fellow with the South Carolina Academy of Authors, a reader for *Kalliope: A Journal of Women's Art,* and an artist-in-the-schools for the South Carolina Humanities Council. She has taught through the University of South Carolina's Creative Retirement Center, as well as the Tennessee Mountain Writers Conference, and the Appalachian Writers Workshop. She says, "I might never have begun writing poetry again (after my teenage poems of angst) had I not gone to the Appalachian Writers Workshop at Hindman [Kentucky], where Jim Wayne Miller saw my poems and spoke to me about them. I feel a heart-connection to Kentucky, which plays itself out in my writing." She has also studied with Fred Chappell and Jonathan Williams at the Atlantic Center for the Arts.

Wildsmith has two chapbooks—*Alchemy*, published by the Sow's Ear Press in 1995, and *Annie*, winner of the Palanquin Press Chapbook Competition in 1999. Iris Press has issued her audiotape of poems and commentary, *Choices* (1997). Her first full-length collection of poetry is *Our Bodies Remember*.

OTHER SOURCES TO EXPLORE

Poetry: *Our Bodies Remember* (1999), *Annie* (1999), *Alchemy* (1995).

ECONOMY

from *Our Bodies Remember* (1999)

The truth is,
love is a tune without words.
For instance, if he's still awake
and you're still awake
from leftover worry or fear,
then one of you
journeys two inches of mattress
to spoon the other one's back;
not for love or for money
could you explain
how a gesture as homely as that
could salvage a hopeless night,
but you know.
As sure as the hum
of your pulse,
you know.

NEW POOR

from *Our Bodies Remember*

First she finds out how much time it takes to be poor.
The path from some to less has to be planned,
even meals. Each meal must bleed to the next:
the whole roast to the hash,
yeast bread with toast,
toast with eggs.

This is a siege. She sits down to take stock, to deal
not with what is gone, but with what is left.
Each thing she names, she owns as a tool.
Milk and eggs can be two meals or
cake once. There is still tea.
In siege time,

old rules flesh out like a starch-fed child. Girls were
once taught to save back a bit to use when need came
(from a quart, the scant cup; from four eggs,
a yolk), to let bread pad out poor meat,
and that a whole sliced thin seems
more than it is.

Meals laid on the best plates take on a bit of grace.
When the siege was new, she mapped these hints as if
they were clues to a code. As if one day at last
each dear act of faith would add up to
some truth less stark than that
there are no tricks to use
on food that has
run out.

A DRY SPRING

from *Our Bodies Remember* (1999)

Tell me the relation between
a May and a June with no rain

and your going away in April.
Today I cut half the grass,
every other blade

dead from drought.
Half the words I would have said
this spring died at their root

or shrank underground
to wait out another dry day,
another night shallow as dust.

I miss you like a shade oak gone.
Having you here was rain, and
the cistern full. I could

live my life twice then:
once in the doing,
once in telling you.

OUR BODIES REMEMBER

from *Our Bodies Remember* (1999)

"You don't have a body; you are a body."

A Habit of the Blood, Lois Battle

Sealed and stamped, but now I'm not sure
what I wrote
or didn't write, so I'm typing your letter over
in blank air
because fingers remember where they've been sent
and will walk
their previous walks when we let them. If we don't
trip them up
with our thoughts, fingers can touch-tone
phone numbers
our minds can't recall, and my grandmother's piano
couldn't care less
if I have a brain, so long as my hands
step lively.

I'm reminded of thirty years back, when
therapists
tested this notion of body memory
as a means
to imprint habits of movement on palsied
muscles. Their
technique, named "patterning," called for
a circle
of volunteers who would position a patient's
arms and legs
to one posture of useful motion, and then
another—

choreographing progressive freeze-frames
of belief in
their power to animate, cell by cell,
tissues dulled
by a mind's misfires. I remember liking
the elegance
of patterning's slow pavane, and I thought then
how pleasing,
in a homey way, must be the patterner's work
of tidying
a jumbled body, as if straightening
bed covers,

the sort of job where you can see
what you've done.
But what had been done? I can't recall seeing
follow-up
stories with photos of birth-harmed children
now rooted
like willows in a neuron stream,
their movements
as thoughtless as wind. Does a body refuse
to forget
its history, even in favor of
a gentler
now? Many's the time I've watched you
flinch
from some teasing comment of mine—I
who love you,
who would no more say you a hurtful word
than I would
lay a live coal in your ear. Why
do you think
I rewrite my letters to you, checking each
gossips bit
for barbs and shafts? Knowing how words have
damaged you,
I keep an intention of placing my words
precisely,
like hands to muscle, hoping to heal your
troubles, but

there is no healing. My job
is not to mend
but to soothe. I remind myself how you'll look
when you open
my letter a few days from now—your legs
stretching out
as you read, your chair tilting back, and
line by line
your strict face relaxing, remembering
how to grin.

FORCE

from *Alchemy* (1995)

You'll be a good driver, he'd say,
when you know how to take a curve.
Just go in to it easy.
Keep your foot away from the brake, see,
and hold off giving any gas
until right when the widening out
starts to elbow in. You'll feel it.
Lean in to it then. Feed the engine
a little, let the curve carry you.
Might as well enjoy these twisty roads.

Halfway home to Georgia she lets off
on the gas to cruise around
another jut of loblolly pines
but the car hesitates
and her daddy's box of ashes
comes sliding across the seat. Too soon,
he'd say. You've got to keep gassing it
until there's bend enough to maintain
the drive. There's more here than just
you and the car, Hon. Listen to the road.

SYLVIA WILKINSON
(April 3, 1940–)

The only writer in this book to have served as a motorsports correspondent for *Autoweek* and as timer/scorer for Paul Newman's race team, Sylvia Wilkinson has impressively diverse interests and talents.

Born in Durham, North Carolina, to Peggy George Wilkinson and Thomas Noell Wilkinson, she excelled in horseback riding and painting as a child and won district tennis championships as a teenager. During her college years, she studied with and received the encouragement of noted writers Randall Jarrell and Louis Rubin. She completed a B.A. in painting and English at the University of North Carolina at Greensboro in 1962, and an M.A. in English and writing at Hollins College in 1963, where she received a Hollins College Creative Writing Fellowship.

She began her second novel, *A Killing Frost*, while she held the Wallace Stegner Creative Writing Fellowship at Stanford (1965–1966). The recipient of a number of literary awards, Wilkinson has twice received the Sir Walter Raleigh Award for North Carolina Fiction (1977, 1968), a Creative Writing Fellowship from the National Endowment for the Arts (1973), and a Guggenheim Fellowship (1977).

She has been a teacher in writers-in-the-schools programs, as well as a visiting writer in college and university classrooms since 1963. In addition to her six novels and three nonfiction books, she wrote a dozen books on racing for Children's Press between 1981 and 1986 and four juvenile mysteries for Grosset & Dunlap. She divides her time between Chapel Hill, North Carolina, and El Segundo, California. Currently she covers auto racing for *World Book Encyclopedia* and is working on a seventh novel.

Her fictional protagonists are usually young girls or women from rural or small town communities who struggle for the freedom to define their own lives. As she explains, "A big part of my motivation to be a writer came from

608

my mother's mother, Mama George. She was a farm woman with a third grade education from Sunday School who listened to soap operas, read newspapers and comic books. But she was a storyteller with a natural sense of form and drama . . . I became a writer out of an oral tradition, knowing I could never equal her standards."

In her first, second, and fifth novels, Wilkinson is particularly interested in the effects of strongly imposed gender roles on her young protagonists. Even in *Cale*, a novel focusing on a young male character, Cale struggles with the expectations his family places on him to farm the land he will inherit.

In *Shadow of the Mountain*, Wilkinson's Jean Fitzgerald, a naive but privileged college girl, joins the 1960s federal War on Poverty by accepting a job with "the Appalachian Corps."

Other Sources to Explore

Primary

Novels: *On the Seventh Day, God Created the Chevrolet* (1993), *Bone of My Bones* (1982), *Shadow of the Mountain* (1977), *Cale* (1970), *A Killing Frost* (1967), *Moss on the North Side* (1966). **Selected nonfiction:** *Dirt Tracks to Glory: The Early Days of Stock Car Racing as Told by the Participants* (1983), *The Stainless Steel Carrot, An Auto Racing Odyssey* (1973). **Selected juvenile nonfiction:** *I Can Be a Race Car Driver* (1986), *The True Book of Automobiles* (1982), *Can-AM* (1981), *Endurance Racing* (1981), *Formula One* (1981), *Sprint Cars* (1981), *Stock Cars* (1981). **Interviews:** In *Images of the Southern Writer* (1985), 90–91. In *Kentucky Review* 2 (1981), 75–81. In *The Writer's Voice* (1973), ed. George Garrett (Morrow, 1973). In *Craft So Hard to Learn* (1972).

Secondary

Fred Chappell, "The Unpeaceable Kingdoms: The Novels of Sylvia Wilkinson," *The Hollins Critic* [Hollins College, VA] 8:2 (April 1971), 1–9. Joyce M. Pair, "Sylvia Wilkinson," *Contemporary Fiction Writers of the South* (1993), 479–93. Review of *Shadow of the Mountain*, *Publisher's Weekly* (24 January 1977), 328.

SHADOW OF THE MOUNTAIN (1977)
from Part III

Two of the local women's club leaders stopped by to welcome me. They were bored and boring. They gave me a bank calendar, a Gideon Bible, and a free set at the local beauty parlor. On the way home I stopped off to see Mollie. We had a good laugh over which one of us should use the beauty parlor coupon, since we both have our thin frizzy hair in braids.

. . .

Today Mollie talked more of her mountain girlhood. She asked me if I was tired of listening to an old woman, that she would know she had run me off when I didn't stop by again. Mollie said she grew up scared of her daddy. She remembered him today, back when she lived in Kentucky, which was really her home, Hazard, Kentucky. There folks didn't think they were too good for her like the ones in Rocky Gap. The residents of that dismal Cumberland town knew they were in Little Hell and the poverty they were born with had sent them there.

Her daddy plowed around the graveyard on the farm they settled for as many years as they thought people in the community would remember there was a family buried up there. Then came the spring of 1900 and he broke the grave-yard land. Time for a new generation, he said, at the turn of the century, so he planted it in corn. If their bones were close to the top, they would be like powder, he figured. There was bone meal in fertilizer and it ought to be good for his crop, he told her with a laugh. If they hadn't been lazy and had planted their kin deep, he'd never reach them with his plow. The Lord would make him pay, Mollie's mother said, and his corn would grow dark green from their bones to spite him and have kernels on their ears as hard as a dead man's teeth. Mollie said her mama had strong feelings about laying aside room for the dead. But the corn didn't grow greener; the corn was the same as in the other fields. All that there was to spite her daddy was his little girl, Mollie, digging around his stalks with a spade. He snatched her up by the back of her dress and it made a tear, out loud, at one of the rotten arm seams. In her mind an animal had grabbed her, and she could never think of her daddy without being afraid to turn her back on him.

"You going to leave the roots bare to the sun." He scolded her and shook her until the spade fell from her hand.

"No, Papa," she said clearly, hiding her fear of him. "I'm going to dig out the grave of the little girl. She was near my age, they say, when she died of the pox and they buried her with a china doll. A real china doll with white slick legs and arms. Her dress might be all gone now in the dirt and even the blue eyes

and red lips a-painted on might be wasted, but I figure that china lasts longer than bones."

"I wanted that china doll bad," Mollie told me seriously, and every spring at land-breaking time she walked the furrows looking for it. She had found it a thousand times in her dreams and it was beautiful. She ran for every white root and cutworm that turned up with the plow, thinking it was an arm or leg of her china doll. She was shamed for telling her daddy. He laughed loudly at her and teased her until he broke her doll dream to pieces in her head and she never had it again.

I looked at Mollie's hands, wondering how she could ever have wanted a china doll or even felt its slickness, how she was once a soft child. The sides of her fingers are crusted from whittling in the winter, making toothpicks and sewing quilts without a thimble, or from pulling husks off corn. She is always doing something with her hands when we talk. Her skin looks like an old piece of wood that the water has run over for years; the hard flesh is left in ridges and the soft has worn away. It appears she could be snapped apart like the sticks she uses to kindle her fire.

The women here are so different from those southern ladies that wear gloves for everything they do, church, washing dishes, gardening, as if their hands must never come in contact with anything coarser than they are. Gay MacKensie's hands were scarred and callused from her jackknife. I watch Mollie use her hands as tools. I've seen my mother buy tools for what Mollie does with her hands. Grandfather Fitzgerald's maids had far more money than Mollie. We used to give them lotions and perfumes for presents. The maids always had extra time to sit around and rest their bodies. I don't think Mollie has ever stopped being busy, even now when there's only her left.

"Women here don't want what they never had because they don't know what they should be wanting," Mollie said. It didn't offend her to talk about being poor. "I'm speaking of the hard-up ones. Some of them in town never wanted a day in their lives." She went on to talk about how radio and television were presenting to people wants and dissatisfactions they never had before. To know that everyone wasn't poor was a bad thing; it didn't give you ambition, just bitterness. All boys wanted now was a fast automobile, and the girls wanted to marry the one with the fastest automobile whether he had a "lick o' sense or a dime in his pocket. They start a-thinking they ought to have what ever'body else has." I listened for the edge in her voice, wondering if that comment was meant for me because I came from outside.

I finally asked her about outsiders coming in, why there was such a resentment towards people from other places, was it because they came in fancy cars wearing nice clothes and built expensive houses? Mollie changed when I ques-

tioned her directly instead of letting her ramble. She tightened up her lip and told me what a fool I was. That it wasn't what the outsiders brought in; it was what they took away. She said the fruit was stripped from the plant and not even a seed was left. Their hills had been plucked clean by outsiders with no respect for who was there first. I felt the fool she called me.

I'm attached to these hills in a different way from hiking. I think the mountain people have to go nowhere else to know that what they have is prettier or just as pretty as anywhere in the world. The Appalachians are special mountains, worn down and covered with vegetation. Often the houses are impractically located—the view from the porch not sacrificed to shorten the walk to the fields. That must be unusual for poor people, to consider the beauty of the surroundings before they consider water, land, wood, and whatever they need to survive. I don't think their placement of their cabins could be by accident, not from what I saw from the house windows in Lost Cove. I said that to Mollie and she just grunted and said, "They wont still there, now was they?" I better keep my idealistic dissertations to myself for a while.

Mollie told me there were seashells printed in the rocks on the plateau, that she wasn't "pulling my leg." This was all once an ocean, and when the ocean went away, it left the coal. Her daddy told her that. He never saw the real ocean and neither had she. But he hadn't told her that when they had taken all the coal away, they would leave the people buried under mud from the strip mine slides. He didn't live to see that. He thought the coal would never run out. Mollie gestured at the coal scuttle beside her fireplace as if the contents were so foul she didn't want it near her, instead of something to bring warmth from the cold. The slag, the mud slides, men coughing till they died, arms and legs gone from the explosions. There is no love from the mountain people for the black mineral.

She told me one horror story after another. I had set her mind off churning up the bad memories she had buried. The men in Kentucky went down in the mines and worked in hell every day of their lives, hating what was bringing them what little they made, hating the coal and hating the owners. The owners took the coal away, and with it went a chunk of the life of the people for good. And in return they got barely enough money to stay alive and keep digging. Every railroad car that went out left the people and the land more wasted. It was hard for her to tell if it was worse after the coal was gone. She had left Kentucky and didn't want to see it again to find out.

As I was leaving, she asked if I'd heard about the Reverend who was snake-bit. I had. He had died because he refused medical treatment. Mollie sat back in her chair at the news and hissed through her teeth without emotion. "The fool. He knowed a snake could kill you."

ℳEREDITH 𝒮UE 𝒲ILLIS
(May 31, 1946–)

Born in Clarksburg, West Virginia, Meredith Sue Willis spent her youth in the coal-mining town of Shinnston, West Virginia, where the residents, she explains, "were as likely to be Italian or Spanish or Lebanese as Scotch-Irish." She has become an articulate, outspoken voice against homogeneous portrayals of Appalachian people.

Her maternal grandmother, Pearl Barnhardt Meredith, was a mining-camp midwife, and her maternal grandfather, Carl Meredith, was a coal miner. Her paternal grandparents tended coal company stores in Coeburn, Virginia; Burdine and Jenkins, Kentucky; and Owings, West Virginia. "This tendency to associate moving on with bettering yourself seems to be a part of my particular family heritage," she admits, but "it is only one aspect of Appalachia" that "ties us to other immigrants."

Her father worked in the mines between college semesters, and both of her parents became teachers. An accomplished teacher herself, Willis is author of three useful and popular books about the writing process, all published by the Teachers and Writers Collaborative Press.

After graduating from Shinnston High School and spending two years at Bucknell University, Willis dropped out to spend a life-altering year as a Volunteers in Service to America (VISTA) worker in Norfolk, Virginia, before graduating from Barnard with a B.A. in 1969 and completing an M.F.A. at Columbia in 1972, where she spent her time studying, writing, and protesting the Vietnam War.

She and her husband, Andrew Weinberger, live with their son in South Orange, New Jersey. In *Contemporary Authors* she explained, "I have done a lot of odd jobs in my life and I value these very highly. I have worked with wheelchair patients, been a disc jockey for a college radio station, and given workshops for teachers and students of all ages in video tape and acting as well as creative writing . . . I have worked in a recycling center, and written painstaking letters in Spanish to dictators and other unsavory characters for Amnesty International. I like seeing everything—teaching, childhood, books I've read, jobs I've had, come together in fiction."

Willis's first novel focuses on the family of a West Virginia preacher; her second introduces Blair Ellen Morgan, a character who rebels against the values of her West Virginia schoolteacher parents. In *Only Great Changes*, Willis continues the story of Blair Ellen Morgan, whose experiences echo Willis's own, as her fictional character travels from a small Baptist college in West Virginia to become a VISTA worker in a black neighborhood in Norfolk.

In the Mountains of America, a collection of eleven stories set in West Virginia, celebrates the art of storytelling. In "My Boy Elroy," a young female narrates her experience and her grandmother's, achieving a memorable balance of empathy and understanding.

OTHER SOURCES TO EXPLORE

PRIMARY

Fiction: *Oradell at Sea* (2002), *Trespassers* (1997), *In the Mountains of America* (1994), *Quilt Pieces*, with Jane Wilson Joyce (1991), *Only Great Changes* (1985), *Higher Ground* (1981), *A Space Apart* (1979). **Books for children:** *Marco's Monster* (1996), *The Secret Super Powers of Marco* (1994). **Nonfiction:** *Deep Revision: A Guide for Teachers, Students, and Other Writers* (1993). "Writing Out of the Region," *Appalachian Journal* 18:3 (spring 1991), 296–301. *Blazing Pencils: A Guide to Writing Fiction and Essays* (1990). *Personal Fiction Writing: A Guide to Writing from Real Life for Teachers, Students, and Writers* (1984). **Autobiographical essay:** "An Inquiry into Who My Grandmother Really Was," in *Bloodroot* (1998), ed. Joyce Dyer, 289–97.

SECONDARY

Thomas E. Douglass, "Meredith Sue Willis" [Interview], *Appalachian Journal* 20 (1993), 284–93. Gina Herring, "Politics and Men: What's 'Really Important' about Meredith Sue Willis and Blair Ellen Morgan," *Appalachian Journal* 25:4 (summer 1998), 414–22. Nancy Carol Joyner, "The Poetics of the House in Appalachian Fiction," *The Poetics of Appalachian Space* (1991), ed. Parks Lanier Jr., 17–20. "Meredith Sue Willis Issue," *Iron Mountain Review*, 12 (spring 1996). Ken Sullivan, "Gradual Changes: Meredith Sue Willis and the New Appalachian Fiction," *Appalachian Journal* 14 (1986), 38–45.

My Boy Elroy

from *In the Mountains of America* (1994)

My grandmother's store sat at a curve in the Wise Mountain road. It was a general merchandise store and mail drop-off for all the farms and hollows and ridges and folds of the mountain community of High Gap. People used to come down near noontime and wait for the mail. The store had so much open space that they pulled the kitchen chairs, nail kegs, and wooden dynamite boxes near the iron stove, even in the hot summer weather, just to localize the conversation.

When I stayed with my grandmother two summers in a row, her main stock-in-trade was Pepsi Cola, pink snowball nickel cakes, and canned lunch meat. She also sold a lot of pressed chewing tobacco: mostly Red Man and Day's Work, which looked like a yellow candy bar to me on some days, and like dried dung on others. She used to have staple goods in her store, too, bags of flour and meal, but over the years she found that the fewer large items she sold, the less she had to enter on her credit books; people tended to pay cash for Vienna sausages and Dreamsicles.

The people waiting for the mail used to tell stories. I loved the slowness of the telling. I would line up coins in the coin drawer, or sit on a sack of cornmeal and look out the window, letting their voices carry me along. They took turns speaking, never interrupting each other, using short blasts of words: quick-speakers, not Deep South drawlers, but mountain talkers, rat-a-tat followed by a space. After a decent appreciative interval at the end of one story, someone else would start. I loved to be a part of those stories. Sometimes I wished I could be big enough to sit on a nail keg and take a turn, but mostly I was a little awed by the people, and happy to watch them from a distance. They had mouths that weren't like people's I knew; cheeks that had collapsed around toothlessness, and the men sometimes wore their bodies bare inside stiff blue jean overalls. The women sat with their knees apart and discreetly waved their dresses up and down for ventilation.

So I stayed at the window, or behind the counter with my grandmother. She always kept a distance herself, never joining them in the circle. People called her Mrs. Morgan, even the ones she called by their first names, and no one ever came into the living quarters in the back of the store. When I asked why, if Mrs. Robinson was a good woman, she never came back into our kitchen, my grandmother said, "Oh, honey, you have to be real careful when people owe you money."

To tell the truth, looking back, I think my grandmother's pride entered into it. She had sent her children to college, and while she didn't boast, people knew my father and my Aunt Ellen were both schoolteachers. My grandmother had a very precise line in her mind between good and bad. Educating your children and paying your bills were on the good side. Politeness was good, too, and she was polite to everyone, but she told me very clearly the difference between good people like the Robinsons who would give you the shirt off their back and the other ones you couldn't turn your back on for three seconds or they'd steal the varnish off the countertop.

And then there were the Possetts, who were in another category altogether. I first heard them mentioned in the course of someone's story around the stove. "Worthless as a Possett," someone said. I asked my grandmother later, just what is a Possett?

"Euh, euh," she said, in her special tone of humorous disgust that was supposed to make me giggle. "You stay away from those Possetts. They have cooties and they marry each other. Euh, euh."

A few days later, Earl Robinson started telling a story about the Possetts, how they'd had a fire and lost a child, or maybe two. "They never could count that good," said Earl. He paused then, and no one haw-hawed, but even I figured out the joke. "The ones that lived got burnt, too," said Earl. "All but that big Elroy. He just hightailed it out of there, didn't lift a finger to help." He went on and on, and then other people turned out to have Possett stories, too, many stories about this family that didn't have sense to pull each other out of a burning house.

One morning, shortly before my mother and father came to take me home that summer, the Possetts came to the store.

"Law, law, here come the Possetts," said my grandmother, who had gone out front to sweep the little square of cement under the step. She ran and put a piece of canvas over the bags of meal. She told me to close the kitchen door and stand by the ice cream freezer. I was not supposed to get close to them, but if any of them wanted an ice cream, I could get it out of the freezer and scoot it across the white enamel lid.

I was as excited as if they had declared Christmas in August, watching through the big plate-glass window as the Possetts came down the yellow dirt road, past the one-room schoolhouse, across the asphalt, barefooted, one after the other: two full-grown men in overalls first, the old one with no teeth and a straw hat (but, to my shame, I couldn't see that he looked all that different from a fine man like Earl Robinson), and the younger one, chubby and round-shouldered, strawberry blond. After him came the old Possett woman, who wore a boat-necked dress with no sleeves or waist, as if she had simply stitched two rectangles of fabric into a garment. The young woman had a little baby in her arms.

"Look at them," whispered my grandmother. "They think that boy Elroy is the smartest thing that ever lived. They buy him shoes in the winter and keep him fat. He got to second grade, too, before he turned sixteen and quit. I just wondered which one of them fathered that baby."

I don't understand that, I thought to myself, but I understood more than I wanted to. I tried to pay attention to the children, counting them, examining them. The little baby, plus a boy, two girls, and another boy. My stomach wrenched and I stopped counting as that last boy came across the road. He seemed to have no chin; I tried to look away. I ran to my station by the ice cream freezer, but when I turned back, the little boy was only four feet from me. He had big eyes that seemed to roll all the time because his face was pulled down by terrible stretching from his cheeks over his lower lip area. His little white bottom teeth were as exposed as a bulldog's and you could see all the healthy red flesh that should have been inside his mouth.

My grandmother said, "Is that your boy that got burned?"

Mr. Possett said, "Ee-ah," or something like that, grinning all the while, reaching behind him and grabbing the boy by the head, tugging him around for my grandmother to see. "Don't talk no more," said Possett. "Still eats, though."

My grandmother grabbed a handful of peppermint balls and maple chewies and gave them to the boy. It was as if her hands had to give to him, just as my eyes had to look. When he couldn't hold any more candy, it started dropping on the floor and the other children ran and picked it up. Mr. Possett bought himself an R.C. Cola, and after a while Elroy whined until he gave him a nickel for one, too. The mother Possett took some of the wounded boy's candy and shared it with the big girl and the baby. They sat on the kegs and boxes and looked at us, at the store. Once in a while Elroy would make a sucking noise with his R.C. Cola. Mr. Possett bought some chewing tobacco and two strips of licorice, which he tore into pieces for all the children, and then they left, back across the asphalt, up the road past the schoolhouse, into the pinewoods again.

My grandmother got a rag and wiped every wooden box a Possett had sat on, and rubbed the plate glass where a Possett had rested his cheek. She moved fast, as if she were doing something she couldn't have stopped if she'd wanted to.

I said, "What did they come down for?"

She said, "They came down to go to the store."

It was almost time for the mail; Mrs. Robinson showed up, and Mary from down the road, and, after a while, Earl Robinson. This time my grand-mother did the talking, more than I'd ever heard her say to her customers. She told about the Possetts coming, about the girl with the baby big as life and Elroy fat as the hog for winter, and the boy with no chin. She went on and on, and there was no climax to her story, just the necessity of telling it.

The next summer, I didn't go down to stay by myself with my grand-mother. I didn't go down until our yearly visit, and everything seemed differ-ent. My grandmother directed all her remarks to my father; she called herself an old widow-woman, and said if things got much worse she was going to end up having to marry that dirty old fellow with the greasy black hat who had the tiny store down the road. "Euh euh," she said. "He's so old and dirty. He sleeps in the same room as the store." It seemed to her, she said, that the boys nowadays were getting worse and worse, and meaner and meaner, and all the time she was getting older and feebler and more of an old widow-woman.

It didn't make any sense to me at all, because she had never looked bigger and better to me. Her hair was still brown, and she moved briskly around the kitchen, and her eyes sparkled. My father didn't take it seriously, either, and he called her by her first name. "Now, Ella," he said, the way he always did when he was being cheeky.

We were sitting around her kitchen table eating an apple pie she'd made for us from a bushel of Rome Beauties someone gave her on their bill. "You don't know," she said.

"Come and live with us," said my mother.

"You know you're always welcome," said my father.

My grandmother said, "I didn't write you about the convicts, did I? I'm getting so forgetful nowadays." My mother and father looked at each other, and then my grandmother settled in and told us about how a few weeks back, folks were sitting around waiting for the mail, and someone told about a certain Hines boy from Jenkins, Kentucky, who had broken out of jail in Pikeville. These Hineses, apparently, were the most evil-hearted bunch who had ever lived. They would shoot up churches and kill off people as soon as look at them. Especially old widow-women.

"Now, Ella," said my father.

Well, anyhow, as it happened, people were worried about the Hineses coming over this way, and Earl Robinson was going to send down one of his boys to sleep in the store, but my grandmother said no, of course not, she was fine. "Well," my grandmother told us, "that very night I had this evil Hines fellow pecking at this very kitchen door. And Elroy Possett the toad-stool, too."

Involuntarily, we all glanced at the door. It was a screen door to a little back porch, also screened, with a rocking chair where I loved to sit and read. She kept her brooms out there, the coal scuttle, and baskets of produce people gave her when they couldn't pay cash: the Rome Beauties, potatoes, peaches in season, and more tomatoes than she could ever eat. This porch had a door and three steps down to the garage and coal house.

The thing that frightened her that night, she told us, was that the knocking was on her back door instead of at the store door.

She had been watching Bret Maverick on television when she heard it, and she walked into the kitchen without turning on the light because she had a bad feeling and wanted to look at who was knocking before they saw her. She passed the telephone, thinking all the time she should call the Robinsons, but she didn't want her imagination running away with her. She didn't want to act like a timid old widow-woman, even if she was one.

"So," she said, "I ended up with convicts at my back door and no help but myself."

"Come and live with us, Mother," my father said, not fooling around now.

"And do what? Set in a chair? No, I'll just keep on working and getting deeper in debt till some convict really does get me."

She had stood in the dark kitchen, peering at the shape on the steps, pressing at her outer door. No friendly voice saying, Hey, Mrs. Morgan. Nothing she could recognize as a Robinson or an Otis. The television was still going in the background, cowboys shooting. She made out another man down on the ground at the bottom of the steps, and at a little distance, by the garage wall, a cigarette ash glowing. Three of them, she thought, and that was when her blood ran cold. Three men, and she was sure they were convicts. She spoke suddenly, harshly, as if the force of her voice could blow the man off her steps. "What do you want?"

"You the store lady?" he asked, without so much as a *good evening*.

"Store's closed," my grandmother answered, working on a plan in her mind. What she wanted to do was ease herself over to the telephone and gently give a message to the Robinsons. It was a party line, and with luck one of the girls would be on the phone already, talking to her boyfriend. She had heard the Robinson's ring just a little while before, and she thought she might be able to whisper that she needed help without these convicts hearing her over the television. "Store's closed, boys," she said again.

The fellow pressed his shadow face into the screen wire, trying to see. He gave a slimy little laugh, and she thought she could smell whiskey. "Aw," he said. "We was wanting something, too."

"Who's we?" said my grandmother. "Do you think I open up to every Tom, Dick, and Harry?"

The snicker again. "I don't think you know us, ma'am." She knew he could break the little hook and eye on the door in no time, and once he did that, once he started breaking her things, she would have lost the chance to do anything but scream.

A voice came from the cigarette glow. "Tell her to give us a drink of water, Ed." She was sure the one staying back so far was the leader. He was the Hines. The dangerous one with his picture in the paper, standing back out of sight.

The third one, the big hulk, at the bottom of the stairs, said, "Naw, you said I could have a R.C. Cola to drink."

My grandmother said, "Elroy Possett, is that you down there?"

A snuffle and a giggle. "Yes, ma'am."

Well, my grandmother saw it all in a flash then. She saw the convicts running across Elroy, who was probably sitting on a rock by the side of the road, and them asking him who had money around these parts, and him saying, Oh, Mrs. Morgan, she owns a big store.

"That's how dumb the Possetts are," my grandmother told us.

"The most money they can think of is me and my poor little in-debt store with nothing but books full of credit." She said it made her so mad to think that Elroy Possett had got her in all this trouble that she threw the light switch, jut hit the whole bunch of them with the spotlight my father had installed so she wouldn't stumble going out to load her coal scuttle. Light all over Elroy, who shaded his eyes. The fellow up on the steps already had a hat pulled low over his eyes, and the one down by the garage stepped back in the shadows, so she never did get a look at him.

"Now, why'd you do that?" said the one called Ed, and my grandmother took a closer look at him; narrow-shouldered, with clothes that didn't fit, like they belonged to another man. Like they'd been stolen, she thought.

"Tell her what we want, Ed," said the man in the shadows.

"Well," said Ed, "we was traveling and we got hungry and this fellow here said you could sell us some lunch meat and bread and pop."

While he talked, my grandmother kept looking at his hat, a man's regular dress hat of a greasy black color, and it reminded her of something, and all of a sudden she was sure it belonged to the old fellow with the little store about a sixth the size of her own. She thought, Lord Lord, they killed that old man who wanted to keep me company, they killed him and took his money and his hat and now they're going to kill me. It was the hat that set her imagination to working. She wasn't the kind of person to imagine out of nothing, but the hat and the grease spots made her see the old bristle-chinned fellow lying with his throat cut in a pool of blood in that store, where, if his head was at the stove, then his feet must be out the door. She saw her own blood then, too, on the linoleum of her kitchen floor. Saw her apron and her plaid print dress. Saw a terrible stillness of sunrise on herself laid out on the floor with no life in her.

She heard another snuffle from Elroy, and it infuriated her that a filthy oaf like Elroy Possett was going to be the death of her. She got so mad, she snarled, "What are you laughing at, Elroy Possett? It isn't funny these poor boys being hungry and thirsty in the middle of the night like this and want-ing a little something, and you know very well I can't open up this store."

"Yes, ma'am," said Elroy.

The one named Ed with the old man's hat said, "Just some lunch meat, lady."

"Can't open the store," she said. You know I'm not one to have wild ideas, she told us; it was something about the Possett that gave her the idea. "I can't open my store, much as I'd like to."

The man in the dark said, "And why's that, ma'am? We surely would like a little something to eat."

My grandmother kept looking at the Possett, the only one of that whole family with any meat on him, no doubt stealing from his mother and the little ones, no doubt giving his sister that baby. She said, "Elroy Possett knows why, don't you Elroy? I can't open up because of my boy Elroy."

There was a little silence, and Elroy Possett said, "Yes, m'am."

She said, "You know all about my poor Elroy, don't you?"

Ed said, "What are you talking about?"

Elroy Possett said, "Her boy Elroy."

"How many Elroys *is* there around here?"

"Two of us," said Elroy Possett, and my grandmother's head began to swim. Some moths and beetles were flapping and flying and banging on the spotlight, and the one named Ed slapped at them.

"Tell us about him," said the one in the dark.

"He's a bad boy," said Elroy Possett.

"Now, Elroy," said my grandmother, feeling a kind of joy; things hap-pening, and she wasn't still yet. "Now, Elroy, don't talk about my poor boy like that. He never hurt me."

"He hurts other folks, all right."

The one down in the shadows said, "Where is this fellow? I'd like to see this Elroy."

"Law," said my grandmother. "I'd never disturb him."

"Don't disturb him!" said Elroy. And my grandmother turned out to have underestimated him, because it was Elroy Possett who made up the next part. "That Elory sets in the store next to the money box with a shotgun, and nobody never gets near nothing."

Ed cursed. "Why the ----"

"Blank," my grandmother said.

"Why the blank did you bring us here then?"

Elroy Possett was having a good time; his imagination was working away. It must have been a real treat for him, said my grandmother, to feel his brain working.

"Yes, sir, that Elroy sets right there with that shotgun and blows folks' heads off. He sleeps in the daytime and shoots burglars at night. He shot lots of burglars."

My grandmother was getting worried that Elroy was going to ruin it by saying too much. "Now, Elroy, you're exaggerating."

"Why ain't he in jail?" asked Ed.

"Well, he never killed anybody," said my grandmother. "He has real bad coordination, my boy Elroy. He never hurt those boys, the time Elroy's talking about. They wasn't supposed to be in the store, after all. The sheriff agreed to that."

The one down in the dark said, "Tell him to step aside then, ma'am, he'll do what you tell him."

"Law no," said my grandmother. "I'm sorry to say that I'm not a trusting woman. I have a suspiciousness in me."

"Let's go," said the one in the dark, and the cigarette went hurling off. "She ain't letting nobody in her store."

Elroy Possett said, "That Elroy is ugly too. And he ain't bright."

Ed cursed again, then cursed Elroy and stomped down the steps, and Elroy went after him. My grandmother said she went around checking all her window locks, then she got out the butcher knife and sat all night in the kitchen with the knife in her lap.

"Why didn't you call the Robinsons?" asked my mother.

"It was getting late," my grandmother said. "Besides, I always like to do what I can by myself."

"We're getting you a gun," said my father.

"I'd shoot my foot. Beside, it turned out those Hine boys got caught earlier that day all the way over in Danville. Those boys weren't the convicts after all," she said. "Although I do believe they were mean as convicts."

I asked, "What about that hat?"

She shrugged. "Two hats. The old man was fine. I got a message from him the next day through the bread boy. He wanted to take me out for a drive on Sunday. In my car."

"Just the same," said my father, "we're getting you a gun."

"All I need," said my grandmother, "all I need is for people to pay their bills."

"Did Elroy come back?" I asked her. "Did you ever see him again?"

"Of course," said my grandmother. "He brought the whole family down again a day later. The whole defective mess of them. They stood around my store for three hours and never bought a thing."

She looked at us. "Do you know what they were waiting for?"

I knew, but I said, "What?"

She gave a nod with her chin. "They were waiting to see my boy Elroy."

ℒEIGH 𝒜LLISON 𝒲ILSON
(October 23, 1957–)

Short story author Leigh Allison Wilson is a native of Rogersville, Tennessee. She earned a B.A., magna cum laude, from Williams College in 1979 and did graduate work at the University of Virginia from 1979 to 1981. In 1983, Wilson received an M.F.A., with honors, from the University of Iowa Writers' Workshop. Her first book, a collection of short stories, *From the Bottom Up*, was awarded the first annual Flannery O'Connor Award for Short Fiction from the University of Georgia Press in 1983.

Wilson's work, which is frequently set in the mountains of East Tennessee, features characters who are endearingly eccentric. Noted one reviewer, "She records not only absurd behavior but the stubborn craziness baked into rural personalities."

Wilson says, "I've recently realized how very much I owe my sense of storytelling and humor to the Appalachian women who raised and nurtured me. I had thought I created my sensibilities and wit out of my own cloth, but now I realize I owe much of it to my family, particularly their ready grasp of narrative and humor."

Responding to critics who insist on labeling Appalachian literature as "regional," Wilson says, "All American fiction, it seems to me, is circumscribed by place; I have the feeling my work ends up being labeled regional simply because fewer people come from my particular place."

The following scene from the short story "The Raising" is from Wilson's collection, *From the Bottom Up*.

OTHER SOURCES TO EXPLORE

PRIMARY

Short stories: *Wind: Stories* (1989), *From the Bottom Up* (1983).

SECONDARY

Contemporary Authors, Vol. 117, 487–88. *Southern Women's Writing* (1995).

FROM THE BOTTOM UP (1983)

from The Raising

Of the eight matrons perched like pigeons around two identical card tables, Mrs. Bertram Eastman was the lone childless woman. Her husband, in whom—she was sure—the fault lay, only confounded this burden she'd borne for thirty years, fixing a funny look on his face every time the subject came up and saying, in a voice soft as solemnity itself, "Spare the child and spare the rod, Mrs. Eastman." But he was like that, a nitwit, and half the time she never knew what he was talking about. Still, being a woman of industry, Mrs. Eastman took up the slack of impotence by becoming an expert on children and motherhood. She was renowned in the gin rummy set, in the Daughters of the Confederacy set, and perhaps in the whole area of East Tennessee, renowned and widely quoted for her running commentary on child-rearing.

"A child is like a new boot," she'd say and pause with the dramatic flair of a born talker. "You take that boot and wear it and at first it blisters your foot, pains you all over, but the time comes it fits like a glove and you got a dutiful child on your hands." What she had missed in experience, Mrs. Eastman overcame with pithy insight; what she lacked as human collateral in a world of procreation, Mrs. Eastman guaranteed with sheer volume. She was a specialist in armchair mothering.

A steady hum of a general nature had settled over the women playing at both tables, punctuated by an occasional snap of a card, but like a foghorn in the midst of a desert the voice of Mrs. Eastman rose and fell in every ear. She was explaining, for the third time since seven o'clock, the circumstances that led to Little Darryl, the melungeon orphan boy, who would come to live at her house the very next morning. A child! In her own home! She couldn't get over it. Her brain worked at the idea with a violence akin to despair turning upside-down and her hair, from some internal cue, dropped onto her forehead a large, stiff curl that flopped from side to side as if to let off steam. Mrs. Eastman, although not fat, was a formidable personage, stout and big-boned and not unlike the bouncer in a hard-bitten country bar. Mr. Eastman was the tiniest man in Hawklen County. Just yesterday he had come home and told her, out of the blue, that he was bringing Little Darryl out from Eastern State and into their home—one two three and like a bolt of electricity she was a mother. She couldn't get over it.

Little Darryl was thirteen years old and of "origin unknown," a poor abandoned charity case dumped from orphanage to orphanage since the day his faceless mother—unfit and unwed, Mrs. Eastman knew for a certainty—dropped him off in the middle of the canned-goods section of the Surgoinsville A&P. He was discovered beside the creamed corn, eating an unhealthy peanut butter and jelly sandwich. The "origin unknown" part delighted Mrs. Eastman: Little Darryl would be *her* child, sprung as mysteriously and as certainly into her care as a baby of her own making. O, she would make a lawyer out of him, distill the taint of his blood like meltwater. She would recreate the boy in her own image and watch him tower among men in her old age.

"Smart as a *whip*, the social worker told Mr. Eastman," Mrs. Eastman said in a loud, confidential voice. At her table were old Mrs. Cowan, the Methodist preacher's wife; Mrs. Jenkins, the wife of the Jenkins Hardware Jenkinses; and Mrs. Talley, wife of Hubert Talley, the local butcher. Mrs. Eastman had given each one advice, off and on, for thirty years, from Mrs. Talley's red-headed boy who was thirty years old and no good, right down to Mrs. Jenkins' six-year-old who still sucked her thumb and was a "mistake."

"You said that ten minutes ago, Eloise," Mrs. Jenkins told Mrs. Eastman, "and you said he was a genius before that." Mrs. Jenkins was playing North to Mrs. Eastman's South. "You said he was a genius that wasn't understood and you ain't even met him yet."

"Made him a lawyer already, too," said Mrs. Talley, looking calmly over Mrs. Jenkins' shoulder, her lips screwed up in concentration.

"Ida Mae Talley!" cried Mrs. Jenkins. "Put you in the East and straightway you cheat left and right."

"For your general information," Mrs. Eastman said and tossed her curl, like a hook, back up into her beehive hairdo, "for your edific*a*tion, Little Darryl scored in the 'excessively bright' range on three different tests."

"I am most certainly not cheating," said Mrs. Talley. "I seen those kings three minutes ago."

"God loves all the little children, smart and stupid, black and white," old Mrs. Cowan said with a smile so bright that her lips appeared to retreat back into her gums. She was the simple-minded member of the women's club although, somehow, her children had grown up to be wildly successful bankers and businessmen in the county, as if to intimate that children, even life, were too muddled a factor to control entirely. For this reason old Mrs. Cowan said nothing that was really heard, did nothing that was really seen, and existed in the main as a hand in gin rummy, or as a how-de-do on the Methodist Church steps every Sunday morning. She was incapable of taking sound advice, given in good faith, by even the best of friends. Deep in her bowels Mrs. Eastman believed her to be the most wicked woman of her acquaintance, the most deceitful as well as the most dangerous, and to hold, somewhere behind her idiocy, a hidden ace in the hole.

"God may be well and good on Sundays," Mrs. Eastman said, leveling her eyes like shotgun bores toward old Mrs. Cowan's western position. "But God Hisself don't have to raise no boy geniuses at a moment's notice. Pass me one of those green mints, Vivian." She stretched her free hand toward Mrs. Jenkins. "The white ones give me the morning sickness."

"They come in the same box, Eloise. Green and white. In the same damn box." Mrs. Jenkins, whose mints and home provided this evening's entertainment for the club, shut her cards with a click, laid them carefully face down on the table, then folded her arms like hemp cord and stared at Mrs. Eastman. She looked ready to pounce in panther fashion across the table, to defend her territory with a beast's wit. Mrs. Eastman had on her patient expression, the one she recommended for children with colic.

"I only meant to point out that I *read* somewheres that they put more dye in the white mints than they do in the green, that's all. They start out gray and add twice't the dye to turn them white. Scientific fact. Twenty school-children alone have died in Detroit, Michigan, from a pound of white mints. Now think about *that*."

"All I know," said Mrs. Jenkins, rising clumsily from her chair, "is we've had these same mints for fifteen years and I never heard a word till now. I'm going to put whip cream on my jello if you'll excuse me."

"I didn't read it till last week," Mrs. Eastman called over her shoulder, then she lowered her voice until only the whole room could hear: "Don't either of you tell a dead man, but she's on par*tic*ular edge tonight strictly because her boy was found pig drunk, with a hair ribbon in his mouth, underneath the 11-E overpass. No clothes on him anywhere."

"O," said old Mrs. Cowan. "He was the finest acolyte our church ever had."

"No more he ain't," Mrs. Eastman said happily. "Comes of no discipline."

"Now, now," Mrs. Talley said, watching herself thumb through Mrs. Jenkins' cards, "You ain't exactly the one, Eloise"—here she paused to exchange one of her cards with one in the other pile—"you ain't exactly the one to pass judgement on a drunk, now are you?"

"Well, Mrs. Ida *Mae* Talley." Mrs. Eastman sneered on the "Mae." "Are you sinuating that my husband is a drunk?"

"That's for you to know, Eloise," she said, "and me to hear over coffee."

ℳary Élizabeth ℳitherspoon
(June 14, 1919–)

A native of Florida, Mary Elizabeth Rhyne Witherspoon graduated from the University of North Carolina in 1941 with an A.B. in drama. "I'd intended to be an actress," says Witherspoon, "but my collegiate studies in drama turned out to be training for writing fiction." She married Jack Witherspoon, an engineer, in 1942, and the couple moved to Knoxville, Tennessee.

Witherspoon built a career as a freelance writer while raising three sons. In 1963, she earned a master's degree in history from the University of Tennessee and later served as a history instructor at the University of Tennessee and Knoxville College. Her work includes two novels, a history of the Breadloaf Writers' Conference, a poetry collection, essays, and short stories.

"My first novel [*Somebody Speak for Katy*] was a case of 'write what you know,'" Witherspoon says. "*The Morning Cool* [her second novel] was a case of 'know what you write,' which is more difficult." Witherspoon's novel *The Morning Cool* focuses on the human cost of McCarthyism in 1950s America.

In this excerpt from *The Morning Cool*, we meet Maggie Cole, a forty-something widow whose husband, Chris Cole, had been active in radical circles during the 1930s and 1940s. An old friend, Joe, comes to visit, along with his mother, and brings Maggie disturbing news regarding Senator McCarthy's crusade to uncover American communists, and Maggie begins her own search for the truth behind her husband's suicide and his political past.

Other Sources to Explore

Primary

Novel: *The Morning Cool* (1972), *Somebody Speak for Katy* (1950). **Nonfiction:** "On Leaping from Rock to Rock with an Intellectual," *Whose Woods These Are, A History of the Breadloaf Writers' Conference* (1993).

Secondary

Thomas Lask, "There's No Place to Hide," *New York Times* (8 April 1972), 27.

THE MORNING COOL (1972)

from Part One

Between Soap Ridge and the Tennessee River lies a narrow strip of highway edged with towns—Tate City, Danzig, John's Creek, Goshen, Holly. There is a look about these towns of unnatural quiet, of complacency, and strangers passing through have sometimes said to themselves: Here lies the tag end of America; the ridge and the river have boxed these people in, walling out change, sealing in old habits and obsolete concepts.

They do not know the whole story.

. . .

Maggie met Joe on the porch. He looked so worried, she said quickly, "She's all right, Joe; just asleep."

"Good. Will you sit down a minute? I need to talk to you."

She sat down; so did he, and began rubbing his hands together; then he sneezed.

"Do you have your pills?" she asked.

He ignored her, and blew his nose. Then he shook his head hard, like a wet dog trying to get dry. He passed one hand across his forehead, and rubbed his hands together again.

"Joe, you're making me nervous. What's on your mind?"

"I ran into Will Green this morning."

"In Nashville? I thought he was in Texas."

"He comes back, now and then. Maggie . . ." He chewed his lip and rubbed his hands again. "I know you don't have anything to hide, but how much do your children know?"

"About what?"

"About their father."

Maggie stopped rocking. When she spoke, her tone sounded stilted and pious. "They know that he was a labor organizer, and they know—that is, Meg and Mark know—that he killed himself."

Joe gave her a long, incredulous look. After a while, he said, "*I* didn't know that, Maggie. You said it was heart trouble, remember?"

"Yes, I remember. But the older children knew."

"Do they know why?"

Maggie stared into the snowball bush. She felt tears rising, and she tried to swallow them before Joe could see. She felt in her pockets for Kleenex.

"*I* don't know why, Joe, for sure. Do you?" She looked at him, pleading, ignoring the tears.

There was a puzzle in his eyes she couldn't solve—something anxious, something gentle, something hurt.

"No, I don't, Maggie," he said. "I really don't." He laid his hand, very lightly, on her arm, then very quickly drew it back. She began to rock again, quiet, and finally she asked, "What was it that Willoughby told you?"

"Oh, he's had people coming around asking questions, and he's been to see a lawyer. He thinks he's gonna be subpoenaed, and that if he is, the rest of us may be, too."

There was still a question in his eyes, and Maggie frowned. "Joe," she said, "Chris wasn't a Communist; he hated the CP with a passion. You know that."

Joe linked his fingers and rubbed his thumbs together. "Yeah," he said. "I guess. But do you remember a guy named Ernest Greeley?"

"Yes. He was a snake."

"He's still a snake, and he's turned witness for the government."

She said, "That damned hypocrite. He's the kind Chris hated the most."

"He hated Chris, too, Maggie."

"Oh, lord. But Joe, surely—even McCarthy won't take the word of a slimy character like that—surely."

"They *are* taking his word, Maggie, about all sorts of things. Besides, he's not their only witness. Do you remember Killion?"

"Of course."

"Well, he's on their staff, now, Maggie; it's Killion's files they're using."

"Oh, Joe." Her tone said very clearly, I was learning to trust you, up to this point, but . . .

He got the implication, and he flushed. "Look," he said. "I'm not making these things up. Don't you read the papers?"

"Yes." (But not really, do I? I open the pages, and I scan, but I lower my lashes when the seeing hurts.) "But, Joe, *Killion*. I mean, I know his views changed a lot through the years, and I'm not sure I ever really liked him. But he was honest; I could swear he was."

"He probably still is, Maggie."

She thought about that, and then said, "Then it's all right."

"I hope so." He looked deflated and embarrassed; he pushed himself up from his chair and started to go inside. "At least," he said, "I can get Ma off your hands."

"No, wait, Joe. Don't change the subject. And don't go, please. I really don't want to be alone right now."

He let out his breath and sat back. He said with his eyes closed, "Thanks. I really don't want to nurse Ma, either, all by myself."

Maggie sat rocking, thinking, trying to be calm. After a while, she said, "What could they do to people like us, even with Killion's files?"

He covered his face with both hands, blew into his cupped palms, and rubbed his eyebrows with his fingertips. "Theoretically," he said, "they can't do anything to you unless you were involved in something criminal like sabotage or espionage or conspiracy—but you know what they do, they just throw out a big net and see what they can haul in. Sometimes they pick up one or two genuine revolutionaries that way, but in the process a lot of ordinary people lose their jobs, their kids get ostracized at school, and all that sort of thing. The trouble is, most of these characters don't know a Communist from a Socialist."

She said, "I never even joined the Socialist Party."

"You didn't?"

"No. I think I might have, back then. But Chris thought they were a bunch of pantywaists."

"What did you join? Did you join any of the front groups?"

"I don't think so. I'm not even sure I know what you mean by 'front groups.'"

"You know, the ones they listed a few weeks ago, eleven or twelve of them."

"I haven't kept up, Joe. What were they?"

"Well, let's see—there's the American Committee for the Protection of the Foreign Born, the Council on African Affairs, the Joint Anti-Fascist Refugee Committee . . ."

"What on earth is that?"

"I don't know, but it's supposed to matter."

"And what else?"

"The Civil Rights Congress, the National Council of American-Soviet Friendship, the United May Day Committee . . . that's all I can remember at the moment."

She wanted to laugh, but she didn't. "Joe, Chris didn't like groups, and we almost never joined things. Especially things with names like that."

"Did you ever give money to organizations, or sign any petitions?"

"We never had any money. We did sign things sometimes. Peace things, mostly, and sometimes civil rights. After Chris died, I did join that one that was started in Atlanta—I think it was called SKY."

"Oh my God; that's the one."

"Why? It was perfectly harmless."

"It *was*, I know. But they claim that it got took, Maggie."

"But Joe, it's dead as a doornail, now."

"That don't make no difference, HUAC's got it on their list, and if you were on its list, you're a clay pigeon."

"Ay-y-y." She bit off a hangnail.

He saw he had her troubled, and he tried to back off. "Look, Maggie," he said, "I didn't mean to upset you; I probably blew the whole thing up too big . . ." He began to fidget, the way he had when she tried to get him to talk about Brother Frank. And she understood one thing that he was saying with his eyes. It wasn't really her connections that disturbed him (she'd done her swimming in the bayou, not the channel); it was Chris.

"Joe . . ." she began, and hesitated.

"Yeah?"

"There are some things of Chris's—two or three packages—in the barn. I'm not sure just what's in them. I glanced through, after he died, but not carefully. I guess I didn't want to face them. Do you think I should go into them now?"

He said very quickly, "Nobody knows that but you."

They were hand-washing, excommunicating words; she could hear a gavel pound on varnished wood. Nobody, nobody else, Maggie Cole; just you.

More Women
Writing in Appalachia
Other Voices to Study

Many other women writers throughout the Appalachian region are worthy of being included in this book, which could easily have been twice as large. Some of the writers have not yet published a book and others are widely recognized. This list of selected titles is in no way comprehensive; it is merely a starting point for further study. New writers are constantly emerging. The voices listed here also deserve to be heard.

Abbreviations

P   poetry
F   fiction
YA   young adult fiction
NF   nonfiction
D   drama
SR   sound recording
VR   video recording

Gail Galloway Adams (1943–) (W.Va.)

F *The Purchase of Order* (Athens: Univ. of Georgia Press, 1988), won Flannery O'Connor Award

Gail Amburgey (W.Va.)

P *We're Alright But We Ain't Special: Poems by three women from Appalachia* [Gail V. Amburgey, Mary Jane Coleman, Pauletta Hansel] (Beckley, W.Va.: Mountain Union Books, 1976)
P *Some Poems by Some Women* [Gail V. Amburgey, Alice May Holdren Oglesby, Bonni V. McKeown, Leslie Thornhill Graham, F. Evelyn Ryan, Pauletta Hansel] (Beckley, W.Va.: Quickprint Center, 1975)

COLLEEN ANDERSON (1950–) (W.VA.)

F & P Stories and poems published in *New Voices, Kestrel, Carolina Quarterly, Redbook, The Sun*

BARBARA ANGLE (MD./W.VA.)

F *Those That Mattered* (New York: Crown Publishers, 1994)
NF *Sexual Harassment in the Coal Industry: A Survey Of Women Miners* by Connie White, Barbara Angle, & Marat Moore (Oak Ridge, Tenn.: Coal Employment Project, 1981)
F *Rinker* (Washington, D.C.: Crossroads Press, 1979)

REBECCA BAILEY (1958–) (KY.)

P *A Wild Kentucky Garden: Poems & Essays* (Ashland, Ky.: Jesse Stuart Foundation, 1998)

JULIE BAKER (W.VA.)

YA *Up Molasses Mountain* (New York: Wendy Lamb Books, 2002)

LOUISE R. BAKER (1868–?) (TENN.)

F *Cis Martin, or The Furriners in the Tennessee Mountains* (1898)

SANDRA BELTON (1939–) (W. VA.)

YA *McKendree* (New York: Greenwillow Books, 2000)
YA *From Miss Ida's Porch* (New York: Four Winds Press, 1993)

MICHELLE BIOSSEAU (1955–) (KY.)

P *No Private Life* (Vanderbilt Univ. Press, 1990)

MARY BRECKINRIDGE (1881–1965)

NF *Wide Neighborhoods: A Story of the Frontier Nursing Service* (New York: Harper, 1952), memoir of its founder

JEANNE BRYNER (1951–) (W.VA./OHIO)

P *Blind Horse* (Huron, Ohio: Bottom Dog Press, 1999)
P *Breathless* (Kent, Ohio: Kent State Univ. Press, 1995)

FRANCES HODGSON BURNETT (1849–1924) (TENN./ENGLAND)

F *Louisiana* (New York: Scribner's, 1880)
NF *The One I Knew Best of All: A Memory of the Mind of a Child* (Scribner, 1893)

BETSY BYARS (1928–) (W.VA.)

YA *After the Goat Man* (New York: Viking, 1974)
YA *The Summer of Swans* (New York: Viking, 1970)

SARA CARTER (1899–1979) (VA./TENN.)

SR *In The Shadow of Clinch Mountain*, Bear Family Records, 2000
SR *Sara & Maybelle Carter*, Bear Family Records
SR *An Historic Reunion: Sara & Maybelle, the Original Carters*, Koch, 1966, 1997

WILLA CATHER (1873–1947) (W.VA.)

F *Sapphira and the Slave Girl*, 1940

GRACE CAVALIERI (1932–) (W.VA.)

P *Sit Down, Says Love* (The Argonne Hotel Press, 1999)
P *Heart on a Leash* (Red Dragon Press, 1998)
P *Pinecrest Rest Haven* (Word Works, 1998)
P *Poems: New & Selected* (Pensacola, Fla.: Vision Library Publications, 1994)

SEPTIMA P. CLARK (1898–1987) (S.C./TENN.)

NF *Echo in My Soul* (New York: Dutton, 1962), memoir of African American teacher/activist affiliated with Highlander Center in Monteagle, Tenn.

SUZANNE UNDERWOOD CLARK (1950–) (TENN.)

P *What a Light Thing, This Stone: Poems* (Abingdon, Va.: Sow's Ear Press, 1999)
P *Weather of the House* (Abingdon, Va.: Sow's Ear Press, 1994)

VERA CLEAVER (1919–) & BILL CLEAVER (N.C./FLA.)

YA *Where the Lilies Bloom* (New York: Harper & Row, 1969)

LENORE McCOMAS COBERLY (W.VA.)

F *The Handywoman Stories* (Athens, Ohio: Swallow Press/Ohio University Press, 2002)

MARY JOAN COLEMAN (W.VA.)

P *Take One Blood Red Rose* (Cambridge, Mass.: West End Press, 1978)

JENNY GALLOWAY COLLINS (1950–) (KY.)

P *A Cave and a Cracker* (Georgetown, Ky., 1996)
P *Blackberry Tea* (Pikeville, Ky., 1988)

Tess (Theresa) Collins (Ky.)

F *The Law of the Dead* (New York: Ivy Books, Ballantine, 1999)
F *The Law of Revenge* (New York: Ivy Books, Ballantine, 1997)

Geraldine Connolly (1947–) (Pa./Md.)

P *Province of Fire* (Oak Ridge, Tenn: Iris Press, 1998)
P *Food for the Winter* (Purdue Univ. Press, 1990)

Grace MacGowan Cooke (1863–1944) (Ohio/Tenn./N.J./Calif.)

F *The Power and the Glory* (New York: A.L. Burt Co, 1910, rpt. 2003)

Cornelia Cornelissen

YA *Soft Rain: A Story of the Cherokee Trail Tears* (New York: Bantam, 1998)

Rebecca Cushman (N.C.)

P *Swing Your Mountain Gal: Sketches of Life in the Southern Highlands*, with illustrations by the author (Boston & New York: Houghton Mifflin, 1934)

Jenny Davis (1953–) (Ky.)

YA *Good-Bye and Keep Cold* (Orchard/Watts, 1987)

Linda Scott DeRosier (1941–) (Ky.)

NF *Creeker: A Woman's Journey* (Lexington: Univ. Press of Kentucky, 1999), memoir of Eastern Kentucky native
NF *Songs of Life and Grace* (Lexington: Univ. Press of Kentucky, 2003)

Hazel Dickens (1935–) (Ky.)

SR *Hard-Hitting Songs for Hard-Hit People* (Rounder 0126)
SR *By the Sweat of My Brow* (Rounder 0200)
SR *It's Hard to Tell the Singer from the Song* (Rounder 0226)
SR *A Few Old Memories*, Rounder Records, 1987
SR *Hazel Dickens and Alice Gerrard*, Rounder, 1976, 1998
SR *Coal Mining Women*, Rounder, 1997
SR *Hazel Dickens & Alice Gerrard Pioneering Women of Bluegrass*, Smithsonian/Folkways, 1965, 1996
SR *Won't You Come & Sing For Me*, 1973
SR *Who's That Knocking?* [with Alice Gerrard, Chubby Wise, and others, Verve Folkways, 1966
NF "Songs: Mannington Mine Disaster and Black Lung," *Mountain Life & Work* 47 (April 1971): 10–13.
NF "As Country as I Could Sing." *Growin' Up Country*, ed. Jim Axelrod. Clintwood, Va.: Council of the Southern Mountains, 1973.

Pamela Duncan (1961–) N.C.

F *Plant Life* (New York: Delacourt, 2003)
F *Moon Women* (New York: Delacourt, 2001)

Eloise Buckner Ebbs (N.C.)

F *Carolina Mountain Breezes* (Asheville, N.C.: Miller Press, 1929)

Kelly A. Ellis (1964–) (Ky.), Affrilachian poet

NF *Womanist Conjure: Voodoo Narratives in the Fiction of Black Women Writers* (Ph.D. diss., Univ. of Kentucky, 2001)

Wilson Gage [pen name of Mary Q. Steele] (1922–1992) (Tenn.)

YA *My Stars, It's Mrs. Gaddy* (Greenwillow Books, 1991)
YA *Journey Outside* (Viking, 1969)

Joanna Galdone (Tenn.)

YA *The Tailypo: A Ghost Story* (Clarion Books, 1977)

Ellen Glasgow (1873–1945) (Va./W.Va.)

F *Vein of Iron* (New York: Harcourt, 1935)
F *Barren Ground* (Garden City, N.Y.: Doubleday, 1925)
F *The Battle-ground* (New York: Doubleday, 1902)

Doris Gove (1944–) (Tenn.)

NF *A Water Snake's Year* (New York: Atheneum, 1991)

Michelle Y. Green (1953–) (Ky.)

SR *Tell It on the Mountain: Appalachian Women Writers* (Whitesburg, Ky.: WMMT-FM, Appalshop, 1995)
YA *Willie Pearl* (Temple Hills, Md.: William Ruth & Co., 1990)

Sarah Ogan Gunning (1910–1983)

NF "My Name is Sarah Ogan Gunning," *Sing Out!* 25:2 (1976): 15–16.

Gail E. Haley (1939–) (N.C.)

YA *Mountain Jack Tales* (New York: Dutton, 1992)
YA *Jack and the Bean Tree* (New York: Crown, 1986)

Alberta Pierson Hannum (1906–1985) (Ohio/N.C./W.Va.)

NF *Look Back with Love: A Recollection of the Blue Ridge*, (New York: Vanguard, 1969), essays
F *Roseanna McCoy* (New York: H. Holt, 1947)
F *The Gods and One* (New York: Duell, Sloan and Pearce, 1941)
F *The Hills Step Lightly* (New York: Morrow, 1934)
F *Thursday April* (New York: Harper, 1931)

Vicky Hayes (Ky.)

P *Night Winds* (1976)

Jane Hicks (1952–) (Tenn.)

P Published in *Now and Then, Wind, Pine Mountain Sand & Gravel, Iron Mountain Review, Red Crow Review, Sow's Ear, Appalachian Journal, A! Magazine for Arts and Antiques,* and *Appalachian Heritage*

Helen B. Hiscoe (1919–) (Ga./W.Va.)

NF *Appalachian Passage* (Athens: Univ. of Georgia Press, 1991), memoir

Juliette Ann Holley (W.Va.)

YA *Jamie Lemme See* (Radford, Va.: Commonwealth Press, 1975)

Elizabeth Howard (1933–) (Tenn.)

P *Anemones* (Memphis: Grandmother Earth Creations, 1998)

Rebecca Dougherty Hyatt (Tenn.)

F *Marthy Lou's Kiverlid* (Morristown, Tenn.: Triangle Press, 1937; rpt. 1963), preserves Tenn. and N.C. mountain folklore and speech from around 1900 to 1910

Dot Jackson (N.C./S.C.)

NF *Keowee: The Story of the Keowee River Valley in Upstate South Carolina* (Greenville, S.C.: Michael Hembree & Dot Jackson, 1995)

Aunt Molly Jackson (1880–1960) (Ky.)

SR *Aunt Molly Jackson* (Library of Congress, 1972)
SR *The Songs and Stories of Aunt Molly Jackson* (1961)

Maggie Pogue Johnson (Va./W.Va.)

P *Virginia Dreams: Lyrics for the Idle Hour, Tales of the Time Told in Rhyme* (John M. Leonard, 1910), published online as part of the Digital Schomburg African American Women Writers of the 19th Century project providing electronic access to collections on the African Diaspora and Africa from The New York Public Library. http://digilib.nypl.org:80/dynaweb/digs/wwm9712/@Generic__BookTextView/130;pt=127

Patricia A. Johnson (Va.)

P *Stain My Days Blue* (Philadelphia: Ausdoh Press, 1999)
P *Spirit Rising* (1999)

JAN KARON (1937–) (N.C.)

F *At Home in Mitford* (Elgin, Ill.: Lion Pub, 1994), the first of the Mitford series of novels

LOU KASSEM (1931–) (TENN./VA.)

YA *Listen for Rachel* (New York: Margaret K. McElderry Books, 1986)

LORETTA LYNN (KY.)

NF *Still Woman Enough: A Memoir* (New York: Hyperion, 2002), written with Patsi Bale Cox

NF *Loretta Lynn: Coal Miner's Daughter* (New York: Warner, 1976), memoir written with George Vecsey

ALICE MACGOWAN (1858–1932)

F *Judith of the Cumberlands* (New York: Grosset & Dunlap, 1908)

SANDRA MASHBURN (1935–) (W.VA.), EDITOR OF *KANAWHA REVIEW*

P *Controlled Flight* (Alms House Press)
P *Undertow* (March Street Press)

MARGARET MCDOWELL [LITTLE] (W.VA.)

P *Dandelions Under the Snow*
P *Our Song, Too* (1974)
P *View from College Avenue* (1973)

BONNI MCKEOWN (W.VA.)

NF *Peaceful Patriot: The Story of Tom Bennett* (Charleston, W.Va.: Mountain State Press, 1980)

P *Pieces: A West Virginia Woman Looks at Love, People, and Politics* (Beckley, W.Va.: McKeown, 1978; rpt. Capon Springs, W.Va.: Partnership Foundation, 1982)

MARAT MOORE (1955–) (TENN./W.VA.)

NF *Women in the Mines: Stories of Life and Work* (New York: Twayne, 1996)

KATHLEEN MOORE MOREHOUSE (1904–2002) (N.C.)

F *Rain on the Just* (New York: Lee Furman, 1936; rpt. Southern Illinois Press, 1980)

SARAH ELIZABETH MORRISON (1833– ?)

YA *Chilhowee Boys* (New York: Crowell, 1893), wagon trip across the Blue Ridge from N.C. to Tenn. in 1811, based on family records

LOUISE [R. SANDERS] MURDOCH (KY.)

F *Almetta of Gabriel's Run* (New York: Meridian, 1917)

PHYLLIS REYNOLDS NAYLOR (MD./W.VA.)

YA *Shiloh* (New York: Atheneum, 1991), winner of the 1992 Newbury Award

VALERIE NIEMAN (W.VA.)

F *Survivors: A Novel* (Midlothian, Va.: Van Neste Books, 2000)

JUDY ODUM (1942–) (TENN.)

P *Blossom & Vine* (Oak Ridge, Tenn.: Iris Press, 1990)
F "The Killing Jar," in *A Southern Appalachian Reader*, ed. Nellie McNeil and Joyce Squibb (Boone, N.C.: Appalachian Consortium Press, 1988)

LISA J. PARKER (1972–) (VA.)

P Published in *Parnassus: Poetry in Review*, *Appalachian Journal*, *PoetLore*, *Now & Then*, recipient of the 1996 Randall Jarrell Prize in Poetry, 1997 Academy of Poets Prize, 1999 Allen Tate Memorial Prize in Poetry

DOLLY PARTON (TENN.)

NF *Dolly: My Life and Other Unfinished Business* (New York: HarperCollins, 1994)
YA *Coat of Many Colors* (New York: HarperCollins, 1994)

EDWINA D. PENDARVIS (1944–) (W.VA.)

P *Like the Mountains of China* (Blair Mountain Press, 2003)
P *Joyride* in *Human Landscapes: Three Books of Poems* (Huron, Ohio: Bottom Dog Press, 1997)
P *Coruscations*, winner of the 1995 West Virginia Writers' Competition

MARIA LOUISE POOL (1841–1898) (N.C.)

F *Against Human Nature* (New York: Harper, 1895), set partly in Asheville, N.C.

BONNIE PROUDFOOT (W.VA.)

F "Watching Baseball, Thinking About Men," best short story of 1995 in *The Best of West Virginia Writers*
F "Goshen Road," M.A. Thesis, West Virginia Univ., 1994

CAROLYN REEDER (1937–) (VA.)

YA *Grandpa's Mountain* (New York: Macmillan, 1991)
YA *Shades of Gray* (New York: Macmillan, 1989)

Rita Sizemore Riddle (1941–) (Va.)

P *Aluminum Balloons* (Blacksburg, Va.: Pocahontas Press, 1996)

F *Pieces for Emma* (Radford, Va.: Radford University College of Arts and Sciences, 1994)

P *Soot and Sunshine* (Radford, Va.: Radford University College of Arts and Sciences, 1993)

Charlotte T. Ross (N.C.)

VR / D *From My Grandmother's Mother Unto Me* (video, Cinema Guild, 1990), with Clarinda Ross-Clark

NF *Bibliography of Southern Appalachia* (Boone, N.C.: Appalachian Consortium Press, 1976)

Gwyn Hyman Rubio (Ga./Ky.)

F *Icy Sparks* (New York: Penguin, 1998)

Brenda A. Saylor (Ky.)

VR *Mountain Shadow: Four Appalachian Artists* (Cincinnati: TV Image, 1997), videotape by Dorothy Weil and Jane Goetzman

P *Poems of My People* (Cincinnati : Riverside Books, 1993)

Alvina Seckar (W.Va./Ohio/Pa.)

YA *Zuska of the Burning Hills* (New York: Oxford Univ. Press, 1952), daughter of immigrant Czech coal miners

Beth Tashery Shannon (Ky./Cal.)

F short fiction in *Chicago Review*

F "Bons," in *The Pushcart Prize, III: Best of the Small Presses*, ed. Bill Henderson (Yonkers, N.Y.: Pushcart Press, 1978)

Susan Sheppard (1949–) (W.Va.)

P *From the House of Heaven and Earth: Poems* (http://home.wirefire.com/pooka, 1991)

NF *The Phoenix Cards* (Destiny Books, 1990)

P *Book of Shadows, Book of Dreams* (Westfield, N.J.: Merging Media, 1979)

Vivian Shipley (Ky./Tenn./Conn.)

P *Fair Haven* (Negative Capability Press, 2000)

P *Crazy Quilt* (Hanover Press, 1999)

P *How Many Stones?* (Univ. of South Carolina Press, 1998)

P *Devil's Lane* (Negative Capability Press, 1996)

P *Poems Out of Harlan County* (Ithaca House, 1989)

P *Jack Tales* (Greenfield Review Press, 1982)

PATRICIA SHIRLEY (1939–) (TENN.)

P *Mary Pearl Kline* (Big Timber, Mont.: Seven Buffaloes Press, 1990)
F *Dear Flora Mae and Other Stories* (Big Timber, Mont.: Seven Buffaloes Press, 1987)
P *Pearl* (Big Timber, Mont.: Seven Buffaloes Press, 1986)

BETTY [NANCE] SMITH (1926–) (N.C.)

SR *With You Again* (Hot Springs, N.C.: Bluff Mountain Music, 2002)
NF *Jane Hicks Gentry: A Singer Among Singers* (Lexington: Univ. Press of Kentucky, 1998)
SR *Both Sides: Then and Now* (Bluff Mountain Music, 1994)
SR *A Bluff Mountain Christmas* (Bluff Mountain Music, 1988)
SR *Psaltry Concert* (Bluff Mountain Music, 1983)
SR *For My Friends of Song* (June Appal Records, 1977)
SR *Betty Smith: Songs Traditionally Sung in North Carolina* (Folk Legacy Records, 1975)

DEBORAH SMITH (GA.)

F *On Bear Moutain: A Novel* (New York: Little, Brown, 2001)

DORIS BUCHANAN SMITH (1934–2002) (GA.)

YA *Return to Bitter Creek* (New York: Viking Kestrel, 1986)
YA *The First Hard Times* (New York: Viking, 1983), ALA Notable Book
YA *Last Was Lloyd* (New York: Viking, 1981), School Library Journal Best Book of the Year
YA *A Taste of Blackberries* (1973), Georgia Children's Book Award

LILLIAN SMITH (1897–1966) (GA.)

F *Strange Fruit* (New York: Reynal & Hitchcock, 1944)

ANNA EGAN SMUCKER (W.VA.)

NF *History of West Virginia* (West Virginia Humanities Council, 1997), written for new adult readers
F *No Star Nights*, illus. Steve Johnson (New York: Knopf, 1989), winner of the 1990 International Reading Association Children's Book Award

DEBORAH HALE SPEARS (KY./OHIO)

P *Between Comets*
P *Rain Dancers, Earth Blankets* (chapbook, 1988)
P *Spring Passages, Unguided Tours*

ANNE BETHEL SPENCER (1882–1975) (W.VA./VA.)

P *Time's Unfolding Garden: Anne Spencer's Life and Poetry*, ed. J. Lee Greene (Baton Rouge: LSU Press, 1977)

MARY JO STEPHENS (KY./OHIO)

YA *Witch of the Cumberlands* (Boston: Houghton Mifflin, 1974)
YA *Moccasin Tracks* (New York: Dodd Mead, 1958)

JULIA MONTGOMERY STREET (1898–) (N.C.)

F *Fiddler's Fancy* (Chicago: Follett, 1955)

JEAN THOMAS (1881–1982) (KY.)

NF *Blue Ridge Country* (New York: Duell, Sloan & Pearce, 1942)
NF *Ballad Makin' in the Mountains of Kentucky* (New York: H. Holt, 1939; rpt. New York: Oak Publications, 1964)
NF *The Traipsin' Woman* (New York: Dutton, 1933)
NF *Devil's Ditties: Being Stories of the Kentucky Mountain People* (Chicago: W.W. Hatfield, 1931; rpt. Detroit: Gale Research, 1976)

ALLISON THORPE (KY.)

P *Thoughts While Swinging a Wild Child in a Green Mesh Hammock: Poems of Rebirth from the Bootheels of Appalachia* (London, Ky.: Janze Publications, 1991), with a foreword by Jim Wayne Miller

JUANITA TOBIN (1915–) (N.C.)

P & F *License My Roving Hands: Poems and Stories* (Boone, N.C.: Parkway Publishers, 2000)
P & F *Ransom Street Quartet: Poems and Stories* (Boone, N.C.: Parkway Publishers, 1995)
P *Four Contemporary Poets: Sharon Olds, Eleanor Wilner, Maddie Gomez, Juanita Tobin* (Flushing, N.Y.: La Vida Press, 1984)

SUSAN O'DELL UNDERWOOD (1962–) (TENN.)

F *Genesis Road* (unpublished novel-in-progress)
P *Light and Sound* (M.F.A. thesis, UNC-Greensboro, 1987)

CHERYL WARE (W.VA.)

YA *Flea Circus Summer* (New York: Orchard, 1997), the first book in the Venola Mae series, all set in West Virginia

EMMY WEST & CHRISTINE GOVAN (TENN.)

F *Danger Downriver* (New York: Viking, 1972)

RUTH WHITE (1942–) (VA.)

YA *Belle Prater's Boy* (New York: Farrar, 1996) Newberry Honor Book
YA *Weeping Willow* (New York: Farrar, 1992) ALA Best Book for Young Adults
YA *Sweet Creek Holler* (New York: Farrar, 1988)

CRYSTAL WILKINSON (1962–) (KY.)

F *Water Street* (London: Toby Press, 2002)
F *Blackberries, Blackberries* (London: Toby Press, 2000)

LANA WITT (KY.)

F *The Heart of a Thirsty Woman* (New York: Scribner, 1999)
F *Slow Dancing on Dinosaur Bones* (New York: Scribner, 1996)

CONSTANCE FENIMORE WOOLSON (1840–1894) (OHIO/EUROPE)

F *For the Major, A Novelette* (New York: Harper, 1883), set in western N.C. in 1860s

KRISTIN CAMITTA ZIMET (TENN./VA.)

P *Take in My Arms the Dark: Poems* (Abingdon, Va.: Sow's Ear Press, 1999)

ISABEL ZUBER (N.C.)

F *Salt* (New York: Picador, 2002)
P *Oriflamb* (Asheville: Groves Print, N.C. Writers Network, 1987)

A SELECTED BIBLIOGRAPHY

Alexander, Maxine, ed. *Speaking for Ourselves: Women of the South*. New York: Pantheon Books, 1977.

Askins, Donald, and David Morris, eds. *New Ground*. Co-published by Southern Appalachia Writers' Co-operative and *Mountain Review*, 1977.

Baber, Bob Henry, George Ella Lyon, and Gurney Norman, eds. *Old Wounds, New Words: Poems from the Appalachian Poetry Project*. Ashland, KY: Jesse Stuart Foundation, 1994.

Baber, Bob Henry and Jim Webb, eds. *Mucked*. Williamson, WV: Southern Appalachian Writers Co-op / Herperus Press, 1978.

Bain, Robert, Joseph M. Flora, and Louis D. Rubin Jr., eds. *Southern Writers: A Biographical Dictionary*. Baton Rouge: Louisiana State University Press, 1979.

Beaver, Patricia D., guest editor. "Special Issue: Appalachia and the South: Place, Gender, Pedagogy." *National Women's Studies Association Journal* 11.3 (fall 1999).

Best, Bill, ed. *One Hundred Years of Appalachian Visions, 1897-1996*. Berea, KY: Appalachian Imprints, 1997. 2nd ed., 2000.

Bickley, Ancella R., and Lynda Ann Ewen, eds. *Memphis Tennessee Garrison: The Remarkable Story of a Black Appalachian Woman*. Athens: Ohio University Press, 2001.

Billings, Dwight B., Gurney Norman, and Katherine Ledford, eds. *Confronting Appalachian Stereotypes: Back Talk from an American Region*. Foreword by Ronald D. Eller. Lexington, KY: University Press of Kentucky, 1999.

Campbell, Diana Kaye. "'Mutual Answerability': Aesthetics, Ethics, Transgredients from Mikhal Bakhtin to Lee Smith to Leslie Marmon Silko." Ph.D. Diss. University of North Carolina, Greensboro. 1999. [Chapter 2 focuses on Lee Smith's *The Devil's Dream*.]

Catching the Crow: a Collection of the 1982 Winning Entries in the West Virginia Writers' Annual Competition [1982]

Chaffin, Lillie D., Glenn O. Carey, and Harry N. Brown, eds. *God's Plenty: Modern Kentucky Writers, a Collection of Short Fiction, Poetry, Essays, by 56 Modern Kentucky Writers*. Greenwood, FL: Penkevill Publishing Co., 1991.

Collett, Dexter. *Bibliography of Theses and Dissertations Pertaining to Southern Appalachian Mountain Literature, 1912-1991*. Berea, KY: Appalachian Imprints, 1994.

Comer, Melissa. "Rob, Mary Call, and Me: The Search for Self in Appalachian Literature." *New Advocate: For Those Involved with Young People and Their Literature* 12 (spring 1999), 141-53.

Comstock, Jim, ed. *Stories and Verse of West Virginia, [Vol.] II.* Richwood, W.V.: Jim Comstock, 1974. [Extends the work of Ella May Turner, an anthology of West Virginia writing since 1935]

Davidson, Cathy N., and Linda Wagner-Martin, eds. *The Oxford Companion to Women's Writing in the United States.* New York: Oxford University Press, 1995.

DeNobriga, Kathie, and Valetta Anderson, eds. *Alternate Roots: Plays from the Southern Theater.* Portsmouth, NH: Heinemann, 1994.

Dyer, Joyce, ed. *Bloodroot: Reflections on Place by Appalachian Women Writers.* Lexington, KY: University Press of Kentucky, 1998.

Elliott, Sarah E. "Dead Bodies, Burned Letters, and Burial Grounds: Negotiating Place Through Storytelling in Contemporary Southern Fiction." Ph.D. Diss. Northern Illinois University, 1998. [Discusses Lewis Nordan, Lee Smith, and Clyde Edgerton. Chapter 2 focuses on Lee Smith's use of folklore. Includes interview with Lee Smith.]

Farr, Sidney Saylor. *Appalachian Women: An Annotated Bibliography.* Lexington, KY: University Press of Kentucky, 1981.

———. "Appalachian Women in Literature." *Appalachian Heritage* 9:3 (summer 1981), 10-18.

Ferguson, Carolyn Sue, ed. *The Best of West Virginia Writers: A Selection of Winning Entries from Five Years—1991, 1992, 1993, 1994, 1995—of the West Virginia Writers, Inc. Annual Awards Competition.* Charleston, WV: Mountain State Press, 1997.

Francisco, Edward, Robert Vaughan, Linda Francisco, eds. *The South in Perspective: An Anthology of Southern Literature.* Upper Saddle River, NJ: Prentice Hall, 2001.

Ganim, Carole. "Herself: Woman and Place in Appalachian Literature." *Appalachian Journal* 13:3 (spring 1986), 258-74.

Gantt, Patricia Miller. "'Appalachia in Context': Wilma Dykeman's Search for the Souths." Ph.D. Diss. University of North Carolina, Chapel Hill, 1993.

Giles, Ronald K., ed. *In Place: A Collection of Appalachian Writers.* Johnson City, TN: Center for Appalachian Studies and Services, 1988.

Guinan, Edward, ed. *Redemption Denied.* Washington, D.C.: Appalachian Documentation (ADOC), 1976. [An anthology of oral histories, poems, essays. A note on the copyright page explains that ADOC "was created to present the authentic voices of the mountain people to a broader, mainly urban, culture."]

Haddix, Cecille, ed. *Who Speaks for Appalachia? Prose, Poetry, and Songs from the Mountain Heritage.* New York: Washington Square Press, 1975.

"Granny Hager, In Memory and Honor." *Mountain Life and Work* 51 : 4 (April 1975).

Hamm, Mary Margo. *Appalachian Women: An Annotated Bibliography,* 1994.

Harrison, Elizabeth J. *Female Pastoral: Women Writers Re-Visioning the American South.* Knoxville: University of Tennessee Press, 1991.

Higgs, Robert J., and Ambrose N. Manning, eds. *Voices from the Hills: Selected Readings of Southern Appalachia.* New York: Frederick Unger Publishing, and Boone, NC: Appalachian Consortium Press, 1975.

Higgs, Robert J., Ambrose Manning, and Jim Wayne Miller, eds. *Appalachia Inside Out: A Sequel to Voices from the Hills.* Vol. 1: *Conflict and Change.* Vol. 2: *Culture and Custom.* Knoxville, TN: University of Tennessee Press, 1995.

Hinsdale, Mary Ann, Helen M. Lewis, and S. Maxine Waller. *It Comes from the People: Community Development and Local Theology.* Philadelphia: Temple University Press, 1995.

Ivie, Doris, and Leslie M. LaChance, eds. *Breathing the Same Air: An East Tennessee Anthology.* Knoxville, TN: Celtic Cat Publishing and The Knoxville Writers' Guild, 2001.

Joyner, Nancy Carol. "Appalachian Women's Writings and Identity Theories." *Gender, Race, and Identity.* Ed. Craig Barrow, et. al. Chattanooga: Southern Humanities Press, 1993. 223-29.

Kahn, Kathy. *Hillbilly Women.* New York: Avon, 1974.

Kendrick, Leatha, and George Ella Lyon, eds. *Crossing Troublesome: 25 Years of the Appalachian Writers Workshop.* Preface by Robert Morgan. Nicholasville, KY: Wind Publications, 2002.

Lanier, Parks, Jr., ed. *The Poetics of Appalachian Space.* Knoxville, TN: University of Tennessee Press, 1991.

Lewis, Helen, and Suzanna O'Donnell, eds. *Telling Our Stories, Sharing Our Lives.* Ivanhoe: Ivanhoe Civic League, 1990.

Lord, Sharon B., and Carolyn Patton-Crowder. *Appalachian Women: A Learning/ Teaching Guide.* Newton: Education Development Center, 1979.

Lyon, George Ella, Jim Wayne Miller, and Gurney Norman, eds. *A Gathering at the Forks.* Wise, VA: Vision Books, 1993.

MAW: A Magazine of Appalachian Women. Huntington, WV, 1977.

McNeil, Nellie, and Joyce Squibb, eds. *A Southern Appalachian Reader.* Boone, NC: Appalachian Consortium Press, 1988.

Miller, Danny L. "The Mountain Woman in Fact and Fiction of the Early Twentieth Century." *Appalachian Heritage* Part 1, 6:3 (summer 1978), 48-55. Part 2, 6:4 (fall 1978), 15-21. Part 3, 7:1 (winter 1979), 55-72.

———. *Wingless Flights: Appalachian Women in Fiction.* Bowling Green, OH: Bowling Green State University Popular Press, 1996.

Miller, Jim Wayne. "Appalachian Literature." *Appalachian Journal* 5:1 (autumn 1977), 82-91.

———. "A People Waking Up: Appalachian Literature Since 1960." *The Cratis Williams Symposium Proceedings: A Memorial and Examination of the State of Regional Studies in Appalachia.* Boone: Appalachian Consortium Press, 1990.

Miller, Jim Wayne, ed. *I Have a Place.* Pippa Passes, KY: Alice Lloyd College, 1981. [A literary anthology with many selections from *Appalachian Heritage.*]

Mitchell, Felicia, ed. *Her Words: Diverse Voices in Contemporary Appalachian Women's Poetry.* Knoxville: University of Tennessee Press, 2002.

Munn, Robert F. *The Southern Appalachians: A Bibliography and Guide to the Studies.* WVU Library, 1961.

North Carolina Fiction 1734-1957: An Annotated Bibliography. Prepared by the Joint Committee on N.C. Literature and Bibliography of the N.C. English Teachers Association and the N.C. Library Association. UNC Library Studies, No. 2 (1958).

Norris, Randall, and Jean-Phillipe Cypres. *Women of Coal.* Lexington, KY: University Press of Kentucky, 1996.

And Now the Magpie: A Selection of Winning Entries from Four Years—1983, 1984, 1985, 1986—of the West Virginia Writers, Inc. Annual Writing Awards Competition. Charleston, WV: Mountain State Press, 1987.

Oakes, Elizabeth, and Jane Olmsted, eds. *Writing Who We Are: Poems by Kentucky Feminists.* Bowling Green: Western Kentucky University, 2000.

Pearlman, Mickey, ed. *American Women Writing Fiction: Memory, Identity, Family, Space.* Lexington, KY: University Press of Kentucky, 1989.

Pennington, Joy, ed. *Selected Kentucky Literature.* Danbury, CT: Archer Editions Press, 1980.

Perry, Carolyn, and Mary Louise Weaks, eds. *The History of Southern Women's Literature.* Baton Rouge: Louisiana State University, 2002.

Quillen, Rita. "Modern and Contemporary Mountain Poetry." *Appalachian Journal* 13:1 (fall 1985), 51-77.

Robison, Lori. "The Re-Construction of Local Color: Writing Region and Race, 1865-1896 (Black Studies)." Ph.D. Diss. Indiana University, 1995. [Chapter 3 discusses Mary Murfree's *In the Tennessee Mountains* in the context of Reconstruction politics.]

Ross, Charlotte. *Bibliography of Southern Appalachia.* Boone, NC: Appalachian Consortium Press, 1976.

Shorb, Glenda Norman. "Identity within Nature: Contemporary Women and Their Fictions of Appalachia." M.A. Thesis. Memphis State University, 1987.

Smith, Barbara, and Kirk Judd. *Wild Sweet Notes: Fifty Years of West Virginia Poetry, 1950-1999.* Huntington, WV: Publishers Place, 2000.

Summerlin, Donna Jan. "A Portrait of the Woman as Artist: Woman's Struggle for Artistic Expression in the Fiction of Six Appalachian Women Writers." Ph.D. Diss. University of Tennessee, Knoxville, 1995. [Discusses writings of Elizabeth Madox Roberts, Olive Tilford Dargan, Harriette Arnow, Mary Lee Settle, Lee Smith, and Denise Giardina.]

Tickle, Phyllis, and Alice Swanson, eds. *Homeworks: A Book of Tennessee Writers.* Knoxville, TN: University of Tennessee and the Tennessee Arts Commission, 1996.

Turner, Ella Mae, comp. & ed. *Stories and Verse of West Virginia.* [Vol. 1, copyright 1923] Richwood, WV: Jim Comstock, 1974.

Walser, Richard, assisted by E.T. Malone Jr. *Literary North Carolina, A Historical Survey, Revised and Enlarged.* Raleigh, NC: Division of Archives and History, NC Department of Cultural Resources, 1986.

Ward, William S. *A Literary History of Kentucky*, with a Foreword by Thomas D. Clark. Knoxville, TN: University of Tennessee Press, 1988.

Williams, Cratis. "Appalachia in Fiction." *Appalachian Heritage* 4.4 (fall 1976), 45-56.

———. "The Southern Mountaineer in Fact and Fiction." Ph.D. Diss. New York University, 1961. Abridged by Martha Pipes in *Appalachian Journal* Part 1, 3:1 (autumn 1975), 8-61. Part 2, 3:2 (Winter 1976), 100–162. Part 3, 3:3 (spring 1976), 186-261. Part 4, 3:4 (summer 1976), 334–92.

Williamson, J.W., and Edwin T. Arnold, eds. *Interviewing Appalachia: The Appalachian Journal Interviews, 1978-1992*. Knoxville, TN: University of Tennessee Press, 1994.

Young, Thomas Daniel. *Tennessee Writers*. Knoxville: University of Tennessee Press, 1981.

Index of Titles and Authors

Permissions

Sheila Kay Adams

"The Easter Frock" from *Come Go Home With Me: Stories By Sheila Kay Adams* © 1995 by the University of North Carolina Press, used by permission of the publisher and the author.

Dorothy Allison

Excerpt from *Bastard Out of Carolina* reprinted with permission from Frances Goldin Literary Agency, Inc.

Lisa Alther

Excerpt from *Five Minutes in Heaven*, Dutton, Penguin Books, 1995, reprinted with permission from the author.

Maggie Anderson

"Ontological," "Long Story," and "Sonnet for Her Labor" from *Windfall* © 2000, reprinted by permission of the University of Pittsburgh Press. "A Place With Promise" from *A Space Filled with Moving* © 1992, reprinted by permission of the University of Pittsburgh Press.

Harriette Simpson Arnow

Excerpt from *Hunter's Horn*, Michigan State University Press, 1997, reprinted with permission from Michigan State University Press, Thomas Arnow, and Marcella Arnow. "The Old Boot" from *Seedtime on the Cumberland,* University of Nebraska Press, 1995, reprinted with permission from Thomas Arnow and Marcella Arnow. "The First Ride," *Appalachian Heritage*, (fall 1989), reprinted with permission from *Appalachian Heritage,* Thomas Arnow, and Marcella Arnow.

Sylvia Trent Auxier

"Neighbors," "When Grandmother Wept," "Cicada's Song," and "Someday in a Wood" from *With Thorn and Stone*, Hilltop Editions, Pikeville College Press, 1968, and "The Stair" from *Love-Vine*, The Story Book Press, 1953, used with permission from Michael T. Auxier.

MARILOU AWIAKTA

Excerpts from *Selu: Seeking the Corn Mother's Wisdom,* Fulcrum Publishing, 1993, reprinted with permission from Fulcrum Publishing, Inc. Excerpts from *Abiding Appalachia: Where Mountain and Atom Meet,* St. Luke's Press, 1978, reprinted with permission from the author, originally published by St. Luke's Press, 1978. Quoted from eighth edition, Iris Press, 1995.

ARTIE ANN BATES

"Belinda, Our Tremendous Gift" from *Appalachian Heritage*, vol. 19, no. 2, reprinted with permission from the author and *Appalachian Heritage.*

SUE ELLEN BRIDGERS

Excerpt from *Sara Will,* Harper & Row, 1985, reprinted with permission from the author.

FLORENCE COPE BUSH

Excerpt from *Dorie, Woman of the Mountains,* the University of Tennessee Press, 1992, reprinted with permission from the University of Tennessee Press.

KATHRYN STRIPLING BYER

"Wildwood Flower," "Bittersweet," "Lineage," and "Easter" from *Wildwood Flower,* Louisiana State University Press, 1992; and "Mountain Time" from *Black Shawl,* Louisiana State University Press, 1998, reprinted with permission from Louisiana State University Press and with permission of the author.

CANDIE CARAWAN

Excerpts from *Sing for Freedom: The Story of the Civil Rights Movement Through Its Songs,* Sing Out Corp., 1990, reprinted with permission from Guy and Candie Carawan.

JO CARSON

Excerpts from *Stories I Ain't Told Nobody Yet: Selections from the People Pieces,* Orchard Books, 1989, reprinted with permission from the author. "Maybe" from *The Last of the "Waltz Across Texas" and Other Stories,* Gnomon Press, 1993, reprinted with permission from Gnomon Press and the author. Excerpt from *Daytrips,* Dramatists Play Service, Inc., 1991, reprinted with permission from the author.

REBECCA CAUDILL

Excerpt from *My Appalachia,* Holt, Rinehart, and Winston, 1966, reprinted with permission from Rebecca Jean Baker.

LILLIE D. CHAFFIN

"The Glad Gardener" from *Appalachian Heritage,* vol. 15, no. 3 (summer 1987) reprinted with permission of *Appalachian Heritage* and Thomas R. Chaffin; and "Second Christmas," "Spending the Night," and "Discipline" from *8th Day, 13th Moon,* Hilltop Editions, Pikeville College Press, 1974, reprinted with permission from Thomas R. Chaffin.

LOLETTA CLOUSE

Excerpt from *Wilder,* Rutledge Hill Press, 1990, reprinted with permission from the author.

LISA COFFMAN

"Maps," "In Envy of Migration," and "About the Pelvis" from *Likely,* Kent State University Press, 1996; and "Tick" from *Meridian* (fall 2000), reprinted with permission from *Meridian* and the author.

AMY TIPTON CORTNER

"The Hillbilly Vampire," "The Vampire Ethnographer," and "No Minority" from *The Hillbilly Vampire,* Rowan Mountain Press, 1990, reprinted with permission from the author.

LOU V.P. CRABTREE

"Homer-Snake" from *Sweet Hollow,* Louisiana State University Press, 1984; and "Sports Widow" and "Sister" from *The River Hills & Beyond,* Sow's Ear Press, 1998, reprinted with permission of the author.

DORIS DIOSA DAVENPORT

"Country" from *Soque Street Poems,* Sautee-Nacoochee Community Association, 1995; "for Dr. Josefina Garcia & the 'Tissue Committee'" from *voodoo chile: slight return,* Soque Street Press, 1991; and "zora neale" from *eat thunder & drink rain,* Soque Street Press, 1982, reprinted with permission from the author.

ANN DEAGON

"Giving the Sun," "The Hole," and "Twins" from *Women and Children First,* Iron Mountain Press, 1976; "Poetics South" and "In a Time of Drought" from *Poetics South,* John F. Blair, 1974; and *Broadside* reprinted with permission from the author.

ANGELYN DEBORD

Excerpt from *Praise House,* Urban Bush Women, 1991, reprinted with permission from the author.

Nikki Giovanni

"Griots" from *Racism 101* © 1994, "Knoxville, Tennessee," "Revolutionary Dreams," and " A Poem Off Center" from *The Selected Poems of Nikki Giovanni* © 1996, reprinted by permission of HarperCollins Publishers, Inc., and the author.

Gail Godwin

Excerpt from *A Southern Family*, Morrow, 1987, reprinted with permission of the author.

Connie Jordan Green

Excerpt from *The War at Home,* Macmillan, Margaret K. McElderry Books, 1989, reprinted with permission from the author.

Virginia Hamilton

Excerpt from *M.C. Higgins, the Great*, Macmillan, 1974, reprinted by permission from Arnold Adoff.

Pauletta Hansel

"To her mother, lying in state," from *Appalachian Journal* (autumn 1982); and "Writing Lessons (I.)," "She," and "Writing Lessons (II.)" from *Divining,* WovenWord Press, 2001, reprinted with permission from the author.

Mildred Haun

"The Hawk's Done Gone" from *The Hawk's Done Gone and Other Stories*, Vanderbilt University Press, 1985, reprinted with permission from Vanderbilt University Press.

Ellesa Clay High

Excerpt from *Past Titan Rock,* University Press of Kentucky, 1984, reprinted with permission from the author.

Mary Bozeman Hodges

"Ms. Ida Mae" from *Tough Customers and Other Stories,* Jesse Stuart Foundation, 1999, reprinted with permission from the Jesse Stuart Foundation and the author.

Gloria Houston

Excerpt from *My Great-Aunt Arizona,* HarperCollins Publishers, 1992, reprinted with permission from HarperCollins Publishers and the author.

LEE HOWARD

"Momma's Letter" and "The Last Unmined Vein" from *The Last Unmined Vein,* Anemone Press, 1980, reprinted with permission from the author.

JANE WILSON JOYCE

"Life and Art in East Tennessee" from *Old Wounds, New Words: Poems from the Appalachian Poetry Project,* Jesse Stuart Foundation, 1994; and "Hooked Album Quilt, 1870" from *The Quilt Poems,* Gnomon Press, 1992, reprinted with permission from the publishers and the author.

MAY JUSTUS

"Weather Rhymes" from *The Complete Peddler's Pack,* the University of Tennessee Press, 1967, reprinted with permission from the University of Tennessee Press.

LEATHA KENDRICK

"The Familiar Level" and "Refusing a Spinal" from *Heartcake: Poems,* Sow's Ear Press, 2000, reprinted with permission from Sow's Ear Press and the author.

BARBARA KINGSOLVER

Excerpt from *The Bean Trees* © 1988, reprinted by permission of HarperCollins Publishers, Inc. and the author. Excerpt from *Prodigal Summer* © 2000, reprinted by permission of HarperCollins Publishers, Inc., and the author.

LISA KOGER

Excerpt from "Extended Learning," *Farlanburg Stories,* Norton, 1990, reprinted with permission from the author.

CATHERINE LANDIS

"On My Way to the Rest of My Life," Chapter 1, from *Some Days There's Pie* © 2002, reprinted by permission of St. Martin's Press, LLC., and the author.

LILY MAY LEDFORD

Excerpt from *Coon Creek Girl,* Berea College Appalachian Center, 1980, reprinted with permission from Cari Norris.

GEORGE ELLA LYON

Excerpt from *With a Hammer for My Heart,* DK Publishing, 1997; and "where I'm from," "Rings," "Salvation," and "Growing Light" from *where i'm from: where poems come from,* Absey & Co., 1999, reprinted with permission from the author.

Linda Parsons Marion

"Good Luck Charm," "Welcome to the Other Side," "To My Daughter Going Off to College," and "Mulberries" from *Home Fires,* Sow's Ear Press, 1997, reprinted with permission from Sow's Ear Press and the author.

Catherine Marshall

Excerpt from *Christy* © 1967 by Catherine Marshall LeSourd, © 1995, 2001 by Marshall-LeSourd L.L.C., published by Chosen Books, a division of Baker Book House Company. Used with permission. All rights reserved.

Belinda Ann Mason

The Gifts of the Spirit from *Appalachian Heritage,* Vol. 16, nos. 2 & 3 (spring/summer 1988), reprinted with permission from *Appalachian Heritage,* Ron Short (Roadside Theater), and Stephen Carden.

Kathy L. May

"Ascension," "Saved," and "Rain" from *Door to the River,* The Panhandler Poetry Chapbook Number 5, (spring 1992), reprinted with permission from the author.

Truda Williams McCoy

Excerpt from *The McCoys: Their Story as Told to the Author by Eye Witnesses and Descendents,* Preservation Council Press of the Preservation Council of Pike County, Inc., 1976, reprinted with permission from Paul R. McCoy.

Sharyn McCrumb

Excerpt from *The Songcatcher* © 2001, Dutton, a division of Penguin Putnam, Inc., used by permission of the author.

Jeanne McDonald

Excerpt from "Up the Hill Toward Home" *Breathing the Same Air: An East Tennessee Anthology,* Celtic Cat Publishing and the Knoxville Writers' Guild, 2001, reprinted with permission from Celtic Cat Publishing, the Knoxville Writers' Guild and the author.

Karen Salyer McElmurray

Excerpt from *Mother of the Disappeared: An Appalachian Birth Mother's Journey,* Hill Street Press, 2002, reprinted with permission from Hill Street Press and the author.

LLEWELLYN MCKERNAN

"Many Waters" and "For My Grandmother Who Knows How" from *Many Waters: Poems from West Virginia,* Mellen Poetry Press, 1993; and "Music," "Mother Milking," and "The Hollow" from *Short and Simple Annals,* Perfect Printing, 1983, reprinted with permission from the author.

IRENE MCKINNEY

"Twilight in West Virginia: Six O'Clock Mine Report," "Deep Mining," "Sunday Morning, 1950," "The Only Portrait of Emily Dickenson," and "Visiting My Gravesite: Talbott Churchyard, West Virginia" from *Six O'Clock Mine Report,* University of Pittsburgh Press, 1989, reprinted with permission from the author.

LOUISE MCNEILL

"The Other Woman," *Appalachian Heritage* (fall 1985), reprinted with permission from *Appalachian Heritage;* "Aubade to Fear (Heavy with Child)," "Hill Daughter," and "Arrow Grasses by Greenbrier River" *Hill Daughter: New & Selected Poems* © 1991, by Louise McNeill, published by University of Pittsburgh Press; and excerpt from "A Patch of Earth" from *The Milkweed Ladies* © 1988, by University of Pittsburgh Press, reprinted by permission of the Universtiy of Pittsburgh Press.

JANE MERCHANT

"Lanterns and Lamps," copyright renewal © 1980 Elizabeth Merchant, "First Plowing in the Hills," copyright renewal © 1979 Elizabeth Merchant, reprinted from *The Greatest of These* by permission of Abingdon Press.

HEATHER ROSS MILLER

Excerpt from *The Edge of the Woods,* Atheneum, 1964; "Breadstuff" from *Hard Evidence,* University of Missouri Press, 1990; and "Seventh Grades" from *Friends and Assassins,* University of Missouri Press, 1993, reprinted with permission from the author.

JANICE TOWNLEY MOORE

"All Those Nights" from *Southern Humanities Review,* Vol. 14, no. 2 (spring 1982); "The Way Back" from *Negative Capability,* Vol. 4, no. 4 (fall 1984); and "Under the Earth" from *Southern Humanities Review,* Vol. 19, no. 2 (spring 1985), reprinted with permission from the author.

MARIJO MOORE

"Solidarity in the Night," "Ahlawe Usv' Tsigesvgi," and "Story is a Woman" from *Spirit Voices of Bones: Poetry,* rENEGADE pLANETS pUBLISHING, 1997; and "Rumors" from *red woman with backward eyes,* rENEGADE pLANETS pUBLISHING, 2001, reprinted with permission from the author.

Elaine Fowler Palencia

"Briers" from *Brier Country: Stories from Blue Valley,* University of Missouri Press, 2000, reprinted with permission from the author.

Jayne Anne Phillips

Excerpt from *Motherkind,* Alfred A. Knopf, 2000; and "The House At Night" from *Machine Dreams,* Washington Square Press, 1984, reprinted with permission from the author.

Lynn Powell

"Nativity," "Echocardiogram," and "The Calling" from *Old and New Testaments* © 1995, reprinted by permission of the University of Wisconsin Press and the author.

Barbara Presnell

"In the Kitchen We String Beans," "Clarissa and the Second Coming," "When You Lose a Child," and "Snake Dreams" from *Snake Dreams,* Nightshade Press, 1994, reprinted with permission from the author.

Rita Sims Quillen

"July 18, 1966," "Woman Writer," and "I Used To Be a Teacup" from *Counting the Sums,* Sow's Ear Press, 1995; "Discovered" from *October Dusk,* Seven Buffaloes Press, 1987; and "How Do You Remember Him?" from *Appalachian Journal* (summer 1997), reprinted with permission from Sow's Ear Press, Seven Buffaloes Press and the author.

Jean Ritchie

Excerpt from *Singing Family of the Cumberlands,* University Press of Kentucky, 1955, reprinted with permission from the author.

Cynthia Rylant

Excerpt from *Missing May,* published by Orchard Books, an imprint of Scholastic, Inc., copyright © 1992 by Cynthia Rylant. Reprinted with permission.

Bettie Sellers

"Liza's Monday," "Pink," and "Mornings, Sheba Combs Her Hair," from *Liza's Monday and Other Poems,* Appalachian Consortium Press, 1986; and "Morning of the Red-Tailed Hawk," "All On A Summer's Afternoon," and "Legacy For Rachel" from *Morning of the Red-Tailed Hawk,* Green River Press, 1981, reprinted with permission from the author.

MARY LEE SETTLE

Excerpt from *Addie*, University of South Carolina Press, 1998, reprinted with permission from the University of South Carolina Press. Excerpt from *The Killing Ground*, reprinted by permission of Carlisle & Company, LLC on behalf of the author.

ANNE SHELBY

"Why I Write" (fall 1997), "Fat Sestina," and "Spellcheck" (fall 1998) from *Pine Mountain Sand & Gravel*, reprinted with permission from the author.

MURIEL EARLEY SHEPPARD

Excerpt from *Cabins in the Laurel* © 1935 and 1991 by the University of North Carolina Press, used by permission of the publisher.

BETSY SHOLL

"Appalachian Winter" from *Appalachian Winter*, reprinted with permission from the author.

ELLEN HARVEY SHOWELL

"What is a Mountain?" "The Trouble with Town," and "Going to the River" from *Our Mountain*, Bradbury Press, 1991, reprinted with permission from the author.

BENNIE LEE SINCLAIR

"Homecoming" from *The Arrowhead Scholar*, Wildernesse Books, 1978; "Kathy" from *Little Chicago Suite*, Wildernesse Books, 1978; and "My Father. His Rabbits" and "Backwoods Haiku" from *Lord of Springs*, Rowan Mountain Press, 1990, reprinted with permission from the Estate of the author.

VERNA MAE SLONE

Excerpt from *What My Heart Wants to Tell*, New Republic Books, 1979, reprinted with permission from the author.

BARBARA SMITH

"Bad News" from *Weeping With Those Who Weep: Poems of Bereavement*, "And This Is The Way To Be Poor" from *Pine Mountain Sand and Gravel: Contemporary Appalachian Writing*, and "The Language of Poetry" from *New River Free Press*, reprinted with permission from the author.

Effie Waller Smith

"Memories of Home" from *The Collected Works of Effie Waller Smith,* Oxford University Press, 1991.

Lee Smith

Excerpt from *Saving Grace* © 1995 by Lee Smith, published by G.P. Putnam's Sons, a division of Penguin Putnam, Inc., used with permission of the author.

Jane Stuart

"Cycles" from *Transparencies: Remembrances of My Father, Jesse Stuart,* Archer Editions Press, 1985; "Where Stuarts Lie" and "Roots" from *Eyes of the Mole,* Stanton & Lee, 1967; and "Composition" from *White Barn,* Whipoorwill Press, 1973, reprinted with permission from the author.

Adriana Trigiani

Excerpt from *Big Stone Gap* © 2000 by The Glory of Everything Company, used by permission of Random House, Inc., and the author.

Dana Wildsmith

"Force," from *Alchemy: Poems,* Sow's Ear Press, 1995; and "New Poor," "Economy," "Our Bodies Remember," and "A Dry Spring" from *Our Bodies Remember: Poems,* Sow's Ear Press, 1999, reprinted with permission from Sow's Ear Press and the author.

Sylvia Wilkinson

Excerpt from *Shadow of the Mountain: A Novel,* Houghton Mifflin, 1977, reprinted with permission from the author.

Meredith Sue Willis

"My Boy Elroy" from *In the Mountains of America* © 1994 by Meredith Sue Willis, published by Mercury House, San Francisco, CA, and reprinted with permission of the author.

Leigh Allison Wilson

"The Raising" from *From the Bottom Up,* University of Georgia Press, 1983, reprinted with permission from the author.

Mary Elizabeth Witherspoon

Excerpt from *The Morning Cool,* MacMillan, 1972, reprinted with permission from the author.

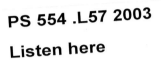